Indians in the Making

AMERICAN CROSSROADS

Edited by Earl Lewis, George Lipsitz, Peggy Pascoe, George Sánchez, and Dana Takagi

Indians in the Making

Ethnic Relations and Indian Identities around Puget Sound

Alexandra Harmon

University of California Press

Berkeley   Los Angeles   London

University of California Press
Berkeley and Los Angeles, California

University of California Press, Ltd.
London, England

First Paperback Printing 2000

Library of Congress Cataloging-in-Publication Data

Harmon, Alexandra, 1945–
   Indians in the making : ethnic relations and Indian identities
around Puget Sound / Alexandra Harmon.
      p.   cm. — (American crossroads ; 3)
   Includes bibliographical references and index.
   ISBN 0-520-22685-2 (pbk. : alk. paper)
      1. Indians of North America—Washington (State)—Puget Sound
   —History.   2. Indians of North America—Washington (State)—
   Puget Sound—Ethnic identity.   3. Indians of North America—Gov-
   ernment policy—Washington (State)—Puget Sound.   4. Frontier
   and pioneer life—Washington (State)—Puget Sound.   5. Puget
   Sound (Wash.)—Ethnic relations.   6. Puget Sound (Wash.)—
   Politics and government.   I. Title.   II. Series.
   E78.W3H37   1999
   979.7′700497—dc21   98-17665
                                                                      CIP

Printed in the United States of America

08   07   06   05   04   03   02   01   00
9 8 7 6 5 4 3 2 1

For my parents

Contents

Maps

Acknowledgments

When I think of the people who made this study possible, my thoughts go first to the governing councils, members, and employees of the Indian tribes for whom I worked during the 1970s and 1980s. My years as a staff attorney at the Skokomish Tribe, Suquamish Tribe, Evergreen Legal Services Native American Project, and Small Tribes Organization of Western Washington were happy ones. Tribal community members made me feel welcome, my tasks were always interesting, and the positions my clients asked me to advocate seemed just. I considered it a privilege to assist the tribes as they effected dramatic, positive change in their communities. If I name some of the people who gave me the opportunity to do that, I will inadvertently slight many more who deserve mention; so I wish simply to express my deep gratitude to them all.

It may be that few of the Indians who enlisted my help in recovering or protecting their resources and developing their community governments will read this book. Some who do may be surprised or disappointed at not finding a straightforward story of tribal continuity and fierce determination to preserve aboriginal traditions. But I hope others will rejoice to read an account that acknowledges the difficulties of defining and preserving Indian identity, as well as the creativity, ingenuity, and resilience of the people in western Washington who have done just that. I am indebted to my Indian clients and friends not only for sharing their stories and memories with me but also for opening my eyes to the complex, ambiguous, and dynamic nature of Indianness in America.

I am also indebted to many talented history scholars. My largest debt is to Richard White, who provided abundant help at every stage of this project. He read numerous draft chapters, returning them promptly with comments that were invariably incisive and wise. While pushing me to produce a higher-quality product, he assured me that the goal was attainable. The extensive comments I received from Peggy Pascoe and Philip Deloria, who read an entire manuscript, were enormously helpful. Russel Barsh earned my admiration and gratitude for generously sharing his census research with me. Tips from Sharon Boswell and Leonard Forsman led me to particularly useful sources of information. I benefited, too, from the sage advice, encouragement, and inspiring examples of John Findlay and Tsianina Lomawaima. Other scholars and friends who contributed welcome ideas and support include Jay Miller, Jane Merritt, Cassandra Tate, Julia Eulenberg, Mary Wright, Kathleen Brown, Brad Asher, John Lutz, John Bower, Barbara Lane, Francis Paul Prucha, Dauril Alden, and Sandra Coffman. My parents, Merle and Sonja Harmon, studied a draft with great care, and their suggestions saved me later embarrassment.

During months of research at the National Archives in Seattle, I took liberal advantage of the cheerful assistance of Joyce Justice and her staff. I also had patient help from librarians at the Washington State Historical Society, the Washington State Archives, and the University of Washington, especially in the university's Special Collections and the Archives and Manuscripts Division. The Suquamish Tribal Archives made an invaluable collection of oral history interviews available to me. And I thank Jack Kidder and Bill Matheson of the Snohomish Tribe of Indians for opening and copying many of the tribe's files. When I sought photographic illustrations, Richard Engeman, Carla Rickerson, Carolyn Marr, Elaine Miller, Rod Slemmons, and Charlie Sigo provided assistance. And finally, enthusiastic and considerate editors at the University of California Press—Monica McCormick, Rose Anne White, and Susan Ecklund—have buoyed and enlightened me as they have transformed a novice's manuscript into a real book.

Financial support from the National Endowment for the Humanities enabled me to work full time on this project for a year. During the long years of graduate study, as always, my husband Jim Douglas was a vital source of moral and material support. All the people I have named and more have helped me to fulfill a cherished dream, and I thank them from the bottom of my heart.

Introduction

In 1980 the Suquamish Indian Tribe brought suit to settle a long-standing dispute about the boundary of its reservation, which is visible from the city of Seattle, across Puget Sound. I took responsibility for the case two years later when I became the tribe's staff attorney. Since the claim derived from a 125-year-old treaty, it presented historical questions as well as legal ones. By arousing in me a desire to address some of the historical questions more fully than court proceedings allowed, the litigation tempted me into writing this book and ultimately into a new vocation.[1]

Our opponents in the suit—the State of Washington and several hundred holders of state deeds—responded in part by challenging our account of the tribe's history. The modern Suquamish Tribe, they argued, is not the entity that concluded the treaty but a recent creation of the federal government; the original Suquamish Tribe ceased to exist a few decades after Chief Seattle signed the treaty on its behalf. To prove this, they planned to call as witnesses a historian and an anthropologist.

If the judge had allowed the witnesses to testify as proposed, they would have stressed that most Suquamish Indians did not honor their promise to move onto the reservation but stayed in their scattered villages or hung around American towns. Thirty years after the treaty, when the government assigned tracts of reservation land to individuals, there were only fifty-one takers; and they were descendants not only of Suquamish but also of Snohomish, Skagit, Canadian, and other Indians, of white and black Americans, and of Chileans. Our adversaries planned to show further that no one formed a Suquamish tribal government until federal funding made it worthwhile in the 1960s. By that time tribe members not only lived among non-Indians, who far outnumbered them on the reservation, but also looked, spoke, and earned their livings like non-Indians.

1

How could such people claim historical continuity with the Indians who signed the treaty?

Answering this question to the satisfaction of a judge and jury would probably have entailed getting them to set aside stereotypes for more nuanced images of Indians. Afraid that such reeducation was not possible in a brief federal trial, we asked the judge to decide the issue as a matter of law, without testimony. He obliged, declaring himself bound by another court's ruling that the Suquamish Tribe in the lawsuit was the legal and political successor to the treaty party of the same name.[2]

I knew that the Suquamish boundary litigation was not the first test of a Washington Indian tribe's historical authenticity; nor would it be the last. A year before my clients filed suit, a different judge refused to recognize five groups as the modern incarnations of aboriginal tribes from the Puget Sound region. All five subsequently petitioned the Bureau of Indian Affairs for such recognition.[3] Their quest was an outgrowth of the same history that prompted our opponents to dispute the present Suquamish Tribe's pedigree. Around Puget Sound for almost two centuries, native people and their progeny have had extensive and intimate relations with immigrants and their offspring, who now constitute the vast majority of the population. As a result, relatively little remains of the characteristics that distinguished indigenous people from Europeans when they first met. Descendants of Indians are inextricably tangled in the cultural, economic, and racial threads of a social fabric designed by non-Indians.

When those descendants nonetheless claim a distinct, enduring Indian identity, they raise intriguing historical questions. If they group and identify themselves in ways that neither their native ancestors nor their non-Indian neighbors would recognize as indigenous, why do they think of themselves as members of historic Indian tribes? By changing their habits and the nature of the groups they affiliate with, have they lost their Indian identity or reinforced it? Have they claimed and maintained an Indian identity in spite of extensive relations with non-Indians or because of those relations? Are non-Indians responsible for destroying Indian communities or for creating and perpetuating them?

As much as I wanted to deflect these questions in litigation, I wanted to address them in another forum. I yearned to tell the story the judge had suppressed. It was my good fortune to begin indulging my desire, as a graduate student of history, at a propitious time. Scholars in several disciplines, I discovered, were confirming that racial and ethnic categories are mutable social constructions and therefore proper subjects of historical inquiry. This discovery bolstered the courage of my growing conviction: a history of Indians like the Suquamish could and should be a chronicle of change over time in Indianness itself.

The view that "primordial" sentiments determine ethnic identity has lost favor among anthropologists and sociologists. Drawing on historical data, they have shown that ethnic groups are born, change, and dissipate as the contexts of human relations change. Among other things, their studies confirm that changes in culture and membership do not necessarily destroy ethnic categories themselves. Concluding that we should conceive of ethnic and racial distinctions as a process rather than an essence, such scholars have concentrated on elucidating the dynamics of group differentiation (Fredrik Barth calls it "boundary maintenance").[4]

American historians have awakened recently to the possibility and potential rewards of taking racial and ethnic categories as their subjects. More often now, they are asking how such classifications have developed and endured. Aware that a sense of group affiliation depends on relations and comparisons with outsiders, historians are especially interested in encounters between formerly separate populations. And those who study the American West, where such encounters have been numerous, are staking a claim to a significant share of this new intellectual territory.[5]

On the other hand, scholars have barely begun to explore the implications of these insights for the history of North American Indians.[6] Too often Indians' history is written as if protagonists, authors, and readers have no reason to wonder who is Indian (or Sioux, Cheyenne, or Cherokee). Since questions about the origins, continuity, distinctiveness, and membership of Indian groups have not been unique to western Washington, this pattern is surprising and disappointing. Arguably more than any other group, Indians depend on representations of history for their identification as Indians; and people who profess to be Indians have had to defend their claims with a frequency and rigor seldom demanded of people in other ethnic or racial classes.[7] Yet scholars of Native America have rarely acknowledged that the definitions of Indian and Indian tribe have histories themselves.

Pioneering studies by James Merrell, J. Leitch Wright, and Richard White point the way that few others have taken. They show that indigenous nations or tribes—shredded by disease and thrown into a bubbling stew of European traders and colonists, African slaves, and displaced aborigines—often disintegrated and fused and dissolved again. But Merrell, Wright, and White recount events that took place east of the Mississippi River before whites subordinated Indians across the continent. Few histories ask how events have affected the salience, content, and expression of

Indian identity elsewhere and more recently, particularly in the twentieth century.[8]

This book does ask that question. Relying on data from the Pacific Northwest, it answers that the marks and meanings of Indian identity have evolved through decades of negotiation between supposed races. Indians and non-Indians share responsibility for creating and repeatedly reformulating a special social category. In 1986 Richard White called for historical studies of the daily relations and symbolic activities that have produced and preserved the many racial and ethnic groups in the West.[9] This is such a study. By focusing on a region where daily relations between Indians and non-Indians have been especially abundant, it allows us to see people continually defining and redefining themselves in contradistinction to each other.

A history of Indians in the Puget Sound region is a history of racial and tribal categories because it is a litany of attempts to draw boundaries, social as well as geographic, around Indians. Occasionally the lines of demarcation have been literal. English explorer George Vancouver described how his men separated themselves from natives who approached them on a beach near Puget Sound in 1792: "On a line being drawn with a stick on the sand between the two parties, they immediately sat down, and no one attempted to pass it, without previously making signs, requesting permission for so doing." A fortnight later, Vancouver's lieutenant sorted out the people at another rest stop by also drawing a line "to divide the two Parties, the Intent of which the Indians perfectly understood."[10]

Locating and marking boundaries between Indians and others has rarely since been so easy, but it has often been that explicit. Even when no one recorded the process as candidly as Vancouver did, we can find evidence of people's sense that they belonged in distinct groups. As anthropologists point out, people develop and express ethnic affiliations not only by names, language, folklore, dress, manners, and social and economic roles but also by actions that are the stuff of historical narratives. For example, Barbara Myerhoff observed Jews at a California senior center who convinced themselves and others that they had a common ethnic heritage, despite their diverse nationalities, by jointly staging historical skits and a political protest.[11] Puget Sound's aboriginal groups defined themselves in analogous conspicuous acts and rituals that dramatized their conceptions of themselves, their histories, and their relations with others.

Fortunately for historians, ethnicity has a strategic function that fosters public dialogues. Distinctions between Indians and non-Indians or between different kinds of Indians have been integral to some people's strategies for survival, economic gain, or self-respect; and groups do not formulate strategy without debate.[12] The emblems of Indian identity have never enjoyed unanimous endorsement. When debating strategy or emblems for Indians in western Washington, many people have put their conceptions of Indianness on record.

On the other hand, people do not all or in every instance deliberately act as agents of an ethnic group. Rather than consciously choosing to be Indian or white, Suquamish or Snohomish, many individuals have simply responded to new and often difficult personal situations. Yet their myriad choices have added up to significant changes in the composition and cultures of their societies. It is the historian's task to suggest how such unselfconscious actions, too, have helped to define or redefine the boundaries and content of categories such as "Indian" or "Suquamish."[13]

To detect and explain evolving notions of Indianness in western Washington, I have searched the historical record for explicit dialogues about racial, cultural, and legal classifications, and I found many. But I have also scrutinized situations and actions that were likely to generate or symbolize a sense of difference. I have perused records of meetings at trading posts, workplaces, treaty conferences, battlefields, trials, and festivals for indications that the participants saw or wanted a distinction between peoples. At such meetings—whether ceremonial or informal, cordial or antagonistic—the affiliations and distinguishing characteristics of presumed Indians were often explicitly or implicitly at issue, and emblems of identity were invariably on display.

Of course, members of an ethnic group do not direct their manifestos of difference or displays of affinity solely at people outside the group. Ethnicity wears two masks, one donned for meetings with outsiders and another presented to insiders. To explain why a Comanche Indian community has persisted despite drastic disruption of the original basis for members' association, ethnohistorian Morris Foster focuses not on how Comanches have defined themselves in relation to outsiders but on their internal mechanisms for generating and preserving a common identity.[14] When explaining the demarcation and evolution of Indian communities around Puget Sound, I have likewise noted internal definition processes. But my priority is to document Indians' relations with non-Indians, which have long been the inescapable context for all relations between Indians.

The most important relations have been economic and political. Ethnic divisions acquire salience especially from disparities in economic and political power. State power to set ethnic policies or allocate economic resources often determines whether particular groups emerge or persist. In western Washington, power relations have been a critical determinant both of reasons and of ways to be identified as Indian. An essential factor in the power calculation has been the relative numbers of people regarded as Indians and non-Indians. Consequently, a distinctive set of demographic, political, and economic conditions frames each of this book's eight chapters. In each successive context, people pondered anew, debated, and revised Indians' relationships to non-Indians and to each other.

This does not mean that everyone thought about those relationships the same way. Culture—the beliefs and associations that seemed right and natural to people—shaped their interpretations of economic and political relations. Western Washington's natives, I argue, interpreted their circumstances in light of beliefs about power that differed from their colonizers' (and from modern scholars') beliefs about the power invested in a coercive state.[15] I therefore assess the shifting balance of power not only as non-Indians have but also as Indians likely have. The fact that these assessments did not always coincide has been as important to Indians' self-conceptions as demographics and policy.

In order to answer my original questions, I could not limit my inquiry to the metamorphosis of the Suquamish Tribe. I have had to analyze the course of human relations in an entire region—an area roughly encompassed by a line running from the Strait of Juan de Fuca at its midpoint along the mountains west of Hood Canal to the southern reaches of Puget Sound, then southeastward to the Cascade Mountains at Mount Rainier, then northward to the Canadian border, westward to Point Roberts, and southwestward to the starting point. Although the Puget Sound proper is only a portion of the sheltered salt water inside that line, I borrow its name, as geologists do, to designate a larger basin carved by the Vashon Glacier a dozen or two millennia ago.[16] The line circumscribes localities united by climate, geology, and political and economic history. But these commonalities are secondary reasons to adopt a regional focus. The primary reason is a habit of the aboriginal peoples—their habit of creating and maintaining links between communities.

I do not mean that the original inhabitants of the Puget Sound basin were one people. On the contrary, they spoke several mutually unintelligible languages, and many were strangers and even enemies to each other. What they shared was a system of communicating and conducting relations with outsiders—a system that drew them all into a regionwide social network.

Early in the nineteenth century, an individual native typically identified his or her group affiliation with a word formed from the name

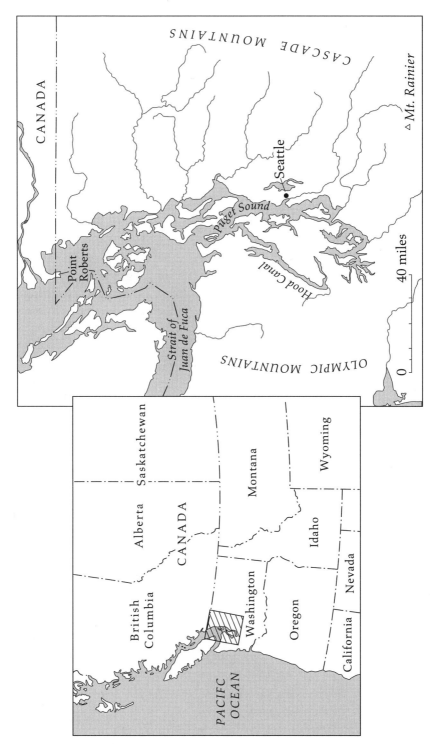

Map 1.   Study area.

of a village and a suffix or prefix meaning "people of." Each of the hundreds of villages near Puget Sound was cohesive and autonomous, even though it was a winter residence only. In some places and periods, villagers also identified with a larger population that shared nearby territory, but the defining characteristics and significance of these larger "tribes" are the subject of vigorous debate among ethnologists. Underlying the controversy is the fact that individual natives had multiple associations, multiple loyalties, and multiple ways to identify themselves to others.[17]

The principal reason for individuals' ambiguous, multifaceted identity was a broad web of family ties. Most people, especially the well-to-do, aspired for economic and social reasons to marry outside their villages, even outside their language groups. Local communities therefore incorporated outsiders and dispersed some members to other communities, with the consequence that most settlements had culturally and linguistically diverse populations. Many people lived in more than one village during their lifetimes, and most people had close relatives residing in other places.

The courtesies of scattered kin enabled people to visit, move into, and use resources in communities where they otherwise would have been unwelcome strangers. On the invitation of relatives, the well-to-do also took part in other villages' ceremonial life, including ceremonies validating their extended families' achievements. Thus, through marriage and a well-ordered system of intervillage relations, the elite of aboriginal societies forged social bonds that transcended local loyalties. Since most familial ties were between communities in contiguous territories, relations with members of distant groups were rare. Yet a complete diagram of kinship links would show an unbroken tangle of lines extending from the southernmost reaches of Puget Sound to and beyond the present international boundary in the north. Almost any attempt to subdivide the linked peoples would fail to account for important social ties cutting across those subdivisions.

As people circulated, so did ideas, technology, and rituals. The resulting standardization justifies ethnographers' classification of the region as a single culture area. But one author who concurs in this classification also asserts that no population of American Indians included a more diverse assortment of peoples. Her explanation of this paradoxical statement has important implications for a history of the Indians in question. Exchanges between communities not only inspired imitation but also introduced variations and encouraged innovations. In addition, contacts between residents of different villages highlighted group differences and stimulated local pride, because they were occasions for self-representation and comparison. At ceremonial gatherings, for example, people from each group in turn performed their own songs and dances and displayed the fruits of their special relations with supernatural beings.[18]

As the following narrative shows, descendants of indigenous people have also cherished ties to outsiders. Their consequent mobility and numerous social options have worked at cross-purposes with U.S. government efforts to sort them into a manageable number of tribes, assign them to a few reservations, and administer their affairs on a tribe-by-tribe basis. If I had taken tribal subdivisions as givens when researching this history, I would have faced analogous frustrations.

A word about words is necessary, since this is in essence a history of the meanings of certain words. From the moment I sat down to write, I have been painfully aware of the limitations and hazards of the lexical tools at my disposal. George Vancouver had a ready-made label for everyone on the other side of the line his men drew. Yet "Indian" was a term unknown to the people he labeled. It does not even denote a category for which they had a word. Although they or their children eventually used the term to identify themselves, its meaning has not since been static or indisputable.[19] That is the point of this book. And writing a story with such a point has sometimes seemed like drawing in beach sand. No sooner have I inscribed a term that delineates my subject than the tides of history have undermined the foundation and blurred the definition of that term. Because of the book's subject and regional focus, I need general ethnic or racial designations for people. But to use words such as "Indian," "tribe," or even "Suquamish" presupposes the existence of the very groups whose creation, transformation, dissolution, or redefinition I must document. Such labels have connotations of naturalness and permanence, and those are precisely the assumptions I want readers to set aside. Yet how can I unseat antiquated ideas about races and tribes without using antiquated language?[20]

A few scholars, seeking to express a pluralist conception of history, have experimented with new terms. In a history of the Marquesas, Greg Dening declares independence from the European colonizers who claimed the power to name the inhabitants of the South Pacific; he substitutes the indigenous people's terms for natives and outsiders.[21] If data for the Northwest permitted, I might emulate him. There is no evidence, however, that indigenous peoples around Puget Sound had a single name for themselves until they or their offspring accepted the name "Indian."

The names that natives pinned on immigrants illustrate the dilemma as well, confirming that any ethnic or racial label can obscure the diversity of the people and the elasticity of the category it designates. By the 1840s indigenous people throughout the Northwest had grouped most colonists into two broad categories—"King George men" and "Bostons"—which historians have translated as "Englishmen" and "Americans," respectively. Among the former, however, were people from Hawaii, Iroquois country, and French Canada. The latter included emigrants from many European countries and eventually from Asia and Latin America.

It is easy to see from this that the terms "King George men," "Bostons," and "whites" are inadequate labels for heterogeneous, changing populations.[22] It takes more effort to keep in mind that terms such as "Indians" or even "Suquamish Indians" likewise refer to heterogeneous collections of people, some of whom have moved into or out of these groups at different times. To remind readers of the need for such effort, I sometimes write "so-called Indians," "people who identified themselves as Indians," or another qualifying phrase. But doing so repeatedly would encumber my prose without relieving me of the need to discuss inchoate, contested, evolving groups in a language that implies certainty and continuity.

Virtually every reference I make to a population's or a person's race or ethnicity has required that I choose from a limited assortment of unsatisfactory terms. For the earliest period of this history, "natives" and "indigenous peoples" are useful terms. After that, ethnic or racial labels are unavoidable. As I apply a label, I try to follow a simple principle: either the people labeled or the labelers I refer to were using the label by then, at least in interracial or intercultural relations. This rule explains why I repeat some epithets, such as "half-breed," that offend modern sensibilities. It also explains my choice of "Indian" over "Native Americans" or other terms fashionable since the 1970s. Most people who base their ethnic identification on descent from western Washington's original inhabitants now call themselves Indians. While bearing in mind the deceptive nature of any collective name, you should therefore construe each mention of Indians as carrying the implicit qualification "people they called Indians" or "people who thought of themselves as Indians." No doubt you will spot a poor choice of terms here or there. But at least you will be approaching this history with the consciousness that it hopes to promote.

This is the first extensive history of Indians in western Washington. The interpretation is necessarily preliminary and general. Although the activities that influence and reflect ethnic affiliations are innumerable, I selected a few subjects for investigation or emphasis. Arguably, I have neglected subjects of equal importance. Given the opportunity to expand this analysis, I would examine four aspects of Indian experience that get short shrift here: family relations and gender roles,[23] aboriginal languages,[24] schooling, and relations with ethnographers.[25]

First and foremost, this is a story of human relations and the effect of those relations on people's self-concepts and self-presentations. From government and commercial records, ethnographies, interviews, periodicals, photographs, diaries, and memoirs, I have spun a tale that begins in the 1820s with the appearance of land-based Hudson's Bay Company traders on the fringe of Puget Sound. The narrative ends in the 1970s with two federal court rulings that resolved some long-standing questions about Indian identity and its perquisites. At either extreme of this period, people known as Indians were likely to identify themselves to outsiders as members of groups that had particular resources, particular ancestors and histories, unique ways of doing things, and special partnerships with beings who had power to ensure their health and prosperity. But in 150 years the resources, histories, customs, and sustaining partnerships that demarcated Indian groups changed as much as the populations they encompassed. The story of those changes has several interwoven themes.

Many of the outsiders who came after Vancouver tried, as he did, to ensure orderly relations with Indians by drawing lines of demarcation. Yet time and again people ignored, moved, or effaced the lines as they approached each other in the hope of benefiting from a variety of relations. While their relations induced the formerly separate peoples to develop some common customs, relations also drew attention to the differences that remained and thus engendered new urges to separate the peoples, to define Indians, and to clarify Indians' status in regional society.

In the interest of orderly relations, people of different cultures often made sincere efforts to discern each other's thoughts. But in order to interpret each other, they could draw only on the concepts and values they regarded as common sense. Although there were congruities in the peoples' concepts and values, there were also important differences; and misunderstandings were predictable. But even misunderstandings fostered mutual activities.

Native villagers of the early nineteenth century believed that contact with beings from a different realm, while dangerous, could be a source of individual power and thus a means to establish an estimable persona. It appears that many of them saw relations with King George men and Bostons as a way to obtain or demonstrate personal power. Instead of treating the intruders as a threat to their existence as peoples, they acted as if they expected relations to validate that existence. Many non-Indians likewise expected to realize power and peoplehood through relations with Indians, but most aimed to do so by breaking rather than tapping Indians' power.

Non-Indian Americans finally acquired hegemony in the region at the end of the nineteenth century. They then had the means to erect important racial boundary markers and to dictate the terms of most relations across those boundaries. Meanwhile, the people who found themselves on the Indian side of the line were growing more diverse. As they tried to understand what the Bostons meant by "Indian," they also tried varied ways of giving that term a meaning more to their liking. Occasionally they were able to win general acceptance of their definitions by seizing and skillfully wielding the very tools—laws and courts, for example—with which America's ruling elite tried to push them into a more restrictive mold.

In 1973 a representative of the Lummi Tribe told a federal judge, "The U.S. has tried to build a glove to fit us into, and we haven't been able to fit because there is a cultural value difference."[26] I like the image of wriggling fingers the Lummi man evoked; for the people whom the United States has tried to stuff into stereotypical Indian garb are many, and they have moved independently of each other. Indeed, they have moved in divergent directions. Moreover, their different digits often touched not an American fist but the fingers of a segmented non-Indian population. When indicating the paths that Indians should take, non-Indian fingers have pointed in different directions. It is no wonder that there have been so many ways to be Indian.

This story of regional ethnic relations is a significant chapter of the American saga. It shows not only that Americans of all races have participated in the creation and preservation of a racial group but also that national and local forces have interacted dialectically to define the group. It reveals the influence of federal law and policy on the ways that descendants of Washington's indigenous people have presented themselves. At the same time, it should dispel any notion that law and policy merely stamped on those people the marks of a nationally standardized Indian identity. Indeed, aboriginal habits and peculiar regional circumstances repeatedly frustrated federal officials' efforts to package Puget Sound Indians in boxes designed with other Indians in mind. But the symbols of identity that Indians of the Puget Sound area preferred to adopt have in turn inspired Indians elsewhere in the United States. No doubt the regional legacy described here is one of many that history has bequeathed to modern American Indians.

1 Fur Traders and Natives

Empowering Encounters

In the 1940s an elderly man explained his identity to ethnographer William Elmendorf by telling a 150-year-old war story. He was a Twana Indian, Frank Allen said, but his mother was not. She was a Klallam Indian who in turn had Skagit Indian ancestry. Allen recounted for Elmendorf how he and his brother Henry came by Skagit ancestors.

> The Dungeness Klallam get ready to go to Skagit. ... They're going to Skagit now for war. Going for women and slaves now. They go and get to Skagit ... at night, and they land away from the village and haul their canoes into the woods and hide.
>
> Next morning they see two little girls playing on the beach. The Klallam catch them and ask them, "Who are your people?" One of the girls says, "My grandfather's name is kʷ 'áɬqédəb." That is the chief of the Skagit people. ... And one man, sxʷilácəm, says, "I'm going to take this girl home, this grandchild of kʷ 'áɬqédəb and keep her for my wife. ... "
>
> And now after kʷ 'áɬqédəb hears that the Klallam got his grandchild ..., he gets ready now for the Klallam, he gets ten slaves ready, preparing for the Klallam when they come to buy his daughter. And ... the Klallam are preparing, too. Gathering slaves and goods, getting ready to go and pay for that girl. My grandfather told me they took more than twenty slaves to buy ma'náyɬ.
>
> Now they are landing, they sing as they show the mask: " ... (I'm the great Klallam)." They are showing off now, showing off the mask, showing they are high-priced people now. ... Now kʷ 'áɬqédəb's interpreter hollers to all the Klallam to come to the chief's house and eat. So they all come. Now cooking, eating, good time. ... And kʷ 'áɬqédəb sings now, he is happy now, with those twenty slaves and that canoe. ... Now he takes ma'náyɬ over to where sxʷilácəm is sitting and seats her beside him. That is marriage now.

And after a while the Skagit bring those ten slaves kʷ 'áɬqédəb had raised from his people. That is all he had to give, those ten slaves; the Klallam beat him there, in giving. Now sxʷilácəm divides the ten slaves to his people, gives one to this man, one to that, gives them to his tribe. ...

That is where we are from. ... So we are related to the Skagit people from that time.[1]

According to Elmendorf's calculations, the Allens' forebears converted war into marriage around the turn of the eighteenth century. By then Europeans and their American descendants had probably sailed the waters between Dungeness and Skagit, although none yet resided in the area. From the Europeans or Americans, directly or indirectly, Klallams and Skagits had acquired desirable new objects but also unwelcome new microbes. A smallpox epidemic had killed hundreds of people, gutting local social structures. Nevertheless, at the time of sxʷilácəm's wedding, the regrouped survivors were still living in an environment and a fashion that had sustained many generations of their ancestors. It was the new couple's descendants who would see the aboriginal world transformed—capsized, Henry Allen said—when many pale foreigners came to stay in the Puget Sound region.[2]

The first pale foreigners who stayed—British employees of the Hudson's Bay Company (HBC)—did not make dangerous waves; but sharing local waters with them was tricky because they were strikingly different from other people the Klallams and Skagits knew. To most Klallams, even the Skagits were strange: their language was unintelligible, and they had distinctive songs and dances, names, and food specialties. Still, Klallams and Skagits observed the same protocol of relations between communities. Neither would be surprised at a proposal to link warring peoples by marriage. Both knew how to conduct themselves at a wedding and would properly reciprocate a gift of slaves. In contrast, Klallams and Skagits could only guess what the Britons expected and would do when approached.

People with gumption like sxʷilácəm's approached the newcomers nonetheless, pursuing the same ends that inspired them to seek out indigenous strangers—hoping to prove their mettle, acquire wealth, or forge new kinship links. Many of the daring people succeeded in these quests. In order to do so, however, they had to discern and indulge some of the newcomers' expectations; and in the process, they gradually modified the pattern and protocol of their relations with outsiders.

From the 1820s to the 1860s, Hudson's Bay conducted modest, land-based commercial trade in the Puget Sound basin. Traders and natives soon developed ways of dealing with each other that usually worked to all parties' perceived advantage. The process of arriving at a common protocol did not require natives to discard the assumptions guiding their conduct. They could reasonably infer that they had incorporated the newcomers into the existing regional network of intercommunity relations. For this reason, it is unlikely that trade with Hudson's Bay Company substantially changed the ways indigenous people conceived of themselves in relation to others, although it probably made many of them more conscious of their own distinguishing characteristics.

Foreigners joined the region's resident population in 1827. That summer eighteen HBC men under Archibald McDonald's command left Fort Vancouver, on the Columbia River, with instructions to erect a post near the mouth of the Fraser River, approximately 250 miles to the north. From the new establishment, to be named Fort Langley, they would promptly begin commerce with inhabitants of the surrounding region, offering British merchandise for furs.

McDonald's itinerary included several days canoeing the deep, sheltered, saltwater inlet he knew as Puget Sound. At a few of the Sound's populated coves and estuaries, his party stopped. Residents of villages that McDonald identified as "Soquams," "Sinahomis," and "Scaadget" greeted the travelers civilly and agreed to exchange deer and salmon for beads, tobacco, mirrors, and knives.[3]

The people McDonald called on already knew something about their visitors. Many had seen a larger contingent of HBC men who made the round trip between the Columbia and Fraser Rivers in 1824. Indeed, McDonald probably chose to stop at villages that had hosted the earlier expedition. Natives around the north Sound had also welcomed trading ships for years, and a few northern villagers had made the long journey to the foreigners' forts on the Columbia. By 1827 native people had sorted the foreigners into two categories—King George men and Bostons—in the apparent belief that those names indicated where the crews of British and American ships were from. Even natives who had not seen the strangers or their vessels were aware of their presence in the region, for exotic objects obtained from them were circulating among the well-to-do in all villages.[4]

To indigenous people, the King George men and Bostons were in many respects repulsive. Some were unnaturally pale; some had hairy faces; none had heads flattened by cradleboards, as befitted freeborn persons. They spoke languages as incomprehensible as birds' chirping. Nonetheless, the villagers respected the newcomers' manifest ability to acquire extraordinary riches and approved their interest in trading.[5]

The foreigners not only traded desirable items for food and animal skins but also bestowed wealth on people who rendered them services. Therefore, when King George men asked at villages for guides and interpreters, someone usually volunteered. Two "Sinnahomis chiefs" who greeted McDonald's party were veterans of such service. The one McDonald identified as "Sinokton" was likely a man who had accompanied the HBC expedition of 1824. The other was so familiar to the King George men that a British doctor in 1825 described him as "a famous chief named Waskalatchy, who had wandered more over the N.W. coast than any Indian upon it."[6]

McDonald's men had little or no experience in the Puget Sound area, but they had well-informed expectations. Like the people they encountered on the Sound, they had gleaned intelligence from company forays into northern waters and from northern natives who came south. Educated King George men were also familiar with English Captain George Vancouver's account of exploring the Sound in 1792. In addition, at least one member of McDonald's crew had made the 1824 trek to the Fraser after living for "some time" among natives in the Chehalis River valley, not far from the Sound.[7]

For these reasons, the voyagers of 1827 knew that dense forests covered most of the land around Puget Sound. At intervals along the convoluted shores, they expected to find collections of large, cedar plank lodges or small, mat-draped lean-tos. They anticipated the fishy stench hovering over such settlements. They were disgusted but not surprised to see inhabitants who covered their brown skin with little more than red- or black-pigmented grease. The traders knew that these people had abundant supplies of salmon and shellfish and that most would exchange such food, as well as mammal pelts, for European manufactures, especially metal. Each village or camp, they assumed, would have men who took the lead in dealing with visitors. And they believed that different tribes, many of whose names they had heard from other natives and travelers, claimed different subdistricts as their territories.[8]

In addition to the reports of Vancouver, colleagues, and natives, McDonald's men had company experience elsewhere in North America to guide them as they entered new territory. During two centuries on the continent, British fur traders had drawn into commerce numerous indigenous peoples, all of whom they called Indians. Although they were not insensible to differences in the habits, structures, and economic orientations of native groups, they assumed that proven methods of dealing with some Indians would serve as well for others. Hudson's Bay employees did take note of local people's peculiarities but always with a utilitarian eye for the customs and beliefs most likely to affect business.[9]

Doubts that they could do business with the people around Puget Sound do not seem to have occurred to the King George men. Even if the natives did not initially want trading posts in their midst, HBC intended to change their minds. Company officers hoped (indeed, expected) to take out of the region far more wealth than they imported. This vision made it worth their while to work out orderly, mutually agreeable relations with the inhabitants.[10]

Those inhabitants had their own time-tested techniques for relating to outsiders, as Frank Allen's tale suggests. Although they regarded strangers as potentially dangerous, they had reasons to risk contact with them in a variety of circumstances. In some cases, the appropriate approach was war or raiding; but peaceful relations, which could pay off in prestige and augmented resources, were usually more desirable.

According to local folklore, Europeans at first seemed so different from known humans that Indians supposed them to be animals or creatures from myth times, but this judgment was probably neither universal nor long in vogue. A history of contacts with strange people gave natives of the Puget Sound basin a conceptual basis to explain the King George men and to formulate strategies for dealing with them. Vancouver found Indians who had never seen Europeans yet were ready to trade; and by the 1820s, natives plainly recognized the King George men as fellow humans, candidates for incorporation into the regional network of human relations.[11]

Strongly attracted to each other yet repelled by each other's alien appearance and behavior, wanting to communicate yet hampered by language and etiquette differences, King George men and natives of the Puget Sound region had to work cautiously toward a mutual understanding of the bases for intercourse. The conventions that eventually governed their relations—gift exchanges and hospitality rituals, marriage alliances, broker services provided by prominent native men—resembled conventions of the fur trade elsewhere in North America.[12] Yet the local practices were not simply HBC imports. They developed from a complex interplay of introduced and indigenous customs, conflicting expectations and complementary goals. The divide between alien societies was bridged in stages by trial and error, as people on both sides signaled their intentions and desires, observed the reactions they got, and modified their signs and behavior to elicit other reactions. Information about this process is essential to discovering how the fur trade affected indigenous people's conceptions of themselves.

When Fort Langley opened for business, there was still a great deal that King George men and natives did not know about each other. Relations required guesswork and improvisation. To keep natives at a safe remove while he assessed their disposition, McDonald had a bastion built. He watched for signs that the Indians had deciphered the intended message: the King George men planned to stay and were strong enough to defeat attempts to deter them. Indians who had come north with McDonald reported that local people were threatening to annihilate the King George men, but the trader shrugged the news off because he saw forty or fifty natives peacefully watching the construction and listening to their leaders deliver speeches with friendly themes. Even though he suspected ill-disposed natives of setting fires that menaced the post the following month, McDonald did not consider leaving. The bastion, he assured himself, commanded Indians' respect.[13]

McDonald had reason to doubt this judgment, however, when he received word a few months later that natives had murdered five of his colleagues. The killings occasioned a confrontation whose violent climax was evidence that HBC's communication with natives was still imperfect. Company officers told themselves that the violence made clear to everyone what the relationship and relative power of natives and traders would be, but they were probably wrong.

The slain King George men—Alexander McKenzie and four subordinates—allegedly died at the hands of Dungeness Klallams in the area where Frank Allen's Klallam grandfather had raided the Skagits. The killers' motives are obscure. According to a Klallam tale recorded much later, the slain men courted their fate by treating natives like slaves. But John McLoughlin, HBC's top officer in the district, told his superiors, "From every information I have been able to collect, they committed this crime without having had the least difference with our people & murdered them merely for the sake of their apparel and Arms. ... " Like Allen's forebear, the assailants seized an important man's daughter—a native woman in McKenzie's party. But events following the second kidnapping then took a different course, in part because the King George men were unfamiliar with the conventions that had allowed Klallams and Skagits to make peace.[14]

In 1828 as in sxⁿiláčəm's time, the Klallams' female captive seemed to them a key to peace, although not as a bride. They reportedly expected HBC to request payment for the dead men and assumed that an offer to release the woman would facilitate a settlement.[15] The King George men took action that initially seemed consistent with these expectations. Four months after the killings they came to Klallam country, intent on settling with the inhabitants and retrieving the woman. But instead of leaving with compensation for the loss of their colleagues, they left behind dead natives, a litter of shattered canoes, and smoldering house timbers.

Whether HBC initially intended to wreak havoc on Klallams is unclear. When mustering sixty-three men for the expedition, Chief Factor McLoughlin told them that "the honor of the whites" and their safety outside company forts were at stake. In the official journal, Frank Ermatinger said that everyone agreed on the need for an expedition "if not as a punishment to the tribe in question, at least as an example, in order, if possible, to deter others from similar attempts in future." Nonetheless the group's commander, Alex McLeod, seemed unsure of his mission. He and his lieutenants squabbled about their objectives and strategy.[16]

After traversing Puget Sound, where they attracted sundry natives who also had grudges against Klallams, McLeod's group rendezvoused with a company schooner and began a vigil in front of the suspects' village at Dungeness. Shortly thereafter Waskalatchy, the well-traveled "chief," arrived with a retinue from Snohomish. It was Waskalatchy who arranged the ransom of the captured woman, but only after days of posturing on everyone's part ended in confusion and cannon fire.[17]

All parties at Dungeness were aware of impediments to communication but tried to signal their desires and intentions in ways they thought unmistakable. They alternately brandished weapons and made conciliatory gestures. One evening, Ermatinger wrote, "a large body of Indians collected, armed, singing and yelping before us." The captain readied the ship for attack, aiming his cannon at a canoe. When McLeod countermanded the order to fire, the Indians went off in apparent triumph. But the next day two men of obvious importance in the village, one "primly dressed in a tensel laced cloth coat," came on board for talks and received a respectful reception.

According to Ermatinger, the effort to reach understanding then went awry. Seeing Waskalatchy's canoe approach, the Klallam men abruptly left in their own craft. When they did not heed calls to stop, McLeod ordered the gunners to fire at them. Some Iroquois who went to ascertain the results returned with one scalp and one wounded hostage. Since firing had begun, Ermatinger wrote, the captain cannonaded the village, destroying it in three shots. While setting the ruined houses ablaze, the King George men discovered and seized a few items belonging to McKenzie's party, plus two small boys, but they did not flush out the killers. Eventually they swapped captives and departed—so far as Ermatinger knew—without even mentioning the reason they had come.[18]

This account of conflict, negotiation, and further conflict belongs to a large body of literature generated by emissaries of expansionist Europe who encountered previously unknown, unlettered peoples. Analyzing the events from the standpoint of the participants who did not write about them requires some speculation; but recent interdisciplinary scholarship elucidates the processes at work in such encounters, providing a basis for inferences about the natives' views.[19]

Analysis can begin with the premise that all actors were equally concerned with projecting images and deciphering the impacts they made. Natives in Klallam territory were thus making efforts that paralleled those of the King George men: guessing not only at the foreigners' intentions but also at the foreigners' interpretation of what natives did. In trying to comprehend their effects on each other, King George men and Klallams alike drew on concepts and patterns of association they regarded as common sense; but they did not draw on the same concepts and associations. What anthropologist Marshall Sahlins calls the "structures of significance" for their respective societies were radically dissimilar. The King George men sensed some of these disparities. They realized that Indians might assign unfamiliar meanings to some actions and gestures. In order to achieve ends dictated by their own norms, the British traders therefore tried to appeal to what Indians understood and valued. It stands to reason that their native counterparts were doing the same.[20]

McLoughlin's account of the showdown depicts Britons consciously trying to get a message across to people with an alien mind-set. To his superiors, McLoughlin first said that his men had done their duty to their murdered countrymen, but ultimately he justified the artillery barrage by its supposed effects on indigenous people. Nothing short of brute force, he said, would project to Indians the image that Hudson's Bay had to maintain.

> To pass over such an outrage would lower us in the opinion of the Indians, induce them to act in the same way, and when an opportunity offered kill any of our people, & when it is considered the Natives are at least an hundred Men to one of us it will be conceived how absolutely necessary it is for our personal security that we should be respected by them, & nothing could make us more contemptible in their eyes than allowing such a cold blooded assasination [*sic*] of our People to pass unpunished, & every one acquainted with the character of the Indians of the North West Coast will allow they can only be restrained from Committing acts of atrocity & violence by the dread of retaliation.[21]

Ironically, McLoughlin was arguing that he could give Indians the right impression of King George men not by acting according to British ideals but by resorting to measures supposedly consonant with Indian standards of conduct.

On the other hand, when McLoughlin assured his superiors that British cannons had spoken a language intelligible to Indians, he affected a confidence he did not feel. In reality, he was uncertain how the Indians understood his men's acts. For five days the traders had solicited signs that Klallams respected their power. Finally, in anger, frustration, or fear, they had displayed that power in what they hoped were unmistakable terms. Yet their reading of native people's reactions was necessarily conjecture.

Even Britons, who presumably fit their experiences into the same structures of significance as McLoughlin, disagreed among themselves about how to interpret the Dungeness encounter. Ermatinger, for example, declared the campaign against the Klallams a debacle. McLoughlin expected that some company servants would fault expedition leaders for hesitating to use force, while others would condemn the leaders for brutality toward "fellow beings." The chief factor himself, in charge of an enterprise that required a state of peace, was ambivalent. On at least one occasion, he voiced doubts that the Klallams' losses would deter attacks on traders. Natives might instead read his employees' violence as an endorsement of war.[22]

Evidence available to modern scholars supports McLoughlin's claim that his men's actions conformed to local patterns of conduct. Ermatinger's report resembles descriptions of ancient warfare in oral histories and ethnographies of Puget Sound's indigenous peoples. The Allens' forebears did not resolve all conflicts by marriage; they also exacted retribution by attacking people besides the actual offenders, recruiting allies from other communities, burning houses, destroying canoes, and taking captives.[23]

Precisely because the King George men's actions fit local patterns, native people probably did not construe them as McLoughlin wished. Rather than inferring that Hudson's Bay disapproved and intended to prevent violence and robbery, Klallams and their neighbors could have assumed that the foreigners shared or had embraced the indigenous social code, which sanctioned some retaliatory raids.[24] Aware of this possibility, the King George men remained leery of Dungeness Klallams for several subsequent years.

The issue that HBC officers most ardently wanted to settle at Dungeness was the relative power of King George men and Indians. By proving their power to thwart Indians' objectionable designs, the Britons expected to win a desirable role and greater predictability in their relations with native people. McLoughlin preferred to construe what transpired in Klallam territory as the proof he needed: his men had shown that "the whites" could marshal power superior to anything "the Indians" had. From a modern vantage point, this interpretation of events seems like common sense. Who would not have reasoned along with McLoughlin that King George men could ultimately have their way in the region, especially after observing the terrible might of their weapons?

There are at least two reasons to be wary of projecting McLoughlin's wishful thoughts into indigenous people's minds. First, the confrontation they witnessed did not pit natives as a group against united Britons. Natives took part in the conflict on both sides. McLeod ransomed the native woman because his superiors feared they would otherwise alienate her father, a vital ally. And the company men could be seen relying on local people as guides and mediators. Moreover, even though McLoughlin exhorted expedition members to redeem whites' honor, he knew that his men were neither all white nor united around a common code of honor. Ventures such as the Dungeness expedition, he said in 1830,

> are extremely difficult to manage Composed as they are of Canadians Iroquois a few Europeans Owhyees and native Indians whose language we do not speak nor they ours and even hardly understand us of hired servants who consider themselves bound to defend our persons and property when attacked but conceive it no part of their duty to go to war and merely go to oblige and of freemen who may be led but will not be commanded.[25]

Second, McLoughlin's interpretation rested on the erroneous assumption that Indians shared or understood his conception of power. Folklore, oral histories, and ethnographies suggest that Klallams and their neighbors instead made sense of events by referring to a structure of significance in which many European ideas about power had no place. For Puget Sound's original peoples, human capabilities and humans' influences over each other had fundamentally different explanations, manifestations, and implications than they did for McLoughlin and other Britons.

Natives were unlikely to conclude that the destruction at Dungeness had settled the question of King George men's and Indians' relative power because they were unlikely even to frame such a question. Rather than thinking in terms of power-wielding institutions or national groups, they focused on individuals. They regarded a person's efficacy in diverse endeavors as evidence of strength, but they expected that efficacy to vary with circumstances. Much as children deciding who goes first know that the sign for rock beats the sign for scissors but scissors beats paper and paper beats rock, Puget Sound natives could acknowledge King George men's advantage in some circumstances while never doubting that eventually, in other situations, various Klallams would also exhibit powers worthy of King George men's respect.[26]

Klallams' powers did not originate in the human realm. They were endowments from a multiplicity of nonhuman beings, both visible and ordinarily invisible, animate and apparently inanimate. In certain settings the spirit of a powerful being might appear to a properly prepared person and offer to enter a partnership. In return for agreeing to perform the apparition's song and dance, the human partner would obtain one or more useful gifts—for example, the ability to acquire wealth, to hunt, to cure or inflict illness, to survive enemy assaults, to speak well, or to win at gambling. Without nonhuman help, a person was weak and poor; with help, he or she could have abilities that other people admired. Virtually all people indigenous to the Puget Sound basin conceived of human agency this way. They construed their own and others' achievements as evidence of good relations with spirits, and people who did attract the favor of powerful spirits expected to be effective in human society.[27]

This theory of power had corollaries with important social implications. Spirits might choose to associate with anyone, even the humble and ill trained. And explicitly mentioning the gifts one had obtained from spirits was improper. Therefore, although most people exhibited abilities consistent with what they had obtained, any person might have undiscerned powers. It was prudent to grant every individual a measure of respect in case he or she "had something." A twentieth-century ethnographer said of people who subscribed to these beliefs, "Coast Salish Indians are ... genuinely afraid of offending those whom they believe have strong spirit powers, because the spirits may take umbrage at the insult offered their human partners and retaliate without the conscious participation of the injured person."[28] Making allowances for other people's power was not inconsistent, however, with deriving self-confidence from one's own endowments. Power or strength was not so much a means to dominate others as insurance against domination.

Prudence induced by these beliefs may explain why some indigenous people fled at first sight of Europeans and why most of them later treated non-Indian immigrants deferentially. It may even explain why there is no record of a Dungeness Klallam counterattack on HBC.[29] However, such cautiousness should not be read as a concession that the foreigners possessed power greater than anything native people had or might later obtain. In local logic, the probability that King George men wielded dangerous powers had its converse: the King George men could assume that the Klallams also included people with formidable abilities yet to be demonstrated.

A related train of aboriginal thought further reduces the odds that Klallams and their neighbors interpreted events at Dungeness as proof of HBC supremacy. The beings who bestowed power allied themselves with individuals rather than groups. Although family or community members sometimes had similar powers and used them in concert, indigenous people were not inclined to think of Klallams and King George men as corporate entities with collective power that could be measured and compared. They had no conceptual basis at all for weighing HBC or British strength against the combined strength of the people McLoughlin called Indians.[30]

Finally, prowess in war was only one of many attributes that commanded respect among Klallams and their neighbors. Early-nineteenth-century Klallams reportedly took pride in their reputation for pugnacity; but in village after village around Puget Sound, the most highly esteemed people were those able to promote peaceful relations, amass wealth, and enhance others' welfare. Much as Hudson's Bay employees understood that company power was based on more than cannons, indigenous people counted on varied talents to help them deal with King George men. Unquestionably, King George men had extraordinary powers, evidenced not only by their deadly weapons but also by their great riches. Nevertheless, many native people were more attracted to than intimidated by the fur traders. They dared to visit HBC posts because they saw opportunities to employ their own powers to advantage there and perhaps to obtain new powers.[31]

The prospect of advantageous trade gave native people and Britons alike such a strong incentive for peaceful relations that they devoted considerable effort to averting conflict. Evidently, they were usually able to convince each other of their benevolent intentions. The violence at Dungeness in 1828 was exceptional: two decades would pass before armed King George men and natives clashed again in the Puget Sound region.[32]

When HBC established a south Sound post in the spring of 1833, people in the vicinity seemed so accommodating that the traders did not hurry to fortify their structures, although they tried as always to project an intimidating image. William Fraser Tolmie, a young doctor new to the Pacific Northwest, initially kept five guns at his bedside for fear of Indian mayhem. He soon concluded that he could relax. Not long after he and McDonald set up shop near the mouth of the Nisqually River, seemingly

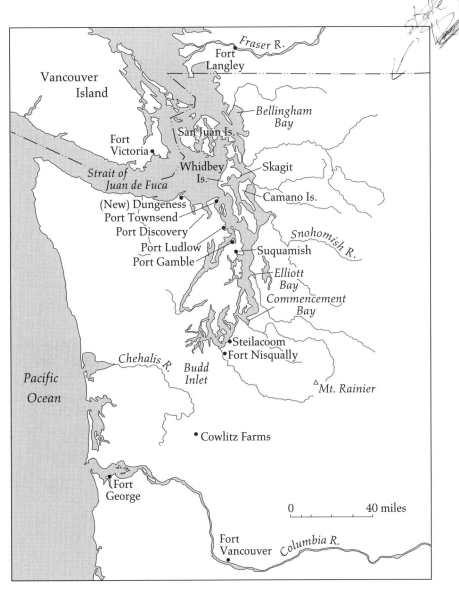

Map 2.   Sites of Hudson's Bay Company activity and early settlements.

friendly Indians were streaming in from all corners of the region. On many days the waterfront bustled with activity so benign that Tolmie compared it to a country fair. In July, when the traders relocated from the beach to the prairie above, two dozen men from several indigenous communities helped to carry goods up the hill, and the Britons rewarded them with tobacco and ammunition. By August Tolmie dared to make a several-day hike into the Cascade Mountains with only native men for company. In his journal he referred to the fellow hikers who gave him venison, dried cockles, berries, and clothing as "my Indians" and "my companions." "Cannot call them my attendants," he added.[33]

While Tolmie and his associates credited themselves with showing Indians that they had more to gain from amicable relations than from robbery or murder, native people likely entertained comparable self-congratulatory thoughts about their effect on King George men. But neither Indians nor King George men made a favorable impression by mechanically counterbalancing displays of power and offers to trade. Members of both groups also worked at ascertaining and catering to each other's desires and expectations.

To obtain beaver and other furs, King George men not only had to appear well-intentioned but also had to provide what native people wanted from them. It was clear that Indians wanted some British manufactures and that many Indians were willing to gather pelts in order to obtain the desired articles. But this appetite for trade had conditions and limits that Hudson's Bay personnel needed to discover. Indigenous people appraised both company merchandise and King George men's conduct according to their own values.

From the outset the patrons of Forts Langley and Nisqually would trade only for particular types of merchandise. On one occasion McDonald noted that the Snohomish would accept nothing but blankets. On another, a man with six beaver demanded shells or, failing shells, blankets of a specific kind. When the man learned that neither shells nor the stipulated blankets were available, he took his skins back and said he would wait. Natives were also disappointed with the first wares McDonald offered at Nisqually. They were less interested in the guns he had stocked than in blankets, textiles, molasses, and rum. They ignored the conspicuously displayed, printed shirts.[34]

Indigenous people also showed that they wanted relations with King George men to involve more than commercial trade. This they did in part by annoying Tolmie and his colleagues "with importunities for presents, before commencing to barter." Early visitors to Fort Nisqually questioned

McDonald's failure to bestow special clothing on their chief men. Trade proceeded more smoothly if such people received gifts. Some Indians also expected ceremonious hospitality, including invitations to eat and smoke with the King George men, and showed no interest in trading until granted these courtesies.[35]

The Indians' expectations could not have surprised Hudson's Bay. Elsewhere in America, gifts and hospitable gestures had become standard fur trade procedure because indigenous people insisted on it. When company personnel saw that similar notions of propriety prevailed in the Puget Sound area, they initiated many encounters with gratuities, received the most reliable native traders with considerable ceremony, and entertained presumed chiefs with food, drink, and tobacco.[36]

These HBC practices, first adopted to suit other peoples, were congenial to inhabitants of the Northwest because they did not conduct trade with a mercantile or capitalist model in mind. Merchants of nineteenth-century Europe tended to conceive of trade as an impersonal exchange of equivalents. In their emerging market economy, the connection between commerce and the social significance of the money generated by commerce had become relatively remote.[37] For the people who brought pelts to Forts Nisqually and Langley, on the other hand, economic activity created, symbolized, and followed from particular social relations. Acquiring precious items was desirable primarily because the items represented desirable personal relationships and afforded the means to establish more such relationships. To indigenous people, social ties were the real indicators of a person's worth.[38]

Commerce with King George men was an exciting avenue to prestige in local societies. Prestige followed from the ability to acquire property but also from ritually redistributing rather than accumulating property. The valuables people obtained in barter attested to their powers, especially if they had traveled and taken significant risks to make the exchanges. When they subsequently sponsored ceremonies where they gave away their acquisitions, native traders also earned coveted reputations for generosity and nobility. In addition, the fact that wealthy, apparently powerful foreigners wanted to associate with them enhanced their social standing.[39]

Indigenous people's skill at communicating what they wanted from King George men prompted McDonald to describe them as practiced traders with a keen eye for their own advantage and a shrewd sense of how to secure it. Again and again he grumbled that troublesome Indian customers subjected him to long harangues about company prices. They also insisted by their actions on helping to define the ground rules of commerce. Their tactics were varied. Two months after natives began bringing beaver to Nisqually, many decided to withhold their skins because the company had hiked its prices. The impasse continued for months.[40] Fort Nisqually staff also witnessed many dramas such as the one a man named Babyar staged when Tolmie refused to pay more than the standard rate for his best beaver. Babyar threw his blankets over the counter and rushed into the back room to repossess the skins he had already traded. Tolmie, by his own account,

> collared and bundled him out—he went to the door and called in his people who were lurking round the house, I now backed by Rendall stood firm, at same time endeavouring by soft words to pacify the savage, which was affected & he at once gave the beaver at the usual barter, his brother who shortly before had gone out in dudgeon now traded without trouble—we taking the precaution of locking them in— our weakness is apparent to the rascals & they take advantage of it.[41]

Although the British traders claimed several small triumphs of this kind, the vulnerability that Tolmie acknowledged constrained them to make concessions in turn. Until the 1840s, employees at regional HBC posts were few and handicapped by unfamiliarity with the country. Not only would they fail in business if they alienated the people around them; they would also go hungry. They needed Indians to supply food as well as skins. After a theft drove McDonald to forbid local people from landing at Fort Langley, he confessed in the official journal, "[T]he want of fresh provisions will compel us to concede a little in regard to this restriction & indulge them with some familiarity of intercourse that they before enjoyed."[42]

Hudson's Bay personnel adjusted to the exigencies of their situation and the desires of their new clientele. They altered their inventories, paid natives for fish and game, and accepted trade items valued solely or primarily by other natives, such as baskets, rush mats, and strings of shells. Both consciously and unwittingly, company traders also enabled their establishments to serve the social ends that prompted Indians to trade. For example, they tolerated people who came empty-handed, merely to pay social calls.[43]

To facilitate and simplify the process of accommodating each other's desires, natives and foreigners relied on intermediaries, such as members of the local elite. It was HBC policy to seek out indigenous men whose interests appeared to dovetail with the company's and to deal with local communities through those individuals as much as possible. McLoughlin therefore instructed his employees "to operate on the hopes and fears of the Native Chiefs by a system of distinctive rewards, bestowed on such as succeed in preserving the peace, and inducing their followers, to visit the Fort ... with the furs in their possession."[44]

At Fort Langley McDonald promptly set about identifying and cultivating the goodwill of influential individuals; he called them "friends" in his journal. Candidates usually nominated themselves, indicating by their behavior that special treatment was appropriate for people of their caliber. Within weeks McDonald had many "friends," including some he identified as Klallam, Snohomish, Skagit, and Suquamish chiefs. When Fort Nisqually opened, several of these men journeyed south, where they received the respectful reception they obviously expected.[45]

In Fort Nisqually's early years, visitors who could count on special attention included Waskalatchy, the mediator at Dungeness in 1828. Also known to King George men as "the Frenchman," Waskalatchy communicated his interest in good relations by emulating European dress and grooming, even sprouting a bushy beard. Another assiduously courted person was Tslalakum, usually identified in company records as a chief of the Suquamish. (Journal keepers spelled his name many ways, including Chilialucum.) Like Waskalatchy, Tslalakum acted as if he deserved special recognition, but he also solicited good relations with King George men by behaving in ways he must have thought consistent with their sensibilities.

Tolmie met Tslalakum a week after arriving at Nisqually. Advised not to interpret Tslalakum's possession of the late Alexander McKenzie's gun as evidence of hostility, Tolmie accompanied the chief to his Whidbey Island residence.[46] Afterward Tolmie wrote:

> This man's lodge presented a greater appearance of plenty than any yet seen—he is a chief of some note & well disposed towards the whites, displaying more hospitality than any other of the Indians met with on our journey, for he requested us to eat, on entering, while the others generally bargained for payment before giving what we asked.[47]

By a gesture that Tolmie interpreted as hospitality, Tslalakum helped to bridge the cultural distance between natives and newcomers. At the same time, he probably confirmed for his countrymen that he had valuable powers to amass surplus food and to command attention from wealthy foreigners.

Despite lingering apprehensions on both sides, the symbiotic relationship between Tslalakum and King George men flourished. At Nisqually a few weeks later, Tolmie gave Tslalakum a capote and trousers "as a reward for his services and general good conduct. Told him to visit the Klalums, and invite the Chief hither to trade their skins which he promised to undertake." During the next decade Tslalakum often undertook services the company needed and rewarded: carrying letters from post to post, offering protection from vengeful Klallams, relaying King George men's words to native people. In 1838 he even presented Fort Nisqually's chief officer with potatoes—a food that Hudson's Bay had introduced—grown by his own people.[48]

Already rich enough to be known in several communities, eager to increase his wealth through reciprocal relations with other rich men, and willing to innovate, Tslalakum epitomizes the natives HBC preferred to deal with. The resulting friendship enhanced the standing of both Tslalakum and the company gentlemen in local society. Even as the foreigners' association with the native man suggested their high estimation of him, it confirmed that the foreigners ranked with the local elite.

Besides men like Waskalatchy and Tslalakum, the intermediaries between HBC and local communities included native women on intimate terms with King George men. Many women became traders' consorts, often by arrangements they regarded as marriage. In their villages nearly everyone aspired to find a spouse outside the village, and the reasons to marry native outsiders also served as reasons to marry King George men. Intercommunity marriages could ease tensions, expand families' resources, and enhance status, as Frank Allen's ancestors knew. King George men, strange and suspect as they were, had access to desirable resources; and anyone whose close relative married one of them expected to benefit materially and socially as a result.[49]

By Tolmie's account, several local men saw him as a desirable in-law. In his first two months at Nisqually, he respectfully declined offers from three "chiefs" who "courted [his] alliance" for their daughters or sisters. Tolmie declared himself untempted by native women's "blandishments," but he understood why one handsome, charming upper-class woman had "made the round of many of the gentlemen." "While living with the whites," he wrote, "she was looked on as a personage of importance & possessing great influence among the Indians."[50]

Some company gentlemen succumbed to native women's "blandishments" or to proposals from the women's fathers more readily than Tolmie did, often with an expectation of collateral benefits. In order to maximize his economic and political leverage, McDonald was eager to create ties that would give local people a family interest in the company's fortunes. Early in his tenure at Fort Langley, he reported, "We have thought it good policy in Mr. Yale to form a family connection with them and accordingly he has now the Chiefs [*sic*] daughter after making them all liberal presents. ... "[51]

McDonald and Yale did not devise this policy. As other historians have documented, it was standard practice for gentlemen at HBC's American outposts to further their business objectives by marrying or consorting with indigenous women. Lower-ranking employees also cohabited with local women, although records of their arrangements are scarcer. Sprinkled through the Langley and Nisqually journals are incidental references to laborers with wives from surrounding populations. No doubt some laborers had briefer sexual encounters that no one recorded, including exploitative ones.[52]

As Hudson's Bay men and local people cohabited, traded, and tried to indulge each other's desires without forfeiting their own, they cleared and gradually expanded a figurative arena for their joint activities—a cultural space where people from dissimilar societies could serve their separate interests by observing common, specialized rules. Richard White has coined the term "middle ground" to describe a comparable culture of relations that developed in the Great Lakes region in the seventeenth century.[53]

The conventions of Puget Sound's trade culture, like most other unwritten codes of conduct, evolved through continuous testing and negotiation. By observing what happened when they hiked prices or boycotted the trading posts, angled for presents or tendered tobacco, the different peoples gradually determined how to act in each other's presence. Testing and negotiation were the order of the day when Tolmie discovered that Tslalakum's slaves had used a company canoe without permission. Tolmie "remonstrated" the chief, threatening to leave the area if Indians did not stop "pilfering." According to Tolmie's interpreter, this tirade provoked Tslalakum to threaten the white doctor in terms too foul to translate. The next day, however, Tolmie took pains to smooth things over in Tslalakum's terms: "Said did not believe him capable of doing the whites harm who looked on him as a brother—gave him some tobacco & the peace was made 'toute suite.' "[54]

The King George men tried to make certain standards of conduct nonnegotiable. Rather than indulging Indian mores regarding homicide and property rights, for example, they proposed to enforce rules of "civilized" society. One Sunday in 1833 Francis Heron, Fort Nisqually's new chief trader, made this intention known in a startling way.

> Mr. H. got Watskalatchet, Chilialucum, Babyar & Sialah (a brawny Soquamish ...) into his room with Lahalet as interpreter and told them to confess to him all their evil actions beginning with the murders &

next the thefts. Chilialucum began & confessed having murdered four men, but pleaded guiltless of any other crime. Watskalatchet none. Lachalet killed the murderer of his uncle & a slave of the former chief's. Scaldh [Sialah] in his youth slew a great chief & stole a fathom of very fine payaquas from the Klalum. Babyar, after coughing, blowing & humming frequently, declared himself guiltless of any evil action but recollecting himself shortly after said that he had killed 5 men & stolen their property, also stole two slaves. Chiatza[s]an being called in said he had for a long time been a physician & conductor of the religious ceremonies, that he had never done any harm, but afterwards acknowledged himself the murderer of five, (besides those killed by his medicines). The enormity of the crime of murder was then pointed out to the worthy assemblage & they were told it was as contrary to the Almighty's express command—they all promised, never again to commit the action, but in self defence & by way of expressing it more strongly on their minds they were made to mark with a pen a sheet of paper on which their names were written.[55]

Heron was one of several company leaders who also labored to change Indian behavior by religious proselytizing. Along with Tolmie, he and some of his successors delivered periodic lectures to crowds of natives at Nisqually, describing "what was proper for them to act in regard to our Divine Being."[56] Yet even this evangelizing was part of a give-and-take process. Heron and others may have preached because they were genuinely horrified at Indians' ignorance of Christian doctrine, but they chose to stress the Christian moral precepts most conducive to trade relations. When Chief Trader Kittson told assembled natives in 1834 "that they should endeavor to keep their hand from killing and stealing to love one another and pray only to the Great Master of Life," Tolmie said Kittson had laid out the "commandments most applicable to [the Indians'] state."[57]

From a modern standpoint, Heron's and Kittson's sermons seem arrogant and even unwisely provocative for members of a tiny crew dwelling in the midst of numerous strangers. For several reasons, however, it would be rash to assume that native people regarded King George men's moralizing either as disrespectful or as a defiant refusal to negotiate a mutually acceptable basis for relations.

First, the words that natives actually heard may have been substantially different from the messages Heron, Kittson, and Tolmie thought they sent. The Britons usually spoke in English to Indian interpreters whose comprehension they could not test. Sometimes their words passed through two translations, as when Waskalatchy claimed to understand the

Spokane language that Heron's wife spoke. At other times the only mutually intelligible language was a crude trade jargon known as Chinook. Tolmie complained that Indians could not understand his explanations of Christian doctrine because Chinook—"a vile compound of English, French, American & the Chenooke dialect"—was "a miserable medium of communication."[58] Rendered first in jargon and then in local languages, traders' sermons could as easily have sounded innocuous as arrogant. It was possible to say in Chinook, "When you come here to trade, do not steal or kill. You want to know about our spirit powers; we will tell you." It was harder, if not impossible, to impart British concepts of sin and barbarism.[59]

Second, people who heard the traders' religious and moral exhortations placed them in a context the speakers knew little about. To natives, the sight of eminent men counseling guests to behave properly was neither novel nor offensive. When a wealthy man invited outsiders to a ceremonial feast or giveaway, he admonished them to conduct themselves civilly, as the King George men did; and it was an honor to be in the audience at such a gathering. Thus, while Heron and Kittson may have intended to scold people they deemed inferior, their listeners may have thought they heard expressions of respect consistent with familiar ceremonial protocol. Even the men whose confessions Heron extracted probably believed themselves honored by their inclusion in a solemn British ritual.[60]

Third, Indians had entreated the King George men to "'wawa sacchali'"—that is, to speak about religion. A fervent interest in spirits prompted their requests. Believing as they did that "[e]very one of a man's characteristics, his appearance, his skills, his abilities, was dependent upon the nature of the supernatural he had obtained," native people undoubtedly wanted to hear about the "supernaturals" from whom Britons obtained their extraordinary wealth and skills.[61] As is evident from statements that Tslalakum made later, some Indians hoped to establish fruitful partnerships with spirits that only the foreigners knew about. In 1840, a few months after receiving religious instruction from French priests, Tslalakum told one of them that he had won a battle because his enemies did not know God, sang no canticles, and did not make the sign of the cross.[62]

The earliest traders induced few, if any, native people to embrace Christianity; but their Sunday rituals did inspire behavior that pleased the King George men and augmented the special protocol of trade relations. Several months after bringing the gospel to Indians around Nisqually, Heron boasted, "I have at length succeeded in altering their savage natures so far, that they not only listen with attention to what I tell them but actually practice it." The new practice Heron alluded to was observance of the Sabbath. Heron admitted, however, that Indians' Sunday observances took the form of dancing and chanting in a manner unknown to English churchgoers. Without the strange dances, he said, "they would think very little of what we say to them." Pragmatically, both Heron and Tolmie lowered their evangelistic sights and declared themselves satisfied that Indians were honoring Christianity in their own way.[63]

Accounts of Indians dancing on other occasions suggest that Tolmie and Heron were thinking wishfully when they characterized the "devotional dances" as Christian practice. One day in 1837, for instance, Fort Nisqually's clerk noted the arrival of Cowlitz Indians who "proceeded to La ah let's [Lahalet's] tent and there danced, receiving in return for the honor done about twelve fathoms of hyoquois [shell money]. They then proceeded to the beach and honored the Frenchman with the same, he gave them an old Blanket." When a Skagit party came in 1839, they danced first at the lodges of other Indians and later before the fort.[64] What motivated the dancers is an unsolved riddle. Maybe they did mean to honor their hosts, but maybe they aimed instead or in addition to attract or placate powerful local spirits or to invoke their own invisible helpers. In any case, the Britons construed the dancing as "a token of peace"; and like Lahalet and the Frenchman, they gave the dancers presents "for their good will." Thus the dancers accomplished something new along with any customary ends they served: they ingratiated themselves with King George men.[65]

However native people made sense of sermons and Sabbath rituals—and they probably did so in assorted ways—their responses became part of the decorum that eased relations between natives and newcomers. Thus, they and King George men gradually constructed a cultural edifice that bridged the gulf between them. It was a bridge fashioned of mutually agreeable etiquette, including gifts and favors, shared pipes and libations, interpreters and the Chinook jargon, bluffs and bargains, Sunday sermons and dances. All architects of the bridge made concessions to the perceived sensibilities of the people across the gulf, yet the result of their concessions was neither a merger of two societies nor the subordination of one to the other. What they built was a specialized, ever-widening structure located between societies. To use the bridge did not require a fundamental change of course; people could approach each other without renouncing their own distinctive habits and values. Strategic congruities in their values enabled them to benefit from each other's abilities and desires while pursuing separate agendas. Beyond either end of the bridge, there remained realms that people on the opposite side saw but dimly, if at all.

Although the people who constructed and used the bridge between cultures did not renounce their own cultures, they made choices that had transformative repercussions in their respective societies. In native societies, the King George men's commercial activities and novel customs inspired some people to rearrange their priorities or to innovate. The change thus precipitated was moderate, however—principally an increase in economic, social, and religious diversity.

Indigenous people already distinguished different population groups by the disparate resources and demands of the territories around their respective winter residences. Villagers on the salt water moved to somewhat different seasonal rhythms and stressed different social relations than did villagers on the mountain slopes. The fur trade exaggerated these contrasts because people along saltwater thoroughfares had more occasions than inland groups to engage in trading and brokering. Residents of the Nisqually area, who could also acquire European goods by providing the King George men with services, had incentives to adjust their habits in ways that differed from people even fifty miles away. As various communities innovated, they also borrowed each other's innovations; but participation in the fur trade probably diversified local practices more than it standardized them.[66]

The new trade also unsettled some social status classifications. Lack of industry, manners, and wealth had long marked a portion of native people as low-class; enslavement had condemned others to a life without honor.[67] But the new wealth that flowed from HBC into local communities lifted some lowly folk to greater social heights. While the company preferred to deal with people who were already well-to-do, it opened its stores to anyone who supplied furs or labor. By enriching humble individuals, this practice probably enabled some of them to escape subordinate positions in their households. Tales featuring characters who rose from humiliating poverty to admirable prosperity were favorites of native raconteurs. As reality more often resembled the folklore, there was reason to rethink some long-accepted relations.[68]

Additionally, Europeans' presence triggered diversification of religious practices and laid the basis for unprecedented conflict about spiritual matters. As Skagit shaman John Fornsby later said, some people believed the Christians, and some did not. Since wealth was a sign of religious fulfillment, the influx of wealth also gave new people a basis for claiming access to powerful spirits. Early in 1835, for example, a young Suquamish man attracted attention when he described receiving a "written paper" and eighteen blankets "from above." Rumors circulated that he had a coat covered with dollars and would distribute blankets annually to followers. The man's influence dissipated when someone discovered that he had gotten his riches not from heaven but from graves.[69]

Potentially the most subversive side effect of the fur trade, because of the new perspectives it gave people on themselves and their societies, was an enlarged regional network of intercommunity relations. Many formerly separate peoples converged on HBC forts, where they had occasion to initiate or expand relations with each other. Inevitably, the various villagers compared themselves to the people they met. Thus, their new and more frequent encounters with outsiders would have made them more conscious both of what they had in common with other peoples and of the traits that set them apart.

Following a day of brisk trade at Fort Nisqually, Tolmie could usually see a string of campfires along the beach. Congregated around the separate fires were groups of people he called Cowlitz, Klallams, Puyallups, Skagits, Suquamish, Snohomish, Twanas, and "petty Indians of the house." At times, HBC officers claimed to see no characteristics except language differentiating the named groups. After listing ten major "communities" in the Nisqually district, James Douglas told his superiors, "Under this variety of names we find no traces of national difference, and identity of language proves, beyond a doubt that they are, with the exceptions of [three groups], one and the same people. . . . " Yet residents of the different communities mistrusted and even waged war against each other, as Douglas lamented. He attributed the friction to specious tribal distinctions, but he was aware that clashes occurred within as well as across the "imaginary lines of demarcation which divide[d] the inhabitants of one petty stream, from the people living upon another."[70]

Before foreign traders appeared on Puget Sound, there were probably few, if any, occasions for large-scale, nonviolent gatherings of people who were complete strangers to each other. Hudson's Bay Company changed that. Visitors to Forts Langley and Nisqually found themselves camping near people from all corners of the district. On August 23, 1833, for example, Heron estimated the multitude around Fort Nisqually at eight hundred souls. They belonged, he thought, to eight tribes. Many times after that the fort's log noted the simultaneous presence of peoples from widely separated territories. On one day in 1835 Indians arrived from Spokane country, three hundred miles to the east, and from the Clackamas and John Day Rivers, south of the Columbia.[71]

The prospect of confronting strangers or enemies worried HBC's customers. Tension mounted in the camps around Fort Nisqually when the Spokane, Clackamas, and John Day groups appeared. Visitors who had friends near a trading post could expect protection, but callers who lacked such connections often stayed no longer than necessary to take care of business.[72] On the other hand, the desire to trade regularly with the King George men was a compelling motive for making friends with HBC's other patrons.

The Nisqually journal affords glimpses of the means that strangers employed to allay their suspicions of each other. Many visitors did not approach the King George men until they had paid their respects in dance and gifts to natives residing in the area. Intercommunity gambling, a regular pastime around the forts, was an alternative to violent rivalries. Even so, smoldering ill will sometimes threatened to flare up. Then ambassadors would shuttle between the antagonists until they agreed on a way to cool off, usually an exchange of property.[73]

Often, too, peace came with an exchange of people. Marriages could be the inception and guarantee of harmonious relations between alien communities, as Frank Allen attested. By acquiring in-laws in foreign territory, a family also gained a safe-conduct pass and the right to gather sustenance there. A Skagit or Suquamish man who wished to trade at Fort Nisqually thus had good reason to marry his daughter or sister to a local resident. Moreover, a man flush with beaver or trade blankets had the means to arrange a good marriage. It makes sense that Lahalet, a prominent Nisqually man, acquired several new wives during the heyday of the fur trade.[74]

As HBC posts attracted throngs of people, they became venues for intertribal diplomacy that often had little or no relation to the fur trade itself. Natives traveled to the forts not only to barter with King George men but also to arrange the ransoms of captured relatives or to negotiate alliances with other village groups. It may even be that some visits to the HBC store were incidental to such maneuvering.[75]

At times, company officers watched with amused detachment the complex interactions going on around them. They knew, however, that Indians expected them to preserve peace among sojourners at their doorstep. Native visitors often asked for assurances that they would not be molested. So the King George men did accept a degree of responsibility for relations among their customers. Although they usually did not grant requests to camp inside company compounds, they otherwise assumed the role played by native hosts at intercommunity gatherings: they tried to ease tensions and ensure safety among those who gathered at their behest. Activated more by a desire to preserve conditions needed for commerce than by a hope of earning their halos, King George men counseled and cajoled people to avoid conflict, intervened to prevent acts of retribution, and encouraged diplomatic missions. Their efforts—especially the goodwill purchased with their merchandise—sometimes promoted new alliances between indigenous groups.[76]

Parochial and divided as native villagers seemed, HBC officers lumped them all in a single category and told them so. When Heron preached to congregations composed of people from various settlements, he addressed them either as Indians or by the Chinook jargon word "siwash."[77] In the face of their diversity and mutual suspicion, these labels urged them to consider that there were only two kinds of people: Indians (siwash) and others. But did this classificatory scheme make sense to the sundry people? Probably not in the way that it does to twentieth-century Americans.

Although indigenous people did distinguish King George men from everyone else in the region, most of what they saw and knew in the 1830s gave lie to the idea that "Indians" constituted a single, contrasting category. The foreign traders' strange habits and the changes precipitated by their presence must have provoked many natives to think in new ways about social categories they had long taken for granted, and their ruminations surely included comparisons of natives' and foreigners' capabilities. But such comparisons did not yet amount to the racialized ranking of peoples that the British traders encouraged by their labels and their sermons.

Some scholars reason that Indians' eagerness to please the King George men and learn about Christianity reflects a loss of confidence in their own ideological heritage and a corresponding acknowledgment of European superiority. Thinking in Europeans' racial terms would follow easily from the adverse comparison. This argument is seductive because Puget Sound natives had recently suffered catastrophes capable of daunting anyone. First, thousands of people had discovered that their powers were insufficient to defeat new agents of illness and death loose in the land. So many natives had sickened and died from imported pathogens that some could not make sense of their afflictions and loss in the usual ways. Mortality estimated at 20 to 80 percent had also disrupted kinship networks and subsistence activities on which individuals' well-being and self-confidence depended.[78] In addition, bellicose outsiders had robbed many local communities of their sense of security. The maritime fur trade had enriched, armed, and emboldened natives of Vancouver Island and regions farther north. Cowichan, Kwakiutl, and other northern raiders descended with increasing frequency on the more pacific peoples south of the Strait of Juan de Fuca. The Allens' ancestors told of a time when Kwakiutl attacks prompted a meeting of warriors from ten places around the Sound. All but two of the communities had lost loved ones and property to the northerners.[79]

The fact that King George men were less vulnerable than local people to epidemics and northern raiders was reason enough to seek the foreigners' advice about spirits. And because the King George men's spirit allies were reportedly capable of causing or curing the new illnesses, some natives deemed it prudent to propitiate the Christians' deity. Not surprisingly, some also appealed to the King George men to treat their illnesses or accepted smallpox vaccinations.[80]

The traders occasionally flattered themselves that sick and fearful Indians could see the superiority of English religion and medicine, but these thoughts were foolish. The people who sought medical help from King George men did so not because they conceded the categorical superiority of English knowledge but because it was their custom to consult doctors outside their communities. In consulting Britons, they did not forsake local shamans. Chief Trader Kittson spent a sleepless night listening to the singing and drumming of natives who were doctoring a company laborer's wife. Afterward he wrote, "Sometime I have endeavored to stop the business but believe to no purpose as she is bent on getting blowed by her countrymen." Although the woman had asked him for medicine, he added, she credited native doctors with any relief she got. The sick woman had good reason to hedge her bets. Kittson appeared to relieve one man's sore throat with Dover's powder, blistering, and foot baths, but he was powerless to prevent the deaths of his two children when disease later scourged the fort. Had he sought the help of native doctors, indigenous people would not have construed his act as an admission that English medicine was inferior.[81]

In sum, neither curiosity about Christianity nor appeals for British medicine constitute strong evidence that indigenous people compared themselves with Europeans in the 1830s and found themselves or their beliefs wanting. It is equally or more plausible that their approaches to the traders were consistent with adherence to traditional beliefs and values. If they sought out Europeans in the hope of learning about spirits with awesome powers, they acted on familiar precepts. Furthermore, their actions are testimony to their continuing self-confidence; for exposing oneself to powerful spirits was not a deed of the fainthearted.

Several other factors make it unlikely that native people compared themselves wholesale with "whites" and judged themselves deficient. The first is that the foreigners, for all their amazing accomplishments, fell short of many indigenous standards of merit. At least one native dialect reflected this judgment. According to a South Puget Sound man born in the 1840s, his people's term for Englishmen or white people derived from the word for "left off" and thus connoted "something lacking."[82]

We can infer some of the King George men's perceived shortcomings from what nineteenth-century indigenous people considered proper. That most of the traders came without wives and families would have marked them as odd. They also lacked knowledge of the country's natural bounty and were unaware of the rules for using and renewing that bounty. Not only were they ignorant of fishing techniques, for example, but until local people educated them they did not understand the importance of ensuring the salmon's return by treating the first fish of the year ceremonially.[83] In other respects, too, the foreigners showed a lack of good advice, the foundation of good character. Their important men often appeared lazy, bossing dependents instead of working alongside them. They did not employ proper, self-deprecating expressions when addressing eminent outsiders. Some did not keep their tempers in check, as well-bred men and women did. Occasionally, Heron and Tolmie flew into rages, beating company workers. These facts should make us wonder why there are no records of indigenous people urging moral reform on the King George men.[84]

Relations with King George men were unlikely to disturb indigenous people's conceptions of themselves for a second reason. Those relations had not thwarted most natives' aspirations but instead had provided new opportunities to show off the abilities they took pride in. Specifically, since anyone who supplied the foreigners with desired commodities or services could tap the fount of wealth they controlled, many indigenous people had become richer than ever before; and wealth, after all, confirmed their status.[85]

Few native people would have worried that they had discovered new avenues to wealth and prestige by turning away from proven, traditional ones. As groups, they had not forgotten the powers and practices that had long sustained them. They had not forsaken fishing, clam digging, berry picking, root digging, and reciprocal feasting in order to trade with King George men. Instead, most people fit calls at HBC posts into time-honored seasonal rounds, swapping beaver for blankets on their way to or from fishing places or ceremonies. Salmon migrations rather than the desires of foreign traders determined when they fished and when they traded. Besides, if some individuals wished to trap beaver or work for the King George men, they could do so without disrupting other gainful family pursuits. Indeed, the wealth they obtained that way could enhance their households' productive capacity by making it possible to add wives and slaves.[86]

Intermarriage was a third factor that discouraged native people from viewing themselves as a single group inferior to the foreigners. By linking the once-separate groups, marriages made it hard to create and maintain a ranked distinction between two races of people. In the eyes of natives at least, the families of King George men's brides acquired a status comparable to that of their new in-laws. Furthermore, amorous ties generated other social ties that were extensive and tangled. McDonald, frustrated when he tried to prevent Indians from entering Fort Langley to visit his men's wives, complained that it was hard to keep the family connections "within due bounds."[87] Marriage alliances also blurred the lines between natives and foreigners when King George men's wives gave birth to children who could identify with either or both kinds of people.

The babies joined a populace that was already heterogeneous, and heterogeneity was a fourth factor deterring comparisons of native people as a whole with the King George men as a whole. Neither HBC staff nor the indigenous population acted as a unit. Although HBC arguably had its own culture, it hardly constituted a cohesive society. The company expected employees to observe a single code of conduct, fit into a well-defined social structure, and interpret events by reference to principles that guided the English elite; but HBC personnel were not all paragons of the British merchant class. King George men differed in place of origin or ethnic lineage, religious persuasion, and economic status, and their differences often set them against each other. John McLoughlin, for instance, had a reputation for abusing the Canadians who made up a majority of his workforce.[88]

Occasionally McLoughlin's restless subjects reached out to native people for leverage against their tormentors in the company. Tolmie once beat a laborer, for example, in the belief that the man had spoken ill of Tolmie to an Indian.[89] Conversely, the indigenous people, with even less reason to unite than the HBC workforce, did not act in solidarity toward the King George men. Events during the 1828 expedition to Dungeness demonstrated that individuals and groups in the native population would create or use ties with the foreigners as leverage in their rivalries with each other.

Both before and long after the first HBC fort went up near Puget Sound, the region's native inhabitants identified primarily with close kin

fellow residents of their winter villages. In many respects, rela-
ng the myriad autonomous villages resembled modern interna-
.... affairs. Both enmities and affiliations were negotiable and fluid.
Even amicable relations involved uneasiness and suspicions that did not
disappear with mutually satisfying trade or intermarriage. Maintaining
amity required recurring tests and reaffirmations of the bases for friendly
association. Understandings had to be periodically renewed in symbolic
ways. This had long been true of relations among Skagits, Klallams, Snohomish, and other natives. After the 1820s it was also true of relations
between indigenous peoples and King George or Boston men.

The evolving rituals of the Puget Sound fur trade were in effect a diplomatic protocol that made regular relations between dissimilar peoples
possible. An eclectic blend of indigenous customs and Hudson's Bay Company practices, the rituals enabled many people around Puget Sound to establish and maintain useful new partnerships. Most people who did form
such partnerships—natives as well as newcomers—had good reason to
congratulate themselves. They had served their respective communities'
perceived interests while meeting their individual needs for status and
material well-being. Paradoxically, by collaborating with exotic people in a
shared arena of activity, they had also reinforced the foundations of their
own community pride and thus their sense of identity. Finally, they had
acquired training that would serve them well during years to come, when
occasions for relations between dissimilar peoples would multiply.

2 Settlers and Indians
Intertwined Peoples

By 1841 large ships were a familiar sight on Puget Sound and the Strait
of Juan de Fuca. When the sloop *Vincennes* entered the Strait in May
that year, natives paddled out to it in canoes laden with items for sale.
The sailors gave them red paint, gunpowder, hooks, tobacco, and clothing
for their fish and venison but did not buy their furs. The sloop's captain,
Charles Wilkes, later remarked, "[These Indians] seem much disposed to
trade and barter and are greatly surprised that so large a ship should
want no furs, and it is difficult to make them understand the use of a
Man of War."[1]

The man-of-war was in use as the flagship of an American exploring
expedition. For two months after this encounter, men on the four vessels
under Wilkes's command inspected and mapped Puget Sound and its environs. Like the English explorers who had done the same thing almost fifty
years earlier, the Americans came at the behest of their country's governors to see whether the Pacific Northwest offered desired opportunities.
But the visions that inspired American leaders in 1841 differed from the
visions that had attracted outsiders to the region since the Britons found
it. Rather than lucrative trade and coexistence with native people, Wilkes's
sponsors foresaw displacement of those people; for the United States was a
nation that had limited citizenship to "whites" and defined itself largely in
opposition to "Indians."[2]

The Wilkes expedition inaugurated the decade when Americans began
settling around Puget Sound. Although most of the settlers dreamed of
installing a white society that would supplant or suppress Indians, their
goal was unattainable during the 1840s and early 1850s, while their numbers were small. Instead, they found themselves drawn into the system of
exchanges and mutual deference that linked the region's assorted commu-

nities without compromising the communities' autonomy or distinctiveness. The settlers' novel activities and attitudes induced changes in natives' activities and views of Bostons; but not until the mid-1850s did Americans' growing population and cockiness generate a need for a new paradigm of human relations in the region.

Although Charles Wilkes was intent on expanding the boundaries of scientific knowledge more than the boundaries of the United States, he represented a restless people who were moving pell-mell from the Atlantic seaboard into far-flung areas of North America. As early as the 1820s some of his countrymen had called for settlement of the Pacific Northwest, touting it as a farmer's paradise. By 1840 several score Americans had migrated to Oregon's Willamette Valley and were encouraging others to follow. Wilkes's sponsors hoped, among other things, that he would identify sites for American commercial ports in the region.[3]

For the sake of prospective colonists, Wilkes noted the disposition of the people they would find in the Northwest. By most accounts Wilkes was a suspicious martinet, not likely to see any fellow humans in a rosy light. His negative preconceptions about "Indians" and the nature of his backers' aspirations further darkened his view of Northwest natives. Where Hudson's Bay Company had seen people eager for profitable commerce, Wilkes saw "poor creatures" who made nuisances of themselves by soliciting favors.[4]

"[F]ew can imagine [their] degradation ... ," Wilkes said of people fishing near Port Discovery. "[T]hey pretend to no decency in their clothing if a blanket alone may be entitled to this name. ... " Their "gutteral language [*sic*]" and "fishy smell" were disgusting. A look at their village convinced Wilkes that they were "lazy lounging & filthy." The Indians around Nisqually, he complained, were addicted to stealing, demanded food as a condition of providing services, and gambled through the night, then slept all day. Wilkes also resented the natives' acumen as traders. "[T]hey are not slow in perceiving your wants, or the dilemma you may be placed in—which they view with becoming sang froid ... ," he wrote. "[They] are beyond measure the most provoking fellows to bargain with that I have ever met. ... "[5]

Wilkes rated Northwest Indians inferior in stature and strength to those east of the Rockies and pronounced the natives of northern Oregon "among the ugliest of their race." The native men who guided him from Nisqually to the Columbia River looked good, however, compared with the naked Port Discovery fishers. They wore faded European clothing, and "their free & easy carriage on horseback with a few ribbons and the cock's feathers stuck in their caps gave them an air of hauteur and self esteem that was not unpleasing."[6]

In turn, at least one native man found the Americans' air of self-esteem pleasing. Slugamus Koquilton watched Wilkes's crew celebrate Independence Day at Nisqually. Fifty years later he recalled the ceremonies in loving detail. First the soldiers fired their guns about ten times; then, dressed in white and stepping as one person, they marched four abreast to the top of the bluff. Behind a man with a flag came others playing drums and horns. More marchers hauled up cannons, pans, dishes, tables, and food. At a place the Indians recommended, the soldiers and other whites feasted, then invited the natives to partake. Koquilton's account differs from Wilkes's in only one significant respect. According to Wilkes, several hundred Indians looked on in wistful silence as the Americans ate; according to Koquilton, the Indians "had a splendid time and went away saying that Wilkes and the Boston men were good."[7]

In the language of pageantry, the Americans had introduced themselves to the local people. Whether or not native witnesses were as amazed as Wilkes imagined, they surely saw the ceremonies as a representation of the Bostons' unique attributes or powers. Yet they could not decipher the Americans' most portentous message because it was encoded in English oratory. Dr. John Richmond, an American missionary living near Fort Nisqually, welcomed the visitors as harbingers of a society that would replace the one the Indians knew. " 'The time will come,' " Richmond reportedly predicted, " 'when these hills and valleys will have become peopled by our free and enterprising countrymen. ... ' " The cities, farms, and factories that Americans built would effect the foreordained expansion of a powerful nation. The premises of American civilization and social order would then preempt all other bases for human relations in the region. By making the truths of Christianity known to the savage children of the wilderness, Richmond said, Americans would " 'fit them to act creditably their destined parts as citizens of the Republic.' "[8]

If Richmond's words had been translated for listening natives, his forecast of drastic change might not have startled them. Rumors of Bostons' impacts on indigenous societies to the east had probably reached the Northwest. However, to make sense of Richmond's vision, native people could refer only to what they knew. They could interpret some of the Independence Day rituals by analogy to displays of power and generosity at their own multivillage ceremonies, but they could not then imagine how the Bostons conceived of power or social relations. The villagers of Puget Sound had no exposure to nation-states, institutionalized religion, law, or race-based privilege. Looking back at 1841 from a world that seemed the fulfillment of Richmond's prophecy, Koquilton said, " 'Long before that time the Indians did not know about anything of that kind. The country did not belong to any nation ... ; it was for all the people.' "[9]

If native people missed the import of Richmond's speech, others in the crowd surely did not. Hudson's Bay officers were present to hear his insinuation that their mission and their arrangements with Indians were obsolescent—a cheeky claim from a man who had HBC to thank for his supplies and personal safety, not to mention that day's dinner of roast ox. For at least another decade, however, the King George men and their native allies could afford to laugh at Richmond's augury. Indeed, it was Richmond who soon abandoned his mission, while HBC and its relations with indigenous peoples continued to thrive.[10]

The American explorers saw, without fully comprehending, many of the protocols that facilitated the relations of British traders and natives. Soon after arriving in the region, Wilkes solicited an Indian's services as a courier. The man knew that the situation called for special etiquette.

> [T]he first thing he did, when brought into the cabin, was to show me a cross and repeat his ave, which he did with great readiness and apparent devotion; but he burst into loud laughter as soon as he had finished. ... He and I made many efforts to understand each other, but without much success, except so far as the transmission of the letter to Fort Nisqually, and the reward he was to receive on his return.[11]

With Christian signs and a few English words, this man invited Wilkes onto the cultural bridge where natives and foreigners usually met. Wilkes and his crew noticed other customs that people observed when on that middle ground: the hospitable acts, bold demands, and pretended indifference of people engaged in trade; the Indians' adoption of European clothing for meetings with whites; the use of names such as King George, Boston, Klallam, or Snohomish to identify group affiliations.[12]

The native courier's availability for hire was a girder of the bridge between cultures. Wilkes, his vision hampered by a conviction that Indians were lazy, failed to note that opportunities for compensated labor were a familiar and expanding basis of indigenous people's association with foreigners. Natives had long known that the King George men at Nisqually would reward them for unloading cargo, cutting wood, constructing buildings, washing clothes, keeping house, or tending food crops and livestock; and three years before Wilkes's voyage, Fort Nisqually's raison d'être had changed to one that required more such labor. Because of disappointing fur intake, HBC had rededicated the post to farming and consigned it to a new subsidiary, the Puget Sound Agricultural Company.[13] After that, natives seeking employment came in even greater numbers from a wider area. Some contracted individually to perform services; others worked in what the traders called gangs or mobs. Annual sheepshearing drew scores of families from as far as the Snohomish River. By the 1840s gang supervisors and the fort's regular staff included several Indians from the Puget Sound area.[14]

The gestures that seemed to identify Wilkes's courier as a Roman Catholic were more recent contributions to the cultural structure linking native and European societies. French priests had opened a mission at Cowlitz Prairie, near the Columbia, in 1839. They attracted so much attention from residents of the Puget Sound area that their rituals were well known there by 1841. Waskalatchy and Tslalakum, among others, went south to hear the foreign shamans' advice and passed the lessons on to friends and relatives at home. Tips from converted Indians, such as traders' wives, also helped natives to ingratiate themselves with the black-gowned men. When Father F. N. Blanchet first visited Whidbey Island in 1840, hundreds of men, women, and children astonished him by crossing themselves and singing hymns.[15]

This lively interest in Catholic rites and talismans initially elated the missionaries, but further contacts with their prospective parishioners were sobering. Blanchet said that he learned not to rely on Indians' first demonstrations of belief because they did not give up the customs of their ancestors. Standing between them and their transformation into Christians, he wrote, were idolatry, superstition, and sinful practices such as polygamy and gambling. The babel of local languages also impeded Indians' reformation. If his words "penetrated into the understanding of the natives," Blanchet noted, it was often through three or four interpreters in sequence. Sometimes the only verbal tool for penetrating natives' understanding was the lamentably deficient Chinook jargon.[16]

The priests' use of the jargon for hymns and biblical history lessons is evidence that they who came to teach savages became students themselves, taking lessons on how to fit into their novices' social world. From indigenous people and Hudson's Bay personnel, the missionaries learned the categories and conventions that ordered the strange society they had entered. Blanchet soon discovered, for example, that one "odd" custom would be an obligatory "ceremony of etiquette" whenever he visited native communities. He had to guess at its purpose.

To honor a person of distinction they line up to offer their hand, one after the other, from the first to the last. I too had to undergo a similar ceremony on the part of about fifty persons, all in full dress, ornamented with feathers of every color, ears and nose adorned with rich haiqua shells, face speckled with red in diverse ways, eyes encircled in various colors, cheeks painted in all fashions. Even the women observe this custom. They carry their children on their backs, and hurry to seize the hand of the little ones as soon as they have touched that of the *chief*, in the conviction that they are transmitting to these an assured blessing.[17]

When Father Modeste Demers unintentionally slighted an eminent Klallam man, his native companions told him how to make amends. Demers declared himself a quick study. "This adventure," he wrote, "made me understand the importance of treating with caution the susceptibilities of the chiefs and to attract their consideration, in order to win to God the tribes that they govern." Blanchet discerned that gifts would attract chiefs' consideration. When he conducted services, he distributed tobacco, rosaries, and crosses "according to the quality of the persons [receiving them]."[18]

Both priests and natives sought to explain the missionaries by reference to known indigenous roles. Blanchet was careful to travel in the company of "chiefs" because "[s]uch a noble escort was well fitted to arouse in the natives a high idea of the distinguished character of the great chief of the French, or *papa le Plete*, as they call him." The same logic motivated some native "chiefs" to associate with the priests. They reciprocated the attention paid to their "susceptibilities" by rounding up escorts, canoe crews, and respectful audiences for the blackrobes. When a wealthy Skagit man recruited two hundred people to raise a structure where a priest could conduct mass, he probably considered himself a cosponsor of ceremonies analogous to the dances and feasts that validated Skagit social relations.[19]

Keeping company with eminent men made the priests eligible for another respected role in indigenous society, that of mediator. Blanchet received on-the-job training in local dispute resolution methods when he visited Tslalakum's village in 1840. Hours before he arrived, Klallam and "Skekwamish" warriors had clashed nearby. As people from various villages gathered to see the priest, a Klallam man initiated reconciliation efforts. After Blanchet also made a plea for peace, the natives included him in negotiations that arranged an exchange of guns to cover the lives lost in war.[20]

In the Nisqually district there were newcomers besides the priests to incorporate and educate during the 1840s. Some were farmers. The Puget Sound Agricultural Company, hoping to increase its output and strengthen Britain's claim to northern Oregon, installed a number of tenants on lands between the Nisqually and Puyallup Rivers. One was Joseph Heath, a middle-aged Englishman who moved into a crude cabin near a village on Steilacoom Creek, six miles north of Fort Nisqually. When Heath appeared in 1844 with a few Indians of unidentified origin, other natives set up camp around him. For the next four years his enterprise, his diet, and often his mental health depended on relations with the people he called "my Indians." Heath's need for native workers and suppliers mixed with his distaste for their strange ways to form a volatile brew of emotions, which he poured onto the pages of his diary. The diary shows that indigenous people's relationship to settlers such as Heath was consistent with roles or social categories they were accustomed to, even though it induced them to alter some habits and learn some new skills.[21]

Joseph Heath sometimes portrayed himself teaching Indians acceptable new habits and roles. He reviled and occasionally punished them for being idle, borrowing his horse without asking, taking in "hangers-on," or gambling. He struggled especially to make their habits conform to his need for labor and his notions about property relations. Early in 1847 he wrote, "Detected two of my people stealing, one (taking) wheat and the other, potatoes. (I) try everything in my power to make them comfortable and pay and feed them liberally and yet cannot prevent them from stealing. But please Goodness, (I) will do it or go without Indian labourers."[22]

However, Heath realized that his workers could do without him better than he could do without them. His dependency was a reason to suppress his urge to dictate the terms of relations or remake Indians in an English image. A typical diary entry reads: "(The) house is full of Indians. (I) shall break out soon and lay my stick about them. They cannot keep away. (I) do not wish to offend them, as they are the only labourers I have to depend upon." For this reason, when his most valuable helper took umbrage at a scolding and threatened to leave, Heath appeased the man. Unable to provide all of his laborers' subsistence, he acquiesced in a schedule that reflected their need to fish, plant their own potatoes, doctor their sick, or adjust affairs with other natives. For the sake of their services and companionship, he often tolerated their invasions of his privacy as well.[23]

The strain of coping with Indians' inconvenient priorities and tests of his power aggravated Heath's irritability, already heightened by ill health. Hardly noticing that his workers likewise struggled to accommodate his strange expectations, he repeatedly lost his temper. Because he regretted these outbursts, however, he learned to make amends as the locals did. One day, for instance, Heath shot an Indian's dog for harassing his fowl and thus provoked a retaliatory slaying of his favorite terrier. He escalated the conflict by going with a loaded gun to the Indian's lodge and commencing to tear it down. The man's father, wrote Heath, "came out and wished us to make peace by an exchange of presents, which I would not accede to, demanding his gun as the only means of satisfying me. Ambassadors ... going between us the whole day. ... " The next day, after refusing to give the younger man a shirt and blanket for the gun and after threatening to withdraw his friendship, Heath received the weapon. He purported to draw from this sequence of events a proper British lesson: in a fight "whether [he] should be their master or their slave," he had shown that he would "not be trifled with." Yet a few days later, not wanting "to drive Matters to extremity," he gave the same Indian a blanket. While he told himself that he had established his right to punish the man as he would a servant, native people would have inferred that Heath had learned the proper way to restore relations of reciprocity.[24]

Heath also learned local methods of conducting relations with outsiders. Animosities between his workers and other natives, usually stemming from murders of or by shamans, repeatedly required his attention. Natives from other districts, bent on vengeance and evidently identifying Heath with "his Indians," threatened his life several times. Twice he armed the people around him against expected attacks. He described how he averted violence in one instance:

> The Snoqualmie Indians arrived upon a war expedition, the same who have so long been talking of taking my head to adorn their lodges. (I) went to them as soon as they arrived, without any arms but a stout walking stick, and told them plainly that if they committed any depredations I should fire upon them. (We had) a long peaceable talk. (I) gave them some tobacco, after which they left, *only* stealing a couple of canoes from the beach.[25]

Heath detected and bowed to other social conventions of his adopted country. He realized that natives—residents of nearby villages as well as his workers—expected him to host a feast when his larders were full. He also learned, to his dismay, that good relations had to be periodically renewed with reciprocal gifts and favors. "(I) don't want to have presents made me," he wrote; "always pay too dearly for them."[26]

As Heath indulged some of his neighbors' desires, he often rationalized his actions in English terms; but because English terms had no meaning for Indians, he also felt free at times to dispense with the usages of his homeland. No doubt Heath's workers understood him in parallel fashion, sometimes comparing him to what they knew, sometimes recognizing his foreignness and realizing that it allowed or required them to depart from custom. Many of Heath's habits would have disgusted or puzzled indigenous people, just as theirs did him. They who bathed every morning would have been appalled that he went five months without a bath. Well-bred natives no doubt sniffed at his angry outbursts, his often-inhospitable treatment of Indian visitors, and his selfish claim to food that others had helped to produce. Nonetheless, they had uses for this strange, indecent man. His ability to organize productive activities, his access to King George men and English goods, and his willingness to protect them and intercede with enemies equipped him to fill a role like that of indigenous leading men. Skagit natives who saw this invited Heath to farm in their country. By remaining at Steilacoom instead, he effectively served as a household head for the people there.[27]

When native people perceived an advantage and no overbalancing disadvantage in doing what Heath wanted, they were willing and remarkably efficient workers. Additionally, in order to maintain their relationship with Heath, they sometimes acted as he required even if it meant departing from custom. On the whole, they could accommodate Heath's needs without surrendering their guiding beliefs and conceptions of themselves. Yet while their motivations were probably traditional, Heath's workers had entered a new relationship. By requiring them to change some habits, that relationship had the potential to change some of their ideas, including their ideas about themselves in relation to others.[28]

By the time Joseph Heath died early in 1849, variations on the themes of his diary were being played out at cabins nearby. Some cabins sheltered former HBC servants, but others housed Americans. A small party of American men and women came to Nisqually in the fall of 1845. The next spring, as the newcomers were building homes in the vicinity, Britain abandoned efforts to preempt American claims there—indeed, everywhere south of the forty-ninth parallel. That June the United States formally assumed sovereignty in the region, which became part of Oregon Territory, organized two years later. These developments encouraged more Americans to scout Puget Sound as a prospective home but did not immediately change relations between natives and immigrants. The prevailing terms of coexistence seemed as applicable to Bostons as to other peoples; so natives and King George men set about making those terms known to the newcomers.[29]

Forty years later A. B. Rabbeson recalled that HBC took advantage of his and other Americans' need for provisions and help by exacting a promise: the new settlers would not abuse or deal unfairly with Indians and would "be guided by their customs and usages." Under pressure from Dr. Tolmie, the HBC officer in charge at Nisqually, the Americans also agreed to pay Indians at the company's rates:

One day's work	1 cotton handkerchief
One week's work	1 hickory shirt
One month's work	1 3-pt. blanket
Use of canoe to Nisqually and back	1 handkerchief
Each Indian in canoe	1 handkerchief
1 deer ham	1 load powder and ball
3 ducks	1 load powder and shot
1 bbs. cranberries	5 yds. white cotton cloth
50 Chinook salmon	1 hickory shirt
1 good horse	1 musket

The only source of merchandise to pay Indians was HBC; and in order to obtain that merchandise, the Americans—their initial efforts to farm frustrated by drought and frost—had to sell shingles or their own labor to the company.[30]

Whether or not Rabbeson's tale is literally true, it embodies an important historical truth. Because the first American settlers on Puget Sound were few, isolated, and needy, they had to accept the region's existing social arrangements. In the wind they may have heard echoes of Richmond's 1841 Independence Day oration. They may have imagined themselves the vanguard of those "free and enterprising countrymen" who would transform the territory and its social categories. But Richmond was no longer there to cheer them on, and from the vantage of their crude dwellings in a land populated by fish-eating Indians and self-satisfied Britons, they may have suspected that Richmond's vision was a mirage. As they bartered for salmon or toiled at Fort Nisqually, the Americans knew that their well-being and probably their lives depended on fitting in.[31]

To native eyes, the immigrants of 1845 and the few score Bostons who came later that decade probably seemed like additional subordinates of the King George men. To envious Americans, on the other hand, it was Indians who appeared to be under the Britons' thumbs. Not only did Indians prize HBC goods, but many also submitted to company discipline in order to earn those goods.[32] With apparent impunity, the company and its tenants also plowed, fenced, and pastured animals on prairies that had long furnished natives with roots, berries, acorns, and grass for horses.

Indian subservience to HBC was largely in the eyes of American beholders. Like Joseph Heath, the King George men were determined to prove themselves the masters of their own establishment, but they still needed and had to earn natives' goodwill. When they caught individual natives killing stock, taking tools, or menacing company personnel, Fort Nisqually's managers imposed corporal punishment and demanded restitution. On the other hand, they continued to distribute gratuities to native workers and to honor friendly "chiefs" with gifts and favors. In 1846 Tolmie flogged and imprisoned two Indians for skinning an ox, but a few days later he yielded to a headman's request that he free the culprits, taking a rifle and pistol in payment either for the favor or for the animal.[33]

Neither floggings nor HBC's use of land provoked organized retaliation from native people. While such docility could indicate fear of British powers, it is also consistent with a perception that the benefits of accommodating the King George men continued to outweigh the drawbacks. Perhaps the prestige of having the rich King George men in Nisqually territory, the wealth earned in trade or labor, and the food received from farmers like Heath made up for forgone natural resources. Perhaps the resources lost to plows, cattle, and sheep were available at alternate sites or through trade with other villagers.[34]

One benefit of the King George men's presence was having their assistance with defense, and neither HBC discipline nor new farms alarmed Nisqually area natives as much as the armed aggression and malevolent magic of other indigenous people. During the 1840s raiders descended on south Puget Sound communities numerous times. Heath and Tolmie identified most of the marauders as Indians from the Snoqualmie and Skykomish Rivers, ninety miles to the northeast. Probably acting on old grudges and new envy of Nisqually villagers' access to European goods, the northerners usually menaced isolated camps and individuals.[35]

By 1848, however, many people believed that aggressive natives were increasingly inclined to turn their weapons against King George men and Bostons. When settlers on the Sound got word that Cayuse Indians had killed and kidnapped Americans at a mission east of the Cascade Mountains, some predicted a copycat uprising of west side tribes. Having heard that the Cayuse blamed Americans for a measles epidemic, settlers grew more fearful when measles appeared in Puget Sound villages. Tolmie was inclined to believe a report that Snohomish and Klallam warriors, thinking whites had brought measles to exterminate Indians, planned to attack the King George men. At about the same time, Rabbeson and a friend claimed to have overheard a Snoqualmie chief urging thousands of assembled Indians to drive whites out of the country. Puget Sound Agricultural Company officers decided it was time to build true fortifications.[36]

The fortifications proved useful, not because Indians declared war against whites but because HBC was entangled in continuing conflicts between native peoples. In July 1848 Tolmie reported that some "Skeywhamish & Snoqualimich" had "with murderous intent pursued a Nisqually Indian right up to the establishment, where he obtained shelter." Tolmie later downplayed the importance of such unpleasantness, but he noted that evidence and rumors of Indian belligerence made settlers more timid. "The Indians ... ," he wrote, "knowing white men better than white men know them ... , became in consequence forward and troublesome. ... "[37]

Many of the settlers left. If any left for fear of Indians, they did not later admit it for the record. According to Rabbeson, poor farming conditions drove some away. Many more caught gold fever, rather than measles, and headed to California in search of the cure. While they were gone, another large party from Snoqualmie came to Fort Nisqually, apparently spoiling for a fight. This time—May 1, 1849—the northerners said they had come to investigate rumors that Lahalet's son was mistreating his Snoqualmie wife. Tolmie suspected that they again planned to "kick up a row with the fort Indians" in order to capture a few. Although he said later that the Snoqualmies also seemed ready to take offense at whatever whites did, he conceded that they resorted to force only when a company employee—an Indian—nervously or carelessly fired his musket. In the ensuing melee, two American bystanders were wounded, one fatally.[38]

Most chroniclers of this affair, while debating whether the Snoqualmies intended to storm the fort, have agreed that the American casualties were an unforeseen incident rather than a calculated affront to Bostons.[39] Nonetheless, like self-centered adolescents, Americans promptly construed the event as an Indian vendetta directed at them. Their reaction shows how insecure they felt. It is evidence, too, that they viewed the population around them through a polarizing lens, seeing but two sets of people—Indians and others—with inherently antagonistic agendas.

According to pioneer mythology, the marauding Indians offered safe passage out of the country to any Bostons who would leave their property behind. This ultimatum was probably an American fantasy; but by acting on the belief that Indians intended to drive them away, settlers began reshaping social reality to match their racialized fantasy. Gathering at hastily erected blockhouses, they beseeched Tolmie for guns. They also appealed for help to their only other possible source of power over the Indian multitudes—the territory's recently installed government. Territorial officials responded with displays meant to teach Indians their place in an American jurisdiction.

A few months later officials pronounced themselves satisfied with the effect of their demonstrations. However, like the British traders who strafed Dungeness village in 1828, the Americans assumed that their interpretation of events was the only sensible one and failed to see that native people probably made sense of Boston actions another way. Natives did not yet share Americans' concept of them as a new class of U.S. subjects called Indians.[40]

The settlers' desperate pleas moved Governor Joseph Lane to head for Puget Sound with an army lieutenant and five of the eight troops in his jurisdiction. En route he received word that two artillery companies had landed at Fort Vancouver, and he turned back to meet them, sending a letter on to Fort Nisqually. Lane's letter asked Tolmie

> to cause the hostile tribes who have committed the outrage to be informed that ... our force, which will be immediately increased, is at this time amply sufficient for an immediate expedition against them; that the moment I am informed that any injury has been committed by them upon our people, they will be visited by sudden and severe chastisement.

Tolmie obligingly assembled "all the natives about the establishment" and translated the letter for them.[41]

The governor had no cause to make good his threats, but the altercation of May 1 motivated American officials to establish a permanent presence on the Sound. In August native people finally saw the forces Lane alluded to. On the land where Joseph Heath had learned to deflect the Snoqualmies' hostility with a confident air and small gifts, Americans built an army fort. At about the same time the region also received its first U.S. agent for Indian affairs.[42]

One of agent J. Q. Thornton's first acts, consistent with long-standing federal policy, was to seek the surrender of those who shot the two Americans. From his comparatively secure southern Oregon settlement, the governor said he planned to "make the Indians know that they should give [the murderers] up for punishment" because "there is no mode of treatment so appropriate as prompt and severe punishment for wrongdoing." Upon seeing conditions at Steilacoom, Thornton was less confident of his government's ability to force Indians to do its bidding. At Tolmie's urging, he tried an inducement instead. He promised to give HBC blankets to natives who brought in the killers.[43]

A month later some Snoqualmies came to settle with the Bostons. By Tolmie's account, "it ended in 6 of the worst being seized and confined.... 80 blankets were paid out to the different chiefs of the tribe." American officials described the payment as a reward for cooperation. The Indians may have likened the exchange to their principal method of defusing a serious conflict, but it differed in an important respect: instead of compensation for their dead, the Bostons asked for custody of the suspected killers. The Snoqualmies had several possible reasons for acceding to the strange demand—desire for the blankets, fear of Boston soldiers, jealousy in their own ranks, and the fact that other natives and Hudson's Bay had allied with the Bostons.[44]

Snoqualmies who stayed to see what would happen to the hostages witnessed something without precedent or parallel in their experience. Bostons converged on Steilacoom to put the six Indians on trial for murder. In order to perform this commonplace American ritual, they went to extraordinary trouble and expense. North of the Columbia, U.S. citizens were so scarce that Oregon legislators had to pass a special act attaching the region to the territory's first judicial district, then pay the judge, lawyers, and most jurors to travel many miles to Steilacoom. After two days of deliberation, the tribunal freed four of the prisoners but sentenced two to death and presided over their immediate hanging.

According to the judge, his time and the public money were well spent.

> The effect produced by this trial was salutary, and I have no doubt will long be remembered by the tribe. The whole tribe, I would judge, were present at the execution, and a vast gathering of the Indians from other tribes on the Sound; and they were made to understand that our laws would punish them promptly for every murder they committed, and that we would have no satisfaction short of all who acted in the murder of our citizens.[45]

The official significance of the trial and punishment, the judge assumed, was as apparent to Indians as to settlers. A powerful state, employing fair procedures, had penalized people within its jurisdiction for violating impersonal general laws.[46] What better way to show Indians that those laws now defined their place in the world than to mount a terrifying public display of the government's might? Like territorial officials, some settlers believed that the ritual had communicated its intended message. A few years after the trial, Arthur Denny heard about the case from Patkanim, brother of one of the men executed. From this conversation Denny deduced that Patkanim had conceived "a wholesome fear of the law and the power of the government...."[47]

Denny was projecting onto Indians thoughts the latter almost certainly did not have. To indigenous people of the Puget Sound region, state power, universal laws, and crimes against society were alien, untranslatable concepts. They viewed homicides not as injuries to an abstract body politic but as manifestations and disruptions of specific personal relationships. The repercussions of a homicide were matters for the affected families and mediators to adjust. Rather than a righteous American sovereign with power to assign them all a new status, native people probably saw only a small, if formidable, tribe of Bostons who had responded in an exotic way to the harm done by particular local people.[48]

Two scraps of data are consistent with this speculation about Indian views of the trial and executions. Tolmie wrote that the family of one hanged man "made away" with an American soldier, who was not seen again; and when Lahalet died that winter, Nisqually friends said that a Snoqualmie shaman had killed him for helping to arrange the defendants' surrender. Evidently, rather than establishing that American rules would thenceforth govern relations between settlers and natives, the Boston ritual of retribution had merely invited further retribution. Even if natives construed the trial and executions as evidence of dreadful Boston powers, they had not discerned what else American law meant to Americans.[49]

For Americans, law was more than an instrument of state power; it was also a means of defining American society and its components. The prosecution of six native men in an American court highlighted the distinction that white Americans drew between themselves and Indians. It dramatized an important part of the content ascribed to two racial categories: Americans lived by laws; Indians were lawless. The trial's ostensible purpose was to draw lines between law-abiding Indians and unacceptable, outlaw Indians. Indeed, subjecting the Snoqualmies to U.S. law incorporated them symbolically into American society, albeit as a subordinate class. Yet in justifying what they did, the governor and judge betrayed a conviction that all the people they called Indians—in their "untamed" state, at least—belonged in a single category separate from and incompatible with Americans. Ironically, the trial itself revealed a contrary state of affairs: the formerly separate peoples were already intertwined.[50]

Inherent in the idea that Indians constituted an alien race was the notion that Americans were themselves one people. Since Oregon's settlers were in reality heterogeneous and often at odds with each other, the most important function of the 1849 prosecution may have been to create an illusion of American unity and perhaps of "white" unity. The proceedings displayed, for British traders and for settlers accustomed to freedom from federal control, the presence and resolve of the brand-new territorial government. That government's spokesmen expected Americans and even Britons to unite on the basis of race when Indians threatened them. The jury trial enlisted assorted white settlers in a ritual enactment of the qualities they presumably shared. It was thus a drama of self-definition.[51] In order to play the role of just and orderly citizens, settlers assigned Indians the role of cruel and capricious savages.

Were white players in the drama satisfied that the actual relationship of Indians to Americans was like the one they enacted? Settlers who stayed in the area frequently told themselves and prospective immigrants that the natives were indeed cowed. Some said they expected to replicate easily the feats of forebears who had pacified or exterminated eastern Indians. Yet Americans' boldness may have had less to do with the 1849 trial than with the presence of soldiers at Fort Steilacoom and the gold rush, which strengthened settlers' desired to stay by creating a market for local timber and food crops. In any case, Americans kept coming to Puget Sound. But there, like Joseph Heath and Father Blanchet, most had to adapt to a social setting that contrasted sharply with the racially defined hierarchy they expected to find or create.[52]

Instead of a country where their welfare depended on good relations with self-sufficient Indians, many of the new settlers hoped to find a place with abundant free land and opportunities for profitable enterprise. Congress seemed to grant their wish for land and tempted hundreds more Americans into the area by passing the Oregon Donation Land Act in September 1850. The statute disregarded a long-standing federal policy of obtaining consent from Indian occupants before issuing land titles in a new U.S. territory. As amended, it promised a patent to anyone who had already claimed land in Oregon and to additional citizens who occupied tracts before 1855 and tilled them. By the law's expiration date, 529 people had filed for tracts bordering Puget Sound, Hood Canal, and the Straits of Georgia and Juan de Fuca. The claims ranged in size from 60 to 640 acres.[53]

Whether or not they expected actually to farm their claims, most early settlers did expect to become prosperous property owners. Editors of the region's first newspaper, boosting the area as a destination for immigrants, predicted in 1852 that any diligent settler could make a fortune. A visitor of 1853 remarked, "They all seem to have the common idea in this country that they can get rich in a few years." Many newcomers were on the lookout for chances to make money trading, speculating, exporting raw materials, and mining. Few were interested in working for someone else.[54]

Although some settlers tried to make their fortunes in commerce with Indians, native people were not an ingredient in the most common prescriptions for getting rich. Would-be tycoons did not even plan to seek natives' approval for their enterprises. Some Americans imagined, as missionary John Richmond had in 1841, that they could persuade Indians to abet or emulate their economic ventures.[55] Others hoped to create a society where Indians were irrelevant. In 1853 the newspaper predicted, "Of the Indians now in our midst and around us in every direction, and in large numbers, but a miserable remnant will remain, and they confined within such narrow limits as Government may allot to them in some obscure locality, will ultimately succeed in dragging out to the bitter end their wretched existence."[56]

Throughout the 1850s, however, Indians were not confined to obscure corners of the Puget Sound basin. While colonists still numbered in the hundreds and native inhabitants in the many thousands, Indians were unavoidably relevant to Americans' lives, and routine relations between settlers and natives bore little resemblance to those enacted in the trial at Fort Steilacoom. Even the trial's outcome, Tolmie said, indicated that Americans had less power to control relations than they pretended. Jurors who lived a safe distance away wanted to hang all six defendants, but those within reach of Snoqualmie avengers vetoed that verdict.[57]

For several years after 1849, other immigrants had as much reason as the jurors to beware of offending Indians, for most lived scattered among native people. Because Bostons prized land with arable prairies, fresh water, and sheltered anchorage, they commonly staked claims in places that natives already used for the same reasons. Some settlers deliberately built homes near native villages, expecting to trade with the inhabitants or hoping for protection from northern raiders. Non-Indian neighbors, by contrast, were scarce and often distant. One pioneer said that Indian midwives had attended his birth in 1852 because the closest whites were six miles away. Even whites who did not choose to live near Indians acquired native neighbors, sometimes in large numbers. Lawyer George Gibbs told U.S. officials, "Whenever a settler's house is erected a nest of Indian rookeries is pretty sure to follow. . . . "[58]

Many settlers considered their indigenous neighbors repulsive and exasperating. Indians, often barely clothed, walked into cabins without knocking and expected to be fed. Their speech seemed a jumble of clicks and growls. They sometimes filled the night air with the eerie noises of pagan rites. David and Catherine Blaine, who lived in Seattle when it was a one-street town "with miserable indian shanties scattered all about and indians meeting you at every step," could find nothing to love in the "coarse, filthy, & debased natives." Although few settlers were as finicky as the Blaines, many shared their disdain for Indians.[59]

Yet early settlers needed native people. They particularly needed foods that only Indians could supply. In reminiscences, nearly every immigrant of the 1850s mentioned fish, game, berries, and potatoes purchased or received as gifts from Indians. During Arthur Denny's second winter on Puget Sound, few sailing vessels visited, and his party's supply of pork, flour, and hard bread ran out. To feed themselves the Americans "had to make a canoe voyage to the Indian settlement on Black river to get a fresh stock of potatoes."[60]

Settlers also relied on natives for services. Even the "comparatively unprofitable labor of the inconstant Indian" was sorely needed, Gibbs admitted in 1854; Indians could be employed "to advantage" as domestics, in sawmills, and on farms. Americans recognized their dependency in the high rates they paid to travel or ship goods by Indian canoe and in the hard bargains Indians drove for their labor. Having tried for two weeks before she found Indians to work in her potato field, Rebecca Ebey yielded to one worker's demand for an extra blanket and settled for grumbling in her diary that he did not deserve more than the coat, hat, boots, and two shirts she had already paid him.[61]

Outnumbered and needy, immigrants to Puget Sound were relieved to find that indigenous people were less fearsome than the Indians of American literature and folklore. Local "savages" seemed mild-mannered and hospitable. Perceptive settlers quickly understood that they could encourage Indians' hospitality by making them gifts, doing them favors, and scrupulously fulfilling promises. Describing an occasion when settlers forced a fellow American to honor his promise to an Indian, Rabbeson said, "We were guided entirely in dealing with the Indians by their own laws & not ours."[62]

Rabbeson's statement is an oversimplification. The code that native people expected Bostons to follow was a hybrid one that had evolved to facilitate the relations of King George men and natives; and while Americans learned that code, they also proposed amendments. Some of the tactics they adopted seemed consonant with native mores but were probably innovations. Rabbeson, for instance, took a headman's horses hostage in order to make the man find out who had burglarized Rabbeson's house. Although this may not have been a negotiating tactic familiar to the headman, he apparently accepted it as a method of conducting relations across cultural boundaries. Rather than threatening to escalate hostilities, he acquiesced in the impoundment until he had fingered the thief.[63]

Like Heath and the French priests, Americans learned the prevailing rules in part from Indian tutors, in part from other whites. A vital subject of instruction was the Chinook jargon. So common were encounters with native people, and so useful was the trade language in those encounters, that in January 1853 the *Columbian* newspaper devoted its entire front page to a jargon dictionary, then ran the feature again in response to readers' demands. Americans often implied that Indian preference compelled them to learn Chinook. George Gibbs, for instance, referred to the jargon as "the Indian language." Indians, on the other hand, let James Swan know that they regarded the jargon "as a sort of white man's talk"— a skill made necessary by the need to deal with foreigners.[64]

A third, hybrid language became the medium of communication between settlers and natives because neither group had the power or inclination in the 1850s to make its dialect the regional language. For that matter, neither settlers nor natives could require changes in any of each other's practices without bargaining. Rabbeson claimed that settlers around Budd Inlet compelled nearby natives to bury their dead and cease killing slaves whose masters had died; but he added, "To satisfy the Indians so they would submit to our demands peacefully, we also agreed to protect them in all cases where the Lower Sound Indians attempted to raid their country." On Whidbey Island a few years later, Indians demanded action from settlers whose cattle had destroyed natives' potatoes. The whites, Rebecca Ebey said, thought it better to pay three hundred dollars "rather than have any difficulty with them now when our settlement is weak. . . ."[65]

In February 1853, when natives and farmers struck this deal, American settlements were still weak. Around Puget Sound and adjacent waters, fewer than two thousand colonists lived among twelve thousand or more indigenous people.[66] On the other hand, two thousand settlers represented a two-hundred-fold increase in four years. Bostons had spread from the south Sound to the Puyallup, Duwamish, and Skokomish River valleys. At Budd Inlet, Steilacoom, Elliott Bay, Port Townsend, and Bellingham Bay, they clustered at town sites and mines; at Port Gamble, Port Ludlow, Seattle, and elsewhere, they operated sawmills; and on Whidbey Island and Commencement Bay, they had launched commercial fishing enterprises.[67]

Even though some of the new settlers encroached on native sources of subsistence, few suffered harm at natives' hands. The Ebeys said their safety rested on Indians' knowledge that Americans "could soon have them all killed and driven off" if they murdered a white person. The Blaines and others thought they were ordinarily safe because Indians were preoccupied with enmities between tribes.[68] But it is just as likely that most indigenous people tolerated early immigration because they expected to turn it to their advantage, as they or their neighbors had turned the King George men's presence to their advantage.

Natives in many locations were willing and sometimes eager to have an American move in, particularly one who proposed to open a trading post, pay for labor, or provide medicine. As Samuel Hancock ventured into valleys where Americans had never gone, his eyes peeled for a chance to make money, he learned to reassure inhabitants by billing himself as a "mah-kook," or merchant man. A headman on the Pacific Coast pleaded with Hancock to stay and build a mill, offering his daughter and laborers as incentives. Hancock feigned acceptance of the deal, he said, because he needed to borrow the man's canoe.[69] What Hancock construed as the price of the chief's hospitality was the kind of reciprocity that often endeared Bostons to native people. Many settlers reported, as did John Roger James, that Indians "were very persistent in declaring the land was theirs. At the same time they liked to have people settling among them and improving the country." Americans who seemed to acknowledge Indians' territorial prerogatives were thus usually welcome. According to pioneer folklore, four men who staked claims at Port Townsend smoothed the way for their families to join them by holding a "pow-wow" with local Indians, distributing small gifts, and promising that the U.S. government would soon pay liberally for lands the Bostons occupied.[70]

In native eyes, Boston immigrants then became identified with the community that had admitted them, and their productive activities were a credit to all in the vicinity. According to Gibbs, Indians did not take offense when settlers erected a sawmill at one of their fishing sites, in part because the mill dam improved the fishery. "[B]ut what afforded the greatest satisfaction to them was its situation upon their property, and the superior importance thereby derived to themselves. They soon began to understand the machinery, and took every visitor through the building to explain its working, and boast of it, as if it had been of their own construction."[71]

The paradigm for natives' assimilation of Bostons was kinship. Emily Denny, born and raised in the settlement that became the town of Seattle, said that Indians claimed brotherhood with white children, telling them, "You were born in our country and are our people. You eat the same food, grow up here, belong to us." Moreover, in numerous instances immigrants became Indians' actual relatives, at least according to native mores. Many a Boston bachelor took a native wife. Because they were ignorant or careless of the social and economic obligations that came with sexual privileges in the women's society, or because they were intent on claiming the privileges that patriarchs enjoyed in their own society, some non-Indian men disappointed their native in-laws. But those who observed natives' norms often gained access to resources and a variety of services as well as companionship. In addition, men who married Indians by American law— an option available until the territorial legislature proscribed it in 1855— were entitled to double the size of their Donation Land Act claims.[72]

Thus did early settlers and indigenous people usually coexist peacefully, even deriving mutual advantage from regular relations. Many of them later reveled in this accomplishment. The pride and relief of managing a risky situation and mastering new customs could temper the disgust that Bostons and Indians aroused in each other. Still, reciprocity was not a guarantee of friendship or comfortable association. Accustomed to assuming that any individual might have the aid of dangerous spirits, Puget Sound natives could not quite banish their suspicions of people outside a circle of close blood relations. Americans likewise could not be sure they knew even the most accommodating Indian's heart or inclinations. Most relations between natives and newcomers remained tentative and uneasy.[73]

Crises in a relationship could raise questions for which Indians and Bostons did not have common answers. One poignant example shows that the intimate relations of immigrant men and indigenous women, while capable of reducing differences between the groups, could also highlight differences. The native wife of a white settler committed suicide. Catherine Blaine, who characterized the couple's marriage as a purchase, related subsequent events in a letter.

> [The man] was left in rather a peculiar position, the indians claiming the body to bury among their own people with their own ceremonies and he unwilling to let it go, but uncertain whether the whites would allow her to be buried in their ground. There was some opposition to it, but they consented, then came the trouble of getting the coffin because she was a squaw, but he got the coffin at last. He came up here this morning to see if Mr. B. would be willing to officiate at the funeral, but Mr. B. told him if they were not married he could not consent to sanction their past manner of living by burying her like other people. He saw the propriety of Mr. B.'s position and did not urge the matter. So they buried her without any service. Indians carried the coffin covered with a blue indian blanket, the man who had owned her, accompa-

nied by one or two squaw men ... and a number of indians followed to the grave, and this afternoon as Mr. B. was passing his house the indians were in it howling and bewailing, as they are accustomed to do. Now what a situation he is in, with his little half breed child, and despised by the whites and hated by the indians who would kill him if they could get a chance in revenge for her death.[74]

Testing remained a necessary part of establishing, clarifying, and reaffirming relations between people bred in the contrasting cultures. Natives occasionally tested immigrants' courage or their willingness to acknowledge Indian prerogatives, as they had done with the fur traders. Many an American would later tell stories like Rebecca Ebey's.

Six large indians came today and crowded in the door so that I could not stand them, and tried to get them out and shut the door but they stood still and sauced me untill I was afraid of them and went and sat down and gave them up. ... I never was more vexed, and still affraid to compel them to go not knowing what so many large indians might do where there was no white man near and they knew no person was here but myself and the children.

Many pioneers would likewise claim to have won Indians' respect by demonstrating their pluck as Ebey did the next day: driving seemingly insolent visitors off by threat of force.[75]

Such jockeying could be perilous and costly. In 1852, according to James McCurdy, settlers near Port Townsend had to call in an American ship to intimidate natives who had forbidden them to plant crops. That year, too, Indians drove all the settlers at New Dungeness into George Gerrish's store and demanded redress for the murder of a Klallam man. To appease them took forty blankets and a promise that the killer would stand trial. Wishing for a society where chancy negotiations with Indians were unnecessary, people like the Ebeys and Blaines anxiously awaited the day when U.S. officials would assume responsibility for Indian affairs. They particularly expected the government to ease tensions by paying Indians for their lands, as settlers familiar with U.S. practices had promised.[76]

Federal representatives did try to take charge of Indians in the Puget Sound area, but their early efforts were feeble ones. In 1851, E. A. Starling assumed the duties of Indian agent for the area north of the Columbia and west of the Cascades. No one had filled a comparable post since J. Q. Thornton left in 1849. Shortly after arriving, Starling reported that "the Indians came by tribes ... all extremely desirous to learn the intentions of the government in regard to purchasing their lands." He endeavored to nurture this apparent interest in good relations by distributing a few gifts.

As a step toward controlling natives, Starling then attempted a census of tribes. However, for the populations of twenty-nine named groups "who frequent[ed] the waters of the sound," he had to rely on estimates supplied by Hudson's Bay and his native visitors rather than head counts. It was out of his power, Starling conceded, to learn their actual numbers.[77]

The new agent found most of his assignments beyond his power. For lack of money, knowledge, and military might, he and his superiors were almost wholly unable to govern relations between settlers and Indians. Although Starling parroted Governor Lane's dictum that Indians must be made to fear Americans' superior power, the only indices of power at his disposal were three dozen soldiers and a few ships that made irregular appearances in the Sound. When Lieutenant August Kautz received orders to lead a twelve-man expedition to "intimidate the Indians" near Camano Island, he thought the mission absurd, considering the natives' numbers. His judgment was sound: the venture proved embarrassing. Hoping to force the surrender of a murder suspect, his men seized a Kikealis "chief," but their hostage escaped easily. When they tried to reach the Kikealis camp, they could not negotiate tidal currents. Finally, Kautz had no recourse but to urge settlers to raise a bounty for the alleged killer.[78]

The fractious nature of the non-Indian population in Starling's jurisdiction made his task doubly difficult. Rather than designating a unified group, the term "settlers" refers to an assortment of people with disparate, often conflicting, interests. Boston squatters clashed frequently with the King George men at Nisqually, Boston traders competed with the King George men and each other for Indian customers, rival town builders vied strenuously for new settlers, and different classes of Bostons resented each other. Observant natives did not see the tight-knit society of later pioneer lore; instead, they saw what Ezra Meeker called "a motley mess" of people. As Catherine Blaine told friends in the east, "Things work strangely here. Nobody has any confidence in anybody else, and there is but little ground for any."[79]

Settlers' attitudes toward and interests relative to native people were as inharmonious as the settlers themselves. The Blaines censured whites who associated with Indians and saw no hope of improving their town's moral climate unless such associations ceased, but most of the whites they scorned were profiting from commerce with Indians. Numerous Bostons sold liquor to natives while conscientious officials, unsure whether they had authority to curtail the traffic, wrung their hands. Some settlers openly resisted government efforts to regulate their relations with Indians. William Bell recalled a time when whites in Seattle let Starling take custody of an Indian miscreant, then fumed at news that the agent had merely escorted the man out of town, given him food and gifts, and sent him home with instructions to behave. After that, Bell said, townspeople dispensed their own justice to Indians.[80]

Natives' diversity and mobility also frustrated American officials' desire to regulate interracial relations. Indians no more constituted a cohesive bloc than did whites. Violence between natives—looting, slave raids, and revenge killings—went on around the settlers throughout the 1850s.[81] Individually and as village groups, indigenous people had varying amounts of contact with and varied ways of dealing with immigrants. Some relished direct encounters; others preferred to avoid them. Some imitated whites, while others showed no inclination to change their accustomed ways. Some listened to the Catholics, some to Protestants, and some to neither. In addition, Indians eluded American control by moving frequently. It was this "disposition to wander" that made it hard to count them, Starling said; seldom was a whole "tribe" together. To settlers, however, it seemed sometimes as if whole tribes were together in their backyards, for large groups often moved into American towns to exploit opportunities for trade and paid work. In 1851, for example, a band of Duwamish River natives wintered in the new town of Olympia, sixty miles south of their home territory.[82]

The Indian camps around Olympia and other new towns indicate the most important reason that government agents could not control relations between Indians and settlers in the early 1850s. Those relations already entailed a myriad of individual encounters, and most such encounters reflected or created a web of ties that few of the interlinked people wished to undo. American families ate well because native women came to their doors peddling fish, clams, potatoes, and berries. Indian families acquired wealth and Boston conveniences because they supplied food to Boston families and even to ships bound for California. Immigrant men parlayed modest investments into substantial income by selling wares or alcohol to Indians, and they usually gained entrée into native communities by consorting with local women. Soldiers at Fort Steilacoom also had native female companions. And some children born of these liaisons became new strands in the tangled skein of ties between the different peoples.[83]

Occasions for relations between natives and settlers multiplied as settlers increased in number. However, by changing the ratio of settlers to Indians, new immigration altered the context of relations and made unpleasant encounters more likely. In a single year, 1853, the immigrant population doubled to approximately two thousand. Americans were then so numerous north of the Columbia that Congress detached the region from Oregon and organized it as Washington Territory. This new political status bolstered the courage that Americans' increase was already inspiring. Especially in the more densely settled areas, newcomers felt freer to disregard Indian sensibilities. It became more common for settlers to move into Indians' territory without permission, to insult or assault Indians, and to cheat Indians out of pay for goods and labor.[84]

Furthermore, Indian conduct that had seemingly pleased King George men and blackrobes did not always charm the newest arrivals. The cloth garments that natives donned for meetings with traders and priests struck some Americans as shabby or comical. The sign of the cross did not impress Protestants or skeptics. English names and certificates of friendship, which some natives had accepted as honors from foreign mariners, now became badges of Indian ignorance. Theodore Winthrop poked fun at Chetzemoka, proud recipient of the name Duke of York. Because he carried papers signed by Yankee and British officers, Winthrop said, the illiterate Duke "deemed himself indorsed by civilization," unaware that the signers were "unanimous in opprobrium."[85]

Rum, once associated with good feelings between Indians and King George men, could also poison relations. If natives had inferred that drinking the foreigners' firewater was a prestigious activity, they had good reason. King George men had dispensed rum to promote or confirm trade and friendship and to celebrate special occasions. Boston leading men and soldiers also drank liberally, sometimes in the company of natives. Many of them looked on in tolerant amusement when Indians got drunk. Yet other Bostons now complained that drunk Indians offended and frightened them. Violence against Americans increased, they alleged, where Indians procured liquor easily.[86]

Whether or not liquor was to blame, the number of violent encounters between natives and newcomers climbed in 1853 and 1854. Natives probably killed James McCormick while he explored Lake Union, and Seattle residents subsequently hanged two Indian suspects. At New Dungeness settlers triggered a battle when they attempted to seize two Indians accused of murder. A deadly affray occurred near Port Townsend for similar reasons. Seattle residents suspected foul play when three Snohomish Indians returned to town without the white man who had hired them as guides. A posse followed the three to their own country, where it provoked or met with violence that left one white and nine Indians dead.[87]

Shortly before the Blaines arrived at Seattle, townspeople lynched an Indian for killing other Indians and threatening to kill whites. Indians appeared indifferent at the time of the hanging, Catherine Blaine told friends; but when some white men later disappeared, Indians said that aggrieved natives had exacted revenge. This and the subsequent altercation over the three Snohomish suspects threw settlers into a frenzy. Men volunteered to organize an attack on the Snohomish, "but upon more mature thought they decided to refer the case to the Governor. ... " Whether the Indians would act against the settlers before the governor could act against them worried Blaine. "[I]f they knew their strength," she wrote, "they might dispatch every white person on the sound."[88]

When Washington Territory's first governor arrived in Olympia at the end of 1853, Agent Starling assured him that Indians of the area did not know their own strength. Instead, Starling told Isaac Stevens, Indians looked up to whites "as superior beings." "They are becoming more and more convinced ... ," the agent continued, "that their destiny is fixed; and that they must succumb to the whites. ... They, therefore, feel every day, more inclined to look to them ... for order, as to what they must do."[89]

The most commonly cited evidence that Starling correctly perceived natives' readiness to accept the status that the United States ordained for Indians is a quotation attributed to Seattle, a man whose strategy of cooperating with American officials has ensured him a prominent place in histories of Washington State. If the quotation is authentic, it is from a speech Seattle delivered to Isaac Stevens in January 1854, when hundreds of indigenous people gathered at Elliott Bay to see the governor for the first time. According to Henry A. Smith, an eyewitness, Seattle spoke the following mournfully fatalistic words:

> The son of the white chief says his father sends us greetings of friendship and good-will. This is kind, for we know he has little need of our friendship in return, because his people are many. They are like the grass that covers the vast prairies, while my people are few, and resemble the scattering trees of a wind-swept plain. The great, and I presume also good, white chief sends us word that he wants to buy our lands but is willing to allow us to reserve enough to live on comfortably. This indeed appears generous, for the red man no longer has rights that he need respect. ... There was a time when our people covered the whole land as the waves of a wind-ruffled sea cover its shell-paved floor. But that time has long since passed away with the greatness of tribes almost forgotten. ... [W]e are two distinct races and must ever remain so. There is little in common between us. ... Day and night cannot dwell together. The red man has ever fled the approach of

the white man. ... It matters but little where we pass the remainder of our days. They are not many. ... [90]

Circumstances make it easy to believe that Seattle expressed such sentiments and that his indigenous contemporaries shared those sentiments. A smallpox epidemic had felled many Indians in the preceding year. This calamity, which prevented many families from meeting basic needs, would also have undermined natives' ability to respond to increasingly frequent affronts from settlers. In the aboriginal way of thinking, the pestilence itself was reason to suspect the presence of powers greater than natives' own spirit partners. In addition, Americans saw the Indian death rate as confirmation of the widely accepted maxim that Indians were destined to vanish as civilized society expanded; and it is likely that they communicated their conviction to Indians, some of whom were inclined to credit the Bostons' gloomy prophecies.[91]

However, the eloquent phrases ascribed to Seattle are poor evidence that Puget Sound natives saw themselves in 1854 as a weak race, doomed to displacement. In fact, the phrases themselves may be fictitious. When Smith published them, three decades after the speech, he purported to render Seattle's words verbatim; but on his deathbed he reportedly clarified that he had merely reconstructed part of the oration from notes.[92] There are several reasons to doubt the accuracy of Smith's reconstruction. As of January 1854 he had been in the region barely over a year. Even if his contact with native people was extensive and intimate, he is unlikely during that short time to have achieved fluency in the dialect Seattle spoke. English speakers thought the language so difficult that very few tried to learn it; the rest got by with the Chinook jargon. Furthermore, although Smith was well educated, he did not prove himself a careful recorder of aboriginal beliefs. An article he wrote in 1873 described indigenous practices—devil worship and human sacrifice—not reported by any other ethnographer or eyewitness.[93]

Several commentators, noting that the images and cadences of Smith's text reflect his culture's literary heritage rather than Seattle's, have granted Smith a license to render the presumably poetic speech in appropriately lyrical English prose. But he appears to have exceeded the terms of his license. Why would Seattle, who had lived all his life in a densely forested country, refer metaphorically to vast prairies and windswept plains? Would he have known the long history of American Indians' flight before oncoming whites? How probable is it that a man who valued his associations with Bostons would speak of two races who had nothing in common?[94]

The heavy-handedness of the speech's vanishing-Indian theme—the very theme that has made it an enduring historical icon—should also inspire doubt about its authenticity. Smith published his account not in 1854, when the region's native peoples still outnumbered American settlers, but three decades later, after the demographic balance had changed drastically. By 1887 events seemed to have vindicated the belief that aboriginal peoples were destined to give way before the advance of civilization, and the image of the pitiful Indian relic had its strongest hold yet on Americans' imagination. As he belatedly reduced Seattle's remarks to writing, Henry Smith doubtless felt the influence of this myth.[95]

Even if Smith did roughly paraphrase Seattle's address, he did not produce a document proving that Puget Sound Indians had conceded the hegemony of American civilization. Descendants of Seattle's peers told ethnographers that verbal deference and self-abasement were conventional conduct for well-bred men of the time, particularly at gatherings of unrelated people. Knowing that strangers might have dangerous invisible allies, men in Seattle's situation spoke humbly but simultaneously suggested nonverbally that they also had powers deserving respect. They described themselves as poor and unworthy while bearing themselves proudly. This etiquette was particularly appropriate for high-class men who had suffered a run of bad luck. Their rhetoric did not concede a loss of status but served to preserve status until their luck turned.[96] If Smith accurately described Seattle's behavior, it was consistent with this remembered code of conduct. The chief delivered his lament loudly, forcefully, and with characteristic dignity; while he talked, he even put his hand on the governor's head.

Rather than proof that Puget Sound natives saw themselves as a single, benighted and bested race, Smith's text is at most the gist of one man's thoughts. That man, old enough to be preoccupied with his own mortality or declining vigor, had some reasons to doubt his power in a changing social environment and to wonder about his community's ability to resist Boston demands.[97] As the next few years would prove, however, Seattle's decision to propitiate the Bostons was only one response in a range of Indian reactions to American colonization.

The Bostons' demands reflected their preferred model for ordering the human world. Even though they realized daily how much leverage Indians had against them, most of them envisioned a different future. From the power of their nation-state, Americans expected to derive power and status superior to Indians. This vision and the political culture that inspired it gave them strength of a kind that native people did not gain from their individual partnerships with powerful spirits. Eventually, lack of an analogous vision would put most native people at an unmistakable disadvantage in their relations with Bostons. But in the mid-1850s, before the Americans were able to activate their political institutions effectively, the original peoples of the Puget Sound area still moved freely in a world ordered more according to their social categories than according to American racial distinctions and hierarchies.

Americans had to bend to Ind. social norms b/c of early weakness

culture clash [?]/pop. growth.

3 Treaties and War
Ephemeral Lines of Demarcation

still a time
of lingering
regionalism

THE

As settlers appeared in new places around Puget Sound and natives encountered them with greater frequency, more people felt a need to redefine
the relationship between natives and newcomers. In the mid-1850s U.S.
officials tried to do this in treaties with several dozen "tribes of Indians."
Eventually the treaties would become a basis and symbol of Indian status,
but initially they were not an effective means to circumscribe and manage
that class of people. Although they provided for government-supervised
Indian enclaves, they did not establish orderly relations. Instead, they provoked some natives to violence. And even by suppressing this violent resistance Americans did not prescribe indigenous people's status in the region. Through the 1860s natives' relationships to immigrants reflected
local conditions and individual predilections more than American policy.
The boundaries between peoples and the terms of their mutual affairs remained tentative and negotiable.

Because the increasing association of Indians and non-Indians threatened to reduce the differences between them, it also focused attention on
those differences. For this reason in tandem with others, both settlers and
indigenous people devoted considerable energy during the turbulent
1850s to affirming and exhibiting what they valued about their respective
societies. Americans often dramatized the qualities they claimed as Americans. Evidence that native peoples engaged in corresponding displays is
scarcer but sufficient to be convincing.

In 1853, when settlers above the Columbia got permission to secede
from Oregon and organize Washington Territory, editors of the area's only
newspaper declared, "[W]e have become 'a people' within ourselves." The
Columbian's owners then dedicated themselves to influencing the new
"people's" character by promoting white immigration and civic pride. To

72

encourage as well as prove the little colony's rapid transformation into a proper American community, they crowed about new schools, courts, church services, sawmills, social galas, and the newspaper itself. They reported with special pride that citizens in several locations had organized lavish celebrations of Independence Day.[1]

The *Columbian* did not mention Indians at Independence Day ceremonies, perhaps because local readers knew that the many native people in their midst were routinely present at such events. Ezra Meeker, who arrived on the Sound in 1853, said of Indians, "They joined in our fourth of July celebrations [and] ... in our religious meetings in numerous instances.... "[2] The effect that patriotic ceremonies and new institutions had on Indians was not necessarily Americans' foremost concern; most were intent on convincing themselves and prospective immigrants that they were creating a civilized society in Washington. Yet settlers knew that Indians witnessed their rituals of self-definition; and if asked, most would have agreed that making Indians aware of American schools, churches, national government, laws, and technology was a way to impress on them the difference between civilization and savagery.

Settlers even staged some displays for Indians' benefit, in effect trying to show what made Americans American and, by implication, what made Indians inferior to Americans. One tactic was to transport individual native men to California, where they could see how numerous, rich, and aggressive Bostons were. Tales of chiefs who visited San Francisco and then persuaded their people not to resist American plans became part of pioneer mythology. Some may be pure myth, but a few Indians did see California in the boom years, and it is plausible that their subsequent accounts aided American efforts to project an imposing image.[3]

Indigenous peoples likewise had ways of flaunting what they valued about themselves. Exhibiting local pride was a central function of their multicommunity ceremonies, for example. When Frank Allen described the memorable gatherings his forebears hosted or attended, he said that residents of different villages took turns showing how they did things. When people from one village danced and sang, displayed masks, fed guests on local delicacies, performed feats of magic, or distributed property, everyone there saw the bases of those villagers' self-concepts and self-respect.[4] Native villagers exhibited cherished abilities and traits when they met violently, too. In war as in ceremonial exchanges, they defined themselves in relation to each other.

Both violent and nonviolent encounters between indigenous groups were apparently on the rise in the 1850s, and the rise was an outgrowth of natives' relations with settlers. Some scholars speculate that Puget Sound villages did not even stage large-scale giveaways—called "potlatches" in the trade jargon—until whites introduced new wealth and new occasions to meet Indians from farther north, who had an elaborate potlatch tradition. In any case, by bringing natives from different places into more frequent contact, whites had given them additional opportunities to display and test their respective powers and sources of pride.[5]

Settlers knew that Indians valued the status they gained by hosting feasts and giveaways. Government agent E. A. Starling said the Indians of his district would part with their last possessions to make an impression on others. He cited "a chief of the Ska-git tribe who … gave away over two hundred blankets; and another of the Sklal-lum tribe" who was preparing to "enhance his importance" by distributing property at "a general collection of Indians." Although some settlers construed potlatches as displays of power directed at whites, there is no reason to believe that the hosts of such events hoped primarily to influence Bostons. Still, the largesse and resulting renown of "chiefs" did impress Americans as well as native people. When U.S. officials sought individuals who could represent Indian communities, they thought of men who had sponsored high-profile ceremonies: Seattle, Patkanim, Chowitshoot, Chetzemoka, and others.[6]

To impress Indians in turn, Americans relied increasingly on their government institutions. By the mid-1850s territorial officials were making concerted efforts to take control of relations and show Indians where they would belong in an American-dominated world. Leading Bostons seemed particularly to expect their courts to teach Indians the social implications of American sovereignty. Washington Governor Stevens's first executive order established judicial districts and designated precinct judges. Shortly after that Starling advised Stevens that the Indians, already inclined to look to whites for protection, could easily be made to obey a simplified code of laws. Perhaps because Starling's was a minority opinion, no such code passed the territorial legislature. But settlers insisted with growing frequency that Indians should obey American laws, at least when dealing with settlers. In an article about Stevens's effort to prohibit commerce between Indians and the Hudson's Bay Company, the *Pioneer and Democrat* declared:

> The Indians too, should be made to understand that it is the
> government of the United States, and not the Chief Factors of the …
> HBC, to whom they are to look for protection when their rights are vi-
> olated, or whom they have to fear when evil councils prevail, and they
> are induced to pass the barriers a wise and munificent government has
> instituted to guard the respective rights of the white man and Indian.[7]

In order to manage race relations, government officials needed to educate non-Indians as well as Indians. Settlers who arrived before 1853 had learned to deal with native people in ways that now seemed ill suited to American ambitions. Accordingly, shortly after Stevens appointed Michael Simmons Indian agent for the Puget Sound district, Simmons began his fellow pioneers' resocialization with a letter to the *Pioneer and Democrat*. Petty disturbances were a chronic problem, he wrote, because settlers furnished liquor to Indians, punished Indians for supposed wrongs without sufficient evidence, and hired Indians without first making enforceable contracts. To produce "an amicable state of feelings between the *red* and *white* occupants of this Territory ... ," Simmons pledged to restrain Indians "within suitable limits and to exact from them an obedience to law in their intercourse with the whites" while also protecting their rights. He could carry out these arduous, delicate duties only if settlers cooperated by bringing their grievances to him or to the courts.[8]

Simmons had trouble fulfilling his pledge, and less-than-complete cooperation from settlers was one reason for the difficulty. In addition, many of Simmons's colleagues in government were themselves early settlers, used to operating outside the law, and the government they staffed was small and poor. Consequently, creating a new territory did not end the era when situation-specific power calculations determined how whites treated native people. Settlers who thought they had the upper hand still resorted occasionally to beating, cheating, or lynching Indians. Where they could get courts or officeholders to remove or intimidate troublesome natives, they did so, although the line between legal proceedings and lynchings was sometimes faint. On the other hand, where settlers feared physical or economic retaliation from Indians, they often calmed stormy relations in native fashion. One pioneer said later, "[W]hen an Indian would steal anything it was our custom to tie him up & lynch him"; but after hanging Masatche Jim, "we had him to pay for, to the Indians. ... We had to do it, or run the chances individually of being served in the same way."[9]

The new courts did assume significant responsibility for defining and adjusting relations between Americans and Indians. During the 1850s cases involving native people fattened their dockets. For example, after each of four notorious killings of white men, settlers hauled Indians before the bar to face murder charges. In at least two of the cases, natives claimed that Boston misdeeds provoked the slayings, but the Americans would not deign to settle the reciprocal grievances by exchanging property, as natives might have done. Instead, they tried the accused men and sentenced them to hang.[10]

In order to bring Indians before courts of law, Americans sometimes used extralegal tactics. An attempt to arrest some Klallams developed into a brief military campaign. The governor mobilized troops and instructed their commander to take all Klallam chiefs hostage. "Should the tribe ... offer any resistance," he added, "a summary course should be pursued, and their towns and especially stockades be destroyed." In addition to seizing four native men, the troops whipped three and shot three more.[11] In the meantime, Stevens was leading an expedition to Snohomish country to hunt other Indians suspected of a white man's murder. His actions hardly showed natives what a law-ordered American regime would be like. They did, however, make it clear that he would insist on new procedures for resolving disputes between Indians and Bostons.

At the town of Seattle, Stevens called together some native men— "Patkanam & part of the Snoqualmies, and Seattle with those of the Dwamish usually at the town, and George Seattle his son ... in effect chief of the Suquamish. ... " When he went on to Snohomish with four boat-loads of soldiers and volunteers, he took Seattle and Patkanim along and assigned them to search parties. A sweep through native camps scared up only a few women and some Skagits, whom the governor threatened with dire consequences unless they produced the murderers. When his threats had no effect, he settled for destroying deserted Snohomish habitations and canoes.[12]

Leaving small groups to continue the hunt, the governor moved on to Skagit country, where he informed natives "that they must have chiefs who should be responsible if any thing [sic] was wrong. They should choose a head chief & he would appoint 15 good men to support him. They must obey the chief & the others stand by him." Because the assembled people would not choose a chief, Stevens appointed Goliah and six sub-chiefs. Eight days after the expedition began, Stevens had to end it with no greater accomplishment than this. He even lost his hostages when they escaped during the last night.

Besides signaling that he would strike back at Indians who killed whites, Stevens had served notice (in Snohomish and Skagit territory, at least) that he intended to deal with the many indigenous communities as if they were organized into patriarchal tribes, whether or not such a model of governance corresponded to theirs. If he hoped at the same time to teach them the difference between American law and their prior methods of ad-justing relations with Bostons, his tactics were ill suited to his purpose.

Territorial officials' preoccupation with Indian relations and the high proportion of early court cases involving Indians reveal how interconnected settler and native societies were. Yet government and courts symbolized for Americans their resolve to replace the Indian world with an American one, and many whites were eager to sort out the entwined peoples. The first territorial legislature therefore began establishing lines of demarcation. For example, when it distinguished people competent to testify in court from those deemed incompetent, it classified Indians and "persons having more than one-half Indian blood" with the incompetents.[13]

People with the two kinds of "blood," who personified the porous boundaries between whites and Indians, became the focus of an extended controversy when lawmakers had to decide whom to include in the territorial electorate. Competing bills in the second legislative session would have disfranchised all so-called half-breeds, half-breeds leading an uncivilized life, or half-breeds unable to read and write English. Eventually the legislature approved, reconsidered, and reaffirmed by close vote a law opening the polls to "civilized" half-breeds, whether literate or not.

The debate about half-breed voting shows how the mingling of natives and immigrants stimulated American settlers to define their society. In deciding whether to count the children of pioneers and Indians as citizens, lawmakers not only proposed to sort the region's population into two racial categories but also hoped to determine the content of the "white" society that would ultimately prevail. Delegate Chenoweth, author of the bill to enfranchise half-breeds who conformed to habits of civilized life, said, "Our legislation should be humanizing and civilizing in its effects. We should encourage this class of men in their efforts in adopting our habits, instead of placing a mark upon them. ... In a short time they will be all that is left to remind us that there once was numerous and thickly swarming tribes of savages all over this country. ... "[14]

Although they mistrusted many half-breeds as much for their presumed political orientation and French-Canadian ancestry as for their "Indian blood," legislators most often argued for or against the vote on the basis of the messages they expected to convey by assimilating people so close to "savagery." According to Chenoweth, Arthur Denny opposed the half-breed vote for fear that people in the States would regard Washington Territory society as degraded, while Chenoweth believed that extending the franchise would prove the settlers' adherence to liberal ideals. Delegate Moseley sided with Chenoweth, saying that he wanted to live in a land where all men stood on the same level.[15]

Did sentiments like Moseley's motivate other delegates who voted to enfranchise half-breeds? Bills enacted in succeeding years suggest that lawmakers' commitment to liberal ideals was less than wholehearted. In 1855 the assembly voided marriages "[t]heretofore solemnized" between whites and persons with half or more "Indian blood." Three years later legislators revised the ban, voiding future marriages only. Apparently they were willing to forgive the earliest settlers for crossing the line between Indians and whites, especially since white communities were growing on land that some of those settlers had claimed; but they wanted to redraw and maintain the race line thereafter.[16]

Responsibility for the most significant effort to separate Indians from non-Indians fell primarily on the governor, who doubled as superintendent of Indian affairs. Anxious to make the territory safe for colonization by minimizing chances of conflict between settlers and natives, Isaac Stevens set his sights on separation soon after assuming his duties. He gravitated to a scheme just then winning the endorsement of national leaders: putting Indians on reservations. This model for Indian relations, previously disfavored, had acquired cachet because Americans' recent westward migrations had invalidated the policy of moving Indians from the colonized East to the unwanted West. In 1850 the Indian affairs commissioner proposed instead to isolate Indians on tracts within new states and settled territories.[17]

The need for an alternative to removal was especially acute in Washington, Oregon, and California. By sanctioning settlement of those regions before it made arrangements for the native occupants, Congress had disregarded legal precedent and risked an Indian backlash. Yet the many settlers there who depended on Indians for labor and trade had as much reason as Indians to oppose removal. Even though treaties creating small reservations in Oregon and California had recently failed to win ratification, Stevens and Commissioner George Manypenny concluded that a similar scheme was the only workable way to manage Indians in Washington Territory.[18]

Soon after arriving in Olympia, Stevens reminded Manypenny of the urgent need to purchase the Indians' lands so that settlement could proceed apace. The commissioner obtained authorization and funding for the treaties Stevens wanted, although he cautioned the governor to save money and appease Congress by creating the fewest possible reservations. With his instructions Manypenny sent some recent treaties from Nebraska to use as models.[19]

Stevens realized that adapting these models to Washington Territory would be difficult because the populations he had to negotiate with were amorphous. West of the Cascade Mountains native people were dispersed, mobile, loosely organized, and interrelated. U.S. hopes for a formal cession of Indian lands and especially for control over Indians' relations with Americans hinged on bringing the scattered bands together under accountable leaders. But even before Skagit villagers had declined to designate a chief, Stevens knew that the leaders he needed did not exist. Starling had told him that the Indians' apparent chiefs had little actual authority beyond a circle of relatives. They commanded no government apparatus and had no power to punish crimes. "Any one who has riches (in their sense of the word blankets & slaves) and is the head of a family," Starling said, "considers himself a chief." George Gibbs added that Americans could unite the independent villages only by consistently helping a few men to exercise authority; in other words, by creating tribes and chiefs.[20]

In December 1854 Stevens kicked off the campaign to restructure Indian societies and their relations with Americans. He set a hectic pace, negotiating the first three treaties in little more than a month—one on Christmas at Medicine Creek, with residents of south Puget Sound; a second treaty late in January with north Sound groups congregated at Point Elliott; and the third just a week later with people who came from Hood Canal and the Strait of Juan de Fuca to Point No Point.

In aboriginal villages, invitations to the treaty convocations must have stirred mixed feelings of apprehension and pleasure. The prospect of encountering numerous strangers was cause for some anxiety, yet the special event would be a welcome antidote to wintertime cabin fever. A council with Stevens raised the additional hope of easing the fears and anger stemming from recent run-ins with Bostons. Specific anticipation that the American chief would finally pay for the Bostons' use of land, as settlers had promised, was probably universal.[21]

People en route to Stevens's "potlatch" knew that it was an unprecedented event and would not have anticipated a facsimile of their own giveaways. Just as Frank Allen assumed he would see strange customs at ceremonies in distant communities, guests at the treaty councils would have expected the Bostons to show their peculiar way of doing things. Nevertheless, to explain the extraordinary gathering, native people would have referred to known parallels. With no history of buying and selling land, for example, they might have understood Americans' purchase offer by analogy to the gifts they made when seeking to assuage bad feelings.

They probably expected the treaty councils to have the same kinds of social repercussions as their own potlatches. By attending the Bostons' ceremonies, natives could enhance their standing with each other as well

as their hosts. In their code of meanings, the Bostons could prove themselves big men by being generous hosts who promoted peace, and anyone
invited to associate with the Bostons would gain stature. If Stevens or his
speakers greeted notable guests by name and called on them to accept gifts,
the recipients would assume that the American chief had acknowledged
their prestige and the value of having their respect.[22]

Intervillage ceremonies were not the only analogues for the treaty
councils. King George men and priests had already presided over large, in-
discriminate assemblies of native people. Anyone who had been at one
would have expected this one as well to feature the ritual and etiquette
that facilitated diplomacy during the fur trade years: ceremonious greet-
ings and speeches, feasting, communication through interpreters speaking
the Chinook jargon, and the reading or marking of books or papers.

In many respects, the treaty councils met these expectations. Mimicking potlatch protocol, the Bostons invited people to the meetings by
sending a runner to each village with bundled sticks equal in number to
the estimated inhabitants. Upon arriving at the appointed place, native
groups greeted each other with elaborate formality. When Snoqualmies
greeted Skagits at the Point Elliott convocation, "[e]ach party drew up on
the beach in single file & marched past the other, saluting with the sign
of the cross & taking off their hats. ... " While camped at the treaty
grounds for several days, natives also danced for each other, gambled, and
held strength and skill competitions, as they did at potlatches.[23]

In the venerable tradition of the U.S. government, Stevens and his advisors negotiated and solemnized the treaties with a decorum they
thought Indians expected.[24] At the governor's prompting, a few Bostons
and eminent natives gave inspiring speeches, which interpreters converted
to the jargon so that other interpreters, in turn, could convert them to
English or to the indigenous languages. Stevens then explained what the
Americans proposed to give for land. After the Indians conferred separately about the proposal, and only after serious bargaining in some cases,
all notable native men, Stevens, and other whites marked the Bostons'
paper. Finally, the governor distributed gifts through the chiefs and fed the
assembled people. Most native headmen declared that the proceedings left
them feeling good toward the Bostons.[25]

Promoting good feelings was one of the Americans' aims. In order to
accomplish this, they had to meet Indians on the cultural bridge already in
place between societies. However, they saw the treaties as a way to assume
control of traffic across the bridge until Indians were fit to be Americans'
neighbors. Therefore, even as Stevens observed the protocols that Indians

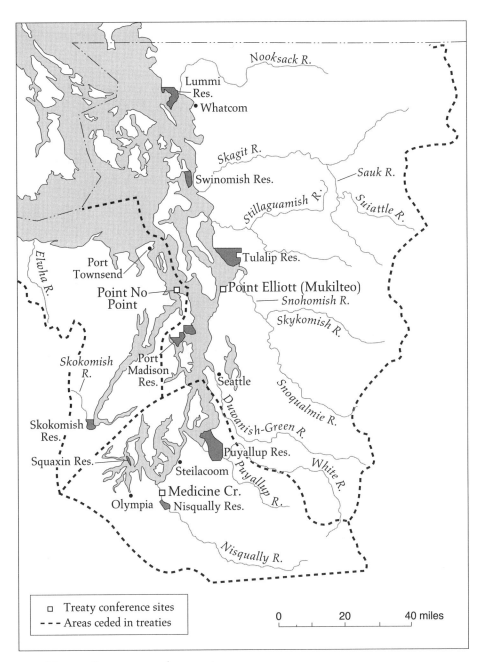

Map 3. Treaty areas and reservations.

seemed to require, he said forcefully that matters could not be arranged between Bostons and Indians except as he proposed: Indians must reside on designated reserves and let U.S. officials guide their relations with outsiders. This demand reflected an American desire to free up as much land as possible for settlement, but it also expressed a general wish to set social boundaries around Indians and to establish the rules for maintaining those boundaries.[26]

According to federal officials, control would be feasible and affordable only if Indians were clustered at one or two sites. To satisfy his superiors and Congress as well as land seekers, Stevens therefore proposed just a few reserves and a treaty clause permitting the president to move Indians onto a single reservation later. But pioneer settlers on the treaty commission argued that more numerous, scattered reserves would be necessary to preserve Indians' access to food and settlers' access to Indian workers.[27] None of the American negotiators intended to cut off relations between white and red people; they simply wanted to limit and regulate relations. The reservations were to be U.S.-supervised homes, not prisons. To people assembled for the first treaty, Stevens described his plan:

> The Great Father has many white children who come here, some to build mills, some to make farms, and some to fish, and the Gr. Father wishes you to have homes, pastures for your horses & fishing places. He wishes you to learn to farm, and your children to go to a good school, and he now wants me to make a bargain with you in which you will sell your lands and in return be provided with all these things. You will have certain lands set apart for your homes and receive yearly payments of Blankets, axes, &c.[28]

Simmons made the Americans' thinking even clearer at the third treaty when one Skokomish man suggested that the Bostons take just half the lands and another asked, "Why not let us live together with you?" If the Indians kept half the lands, Simmons replied, the Americans would insist on strict segregation of the peoples; but if the reserves were small, Americans would let Indians go where they wished in order to fish and work for whites. Indeed, the draft treaty that Stevens brought to every conference included a clause securing the Indians' right to fish at all their customary places.[29]

While the treaties embodied Americans' hopes for well-defined lines between Indians and citizens, they also constituted a scheme to bring Indians into the American polity, where they would occupy a subordinate position. A transaction that native people probably understood as a reciprocal affirmation of the participants' status and friendship thus seemed to

Americans like quite a different accomplishment. They imagined that they had confirmed Indians' subjection to U.S. authority.

To explain the new relationship and make it palatable, American negotiators used the language of kinship. The governor, surrogate for "the Great Father" in Washington, D.C., called himself a father, his aides elder brothers, and the Indians children. When he addressed the multitude at Point Elliott, Stevens explained:

> You are not my children because you are the fruit of my loins but because you are children for whom I have the same feeling as if you were the fruit of my loins. ... What will a man do for his own children? He will see that they are well cared for, that they have clothes to protect them against the cold and rain, that they have food to guard them against hunger. ... I want you as my children to be fed and clothed, and made comfortable and happy.[30]

As if to prove that this metaphor was apt, the governor and his colleagues expressed pity for Indians' helplessness. Indians, they said bluntly or insinuated, were unable to control the power in liquor, unable to cure white men's diseases, unable to keep bad whites from beating them and taking their lands, and therefore unprepared to deal with the consequences of further immigration. "Elder brother" Simmons argued that hope for relief from these tribulations lay in learning to be like Americans. As a father teaches his children how to live, Simmons and Stevens suggested, Americans would teach Indians.

Such paternalistic rhetoric was standard fare in American dealings with Indians elsewhere—a convention dating from the seventeenth century. And even though real or fictive kinship was the basis for most friendly relations among Puget Sound natives, parent-and-child roles were probably the Bostons' idea. Some native leaders do not seem to have relished the role Stevens offered them. In the minutes of the three Puget Sound treaty conferences, only Seattle's speeches make liberal use of the suggested kinship terms. At Point No Point, Chelantehtet and two other men were reluctant to say they regarded Stevens as a father until the governor satisfied them that he offered an advantageous bargain. They and other native speakers seemed less interested in acquiring a father-provider than in getting Stevens to acknowledge the value of their resources and goodwill. They spelled out what the Bostons could do to establish good relations: guarantee Indians continuing access to fish and the other resources that sustained them, allow them to consult good American doctors, and make the promised payments.[31]

Indian negotiators did use self-deprecating rhetoric, as expected of well-bred men. Yet some denied that the American incursion had disabled and impoverished them, declaring instead that they were equal to the challenges and opportunities of their new circumstances. "Before the Whites came we were always poor," said Duke of York. "Since then we have earned money and got blankets and clothing." Nah-whil-luk maintained that he understood how the Bostons thought about land and was prepared to deal with them on their own terms. "Formerly the Indians slept," he said, "but the Whites came among them and woke them up and we now know that the lands are worth much."[32]

To people at the treaty councils, the governor's offer to take care of Indians may have seemed more an expression of goodwill than a guarantee of material support, especially when they saw the meager quantity and quality of the gifts he distributed and heard him warn that further distributions depended on presidential approval. Several men at Point No Point were more interested in whether the governor had power to keep settlers from abusing them than in whether he would supply their material needs. Once Stevens pledged that selling the land would not cut them off from fishing grounds, work sites, and other sources of money and food, they were sure they could provide for themselves and were ready to sign.[33]

The Bostons' parting gifts were far from lavish, but to express disappointment by retracting the good words just spoken was unthinkable. Native people deemed it rude to comment unfavorably on a host's actions and dangerous to criticize people who were not blood relatives. Besides, some indulgence of the Bostons was clearly warranted on this occasion. By their rapid increase, willingness to use deadly force, and political organization, Americans had shown themselves the most formidable people in the region. Especially when contemplating the differences between Bostons' customs and theirs, natives probably saw no alternative to hearing out the Bostons and hoping that their promises were good.[34]

Afterward, some Indians justified their endorsement of the treaties by referring to the Bostons' overawing power. Tyee Dick, for example, told Ezra Meeker that he signed the Medicine Creek Treaty because he knew it was folly to fight American soldiers. But even if others thought as Tyee Dick did, natives also had reason to consider themselves honored by the treaty councils. Construing the Bostons' promises as flattering recognition was not self-delusion; indigenous beliefs supported such a construction of the treaty councils. To Indians, the gatherings established and symbolized bonds of friendship—prestigious bonds—with illustrious men.[35]

Americans characterized the relationship established by treaty as one between all the Indians on one hand and all the whites on the other. At the councils Boston orators referred to natives as a single category of people and explicitly contrasted them with whites. The enormous assemblies, with their focus on concluding a bilateral agreement, gave this message a visual and probably an emotional content. Understandably, after Stevens and Simmons had addressed the crowds as Indians or siwash, the designated chiefs responded in kind. Nonetheless, treaty records show that the category "Indians" was more an American hope than a reality. The proceedings confirmed that Puget Sound's indigenous peoples were still many and diverse.[36]

Although Stevens appointed or acknowledged only a few head chiefs for aggregations he called tribes, the documents he prepared named dozens of autonomous groups as parties to the treaties. For some of the named bands, no one signed; and yet the men who signed outnumbered the bands, probably because the heads of different households expected separate recognition. Furthermore, after proposing two or three reserves around the Sound, Stevens agreed to eight because his advisors warned that villagers would balk at moving into other groups' territories. In other words, subdivisions of the populations encompassed by the treaties were far more numerous and ambiguous than the Americans wanted to admit.[37]

Natives' diversity was evident, too, in their reactions to the Americans' plans. Some witnesses said that Nisqually subchief Leschi refused to sign the Medicine Creek Treaty, and a similar story circulated later about men from upland villages in the Point Elliott Treaty area. Although the minutes do not corroborate these claims, they do document a multiplicity of Indian perspectives on the treaties. The concerns that native spokesmen emphasized at the councils varied considerably. When the people that Americans lumped together as Indians thought about themselves in relation to Bostons, they did not think in unison.[38]

Even in the linguistically homogeneous population assembled at Medicine Creek, the distinct communities had different economic and social orientations, and those differences contributed to disparate feelings about the treaty terms. Especially salient were distinctions between people who resided near salt water and those who lived inland. People in upriver settlements counted their wealth in horses before canoes. Whereas their downstream neighbors usually found spouses and trading partners in other Salish-speaking communities on the Sound, inland villagers often had close relations with people east of the Cascade Mountains—Sahaptin speakers who were known to the Bostons as Yakima or Klickitat Indians.[39]

Because of their orientation, some upriver people soon grew anxious about the treaty concluded at Medicine Creek. The plan to locate them on small, forested, beachfront reserves meant leaving the prairies where they planted crops and pastured horses. At their uninviting new homesites, they would also be farther from eastern kin. Because they communicated regularly with such kin, they learned in the summer of 1855 that Stevens had angered Yakimas by bullying them into a treaty. And Yakima grievances multiplied when gold seekers headed northeast from Puget Sound to the Colville district, streaming through Indian lands east of the mountains before the United States had paid for them. Some natives in the Medicine Creek area felt their qualms about American intentions grow along with the anger and suspicion of their Sahaptin relatives.[40]

Anger and suspicion also mounted in other Puget Sound homes as 1855 passed. Indians who hoped the treaties would enrich them and end whites' harassment were disappointed. Congress ratified only the Medicine Creek Treaty that year, and even ratification did not bring prompt payments or protection from malicious settlers. A rumor flew through camps and villages that the Bostons' real plan was to transport all siwash to a distant land of perpetual darkness. Meanwhile, the government's inaction also dashed settlers' hopes. Whites who expected the treaties to relieve them of the Indians in their midst grew restless as the months wore on without change. Like many others, David Blaine first rejoiced at news of the treaties, which included reports that the Indians were satisfied. "Could the indians and alcohol be removed this would be in most respects one of the most delightful regions of the country in the world," he told his parents. But he added in the same letter, "Since the treaty we are blessed with the presence, dwellings, noise, filth, vileness, & all manner of obscenity of more indians than ever before."[41]

By late summer many people could feel tension in the air. Leschi, a Nisqually subchief, was vociferously unhappy with the reserve selected for his group. He was also on edge, he told W. F. Tolmie, because other Indians reported that territorial officials found him obnoxious and planned to jail him. A native doctor, back from a meager government "potlatch," complained bitterly to Emily Denny's parents. The stingy white people were few and their doors were thin, Dr. Choush rumbled; Indians could easily kill them all. Perhaps settlers projected onto Indians the rancor they would have felt toward anyone who demanded that they relinquish their homes and habits. At any rate, in mid-October, upon hearing a rumor that Yakimas had killed a government agent, many whites voiced an expectation they had had for months: an Indian war was imminent.[42]

The war—Americans' next major effort to subordinate and isolate Indians—was on by November. A week after confirming the rumor about agent A. J. Bolon's death, the *Pioneer and Democrat* called for a crusade to blot out the Yakima tribe. Army officers urged the formation of a volunteer militia. Since Stevens was in Blackfeet country on his treaty-making tour, Acting Governor Charles Mason fielded these demands. Besides mobilizing the militia, Mason summoned Leschi and his brother Quiemuth to Olympia, planning to hold them there lest they emulate or ally with Yakima warriors. The brothers, either mistrusting Mason's claim that he wanted to protect them or having already decided on war, left their farms in haste and vanished from American view. Armed volunteers searched the foothills for the missing men and other possibly hostile Indians. Shortly thereafter, during the last days of October, Indians killed two militiamen in ambush and besieged their comrades. Other Indians raided American claims on the White River, slaying men, women, and children.[43]

Many Americans leaped immediately to the conclusion that Indians on both sides of the mountains had organized a monstrous, antiwhite conspiracy. The captain of the navy sloop *Decatur*, anchored in front of Seattle, believed rumors that "Quiemuth's tribe" had united with the Klickitats in a campaign to exterminate all Americans in the territory. Chiefs Seattle and Patkanim still asserted their friendship for whites, the captain noted; but "[e]very tribe is more or less connected, that is, every tribe has relations and friends in the adjoining ones, and the bad Indians are trying to corrupt the good ones."[44]

West of the mountains, the ensuing war was hardly worthy of the name. At most, a few hundred natives from the area took up arms or abetted those who did. Over a five-month period they fought regular troops and militia sporadically and in a limited area. Most clashes were short and involved few casualties. Except for a daylong battle at the town of Seattle in January, all fighters lay low through the harsh winter. In March territorial forces again engaged Indians in battle and claimed a decisive victory, but there was no Indian surrender. Instead, native warriors and their families slipped over the Cascades or straggled into American forts and the camps established for noncombatants. Although it was August of 1856 before Stevens announced that war had ended in the Puget Sound basin, soldiers realized that west side Indians had ceased hostilities as early as April.[45]

For settlers in western Washington, the brief and apparently vain armed resistance of some Indian neighbors immediately took on a significance out of proportion to its scope or length. They seized on the little war as a symbol of their destiny and the destiny of indigenous people. However, because they did not agree on how those destinies should unfold, they competed to assign meanings to the war. In particular, the war's causes soon became and long remained a subject of heated debate. Even before hostilities erupted, political factions argued about the reasons war seemed likely. Isaac Stevens's critics damned him for strong-arming Indians into unworkable treaties. Supporters of the governor, calling the treaties the best hope for Indians, blamed tensions on a few dishonorable natives and HBC men who had allegedly aroused Indians' discontent with rumors and lies. Although the rivals in this debate called in unison for the subjugation of hostile Indians, they never agreed on whether the native resistance represented unforgivable treachery, an understandable response to American abuses, or the inevitable last stand of people who saw that their way of life was doomed.[46]

This contention colored all contemporary inquiries into the motives of native fighters. The least tainted evidence of those motives comes from men whom the rebels regarded as potential mediators. Leschi, who assumed leadership of some combatants, confided in Tolmie at the Puget Sound Agricultural Company. He and other warriors also explained their actions to some former HBC servants living in the upper Nisqually and Puyallup Valleys. The fighters' litany of grievances included the reservations' unsuitability, the rumored plan to deport them to a land without sun, encroachments on their land and fishing sites, and Mason's scheme to detain Leschi and Quiemuth.[47]

Many commentators then and later interpreted the Indians' resort to violence as a repudiation of the changes wrought by white immigrants—a rage against all things American.[48] But there is little in the rebels' lives or recorded thoughts to support this interpretation. When Leschi made peace overtures, he stressed that he had previously been friendly to whites. And indeed, he and other prominent rebels had maintained close and apparently amicable relations with non-Indians for years. Several had white in-laws or ancestors. All were well known and welcome at Fort Nisqually and American settlements. All had enhanced their status among Indians and non-Indians by emulating European-American means of acquiring wealth.[49]

Men like Quiemuth and Leschi may have felt increasingly threatened by Americans precisely because they emulated whites, at least in their economic pursuits. Unlike natives nearer the salt water, they wanted arable land and pasture as much as settlers did. The demand that they abandon their fenced and cultivated fields rankled. Men so familiar with whites may also have sensed that Americans' growing stress on the differences between Indians and whites was a rationale for pushing Indians aside. Stevens affected surprise that the west side war leaders were men the whites had especially trusted, but his observation reminds us that tensions between ethnic groups have often been greatest along the frontiers where they meet and influence each other.

Paradoxically, war seemed to offer Americans some relief from the tensions attending their relations with Indians. Relations that had been varied and equivocal now seemed clearly and simply defined. As Arthur Denny later recalled, whites "who, a short time before, insisted that the Indians were all friendly, would now declare most vehemently that all were hostile, and must all be treated as enemies."[50] In one sense, war is the starkest possible representation of difference, and the conflict of 1855–56 did confirm that divisive differences persisted between natives and immigrants. Nevertheless, in order to construe the war as a contest between whites and Indians, Americans had to reinterpret and reorder a world that was not so clearly polarized.

On one hand, whites and Indians remained so different that they even thought about the war in dissimilar ways. Unlike Americans, indigenous peoples did not conceive of war as an institutionalized tool of political domination. Historically, they had used deadly force to avenge personal injuries or to seize slaves and property. Rather than conducting sustained campaigns, they commonly made isolated attacks against individuals or small groups, sometimes long after the provocation they had in mind. Such encounters involved the spontaneous use or display of individuals' nonhuman powers, and those powers also made it possible to intimidate foes, avenge insults, or acquire another's property by means other than war.[51] Conduct consistent with these views baffled or amused Americans during the winter of 1855–56. Settlers could not fathom why Indians would slaughter some farm families but leave others unmolested. A naval officer at the daylong siege of Seattle thought it comical when one well-known native man, smeared with paint and yelling, zigzagged across the line of fire with arms and legs extended, sprang into the air, and disappeared behind a house, "highly satisfied with his display of prodigious valor."[52]

On the other hand, to express differences by war is nonetheless to engage in relations; and even to fight each other, Indians and Americans moved onto common ground. In the heat of battle they communicated in the trade jargon. They adapted their tactics to what they knew about each other. Except for the Indian raid on White River homesteaders, the violence usually conformed to American expectations that designated warriors would meet in battle at strategic locations; yet army officers copied some Indian fighting techniques as well. Militiamen also mimicked native custom, as they understood it, when they took revenge on Indians at random or on the relatives of warriors. By recruiting native auxiliaries, Americans further smudged the presumed racial-cultural line between foes.[53]

The war that supposedly arrayed red men against whites in fact revealed that western Washington's population was arranged in a complex mosaic of many hues. When the *Pioneer and Democrat* identified the first Indians to ambush the militia as "our own *dear* Nesqually neighbors," it added, "Beyond a doubt, all the Indians of all tribes on the Sound and Straits are confederates."[54] But in reality, the rebels were a tiny minority of native people. The thousands of other indigenous people around Puget Sound either aided American troops or sat out the conflict. Many followed officials' instructions to move to temporary reservations well away from the theater of war.

Contrary to some of Governor Stevens's claims, whites did not unite reflexively either. Their diversity and their links to native people deterred some whites from seeing race as the basis of a natural alliance. Those with native kin had conflicting allegiances. Many of them, along with others, tried to remain neutral. Unnerved at the way biracial couples and their progeny obscured the presumed line between warring races, Stevens pressured such people to choose sides, even charging several with treason. In defense of this tactic and a related declaration of martial law, he said, "There is no such thing in my humble judgment as neutrality in an Indian war, and whoever can remain on his claim unmolested, is an ally of the enemy. . . . " But this amounted to an admission that white solidarity was a fiction and that hostile Indians could spot friends among the whites.[55]

For all these reasons and more, war did little to clarify the relationship of natives to settlers. Whites who saw the conflict as a confirmation of the races' incompatibility thought that Indians, facing defeat, had finally conceded Americans' right to dominate and quarantine them. But this inference had a shaky foundation. Only if the uprising was indeed an Indian attempt to drive settlers from the Sound did the cease-fire have such humiliating implications for Indians. If the rebels' aims were more consonant with indigenous traditions, they and other natives could construe the war's results in less degrading terms. By their standards, the warriors had demonstrated impressive powers. They had terrified settlers, avenged some injuries, and forced Americans to acknowledge their pride and strength. Most had also proven themselves invulnerable to Boston bullets.

Furthermore, it appeared that the rebels had compelled Stevens to revise his plans for Indians in the area ceded at Medicine Creek. The governor consented to renegotiate that galling treaty. At Fox Island in August 1856, he met a congregation of formerly hostile natives and asked them to say how they wanted the treaty carried out. Acknowledging that dissatisfaction with the original reservations had spurred most of them to fight, he promised them larger tracts with ground enough for horses. He also pledged to add a reserve on the White and Green Rivers.[56]

For American officials, the Fox Island conference was another opportunity to describe the relations they envisioned between siwash and Bostons. Sidney Ford, supervisor of the relocation camp on the island, introduced the governor and his Indian agent by saying "They have come to act the part of white men towards the poor Indian." Ford closed the meeting with the lesson that he and his colleagues wanted Indians to draw from the war.

> [Y]ou were told that the whites were weak & that by one united effort you could rid the country of the Bostons. You now see that you have failed. You now see that where one white man is killed ten more come to occupy his place. I say not this with feelings of enmity. The whites pity your ignorance & for that reason are the Tyees of the Bostons here to-day. . . .

According to conference minutes, the Indians then gave three hearty cheers for the advice they had received. But the minutes as a whole warn us not to assume that the cheering men endorsed Ford's patronizing views. Native speakers neither acknowledged defeat nor explicitly confessed to weakness, ignorance, or dependency on Bostons. Instead, each carefully identified his home ground and expressed pleasure at Stevens's new willingness to create a suitable reservation. Like Indian Sam, who declared himself proud that the governor had visited them again, the native men apparently construed their inclusion in the meeting as an honor. In their terms, the conference renewed mutually respectful relations between peoples who were there to acknowledge each other's distinctive domains and powers.[57]

To show Indians how they should interpret the war, Americans did more than moralize at the Fox Island council. They also dramatized the purported hierarchy of power by prosecuting native men who fought on the wrong side. Beginning early in 1856, hundreds of Indian warriors went on trial for murder and other crimes. The most conspicuous case with the greatest symbolic freight was Leschi's, but a variety of civil and military tribunals considered charges against numerous other Indians. Some defendants, like Leschi, they convicted and punished; many others they acquitted.[58]

If there had indeed been a war between distinct peoples, it made little sense in either native or American terms to charge Indian fighters with breaking U.S. laws. Americans who opposed Leschi's prosecution—no doubt feeling that it cheapened their own military feats to label their enemies common criminals—pointed this out. Nonetheless, Stevens and judges strained to interpret the hostilities as an Indian transgression of domestic rules. Without warning, Stevens argued, Leschi and other "monsters" turned on friends and neighbors who had always treated them with kindness. Such perfidy was not warfare but base murder.[59]

In the eyes of many settlers, Stevens's handling of the treaties and war was implicitly on trial along with the Indians. Leschi's case in particular became the occasion for a bitter contest between white political factions.[60] By treating the rebels as criminals, Stevens aimed to disarm his non-Indian critics while teaching natives their place in an American-controlled world. But to advance the latter aim, convictions were not essential. Simply by holding trials Americans might show that they had established meaningful authority over Indians. Some Americans convinced themselves further that their own fairness entitled them to such authority. Leschi's prosecutor, noting that the accused man had two zealous lawyers, declared that no criminal had ever enjoyed a fairer trial. And the judge who sentenced Leschi to hang told him,

> Whatever may be said of the probability or possibility of your innocence one thing is quite certain you have had the benefit of all the forms of law that the most favored of our own raice [sic] have in trials for murder. . . . Unlike those of our own race with whoes [sic] murder you are charged the law is not vindictive punishments are instituted for the protection of society.[61]

Indians who tried to understand the war from the Bostons' point of view had more than trials and councils with Stevens to consider, however. Claims that Americans sought justice rather than vengeance were hard to interpret when Bostons took revenge on individual Indians and suffered no consequent disgrace in their communities. To Stevens's "mortification," for instance, Quiemuth no sooner committed himself to American custody than he was murdered in the governor's office. Officers arrested a settler who blamed his brother-in-law's war death on Leschi, but no whites would testify against the man.[62]

How did indigenous people interpret such incidents and the postwar trials? The available clues consist mainly of beliefs about war and homicide, passed from Leschi's generation to children and grandchildren who described them later for ethnographers. To their ancestors, Indians recalled, homicides were not crimes that imperiled an abstract public order; they were injuries to and by individuals and their families, who had responsibility for rectifying the social consequences. Personal losses and relationships were likewise the motivations for acts of war and arrangements to end war.[63]

These beliefs afforded a basis for understanding not only the inland Indians' war venture but also succeeding events. Indigenous people could assume that Leschi, Quiemuth, and their associates had acted on particular loyalties and grievances against certain Bostons. The rituals and concessions needed to restore peace also pertained primarily to the erstwhile foes. If other natives took an interest in the terms of peace, they were not necessarily acting in conscious solidarity with fellow Indians; more likely they had ties to the warriors or relished the mediator's role.[64] Headmen from many bands did petition the Bostons to spare Leschi's life, but even this gesture does not mean that they saw Leschi as a symbol of all Indians, now subordinated to American will. Rather, Indians told Sidney Ford that Leschi's execution was unnecessary because Quiemuth's murder had made things even between the former enemies.[65]

These conjectures about native perspectives on the war are less fanciful than retrospective assertions (heard from Indians and non-Indians) that Puget Sound Indians saw Leschi as a martyr for their doomed way of life. The conjectures are also consonant with the account of Leschi's death that Nisqually fighter Wahoolit (waxʷelút or Yelm Jim) offered some years later. Retold by Frank Allen, Wahoolit's grandnephew, the story is the only published record of what Leschi's peers said to each other about his fate.

> Now Leschi was in jail at Steilacoom for a long time. . . . But a mob came along and fixed up a place to hang Leschi. So Leschi's power came one day and said, "They're going to kill you. White people are going to kill you now." So Leschi said to the watchman, "I want all my people to come and see me, before you people are going to kill me." And they let waxʷelút and lúkʷ come to see him. . . .
>
> And Leschi said, "As soon as they hang me, loosen the rope from my neck, and put me on my horse, and take me home quick! I'm not going to die. My power is going to help me." . . .
>
> They hoisted him, and when he was hanged the poor Indians took him down. . . . They put him on his horse to take him away, and they ran his horse to his house. . . . And when they got there they saw that

rope and took it off. Now when they took that rope off, Leschi came to and he breathed, gasping for breath. And then Leschi sang his tamanamis, and everybody helped him sing. His power was going to help him.

Now three or four doctors went outside and talked together, and they said, "We'll kill Leschi with our power." Those bad doctors agreed to kill Leschi. "If Leschi lives, he'll fight the white men again, and all the Nisqually will be killed. We'll all die. So it's best that we kill Leschi now. . . . Now we'll look for Leschi's big power, and we'll kill Leschi's power."

So they say, Leschi lived for quite a while, but he missed his big power now, his power that those doctors killed, and so he died, no more power. It wasn't that hanging killed him, it was those bad doctors killed him.[66]

Wahoolit's tale would have confounded Isaac Stevens, who wanted Indians to believe that Americans, not Indians, had destroyed the power of men like Leschi to thwart American goals. To be sure, the story obliquely acknowledges whites' greater military power, and it is consistent with reports that Indians had lost faith in their supernatural helpers' power to affect whites.[67] But even if Wahoolit knew how Americans analyzed relations between Indians and whites, he had little interest in following suit, because the way he had learned to think about relations still enabled him to make sense of his and other natives' experiences. For Wahoolit and many of his contemporaries, their inability as Indians to match Americans' military and political strength was far less important than their ability as individuals to use their powers effectively in pursuit of personal ends. And neither the treaties nor the war had robbed all indigenous people of that ability.

Through the 1860s Americans could muster precious little evidence that the war had put them in control of Indians. Events during and after the war did weaken indigenous communities, but they took a toll on settler society as well. In addition, national conditions thwarted plans to strengthen the American community in Washington Territory. For years, therefore, neither the treaties nor the apparent American triumph over Indian rebels limited Indians' sphere of operations as Bostons intended. In such circumstances, natives who had found ways to use their personal powers advantageously were often able to do so still or again.

At war's end many native people were poor, hungry, and sick. Families who fled to the hills had forfeited homes, horses, access to some foods, and opportunities to work for and trade with whites. After fighting ceased, well-founded fears of Boston vengeance kept them close to Fort Steilacoom or the reservations and dependent on government aid.[68] People who had moved instead to temporary reserves and some who had stayed in their villages suffered from food shortages as well. Simmons had enjoined them from traveling and promised them rations to make up for forgone subsistence, but the rations were inadequate. Crowded together and undernourished, many in the relocation camps sickened and died. Even after Indians returned to their usual subsistence rounds, hunger and disease dogged them. During 1857 and 1858, salmon runs failed, and drought killed potato crops. Destitute natives camped outside Simmons's office in Olympia, petitioning for the help he had pledged.[69]

The war cast a long shadow on American society as well. Most settlers fled to blockhouses, and many did not go home for months or years. Some left the territory for good. During a visit in August 1857, government inspector Ross Browne saw deserted houses, neglected fields, and wagon-loads of people heading for Oregon. When agriculture around Puget Sound slid into a decade-long depression, some people blamed the war and its aftereffects. Feelings of insecurity helped to keep settlers' social life nearly as depressed as farming. And Stevens's prediction that the Great Father's white children would soon overrun Indians' lands proved erroneous. Except when the Fraser River gold rush briefly swelled the population around Bellingham Bay, immigration came to a virtual standstill.[70]

Whites in the little American colony often felt far from powerful. They begged the federal government for protection from northern Indians who crossed the international border to raid. Behind their exaggerated claims of helplessness lay a desire for the money and markets that came with troops and naval vessels. Nevertheless, some local natives sensed real weakness. According to an agent on Whidbey Island, Indians there said that Bostons did not stop the northerners' plunder because they had "no strong hearts."[71]

Unable to count on American protection, natives around the Sound organized their own responses to threats from the north. In 1857 Michael Simmons told Stevens:

> I am informed by Mr. Fitzhugh ... that there had been a large pot-lach, given by the Lummies on the western side of the bay ... , and that there had been the large[st?] attendance, ever known in that part of the world. The Frasier river, Victoria, Sanich, Nanaimo, Cowegian, Scatchetts, Snohomish, Stilagamish, Clalams, Samish & other tribes were represented on this occasion. The pot-lach was gotten up for the purpose of having an understanding among themselves, in regard to the Northern Indians. ... [72]

When potlatch participants announced that they had made peace with the northern tribes, settlers feared that local natives would join the northerners' raids on whites.

American officials were powerless to orchestrate relations with Indians as sketched out in the treaties. Only the treaty at Medicine Creek won prompt approval in Congress. Unable to honor pledges made at the other councils, Simmons grew nervous. In December 1857 he asked the new superintendent of Indian affairs to imagine how odd the government's conduct appeared to native people: Indians who had waged war received treaty annuities, while those who had sided with Americans were paid only in promises. Two thousand whites lived among ten thousand Indians, Simmons observed, and relations would remain "on a very precarious basis" as long as Indians believed the government was ignoring them. After another year's delay, Simmons tried a new line of argument: "This is Indian country and it is not. Towns now stand upon ground where the Indian title is not extinct. . . . I am agent for the whole Puget Sound district, have thousands of Indians to look after and be in some measure responsible for, yet I actually only have an agent's power on three small reservations and over one thousand Indians."[73]

To the end of his tenure in 1861, Simmons complained that lack of funds and personnel undermined his authority.[74] Without money or permission to set aside reservations, he could do little more than make periodic appearances in Indian communities, reassuring residents that the Bostons would keep their word. Unconvinced, some natives chased settlers and surveyors off land they had ceded in the unratified treaties. Others threatened to renege on the treaty agreements. All were aware that they had no obligation to Boston leaders until their payments came.[75]

The first of the payments promised at Point Elliott and Point No Point did not reach native hands until 1861, two years after Congress finally ratified the treaties. Even then government agents were ill equipped to impress Indians with their wealth and power. Since the number of people entitled to share in each payment was double or triple the initial estimate, treaty annuities amounted at most to a few dollars per person; and officials often did not have even that sum to distribute. Instead of cash, they usually handed out goods worth less than the debt owed. One subagent warned his superiors that to give Indians "cultus [worthless]" blankets was to be humiliated before them.[76] If so, the Civil War added to the humiliation by keeping the government poor. In 1862 the newest superintendent of Indian affairs had to carry on for five months without a dollar of federal funds. And even after Appomattox, appropriations for Puget

Sound's Indian agency did not increase. When Samuel Ross took charge in 1870, he found dissatisfied Indians who had received no annuity goods and no attention to their complaints for several years.[77]

Years also went by before officials marked the boundaries of the Indian reservations. Hoping to deter squatters, Simmons asked the *Pioneer and Democrat* to publish descriptions of the planned tracts in 1859, but formal dedication was at least a decade away for most. Even marking the enclaves did not empower agents to force Indians into them. To persuade native people that living on a reservation was the way to manage relations with Bostons, officials had to make reservations as alluring as the bustling American towns or the districts where Bostons had not yet settled. This they could not do.[78]

In 1863 the Indian superintendent admitted that his office had not done what was needed to attract people to the reserves. In some places, he added, anyone settling on reservation would have died of starvation. At Tulalip, where Stevens had promised to put agricultural and industrial training facilities for all Indians of the region, the only draw for years was a tiny Catholic school—an operation so penurious that Father E. C. Chirouse could not house and feed his students adequately. Each year some children died, and others left to fish and forage with their families. In 1865 Chirouse's pupils complained that they worked hard without reward while their friends made money among the whites.[79]

Hoping to gain influence over natives near Bellingham Bay, subagent Edward Fitzhugh went to their camps with gifts and offers to intercede when whites cheated them. Even so, he persuaded few people to move to the reservation. Stationing a physician, blacksmith, and carpenter at the bleak Squaxin Island Reservation did not bring Indians in there either. Moving those attractions to the Puyallup Reservation, which also offered good fishing and farmland, got better results; but the only way to draw Indians to other reserves was to pay them for clearing land, building houses, or transporting supplies. Like Chirouse, however, reservation supervisors usually could offer only the prospect of uncompensated labor. And as long as American officials did not take the role of provider, most native people saw no reason to defer to them. Lamenting that the agent for the Nisqually Reservation had no control over his charges, Ross Browne added, "In these respects, the Nisquallys resemble all the rest of the Sound Indians...."[80]

Since few Indians moved to Puget Sound reservations during the 1850s or 1860s, the government did not even know who or where all the people encompassed by the treaties were. Again and again, men assigned to oversee Indians admitted that they could not name or count their charges. R. C. Fay told Simmons why he could give only a general report on the Indians for whom he was responsible in 1860: "[T]hey are scattered over a large extent of country, and although I am travelling nearly all the time, they too are travelling continualy [*sic*] changing their camps, as the seasons differ affording them fish of different kinds peculiar to each season, causing an interval of two or three months sometimes that I do not see portions of some of the tribes."[81]

To the dismay of officials who hoped to influence Indians' behavior by giving them advice and farm tools, some natives would not even come to annuity distributions. Those who did stayed only until they wished to go elsewhere. "If their supervisors insist upon anything that they do not fancy doing," Simmons observed, "they can leave the reservation, and have any quantity of excuses ready for having done so on their return." The excuses included opportunities to work, trade, buy whiskey, and sell sexual services in the American settlements.[82] Virtually all but the feeblest of Puget Sound's native people thus continued to provide for themselves. They fished, hunted, and harvested berries and roots as their ancestors had done; but they also sold what they caught or gathered, hired out as domestic servants, ferried passengers and cargo, and labored at mines, mills, and farms. As before the treaties, their activities included frequent, varied, increasing, and diversifying transactions with settlers.[83]

According to contemporary and retrospective descriptions, western Washington settlers could not avoid rubbing elbows with Indians during the 1850s and 1860s. They met Indians in the saloons of gold rush towns on Bellingham Bay, on the docks of boisterous Port Townsend, in the muddy streets of Olympia, in homesteaders' shacks and fields, and at Fourth of July picnics. In many settings the Indians, still more numerous than settlers, had power to structure the physical and social environment. At Port Townsend, for instance, public spaces were used for Indian activities as often as for non-Indian. At the end of a week in 1859 when natives had monopolized the town's beach for a secret society initiation, James Swan wrote in his diary, "Yesterday there was quite a variety of performances, first the Indians, then a fight between two rowdies, then a sermon by Father Rossi."[84]

Settlers rubbed more than elbows with Indians. Especially in the absence of white women, contact with Indians made many a white male's heart grow fond of native women. Neither the legislature's 1855 ban on mixed marriages nor a few prosecutions for illegal cohabitation reduced the number of "squaw men." What John Fornsby recalled about settlements along the Skagit River in the 1860s could be said about other places around Puget Sound: "The first White men to come in the river all got Indian women. . . . "[85]

Although pioneers would later describe a society where Indians and whites coexisted amicably, many sources of friction remained. Indians frequently suffered indignities and worse when encountering settlers. An 1861 incident at Whatcom so excited natives that they appealed to the superintendent of Indian affairs through a literate settler, who wrote:

> A few days ago, to wit, on the 5th Ins a chief of the Lummis visited Sehome with a load of potatoes, and a man, being drunk, wished to take his women from him and on the Indian asking him to not do so he made a violent attack on him with a loaded pistol and tried to shoot him, the Indian took hold of his hand and held on to it, when three other men came up and beat and abused the Indian shamefully.[86]

But Indians were not always the ones to complain of harassment. The governor and Indian superintendent received more than one appeal like the following from a Whidbey Island settler:

> [W]e are in the midst of a great number of Indians who are dayly stealing & robing braking open houses & destroying houses & other property, there are a great number of strange Indians on the Island at this time from the River who are very saucy and make a great many threats, and as there is but few white men on the island we are wholy in their power and if there is not something done we will have trouble with them.[87]

Because the government was weak, appealing to territorial officials was still not the recourse of choice every time Indians and settlers clashed. Threats, violence, mediation, and compensatory payments served to adjust relations as often as they had before 1855. When Indians assaulted settlers, Bostons usually demanded swift trial and punishment. But for all the Bostons' boasts about bringing law to the wilderness, their justice system was of little use to Indians who suffered harm from settlers. Efforts to prosecute whites for murdering Indians or selling them liquor taught Indian Office personnel that judges and jurors would not apply the law evenhandedly. One agent said in 1864, "There is very little hope of a conviction, especially when venerable, grey-headed men . . . will arise in their place in the jury box . . . and say that it would require far more evidence to convict a white man for killing an Indian, than though it was a white man that had been killed."[88]

Thus, in the postwar decade natives and immigrants met and mixed on terms that were constantly in the process of definition. Lacking power to dictate social roles and relations, Americans tried at least to communicate what they expected of Indians. When possible, officials and missionaries told Indians how to behave. An agent in charge of the Nisqually Reservation reported:

> I have had a long talk with this tribe, in council assembled, at which time I endeavored to point out to them the evils arising from the practice of drinking whiskey, of indulging in polygamy, the art of necromancy in the healing of their sick, of flattening the heads of their children, &c., all of which practices they promised to abandon as soon as they possibly could, remarking at the same time that it would take some considerable time to effect such a radical change ... as it was disposing of an old heart or mind and adopting a new one.[89]

To some white observers, advice of this kind seemed to have a salutary effect on Indians' behavior; so when the same Indians resumed old practices, the observers usually blamed wicked whites who set a contrary example. And if Indians were to deduce from Bostons' conduct how to ensure good relations, they did indeed have conflicting models. Besides government agents and priests, there were soldiers, miners, and mill workers they could emulate. Many such men encouraged Indians to drink and to prostitute their women. Moreover, officials and missionaries did not always provide examples of the conduct they advocated. Most agents counseled against drinking liquor, yet some were drunks; most condemned illicit sexual relations, yet several cohabited with native women; and some judges and officials who exhorted Indians to obey the law broke the law themselves. Chirouse promised a better life for Christians, but life at his mission school was a hardship.[90]

Hearing ambiguous and divergent messages from Bostons, native people came to varying conclusions about the roles they should play vis-à-vis whites. As Indians at the Tulalip mission tried to follow the priest's prescription for pleasing the whites' God, other whites and natives handed them different recipes for good relations. In 1859 they voiced their confusion in a petition to Michael Simmons:

> Some whites are anger against us because we do not want give to them our girls as we did heretofore, or because we do not sell a large portion of our fish oil ... for their Whisky. Those whites say that we are very foolish to believe what Mister Simmons says and what the priest says that Mister Simmons is a liar and the priest a monster from kikoola fire. They tell us to that very soon we shall be compeld to desert our religion to follow some other better priest who will give us plenty goods and who shall also show to us the real truth and lead us to

heaven without any trouble of prayers nor privations. ... Those bad indians our brothers do all they can to carry us towards their own way
of rebellion and brutality. ... It is reported by those troublesome
[indians] that you will tie and hang the innocent and good chiefs
because they do pray God ..., and we are very hurry to inform you
that we fear to see the number of the bad indians become very soon
larger and follow the exemple of those bad Nooxak who never did keep
company with us. ... [91]

Native people adopted diverse strategies not just because they heard
contradictory advice but also because immigrants' activities offered a
growing variety of ways to achieve what most natives ardently desired—
status in the eyes of high-status people. An extensive record of Indian
giveaways, marriage exchanges, and initiation rituals proves that old notions about status had continuing vitality during the 1860s. [92] Although
native people were acquiring status-enhancing wealth in new ways, such
as working in sawmills, they used their earnings to perpetuate aboriginal
customs. To Father Chirouse's dismay, Klallams often gambled their wages
away.

> Whenever they do spend their money for useful articles of any kind
> they are generally kept for purposes of display till a sufficient quantity
> has been accumulated, when the whole is given away at once at a grand
> feast made for the occasion, and the Indian who was worth hundreds in
> the morning thus beggars himself before night; the person who can
> give the greatest amount being considered the greatest man.

Thus, in 1865 Indians planned a potlatch at the coal mines where many of
them worked. Along with blankets and canoes, they would give away tin
pans, guns, and cash. [93]

Government officials offered Indians other new avenues to prestige or
influence. The men whom Americans recognized as "chiefs," for instance, included some who had previously had negligible importance to natives.
Goliah, appointed Skagit chief during Stevens's 1854 expedition against
the Snohomish, was one such man. Contemporary records support the
oral tradition that Goliah was of humble birth; yet he became "head chief
for the White people" because he could talk well. [94]

The elevation of humble men such as Goliah was the exception, however. As long as relations between Indians and Bostons were fluid and
under neither group's control, American officials needed chiefs "for the
White people" who could also command respect from their own people. [95]
Duke of York was one of many such chiefs. His role during a disturbance
in 1860 confirms that treaties and recent war had wrought little change in

the social structure and the terms of settler-Indian relations in western Washington.

A Chimakum shaman broke out of the Port Townsend jail, still wearing leg irons. The headman of his band returned the irons the next day, saying that his people were anxious to pay for the Bostons' loss. The Bostons, however, wanted the escapee. Two days later, Duke of York told James Swan that the shaman was in a Klallam lodge, "face painted black and threatened to kill any white man who should attempt to arrest him." When the shaman tried to make good his threat, the town watchman shot him dead. Chimakum villagers then demanded Duke's life for his part in the shaman's death, and Duke enlisted Swan's help in pacifying them. At the funeral, while Duke of York offered to fight his accusers, Swan explained that the man had been shot for resisting an officer who was doing his duty under Boston law. This seemed to satisfy the Chimakums, who then confessed that they did not regret the slaying, since they suspected the shaman of several murders. Whites also eased the Chimakums' minds by giving their headman a blanket and cap.[96]

In such a fashion, for at least a decade following this incident, Bostons and Indians continued to arrange many matters between them with only haphazard government help. Rather than achieving a clear separation and hierarchical ordering of native and immigrant societies, the treaties and limited war of the 1850s had only confirmed that the two societies were entwined in complex ways. Although Americans claimed victory over Indians and called it proof of their superior power, they had neither destroyed the bridge linking their communities to Indian communities nor fully commandeered that bridge.

— Setting up puppet gov't
— meeting + making treaties appeared to Inds to have egalitarian symbolism

4 Reformers and Indians
Reservations about Reservations

After the U.S. Civil War, national expansion and economic integration drastically altered the context of human relations around Puget Sound. Railroads reached the area, and immigrants rode in on them by the thousands, abruptly and decisively tipping the balance of social and economic power in favor of American colonists. Parallel developments across the continent made it possible to redirect federal Indian policy. As implemented in western Washington, the revised policy was the most energetic attempt yet to establish clear lines of demarcation around Indians and then to remake those Indians in a white American image.

Although the attempt to isolate and resocialize Indians was not entirely futile, Indian affairs hardly proceeded according to policy makers' plans. In combination with demographic and economic changes, reforms of the 1870s and 1880s put unprecedented pressure on the descendants of Puget Sound's aborigines to accept American terms for relations, and many yielded in some degree to that pressure. Specifically, more went to Indian reservations, where government agents conditioned their receipt of land and services on compliance with new rules. Nevertheless, many people of native descent still eschewed reservation life, and many more took advantage of opportunities on the reservations without conforming in all respects to their supervisors' expectations.

Rather than isolating Indians and standardizing their status, events of this period impelled indigenous people and their offspring to adopt more diverse cultural, social, and economic strategies. Many of the strategies involved associating with whites. Exposed to whites' disdain for Indians, some people of native descent lost faith in the methods their indigenous ancestors had used to become effective and respected. But when one native man had a religious vision in the 1880s, he inspired an Indian movement that enabled many of the confused people to draw new confidence from selected aspects of their aboriginal heritage.

By 1869 many whites around Puget Sound thought the train of national progress was just over the eastern horizon, headed their way. Secretary of State W. H. Seward claimed to hear it coming when he toured the Sound by ship that year. At Port Townsend he advised a welcoming crowd to extend their hospitality to all newcomers, be they Bostons, Irishmen, whites, blacks, or Chinamen; for all could help to cut down the forests and make the area prosperous. A passenger on Seward's vessel, Thomas Somerville, relayed this assessment of western Washington's potential to readers of *Harper's New Monthly Magazine.* Even though Indians still wallowed there in filthy "rancherees" and lumber workers bunked in crude cabins "with their squaws hanging around," Somerville saw signs that Washington's rough mill towns would soon become premier shipbuilding sites. The village of Seattle, expecting to capitalize on recent coal discoveries and the coming railroad, had doubled its population of five hundred in nine months. Speculators had snapped up land for miles around and put it on the market throughout the West. Meanwhile the Indians, reportedly declining by 10 percent each year, were "letting their time-cherished customs drop as things of death." It was thought-provoking, Somerville concluded, to see the dying race strangely intermingled with the growing one.[1]

Whether or not they consciously heeded Seward's advice, Puget Sound communities did soon receive many newcomers. The area's immigrant population grew at a robust rate in the next two decades. West of the Cascades the number of settlers, which was under five thousand in 1860, swelled to twenty-five thousand by 1880. Ten years later the number had nearly quadrupled again. As Seward had foretold, people from Boston, Ireland, China, and other distant lands were coming to cut down trees and cash in on an economic boom.[2]

Immigration to Washington Territory picked up momentum after the Civil War because entrepreneurs activated old plans to connect the Northwest and Midwest by rail. Puget Sound's direct link to the central states took decades to complete; but a trunk line in Oregon sprouted a northbound branch during the 1870s, and clusters of speculators and new laborers attached themselves to it. Together with technological innovations of the 1880s, railroads also nurtured population growth by making it possible to log inland forests on a commercial scale.[3]

To most contemporary observers, as to Thomas Somerville, the increase in immigrants seemed paired with a decrease of the indigenous population. Pioneers declared that they had lived among twice as many Indians in the 1850s, and censuses appeared to corroborate their claims. In 1877 the agent responsible for Indians of the Point Elliott Treaty area estimated that they had dwindled from seven or eight thousand to three thousand in twenty years. Such reports were mere guesses by men predisposed to see Indians as a dying race, but they reflected and perpetuated a belief that had foundation in some facts. Periodic epidemics took high tolls in native settlements, particularly among children. The demographic crisis was evident from Indian reservation head counts—first undertaken in the 1880s—which showed the number of children at barely half the number of families. And even if they were not dying off, natives and their offspring were indisputably declining in proportion to non-Indians. As late as 1860 they were still roughly half the inhabitants of the Puget Sound basin; by 1890 immigrants outnumbered them about twenty to one.[4]

The overwhelming majority of newcomers congregated in towns, especially east of the Sound. Between 1870 and 1890 Seattle's population mushroomed from 1,107 to 42,837, and Tacoma—founded in 1868—became a city of 36,006. But as strangers flooded in, diluting the color of the human streams flowing through urban streets, they also resculpted the surrounding landscape. By clearing rivers of debris, they opened upper valleys to homesteaders, loggers, and city builders. They farmed more of the region's scarce bottomlands, built more and larger sawmills, dug new mines, experimented with oyster culture and fish packing, and loaded lumber and produce on an increasing number of ships bound for California, South America, New England, and the Orient.[5]

The stream of immigrants touched previously secluded indigenous communities, sometimes sweeping the residents off their foundations and depositing them at new locations. Confident that they and their government could overwhelm any resistance, settlers expropriated more and more lands where Indians lived or grew food. Jerry Meeker was living in the Puyallup Valley in the 1870s when whites destroyed his relatives' cedar plank lodges on nearby Minter Creek, replacing them with their own houses. The whites left room at the Glen Cove fishery, said Meeker, where the Indians rebuilt.[6]

At other creeks and coves around the Sound, natives returned from seasonal subsistence rounds to find charred ground or Boston homes where their own longhouses had been. Sometimes, like the Minter Creek villagers, they withdrew to sites the Bostons did not yet want; sometimes they moved to Indian reservations; but sometimes they stayed around the new settlements. Skagit Indian John Fornsby said the first loggers to appear near his village "rolled the logs right close to their homes. sikwigwílts tribe gave them a chance; they gave them room to work there."[7]

Native people did not all run for higher ground when the immigrant stream swirled around them because the flood that swept away some resources also delivered others to their doorsteps. Settlers brought new opportunities for barter and employment. Logging camps sprang up in Skagit country about ten years after John Fornsby was born, and soon he was working in them. Meanwhile, his father sold the newcomers fish and the animal skins they needed "to sew up the belts" at sawmills. When settlers opened fish canneries in the 1870s, they gave Indians processing jobs as well as new markets for their catch.[8]

Hop culture, which began as an experiment in 1865 and covered several thousand acres by 1890, provided paid work at a convenient time in native families' usual schedules. Farmers recruited Indians by the hundreds for the brief fall harvest, dealing with native labor contractors as well as reservation agents. Puyallup Valley hop ranchers expected fifteen hundred Indians to answer their call for help in 1876. Growers were so dependent on Indian pickers, the *Washington Standard* reported, that even after some Chinese hired on for $.90 a day the Indians demanded and received $2.50.[9] In 1872 the superintendent of Indian affairs reported many Indians logging, working at mills and mines and farms, "getting the highest wages paid to whites," and enjoying "an abundance of the necessaries of life." Among the Indians happy with the opportunities available in towns was Jim Lightner. From Olympia in 1873, he dictated a letter to a friend at the Tulalip Reservation: "I have got a $100 job of grubbing stumps that will take me about one month to finish. I have bargained for a lot in Swantown for $80, and am going to improve it and live on it like a white man. Susan gets plenty of washing to do and we are getting along very well."[10]

As the pace of colonization picked up and newcomers encountered Indians in a variety of situations, the question of how to manage relations with Indians regained urgency. To many recent immigrants, relations seemed too unstructured. In 1869 E. C. Johnson of Steilacoom lodged a complaint with Thomas Chambers, veteran of nearly two decades in the territory:

> I am at a loss how to protect myself and my home from the intrusion of *Drunking* Indians. I am a Stranger not to your *laws But* to the minds of the Inhabitants of this place. It seems strange such disapation should be allowd to exist amoungst so small a Community and it is dettermental to its prosperity if there is a *law* to stop it by all means enforce it. . . . Ladys who visits Mrs. Roes has to seek a protector or weight untill the Indians Leave the Street—terable to think off A move *must* be *made*.[11]

Many advocates of growth agreed on the need to keep the "intrusions" of Indians from driving away recruits such as Johnson. In 1870 the editors of the *Territorial Republican* blasted the government for permitting Indians to annoy whites and thus impede settlement. It made no sense, they said, to reserve the best land for Indians, grant them annuities and educational benefits, and still let them wander at will, with little to fear if they broke the law. A longtime resident opined that new conditions made it imperative to bring Indians under more exact control by requiring them to live on the reservations and giving their agents judicial powers.[12]

White sentiment for strict segregation and supervision of Indians was by no means universal; witness the tug-of-war over a band of natives living on the Black and Cedar Rivers. Late in 1869 thirty-one settlers petitioned the government to remove the Indians, charging that they filched farmers' produce and debased the morals of whites who associated and cohabited with them. However, when the Indian superintendent arrived at the natives' camp, intending to take them to a reservation, the land's white owner asserted their right to stay. Not long after, the superintendent received a "remonstrance" from more than a hundred settlers who "declared their preference for the Indians to remain as ... situated." More such correspondence prompted superintendent T. J. McKenney to complain that Indians were reverting to uncivilized practices because citizens did not cooperate with official efforts to control them. "In fact," he told his boss, "many of the people of this Territory contend that no superintendent or agent has any right to interfere with the customs or tribal habits of the Indians."[13]

Those settlers who favored stricter control of Indians were in luck: national policy makers had aims that dovetailed with theirs. President U. S. Grant, hoping to end bloody conflicts on the Great Plains, had decided to punish Indians who did not withdraw to reservations. At the same time, he promised reforms that would make reservations more palatable to Indians (and to non-Indian critics). Bending the president's ear were philanthropists with religious motivations. By the 1870s religious reformers had infused Indian policy with evangelical fervor. Under their influence, Grant declared reservations the foundation of a campaign to prepare Indians for citizenship. On reservations, his advisors said, Indians could be protected from debilitating contact with frontiersmen while learning Christianity, agriculture, and other fundamentals of civilization.[14]

The reformers and their allies seized on a common metaphor for Indians' situation, reinterpreted it, and made it the paradigm for Indians' relations with whites. At least since Supreme Court decisions of the 1830s, American leaders had likened encircled tribes to wards and the government to their guardian. In the 1870s, when American domination of the whole continent seemed assured, U.S. officials invoked the guardian-ward analogy to justify more intrusive methods of resocializing tribal Indians. The government, they said, should take a parent's role, teaching Indians how to live as individuals within American society. A Washington settler endorsed this view in an 1871 letter to the *Daily Pacific Tribune*. Indians could learn to be diligent and honest, he wrote, if confined to reservations and subjected there to a system of rewards and punishments. Government must become their just and wise guardian, rewarding compliant wards with certificates of citizenship.[15]

Reformers also argued that Indian policy would achieve its humanitarian ends only if government personnel modeled civilized virtues for Indians. In 1869 a delegation of Quakers persuaded Grant that he could provide appropriate models by assigning each Indian agency to a Christian denomination to run. In Washington Territory Roman Catholics consequently assumed responsibility for north Sound reservations administered from Tulalip, and Protestants received appointments to south Sound agencies at Skokomish and Puyallup. Although the policy of allocating reservations to churches lost favor before 1880, the drive to raise the caliber of Indian Office employees continued. During this period western Washington acquired several agents whose professional dedication, crusading zeal, and longevity in office enabled them to exert unprecedented influence over indigenous people's relations with settlers.[16]

Most reformers of the 1870s maintained that it would take more than good examples and fatherly exhortations to convert tribe members into American citizens. They called for a radical restructuring of Indians' relations to American authorities, to each other, and to economic resources. In 1877 Indian Affairs Commissioner E. A. Hayt wrote his prescription for Indians' transformation: gather them on reservations, give them Christian preceptors, compel them to attend school, subject them to laws enforced by Indian police, assign them individual plots of their common land, and refuse to pamper them economically. Another decade passed before Congress decisively endorsed a similar program of education, law enforcement, and land allotment; and then the aim was to dismantle rather than improve Indian reservations. But early in the 1870s reform-minded agents in western Washington were already acting on their belief in such a program's power to solve the "Indian problem."[17]

In 1871 a federal emissary arrived at Puget Sound to spread the gospel of reform. Felix Brunot, chairman of the recently created Board of Indian Commissioners, called Indians together to explain what the government's

During a visit in 1847, Paul Kane depicted "Nisqually, a village on Puget Sound" as a placid, multiethnic settlement. Near the unfortified buildings of the Puget Sound Agricultural Company were the cedar plank houses and mat-covered camp shelters of natives from around the Sound and the conical teepees of Indians from east of the Cascade Mountains. Watercolor on paper, $5\frac{3}{8}'' \times 9\frac{1}{4}''$ (13.6 × 23.5 cm); Stark Museum of Art, Orange, Texas.

Because Henry Yesler hired natives to work at his sawmill in the town of Seattle, he resented government plans to move Indians to reservations in the 1850s. These nattily dressed Indians in front of the mill's cookhouse may have included Yesler employees. According to pioneer Thomas Prosch, the street and mill buildings "looked as here shown in the 60's." Unknown photographer; Special Collections, University of Washington Libraries, Native Americans no. 1389.

During the 1860s, when W. F. Robertson took this photograph, Catholic missionary E. C. Chirouse (holding the cross) and pupils from his Tulalip Indian Reservation school traveled to nearby towns, where the children amused settlers with displays of their talent and learning. Special Collections, University of Washington Libraries, Native Americans no. 1499.

Charles Graham's sketches of a Puyallup Valley hop ranch accompanied a
Harper's Weekly article about the rising fortunes of growers in Washington Territory (October 20, 1888, pp. 795, 801). The workers were Indian families, who
came by the hundreds in canoes laden with household effects and camped at the
ranch through harvest time. Special Collections, University of Washington
Libraries, Native Americans no. 4015.

Indian Shakers furnished their churches austerely with crosses, bells, and benches. When sitting for a portrait, however, many of these Shakers (probably at the Jamestown Klallam settlement) donned furnishings as fancy as their respectable non-Indian neighbors would have worn. Photographer Albert H. Barnes, ca. 1895–1910. Special Collections, University of Washington Libraries, Native Americans no. 1121.

Well into the twentieth century, Indians' habitual subsistence pursuits took them to western Washington cities and towns, where they often found not only fish and shellfish but also merchandising opportunities and temporary wage labor. This late-nineteenth-century camp was on the beach fronting downtown Shelton. Washington State Historical Society (Indians—Culture—Communities no. 3.03.008).

Indians could adopt the architecture, conveniences, and dress fashions of whites without abandoning aboriginal means of subsistence. On the Puyallup Reservation at the end of the nineteenth century, native and new lifeways appeared to blend comfortably. In the stream near their American-style frame house and fenced yard, this family operated a traditional fish trap. Mitchell Photographers, Puyallup, Washington; Washington State Historical Society (Indians—Food Processing—fishing no. 4.03.003).

When residents of the Nisqually Reservation moved Leschi's body in 1895, hundreds of Indians and a trainload of white observers attended the ceremony. For these descendants and confederates of Leschi, as for the whites, it was an opportunity to discuss the modern meaning of Leschi's futile armed resistance to government plans. Paul Leschi identified the men, left to right, as Bill Quiemuth, Luke, unknown, George Leschi, and Yelm Jim. A. C. Carpenter, photographer; Washington State Historical Society (Indians—Nisqually no. 1.04.001).

On this Whatcom County hop ranch at the turn of the nineteenth century, Indians worked alongside non-Indians. Many all-Indian harvest crews also posed for photographic portraits among the hops, often in good clothes and arrangements as formal as this one. Unknown photographer; Special Collections, University of Washington Libraries, Native Americans no. 887.

Indian hop pickers were the subject of numerous articles and photo essays in Washington newspapers and magazines at the turn of the century. Entrepreneurs also turned many portraits such as this into postcards. John P. Soule, photographer; Museum of History and Industry, Seattle, Negative no. 1052.

WASHINGTON TERRITORY AND OREGON VIEWS.

When they gathered for the hop harvest or converged on Puget Sound cities for other reasons, Indians from different districts could socialize or gamble in traditional ways, as these men did. Because white city dwellers found them picturesque, many Indians also turned their urban sojourns into opportunities to earn money posing for pictures and selling crafts. C. E. & Hattie King, photographers, Tacoma; ca. 1900; Museum of History and Industry, Seattle, Negative no. 3488.

At the main entrance to Frederick and Nelson Department Store in downtown Seattle, Indian women sold baskets to white shoppers. Webster and Stevens, Commercial Photographers; ca. 1900–1910; Museum of History and Industry, Seattle, Negative no. 83.10.7929.

A Seattle commercial firm thought this scene worth a photograph, on the back of which Thomas Prosch wrote, "After a day in town these old Indians are on the Colman warf [*sic*] waiting for the steamer to take them back to Eagle Harbor (left to right, Doctor Peter, Charlie Yukon [*sic*], Mrs. Chief Jacob, Chief Jacob Wahalchu, unknown, Mary Adams)." Webster & Stevens; ca. 1900–1910; Museum of History and Industry, Seattle, Negative no. 83.10.7723.

One of Puget Sound's many off-reservation Indian settlements was at Eagle Harbor, across from Seattle on Bainbridge Island. "The people are half civilized," Thomas Prosch wrote circa 1900–1910. "The things on the line are fish. ... These people are well dressed, comfortable and happy as Indians usually are or can be." Webster and Stevens; Museum of History and Industry, Seattle, Negative no. 83.10.6950.

By the turn of the nineteenth century, observers at Indian potlatches often included sympathetic journalists and amateur ethnographers. When Indians gathered for an off-reservation potlatch on Whidbey Island in April 1904, photographer O. S. VanOlinda documented the activities, including a men's strength competition. Special Collections, University of Washington Libraries, Native Americans no. 861.

Early in the twentieth century, the converging interests of town and tourism boosters, aging Indians, new and nostalgic white residents, historians, and ethnographers inspired numerous, selective displays of Indian culture. In 1911 and for several subsequent years, Indians and the government agent at the Port Madison Reservation collaborated with local businessmen to mount a summer festival called Chief Seattle Day, where activities included this dance. William R. Cowan, photographer; ca. 1912; Special Collections, University of Washington Libraries, Native Americans no. 1950.

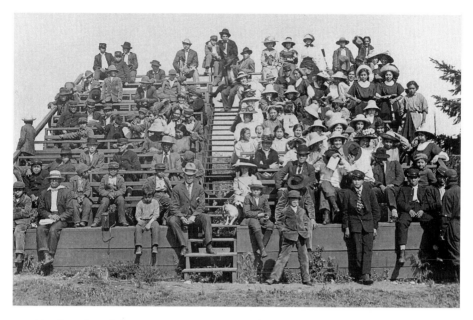

Pupils at the Tulalip Reservation government boarding school learned to think of themselves all as Indians, despite their varied backgrounds and the school's effort to transform them into civilized Americans. When they watched ceremonies and athletic competitions from school grandstands, students and their families and visitors saw Indians cast in a new mold. Ferdinand Brady, photographer; 1910; Museum of History and Industry, Seattle, Negative no. 88.11.64.

FACING PAGE: *(bottom)* To support a claim that she and her children were Klallam Indians, Susan Frances Baker gave enrolling agent Charles Roblin this family photograph, which also documents intimate ties between Indians and whites. Baker identified the people as: "No. 1 my mother Susan Myers, No. 2 my grand-mother Elizabeth Keymes, No. 3 my aunt Mary Keymes, No. 4 my aunt Elizabeth Keymes, No. 5 my son Claude V. Baker, No. 6 my son Gerald M. Baker, No. 7 my daughter Dorothy E. Baker." Applications for Enrollment and Allotment of Washington Indians, 1911–1919, National Archives, Record Group 75, Entry 613, Keymes Family no. 20, Clallam Tribe, file 11E2/23/13/2/Box 1.

The Tulalip school aimed to eradicate its pupils' Indian traits. Yet on school grounds in 1912, families who were present for the commemoration of local Indian treaties had an opportunity to play or observe "old time games." Ferdinand Brady, photographer; Museum of History and Industry, Seattle, Negative no. 88.11.65.

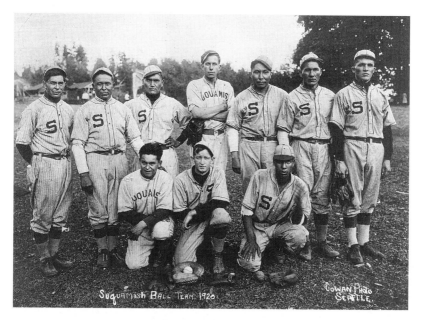

During the teens and 1920s, the Suquamish Indian baseball team played teams from Seattle and other nearby towns; they even toured Japan. Players' faces reflect their native ancestors' other interactions with non-Indians. Gowan Photo, Seattle; 1920; Suquamish Tribal Archives no. 1843.

In the 1950s, as Indian participation in spirit dancing increased, Swinomish Reservation resident Tommy Bob had new occasions to sing the song of the spirit that had empowered him to cure the sick and confuse enemies. John W. Thompson's interest in this power induced Bob to show the white teacher and naturalist how he sang to invoke the sgʷədílič power. January 10, 1955; Special Collections, University of Washington Libraries, Photograph no. 17765.

FACING PAGE: *(bottom)* "Chief Shelton and family from the Tulalip Reservation before appearing on a visual-radio programme in Seattle's Volunteer Park," wrote Norman Edson on his photograph of 1938. "Left to right: Mrs. Annie Frederick, Mrs. Shelton, Chief Shelton, Wayne Williams (grandson), Silas George (drowned), Harriete [*sic*] Shelton Dover." By then a practiced spokesman for Indians, Shelton chose regalia that symbolized admirable Indian traits for most non-Indians—feather bonnets and fringed, beaded buckskin—even though his Snohomish ancestors did not wear them. Special Collections, University of Washington Libraries, Native Americans no. 657.

During the 1950s and 1960s, Bob Satiacum was among the Indians who asserted a treaty right to fish by deliberately and dramatically defying Washington law. Such actions, plus state reactions, prompted national Indian organizations and celebrities to join the Northwest fishers' campaign. On March 2, 1964, actor Marlon Brando and an Episcopal clergyman successfully courted arrest and press attention by joining Satiacum in fishing contrary to state regulations. Officials released them a few hours later. *Seattle Post-Intelligencer,* March 3, 1964; Museum of History and Industry, Seattle.

Indians' campaign for state recognition of treaty fishing rights included a mass rally at the state capitol, picket lines at courthouses, and other tactics favored by advocates of civil rights. These Indians and their allies trekked through south Seattle on July 13, 1966, headed for the trial of four Muckleshoot men charged with fishing illegally in the Green River. *Seattle Post-Intelligencer,* July 14, 1966; Museum of History and Industry, Seattle.

new policy would require of them.[18] But Brunot's words may not have had the intended effect, because they did not have the same meanings for native people as for him. When he referred to treaty promises, he and they probably thought of different obligations; and when he exhorted Indians to be good, he and his audiences likely imagined different scenarios. Brunot's imperfect communication foreshadowed the imperfect results of the reform program in the Puget Sound area.

Brunot's schedule included meetings at the Tulalip and Skokomish Reservations. At Tulalip, where "all the minor chiefs ... and a large number of the men and women of the tribe" assembled for the occasion, Napoleon opened the dialogue by remarking that he was the only chief there who had taken part in the treaty. Brunot replied that he had come not to make a new treaty but to warn that the period of treaty payments was half over. "[I came] to see whether you will be able to take care of yourselves when the time ... is up," he said; "to see, if you have not done right in the past, whether you want to do so now. ... " Since Indians were far fewer than when the treaties were made, he assumed that they had not done right. "If you want your race not to die out," he admonished, "you must live like good white men." While conceding that white men set conflicting examples, Brunot asserted that the assembled people knew which example they had to follow. Rather than spending their money for whiskey, they had to spend it making the reservation a home. "[T]he reservation belongs to all of you," Brunot elaborated; but "[i]f this reservation belonged to me ... ,"

> I would go somewhere and work a week or two, and get a little money and buy something to eat with it. Then I would take my blanket, ax, and shovel, and I would go to the Beaver Meadow Swamp and begin digging a ditch. As long as my provision lasted I would dig at it. Then I would go and earn more, and I would keep on digging til the marsh was drained, and when it was drained I would cut the hay, and soon be as rich as the President.[19]

Brunot invited reactions to his remarks but limited the time he would listen and required the Indians to choose a few spokesmen. Without hiding their disapproval of this unmannerly impatience, the designated speakers applauded Brunot's desire to set the relations between Indians and Bostons aright.[20] Good relations, they agreed, would depend on fulfillment of the treaties. But rather than confessing dereliction, they boldly blamed the unsatisfactory state of relations on Bostons who had betrayed treaty pledges. Government men who were supposed to give them good advice had instead denied them tools, brought whiskey onto the reservations, enriched themselves selling reservation timber, and distributed goods worth less than the amount due by treaty. At Tulalip Hallum countered Brunot's claim that Indians were not doing right unless they settled on the reservation:

> Father Chirouse talks to the Indians who are not Catholics; they don't know what to do, and it scares them away; some of the Indians think they must not do what they have been accustomed to do in their Indian ways, so they go away. There are only a few Indian homes here, they are scattered everywhere. If you will do what is right all the Indians will settle on this reservation.[21]

By restating their understanding of the treaties, Hallum and other elders indicated what they thought it meant for the Bostons to do right. At Skokomish Big Frank recalled:

> Governor Stevens said all the Indians would grow up and the President would make them good. He told them the Indians would become as white men; that all their children would learn to read and write. I was glad to hear it. Governor Stevens told them, "I will go out and have the land surveyed, and it will be yours and your children's forever." I thought that very good. He said a doctor and carpenter and farmer would come. The chiefs thought that was good, they thought the President was doing a kindness. ... [22]

Pleased that the president had sent Brunot, Big Frank evidently wanted to construe the visit as a renewal of the treaty pledges, but he could not suppress doubts. "All the Agents talk differently," he fretted. To hear Brunot talk differently than previous agents could not have been reassuring. Stevens had promised money and advice so that Indians could become as good as white men, but Brunot intimated that Indians must be good before they could expect respectful attention from American leaders.

Brunot and the native men thus talked about the treaties as if they were scripts for everyone's behavior and charged each other with failing to play the roles scripted. But their recriminations derived from divergent constructions of the text and of the word "good" in particular. To Brunot a good person was one who adopted the work ethic of a yeoman farmer and the moral ideals of a pious American Protestant. He urged Indians to show by their conduct, without preconditions, an intent to be good in this sense. But the people in his audience used the word "good" in another way. For them "good" meant prosperous and honored. The best evidence that a man was good—that is, agreeable to the spirits and therefore endowed with admirable qualities—was the respect and wealth he won. By this logic, the recognition and payments that Stevens had offered would affirm Indians' goodness.[23] Without the promised favors, Indians could not manifest their goodness as expected. Big Frank said, "Perhaps the President thinks all the Indians are good, as they were to be under the treaty, but they are not. They are Indians still." While Brunot no doubt took this as an admission that the Indians had not fulfilled their pledge to advance in civilized virtues, Frank may have meant it as a comment on the government's failure to give Indians the things that made whites good in his sense.

The native spokesmen suspected that the Bostons disdained "Indians." Generous payments and uncoercive instruction, which natives would have construed as recognition of their status, might have reassured them. For Brunot, however, the favors that the Indians expected would only have confirmed their inferiority. He saw federal paternalism as necessary *because* Indians were inferior to Americans. Convinced as were virtually all his peers that white American Protestant culture represented the pinnacle of human development, Brunot wanted to see Indians act like whites before they were honored. For him the Indians' shame was having waited for the government to do something for them; for Big Frank and his contemporaries, the shame was not having received the goods and advice that would affirm their respectable standing and their ties to high-ranking Bostons.[24]

Brunot had not come solely or even primarily to scold Indians; his mission was also to push the Office of Indian Affairs (OIA) into playing its role, as he interpreted it. Although he regretted his government's former policy of negotiating with Indians as fellow sovereigns, he urged that existing treaties be honored. By fulfilling promises to furnish schools, land for homes and farms, and agricultural instruction, the government would not only do right by Indians and thus allay their discontent; it would also justify its plans to keep them on reservations.[25]

Ironically, when Brunot exhorted people at Skokomish and Tulalip to stay on the reservations, he was probably preaching to the choir. Either because those reservations encompassed their ancestral villages or because they spotted opportunity at the reservations, most people at the meetings of 1871 had apparently decided to locate their homes there, at least provisionally. But they told Brunot that many other Indians had not yet made the same decision.

If agent Edwin Eells accurately described conditions on the Skokomish Reservation when he arrived in 1871, it is a wonder that as many as two hundred people did choose to live there. Of the hundred acres once cleared for crops, half were overgrown. Residents were hungry and discouraged, they said, because recent military overseers had usurped their improved lands. The reservation school was so badly managed that its five remaining pupils were nearly destitute of clothing. Elsewhere around Puget Sound new administrators echoed Eells: the government had done almost nothing to make the reservations into havens for citizen-trainees.[26] Eells began a two-decade campaign to turn things around.

Despite the labors of Eells and like-minded colleagues, the reservation program in western Washington fell substantially short of reformers' ideal. One reason was government neglect. The OIA posted a mere handful of men to oversee all Indians in the region. Inadequately paid and trained, these men were often demoralized, ineffective, or worse. Employees at Tulalip went at least seven months without pay in 1879. It was the 1880s before national officials backed up reform rhetoric by centralizing appointments, imposing civil service rules, and instituting regular supervision of field personnel. Even then improvements in the Puget Sound district were halting, and staffing was ill suited to the OIA's mission. Reorganizations shunted Eells to three new positions in three locations during the same year. In one position he was responsible for ten reservations. The Port Madison, Squaxin Island, Nisqually, and Muckleshoot reserves had no resident personnel during this period. There was never money for more than a few small schools, and those had trouble finding and keeping staff.[27]

The local civilization program also deviated from the national model because conditions around Puget Sound differed from those that inspired national policy. The violent resistance of Plains tribes had motivated President Grant to quarantine Indians, but Indians in western Washington showed little inclination to take up arms. Besides, American treaty negotiators had assured Puget Sound natives that they would be allowed to work or gather foods off the reservations, and they remembered and unhesitatingly acted on this assurance.

Despite the distinctive circumstances in western Washington, OIA personnel there tried to move in step with the national drumbeat. In 1873 Superintendent R. H. Milroy advised Father Chirouse, the agent in charge at Tulalip, that he should confine his Indians to the reservations and issue passes only to those with outside employment or other legitimate errands. Edwin Eells went further: he tried to force Indians onto reserves. At his request in 1871, city officials demolished Indian houses at Port Townsend. As Eells escorted the dispossessed people up Hood Canal toward the Skokomish Reservation, he noted other renegade communities. "At Seabeck," he reported, "I found some drunken Indians whom I punished severely and ordered them to move to the Reservation immediately on pain of being burnt out."[28]

Many people defied or evaded such measures, often with help from white employers. Moreover, as Eells admitted, Washington Indians always had a legitimate reason to be off the reservations, since they could always go fishing. Consequently, officials soon renounced coercive methods of populating the reservations.[29] In lieu of sticks, agents needed carrots to coax people into federal Indian enclaves.

One intended carrot—an essential ingredient of reformers' recipe for civilized Indians—was a secure land base. But for many western Washington natives, the land lure had little appeal, in part because Bostons seemed unsure whether to offer it to Indians or swallow it themselves. Even as they demanded that Indians be confined to reservations, whites lobbied to reduce the number and size of reservations. Although plans to shrink or abolish Puget Sound reserves did not materialize, residents repeatedly heard that their eviction was imminent. These rumors, Milroy reported, stymied efforts to sell them on the farmer's sedentary life. He cited a petition from chiefs of the Medicine Creek Treaty bands.

> They said that they and their people desired to build houses, make farms ..., and live like white men, but that no one knew where his land was, or had a paper showing that he owned any land at all; that neighboring white men frequently told them that the Government would soon take their reservations and sell them ... and hence they had no heart to work and make permanent improvements.[30]

By deluging his superiors with such testimonials, Milroy secured overdue surveys and orders defining the boundaries of all reservations under his jurisdiction. He used the surveys to alter the character of the reservations. Citing a treaty clause that allowed the president to assign small tracts to individual Indians, Milroy and his colleagues subdivided some of the reserved lands. Certificates of Indians' rights to the individual lots would guarantee their tenure, Milroy argued. At the same time, he endorsed reformers' theory that this land allotment would break Indians' attachment to tribal groups and instill pride of ownership, the hallmark and driving force of American civilization. Giving an Indian separate property and a fixed home would teach him that he could surround himself with the comforts of civilization "by increasing and gratifying his wants, which constitute the grand difference between the savage and the civilized man." Milroy acted on this belief more than a decade before Congress mandated the subdivision of all tribal lands in the General Allotment Act of 1887.[31]

The promise that title to individual tracts would protect them from dispossession roused many Indians to petition for allotments. So long as they held their land in common, agents explained, the president had authority to reduce or eliminate the reserves and distribute proceeds from the land to all people covered by a treaty, even those who did not live or work on reservation. Chirouse made allotment more attractive when he announced that he would collect stumpage fees from Indians logging at Tulalip because other Indians of the Point Elliott Treaty area had equal rights in that land.[32]

Subdividing reservation land did not give Indians a sense of security, however. Some were upset when they learned that allotment would mean relinquishing fields they had cleared to people who had done nothing. More important, national officials withheld for years the certificates that Eells and Milroy had promised to individuals who accepted land assignments. As a consequence, Eells reported in 1878, some nervous and disappointed Indians had left their houses and fields on the reservation to take homesteads on the public domain, where they would not face the vicissitudes of reservation management. Many reservation tracts went unclaimed or unused. Uncertainties about the status of reserved land thus frustrated reformers' designs well into the 1880s.[33]

Like land allotment, the services intended to entice Indians onto reservations sometimes backfired. Governor Stevens's 1855 promise to send farmers, doctors, carpenters, and teachers had impressed Big Frank as a kindness; and men like Brunot planned to play to such sentiments. Rather than attracting and inspiring Indians, however, some reservation personnel repelled them. At the meeting with Brunot, native speakers accused a Tulalip employee of brutality. According to Henry Allen, no one at Skokomish liked missionary Myron Eells. "I used to have to read the Bible with that awful man," Allen said, "used to have to go to his church. . . . After I got through with all that I never went to church again. . . . "[34]

Government agents realized that the best way to boost a reservation's population was to create opportunities to earn money there, either by promoting enterprise or by paying prospective residents to clear forests, build houses, and care for crops. "Since I took charge," Chirouse reported in 1872, "a great number of Indians are continually arriving to Tulalip from every part of this agency and finding the means of making a good living in cutting logs for sawmills they seem very happy to stay there. . . . " Chirouse took credit for organizing fifteen logging camps, each employing eleven Indians under a white foreman, and for securing a just price for the logs. As work opportunities fluctuated, however, so did reservation populations. When an order from the national office halted the logging in 1873, Chirouse deluged his superiors with panicky protests. Because the Indians were unable to support their families as they had expected, he said, they were preparing to leave again.[35]

Although Puget Sound reservations did not attract and support as many people as administrators expected, they did harbor gradually growing numbers. A census of 1885 found 527 Indians at the Puyallup Reservation, 162 at Skokomish, 167 at Nisqually, 112 at Squaxin Island, 467 at Tulalip, 222 at Swinomish, 234 at Lummi, and 142 at Port Madison.[36] It was on these people that Americans focused their hope of remaking Indians. Although Indian agents tried to influence the conduct of people elsewhere, they had their most frequent contact with and their clearest jurisdiction over residents of the reservations, who therefore felt the brunt of government efforts to teach Indians what it meant to be good.

Before the 1870s were out, Edwin Eells claimed success. Virtually all Indians on his reservations, he exulted, subsisted without government aid, most by cultivating some land and engaging in other "civilized" pursuits. He took heart at the enrollment in reservation schools—approximately three hundred of seventeen hundred eligible children attended at least part of the year—and at the number of Indians who were thrifty, industrious, lawabiding, and apparently content with government actions on their behalf.[37]

Some of the intended beneficiaries saluted the reform efforts, too. A proposal to shift responsibility for Indians from the Interior Department to the War Department brought Eells this compliment from Skokomish chief Dick Lewis in 1878: "We knew very little when [our present agent] came, but we have learned and improved very fast since. ... We now have good houses, chairs, bedsteads, tables, stoves, dishes, etc. and do not eat on the floor as we used to. ... He has come and taught us about God, and this is another reason we want him to stay with us." Chehalis Jack added that Eells was the first agent to show them the right way and to treat them as Governor Stevens had promised. Even Hallum, so disgruntled when Brunot visited Tulalip, seemed to accept the government's plans by 1879. Through agent John O'Keane he wrote to the president, "You make good laws for us Indians and I will accept that law."[38]

Administrators' favorite exhibits of their influence were pupils from reservation schools. Chirouse initially sought support for his mission school by taking the schoolboys to towns, where they marched in military formation and performed for crowds of curious settlers. By the 1870s Chirouse regularly invited potential sponsors to witness ceremonies at the school. A recital in 1871 impressed one observer with the students' "astonishing facility for embryo savages." The children's appearance attested to their ongoing transformation. "[A]t present," Chirouse wrote in 1872, "they look more like good and industrious Yankees ... than Indians."[39]

Although many youth and some adults appeared eager to follow government agents' advice, officials could not transform all Indians into good and industrious Yankees. Indeed, rather than molding Indians to fit a single frame, federal reform measures had the effect of diversifying indigenous people's social and cultural strategies. This is evident from the record of government efforts to eradicate "uncivilized" behavior. During the 1870s and 1880s, Indian agents around Puget Sound devoted considerable attention to this aspect of their duties, with mixed results. In the face of attempts to remake them, the descendants of natives had a variety of options. The Indian Office did not so much stamp out unwanted practices as promote alternatives in some populations and settings.

Reservation supervisors ordered their charges to give up aboriginal healing rituals, potlatches, gambling, liquor, cohabitation, and polygynous marriage. When a new Tulalip agent found unmarried men and women living together, he threatened to separate them. During John Fornsby's adolescence, the agent banned ceremonial giveaways at Tulalip. "They had a few potlatches among themselves after that, but not a big time."[40]

To enforce their standards of civilized conduct, agents used any means in their power. Due process of law was often a casualty. Because he had no employees at Port Madison, Superintendent Milroy deputized trader William DeShaw to oversee Indians there; and when some of the Indians behaved in what DeShaw considered "an outrageous manner," defying his orders in "extremely vulgar language," Milroy told Chirouse to take them in irons to Tulalip for hard labor. With no more authorization than this, agents detained, judged, and punished Indians not only for conjuring, potlatching, and "outrageous" behavior but also for thefts, assaults, and even homicides.[41]

In 1877 Eells took the case of Billy Clams as a test of his power to control and remake Indians on the Skokomish Reservation. Clams had been disorderly, abusing his wife and drinking, Eells told the commissioner. When Clams fled to avoid incarceration, Eells procured his surrender by taking some Clams "allies" hostage. Several months of "severe punishment" seemed to have corrected Clams's behavior until he eloped with a new woman and left the reservation in an allegedly stolen canoe. Eells then prevailed upon soldiers to arrest the fugitive near Port Madison and jail him in Port Townsend. "The point to be made by his punishment ...,"

Eells wrote, "is not simply for adultery and theft, but disobedience to ... the authority of the Agent and the bad effect of such a crime going unpunished, in its influence on the other Indians here."[42]

Cases like the Clams affair taught people that it was prudent, especially while on a reservation, to renounce or hide activities condemned by reservation supervisors. But the "quasi-martial law" that Eells imposed could not make all people of native descent conform to his code of conduct. Those who wished to hold potlatches, spirit dances, or healing ceremonies could usually avoid repression by leaving the reservations. Eells's authority to use soldiers against off-reservation Indians was dubious, and he knew it. Eventually, court decisions and executive directives confirmed that agents had minimal jurisdiction outside reservation boundaries. And whether or not they had the sanction of law, agents rarely had the resources to pursue people beyond the reservations.[43] Natives may have obeyed orders to stop potlatching at Tulalip; but many of them, like John Fornsby, attended potlatches at off-reservation sites. Even on the reservations, agents could not detect and suppress all forbidden practices, and most did not try. Some evidently tolerated pagan ceremonies, knowing that a total ban would just drive people away.[44]

The off-reservation escape valve was part of a complex of reasons that Indians could resist some pressures for change or win concessions from their appointed overseers. As French historian Michel Foucault observes, power is not a commodity that one person has and another does not; all people simultaneously exercise and yield to power. In order to exercise power over Indians, agents had to tap Indians' own power.[45] Indeed, Eells and his colleagues wanted Indians to help them govern Indians. They therefore designated chiefs or approved the Indians' designation of chiefs who made and enforced rules for reservation residents. By the end of the 1870s, they also appointed Indian police.[46]

Federal officials reasoned that guided self-government was good training for citizenship, although they taught Indian chiefs and policemen some practices that had no place in American civics classes. Among other things, they overruled or bypassed the apprentice officers at will. Yet Indian agents were not puppet masters. There was both a grain of truth and a dose of self-delusion in Eells's claim that "a little dextrous management" enabled him to fill the tribal offices with men who meekly directed the Indians toward civilized behavior.[47] While some appointees did seek mainly to please their white patrons, others more often advocated for their own substantial constituencies. In fact, Chirouse complained that giving the "old chiefs" commissions merely fed their arrogance, making them think they could defy him and stick to wild habits and superstitions. Because agents needed such men's help to influence other Indians, reservation residents could sometimes influence the actions of their chiefs, who in turn could influence agents.[48]

Agents acknowledged Indians' leverage by observing time-honored local protocol in some official affairs. For example, after disciplining people on the Chehalis Reservation, Edwin Chalcraft tried to restore goodwill by hosting a "feast," which he called a "potlatch." Federal officers did not interfere when the chiefs handled supposedly trivial matters according to "Indian customs of law." Some such matters were far from trivial. In 1879 chiefs from several reservations came together to discuss a retaliatory murder. Superintendent Milroy granted their request that "the Indians be permitted to settle the matter in their old way to stop further killing."[49]

Repressive as federal officials were, then, they could not unilaterally determine how the descendants of indigenous people organized themselves or their external relations. Such people had been redefining their communities, leadership, and individual roles since they first encountered Bostons. Their redefinition efforts accelerated when American leaders got serious about the Indian reservation system. But like all strategies of control, the reservation system provoked a welter of counterstrategies in the targeted population.[50]

Instead of forcing native people into a prescribed relationship to Americans and to each other, events of the 1870s and 1880s stimulated them to experiment with and debate a variety of relationships. Federal records, such as a letter from Chirouse to the Indian commissioner in 1874, afford glimpses of the debates.

> The Port Madison Indians are not doing as well as might be desired which is chiefly to be attributed to their head man or chief who latterly has fallen back to his old Superstitious practices and is doing all in his power by work and example to retard progress and civilization among his people. There are some very well disposed Indians residing on this reservation who are most anxious to have another and better man appointed ... and thus be relieved of the evil influences of their present leader.

In 1886 a man—apparently Indian—warned the Tulalip agent that granting Snohomish Joe's wish to be chief at Muckleshoot would cause trouble with supporters of Peter. Peter's backers included three longtime chiefs, the correspondent said, while Joe's friends were the kind who turned away their wives.[51]

Indian criticisms of chiefs' behavior and rivalries for office could reflect differences of opinion about a broader issue: what was the most desirable way to live and to deal with Bostons. By the 1880s such differences of opinion were gaining visibility and intensity because the variety of ways to live was growing. While American officials pretended that a reservation-based political guardianship defined Indians and their place in Puget Sound society, the descendants of indigenous people were trying out various places and creating a wider range of categories for themselves.

Even in the places ordained for Indians—the reservations—natives' descendants adopted varied roles. Their circumstances differed considerably from reservation to reservation. The amount and quality of reserved land, the availability of government services, the proximity of towns and wage work opportunities, the activities of nearby non-Indians, and the religious affiliation of white overseers all had a bearing on reservation residents' cultural and economic orientations. Thus, while Indians on isolated Squaxin Island reportedly survived solely by fishing and occasional work for settlers, many residents of the large Puyallup Reservation built farms and single-family homes rivaling those of whites in size and value.[52]

Many other people of indigenous descent shunned the reservations. In 1887, by one investigator's estimate, no more than three-fifths of Indians who belonged on south Sound reservations were actually there. The rest were scattered, living where they pleased. Data concerning the latter people suggest that opportunities for self-support had more impact on the lifestyles of natives' descendants than government programs did. Indeed, the data undermined reservation administrators' attempts to take credit for Indians' reformation. As a federal inspector remarked in 1881, Indians living off the reserves appeared nearly as civilized as those on reservations. Inspector J. Pollock doubted that the agencies benefited Indians at all, except in providing education and moral influence; and many Indians resisted both. The agencies' agricultural instruction was hardly worth mentioning. Puget Sound would never be farm country, Pollock said, and besides, "Indians off reservations [were] doing as much in that line as those under the fostering care of the Government."[53]

Off reservation the cultural and economic choices open to people of indigenous descent were even more numerous than on the reservations. Along the Hood Canal and the Strait of Juan de Fuca, for example, natives had made diverse adjustments so they could support themselves without moving to the Skokomish Reservation. In his 1887 report on the Klallams, Myron Eells described families on the Elwha River who had taken homesteads, denizens of Port Townsend and Sequim who lived by eating and selling fish, other Indians who were squatting across from three sawmills where the men worked, and residents of Jamestown village, who had bought their land and added farming to the usual Indian occupations.[54] At numerous locales around the Sound, other people clung to lands their indigenous ancestors had occupied, sometimes asserting a right to exclude settlers. Indians in the Skagit River watershed, for instance, refused to move and chased surveyors away, saying that they had not signed the treaty.[55]

Many people of native ancestry also gravitated to non-Indian settlements. A government farmer at the Lummi Reservation lamented in 1874 that Indians from several tribes were wintering in the town of Whatcom, where they had access to intoxicating drink, customers for sexual services, and opportunities to discuss their grievances against whites at numerous potlatches. Louisa Sinclair's Skagit mother seized a common option: she ran away to avoid an arranged marriage and eventually wed the white man who hired her to work in his tavern and trading post.[56] Some native people felt so confident of their ability to maneuver in Boston society that they sought American citizenship. In 1875 thirteen men petitioned the commissioner of Indian affairs to call off attempts to put them on reservations:

> Your petitioners respectfully represent that they are Indians of Washington Territory that they are not now connected with any tribe of Indians, but that they are performing the duties of civilized men—some of us are owners of land, some are laborers upon lands of others—that they are peaceable quiet and industrious, that they receive nothing from the government of the United States, nor do they claim anything by treaty or otherwise and desire to become citizens of the United States. ... [57]

Despite the adaptability such people demonstrated, officials often accused them of resisting the changes that would transform them from Indians to civilized Americans. Chirouse charged that young men on the Nooksack River, "well dressed but still very wild," were trying to incite their tribe to expel white settlers so that Indians could congregate there in communal lodges and carry on pagan rites, potlatches, and gambling. Yet in many cases the strategies of off-reservation Indians confounded officials' efforts to characterize them as untamed. Jamestown Klallams placated white neighbors and thus avoided removal to the reservation by consciously conforming to Boston notions of respectability. They enforced a ban on alcohol, built a church, and established a school. Even the "wild" Nooksacks were able to stay in familiar territory by meeting one of the most important criteria of civilized status: they became property owners under American law.[58]

The contrast between Indians on and off the reservations should not be overdrawn, for people identified as Indians did not sort themselves into mutually exclusive groups on this basis. As officials noted again and again, most people with homes on reservations still left for long periods to fish or pick berries, to visit relatives, and to work in mills, logging camps, hop fields, and the homes of white settlers. During their migrations they met and mingled not only with Bostons but also with residents of other reservations and with Indians who had homes off the reservations. Often the people they met were or became their relatives. The extent of intercourse between off-reservation and on-reservation Indians can be deduced from Indian censuses and genealogies which show that many people born during these years had one Indian parent from a reservation community and one from outside.[59]

Jerry Meeker and John Fornsby illustrate Indians' movement between reservation and off-reservation milieus. Meeker was born on the white settler's farm where his Indian father had worked since childhood. As a youth he spent summers on the farm, which he considered his residence. Yet he also lived a few months each year on the Puyallup Reservation after his father acquired a farm there. Fornsby resided at times during his boyhood with relatives off reservation and at other times on two different reservations. For Meeker, Fornsby, and other people of native descent, reservations were just some of many places they could choose to live, and choosing to live on a reservation was not necessarily a permanent or exclusive choice.[60]

Indian agents of the 1870s and 1880s may have induced additional people to establish residences on Puget Sound reservations, but they did not succeed in separating all such people from non-Indian society. Settlers and Indians reminiscing about this period invariably mentioned the ways their lives intersected with each other's. Their stories featured biracial families, Indian and white children playing together, Indians shopping and hawking their wares in town, Indians working for whites, Indians participating in Boston festivities, and whites watching or assisting in native ceremonies.[61]

In many of the retrospective accounts, Indians and whites are surprisingly unstereotyped. Jerry Meeker named whites who were his employers, friends, teachers, and fellow workers. Fornsby wielded a traditional shaman's power but also became a Catholic, worked for white loggers, had a white in-law, and married a woman whose previous husband was white. He spoke without apparent surprise about a white man who sang ghost power at spirit dances and a white man who honored his Indian wife's notions of responsibility by avenging the death of her cousin.[62]

Images that emerge from contemporary records match the sketches done from memory. In his diary of the 1870s and 1880s, Mason County farmer John Campbell noted matter-of-factly the many times he hired Indians for short-term labor, sold them livestock and equipment, and hosted his white neighbors' "squaws." Government investigators reported 282 whites and 221 Indians living and working together along the Skagit River above Mount Vernon in 1881. At "Ball's camp," five cabins housed twenty-two white and sixteen Indian loggers. Indians also appear as workers and neighbors in county court records. Several men, including Yen Tey (presumably Chinese) and Indians Jimmie and Charlie, sued W. B. Moore for logging wages in 1879. Three years later Mary Hazeltine, a white woman, testified in a murder trial that the Indian victim and defendant and several other Indians had lived ten or fifteen yards from her house near Seattle for at least two years. On the day of the killing Mrs. Hazeltine had sent her young daughter to town with one of the Indian women to see the Fourth of July festivities.[63]

Another gauge of the continuing commerce between Indians and non-Indians is the ubiquity of the Chinook jargon. Some students of the jargon believe that its use peaked in the 1870s and 1880s. Their conclusion jibes with memoirs, which rarely fail to mention that the jargon was an essential medium of communication during this period. In 1883 a government inspector recommended dispensing with the Tulalip agency's staff interpreter not because the Indians had learned English but because the agent, employees, and Indians all spoke the jargon. Interpreters were still indispensable when Indians were parties or witnesses in court cases, but their assignment was to interpret to and from Chinook.[64]

The persistence of the jargon—a medium of communication for distinct peoples not inclined to learn each other's language—is a reminder that many traits and habits continued to distinguish Indians from non-Indians despite their abundant contacts. Reminiscing settlers emphasized their frequent, friendly association with Indians not because they saw few differences dividing the races but because association made them conscious of differences. Around Puget Sound they discerned two kinds of people, Indians and non-Indians, and their dealings with Indians confirmed and intensified their sense that the Indians remained aliens. Myron Eells expressed this sense vividly in an 1887 article entitled "The Indians of Puget Sound."

> I should say of the greater part of those under forty-five years of age, that if they had white skins, talked the English language,—and if a part of them had abandoned their belief in their medicine men,—as some

have not done,—if they travelled in boats instead of canoes, if their women wore hats or bonnets on their heads, and if they were neater, they would be called civilized, at least as much so as the lower class of whites.[65]

Because the still "uncivilized" Indians of Puget Sound persisted in entering various unscripted relations with non-Indians, officials who had assumed the role of guardian for those Indians had to reinterpret their role and ad lib. Since they could not keep Indians within clearly bounded areas, they devoted much of their energy to preserving peace along cultural frontiers. Positioning themselves between their presumptive wards and settlers, they played to both by styling themselves more as interpreters and intermediaries than as border guards.[66] As Chirouse remarked after touring his jurisdiction in 1872, there were many difficulties to settle between whites and Indians. United States agents received appeals for help from both sides. When a citizen appropriated money that Klallams had entrusted to him, the Indians turned to Edwin Eells, and he pleaded their case to local officials. If Indians owed settlers money, the settlers might likewise ask U.S. agents to intervene.[67]

Because OIA officials were shorthanded, they also devised techniques to prevent trouble from developing. When groups left the reservations to work or fish, agents sometimes sent reservation police with them or gave them documents certifying their right to be at large. Agent Patrick Buckley addressed a warning to "Whome [*sic*] this may concern": "Indian Sam has made complaint at this office that some parties have been tearing down his salmon house and packing away the lumber. It is to be remembered that although Sam is an Indian, yet he has certain rights and those rights must and will be protected."[68]

In addition to contacts between Indians and non-Indians, agents monitored and mediated relations between Indians. When a score of people from Tulalip came to Olympia for help collecting back wages, Superintendent Milroy wrote to the Indian couple who had employed them. The couple responded in a letter written for them by Chirouse, and Milroy answered, "These Indians may be drunkards, liars, polygamists and thieves as you say, but still they have rights that every good man should respect." Eells even received a request from a Skokomish man for permission to present a marriage proposal to the father of a girl on another reservation.[69]

In the Puget Sound region, the institutionalization of agents' roles as mediators and arbitrators was perhaps the most significant short-term consequence of the reservation policy implemented during the 1870s and

1880s. Government mediators were in a position to adjust and often to structure Indians' interactions with other people. Increasingly, non-Indians looked to agents to explain and control those people whom they regarded as Indians, whether or not the latter fit cleanly into official administrative categories.

Although agents could help to resolve conflicts, they could not insulate native people from the contempt that many Bostons felt for Indians. In fact, government employees typically shared that contempt. Even Indians who tried to meet American standards of respectability found that the praise they earned was often qualified. When forwarding a day school teacher's letter to the commissioner, agent Alfred Marion urged indulgence of the writer's odd style because he was "only an Indian." Children in reservation schools learned along with their ABCs that such condescension was common among whites. Marion overheard a pupil at the mission school respond to a white child's insult with " 'I may be an Indian, but I have a soul to be saved as well as you.' " Although the agent related the incident as proof that Indians could learn Christian precepts, it is better evidence that the boy had learned to see himself as a member of a group ranking low in Christians' social hierarchy. Chirouse, conceding that Indians had not always received justice at the hands of whites, said ruefully, "It is very difficult to make them believe that the whites are their friends."[70]

To live among people who despised Indians without losing self-respect was not easy. Techniques that indigenous people had long used to earn respect were not forgotten—intercommunity giveaways were still common, for instance—but they were no longer reliable routes to high status. Sponsoring a potlatch, winning a gambling game, or wielding a shaman's power could still win the admiration of some Indians; but the same practices lowered a person in the eyes of most Bostons and confused, alarmed, or failed to impress a growing number of natives' descendants. Potlatches and spirit dances could not ease the tension that many Indians—particularly younger ones—felt when they compared the achievements of Indians and whites. For this reason, the old rituals did not unite an indigenous community as surely as in the past.[71]

Some Indians accordingly renounced or declined to learn aboriginal means of achieving status. At Port Madison, according to William DeShaw, residents had split into factions: ranged against "the Tomanamoos part of the Indians" (those who relied on spirits for efficacy) were people who planned to try farming, as DeShaw urged.[72] Myron Eells had an explanation for the fading glory of the potlatches:

Many of the younger people, who have been in contact with the whites for the past twenty-five years, have become ashamed to go through many of the practices, which were formerly the most savage and the most interesting; they have invented nothing new to take their places, so that the last one which I attended was called very dry by the chief.[73]

Whether or not they were ashamed of the old beliefs, more and more young people did not seek or find the nonhuman help their native ancestors considered essential for achievement and community esteem. John Fornsby recalled of his friend Paul Jesus, "I thought he was going to be tough, but he played cards all the time and gambled when the Whites came. He never saw anything [guardian spirit]." Jerry Meeker dashed his parents' hopes that he would acquire a spirit power. Nevertheless, Meeker enjoyed prosperity and the esteem of whites as well as Indians, probably to the bewilderment of many other natives trying to chart a course through life.[74]

John Slocum was among the bewildered people. Like many of his contemporaries, Slocum had slipped the social and economic moorings that anchored his indigenous ancestors' lives, and he found himself adrift in new cultural waters that were both alluring and dangerous. Yet in the 1880s Slocum seemed to acquire the power to navigate safely. His power came in an encounter with a supernatural being, but he neither undertook a vision quest nor met a spirit known to his ancestors. Instead, he saw the spirit most revered by Christians. Slocum's vision of God inspired a movement, now called the Indian Shaker Church, that offered many people of native descent a way to draw strength from the contradictory forces around them.

The Indian Shaker Church germinated and grew in the thicket of emotions that native people felt as they surveyed conditions of the 1870s and 1880s. They had many reasons to despair. A swelling settler population had altered their world with dizzying speed. Practices that had once ensured high status in native societies and practices acceptable to early settlers no longer brought reliable rewards and could even undermine health and economic well-being. The government and missionaries were trying to dictate Indians' activities and beliefs. As a consequence, the circumstances of people on the reservations were diverging from the circumstances of their off-reservation kin. These conditions presented dilemmas that admitted no simple solution, and the Shakers' response to them was complex; but one of its most significant aspects was an effort to fashion an Indian identity that allayed whites' criticism without buying into a demeaning conception of Indians.

John Slocum was one of the many indigenous people who declined to move to a reservation. A Sahewamish speaker from the southern extreme of Puget Sound, he was entitled to live on Squaxin Island or other land reserved by the Medicine Creek Treaty. Alternatively, he could have moved with relatives to the Skokomish Reservation. Instead, Slocum resided in his native district and logged a nearby preemption claim. Relatives later described him as the boss of a sizable logging operation and the scion of well-to-do people, suggesting that he could have claimed high-class status in aboriginal society. However, by the time Slocum reached middle age, his penchant for firewater and gambling had reportedly made him unhealthy and insecure. Anthropologist Homer Barnett infers from relatives' accounts that Slocum was also caught in crosscurrents of hatred and suspicion within his family—circumstances that made him fear lethal sorcery.[75]

Whether from sorcery or other causes, Slocum died in 1882. Or so it appeared until he sat up and told startled mourners that he had journeyed instead to a beautiful country. There he met the Big Father, who excoriated him for his vices, taught him to pray, and instructed him to build a church. Family and friends from several locations soon converged to erect the church, where Slocum preached that Indians must renounce alcohol, tobacco, gambling, swearing, shamanism, and property not acquired by their own labor. However, unable to practice what he preached, he resumed carousing, fell ill, and seemed again on the verge of death.

The ministrations of Slocum's wife Mary made possible a second miraculous revival, which inspired the new religious sect. A powerful spirit that Mary identified as God took possession of her, causing her to shake and directing her to pray, dance, sing, make the sign of the cross, and brush the evil from John's body. Thanks largely to Mary and Mud Bay Louis (Yowaluck), word of John's recovery spread, along with the belief that other Indians could likewise cleanse themselves and acquire healing power. Pike Ben welcomed the news. Feeling dirty and bad from his work for whites, his gambling losses, and his debts to Indian doctors, he converted because he wanted to be clean inside and out. Hundreds of people like Pike Ben gathered for days at a time at the Slocums' Mud Bay camp, where they held ceremonies that made liberal use of bells, crosses, candles, dancing, and prayer. As in traditional spirit dances, they also helped each other with spontaneous displays of the power and songs that the holy spirit gave them.[76]

The Slocums discovered God's power to heal Indians at a time when physical and psychological distress afflicted many people they knew. A series of epidemics had ravaged Indian communities in 1881. Friction and strife, much of it reflecting religious dilemmas, plagued the communities as well. At the Skokomish Reservation for a decade, the Eells brothers had waged holy war not only against aboriginal "superstitions" but also against vestiges of Catholic missionary influence. In fact, the Eells had targeted Billy Clams in the 1870s because they identified him as leader of a Catholic faction. Such persecution may have driven Clams and many of his peers to seek a syncretic resolution of competing claims for their spiritual allegiance. In the message of John and Mary Slocum, they apparently saw promise of relief. At least half the residents of the Skokomish Reservation—Clams, Big Frank, and Big John among them—were swept up in the wave of excitement flowing from the Slocums' camp.[77]

Although Shakers renounced practices condemned by pious whites and gave other signs of wanting to please non-Indians, officials and clergy were unsure whether the spiritual ferment represented " 'good providence' " or danger. According to Edwin Eells, a minister in Olympia invited some of the inspired Indians to hold services in his church, hoping that such kindness would induce them to give up the "peculiarities" of their ecstatic faith in favor of orthodox Christianity. Whether in response to this invitation or for other reasons—no two versions of the story offer the same details or explanation—Indians came into town in parade. At their head rode Big John, calling himself Jesus and mimicking his namesake's posture on the cross. Behind John walked his wife, renamed either Eve or Virgin Mary, her hand extended toward heaven. By Eells's account, the Indians conducted ceremonies and departed as they had come, "leaving behind them such an odor from their smoked fish and clams and their not overclean bodies that the minister who had invited them failed to get the sympathy from his people that he had desired."[78]

The Shakers initially got little sympathy from other whites. Big John was jailed, either for his outrageous impersonation (according to Erna Gunther) or for refusing to stay on the reservation to face government employees' ridicule (according to Homer Barnett). Agent Eells, suspicious of Shaker healing and the similarity of Shaker and Catholic rituals, instructed his employees to suppress the new church. On the Chehalis Reservation, teacher Edwin Chalcraft convened a hearing to determine whether Shaker worship was shamanism. One witness swore that Slocum was as much God's man as the missionaries were; his newfound ability to be good was proof. Chalcraft nonetheless banned Shaker meetings and forbade Indians under his supervision from going to Mud Bay without a pass. The failure of these measures to discourage all Shaker worship did

not discourage Chalcraft: a few years later he had ten men arrested for
Shaker doctoring.[79]

Like many early critics, some modern scholars have described the
Shaker movement as a ploy to preserve aboriginal practices by disguising
them as Christianity. The suspicion that shamans merely became Shakers
had facts to feed on, especially the sect's focus on curing with power endowed by a spirit.[80] However, the Shakers paired their enthusiasm for
faith healing with a condemnation of shamanism, and this censure was
not merely hypocrisy intended to deter repression. Rather, the attack on
shamans was part of a struggle for a new consensus on the norms of social
relations and the best means to enforce those norms.[81]

Shakers abhorred shamans as much because they often abused their
power as because whites denounced them as sorcerers. Native doctors' impotence against new diseases, along with the availability of alternative
medicine, probably emboldened the Shakers to repudiate shamans. But
the main target was shamans' pernicious effect on social relations. The
number of men claiming shamanic powers and using them maliciously
seemed to increase as people from previously separate villages crowded
into reservations or off-reservation camps. Mutual suspicions often fes-
tered in these conditions, especially as epidemics and economic stress took
their toll. At the same time, shamans had fewer reasons to hesitate before
using their powers for ill. By making it possible for people to sustain
themselves individually, the colonial economy had rendered social pressure and ostracism less effective in controlling such antisocial behavior.
American authorities had also weakened traditional sanctions against
malevolent magic by prohibiting and sometimes punishing the murders
of shamans and by undermining the influence of many native mediators.[82]
Anxious about the resulting disorder, many people understandably welcomed the Shakers' discovery that participants in an Indian Christian fel-
lowship could rid themselves of bad spirits and obtain the power to be
good directly from God.

Shaker beliefs eased other tensions, too. Shakers encouraged work in
enterprises introduced by non-Indians; yet in a world where the old correspondence between religious devotion and prosperity had dissolved, they
did not require wealth as proof of good relations with the supernatural.
Instead, they offered all pious people a prestigious power that had formerly come to very few—the power to cure. The Shakers' large assemblies also filled a need to link the diverse and changing social units where
Indians could be found. In church ceremonies the descendants of natives
could meet and affirm their affiliation with a community that transcended

the differences between reservation and off-reservation groups. At the same time, consistent with an aboriginal respect for and delight in individual differences, Shakers encouraged spontaneity and variations in expressions of faith.

Shakerism emerged during a period when Indians elsewhere in the United States were also flocking to new messianic faiths. While all such movements sought to revitalize indigenous societies, they varied in content from region to region. Most advocated a return to aboriginal customs and predicted the annihilation of whites, but a few preached accommodation with whites.[83] The Shakers, who belong in the latter category, gave revitalization a Northwest flavor by incorporating and reworking local notions about personal power and intercommunity relations. They perpetuated or revived the belief that they could acquire power from nonhuman beings. They also sought, as their ancestors had, to define their relations with other humans by displaying their new powers, thus inviting respect both for what they shared with those humans and for their unique traits and practices.

From the man who brought the new faith from Mud Bay to Chehalis, Chalcraft took a statement that reveals the Shakers' effort to explain their ascribed Indian identity in terms that both non-Indians and Indians would esteem. Being a Shaker did not mean he was no longer a Presbyterian, Smith said. The Bible told whites what to do to be saved; but because "Indians were different" and could not read, God had given Slocum additional instructions for them to follow.[84]

On an indigenous foundation the Shakers fashioned a new self-concept. In one respect they thought about themselves much as their indigenous ancestors had: their personal effectiveness attested to a special relationship with a powerful spirit. Like their ancestors, they expected to earn the esteem of outsiders by exhibiting the effects of their special relationship. However, they invoked these traditional ideas in a new context, with the result that they redefined themselves and their relations to the people who had created that new context.[85] Viewed together, the Shakers' rejection of practices offensive to whites, Big John's urge to display his new identity to whites, and John Smith's assertion that Indians could be both Christians and essentially different from whites suggest that Shakers combined an initial desire to impress or please whites with a desire to affirm their special powers and unique nature as Indians. Shakers thought they had identified both a vital congruence of native and Boston beliefs and an essential distinction between whites and so-called Indians. Therefore, while echoing whites' criticism of some practices that had initially distinguished Indians from whites, they neither attempted to erase all the characteristics that marked them as Indians nor internalized a negative image of themselves as Indians. Instead, they found a basis for asserting and taking pride in their ascribed Indian identity.

For almost a decade after John Slocum's resurrection, Shakers' relations with outsiders did not match their hopes. Miracles at Mud Bay and Big John's revelation did not spur leading whites to acknowledge their powers. Instead, Big John's arrest and the initial repression of Shaker worship reinforced a boundary between Indians and whites without revealing a way to conduct satisfying relations across that boundary. Furthermore, although the Indian Shaker movement flourished and spread throughout the Northwest after 1892, it never attracted all the people in the region who considered themselves Indians. Indeed, in some Indian communities, Shakers faced bitter opposition from friends and relatives.

Nevertheless the Shakers had tried, with considerable success, to retake the initiative in the process of drawing boundaries between Indians and non-Indians and defining the character of society on the Indian side of the boundary.[86] In this they were not alone. Other descendants of indigenous people had also refused during the 1870s and 1880s to define themselves solely in the terms suggested by their American colonizers. For this reason, by the end of those decades there were many ways of being Indian besides the one the government had tried to institutionalize.

5 Indians

Dialogues about Definitions

On May 22, 1892, the *Seattle Post-Intelligencer* reported the outcome of a lawsuit arousing "considerable commotion." A Kitsap County Court had awarded Charles Kelley the estate of Michael Kelley, which the county had held since 1869 in the belief that Michael died without heirs. The *Post-Intelligencer* deemed the case the most important ever heard in the county and perhaps in Washington State, not because Michael Kelley had been a county commissioner, nor because his estate was worth more than two hundred thousand dollars, but because Charles Kelley was Michael's son by an Indian "house companion."

The issue in court was whether Michael Kelley had fathered Charles during a valid marriage. Testimony persuaded the jurors that Michael had observed Indians' "ancient" marriage rules, and the judge consequently declared Charles legitimate "though Indian." Since "it was the admitted custom of many of the old settlers to take Indian women and live with them as wives," and since many children born of such arrangements were "still living in the several Sound counties and just reaching their majority," the *Post-Intelligencer* expected this decision "to disturb the titles of the most valuable land through the western part of the state."[1]

The census of 1900 confirmed that the intercourse of settlers and natives had produced many persons of ambiguous identity like Charles Kelley. In the counties surrounding Puget Sound, at least 1,305 residents had both Indian and non-Indian progenitors. Not all these hybrid people were reminders of the pioneer past, however. Census takers identified 136 households where a non-Indian and someone with at least one Indian parent were cohabiting.[2]

Census rolls also showed that there was no local consensus supporting the Kitsap County judge's conclusion that Charles Kelley was an Indian.

When deciding how to list individuals of dual ancestry, neither enumerators nor the enumerated applied consistent criteria. Some of the people identified as white had parentage comparable to people on the Indian rolls. The race ascribed to "mixed bloods" apparently depended on self-identification or reputation, census takers' biases, and precinct policies. Enumerators did not even agree how to count people with unadulterated native ancestry. Of 4,178 individuals who fit this description, only 1,833 were on Indian reservations. When such people paid taxes, voted, or lived and worked with non-Indians, they often went on white census rolls.[3]

Although persons of mixed ancestry were numerous and increasing in number at the turn of the century, they and the indigenous people from whom they descended were a tiny and shrinking portion of the population around Puget Sound. Nonetheless, the legal and racial status of Indians and their offspring was a matter of intense public interest; for their status would determine whether they could share resources that were becoming more precious as the region's population grew. If classed with white citizens, they might lay claim to wealth for which whites were already competing. If classified as Indians, they would crowd the field of those vying for even scarcer assets reserved to Indians.

Thus, as the nineteenth century closed, demographic and economic developments confronted people around Puget Sound with the fact that earlier attempts to separate Indians from non-Indians had been ineffectual. Mounting pressures on resources touched off new efforts to define Indians and spell out their rights and liabilities. Questions about Indians' identifying characteristics arose in many forums—in courtrooms, administrative offices, historical society meetings, publications, and schools. Although some of the forums were racially exclusive, no group could draw the boundaries between races unilaterally. In order to develop workable definitions, they had to take each other's ideas into account and even consult each other. The salient feature of Indian-white relations at the turn of the century was an explicit, multiparty discourse about the nature and consequences of Indian identity.

The immigrant tide that had been flowing into Puget Sound since the 1860s surged between 1880 and 1910. During the 1880s, 155,000 newcomers boosted the population 600 percent. Together with farmers settling on the Columbia plateau, this accumulation of inhabitants earned Washington Territory its statehood in 1889. Statehood enhanced the region's appeal to investors and settlers, encouraging further growth until the depression of 1893. In the wake of the Klondike gold discoveries of 1897 came another tidal wave of immigrants—a bonanza for merchants

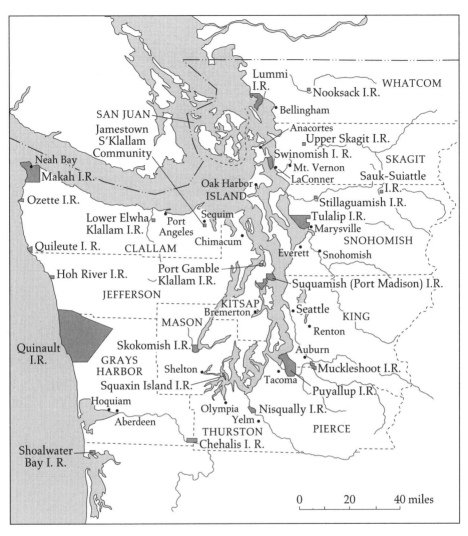

Map 4. Twentieth-century reservations, cities, and counties (County names are set in all capital letters).

and promoters in Puget Sound ports. By 1910 the area's population had leaped to 600,000.[4]

The value of land ballooned as settlers claimed the remaining public domain and lumber companies bought millions of acres. Speculators who correctly foresaw the locations of new ports and rail routes could parlay modest investments into fortunes overnight. Competition was especially intense for the kinds of lands reserved to Indians—waterfront, tidelands, and river valleys. Entrepreneurs with access to strategically located shoreline could invest in wharves and log booming yards or in structures that trapped salmon by the hundreds of thousands. By 1900 commercial oyster culture was paying well, too.[5]

To people with a feverish desire to profit from such opportunities, many of the lands and resources allocated to Indians seemed like medicine. Some whites decided, for instance, that the Puyallup Reservation was the remedy for what ailed them. Bordering an ideal harbor, it lay between the burgeoning city of Tacoma and proliferating farms and mines to the east. Under the headline "Rich Puyallup Indians," an Olympia newspaper estimated in 1890 that reservation lots were worth $50,000 to $250,000 each. But whites could not bottle and sell this elixir of wealth because a treaty clause prevented them from taxing or buying reservation land unless Congress consented.

County and city authorities therefore petitioned Congress to let Puyallup Reservation allottees use or dispose of their land as they wished. Where there was a comparative wilderness, Tacoma's mayor and council declared, there could be vast gardens. Frank Ross saw no reason to wait for congressional action before planting his money tree in the Puyallup garden. While backers of a Puyallup Valley railway followed federal rules for obtaining a right-of-way through the reservation, only to see a council of Indians veto their plan, Ross cut private deals with allottees for a route across their lands.[6]

These schemes to eliminate or evade the legal constraints on Puyallup land stirred up provocative questions about ethnic categories. When Indian Agent Edwin Eells sued to nullify Frank Ross's deals, a federal judge upheld them on the ground that the allottees were no different in law from non-Indians. Upon receiving land patents in the 1870s, Puyallups had become U.S. citizens with a citizen's right to manage their property. A higher court reversed this decision in 1894 because it had a different conception of the Puyallup allottees. Abolishing Indians' distinct status was the government's ultimate goal, the court acknowledged, but that goal would "not be soonest realized by attributing fanciful qualities to the In-

dians or by supposing that their natures can be changed by legislative enactment." Before the appellate court ruled, however, Congress had yielded
to pressure and authorized government-supervised sales of Puyallup
Reservation allotments. Under the legislation, all remaining legal constraints on the lands lapsed in 1903. Many people—Puyallups as well as
whites—then announced that the Puyallup Indian tribe had ceased to
exist.[7]

In venturing onto Puyallup lands, non-Indians were bypassing or top-
pling boundary markers—geographic and legal—that an earlier generation had erected around Indians. There were many such incursions during
the twenty years straddling the century point. Whites demanded opportunities to acquire property inside several other western Washington reservations. They also appeared frequently along reservation borders, claiming
the right to take fish, shellfish, and water there. The two dozen residents of
the Squaxin Island Reservation, who depended on the fauna of surrounding tidelands for food and income, were alarmed to learn that the
state was selling those tidelands to whites. In 1903 a U.S. court halted the
sales with a declaration that the reservation's boundary was the line of
low tide, but that did not discourage non-Indians from locating fish traps
and hauling seines on the shores of other Indian reserves in the region.[8]

Lawyers and judges enabled whites to gain control of many of the assets they coveted. In some cases, as at Puyallup, they did so by disre-
garding or erasing boundaries between Indians and non-Indians, but in
other cases they reinforced old dividing lines. The first stratagem permitted speculators to pry Ezra Hatch's homestead out of his Indian
widow's hands and profit from its location in the path of a projected rail
line. Josephine Hatch was illiterate and unable to converse in English. The
men who persuaded her to sell them the land promptly resold it for one
hundred times their cost. Yet according to the judge, these signs that
Josephine was a stranger to American ways were no reason to invalidate
the sale. Marriage to Hatch made her the legal equal of white females—a
citizen with the right to inherit and dispose of property.[9]

On the other hand, when the verdict for Charles Kelley raised the
specter of Indians taking valuable land from whites, judges on the state
supreme court hastened to restore some lines around Indians. They declared that Michael Kelley's domestic arrangement—paying a woman's
sisters a few dollars and living with her briefly—could not possibly
amount to marriage; and they reversed the trial court's decision. Even
people with more formal and permanent ties to whites found themselves
on the other side of the legal line. Kitty Wilbur had gone to live with set-

tler John Wilbur only after he observed her Skagit family's strict rules of
courtship. Wilbur had called Kitty his wife for years and had fathered her
three children before putting her aside. Yet his white heirs thwarted her
bid for a share of his estate by relying on a historic attempt to separate Indians from whites. John and Kitty had contracted a real marriage, the
judges agreed, but had done so at a time when laws of the territory forbade whites to wed Indians.[10]

Thus, by depicting Indians as people who operated outside the rules of
American society, whites achieved the same results in the Kelley and
Wilbur cases as they did by denying in the Puyallup and Hatch cases that
Indians were different. The *Post-Intelligencer* warned in 1892 that Charles
Kelley was the tip of a sizable iceberg adrift in the regional economy. But
within a decade the courts had substantially reduced the danger that In-
dian consorts and their progeny would emerge from the foggy past to sink
whites whose boats were rising with Puget Sound's economic tide.

As whites used law to pare down the economic opportunities available
to people of indigenous descent, more and more of those people focused
their hopes on land and resources reserved for Indians. The scarcity of affordable land motivated whites to displace Indians who had squatted or
homesteaded outside reservations, and some of the displaced families
sought homesites on reservations. There they had to get in line with assorted other people who hankered for land. Government files from this
period contain numerous inquiries and complaints from individuals who
thought their ancestry or social ties entitled them to reservation lots.
Mindful of this interest and of simultaneous developments conducive to
farming, government agents soon parceled out most remaining, common
Indian lands and unoccupied lots. As provided in the treaties or the Dawes
Act, the new allotments could not be taxed, mortgaged, or transferred
without federal consent.[11]

Many applications for new allotments presented officials with a question they were ill prepared to answer: What characteristics entitled a
person to land reserved for Indians? Some applicants had tenuous or multiple connections to indigenous communities, and many had non-Indian
ancestors or kin. In 1901 the government farmer at Muckleshoot asked his
supervisor whether he could assign land to a man who claimed to be a
Puyallup Indian but did not appear on any Indian census. "He has not
been considered a Muckleshoot Indian but would like to belong to this
tribe," the farmer wrote. "He is a citizen Indian and has never held land at
Puyallup or elsewhere." Requests from women married to whites were
also puzzling. Agent D. C. Govan asked in 1895 whether he should distin-

guish women whose parents or grandparents had been on the reservation from those whose families "failed or refused to avail themselves of the benefits of the treaty of 1856 [*sic*] and belong to that class which has always lived outside the reservation."[12]

The responsibility that Indian agents bore in these circumstances was heavy with irony. Their predecessors had assumed not only that Indians should be segregated from other people but also that Indians could easily be distinguished from others, yet their own efforts to identify Indians revealed that the second assumption was foolish. Moreover, government officials had contributed to the difficulty of differentiating and isolating Indians when they revised federal policy and changed the status of many presumed Indians. Rather than accomplishing a clear division of Indians and non-Indians, U.S. law and policy had generated a need to define Indians.

When Washington Territory's first governor urged all Indians to settle on reservations in the 1850s, he did not anticipate problems identifying Indians. Isaac Stevens drew up treaties that designated reservations for listed tribes, apparently without wondering how to determine the membership of those groups. And before the 1880s administrators left almost no record that they tried to sort individuals by tribe. Agents occasionally worried that people were claiming treaty benefits not rightfully theirs, but more often they worried that paltry payments and the fear of encountering enemies kept eligible Indians from coming to get treaty payments and the accompanying government advice. Glad to have any Indians gather around them, agents rarely questioned the identities of the people who came in. Thus, indigenous people initially sorted themselves into administrative units by going where they willed, and those who settled on the reservations appeared on the first Indian censuses.[13]

Records of the earliest individual land assignments are similarly short on evidence that eligibility was an issue. Agent E. C. Chirouse once inquired whether Indians from outside the Point Elliott Treaty area could live at Tulalip. Superintendent R. H. Milroy answered that they could settle there so long as no Indian from the area objected, although they could not claim "rights or benefits." Probably in most cases the first inhabitants of reservations decided whether to make others welcome; and the latecomers received land, if land was available, alongside their friends and kin.[14]

However, the kin networks that drew some people onto reservations also portended problems for the government's plan to group Indians and allot land by tribe. Myron Eells documented those networks during the census of 1880 when he asked Indians to name their grandparents' tribes. Almost half of those he listed as Klallams were "intermingled with eighteen other tribes," and many had the "blood" of three or four tribes. Among 242 Twanas, Eells found only 20 who did not identify at least one grandparent as Klallam, Squaxin, Chehalis, Samish, Nisqually, Snohomish, Port Madison, Puyallup, Chemakum, Duwamish, Skagit, Victoria, Klikatat, "Skewhamish," or Snoqualmie. Twenty-four Twanas and fifteen Klallams had white ancestors. Although other agents were vaguely aware of such family ties between the presumed tribes and races, none betrayed concern that the ties could trip them up as they allocated Indian property.[15]

The government made it still harder to compartmentalize Indians in the late nineteenth century when policy shifted from minimizing contact with whites to promoting beneficial intercourse. Proponents of rapid assimilation wanted Indians to associate with white exemplars; some even advocated intermarriage as a means of absorbing Indians into American society. Nevertheless, whites were unsure how to classify people of dual ancestry or Indians who obligingly imitated whites. What did such people mean for racial categories? While some policy makers pointed to them as evidence that Indians could become non-Indians, judges were pronouncing many of them Indians.[16]

Grants of citizenship further complicated the business of drawing and patrolling boundaries around Indians. Until 1906 Indians became citizens as soon as they acquired private lands. The Dawes or General Allotment Act of 1887, keystone of the assimilation program, conferred citizenship on all Indians who accepted allotments and renounced tribal ties. Although many Indians on western Washington reservations received land patents authorized by treaty instead of the Allotment Act, they too became citizens. In reform theory and under federal law, they were no longer Indians for most governmental purposes. According to Congressman John B. Allen (whose ulterior motive was persuading lawmakers to lift restrictions on Puyallup Reservation lands), bestowing citizenship on allottees "suddenly and forever wiped out every vestige of racedome or Indianship in their case. You may make a citizen out of an Indian, but you can not [sic] make an Indian out of a citizen."[17]

When many allottees promptly asserted their rights as citizens, Edwin Eells reported that the civilization program was achieving its end, solving the Indian problem by eliminating the special class of people called Indians. However, when some of the new citizens proclaimed themselves exempt from Indian agents' moral code, Eells wanted to redraw racial boundaries. Eells complained about a court ruling in 1891 that citizen Indians did not fall under his jurisdiction. It left them free, he said, to indulge in liquor, hold heathen rites, and take their children out of school on any pretext. Evidently Eells found it difficult to reconcile law and the prevailing theory of Indian assimilation with his perception that the new citizens were still more Indian than non-Indian. He was not alone.[18]

Among the citizens who still seemed like Indians were some who had never lived on reservations. Notwithstanding the directives and court decrees that limited Indian agents' off-reservation jurisdiction, some of the stray people were within the official Indian pale, thanks to two acts of Congress. The first act, in 1875, allowed Indians to take advantage of general homestead laws; nine years later the second law permitted Indians to select off-reservation allotments. While both statutes conferred citizenship on the landowners, both also marked the new citizens for special treatment by prohibiting the sale and taxation of their land for specified periods and by placing the allotments in a federal trust. Off-reservation homesteads and allotments thus further muddled the distinction between Indians under federal protection and people who could be treated as non-Indians.[19]

Scores of people around Puget Sound claimed land under one of these laws, often without the initial knowledge or aid of the Indian Office. As contests for land heated up, Indian agents received more requests to account for and help homesteaders and off-reservation allottees. These requests highlighted the indefinite and paradoxical status of many people with native ancestry. They could be citizens by virtue of land ownership but government wards by virtue of "blood" and legal restrictions on their property. The government's focus on managing Indian land also meant that some citizens received more attention from Indian agents than did other people who seemed less "civilized" but had no property under Indian Office protection.[20]

In sum, the premise of the reservation system was that Indians were readily identifiable people, each born into a known tribe. Yet by the 1890s, the officials who had to apportion property earmarked for western Washington tribes faced a bewildering task. Because administrators had applied the treaty reservation plan haphazardly, because policy makers had tinkered with the plan itself, and because the plan was a poor fit for the interconnected native groups of Puget Sound, it was not easy to identify tribe members. The traits that might mark people either as members of Indian tribes or as nontribal citizens were numerous and ambiguous.

In 1901 Charles Buchanan took charge of the Tulalip Indian Agency, where he would direct a boarding school and oversee land and funds intended for Indians in the Point Elliott Treaty area. A physician with a systematic mind, Buchanan promptly asked the Indian commissioner for guidance in admitting pupils and allocating unallotted land. Please tell me, he wrote,

> Who and what is an "Indian"? What is a "tribe"? What are "tribal rights"? ... In what manner and by what methods can mixed bloods acquire tribal rights ... ? Can an Indian of the mixed blood, one who is white, Yakima and Snohomish maintain a status, tribal or otherwise, as all three? Can he homestead land and also exercise tribal rights among the Yakimas and at the same time maintain tribal rights with the Snohomish?[21]

As guidance from the national office dribbled in, Buchanan and his staff struggled to apply it. When the government farmer at the Muckleshoot Reservation received forms to use in gathering data on Indian families, he asked Buchanan to explain the terms "Blood or Nationality" and "Tribe or allegiance by Citizenship." Edward Bristow asked whether to include on the Swinomish Reservation roll one allottee who had moved to Tulalip and another—a "half breed"—who was living with his white wife among whites. A third employee, himself the son of a local Indian, complained that Bristow produced a Lummi roll laden with errors, particularly in attributions of tribal identity and "blood."[22]

Indian habits compounded the difficulty of identifying Buchanan's charges. Because Indians moved around, he said, census rolls did not necessarily show who belonged on a reservation. He later elaborated:

> It not infrequently happens that relatives or visitors (or those who hope to be either or both) appear upon the reservation at various times for visits ... indefinitely protracted, at the same time claiming residence rights through ... personal relationship, or tribal affiliation, and thus become enrolled on the annual census for that year, but afterwards go out to their former or other haunts, and thus disappear from the census for such period, or may even be lost track of entirely.[23]

Buchanan knew from experience how hard it was to apply the principle that each Indian belonged on a particular western Washington reservation. In 1908 a federal inspector chastised him for enrolling a Puyallup allottee's children at the Tulalip school instead of sending them back to Puyallup. Rejecting Buchanan's argument that the mother was born on a reservation in the Tulalip jurisdiction and was planning to resume relations there, the inspector declared that her allotment fixed her tribal membership.[24] But there was a catch in the inspector's rule: the right to an allotment depended in the first place on membership in a tribe. And tribal membership was an elusive phenomenon, as Buchanan knew. A family had sued him for denying them land at Tulalip, and he had failed in a bid to prove that they were not tribe members. He remained unsure how to reconcile actual social relations with the notions of Indian and tribal identity that were embodied in law and policy.

Buchanan's litigation with the Spithill family about their eligibility for allotments shows how interethnic marriage, mobility, and erratic government practices combined to muddle some people's status. The case drew the descendants of indigenous people, who had varied and inchoate ideas about tribal membership, into a dialogue with whites who were themselves uncertain how to recognize members of an Indian community. The issue was what made someone a Snohomish Indian, entitled to land at Tulalip. Buchanan thought he knew what the criteria were, but in order to apply them he needed information from Indians. Indians, straining to understand what Buchanan meant and how their own ideas fit into white categories, gave him vague and varying answers.

The Spithill applications had troubled agents for years before Buchanan considered them. They came from the wife and children of Alexander Spithill, a Scottish immigrant who had briefly been an unpopular employee at Tulalip. In 1885 Spithill's two sons by a Stillaguamish woman, his second wife Anastasia, and her six children requested allotments. Anastasia, the daughter of an unidentified white man and a native woman, had grown up in the household of her maternal grandfather, known to all as Snohomish Chief Bonaparte. Informed that the Spithills lived on Alexander's valuable homestead, agent Patrick Buckley first denied their request for reservation land, but he relented after the commissioner ruled that Indian women with white husbands were eligible for lots. Fifteen years later the Spithills complained that Buchanan was locating other Indians on tracts they had selected. A seven-year dispute ensued.[25]

Buchanan's predecessors had engendered confusion about the Spithills' status by failing to take a complete census of Indians and allowing reservation land records to get "badly messed." Buchanan doubted Anastasia's membership in part because he could not find her name on a Tulalip census or the original allotment schedule, although it did appear on a map of assigned land. Former agents testified, however, that these facts were better evidence of their own sloppy practices than of Anastasia's absence from the Indian community.[26]

The government had also contributed to its own dilemma by revising the criteria of eligibility for allotments. In the 1880s Buckley did not ques-

tion Anastasia's designation as a Snohomish Indian even though her father was white; he merely asked whether he should assign land to a white
man's wife, and the acting commissioner replied that the only criterion
was membership in the tribe. Between Buckley's time and Buchanan's,
however, Congress provided that half-breeds could enjoy the status of
their Indian mothers only if they were conceived during formal marriage.
For this reason the court ruled that Anastasia's stepsons were not Indians.
As instructed by his superiors, Buchanan acknowledged at trial that the
stepsons and Anastasia were entitled to reservation land by inheritance
through their mothers, but he denied that they had an independent right
to allotments. To establish a right, he said, they had to show membership
in an appropriate tribe by proving descent from Indians named in the
treaty, residence in the reservation community, and continuing association with Indians there.[27]

Buchanan's criteria proved difficult to employ. Like many presumed Indians in the area, the Spithills did not stay put, identify consistently with
a single group, or restrict their social relations to treaty Indians. According
to testimony, they neither lived continuously on the reservation nor left it
for good. In sojourns of varying lengths, they attended to economic interests and visited friends and relatives at Tulalip. Young Spithill men circulated between the reservation and several towns. Witnesses, including
Buchanan, said there were numerous Indians as peripatetic as the Spithills. As Anastasia saw it, the issue was whether she lived on her allotment
any less than other Indians.[28]

To support the contention that Anastasia did not meet his tests of tribal
membership, Buchanan needed information from people whose place in
the tribe seemed undisputed. Although he professed to know that "an Indian uses a white man's terms of relationship in a way very uncertain,"
calling people "grandfather" and "uncle" without regard to actual kinship,
he knew little about Tulalip Indians' actual lineages and affiliations. He
was not even aware that Anastasia's grandfather had signed the treaty.
Based on sources he refused to identify, Buchanan asserted that Anastasia
had "Indian blood to the tribes belonging on the Tulalip Reservation" plus
"alien blood to our tribes"; however, he and other white witnesses were
unable either to corroborate this allegation or to explain its significance
for the issue before the court.[29]

The natives Buchanan consulted did not give clear answers to questions
about Anastasia's tribal origins. Charles Jules, who knew Anastasia's
grandfather, said that Bonaparte did belong to the Snohomish Tribe; but
he qualified his statement by explaining that Indians' custom of marrying

into adjoining tribes had also given Bonaparte "little different connected to other nations of people." Bonaparte's grandnephew identified the chief's tribe as Statan or Skagit Head. A third Indian witness, when asked whether reservation residents were from different tribes, said, "No. All that belongs to Tulalip." Tulalip, however, was not a tribal name listed in the Point Elliott Treaty; it was simply the name of the reservation's locale.[30]

Before trial Buchanan put the question of Anastasia's tribal affiliation to adults on the reservation, assembled in council. They voted not to recognize her as a member of their community, but a summary of their discussion suggests that they were neither certain nor of one mind about what made someone a Snohomish or a Tulalip Indian. When considering Anastasia's heritage and associations, some referred to the bloodline and pale skin that prompted them to call her Little Boston. Others spoke of her mother's Klallam ancestry. However, according to a man who interpreted at the council, Anastasia's ancestry mattered less to the old people than the way she snubbed them after her marriage. Perhaps when they disowned her they also had in mind that a different decision could entitle seven people to eighty acres each of reservation land.[31]

Competition for land stimulated a similar public dialogue about tribal membership at Puyallup. When a real estate dealer learned about the diverse ancestries of Puyallup Reservation allottees, he protested that government agent Edwin Eells had allocated valuable resources without regard for proper criteria of Puyallup Indian identity. James Wickersham claimed that sixty-eight of ninety-eight reservation landholders were not true Puyallups. The sixty-eight, he reported to Congress, included half-breeds, full-bloods from nearby tribes, a Mexican, a Sandwich Islander, a British Columbia half-breed, and a Bad River Indian from Manitoba.[32]

At a Senate hearing on these charges, the principal witness against Eells was Tommy Dean, who had helped Wickersham compile the list of dubious Puyallups. Eells suggested that Dean was no less a foreigner at Puyallup than others on the list, because Dean's mother described herself as half Snohomish. Dean replied that he at least had been born on the reservation, although he promptly conceded that his birthplace was actually a few miles beyond the reservation boundary. Joe Taylor, chief judge of the Puyallup court, readily admitted that his mother was not a Puyallup; she was half Klallam, half Skagit. Taylor, however, did not assume as Dean did that birthplace defined a person's tribal identity. No one had ever explained tribe membership to him, he said, but he was inclined to call anyone on the reservation a member. When given the names of several individuals, he could not say whether they were Puyallups. But including them made sense, Taylor reasoned, "[b]ecause when a person joins a tribe he is a member. ... It is all worked by marriaging and relations."[33]

Clearly, deliberations about the composition of Indian communities did not pit united non-Indians against teams of Indians. Rather, while non-Indians proposed various tests of community membership, people who thought of themselves as Indians also suggested divergent characterizations of their relations with each other. Although whites presided at trials and hearings and then decreed which traits would mark people as tribe members for legal and administrative purposes, records of the Spithill and Puyallup controversies show that the official formulations of Indian identity emerged from complex, cross-cultural and intracultural dialogues.[34]

When judges and litigants expounded on the traits they associated with Indians, they lent their voices to a chorus rising outside their courtrooms. The turn of the century is remarkable not only for the many legal and administrative efforts to define Indians but also for the prominent place that Indians and Indian characteristics occupied in a wider public discourse. Journalists, educators, civic leaders, and pioneer settlers joined the discussion. These whites often seemed less intent on defining and controlling Indians than on using images of Indians to score points in internecine contests. Nevertheless, they did catch the ears of people they regarded as Indians, who in turn had to take the non-Indians' views into account when deciding how to represent themselves.

Demographic change accounts in part for whites' interest in Indians. By the 1890s the overwhelming majority of western Washington residents were recent arrivals, unfamiliar with indigenous people and likely to see them as exotic curiosities. Thousands of whites, especially in the cities, had had little or no personal contact with Indians. To them, local natives must have seemed like colorful vestiges of the fabled Wild West.

Periodicals catered to the fascination with Indians. Between 1890 and 1910 scarcely a month went by in which newspapers and regional magazines did not cover Indians in the vicinity.[35] Besides monitoring Indians' claims to lands and resources, journalists reported on Indian street vendors, Shakers, hop harvesters, marriages, funerals, citizenship, mortality rates, shamans, fishing, schools, legends, and crimes. They also introduced readers to Washington tribes and to the laws and institutions that set them apart. In 1905 historian Edmond Meany supplied the *Seattle Post-Intelligencer* with a series of profiles of nearby Indian communities, recapping in each the statements he had taken from elderly Indians about their concerns and histories.[36]

Correspondents also churned out sketches of Indians they deemed picturesque or droll. Indians on city streets and waterfronts were particularly amusing. A *Post-Intelligencer* piece of 1904 began, "Under the influence of the summer sun the siwashes have thawed out from their winter hibernations and run out over the city sidewalks, collecting here and there in little pools." Variations on the *Post-Intelligencer*'s ensuing description appeared frequently in that paper and others for several subsequent years: Indians in dirty blankets parading mournfully through town, barefoot women squatting stolidly in the rain, children gazing wistfully at store window displays, wrinkled crones jabbering in dialect, girls sporting gaudy costumes that "approached the modern."[37]

The discovery of Indians as local exotica coincided with, reflected, and perhaps furthered a national fad. Historians have traced the vogue for Indians in this period to a sense that America had just closed the chapters of its history in which Indians were important characters. The Indian wars had finally ceased; the Indian barrier to expansion was gone. With this closure came pride in whites' accomplishment but also—among many Americans—nostalgia for what had been sacrificed to progress.[38]

Washington pioneers responded to and fostered the nostalgia about the era when Indians had tested Americans' mettle and found it formidable. In 1893 eighty old settlers submitted entries in the *Tacoma Ledger*'s contest for the most interesting story of early days in the Northwest. A generous handful of their contemporaries published longer memoirs. These and other reminiscences of early colonists—from the recollections that Hubert Howe Bancroft solicited in 1878 to personal histories that the Works Progress Administration collected in the 1930s—contributed liberally to the regional literature about Indians; for adventures involving Indians were de rigueur in narratives of pioneer life. It was impossible, Ezra Meeker declared, "to write of the white race ... of that period without reference to the Indians ... whose everyday life was so intimately connected. ... "[39]

Yarns about encounters with Indians became a standard part of old settlers' repertoires because opportunities to reminisce at reunions and pioneer clubs gave them a collective sense that such encounters established their credentials as white pioneers. Emily Denny's parents dusted off their credentials for their wedding anniversary celebration in 1895. At the party's high point, Emily said, sixteen young people "gorgeously dressed as Indians" entered in "true Indian file," formed a circle on the floor, and beat out Indian songs on their "tamanuse" boards. Then their "chief" addressed "white chief Denny" in Chinook, wishing him many happy returns. Whether the Indians they depicted were friendly and helpful or obnoxious and dangerous, people like the Dennys proved that they had been in the vanguard of Washington's civilized inhabitants by their eyewitness accounts of the Sound country when it was "swarming with Indians."[40]

Reminiscing pioneers were usually grinding axes besides the ones they had used to clear the wilderness. Through accounts of the adversity they had overcome—including Indians who bullied women, plotted to kill well-meaning men, and abruptly declared war on the white race—they sought to impress newcomers with the sacrifices that had made it possible for everyone in Washington to enjoy the amenities of civilized life.[41] Some old settlers were also honing their blades for use in a spreading conflict about the nature and repercussions of their past dealings with Indians. The conflict, probably touched off by the Squaxin Island tidelands case or other Indian lawsuits based on the treaties, spilled out of the courtrooms and into historical societies, editorial boardrooms, and other non-Indian arenas.[42]

Because whites were looking to the past to explain and resolve issues that divided them in the present, they debated the Indian treaties and war as bitterly in 1900 as they had in the 1850s. Many faulted territorial officials for bequeathing them a divided society, some arguing that the mistake had been granting Indians an anomalous special status, others citing a failure to honor the special relationship with Indians. Ezra Meeker held Isaac Stevens and his treaties responsible not only for the war of 1855–56 but also for turn-of-the-century disputes over reservation tidelands. In Meeker's view, Stevens had driven peaceable Indians to fight by pressuring them into treaties that reflected national policy rather than local conditions. For settlers' common sense the government had substituted the judgment of men familiar only with Indians entirely unlike those of Puget Sound. This stupidity had disrupted an integrated community where "the leaven was at work that would have gradually elevated the natives far above their original position. . . . "[43]

Other whites lauded the treaty makers as visionaries who knew what it would take to free up Indians' land for American use. Meany argued that the treaties, although "little thought of" in 1897, were Stevens's greatest work. Benjamin Shaw, an interpreter at the treaty conferences, derided treaty critics for believing stories told by "a lot of Indomaniacs" and by Indians who sought to excuse their decision to initiate the war. Shaw scoffed at Meeker's claim that Stevens had imposed terms on disgruntled Indians. The governor and his aides had had the natives' confidence and apparently unanimous agreement, Shaw said, until other scheming whites planted seeds of discontent.[44]

While deflecting blame for poor relations with Indians from themselves to other whites, the old settlers generalized about Indian traits. Shaw justified the reservation system by saying that Indians of the 1850s knew nothing about religion or law and had no check on their conduct except superstitious fear. He characterized the Indians who waged war as treacherous and vengeful (albeit foreseeable) foes of civilization's preordained advance. Pioneers who disavowed views like Shaw's commonly depicted local Indians as harmless, honest, hard-working, loyal friends of good whites. Emily Denny, ostensibly debunking stereotypes by describing individuals she knew in her youth, declared that the many "types" of Puget Sound Indians included sociable, humorous, and justice-loving Indians. However, the purveyors of stereotypes probably approved of her claim that Indians were "like untaught children in many things."[45]

As pioneers and other whites scrutinized the past in the light cast by contemporary conditions, they spotted individual Indians who could serve as symbols of the lessons they drew. Most were men they regarded as chiefs. To Seattle and Leschi in particular, they attributed traits consistent with their views on Indians. Those who portrayed the natives as amenable to white guidance were partial to Seattle, an alleged champion of peaceful coexistence. Those who emphasized the incompatibility of Indians' cherished ways and whites' ambitions used Leschi's story to make their point.

Emily Denny described Seattle as mild-tempered and merciful and pronounced him "the noblest of his race." To many commentators, Seattle's most significant virtue was the respect he showed whites by his unwavering friendship. When depicted as a man who understood the need to accommodate American settlers, Seattle implicitly exonerated whites of charges that they had mistreated Indians. Probably for this reason, his popularity as a symbol of Washington's colonization increased with the passage of time. The more whites studied Seattle's life, Edmond Meany said in 1905, the more they respected him. Members of the white elite showed their respect for Seattle and other "friendly" chiefs by writing adulatory essays, erecting monuments to them, and featuring them in historical pageants.[46]

Ezra Meeker, on the other hand, declined to fuss over Seattle, even ridiculing him for allegedly expecting tribute for the use of his name. To Meeker the better symbol of local Indians was Leschi, a patriotic martyr to Stevens's political ambition and ill-conceived policies. In Meeker's iconography, Leschi and Stevens "were representatives of their respective races." When he learned in 1895 that Indians at Nisqually planned to rebury Leschi's body with elaborate ceremony, Meeker seized the opportunity to promote his version of history. He escorted white Tacomans to the services in a chartered train. Even whites who did not know the Nisqually language, he wrote afterward, could see from a thousand Indians' grief how much they adored the fallen leader who had won them a reservation they "could live on."[47]

It was not as hard in the 1890s as in the 1850s for whites to see Leschi as a tragic hero. At last in control of the territory that Indians had formerly claimed, they could safely indulge their pity for a chief who had fought in vain to keep his beloved home. By praising Leschi they atoned for the suffering that American colonization had inflicted on Indians and at the same time conveniently discredited the reservation policy. By attending Leschi's reburial, some whites (including Meeker, who had voted to acquit Leschi at his first trial but later declined to block his execution) probably hoped to lay to rest the ghosts of all the Indians by whom they or their forebears had not done right.

There was indeed a ghostly pallor to Indians in the books, articles, and pageants that whites produced during these years. Living Indians, many whites believed, were but shadows, following their forebears into oblivion. The conviction that Indians were dying off inspired the hurried effort of Seattle-based photographer Edward Curtis to compile a comprehensive pictorial record of Indians in aboriginal garb and settings. It imbued whites' writings and speeches about Indians with pathos. "So to-day," Charles Buchanan lamented ritualistically in 1900, "this great and once-powerful race remains little else than so much flotsam and jetsam upon the tides of time. . . . "[48]

The myth of Indians' imminent extinction, along with nostalgia about the past, explains the attention lavished on individual aged Indians during this era. Seattle's daughter Angeline attracted a disproportionate share of the attention, both because she lived in the city named for her father and because she was a surrogate symbol of his acquiescence in the changes whites had wrought. Angeline, said Emily Denny, had seen all the progress of modern civilization and the subjugation of the original, inferior race. Repeatedly photographed wearing shabby clothes and in a waterfront shack, presented in bare feet to President Benjamin Harrison, buried with elaborate ceremony at whites' expense near city founders, Angeline was one of many old people who represented for whites the stoicism and dignity with which Washington's aborigines faced their demise.[49]

It is a happy irony that people who thought they were preserving images of the last true Indians documented societies that were far from moribund. News and magazine articles often belied their own announcements that Indians were vanishing. Like the account of Leschi's well-attended re-burial, they provide evidence that Puget Sound was still home to a variety of visible, dynamic populations whose Indian character no one questioned. A superb example is the *Post-Intelligencer*'s 1907 coverage, in text and photos, of a "Siwash" village on the Tacoma tideflats. Sandwiched between reminders that the village afforded a glimpse of Indians' last stand against civilization, long passages of the story evoked the sights and sounds of a dense and lively modern settlement. The old Siwash fishermen scorned work, the author said, but their sons labored in the mills, their daughters sold baskets to white visitors, and their grandchildren played in the mud, astonishingly free of disease. The Indians had houses styled after white dwellings, sewing and washing machines, store-bought clothes, and cat-boats or sloops instead of canoes. Rather than admit that the people he saw were prospering, however, the reporter argued from these observations that "[s]tep by step the Indian is giving in to the white man as the battle for supremacy continues. . . . "[50]

Residents of the tideflat village may not have read the article declaring them an endangered species, but they surely had an inkling of the way a white reporter would portray them. Many non-Indian assertions about Indians, although directed to other non-Indians and made without in-volving Indians, were audible across the racial and cultural border. Most people of native descent, even those who did not read or attend trials, had occasion to hear what whites were saying about Indians. What they heard in turn provoked them to debate and to communicate to whites how they wanted to be seen.

Government personnel consciously exposed people on reservations to prevailing images of Indians. At councils, holiday celebrations, school exer-cises, and athletic competitions, agents and missionaries often alluded to the regrettable qualities that supposedly characterized unreconstructed Indians. In day schools and boarding schools, teachers spelled out for their impres-sionable, captive audiences the aboriginal traits they abhorred and described the civilized citizens they were endeavoring to mold from Indian clay.[51]

The light that whites shined on Indians could be flattering as well as unflattering, however. While some whites deprecated Indians' inherent tendencies and history, others seemed favorably impressed with Indians' heritage. Scholars like Edmond Meany politely invited tribal elders to re-call and exhibit ancient customs. Even government agents encouraged the old Indians to put themselves and their heritage on display: it was usually the agents who nominated people (almost invariably men) for Meany, other scholars, and reporters to interview.[52]

Thanks to whites' fascination with old Indian customs, turn-of-the-century potlatches were less likely to attract censorious authorities than to draw a pack of delighted journalists. When Indians named Patsy and Prince of Wales hosted a potlatch across from the picnic grounds at Hadlock in 1891, press coverage was copious and nearly free of disparaging comments. The *Post-Intelligencer* reported that streams of palefaces joined native guests, thus fulfilling the hopes of an "intelligent" Indian woman who said, " 'The Indians wanted to come over and celebrate the Fourth of the July with the whites, so that the whites would come over and help us celebrate the potlatch.' " During the next two decades, whites publicized and helped Indians celebrate many other potlatches. The *Post-Intelligencer* claimed to detect waning interest in such events, but under the headline "Last Potlatch of the Nisquallies," it described festivities in 1907 that drew several white pioneers as well as a thousand prosperous-looking Indians.[53]

Non-Indians did not just tolerate and attend some displays of Indian culture; they solicited and produced them. In 1902 Charles Buchanan and a former Tulalip agent arranged for "Indian boys" to stage a "really, truly" canoe race "for the gratification and edification" of visiting President Theodore Roosevelt. Sponsors of a 1903 "labor carnival" at the University of Washington recruited people from the Port Madison Reservation to set up an Indian village, where a *Seattle Times* correspondent saw them "decked out in gay and brilliant costumes," demonstrating beadwork, basketry, and "war" and "medicine" dances.[54]

Buchanan claimed credit for assembling a large number of Indians to commemorate the Point Elliott Treaty on its fifty-fifth anniversary. "After dinner," he wrote in his diary, "speeches were made by the old men; old time songs and dances were given and general good old time reunion was held." Buchanan made sure that journalists were present to film and "write up" the fourth annual Treaty Day ceremonies. During the same years local businessmen and a reservation employee worked with Port Madison Indians to mount a summer festival they called Chief Seattle Day. On the Chief Seattle Day program in 1911, along with a navy band concert and a priest's address in Chinook jargon, was eighty-year-old George Ewye's rendition of a legend in his native Lushootseed.[55]

When whites encouraged native people and their descendants to revive certain traditions and memories, they undoubtedly elicited selective depictions of Indians.[56] As one observer of the Squaxin Island tidelands litigation remarked, the old people who talked about ancient Indian practices likely had their "memories brightened by the exigencies surrounding them." The questions whites asked and their reactions to the answers they got could affect what Indians emphasized about themselves. To Ezra Meeker, Wahoolit described Leschi as rich, strong, wise, and kind to all people. But absent Meeker's obvious sympathy, would Wahoolit's words for the once-hated rebel have been the same?[57]

It would be wrong, however, to infer that men such as Wahoolit or the Treaty Day speakers merely performed at whites' behest, tailoring their representations of Indians entirely to white sensibilities. By granting and even requesting interviews with writers or by participating in fairs and festivals, descendants of native people joined and influenced the public discourse about Indianness. They thus helped to reshape perceptions of Indians and their past.

From different accounts of the decision to resume aboriginal dances on Tulalip agency reservations, it is apparent that collaborative celebrations of Indian tradition were possible because distinct Indian and white agendas converged. On one hand, Superintendent Buchanan said that he did not intend to perpetuate deplorable aspects of Indian culture when he allowed the dances: he had authorized only innocent social activities and drawn the line against superstitious conjuring. He explained to the commissioner why he gave Joseph Solomon permission to lead dances at the annual Lummi picnic in 1914:

> In the last four or five years, in return for the courtesy and hospitality of the young folks, the folks have attempted to show them some of the customs and habits of ancient days, not seriously nor with any intention of teaching the children the olds [sic] ways but by way of giving them a page out of the past Indian history in order that they might realize the progress that had been made by the race.[58]

On the other hand, the "folks" Buchanan referred to put a different spin both on the decision to allow the dances and on the dances themselves. Shaman John Fornsby boasted of a key role in Buchanan's change of heart. Everyone was searching for a missing Indian, Fornsby recalled, when Buchanan said, " 'If John finds that man, I'll let them use all the power they want and have a time.' " After Fornsby's "guarding" power led him within sixty feet of where the body was found, Buchanan invited John to sing wealth power for the white people. "Dr. Buchanan liked it," Fornsby said. "Dr. Buchanan didn't want the Indians to have the old time way. But that time they saw how the Indians fixed power. And he saw the guarding power shake right in the room. . . . That is why those folks have a time now on Treaty Day." Much later Dora Solomon credited a younger

Indian, William Shelton, with persuading Buchanan to "set the powwows free." Shelton's perspective differed from Fornsby's as well as Buchanan's. He took responsibility for managing the first Treaty Day celebration, Shelton said, "to make our old people feel good instead of discouraged."[59]

If a message from one official about one feature of aboriginal culture got varied readings and responses from people who considered themselves Indians, the conflicting and ambiguous messages of other whites were sure to draw an even richer variety of responses. By the end of the nineteenth century, people of native descent knew that Indian identity was a mix of sweet and sour ingredients. Being labeled Indian might garner them the attention of whites interested in Indian traditions or entitle them to such benefits as tax-free land and medicine, but being labeled Indian might also subject them to demeaning rules that restricted their use of property and ordained which beliefs they could honor without fear of punishment. Understandably, most of the people identified as Indians tried to pick and choose from the mix that whites served up.

Thus, some parents pleaded with Indian agencies to admit their children to boarding schools, while a citizen at Puyallup sued to keep officials from forcing her son back to an Indian school, and a man pulled his family off the Port Madison Reservation rather than put his children in school.[60] In 1892, 104 Puyallup Reservation residents signed a petition to terminate their peculiar status as Indians, declaring, "We are citizens of the United States ... and we demand that our rights as citizens be no longer abridged or out [sic] lives and liberties harassed by an agent hostile to our interests. ... " But within the same year, people in the Sauk River Valley asked the Tulalip Agency for help securing a government-supervised reservation.[61]

Even if non-Indians had consistently advanced a single idea of what it meant to be Indian, they would have gotten a wide variety of responses from native people and their progeny; for those people were more diverse than ever. Some had staked their social and economic status on government promises to protect them and their resources, while others lived outside the protected enclaves with little or no help and interference from government. Some had spent years in Indian boarding schools; others had attended public schools; still others had never seen the inside of a schoolhouse. Some counted no non-Indians among their kin, but some had as many non-Indian as native ancestors. Presumed Indians also included Catholics, Protestants, Shakers, spirit dancers, and people who participated in the rites of several religions.[62] Such widely varying experiences and beliefs help to explain why Indians tried many different ways to make sense of themselves and the identity ascribed to them.

Contrary to a common assumption of the time, age did not determine Indians' views of themselves. Young people were indeed coming of age in a society drastically different from the one that had reared their elders, and some Indian parents declined to teach the old ways. But other parents of the same generation passed down family lore and trained their children in ancestral mores. At the turn of the century many Indian children attended school, but almost as many did not. In the same generation were women whose families arranged their marriages according to ancient custom and women of comparable class backgrounds who chose their own spouses without concern for traditional social networks.[63]

By the turn of the century, several thousand people in the Puget Sound area knew that white Americans considered them all Indians, whether or not they had acquired a spirit power, married by aboriginal custom, lived on a reservation, or enrolled in an Indian school. While most did not doubt that they were Indians rather than non-Indians, they were not sure in many instances what they had in common with other people in the same broad category, as testimony in the Spithill and Puyallup cases revealed. Outsiders had lumped them all together and pushed them onto the same broad roadway, but their varied orientations and strategies ensured that they would then head in different directions and occasionally collide.

Any of the factors that made them diverse could set Indians on a collision course. At various times and places, they appeared to line up by age, family, village, religion, moral inclination, or economic orientation. After Puyallups became citizens, Jerry Meeker said, the older ones mostly voted Democrat, while the younger men were Republicans. In subsequent years land sharks exploited differences in ancestry to divide Puyallups further. A priest observed that the election of a judge pitted Indians on the Lummi Reservation against each other because "the whiskey element ... naturally [wanted] a judge likely to sympathize with them, were they to get into trouble." Later, a proposal to give Lummis unrestricted land titles divided them again. According to the resident government farmer, the issue was the greed of the plan's Indian sponsors; but according to the sponsors, the issue was whether Indians should regard themselves as less capable than whites of managing their property.[64]

Occasionally, clashes between Indians turned violent. The murder of David Teuse in 1900 was the fourth slaying at Tulalip in a few years.[65] While trying to build a case against Indians they suspected of the crime, agent Edward Mills and physician Charles Buchanan exposed widespread animosities and suspicions among reservation residents. The bad feelings had roots in a variety of soils, including family loyalties, desires for land

and government favors, and competing economic strategies. Ironically, for many non-Indians and probably even for feuding Indians, the Teuse murder case nevertheless afforded a measure and a symbol of enduring differences between Indian and non-Indian societies.

Mills and Buchanan suspected that young William Shelton had assassinated seventy-year-old Teuse with the help of an uncle, Charlie Hook. Informants told the investigators that Shelton had a host of motives for murder. The Shelton family, originally from south Whidbey Island, had a long-standing feud with the Teuse family, which hailed from "up the river." Shelton was angry that his Klallam-Samish wife, supposedly at Teuse's instigation, had moved her son by a white man onto her allotment, which Shelton had improved and expected to occupy. He was bitter that Teuse, a judge of the Indian court, had punished him and his relatives. Shelton blamed the recent loss of his job at the agency sawmill on Teuse. And Shelton and his associates were desperate for money to pay the lawyer they had hired to procure an end to restrictions on the sale and logging of reservation lands—a move Teuse opposed. From other people, however, Buchanan and Mills learned that Shelton was not the only Indian who had threatened Teuse.[66]

The evidence that Buchanan and Mills collected induced prosecutors to convene a grand jury; but most of the people called before the jury would not talk, the jury failed to return an indictment, and the case closed. Although records of the agency inquest show that most witnesses held their tongues for fear of Hook's shamanic powers, Buchanan and Mills construed their reticence as an Indian conspiracy to thwart white authorities.[67] One of their informants—a "squaw man" who claimed that he was present at incriminating conversations because the Indians thought he was "just like an Indian"—said that Shelton's people had rallied support by promising to expel white overseers so that Indians could do as they liked. Mills therefore downplayed evidence that Indians were sharply at odds with each other on several fronts and excused his failure to muster evidence against Shelton by publicly accusing the Indians of closing ranks to protect their own. "[T]hey can not understand that a murderer should be hung as a matter of protection to the tribe," he wrote. "The greater the guilt of the suspected man, the greater the obligation on the part of relatives and friends to stand by him. That is the Indian idea."[68]

For the *Post-Intelligencer*, likewise, the case provided an occasion to expound on "the Indian idea." Cowardly assassination, the paper said, was typical of Indian murders in the West and the basis for a truer image of the red man than James Fenimore Cooper had evoked in his novels. In the

Indians' unwillingness to finger the killers, the *Post-Intelligencer* saw ignorance, superstition, indifference toward life, and secretiveness "almost beyond belief." The case showed "how very superficial is the veneer of civilization the average reclaimed Indian wears, and ... how strong in comparison with the laws of the white man is the unwritten criminal code of the red man." (The paper speculated that the "unwritten code" had been enforced, with the dead man's kin exacting payment from the murderer's family.)[69]

The commentary of Mills and the *Post-Intelligencer*—racist though it may be—points to an important truth: the need to deal with whites and white-imposed circumstances simultaneously pitted people of native descent against each other and prodded them to conceptualize an Indian society that was distinct from non-Indian society. Even though the Teuse case exposed antagonisms that would not have existed but for whites' presence and action, and even though Indians like Shelton benefited materially from their relations with whites, whites' meddling also provoked Shelton's diverse neighbors to think about themselves collectively in contrast to whites.[70]

Events at the Muckleshoot Reservation in 1903 had similar repercussions. A government decision favoring one faction prompted another faction to rally people behind a broad Indian banner. Just nine months after the resident farmer informed Buchanan that Muckleshoot Indians had had no chiefs or tribal relations since 1883, Buchanan received a protest from "Chief" George Nelson and other men on the reservation, who purported to speak "in the name of all the Indians of this place." They objected to the farmer's choice of a "half breed" as Indian court judge, arguing, "[W]e are always told By a great number of white mans and some Government officials, that a half Breed is not honest man to Carry on office. ... " Paradoxically, in support of the right of "all the Indians of Muckelshoot" to elect their judges, the protesters cited the disappearing differences between them and whites. "[T]he Indians of Muckelshoot ... ," they wrote, "are now in path of a new law lighted on all sides so that they can see what is Just and So Be not wild any more But Civilized like the whites forever."[71]

The same forces that brought assorted people of native descent into new, often abrasive, contact with each other thus provided them with more occasions to see and articulate some bases for unity. As the nineteenth century drew to a close, most people who had reason to think of themselves as Indians—people from different districts, families, and generations—associated with each other in a variety of combinations and contexts, both voluntarily and involuntarily. Often they assembled explicitly as Indians. At these gatherings they were gradually working out a shared conception of the identity ascribed to them.

The mobility that government agents so often deplored took Indians to common work sites, fishing and berrying grounds, Fourth of July and Christmas celebrations, gambling contests, and religious observances. In the hop fields, thousands of Indians from widely dispersed settlements not only worked together but also relished the chance to socialize and gamble. Gatherings for funerals and weddings were vital to a Nooksack Valley man's understanding of his Indian identity. George Swanaset admitted to anthropologist Paul Fetzer that his family did not follow all the old customs at their funerals and weddings, but he delighted in reciting the names of the many native communities that sent guests.[72]

Assemblies of Indian Shakers likewise contributed to a broadly inclusive conception of Indians, even though Shaker practices also provoked controversies that split many communities. The *Post-Intelligencer* alluded to the sect's wide embrace when it reported in 1898 that Puget Sound Indians were preparing for a religious festival whose aim was the union of all "tribes" subscribing to Shaker tenets. For a convocation at Quinault, couriers were delivering invitations at Lummi, Muckleshoot, Puyallup, Neah Bay, Nisqually, and Mud Bay. Despite their lack of a formal membership, the Shakers thus created and preserved links among many scattered people, all of whom identified themselves as Indians.[73]

Even at federal and mission schools, whose ostensible goal was to replace the ideas and habits of Indians with the ideas and habits of white people, the pupils' interaction helped them formulate a common Indian identity. Diverse as they were, the children were at the schools because the administrators regarded them all as Indians. Louisa Sinclair, whose father was white, sensed this and resented her forced association with full-bloods. William Shelton's daughter Harriette, who attended the Tulalip school in the late teens, recalled that one staff member invariably greeted pupils' minor infractions with, " 'Isn't that just like an Indian?' " Harriette also expressed pride, echoed by many other alumni of Indian boarding schools, in her schoolmates' ability to emerge from such an institution with a sense of their original selves intact.[74]

Some gatherings afforded people of native descent the chance to do what whites did at pioneer picnics and historical pageants or in the pages of their publications: to pool memories and myths and thus to develop a standardized lore that became a common heritage. Contemporaneous documentation is scarce, but surely Indians created and preserved traditions by trading and building on each other's reminiscences, just as old settlers did. A generation later many Indians recalled their elders discussing such topics as the treaties and the bitterness they felt about having received so little of what they expected from Bostons.[75]

By means of such conversations, the diverse people who bore or sought the label "Indian" probably devised ways of identifying themselves to each other that were different from the traits they emphasized to outsiders. Yet this internal process of group self-definition was inseparable from ongoing dialogues with people who stood outside the Indian circle, however defined. Even inward-directed displays of Indian identity derived their importance and much of their symbolic code from relations with non-Indians.[76] Indian Shakers' solidarity and self-definition, for example, developed in a context of contradictory non-Indian reactions. On one hand, they had to respond to government harassment. At a convention in 1912, their response was to call on far-flung Shaker churches to support each other. On the other hand, Shakers received outside support that also influenced their self-characterization. A white friend helped the group to incorporate in 1910 and drew up a constitution and bylaws, which declared that the Shakers' aim was the "elevation of the Indian race of this State and of the Northwest."[77]

Sometimes non-Indians' actions stimulated Indians to put aside differences and present one face to the outside world, as Tulalip agent Mills thought they did in the Teuse murder case. One such instance—a lawsuit that Lummi Reservation fishermen prosecuted with government aid—would have long-term significance as Indians in the Puget Sound area continued exploring ways to identify themselves to whites and to each other.

The fishers' grievance was against the operators of a salmon cannery at Point Roberts, near the reservation. After a few years of contracting with Indians to supply the cannery with fish, the operators had built their own traps at reefs where Indians had hitherto set nets. The result, said the Lummi men, was a reduction of their catch to almost nothing.

To support the complaint they filed in federal court in 1895, the Lummis relied on the pooled memories of several old men who had attended the treaty conference at Point Elliott. The elders' affidavits recited, among other things, that Governor Stevens had explicitly promised the Indians to "put it in the paper and they could fish and hunt wherever they have done before. . . . " Judge C. H. Hanford rejected the claim that the cannery traps and state permits for the traps breached this promise, but he did so without discrediting the old men's stories. He merely said that the traps did no harm because the Indians could still fish at remaining places and sell their catch to the cannery.[78]

Clearly influencing the judge's decision was evidence that people on the Lummi Reservation were not the "primitive" fisherfolk who had made the treaty forty years earlier. According to defense witnesses, the Indians had adopted white habits, and most supported themselves by farming on individual lands. The minority who fished did so for profit. Afraid that this testimony would undermine their reliance on promises made in another era, the plaintiffs responded with witnesses who swore that reservation Indians were still "a race of fishermen" and pitifully poor.

The fishermen also had to fend off efforts to discredit their identification of themselves as Lummi Indians. Witnesses for the canneries contended that nearly all Indians who fished at Point Roberts were from British Columbia. Fear of the King George Indians, they said, had kept most Lummis away from the reefs. One of the few Lummis who fished at Point Roberts—a plaintiff named Captain Jack—dared to do so "because he was a relation by marriage of one of the leading Cowichan Indians."

It was awkward for the plaintiffs to address the implications of this argument. To prove that Lummis could fish in territory where King George Indians outnumbered them, they had to affirm that Lummis, Saanich, and Cowichans had intermarried. However, in a suit to enforce a treaty that named Lummi but not Cowichan or Saanich Indians, they could not concede that intermarriage meant an attenuation of tribal identities. They asserted unequivocal membership in what they called the tribe or nation of Lummi Indians. The affidavit of Harry Sealton incorporated this concept of a distinct, autonomous tribe, but it also revealed that the concept was a simplistic characterization of relations among the men who fished together. Since the treaty, Sealton said,

> the LaConnors [*sic*] of Skagit county. ... , the Tulalips and other tribes of the state and territory ... also annually fished at said Point. ... [T]here have been numerous disputes between said indians regarding locations on said reef and sometimes struggles in which lives were lost including the lives of some of the said Lummi Indians, but ... said struggles did not grow out of any tribal hostilities.

As Sealton suggested, personal relations linked men of the Lummi Reservation to people in other communities as well as to each other; but multiple loyalties or affiliations could also pit some of the same men against each other. The desire to protect an economic resource, however, prompted Sealton and his fellow fishers to present their complex web of social relations in simplified form. For the purpose of fighting white profiteers' threat to their livelihood, they would be just the Lummi Tribe.

When the judge accepted the Lummi plaintiffs' representation of themselves as a tribe of treaty makers and fishers, he made a significant addition to a slowly rising structure of Indian identity. As is evident from this review of events at century's end, the structure was a collaborative project of people from a variety of backgrounds and social settings. Although powerful non-Indians claimed authority to erect the framework, they neither followed a single plan nor supplied all the building materials. In a haphazard and sometimes acrimonious process, they worked on the edifice with indigenous people and their descendants. Mixing such elements as kinship, lineage, property law, social relations, and residence, they produced a rambling and unsteady edifice. As of 1910 it remained a work in progress. In the years to come it would offer some people welcome shelter, trap others against their will, and shut out still others who wanted in.

6 Indians and the United States
Wardship or Friendship?

At the heart of late-nineteenth-century U.S. Indian policy was a contra-diction. Policy makers promised to solve "the Indian problem" by pro-moting Indians' absorption into the general population. Although they proclaimed that race was no barrier to this absorption, they conceived of Indians as a distinct race of people whose customary lifeways were incompatible with American civilization. Special laws and institutions seemed necessary for Indians' protection until their anomalous traits disappeared. Yet those laws and institutions tended to perpetuate the racial category they aimed to eliminate.[1]

The contradictory premises of national policy played themselves out in curious ways after the turn of the century. Through the 1920s, while professing an abiding desire to make Indians indistinguishable from other Americans, lawmakers and bureaucrats reinforced the basis for a separate, subordinate class of people called Indians. While ostensibly trying to free Indians from federal control, they augmented government's role in Indians' affairs.

More than ever before, the descendants of indigenous Americans had to define themselves by reference to federal laws and institutions for Indians. In western Washington this was a perplexing task. Many people of native ancestry remained away from Indian reservations, and almost none depended on government for their sustenance. But whether classified as emancipated citizens or federal wards, most of them occupied an ambiguous status that entailed unwanted liabilities.

Unwilling or unable to disavow either their Indian heritage or their rights as Indians under U.S. law, many people around Puget Sound collaborated to present an alternative explanation of their relationship to non-Indians. In congressional hearing rooms and courtrooms, they recounted a

160

history that emphasized treaty relations with the United States. They thus began to fashion a common Indian identity that was more to their taste.

These efforts to enhance Indians' status took place during a time when whites nursed growing doubts that Indians could or would shed the characteristics impeding their "advancement." Assimilationist reformers of the 1880s had expected to turn Indians into citizen Americans with a wave of the legal wand. A belief in humans' psychic unity and unilinear social evolution fostered their optimism. Some reformers had predicted that landownership and law would elevate Indians from a savage or barbarian stage to a civilized stage of development within a generation. After 1900, however, faith in the transformative power of the assimilation program waned, and many American leaders concluded that Indians would require a lengthy apprenticeship before taking their place in U.S. society. Some predicted that the place Indians took would be a humble one. By 1917, says historian Frederick Hoxie, "Optimism and a desire for rapid incorporation were pushed aside by racism, nostalgia, and disinterest. Total assimilation was no longer the central concern of policy makers and the public."[2]

Francis Leupp and Charles Buchanan exemplified the shift in white attitudes, which reflected several intellectual and cultural trends, including the ascendancy of racial determinism.[3] As a spokesman for the Indian Rights Association in the 1890s, Leupp advocated immediate Indian emancipation; but after becoming Indian commissioner in 1905, he argued that the government should tailor its program to persistent Indian traits, such as an aversion to labor and discipline. At Tulalip, Washington, Buchanan's thinking evolved in the same direction. In 1900 he described the Indian as an edition of man bound in red, lacking only the acquired culture to which a civilized man subordinated primitive emotions. Fourteen years later, explaining his reluctance to let most Indians in his jurisdiction control their property, Buchanan voiced a different theory of Indians' nature. Many Indians had proved unable to manage assets wisely, he said, because of conditions inherent and instinctive in the aborigine. Centuries of heredity as well as environment had forged a temperament that could not be uprooted in a single generation.[4]

Writing off older Indians as set in their ways, Indian Office personnel focused their hopes on the young. Their recommendations justified a dramatic expansion of federal schooling for Indians. Buchanan thought a government boarding school would be needed on Puget Sound at least until it housed a generation whose parents had all been educated and civilized. Yet officials' hopes for young Indians sagged under the weight of the ideological baggage they carried. No longer did they think of Indian youth as blank slates on which teachers could inscribe a middle-class American image. Instead, like most whites, they now expected that inherited tendencies would perpetuate some of the attributes that marked the children as inferior.[5]

During the first decades of the century, these racialist assumptions took up uneasy residence in a legal-political structure still dedicated to the cause of Indians' assimilation. Officials stepped up efforts to push Indians into the mainstream, but they also endorsed the idea that Indians' backwardness would oblige the government to supervise many of them indefinitely. Lawmakers and administrators simultaneously devised ways to remove people from the ranks of government-supervised Indians and increased the oversight of people who remained in those ranks.[6]

The Burke Act of 1906 embodied and furthered this double-edged stab at the Indian problem. Congress amended the General Allotment Act of 1887, which had granted citizenship to all allottees, by postponing citizenship for new allottees until the government no longer held their land in trust. In addition, it allowed the president to extend the trust period, originally set at twenty-five years. At the same time, by permitting the Indian Office to terminate the trust whenever an Indian seemed ready to manage property, lawmakers sought to reduce the number of people in the peculiar legal status reserved for Indians.[7]

Subsequent acts of Congress enlarged administrators' responsibilities for those Indians who remained under federal supervision. The new laws authorized the Indian Office to sell the lands of Indians classified as noncompetent, to lease trust allotments, to approve allottees' wills, and to probate and administer deceased allottees' estates. Largely as a result of these proliferating property management duties, the number of employees in the Office of Indian Affairs doubled between 1900 and 1913.[8]

Meanwhile, federal judges decided that the government could retain its legal hold over Indians even after they became citizens. In 1909 the Supreme Court held that citizenship did not by itself end a person's subjection to special laws for Indians. A federal court could try a citizen allottee for a murder on the Tulalip Reservation, the justices said, because both the defendant and the victim were "Indians by race." Five years later the Court squelched any lingering doubts that citizenship and Indian wardship could coexist, ruling in *United States v. Nice* that citizenship did not exempt Indians from federal regulations meant for their protection.[9]

Thus, thirty years after reformers set out to erase the factors that distinguished Indians from other Americans, the program they initiated had achieved the opposite. Allotment of tribal lands had become the basis for an enduring special status. Congress, the Indian Office, and the courts had jointly forged legal instruments that branded thousands of people as Indians. In theory, the brand was not a racial designation but one that indicated individuals' lack of preparation to cope with American society. In practice, officials often assumed that personal capabilities correlated with ancestry. For instance, the Omnibus Act of 1910 specified that education and experience dealing with whites should determine whether an Indian was ready to graduate from federal wardship; but in 1917 Commissioner Cato Sells declared his intent to issue unrestricted property titles to all allottees and heirs of less than half "Indian blood."[10]

The legal scheme peculiar to Indians was bound to have a significant impact on many people's self-conceptions. In western Washington the scheme's contradictory thrusts exacerbated long-standing uncertainties about what made someone an Indian for government purposes. By the 1920s many descendants of Washington natives were still unsure whether their notions of their status coincided with Indian Office ideas. On balance, however, federal policies and practice taught or invited most of those people to believe that their indigenous ancestry made them members of the unique legal class known as Indians.

Early in the twentieth century it became clear that citizenship would not move many Washington Indians into the same legal class as whites. Not only did the Supreme Court and Congress confirm the federal government's authority over citizen allottees, but local government also devalued Indians' citizenship. The state legislature provided in 1901 "that Indians not taxed shall never be allowed the election franchise." Fourteen years later Charles Buchanan blamed this law for cutting the voting rate of Indian citizens to less than 10 percent. Even though the state attorney general subsequently advised against a restrictive reading of "Indians not taxed" and some counties did let Indians vote, Buchanan had good reason for saying, "Our Indians are not locally regarded as 'citizen Indians.'" In 1909 Washington lawmakers again distinguished Indian citizens from other citizens when they prohibited liquor sales to all persons of one-eighth or more Indian ancestry.[11]

Some Indians became disillusioned with their citizenship as well. In 1903 the *Seattle Post-Intelligencer* reported that newly emancipated Puyallups were already tired of citizenship and requesting restoration of their former "privileges and immunities" as wards. During World War I, when citizens were subject to conscription, many people of native descent were eager to forgo the prerogatives of citizenship for the privileges of wardship. For instance, eighteen men and women on the Muckleshoot

Reservation petitioned the Cushman School superintendent to inform military officials that their boys were not citizens.[12]

The national campaign to identify "competent" Indians and end federal control over their property was no more effective than citizenship in reducing the number of people around Puget Sound who were classed as government wards. Local Indian agents bestowed relatively few certificates of competency. As late as 1933 only 39 of 450 Tulalip Agency allottees had been certified "competent."[13]

Other than Buchanan's comments about Indians' lack of aptitude for property management, there is little evidence that beliefs about race-linked traits explain the low number of competency findings. Puyallup superintendent H. H. Johnson, pointing to two "full-bloods" who were wealthy businessmen, declared that lack of "white blood" did not make an Indian incompetent. Both Buchanan and Johnson were as likely to issue competency certificates to "full blood" Indians "of the old type" as to educated "mixed bloods." One certificate went to sixty-year-old John Fornsby, who had recently paid an Indian court fine for conjuring; another went to Billy Clams, whose resistance to the civilization program had twice landed him in jail. Meanwhile, the Indian agencies were managing the land of many young boarding school alumni.[14]

Competency certificates were probably rare in western Washington because there was relatively little incentive to make allotments marketable. Few allottees had potential buyers or renters for their lands, particularly when regional economic growth slowed between 1909 and 1914. Aside from Puyallup lots, waterfront, and fertile bottomlands, reservation property around Puget Sound was not especially attractive to whites. Much of it had already been logged yet was worthless for farming.[15]

Perhaps local agents lacked enthusiasm for lifting restrictions on Indians' land because they expected to lose control of activities there as a consequence. Shortly before the Supreme Court's decision in *U.S. v. Nice*, Buchanan reported that Indians with competency certificates were giving refuge to "drunken characters" and people previously ejected from his reservations. After one certificate holder assaulted the Indian police who tried to arrest him, a federal judge dismissed charges, ruling that the government no longer had jurisdiction on the man's property.[16]

Certificates of competency did not shrink the class of government wards in Washington for another reason: the Indian Office continued to hold property in trust for many of the people it declared competent. Although Buchanan encouraged allottees to view competency rulings as favorable comments on their character and abilities, administrators and courts agreed that a certificate pertained only to the land it designated. When the agent issued a certificate for just one of an Indian's multiple holdings or excepted a homesite from the land described in the certificate, the person in effect was "competent" with respect to one tract and "noncompetent" with respect to another.[17]

In sum, the national campaign to push "competent" Indians out of the federal nest did not shoo many Puget Sound allottees into the population of legally emancipated Americans. Moreover, by arrogating the right to judge Indians' competency, the government affirmed the peculiar, childlike status of the people it judged. Those judged noncompetent then became further isolated, as bureaucrats made a growing number of decisions on their behalf. In addition to deciding whether to sell or lease their land, the Indian Office regulated its wards' timber cutting and controlled the money in their trust accounts. Lyman Siddle of the Muckleshoot Reservation needed approval just to spend seventy-five dollars of his trust money on a piano in 1917.[18]

More than any aspect of the federal guardianship, the handling of allottees' property after death contributed to the delineation and preservation of a class of patronized Indians. When an allottee died without a will, the Indian Office probated the estate, which descended according to state rules. Numerous heirs—not only a spouse and children but also siblings, cousins, in-laws, and more remote kin—might thus acquire interest in federally supervised land and a place on the roll of government wards. In this respect, identification as an Indian ward depended not on participation in an Indian community but on white probate law and fate.

As a result of probates, many descendants of Washington Indians found themselves in new relationships to government officials and each other. Because marriages linked people in scattered locales, allottees' relatives often inherited land on reservations where they did not live or work. Skokomish Reservation records hold one of hundreds of examples. The heirs of Andrew Johnson, as determined in 1915, were not just his son and daughter, who inherited 53/162 and 65/162 of the allotment, respectively, but also his widow's widower and his daughter's widower, who were at Puyallup. Federal regulations prevented an heir from partitioning or using the land without the consent of other heirs. When heirs could not agree, were out of touch, or were still unknown, the management of trust estates defaulted to the government. In western Washington hundreds of allotments went unprobated for years.[19]

This increased responsibility for individuals' property reinforced Indian agents' conviction that they were Indians' social and moral caretakers as well. Buchanan and his successor, for example, kept up efforts to discredit the Shakers, accusing them of perpetuating pagan rites in the guise of Christianity.[20] During the same period Buchanan reversed his decision to allow Treaty Day dances because he suspected participants of including "old forbidden practices" in the ceremonies. Exploiting dissension between Indian conservatives and advocates of change, he prosecuted dancers in the Swinomish Reservation court. The commissioner backed him, turning down a request for dances at Lummi because dancing was inconsistent with government efforts to educate Indians and improve their "industrial condition." Harriette Shelton recalled this as a time when everyone at Tulalip was under the agent's thumb, afraid to hold any meetings without permission.[21]

Families around Puget Sound no doubt detected the invigoration of the federal guardianship when agents shipped their children off to boarding schools. In contrast to the 1800s, when meagerly funded residential schools had accommodated only a tiny percentage of Indian children, few Indian youth could avoid boarding school in the early twentieth century. By 1910 the Indian Office had taken over the Tulalip mission school, replaced it with a larger facility, and dedicated a new institution at Puyallup for more than three hundred boarders. Buchanan said the Tulalip school would fulfill Indians' desire—memorialized in the treaty—for a central industrial school. But he was not inclined to honor the desires of Indians who did not want the service. Even before the Indian Office made attendance compulsory in 1920, agents used coercion to put and keep children in school. Apprehended runaways faced harsh punishment, and Buchanan regularly denied parents' pleas that he send children home to help with chores or nurse sick relatives. Although day schools operated fitfully in several Indian communities and some Indians attended public schools, most children of native descent spent time in the boarding schools, isolated for months from their families and under tight government control.[22]

Boarding school expansion enlarged the number of people within the purview of Puget Sound Indian agencies. School administrators construed Indian status broadly, enrolling not only children from reservations but also "unattached Indians." They took some of the off-reservation children in response to requests from parents who claimed Indian identity, and they actively recruited others even though they had previously provided no services to the children's families.[23]

Indian agents moved to extend their reach in other matters as well. In 1913 the national office instructed Buchanan to regard all the scattered, off-reservation Indians in Whatcom, Skagit, and Snohomish Counties as attached to his agency. Indians farther south would be the responsibility of Buchanan's counterpart at Puyallup. Buchanan then asked whether he should oversee people in San Juan, Island, Kitsap, and King Counties whose ancestors had also endorsed the Point Elliott Treaty. When the commissioner responded by adding those counties to his bailiwick, Buchanan pleaded for more staff. The number of Indians never enumerated or included on government rolls, he stressed, could top two thousand.[24]

Buchanan tried, as directed, to find Indians living outside the reservations. In the agency newsletter of November 1917, he asked for readers' help under the headline "Where Are Our Indian People?" The government's original policy, he explained, was to segregate Indians in communities of their own, each attached to an agency. But as the years passed, officials discovered Indians who were away from the reservations, often on homesteads or purchased lands. Although many got along nicely, Buchanan conceded, they had nowhere to go if harassed, as reservation residents did. A desire to give all Indians the same opportunity for help now motivated him to get to know the missing people.[25]

This search for stray Indians was not a shameless grab for greater power. It came about through give and take between self-identified Indians and officials who were ambivalent about expanding the rolls of federal wards. In 1910, when the Puyallup superintendent learned of a proposal to allot additional land, he protested that it would induce some Indians to leave the communities where they had become "further advanced in civilization than those of reservations." He and his colleagues also shied away from added responsibility that would strain their budgets.[26]

Some "unattached Indians," however, were soliciting federal attention. Besides seeking school berths for their children, they commonly wanted to secure or preserve tax-exempt property. Robert Sulkanon, for example, asked the commissioner to extend the trust period for eighteen homesteads along the Nooksack River. "I have a hard time here . . . ," he pleaded. "I know I am an Indian that God created and I am a decendent [sic] of other Indians before, that is why I do not want to pay tax on my land. Some of my people are poor and cannot pay the tax." In the teens, thirty years after Indians chased surveyors out of the Upper Skagit watershed, saying that they had never signed a treaty, their beleaguered children successfully petitioned the Tulalip agency to help them secure trust allotments.[27]

Thomas Bishop insisted that the United States had unfulfilled obligations to him and hundreds of other landless Indians. The son of a Snohomish woman and a white man who lived near Port Townsend, Bishop learned that land might be available on the Quinault Reservation.[28] He collected a batch of applications for allotments at Quinault and sent them to the commissioner of Indian Affairs in 1916. The applicants' statements linked them by ancestry or association to more than forty Indian tribes. Bishop warned that there were two or three thousand Indians of western Washington in similar need of land.

Although a Quinault Reservation council was initially receptive to this request for allotments, an Interior Department solicitor advised that Quinault land was intended solely for Indians on the Pacific Coast. The commissioner then appointed a special agent to locate landless Indians elsewhere in western Washington and to help them prepare formal requests for enrollment. The result, in 1919, was Charles Roblin's list of more than four thousand names, most of which had not appeared before on Indian rolls.[29]

The people who came to Indian Office attention in this manner could hardly have been more diverse if Roblin had picked them at random. They apparently shared only the belief that at least one ancestor was an Indian. Many had not previously proclaimed or emphasized their Indian identity; others had no basis for claiming to be anything other than Indian. Some had a lifelong attachment to an aboriginal community where both parents were raised, while others had drifted from place to place.

Roblin divided the people on his roll into three rough categories: those who had stayed in ancestral territory instead of settling on a reservation, allottees' offspring who lacked allotments of their own, and descendants of women who had married pioneers. Indians in the first category came in several varieties. Nooksack and Skagit River groups, made up largely of "full bloods," had some land and seemed to be doing well. Klallams along Hood Canal and the Strait of Juan de Fuca elicited Roblin's sympathy because they lived as squatters on sandspits and beaches. Scattered through the San Juan Islands were people whose Lummi, Klallam, and Samish ancestors had mixed "inextricably" with Europeans and with Indians from the Columbia and Cowlitz Rivers, Canada, and Alaska. They called themselves the Mitchell Bay Tribe. Of people in the third category—descendants of women who had married pioneers—Roblin said, "In many cases these applicants and families have never associated or affiliated with any Indian tribe or tribes for several decades or even generations."

Following guidelines from the commissioner, Roblin listed everyone who alleged a possible basis for claiming benefits under the nineteenth-century treaties. Besides possession of "Indian blood," an applicant was supposed to prove membership in a treaty tribe or descent from an acknowledged member. But Roblin did not articulate a test either of tribal existence or of tribal membership. For information regarding a person's ancestry and tribal connections, he relied on Bishop or on elderly natives, many of whom Bishop identified as tribal leaders or historians.[30]

Samuel Eliot reported to colleagues on the Board of Indian Commissioners that Bishop had set aside selfish interests to help the lost Indians, but Roblin was more cynical about the motives of the people asking to be counted as Indians. A probable reason for the "sudden interest of persons of mixed Indian blood, in obtaining their 'rights' and 'what is justly due them,'" Roblin said, was a widespread belief that any person with Indian ancestry would receive six thousand dollars. Blaming people who had stayed off the reservations for their own predicament, Buchanan similarly charged them and their advocates with intent to profit from claims against the government. An occasional claim would have "personal merit," he conceded, but "[d]eserving, landless Indians with treaty guarantees of land" should get allotments only if they agreed to reside there.[31]

Since there was no land or money to allot, few, if any, people benefited immediately from inclusion on Roblin's list. In 1922 the unattached Indians still did not appear on Tulalip agency rolls. Despite some increased government attention to their conditions, they mostly continued to fend for themselves, their status with respect to Indian programs as uncertain as ever.[32]

In fending for themselves, the unattached Indians were not much different from their cousins who were technically under federal protection. Virtually all western Washington Indians were self-sufficient, and their self-sufficiency complicated both their own and government efforts to determine what federal guardianship meant for them. It was hard to make sense of statements that Indians were wards of the government when very few of the supposed Indians depended on government for support or for help coping with non-Indians.

Officials had long marveled, as a field inspector did in 1890, at the ability of western Washington Indians to support themselves.

> These Indians are workers and not lazy or leading lives of idleness and dependency. Numbers of them are working in the woods, and at the various saw mills on the Sound, and as they are good workers they receive the same compensation as white laborers. Those who do not work regularly in the mills farm to a limited extent and cut cord wood for sale to steamers on the Sound. Their greatest source of revenue is from fish which they obtain in large quantities, and utilize for home consumptions and sale to canneries and individuals. These Indians are

apparently well to do. They dress well, have an abundance to eat, and the majority of them have more or less money.[33]

Wage work and their own industry still sustained most people of native descent in 1921, when Malcolm McDowell investigated conditions around Puget Sound for the Board of Indian Commissioners. McDowell concluded that Indians were "of considerable importance in the manufacturing, commercial, and transportation industries of western Washington." "In every city and town," he wrote, "I saw Indians at work and talked to a number, who told me that Indians, like white men, are leaving the rural districts in increasing numbers for the cities." McDowell found Indians on city docks, in railroad yards, in logging camps, at sawmills, and in canneries. He met Indian auto mechanics, gas station attendants, and truckers. On steamers he saw Indian petty officers, engineers, firemen, and deckhands. Reports like his were too common to be dismissed as the puffery of assimilation's official salesmen. Besides, reports to the opposite effect were nonexistent.[34]

Charles Roblin's roll also attests to Indians' confident involvement in the general economy. Applicants for enrollment identified themselves as loggers, stevedores, sawyers, farmers, fishers, clam diggers, and general laborers. They included a cook, a farm labor contractor, a tailor, a bridge builder, a blacksmith, and a steamboat fireman as well. Jennie Harmon, born to two "full Duwamish" Indians in 1865, listed the occupations of her five children: George worked in the logging camps, Frank was a laborer, William had a job in a Seattle candy factory, Hattie was married and keeping house at Suquamish, and Henrietta worked at St. Joseph Hospital in Tacoma.[35]

Most people of Indian ancestry were far from wealthy. Few, Eliot said, rose above "the lower grades of an industrial society."[36] Yet there is anecdotal evidence that the ability to earn money was still a source of pride for Indians. When asked to tell their life stories, Indians who reached their prime between the 1880s and the 1930s talked at length of the work they were paid for. Jerry Meeker said that in 1882, at age twenty-one, he began farming at Puyallup. Over the next three decades he also worked as a carpenter and contractor, reservation policeman, school disciplinarian, and real estate broker. Nooksack Valley resident George Swanaset, Meeker's junior by a decade, recited the opportunities he found to make money on both sides of the Canadian border, fishing for canneries, cutting wood, driving shingle bolts downriver, baling hay, working on steamboats, and raising stock. Still younger Indians had similar résumés. In 1911 ten-year-old Emma Tom hired on at a cannery, where she and five other Indian girls earned ten cents an hour. By the time she retired in the 1970s, she was a hand packer earning considerably more. When Lawrence Webster left Indian boarding school in 1916, he tried successive jobs in a bakery, laundry, and hardware store. Realizing that he preferred outdoor work, he spent most of the next decade either longshoring in Seattle or logging.[37]

If wage work was unavailable, Webster usually went home to the Port Madison Reservation to dig clams and fish. And fishing remained as vital to most other Indians' well-being and self-image as it did to Webster's. For generations, despite the disruptions associated with American settlement, their ancestors not only had subsisted on fish but also had harvested enough for commercial trade. Since the 1890s, fishing and canning fish for white-owned companies, particularly in north Puget Sound, had given many of them an additional source of income. Well into the twentieth century, therefore, fishing complemented intermittent wage work in the economic strategy that most western Washington Indians pursued.[38]

The strategy had dangers, which gave Buchanan an excuse to repeat Indian Office dogma that Indians would be more secure if they farmed. Big investors and machines, he warned, were displacing small entrepreneurs and laborers in the industries that most Indians relied on.[39] Relying on fish appeared particularly perilous. As whites moved into commercial fishing and canning, they eliminated more opportunities for Indians than they created. Close behind the white fishers came state regulators, who enforced limits on Indian harvests but allowed whites to build traps that preempted aboriginal fisheries. Non-Indians also built dams and undertook other engineering projects that obliterated fishing sites and jeopardized salmon survival. For example, a new canal from Lake Washington to the Sound lowered the lake's surface in 1916, eliminating the Black River. As the obstacles to fishing in traditional places and manners increased, federal officials heard more complaints from Indians who were surprised and dismayed to be pushed out of an economic sphere they had long monopolized.[40]

Another latent threat to Indians' economic arrangements—race prejudice—had little recorded impact on their ability to find employment until mechanization and depression changed the labor market. The prejudice that whites directed at Indians in public schools is well documented.[41] There is almost no evidence, however, of bigots refusing to hire Indians before the 1920s or 1930s. In 1909 H. H. Johnson said, "Employers report to me that their Indian laborers are fully as satisfactory as the whites." He even claimed that Indians received preference for some jobs. And the memoirs of Indians who sought work just before and after World War I are remarkably free of complaints about discrimination. Lawrence Webster attributed the cold shoulders he sometimes received as much to bias against loggers and Wobblies as to anti-Indian sentiment. He said in 1982 that he figured out quickly "how to deal with the non-Indian problem" and succeed in the working world. Although a few dozen interviews that lack references to discrimination do not prove an absence of discrimination, it seems safe to conclude that systemic racism did not keep many Indians out of the labor force in the first quarter of the century. As long as businesses needed numerous unskilled and semiskilled seasonal and temporary laborers, there were openings for Indians.[42]

Openings were particularly abundant during World War I, when Washington industries and agriculture profited from demand for lumber, ships, and food. The Puyallup superintendent reported in 1918 that all but the oldest Indians in his area were gainfully employed. While high wages drew many Indians out of their fields and canoes, high prices for fish, timber, and produce lured others back to farms and fishing grounds. At Tulalip, Superintendent Buchanan and the Fidalgo Island Packing Company found themselves pulling in opposing directions on Indians' arms. The cannery was desperate to hire packers, while Buchanan was avid to wean Indians from fish-related pursuits and saw the wartime market for farm products as his chance. The opportunities for Indians to work persisted into the 1920s, at least in some industries and locations. In 1927 Tulalip superintendent Walter Dickens remarked that he had never been at an agency where employment was so plentiful.[43]

When the jobs that Indians preferred grew scarce, however, Indians could not prevent employers from favoring whites. According to ethnohistorian Daniel Boxberger, the Carlisle cannery in Bellingham instituted a whites-only hiring policy during the 1920s. A barber's refusal to serve the Indian principal of the Tulalip school convinced Dickens that prejudice was rampant. Prejudice fed on a desire for economic advantage, he said, because Indians of his region were not isolated or pitiable curiosities but serious players in the general economy. "The door of the lower round of the social ladder is easily opened to [the Indian]," Dickens wrote, "but ... pretty firmly closed a short way up and only thru the assistance of friends can he rise to the social level of decent society."[44]

By the time that economic change and discrimination were undermining Indians' niches in the economy, Indians' legal status was again in question too, thanks in large part to World War I. Events during the war stimulated many people, especially Indians, to rethink Indians' status. Scores of Puget Sound Indians—noncitizens as well as citizens—served in the military. When they returned, particularly from the East Coast or France, many had new perspectives on their communities and themselves. William McCluskey reported from the Lummi Reservation in 1919, "The boys [sic] experience over abroad and at camps are the frequent subject of our people." What the people said when reviewing wartime experiences McCluskey did not reveal.[45] But during the war several of them were not reticent about voicing their views; for pro-war propaganda and conscription provoked a lively debate about wardship, citizenship, and Indians' proper relation to the government.[46]

According to Charles Buchanan, some residents of the Lummi, Swinomish, and Port Madison Reservations "were particularly contumacious" when the draft registrars came. Three of the "contumacious" men showed up at an army training camp near Tacoma, telling Indian recruits they had no right to be there. Buchanan responded by pressing sedition charges. For the accused men, the issue was not whether they had subverted the U.S. war effort but whether the government was subverting Indians' special status. In response to the charges, Lummi Thomas Jefferson made the paradoxical argument that military service was inconsistent with Indians' subordination to the United States. It was at odds with the role American leaders had assigned his people. At the treaty conference Stevens had made Lummis promise to stop fighting, both with whites and with Indians, and Jefferson would not renege on his parents' promise. Instead, he declared, he intended to play the role Stevens had given Indians. And he would keep waiting for the government to fulfill the role of protector and provider in return.[47]

Chief Charles Jules of Tulalip, who consulted frequently with Buchanan, thought otherwise: Indians belonged in the U.S. military. Like Jefferson, Jules drew on memories of earlier times to form an opinion about Indians' proper role, but Jules remembered different events of the past. In olden times, he said, Indians had to fight to save their wives and children from enslavement by enemies. If a hostile tribe was large and powerful, other tribes united to preserve their liberties. The German threat to the liberties of Indian women and children, Jules concluded, called for the same kind of response.[48]

To drum up enthusiasm for the war, federal officials exhorted Indians to reject reasoning like Jefferson's. Far from neglecting Indians, they argued, American leaders had included Indians among the people who enjoyed all the benefits of citizenship. In a eulogy for a Suquamish soldier, Buchanan cited Father Chirouse's labors among Indians as a reason for those Indians' descendants to help the French in the war. The Suquamish man, Buchanan wrote, "requited by service and sacrifice even unto death, the supreme debt of his people."[49]

Wartime conditions sapped the influence of people who argued for continuing Indian wardship and energized the proponents of citizenship and integration. While Indians gained economic clout, their official guardian lost it. Employees as well as students left western Washington Indian schools to take high-paying jobs or join the armed forces. Staff vacancies, inflation, and reduced funding, aggravated by successive epidemics, sent the boarding school at Puyallup into an irreversible tailspin.[50]

Inspired by Indians' support for the war and integration into white military units, the champions of assimilation—Indian and non-Indian—rededicated themselves to ending Indians' legal disabilities. After prevailing on Congress to offer citizenship to Indian veterans, they introduced a bill for universal Indian citizenship. Thomas Bishop, advocate for Washington's landless Indians, was a prominent lobbyist for the measure. Historian Brian Dippie calls the resulting Indian Citizenship Act of 1924 "the symbolic high point of the assimilationist era."[51] Typical of people who viewed the act as confirmation that Indians had adapted completely to American life was F. S. Hall, director of the Washington State Museum. Hall said of western Washington Indians in 1924:

> All signs of the aboriginal inhabitants have disappeared except in certain allotted reservations and the occasional visits to our cities of the wrinkled-faced old basket sellers and of members of the younger generation, who are as much Americanized in dress and appearance as their white neighbors. ... Practically all the ancient tribal customs and observances have disappeared except in a few isolated cases.[52]

The federal wardship apparatus nevertheless survived, exerting drag on assimilationism's renewed momentum. Influential people thought that some Indians still needed protection and supervision. For a decade after the war, therefore, government practice in western Washington was nearly indistinguishable from prewar practice—a capricious mix of paternalism and neglect. In 1922, for example, Superintendent Dickens used the proceeds of timber sales at Tulalip to clear individuals' land, build homes for them, and buy them farm equipment. He also reported that he was attending to the needs of some off-reservation Indians. In the next breath, complaining that Indians had "been paternalized to the extent that they are almost without character," Dickens said he was encouraging them to become taxpayers.[53]

One service that Indians repeatedly requested from their federal guardian—preservation of their access to fish—the government did not reliably provide. Before the war Buchanan at least championed Indians' right under the treaties to fish for food without interference. He pleaded with state lawmakers to exempt Indians from some fishing regulations, denounced state harassment, and prevailed on federal lawyers to represent Indian fishers who resisted prosecution and non-Indian incursions into reservation waters. Even before Buchanan's death in 1920, however, adverse court decisions prompted him to advise Indians that they would have to obey state fishing laws. His successors, claiming that the courts had tied their hands, offered harried fishers negligible aid.[54]

Understandably, many people continued fishing for advantages from their status as federal wards and steering around the disadvantages where possible. Inspector Flora Seymour was amused and encouraged by one man's reaction when the superintendent denied him permission to spend trust funds on a car: he contracted to do some logging and soon bought a fifteen-hundred-dollar automobile with his earnings. Dickens, on the other hand, was unhappy when three educated allottees realized that they could rely on federal law to keep state authorities from entering their lands to collect judgments. Like others here, Dickens said, one of the men "disregards and questions Federal authority and seeks its protection according to the personal desires of the moment."[55]

Dickens was almost comically ambivalent about whether such Indians needed a guardian. His ambivalence reflected both the contradiction embedded in federal policy and his own contradictory impressions of the Indians he supervised. He could not match the enterprising people of his area with the images of Indians that justified either wardship or complete emancipation. In Dickens's view, Puget Sound Indians were at once the most progressive in the United States and maddeningly resistant to important civilizing influences. None of the twelve tribes he had worked with before Tulalip, he said, were so like non-Indians in manner, dress, and willingness to work hard. Young Washington Indians had constant contact with whites and adopted whites' economic practices, even in the heart of large reservations. Yet no apparently civilized Indians in Dickens's experience had retained "the traditional traits of the original aborigne [*sic*]" as these had. (What those traditional traits were Dickens did not say.)[56]

If Dickens was uncertain whether the people in his charge were moving into white society or remaining Indians, so were many of those people themselves. By then the meager advantages and considerable problems associated both with wardship and with legal emancipation were fully apparent to the descendants of western Washington natives. Equally apparent was whites' ambivalence about each status and their reluctance to let Indians choose one. For the people already identified as Indians, this situation was uncomfortable at best. If they were to be Indians in a society dominated by whites, they needed to define that identity more clearly and less demeaningly.

Between 1910 and 1930, an alternative interpretation of Indian identity did gain the approval of most Indians around Puget Sound. Transcending significant differences in perspective and experience, they reached agreement that the treaties of 1854 and 1855, more than either citizenship or wardship, must be the basis for their relations with whites and hence for their distinction from whites.

It is worth emphasizing that the people who forged this apparent consensus were far from homogeneous. Profiles of populations at the different reservations—residents' occupations and economic conditions, their uses of land, the extent of their ties to non-Indians, and their relations with outsiders and with government—varied considerably. Off-reservation populations added to Indians' diversity. Fifty years of radical change had produced different occupational, educational, social, and legal profiles for successive generations of Indians as well.[57]

Acutely aware of their diversity and the tensions it generated, some descendants of indigenous people consciously looked for commonalities. An incident in the Nooksack Valley exposed both the tensions between dissimilar Indians and the desire for emblems that all Indians could display with pride. Three men led by George Swanaset, billing himself as chief of the Nooksacks, complained in 1928 that Upper Skagit, Swinomish, Lummi, and Canadian Indians had recently held a two-day "war dance," over their objections but with the protection of Tulalip agency police. The three men's letter to the commissioner read:

> The Nooksack tribe, as you know, have had their citizenship restored to them and are not living on a reservation and have always followed the more civilized way and desires [*sic*] to continue to advance themselves and keep progress with the white men's civilization and an affair of this nature conducted in our community leaves the wrong kind of an impression to the outside world.[58]

Based on interviews and his officers' observations, Tulalip superintendent F. A. Gross concluded that the supposed "war dance" was a social event rather than a pagan rite. Sponsors of the gathering, he said, had acted on a felt need to commemorate their Indian heritage. Other Indians of the Sound regularly brought their old people joy by celebrating the treaties with songs, dances, feasts, and speeches from Indian and white friends; but because the Nooksacks had not entered a treaty, they had no such celebrations. Gross thought the protesting chiefs were miffed not by the dancing but by the young people's failure to consult them.[59]

Gross's interpretation of the dances may have been naive. Two ethnographers have noted a surge in the number of north Sound Indians singing warrior power after the turn of the century. If the people who danced in 1928 were included in that number, they could have riled Swanaset—a devout Methodist—whether or not they consulted him. But the superintendent's comment on the Indians' aim was perceptive. Both dancers and the old chiefs wanted to identify features of Indian life that had positive meanings for most Nooksacks and for outsiders.[60]

Gross stimulated another discussion about bringing diverse Indians together when he called a meeting of Swinomish Reservation residents and asked them to decide whether to rebuild a burned community hall. Several people backed his contention that the hall would symbolize the desire of people from formerly separate bands to unite for progress. But an old chief and "leader of the 'smoke house' faction" spoke against the proposal. Several people then told Gross that they did not want to choose between the factions favoring and opposing the hall.[61]

Sometimes Indians found new ways to symbolize and celebrate their past without having to choose between competing factions. Ironically, even non-Indian traditions offered themselves for this purpose. American holiday observances, for instance, did not invite government repression or upset Indians who objected to aboriginal ceremonies, yet they could take on positive connotations for Indians of various persuasions. At Memorial Day services on the Swinomish Reservation in 1925, a speaker explained "that while they celebrated the Memorial Day of the white man, they combined with it a much older Indian custom of tribute to their dead."[62]

The white promoters of a 1926 Northwest Indian Congress agreed that some images of the past could inspire Indians to unite for progress in the future. Hoping to demonstrate the Indian race's ability to "take on culture and civilization," they invited mostly young, well-educated people to the conference, but they also moved to forestall discontent by including some "old Indians." In the latter category Walter Dickens nominated William Shelton to represent Tulalip. Shelton, Dickens wrote, was "one of the outstanding characters of the Sound country, being an original aborigine, a maker of totem poles, the author of a number of Indian legend stories, *progressive* and one of the most honorable Indians I ever knew."[63] Perhaps unwittingly, the Tulalip superintendent had nominated a man who thought he knew which symbols of Indian identity would have broad appeal among the diverse descendants of Puget Sound natives, young as well as old.

Late-nineteenth-century reformers would have considered Dickens's characterization of Shelton a contradiction in terms. But Shelton was indeed both an old Indian—born in 1868—and progressive in assimilationists' sense of the word. His parents had sponsored potlatches at their Whidbey Island home and taught him other traditions of the indigenous upper class, but he entered the Tulalip mission school as an adolescent because he saw a need to learn white ways, and he worked many years as the agency millwright. According to his daughter, Shelton advocated using whites' knowledge to elevate Indians, as Indians, to a status they could be proud of. In this respect Shelton was in tune with an assortment of his contemporaries, around Puget Sound and nationwide. In western Washington it was this cohort of "progressive" older Indians who led organized responses to the confusing conditions of the teens and 1920s.[64]

The most important organized response was the Northwestern Federation of American Indians (NFAI). The federation's architect and first president was Thomas Bishop, the man who urged the government to enroll and allot "unattached Indians." Bishop and the NFAI's other early leaders had come of age during the years when the promise of citizenship for Indians was new and largely untarnished by demeaning conditions. Like William Shelton, all had spent some time in school, where they must have heard hope-inspiring rhetoric about human progress and equality. Many had also heard their elders speak of Isaac Stevens's treaty pledge to provide the homes, schools, doctors, and money that would make Indians as good as whites. But after a youth full of promise, organizers of the NFAI found in middle age that their status was problematic and their economic opportunities were eroding.[65]

A similar blend of hope and disappointment, of positive and negative feelings about being Indian, motivated people who initiated a national movement for Indian advancement during the first decade of the century. Desiring the benefits of American prosperity and citizenship but also needing to take pride in their heritage and fearing that government policy condemned Indians to poverty and second-class citizenship, educated men and women from numerous tribes founded the Society of American Indians (SAI) in 1911. The SAI was the hardiest of several pan-Indian organizations born during the same period. SAI members aimed to resolve the tensions they felt by making a place in American society for a redefined Indian, one who combined the best of aboriginal and white American cultures.[66]

National meetings of pan-Indian groups inspired several people to organize Indians in Washington State on the same basis. After attending a conference of the Brotherhood of North American Indians, Chief Mason of the Quinaults professed an intent to devote his life and fortune to the organization's goals: unifying Indians, perpetuating aboriginal traditions, and securing personal rights and liberties "equal to all people and inferior to none." Mason sent circulars about the Brotherhood to all Northwest tribes and set up meetings with Indians in Clallam and Whatcom Counties. Thomas Bishop joined the pan-Indian movement and, in 1916, moved to Washington, D.C. In 1920 he became secretary-treasurer of the Society of American Indians.[67]

The ideological debt that Bishop and his NFAI associates owed to the national movement, as well as to nineteenth-century assimilationism, is apparent from the NFAI constitution, adopted in 1914. Copying nearly word for word the provisional constitution of the SAI, NFAI founders declared that the honor of the race and the good of the country were paramount. They gave themselves the following mission:

> 1) To promote and co-operate with efforts looking to the advancement of the Indians in enlightment [*sic*] which leaves him free as a man to develope [*sic*] according to the natural laws of social evolution. 2) To provide, through our open conference, the means for a free discussion on all subjects bearing on the welfare of the race. 3) To present in a just light a true history of the race, to preserve its records and to emulate its distinguishing virtues. 4) To promote citizenship among Indians and obtain the rights thereof.

The NFAI also adopted the same membership criteria as the SAI, thus endorsing explicitly the notion that Indians were a single race defined by biological ancestry. Active membership was open to all adults "of Indian blood." "Indian associate" status was for Indians from countries besides the United States and for persons of less than one-sixteenth Indian blood not on any tribal roll.[68]

The identical wording of their membership requirements masked an important difference between the SAI and the NFAI. Indians participated in the SAI as individuals rather than as members of tribes, but the NFAI organized its membership by tribal groups. The NFAI had active chapters at all Tulalip agency reservations and in several off-reservation communities. By the 1920s it was dealing with government officials principally through representatives of those chapters, which it equated with tribes.[69]

The NFAI's form was dictated by its most important focus—claiming and clarifying members' treaty rights. Although various NFAI spokesmen later had different memories of the group's original purpose, all recalled that they resolved early to investigate their rights under the treaties and to get what the government owed them. Since the government conceived of the treaty parties as tribes or bands, it would consider individuals' claims only as derivatives of tribal claims. Therefore, by the time that special enrolling agent Charles Roblin was asking landless Indians about their tribal affiliations, the need for tribe-by-tribe organization of the NFAI was clear. Around the Sound people responded by holding councils and choosing men to represent them as tribes at regional meetings. Some Indians later described the resulting organizations as their reservations' first formal governments.[70]

NFAI affiliates did not consist of reservation groups only. The 1915 meeting to select a board of directors for the Duwamish Tribe took place in Tacoma. The board included NFAI activists Peter James and Charles Alexis, who lived on and sometimes represented the Lummi and Port Madison Reservations, respectively, but it also included Joseph Moses from the town of Renton and James Tobin of Olympia. In 1916 seventy-five people calling themselves the Snoqualmie Indians gathered at Tolt in the Cascade foothills, and several voiced a desire for land in that vicinity. The Duwamish and Snoqualmie organizations compiled membership lists that contained some names already on reservation censuses, plus the names of hundreds more people in small towns throughout Puget Sound country.[71]

The need to sort NFAI's individual constituents by tribe presented a hefty challenge, as is exquisitely clear from the data Roblin collected. Roblin's seemingly simple test of a person's eligibility for treaty benefits— membership in a tribe or descent from a tribe member—was rarely simple to apply. Most of his applicants had ancestral and social connections to several groups. Even a single Indian ancestor could have more than one possible tribal designation—the name for the village or extended community where she was born, the group she lived with as an adult, or a parent's tribe. Catherine McKinney, wife of a Swinomish "half breed," could have called herself a Mud Bay Indian, because her father was born at Mud Bay of Mud Bay parents. She could have enrolled as Squaxin, because Squaxin Island was the reservation intended for Mud Bay Indians, or she could have enrolled with her husband. Instead, McKinney sought membership in the Puyallup Tribe, saying that her mother (who had a Yakima father and a Cowlitz mother) was born among the Puyallups.[72]

When they designated their tribes, most Indians probably applied some general principles; but it appears from Roblin's records that different people applied different principles. Peter Rogers determined his tribe by his father's community of origin (Duwamish), not by his mother's ascribed parentage (Suquamish and Skykomish), nor by his residence at Suquamish. But Edward Davis claimed membership in the Snoqualmie Tribe through his mother's father, even though he identified both his parents and his birthplace as Duwamish; and James Thomas identified with the community of his birth and lifelong residence—Snohomish—rather than with the Yakima and Duwamish communities where his parents were born. On Roblin's list were people who claimed affiliation with an ancestor's original tribe even though the ancestor had left that tribe at a tender age; but there were also people who claimed affiliation with a Puget Sound tribe solely because a kinsman had joined the group as an adult.[73]

Many of the people who contacted Roblin had vague ideas about tribes and tribal makeup. Some identified their tribes by naming villages or small bands—Slo-slo-ose, LaQualah, Smalk-kamish, Nookachamps—rather than the larger aggregations on the Indian Office's list of tribes. Members of a nuclear family did not always agree on tribal designations for each other. In fact, a measure of the ambivalence and flexibility with which people approached the question of tribal membership is the sizable number of siblings who claimed or accepted different ascriptions. Julia Barkhousen, listed as an unallotted Klallam, had one sister on the Tulalip roll and another on the Lummi roll.

The people who joined the NFAI, contacted Roblin, or otherwise asked to be included on Indian rolls during the 1920s had a new motivation to identify themselves as Indians. They wanted to be counted because they wanted to share in what the government owed Indians of the treaty tribes—perhaps allotments, perhaps cash, perhaps respect.[74] They did not have strong incentives, however, to identify with one Indian tribe rather than another. If they believed that land or money would be awarded in uniform amounts per capita, as Roblin surmised, no particular tribal designation seemed to offer a material advantage over other designations. The effort to compile tribal rolls encouraged people of native descent to document their lineage, and it got them thinking about the basis and significance of group affiliations; but it did not draw impassable boundaries between the several interlinked communities that could claim their loyalties. Indeed, the need to divide Indians into tribes had a powerful counterweight in the treaties themselves. Except in their descriptions of land ceded and reserved, the treaties of the 1850s were virtually identical. It made sense to mount a regionwide, pan-Indian campaign to redeem the promises made in those treaties.

Thus, by the 1920s many people of different communities and ancestries had pinned their hopes for the future on decades-old treaties. In retrospect it seems as if the strategic choice they made was an obvious one, ordained by the treaties themselves. That the choice was not inevitable, however, is evident from the history of NFAI demands and decisions. It took a decade for Indians of western Washington to develop and organize around a coherent chronicle of broken treaty promises. Recalling how NFAI leadership galvanized communities to define themselves by their treaty rights, Lawrence Webster said, "History could have died if Tommy Bishop did [not] start asking questions."[75]

The origins of the NFAI campaign may include fireside tales told by Indians who remembered the treaty conferences. According to one account, for instance, the native man who interpreted at Point Elliott called Indians together shortly before his death in 1881 and exhorted them not to forget Governor Stevens's unfulfilled promises. In any case, when whites displaced some Indian fishers during the 1890s, aging natives did remember Stevens's 1855 promise to permit fishing, and they protested its breach. But non-Indians share the credit for perpetuating interest in the treaties after that. At the behest of aggrieved hunters and fishers, government lawyers invoked the treaties in the Lummi fish trap and Squaxin tidelands litigation. Officials also promoted Treaty Day celebrations and described the new Tulalip school as a belated fulfillment of treaty promises. Not surprisingly, when the Board of Indian Commissioners sent Samuel Eliot to western Washington in 1915, many Indians wanted to tell him about other treaty promises that were yet unfulfilled.[76]

By 1915 Thomas Bishop was recording elderly Indians' memories of U.S. promises and comparing them to the text of the treaties. That year Bishop published "An Appeal to the Government to Fulfill Sacred Promises Made 61 Years Ago." There he reproduced a copy of the Point No Point Treaty, a letter about his interviews with "the few remaining Indians who were present at the signing of this treaty," and affidavits from two men who said they had heard Stevens promise two buckets of gold and land for every person in the Duwamish Tribe. Bishop's stated aim was to educate officials who had either forgotten the treaty promises or ignored the troubles plaguing Indians sixty years later.[77]

The grievances Bishop recited in 1915 were eclectic: the state legislature had curtailed Indian hunting and fishing privileges, the government had given Indians fewer and cheaper presents than they expected, whites had razed Indian homes and disturbed burial grounds, the reservations did not encompass land enough for all Indians who desired allotments, and red tape prevented Indians from using their trust lands and moneys. As late as 1922, Tulalip superintendent Dickens said that there existed among Indians "a hodge podge of ideas as to the promises of the government." By that time, however, NFAI leaders had settled on a strategy of suing the government and were recasting their memories to fit the required legal mold.[78]

Once again Indians confronted the contradictory consequences of federal guardianship. Federal law precluded suit unless Congress gave the Court of Claims jurisdiction. So Bishop asked congressmen for help. In 1919 Washington representative Lindley Hadley obliged Bishop by proposing the authorizing legislation, but it took six more years and cooperation from the Indian Office to get a bill passed.[79] Cooperation was hard to come by because OIA personnel were initially hostile to the NFAI. Besides privately impugning Bishop's motives, Buchanan publicly criticized him for publishing false allegations that the government had neglected particular Indians. Buchanan's successor also belittled the NFAI. How could Bishop represent people who had conflicting claims and no unity of interest? Walter Dickens asked.

Yet Dickens could neither deny nor dampen the widespread interest in the federation's agenda. Late in 1921 he acceded to an NFAI request that he call a meeting for Indians of the Point Elliott Treaty tribes, and five hundred people came. They resolved to back Bishop's bill, thanked him for his help, and left further lobbying to him. Dickens consoled himself with a passage in the resolution that conceded Bishop's fallibility and excessive zeal. The resolution took this swipe at Bishop because other NFAI officers wanted Indian Office help and knew that Bishop's affiliation with the Society of American Indians was a deterrent, since some SAI leaders wanted to abolish the OIA. In 1923, after Bishop died, NFAI representatives from Swinomish and Tulalip told Dickens they had lost hope of pushing a bill through Congress without Indian Office assistance. Once assured that the organization would not call for an end to federal wardship, Dickens and his superiors cooperated with the NFAI.[80]

Dickens contended that the OIA's "position of technical guardianship, possible donor and 'Big Brother'" entitled him to attend NFAI meetings and to demand evidence that the federation actually represented a majority of the people it claimed as constituents, even if those people had neither trust land nor other relations with an Indian agency. After Congress authorized suit the Tulalip agency assumed an even more intrusive role, claiming power as guardian to limit, direct, or dismiss the tribes' lawyers. The irony of looking for help to the same people they intended to sue was not lost on NFAI leaders. Harriette Shelton later said, "We were wards of the government kind of, they're supposed to take care of us ..., and in the court our adversary is the same attorney."[81]

The effects of this OIA meddling and assistance are difficult to discern, but they included some influence on the ways Indians depicted their past. According to George Swanaset, Dickens "was the one to tell us that the Nooksacks weren't treaty Indians. He thought the treaty Indians should form a separate case altogether."[82] Surely the government's most important means of shaping the Indians' story was to send them into the Court of Claims, where statutes and judicial precedent focused their attention on the actions and events that might entitle them to cash compensation.

When Congress finally gave the green light for a lawsuit, the road it opened seemed broad. It permitted the court to hear "all claims of whatsoever nature" from Indians named in four Washington treaties and from several tribes "with whom no treaty has been made." (It excepted only Klallams, who had arranged both separate counsel and a separate statute awarding them four hundred thousand dollars.) However, attorney Arthur Griffin ultimately steered his clients into a narrower lane. Claiming that the Muckleshoot, Nooksack, Chinook, Upper Chehalis, and San Juan Islands Indians had not endorsed a treaty, he petitioned only for the value of their original lands. On behalf of fourteen other plaintiffs, twelve of them from the Puget Sound area, Griffin charged the United States with violating specific treaty clauses. The government, he alleged, had not paid Indians all it had pledged for their lands, had not compensated them for having to abandon off-reservation property, had not reserved all the land it had promised, had not financed the clearing and fencing of the reservations, had not promptly built an industrial school or provided farmers and physicians, and had not consolidated Indians on a central reservation. In other words, the lawsuit emphasized those treaty provisions that embodied a desire to make Indians more like whites.[83]

In his 1915 "Appeal" Bishop had drawn attention to a treaty provision of a different sort. He had urged the commissioner to ask the courts for a "humane and logical interpretation" of the promise to let Indians continue their customary hunting, fishing, and gathering. However, by the time the tribes were in the Court of Claims, Indians had cited that promise in state court as a defense to charges of illegal fishing and had lost. When Griffin and his clients opted to focus on provisions for land, schools, and annuities, they may have had these losses in mind. In addition, it was easier to assign compensable values to land and schools than to fishing and hunting privileges.

Despite the unfamiliar and inhibiting rules of the legal forum, the treaty claims case gave Indians a welcome opportunity to describe and invite public respect for their heritage. Preparing and prosecuting the claims involved scores of people in re-creating their history. Indians appeared twice before congressional committees: in 1922 Bishop testified, and in 1924 the witnesses were NFAI activists Wilfred Steve, Peter James, Charles Wilbur, and Charles Alexis, plus Nooksack spokesman George Swanaset. In 1923, with the help of interpreters William Shelton and Henry Steve, Dickens preserved testimony by taking statements from seven old men. Finally, for the Court of Claims itself, 113 additional men and women from the Puget Sound region gave depositions in 1927.

The questions these witnesses responded to obliged them to present their history not as a complex drama but as a skit with a simple moral. Dickens and attorney Arthur Griffin wanted only vignettes on a few subjects. Dickens focused on land, asking whether the old men had received allotments, knew Indians who had not received allotments, or knew Indians who had tried to keep their off-reservation land instead of coming to reservations. Griffin guided his witnesses through descriptions of cedar houses destroyed by settlers or abandoned when the occupants removed to reservations. He prompted elders to delineate their tribes' territories, and he invited general statements that Indians' numbers had declined steeply since treaty time.

Although such questioning may have induced people to caricature their history, it did not get them to recite a standardized text composed just for judges. In fact, the stories that witnesses told were hardly uniform. People from the different communities took pains to distinguish themselves. Witnesses routinely said that their knowledge was limited to their own families' traditions and that other people's territories and customs were for those people to describe. Indians of the Nooksack Valley, Muckleshoot Reservation, San Juan Islands, and Sauk River explained in varying ways why their ancestors did not sign a treaty.

Furthermore, not everyone gave testimony advancing the story that NFAI leaders and lawyers had sketched out. While many witnesses did swear that the government had given them little or nothing since the treaties, others recalled regular distributions of tools and supplies. Jack Wheeler accused American officials of lying—promising Indians houses, cows, sheep, and the lands they "hollered out" but leaving most Indians landless. But at the same hearing, Snoqualmie Jim asserted that Indians had received what they were promised. "It isn't the white man's fault," Jim said. "It is the Indians [sic] fault that they didn't get land." Even when

Griffin orchestrated trial testimony, occasional witnesses failed to follow the score. A few people, expected to say that they had waited anxiously for their own plots of land, said instead that they had come away from the treaty unaware of the government's plan to assign them individual tracts.[84]

Most significantly, many witnesses used their time in the spotlight to expound spontaneously on aspects of their history that were important to them. For Jerry Meeker, it was Leschi's refusal to approve a reservation with insufficient pasture. For William Shelton, testifying was a chance to mention a potlatch house where high-class Indians gave things away to the poor, and to recall old chiefs who counseled parents to promote good relations with whites by declining to teach their children "what Indians teach."[85]

Many people wanted especially to talk about hunting and fishing. Again and again, whether or not Griffin gave them an opening, witnesses lamented that whites were driving Indians out of their "natural grounds." Among those who declared that Isaac Stevens had promised Indians' their accustomed foods was eighty-seven-year-old William Kanim, who recreated at length his uncle's exchange with the governor:

> "I want all the game, such as elk and deer, ducks, clams, fish, berries; until you agree to grant us all these I have just named where we make our livelihood, then I will answer to your proposition of buying our land. I want the dry cedar which I could use to make canoes and to make lumber; I want the dry fir for its bark. I am telling you what I want and then I will answer what you want." Then Governor Stevens answered that it would be all right, that he could have all he wanted to reserve.[86]

Yet even with respect to fish and game, these diverse people told stories with varied twists. Kanim was intent on preserving access to a stretch of the Snoqualmie River and the place where his people dried their catch. Annie Lyons was upset to be driven away from shellfish beds near her Samish village and obliged to labor in canneries. William Rosler, a San Juan Island farmer, was concerned that trapmen and canneries were depleting salmon runs. August Martin gloried in the time that a judge had listened to Henry Kwina describe the treaty fishing clause, then "opened the book and he find this was correct."[87]

In the end, the process of re-creating Indians' history for the claims litigation was more rewarding than the litigation itself. The plaintiffs sought money that might raise them to the status their forebears expected as a result of the treaties. But in 1934 the Court of Claims dashed their hopes. Although it did not wholly repudiate either the history they told or their argument that certain government lapses were violations of the treaty, the court decided that the United States owed the plaintiffs nothing. The bases for this judgment were several technical interpretations of the law, a refusal to assign monetary value to some treaty violations, and a finding that government spending on Indians' behalf had far exceeded any losses they could quantify.[88]

The plaintiffs had accomplished something significant nonetheless. They had collaborated in composing a narrative that could serve as the basis for a common, honorable identity. As Harriette Shelton said, the Indians lost, but at least there were a lot of meetings. At those meetings and later during their case, many individuals from many communities described for each other who they had been and who they had become during eighty years of interaction with Americans. The lobbying and litigation meant putting people who asserted an Indian identity on display and allowing them to articulate what made them Indians. The various hearings thus became what anthropologist Barbara Myerhoff calls "definitional ceremonies" in which people could "show themselves to themselves."[89]

Many witnesses in the lawsuit consciously displayed marks of the Indian identity they embraced. The "old Indians" testified through an interpreter. Several stated explicitly what made them "real" Indians: they could not give dates or they could not read or write, they said, because they were Indians. Asked how he knew about methods of building longhouses he had never seen, Charley Blowl (Belole) said, "The Indian is not like you white men; you write down what your fathers used to do a long time ago. The Indian, his father takes his son and he tells him all the history of the tribe. ... "[90]

On the other hand, participants in the litigation did not reach a comprehensive consensus about how to characterize themselves. Even though they agreed on a historical backdrop for their Indian identity, their "definitional ceremonies" did not produce a single picture of Indians so much as a collage of images. At the various hearings each speaker could show a different picture and suggest different symbols around which Indians should rally. For many of them land—the land Indians had lost and the land they had intended to reserve—had taken on greatest symbolic value; for others the more meaningful emblems of Indianness were the foods they now had trouble obtaining. Some witnesses—although they identified themselves as Indians by participating in the lawsuit—even referred to Indians in the third person, as if Indians were from another culture or time. Most such witnesses were young and educated, but several elderly people also spoke of Indians as if the young were not included in that category. Skookum George was blunt. "What the Government ought to do," he said, "is to fulfil [sic] their promises that they made to the Indians because the Indians will soon all be gone."[91]

All who participated in the ceremonies believed that they were entitled to do so because they shared with the others a history of disappointing relations with non-Indian Americans. Most also believed that the old treaties symbolized their hope of better relations in the future. To Lawrence Webster, this was the primary import of the movement that the NFAI started. "The tribes up here didn't have nothin' goin' for 'em where they could get together, except their treaty," he said in 1982. Even people who thought their ancestors had not signed treaties included themselves in the movement by asserting that those ancestors deserved and would have accepted a treaty acknowledging their status as distinct peoples.[92]

Implied in the suit, then, was a belief that the treaties expressed a relationship between Indians and non-Indians less demeaning than the wardship of the 1920s. Even so, the plaintiffs did not agree on whether to speak positively of the treaty terms or of the Indians who acceded to them. Were the Indian negotiators naive victims of American duplicity or shrewd and foresighted people who exacted a respectful acknowledgment of their abilities and needs? Snoqualmie Jim said, "I believe the bargain was a good one for the Indians because the old Indians were smart and knew what they were doing." Many other witnesses were equally eager to say that the ancestors who entered into the treaties were dignified and knowledgeable. In contrast, Bishop and other NFAI leaders depicted the native treaty signers as ignorant of white ways and so weak that they had no choice but to concur. William Wilton, born in 1862, testified, "I pity those old people. If Mr. Stevens had written 'In 75 years your offspring will be exterminated,' they would have signed that, with all the knowledge they had about transacting business."[93]

Whether they praised or doubted their ancestors' acumen, the plaintiffs agreed on the need to pity and help surviving Indians who had not received their due. They wanted what the government had promised, many witnesses said, so that the old Indians would not live their last days in poverty. For young Sam Kadim, secretary of the Swinomish Tribe, the government's failures were "very embarrassing for the Indians." If the government had lived up to its promises, he said, "the Indians would have been far more progressive today than they are."[94]

Most of the Indians Kadim knew were indeed people in an embarrassing situation. Disabled by law and racial prejudice from demonstrating fully the kinds of power that had won their ancestors respect, they had sought or submitted to government protection. But instead of lending them strength, that protection had ensured and signified their weakness and low status. A desire to redefine this humiliating relationship energized the campaign and litigation that the Northwestern Federation of American Indians initiated. By calling attention to the old treaties and insisting that the government honor them, NFAI members suggested a more palatable way to conceive of Indianness. They constructed a collective history that acknowledged their indigenous forebears but offered people like Sam Kadim the hope of leaving those forebears' world behind. In effect, while unapologetically acknowledging that Indians were different from non-Indians, they demanded legal and economic parity with other Americans. By differentiating between old Indians and Indians of the future, they could proclaim pride in their Indian heritage.

7 Tribes
New and Old Organizations

Between 1930 and 1960 national economic and political trends reversed course twice. Each time they did, policies toward Indians changed as well. First, the Great Depression and Indians' especial poverty motivated lawmakers to listen to critics of the fifty-year-old assimilation policy, and Congress acquiesced in a new program aimed at protecting rather than eliminating Indian enclaves. Little more than a decade later, World War II and postwar prosperity provided a rationale for recanting the Depression-era deviation. By the 1950s the government once again planned to abolish the institutions and laws that set Indians apart.

In part because these dramatic shifts in policy came with a dramatic increase in federal power, most histories of Indians in this period focus on national policy and assume that it largely determined how Indian communities structured their internal and external relations at the time. In part because many enduring Indian organizations originated during the period, historians have also assumed that midcentury policies account for the tribal affiliations and legal identities of most Indians today.[1]

Events in western Washington undermine these assumptions. There was no direct correspondence between the ways that Indians of the region defined or grouped themselves in 1960 and the chief federal policies of the preceding three decades. Neither the Indian New Deal of the 1930s nor the termination policy of the 1950s did much to change or to clarify the indices of Indian identity in the Puget Sound area, at least in the short run. The descendants of western Washington Indians remained diverse, dispersed, and of many minds about government conceptions of them.

Although Indian policy fashions for the 1930s and 1950s were not designed to fit the people in western Washington who considered themselves Indians, some of those people borrowed pieces of the new political attire to dramatize their self-conceptions. Dressing up their actions with modish rhetoric about self-government or freedom, they formed and re-formed Indian tribal and intertribal organizations of several types. But in doing so, they perpetuated the diversity and ambiguity that had long characterized Indian identity in their region, and they ensured that debate about the defining marks of that identity would continue unabated.

United States Senators Burton Wheeler and Lynn Frazier saw the diversity and ambiguous status of some western Washington Indians in 1931, when they held hearings in Tacoma to investigate Indians' conditions. The concerns of witnesses from the reservations were varied: they complained of delays in the probate and partition of trust property, outmoded and nonexistent health care, inadequate educational facilities, polluted shellfish beds, discriminatory hiring at the Indian hospital, limitations on their self-governance, and incomplete Indian rolls. Three additional witnesses said they represented Indians the government had never accounted for or installed on trust land. Under questioning, one of them conceded that her people were doing better than Indians on the reservations.[2]

Elsewhere in the United States the Great Depression had reduced thousands of Indians to beggary by 1931, but there is no evidence that the same was true around Puget Sound. Unquestionably, Indians had lost income as shrinking demand forced Washington fish canneries, logging camps, and sawmills to curtail operations.[3] Yet the people who appeared before Wheeler and Frazier did not seem preoccupied with hard times. A letter from the Port Madison Reservation was the only Indian testimony to mention the depression and request relief.

Tulalip agency superintendent August Duclos, on the other hand, did want to talk about Indians' economic prospects, because nearly half the families who belonged on his reservations had scattered to cities and logging camps in search of work. "The present generation are untrained," he observed, and "there are a great many more laborers than there is labor." Because work was increasingly scarce, the itinerant Indians' condition was deteriorating. Nevertheless, Duclos thought that the downturn's effects were no worse for Indians than for non-Indians. Prosperity during the 1920s had enabled some Indians to buy as many luxury items as middle-class whites, he said, and even poor Indians had salmon and potatoes to stave off hunger.

Indian vulnerability was more apparent to Duclos's successor, O. C. Upchurch. Because a majority of Indians lived by day labor, Upchurch noted in 1934, the dearth of jobs "wrought a particular hardship" on them. Even so, their situation was not hopeless. During the first year of hard times, "with marked resourcefulness, they turned to individual fishing, wood cutting, both for fuel and pulp wood, and with a minimum of gratuitous assistance subsisted themselves and their families." The second year a ninety-thousand-dollar road fund enabled the Tulalip agency to employ those Indians who lacked other sources of cash. Only in the third year did some Indians go on relief.[4]

Upchurch's observations corroborate Lawrence Webster's memory that 1930 was the first of three hard years, especially for men who had worked in the woods and on the docks. Jobs were so scarce and wages so low that Webster turned to fishing for cash as well as for food. In one low tide he could bag two hundred pounds of clams, which he sold for three or four dollars. This ability to exploit natural resources enabled him and other Indians to weather the depression better than some whites and even to help white friends, Webster said. Bernard Adams, whose Suquamish family dug clams and sold bait herring to halibut boats, remarked, "[R]eally here ... we didn't suffer like some places durin' the Depression."[5]

Government statistics cannot validate Webster's and Adams's impressions, but neither do they contradict them. For 1929 the Bureau of Indian Affairs (BIA) at Tulalip estimated that three thousand Indians had income totaling $302,990—about $100 per person. The next year's income estimates yield a per capita income figure of $63, but proceeds in trust accounts brought the cash available to the average Indian up to approximately $180. Although this amount looks pathetically small next to the average income of all Washington residents—$657—the latter number probably includes some off-reservation Indians; and the BIA estimate does not take into account the value of fish, game, berries, and farm produce that Indians ate and bartered. BIA personnel concluded in 1934 that a Puget Sound reservation dweller needed no more than $210 or $240 annually "to attain the same approximate standard of livelihood that his or her white neighbors attained about 1926."[6]

Data gathered when the depression was deepest, including surveys of several hundred families on and off the reservations, show that Indians of western Washington felt the downturn in diverse ways. Most Indian households still had at least one member working in private enterprise part of the year, often logging or processing lumber. But annual family incomes ranged from $20 to $2,250. While most men at Squaxin Island were unemployed and many employable adults at Muckleshoot needed aid, a large number of Indians in Kitsap County had high-paying jobs at three places—McCormick Lumber Company, a naval munitions plant, and a shipyard. No one at the Swinomish Reservation was on relief, because the men logged or cut stove wood in winter and made as much as forty dollars a week fishing in the summer. Farther up the Skagit River, where fish were less abundant, six families received local relief.[7]

The nationwide economic crisis soon catalyzed innovations in federal policy. For Indians as for other suffering populations, lawmakers were willing to try a new tack. Armed with evidence that land allotment had bred poverty, critics of the assimilation policy persuaded Congress to halt the subdivision of Indian reservations. Taking the depression as proof of unorganized individuals' vulnerability, they resolved to protect and even to strengthen Indian communities. As a result, the Indian New Deal—a combination of reservation-centered relief programs and federal support for tribal self-governance—was born. Its sire and midwife was Franklin Roosevelt's commissioner of Indian affairs, John Collier.

The work programs appeared first. In 1933 Collier persuaded the president to earmark a portion of national emergency relief funds for Indians. In western Washington as elsewhere, the BIA used such funds to create temporary jobs. Many of the jobs for residents of Puget Sound were on the Pacific Coast, where Indian Emergency Conservation Work crews built fire lines and trails in forests of the Quinault and Makah Reservations. Between 1934 and 1941 the Works Progress Administration (WPA) and other New Deal agencies also funded smaller projects at reservations around the Sound. Hundreds of people of indigenous descent, to whom such short-term work was as familiar as it was welcome, promptly enrolled. Lawrence Webster joined WPA crews who cleaned up a cemetery and baseball field and built a dock at Port Madison. Bernard Adams spent more than a year in a Civilian Conservation Corps–Indian Division unit, planting trees and clearing ground for the community center on a new reservation at Port Gamble.[8]

Commissioner Collier viewed the work programs not just as a way to put cash into desperate Indians' pockets but also as a chance to get Indians thinking affirmatively about themselves and their communities. Along with wage-work experience and marketable skills, program participants might gain new self-respect. More important, Collier thought of work projects as spotlights with which he could draw Indians' collective gaze toward the resources he deemed vital to their existence. By hiring them to conserve and improve the range, soil, and forests of their reservations, he intended to focus their hopes for survival on their common estates. Indians earned less than other relief workers, supposedly because their work enhanced the value of their own property. But even when conservation work did not immediately boost the value of Indians' estate, Collier believed, it could clue them into their reservations' capacity to sustain them economically and culturally.[9]

In western Washington, however, emergency work relief had little power to influence Indians' thinking in these ways. Wage labor was nothing new for Indians there, and few of the New Deal projects showcased Puget Sound reservations as sites with significant economic potential. Except for timber conservation at Quinault and Neah Bay, most relief projects involved small-scale improvements to facilities such as roads and government buildings. Rather than developing valuable resources, workers dug drainage ditches or wells, took surveys, and rehabilitated clinics. Besides, Indians from Puget Sound were as likely to work on other people's reservations as they were to work at home. While programs for Indians did attract additional people of aboriginal descent to the reservations, state-administered programs also enrolled some acknowledged Indians for work outside the reservations.[10]

Tulalip superintendent Upchurch worried that federal relief and "communistic whites" were teaching his previously self-sufficient Indians to expect support from the government. But able-bodied people in his jurisdiction continued throughout the 1930s to support themselves with little federal aid. Most transfer payments to Indians were Old Age Assistance checks. Harriette Shelton remembered the Roosevelt administration not for subsidizing the penniless or even for putting them to work but for finally addressing Indians' need for health care.[11]

Health care was uppermost in the minds of Indian witnesses when Burton Wheeler's Senate subcommittee returned to western Washington in 1933. For people whose elders had judged someone's powers in part by his or her health, it was humiliating that disease felled so many friends and relatives. It was doubly galling that the government provided only one doctor—a doctor who allegedly swore and pointed guns at his patients—for more than thirty-four hundred Indians in an area one hundred miles square. Four of six witnesses therefore urged the senators to make medical care a priority.

The witnesses' unusual unanimity probably reflected their involvement in the Northwestern Federation of American Indians (NFAI), which had emphasized health care at its convention that year. The first witness, Don McDowell, identified himself as president of the NFAI, a group of thirteen tribes. McDowell's colleagues Martin Sampson, Victor Johnson, and Wilfred Steve spoke for NFAI chapters on the Swinomish, Lummi, and Tulalip Reservations, respectively. They depicted themselves as willing and qualified to cooperate with the government as representatives of their communities and of Indians in general. The men and women on the Lummi council, Victor Johnson said, hoped that the government would recognize them and their interest in the reservation by calling them together more often.[12]

Commissioner Collier approved of aspirations like the Lummi council's and planned to encourage them. A few months after the hearing in western Washington, Collier sent Senator Wheeler a proposal for legislation that would allow Indians at Lummi and elsewhere to take over the management of their reservations. By June of 1934 Wheeler's name headed a new statute that incorporated key elements of Collier's proposal.

The Wheeler-Howard Act, also known as the Indian Reorganization Act (IRA), permitted tribes to establish formal governments with limited powers. It provided, too, for federally chartered Indian corporations with authority to manage common tribal assets. In order to secure passage of the act—the second component of his Indian New Deal—Collier retreated from his most radical proposals and watched Congress rewrite or lop off other provisions dear to his heart. In part because of Wheeler's opposition, for instance, the final bill did not endorse Collier's plan to relinquish BIA functions to organized tribes. Nevertheless, Collier rightfully claimed that the Reorganization Act represented a significant shift in federal policy. Instead of destroying tribal formations in order to force Indians' assimilation, the government now pledged to preserve tribal assets and foster tribal organizations.[13]

With help from the White House and other allies, Collier persuaded Congress to change direction primarily because he had proof that the laws enacted by assimilationists had backfired, ensuring rather than eliminating Indians' dependency on the government. Although he denied that he wanted to abandon the goal of assimilation, Collier argued that federal programs should enable Indians to live decently whether or not they chose to assimilate. His personal agenda, however, was more ambitious and radical than the one he got Congress to endorse. He was bent on preserving or reviving indigenous cultures and communal life.[14]

Collier's fondness for Indian culture was the flip side of his disgust with the effects of industrialization and urbanization in the United States. His hopes for reforming Americans' chaotic economic and social life had come to rest on community organizations. In the New Mexico Pueblos, which he visited during the 1920s, he perceived ideal communities, cohesive and spiritually healthy. He leaped to the conclusion that Indians in general had little inclination to settle in cities because they held values antithetical to those of the competitive minions of capitalism. To thrive, Collier believed, Indians should remain on their own lands among their own kind. This conviction inspired both the bill he proposed and his implementation of the less utopian legislation that emerged from Congress. During more than a decade at the BIA, he tenaciously promoted the idea that Indians' prospects would be brighter if they acted collectively to conserve and manage reservation resources.[15]

Collier pitched his ideas in Indian country even before he unveiled his draft Indian Reorganization Act. In January 1934 he sent to agency directors, tribal councils, and selected individuals a circular entitled "Indian Self-Government." He stressed the need for property relations that would "'assure all Indians born on the reservation a fair share of land.'" He advocated the transfer of individual property to tribal corporations and suggested that tribal governments control the expenditure of tribal funds, engage in cooperative marketing and purchasing, and require community labor. BIA personnel, under instructions to promote Collier's ideas enthusiastically, circulated among the Puget Sound reservations to discuss his memorandum.[16]

With the unprecedented intent of proposing legislation that Indians wanted and recruiting Indians to lobby for the legislation, Collier convened a series of regional Indian congresses. The Northwest congress took place at Chemawa boarding school in Oregon on March 8, 1934. In his stead the exhausted Collier sent such high-level officers as Assistant Commissioner William Zimmerman and Solicitor Felix Cohen. BIA-subsidized delegates—a few per tribe or reservation—and other interested Indians came from Oregon, Washington, Idaho, and western Montana. In the general assembly five men spoke for Indians around Puget Sound: George Adams from Skokomish, Joe Campbell from the Upper Skagit district, and three stalwarts of the NFAI—Don McDowell, Peter James, and Wilfred Steve.[17]

The Chemawa conference agenda prompted participants to ponder and debate the bases and implications of their identification as Indians. All speakers evaluated the proposed law by its consistency with their characterizations of Indians and the status they envisioned for Indians. Collier's staff described modern Indians primarily as victims, impoverished, infantilized, and demoralized by wicked laws. "Indians have been taught," Zimmerman said, "that they had to choose between remaining like so many slaves, being taken care of by the Indian bureau or else thrown to the wolves." The self-government proposal he had come to discuss would teach Indians instead that they could be free, thanks to the power inherent in organization. Henry Roe Cloud, introduced as "a man of your own race ... who is 100% American," said Collier's program would "relight the spiritual fire that burned in the hearts of the Indian people in ancient times," empowering Indians by bringing the old culture back to life.

Tribal delegates in turn invoked varied images of Indians. Some spoke of poor and ignorant people who necessarily deferred to federal advisors. A man from Fort Hall, speaking through an interpreter, said, "You know things. We, as Indians, do not seem to know anything." Others developed the motif of Indians as victims but warned fellow delegates that their past mistreatment was reason to distrust yet another government promise of salvation. Several speakers depicted their tribes not as the cohesive communities Collier imagined but as populations divided along generational and racial lines.

For the delegates from western Washington, the meeting was an opportunity to emphasize their distinctiveness. Explicitly differentiating themselves from the generic Indians that men at the podium had described, they pointed out their dependence on fish and forests rather than farms and range. Some of them emphasized that they had no land. More remarkably, they were eager to appear competent, confident, and ready to take responsibility for their economic and political affairs.

Moments after Bob Marshall opened the meeting, Skokomish representative George Adams interrupted to ask whether Marshall knew the cost of launching a logging enterprise. Marshall's answer evidently qualified him to continue, for Adams said, "I just wanted to satisfy myself if you were really acquainted with the amount of money. I am from Puget Sound and I was raised in the lumbering communities and I feel that you can go ahead and continue successfully your speech on logging operations." Later Adams declared that Indians of his region would have no trouble running profitable salmon and timber businesses. "So the State of Washington," he concluded, "can take care of itself if the Indians were given a chance." Wilfred Steve also wanted the commissioner to know that Puget Sound Indians were a competent breed. He followed a description of the NFAI with the observation that self-government was not new to the people he represented: they had been working on it for over twenty years.[18]

This sense of themselves as self-sufficient, self-directed people influenced the responses of other western Washington Indians to the Indian Reorganization Act, as it had influenced responses to the depression. Self-confidence prompted fifty residents of the Skokomish Reservation to support Collier's plan in January 1934. They had worked hard to clear and improve their lands, Skokomish spokesmen told the superintendent, and wanted to continue profiting from their labor. Recalling that they had once administered law effectively with their own police and judges, they felt they could do so again.[19]

A tradition of autonomy was also the rationale for negative comments on Collier's bill. Some Muckleshoots disliked the bill because they had been "rather independent and self-supporting for years," receiving their first significant government help only under the New Deal. "We feel that instead of making us independent, we would be more dependent on the government," they concluded. Tulalip council members liked Collier's idea of "social and political union" but feared that pooling their economic interests would eliminate incentives that had motivated Indians to advance. One Tulalip man preferred to imagine a future when they "would see little distinction among our people and white neighbors; that 'instead of being called Indians they would be called Mr. Steve, Mr. Williams, etc., just folks.'" Only at Nisqually did Indians reportedly lack confidence in their ability to manage economic and political affairs. There it was the superintendent who pointed out that they had governed themselves for years, "particularly in so far as the fishing industry was concerned."[20]

The Reorganization Act departed from precedent most dramatically by permitting Indians to vote on whether it should apply to them. When people around Puget Sound had the opportunity to vote, many did not take it, but a convincing majority of the ballots cast were favorable. In rapid succession during 1934 and 1935, Indians of the Skokomish, Nisqually, Squaxin Island, Tulalip, Port Madison, Puyallup, Muckleshoot, and Swinomish Reservations and the Skagit-Suiattle and Nooksack districts decided by referendum to accept the IRA. Only at Lummi did the negative ballots outnumber the affirmative.[21]

If referenda on the IRA provoked sharp controversy in Puget Sound communities, as they did elsewhere in the United States, the controversies did not generate records that survive in archives. The motivations of most voters are lost to historical view. It is likely that people who opposed the IRA had reasons like those voiced by Indians elsewhere: they feared it would force them to relinquish private land to a tribal corporation, thought it would prevent their integration into American society, doubted their own or other Indians' political savvy, or mistrusted schemes hatched by whites. Unresolved claims against the United States also made some western Washington Indians reluctant to consider new federal proposals. Several councils declared that they would listen to professions of desire to save Indian lands only after the government paid for lands already taken.[22]

From referendum tallies it appears that many doubters, including the Muckleshoot council and Nisqually residents, soon found things to like about the IRA. NFAI activists and others who thought the government owed them land must have welcomed the act's provisions for acquiring, consolidating, and preserving tax-exempt acreage. The act also offered Indians the hope of controlling more funds and obtaining loans for education and development.[23]

Perhaps the IRA also won acceptance around Puget Sound because Indians there did not expect it to work a radical change in their lives. Indian self-government had a variety of precursors in the region. For several years the BIA had promoted or approved local councils, courts, and community improvement associations. In addition, Indians on their own had convened to discuss and take action on common concerns.[24] Thanks to these experiences, plus two decades of NFAI agitation, some people saw Collier's plan for self-government as permission to follow a trail they had already blazed. In Joe Hillaire's view, the IRA offered the equality and emancipation that were Indians' due. When he sent Collier detailed suggestions for rewording several sections of the original bill, Hillaire wrote: "Personally, it is the very thing, I have been hoping for, in the last few years."[25]

While experience in the NFAI and other organizations may have helped people to make sense of Collier's proposal for self-government, it could not fully prepare them for his conception of Indian communities and their defining characteristics. The IRA embodied simplistic and inflexible notions about Indians, tribes, and tribal membership—notions that had little relevance to the diverse, scattered, and interconnected people around Puget Sound who considered themselves Indians.

Conceiving of Indian identity as rooted in lands that the United States administered for Indians, Congress aimed the IRA at reservation residents. The question whether to invoke the act was addressed to Indians on reservations: by its terms the IRA would not apply where a majority of them voted it down. The statute identified eligible voters—that is, Indians—as persons of Indian descent who were members of a recognized tribe under federal jurisdiction, descendants of tribe members who lived on a reservation as of June 1, 1934, and persons of half or more Indian blood. It further defined a tribe, in circular fashion, as "any Indian tribe, organized band, pueblo, or the Indians residing on one reservation."[26]

Collier anticipated problems in applying these definitions. In a 1934 circular that noted the various kinds of existing Indian rolls—allotment, annuity, per capita, census, and final rolls—he asked superintendents to describe the difficulties they would face when compiling lists of people eligible to vote on the IRA. Hoping to maximize the number of voters, he advised them to construe terms such as "reservation" liberally.[27]

For officials who applied the IRA in western Washington, the questions regarding Indian and tribal identity were tougher than Collier could have foreseen. By the 1930s the local BIA regarded as Indians many people who did not fall cleanly into or outside the IRA categories. In 1929, for example, Superintendent Duclos sent state officials a list of 180 people—none of them on reservation censuses—whom he identified as Indians entitled to "special fishing privileges." The next Tulalip superintendent told Congress in 1933 that he knew of 113 allotments on the public domain whose owners were presumably Indians. He also took responsibility for some people outside reservations who had no land or insignificant shares of land. In the Nooksack district alone, he said, there were 126 such people. In order to hold referenda on the IRA, officials in western Washington had to determine whether the act applied to people like the scattered fishers, off-reservation allottees, and landless Nooksacks.[28]

Usually without recording its rationales, the BIA allowed some people who were not on a reservation to vote but denied others the chance. It arranged a referendum on the IRA for Indians of the dissolved Puyallup Tribe because sixty acres of their reserve—the former school site—remained in federal trust. The fact that some off-reservation residents of the Nooksack and Upper Skagit districts had allotments may have influenced the decision to hold referenda there. Why some other groups did not have the same opportunity is unclear, however. Left out were people who called themselves Snohomish, Stillaguamish, Snoqualmie, and San Juan Indians, plus the hundreds of Klallams who had accepted a cash award from the government in 1928.[29]

Difficult questions about Indian identity arose at the reservations as well. Holding referenda there was not as simple as giving ballots to all adult residents. According to Assistant Commissioner Zimmerman, voters had to have a "demonstrable legal interest in the property or other affairs of the tribe"; they had to "'belong' on the reservation." On each western Washington reservation, however, were people of Indian descent who did not officially belong there. Some were on the rolls of other reservations, in most cases because they or their relatives had allotments at the other locations, and they were supposed to vote where enrolled. Conversely, every reservation roster included the names of people who were not in residence. When compared against tribal population figures, the number of people declared eligible to vote at each Puget Sound community suggests that the

BIA pared few absentees from voter lists but chose instead to consider them constructive residents. Some potential voters, however, must have been lost to BIA view.[30]

Once the IRA did apply to a reservation or a community, members of the community could vote to organize a government. This option raised new questions about the makeup and status of groups that identified themselves as Indian. Section 16 of the Wheeler-Howard Act provided, "Any Indian tribe or tribes, residing on the same reservation, shall have the right to organize for its common welfare. ... " Again because Indian organizations in the Puget Sound region were diverse in nature, because the BIA responded erratically to differences among the groups, and because members of the different groups were interrelated, implementing Section 16 was a more capricious process than its succinct phrases predicted.

One dilemma arose because some people around the Sound had already organized as Indian tribes on a basis besides their association with a reservation community. In the 1930s there were still tribes with governing councils and membership lists but no reservations. The constituencies of such tribes and of the reservation governments overlapped but did not coincide. In several instances, a tribe that had organized as a chapter of the NFAI used the same name as a reservation government but had a membership based on family lineages rather than connection to the reservation community. Such groups, some of them quite cohesive, did not meet the criteria for self-government under the IRA. Conversely, other groups that fit the act's criteria did not command their members' sole or principal loyalties. Given the challenges of applying the IRA in these circumstances, it is understandable that BIA officials did not distinguish themselves by their consistency. They applied the act differently to apparently comparable groups.

At Tulalip, as on several other reservations, the BIA had for several years referred questions regarding common property and issues of general interest to a council elected at an annual assembly of adult residents. Tulalip council members ostensibly represented two bands—Snoqualmie and Snohomish—which had contributed the bulk of the reservation population. In the BIA's view, by approving first the IRA and then a constitutional government, band members with homes on the reservation transferred their political loyalty to a new entity called the Tulalip Tribes. However, the Snohomish and Snoqualmie Tribes, which claimed many additional members outside the Tulalip Reservation, had organized separately to press claims against the United States in the 1920s, and they did not disband after 1934. Indeed, Snoqualmie chief Jerry Kenum informed the BIA that his tribe also wished to form an IRA government.[31]

Officials acknowledged Kenum's request but said that the IRA barred them from helping the Snoqualmies to organize unless and until they had a reservation. When Tulalip agency staff prepared a plan for future land acquisitions, they included a large tract for the Snoqualmies, adding the curious suggestion that it be "designated for all homeless Washington Coast Indians not otherwise provided for, but to be governed by the unalloted [sic] Snoqualmie band." However, the BIA did not follow through on this recommendation, and the Snoqualmie organization, like several others in similar circumstances, remained in political-legal limbo.[32]

In the case of two Klallam bands that also lacked reservations, the BIA took a different tack. Even though it had terminated relations with Klallams and overlooked them when holding referenda on the IRA, the BIA promoted their organization during the late 1930s. The Tulalip agency, responding to county officials' desire to clear Indian squatters from prime waterfront, pressed Collier to create reservations for the Klallams at Port Gamble and the Elwha River. Collier urged the agency to set up Klallam governments first.[33] The BIA bought land for both bands in 1936, but achieving the organization Collier desired took several more years because his advisors questioned whether Indians who had not voted on the IRA were eligible to organize under it, especially in the absence of a formally proclaimed reservation. On the other hand, Superintendent Upchurch and field agent George LaVatta did help Nooksack Indians to draft a constitution as provided in the IRA, even though they also lacked a reservation. "These Indians are organizing," LaVatta reported, "as a recognized tribe living within Whatcom County. ... "[34]

People who called themselves Steilacoom Indians, hoping to secure a reservation on the salt water, presented both the BIA and other Indians with more difficult questions about whether and how to apply the IRA. Although some of the Steilacooms appeared on BIA rolls "as being Nisqually Indians," most were unenrolled residents of towns in the vicinity of the Nisqually and Puyallup Reservations. Many, their lawyer said, had sent their children to Indian schools and received services at Indian medical facilities. But a warning from BIA personnel that they could reap IRA benefits only if they had half or more "Indian blood" apparently discouraged the Steilacooms.

Instead of pursuing plans for a separate government, the Steilacooms met with Indians of the Nisqually Reservation to consider establishing a single government for the two groups. The Nisquallys could have brought the Steilacooms into the IRA tent by adopting a constitution that made them eligible for membership in a new Nisqually organization, and some Nisquallys reportedly seemed interested in doing so. According to the Steilacooms' attorney, the proposal foundered because old, uneducated Nisquallys could not "grasp the significance of the new Act." But according to BIA officials, the Nisquallys did not frustrate the Steilacooms' plans so much as the Steilacooms stymied efforts to get the Nisquallys organized, injecting "disturbing claims" into the discussion about how to constitute a tribal government.[35]

By itself the Steilacoom issue does not explain why Nisqually Indians remained unorganized long after accepting the IRA, but such vexing questions about tribal membership were certainly deterrents. In 1937 negotiations with the Steilacooms took a back seat to developments that raised the membership issue in a different way. Some Indians sued in federal court to stop state game officers from interfering with fishing on the Nisqually River. When they won a temporary restraining order, their victory triggered questions to which Nisqually Reservation Indians gave conflicting responses: What made someone eligible to fish as permitted by the Medicine Creek Treaty? Were spouses of Nisqually Indians eligible? What about Indians from other bands named in the treaty?

A BIA agent told fifteen people at a meeting in 1940 that they could form an IRA government with power to answer these questions, but their answers would settle matters only on the reservation. A Nisqually government would lack power to regulate fishing outside reservation boundaries. Moreover, in order to organize a government, they would have to wade into a thicket of issues as thorny as those surrounding eligibility to fish. They would have to decide who was a Nisqually Indian entitled to help charter a government. The foundation for a tribal roll, BIA employees said, would be a census of 1905. However, some people on that census disputed the right of others on the list to call themselves Nisquallys. Apparently unable to move toward formal government either with or without the participation of the doubtful Nisquallys, and perhaps convinced that no government could control the activities that mattered most, Indians at Nisqually did nothing for several years.[36]

As the Tulalip and Nisqually cases show, the conception of Indian tribes embodied in the IRA did not allow for the multiple loyalties and interests that underlay the personal and political relationships of Indians' descendants in western Washington. In particular, the law disregarded kinship ties that crossed the boundaries of the reservations. Because the kinds of associations promoted in the IRA were tangential to many Indians' most

important affiliations, and because Indians had few incentives to emphasize associations of the IRA type, the act's self-government provision had
little initial impact on Indians' conceptions of themselves or on community relations around Puget Sound.

In many places there were no compelling reasons to set up a formal
government. Common resources were few and low in value, people with
legal interest in those resources were scattered, and there was little for a
government to do. To individuals intent on surviving the depression, tribal
governments were inconsequential unless they could organize the use of
wealth-generating resources. For this reason, several groups of Indians besides the Nisquallys—Lower Elwha Klallams, Nooksack and Skagit-
Suiattle public domain allottees, and residents of the Port Madison,
Squaxin Island, and Muckleshoot Reservations—declined for several
years to adopt IRA constitutions.[37] On two reservations—Swinomish and
Tulalip—residents did establish governments that took an early interest
in managing property and regulating the use of fish and game, but they
were unusual. The dominant concern of the new Puyallup government
was to dispose of remaining tribal lands and disburse tribal funds to members. In the words of Superintendent Upchurch, the Puyallup tribe was "a
very loosely integrated body" that had lost "the initiative for collective action ... in their scattered individual fight for existence."[38]

The organizers of IRA governments usually adopted boilerplate constitutions supplied by BIA staff. For the most part the constitutions reflected
officials' belief that small tribes with little or no land had few powers to
wield. When the national office disapproved the first Nooksack constitution, for instance, its memorandum explained, "The article on powers is ...
needlessly complicated and might actually lead some of the Indians to believe that they might exercise powers which, as a matter of fact, are nonexistent at the present time." The IRA, a BIA officer wrote, precluded a
Nooksack government from asserting any jurisdiction over its members'
public domain allotments. BIA lawyers and officers sent other proposed
constitutions back with instructions to change the political bodies' names,
membership provisions, and forms of organization.[39]

Moreover, written constitutions could not answer some ubiquitous and
intractable questions regarding tribal identity. Although the constitutions
spelled out qualifications for membership in the tribes, people both inside
and outside the tribal governments found such provisions hard to imple-
ment. As late as 1960, the BIA in western Washington reported that most
of the organized tribes under its supervision had not prepared rolls of
members. The multiplicity of individuals' affiliations was a major obstacle

to progress on the rolls. On the Tulalip Reservation, for instance, the BIA noted at least four active tribal groups besides the Tulalip Tribes, Inc. In other words, years after most Indians in the region had officially endorsed the IRA, many were still likely to identify themselves as members of tribes other than those organized pursuant to the IRA.[40]

Rather than settling questions about Indian identity and tribal boundaries, the Indian New Deal thus generated new questions. After organizing a reservation government, it was no easier than before to draw clear lines of demarcation around Indians who had complex and intimate relations with people beyond their reservations. Indicative of the uncertainties was Victor Johnson's answer when a congressman asked in 1944 how many Lummi Indians there were. "About 700," Johnson said, but added, "1,000 counting Nooksack and local scattered families." The IRA did not clarify the status of the "scattered families" or other people who identified with each other as Indians on a basis other than residence at the same reservation.[41]

The IRA and the tribal organizations it authorized had a negligible impact on the lives of most western Washington Indians at least through the 1940s. The new governments remained weak in part because John Collier's enemies gained power in Congress and frustrated his plans. Accusing him of the high-handedness he had criticized in his predecessors, they choked off funding for his programs and kept him under siege. By 1945 national political and economic developments had dealt Collier's opponents such a strong hand that they could immobilize him, so he resigned.[42]

One development that fortified Collier's critics was World War II, which reprised the effects of World War I. Again a high demand for labor and raw materials created opportunities that Indians were quick to seize, in western Washington as much as anywhere. Around Puget Sound, Indians streamed back into the lumber and fishing industries. They also leaped at the chance to earn high pay at naval shipyards, the Boeing airplane company, and the many other jobs that mobilization created. Again, too, the military took Indians—a higher proportion than in the earlier war—away from home to serve alongside non-Indians. After the war Tulalip superintendent F. A. Gross estimated that 297 Indians from his agency area had been in the armed forces.[43]

Wartime conditions gave Indians more reasons than ever to focus their aspirations on the world beyond reservation boundaries. Defense production jobs, like military service, brought them into new or increased contact with outsiders. Harriette Shelton found her three years on the Boeing assembly line "fascinating" because she worked with exotic migrants from

Texas and Kansas. A member of the Lummi business council, himself a veteran of overseas combat, noticed changes in Indians who had been "outside." They began to want what everyone else had, he said.[44]

Meanwhile, the nascent reservation governments labored under multiple handicaps. Both the BIA and tribe members expected the new councils to serve as conduits for communication between Indians and the federal government, but neither the BIA nor Indians could give the councils financial or technical support. War-related demands on members' time and gas rationing made it hard for councils to get quorums. In 1944, when the House Subcommittee on Indian Affairs held a hearing near Swinomish, the Puyallup Tribe's elected leaders could not attend because they were at work in defense jobs.[45]

The subcommittee came west in 1944 to investigate "whether the changed status of the Indian require[d] a revision of the laws and regulations affecting the American Indian." As a Senate subcommittee had already done, the House panel answered this query in the affirmative. It found that federal policy and programs operated "too much in the direction of perpetuating the Indian as a special-status individual rather than preparing him for independent citizenship." Lawmakers who agreed with this assessment set the direction of policy from the mid-1940s into the 1960s. As a result, the outlook for the New Deal tribal organizations remained cloudy.[46]

The word "termination" now stands for U.S. Indian policy in the postwar era because policy makers' goal was to terminate federal responsibility for Indians. Many Indians at the time decried some of the measures taken with that goal in mind, and virtually all Indians have since viewed termination policy as a symbol of federal perfidy. However, the diverse laws and administrative actions of the termination era proceeded from varied motivations, including some that Indians approved. Congress repudiated several of John Collier's cherished aims, but it also passed legislation that Collier and Indians supported, such as the act creating an Indian Claims Commission (ICC). Moreover, advocates of termination appealed to ideals that resonated with the values of many Indians. They talked of freeing Indians from oppressive paternalism, granting them equality with other citizens, and repealing discriminatory legislation. For these reasons some Indians, at least in western Washington, were not sure initially whether the postwar political wind was an ill one or even a new one.[47]

Lawrence Webster said in 1982 that it seemed as if he had heard about termination even in the 1930s. By 1944, when Webster appeared before the House subcommittee on behalf of Port Madison Indians, the voices of those who wanted to abolish the BIA were loud enough for all Americans to hear. Nonetheless, nearly a decade more passed before Congress went on record favoring total federal withdrawal from Indians' affairs. Thereafter the pace of change quickened. On instructions from the secretary of the interior, the BIA compiled reports for the different Indians in its care, evaluating their readiness to survive without supervision. The reports described western Washington Indians as competent people who had long managed their own affairs. By the end of 1953 Commissioner Glenn Emmons was soliciting comments on a draft bill to terminate the federal guardianship of twenty-one Puget Sound tribes.[48]

Three times—in 1953, 1955, and 1956—Emmons met with Indians in the region to talk up the new policy. On those occasions and others, competing conceptions of Indians underlay people's positions on termination, as they had underlain positions on the IRA. When federal officials referred to selected characterizations of Indians in order to explain and justify their proposed withdrawal, Indians explained their reactions by presenting alternative images of themselves. Historically determined self-images influenced Indians' responses to termination, but the prospect of termination prompted them to emphasize some traits more than others.

Advocates of termination could make sense of their plan to end federal tutelage and protection only by displacing a common presumption that Indians were not suited to participate in American economic life. Much like earlier prophets of rapid assimilation, they therefore stressed Indians' fundamental likeness to other competent Americans. On his visit in 1956, Emmons told assembled tribal delegates, "I want to see our Indian children ... be inspired with the thought that just because I am an Indian, it doesn't mean that I can't have ambition." Skeptics, Emmons added, "don't think that the Indians have the ability to do things or they think it will take one hundred years for an Indian to reach a point of development the same as any other people. Those people have never seen Indians."[49]

Some Indians who had responded to the IRA by emphasizing their historical autonomy and competence still had leadership roles in western Washington during Emmons's administration, and they took a prominent part in the deliberations regarding termination. Even when they realized the new implications of references to Indians' competence, they did not entirely change their tune. They continued to sing about their own powers, but they added some lyrics about other Indians who were weak and in need of protection.

When Wilfred Steve heard in 1952 that Congress was pressuring the BIA to relinquish control of tribes, he seemed pleased. The Tulalip council, he remarked, had submitted a proposal to take over BIA functions about fifteen years earlier. Later Steve told a gathering of tribal representatives that assimilation of Indian boys and girls into Washington society had long been Tulalip leaders' goal. Arguing that Indians must prove their competence, he said, "I don't want to be classed and you don't want to be classed as a degraded Indian."[50]

George Adams, a member of the Washington state legislature by 1954, was even more inclined than Steve to depict termination as the logical consequence of some Indians' proven ability to take care of themselves. But Adams also argued that Indians fell into two classes, and one consisted of people who still needed government care. He called upon "white Indians" to give up their protected status and leave declining federal aid for "poor Lo," the Indian who was unprepared to handle economic matters. Adams's willingness to push people with less than half Indian ancestry across the race line into the white camp and his insistence that Indians could trust federal officials to do the right thing infuriated spokesmen for other tribes. Nevertheless, many of his critics echoed his argument that certain Indians, especially the young ones, were more competent than others.[51]

Bennie George told Emmons privately that laziness, a fondness for alcohol, and a reluctance to mingle with whites made many Indians backward. The delegate from the Port Gamble Klallam band so impressed Emmons by reciting his own work history that the commissioner said, "If you were an example of your people on the reservation, you would be a wonderful group of people." George insisted, however, that he was different from most of the people he represented, and that they were still unfit for life without federal assistance.[52]

According to Joe Hillaire, the government could blame itself for the fact that some Indians were powerless to deal successfully with non-Indian society. The Lummi Reservation, he told a panel of lawmakers, was far smaller than required to fulfill Governor Stevens's 1855 promise of an allotment for every Indian. "We feel that we have been so badly abused, that we would be entitled to ask the great government of our country to forever leave the remaining land of the Indian tax-exempt; that it might be a haven, a refuge, for the less fortunate of our people."[53]

Images of victimized, culturally handicapped, habitually dependent Indians were useful in arguments against rapid termination. But in one-on-one encounters with federal officials, representatives of Puget Sound tribes, like Bennie George, were wont to dissociate themselves from such images and stress their individual or even their group strengths. When

Martin Hopie had his turn to meet with Emmons, the Lower Elwha band chairman said, "We are different from a lot of the Indians. We all went to school in the public schools. We have been paying taxes. We have had experience in every which way." That same day Emmons held separate brief conferences with delegates from seven other tribes, most of whom also indicated that termination did not frighten them because they were different from other Indians.[54]

After meeting with Indians around the country, Emmons conceded that Indians' diversity would require a variety of termination plans. Even so, he may have been surprised at the extent to which Puget Sound tribes' views on termination varied. When first informed of the new policy, members of the Duwamish Tribe, which had no reserved land and almost no government services, opposed federal withdrawal as contrary to the special relationship established by treaty. In contrast, Lower Elwha Klallams, who had only recently obtained the land and services they expected after the treaty, announced that they were prepared to dispense with federal protection. Squaxin Island and Nisqually councils, both speaking for tiny communities long neglected by the United States, came to opposite conclusions about termination. Squaxins found it acceptable so long as they could continue to hunt and fish, but Nisquallys adamantly opposed it for fear of losing their lands and fishery. While complaining that the BIA stifled their progress, Lummi and Tulalip reservation leaders also balked at the prospect of termination.[55]

After further meetings with federal officials and with each other, the different tribal organizations developed some common responses to termination policy. By 1955 all of them imposed two conditions on their willingness to contemplate federal withdrawal: preservation of some treaty-guaranteed rights and payment for rights already violated. The Lummi, Swinomish, and Tulalip councils soon took virtually identical stands against termination, probably because their spokesmen played leading roles in intertribal forums. Still, throughout the 1950s there remained considerable diversity in the answers Indians gave when asked whether and when their tribes could be terminated.

The most positive responses came from communities that were small, poor, and unorganized. Although they were presumptively the Indians most in need of federal protection, their responses were not irrational. People who had barely felt the BIA's hand in their daily affairs did not expect to miss it. When the Lower Elwha Klallams resolved to forgo U.S. guardianship, they noted that they had lived for generations with almost no services from the government. According to Lawrence Webster, there was no federal activity on his reservation at Port Madison in 1944. A local BIA official excused his inability to report on juvenile delinquency by saying that his employees were not in close touch with Indians. Indeed, the Indian bureau in western Washington was so shorthanded that it did not discharge even its primary duties properly: by the 1950s it had a huge backlog of probates and real estate transactions to process. Services such as law enforcement and health care were wholly beyond its capabilities.[56] No wonder plans for federal withdrawal rang few alarm bells in the smallest, most remote Indian communities.

On the other hand, in tribes with active governments and some revenue sources—tribes that arguably had the means to function without BIA supervision—resistance to termination was the norm. Although the councils of those tribes chafed at the BIA's heavy hand on their reins, they did not want to slip the federal bridle completely. They understood that common trust property, which tribe members would divide among themselves upon termination, was the principal reason for their existence. Without the common property, they could not finance services to replace those that would end when the BIA withdrew.[57]

In a bid to preserve the raison d'être for the reservation government he headed, Tandy Wilbur declared that federally protected assets were the source of Swinomish Indians' ability to conform to American values. By chartering a corporation and borrowing from the government, they had developed enterprises that had made them "independent citizens"— "people that can go around ... with the outside world ... with their heads up instead of hanging down as they used to in the past." "Just like another human being in this country ... ," Wilbur was disgusted with the BIA for blocking progress. However, he continued, "[w]e can't have anything as a corporation, as a tribe, or as an independent, or as an individual, if those tribal assets of ours are liquidated. ... "[58]

While nominally endorsing the termination bill's long-range goals, Wilbur and his allies raised several specific objections to rapid BIA withdrawal. Their most sophisticated and telling arguments reveal one of the reasons that termination plans for western Washington foundered. The government first had to identify the Indians to be terminated. Joe Hillaire brought this hurdle to Congress's attention in 1953. The Lummis he spoke for, Hillaire said, had long enjoyed the freedoms contemplated in the termination legislation. In fact, the only services connecting them with the BIA were those pertaining to land. But land services were "in a most deplorable state of entanglements." The bureau had not identified all the owners of Indian land. Although Indians were capable of managing their lands better than the BIA, only a twenty-five-year effort to straighten out titles would put them in a position to do so.[59]

Even if comments like Hillaire's were merely a clever stalling tactic, they indicated why the BIA could not hurry away from Puget Sound. Although bureau staff did not concede that they would need twenty-five years to sort out land titles, they knew they could liquidate and distribute the assets of Puget Sound Indians only after completing that forbidding task. They also needed rosters of people eligible to share in the tribes' assets. But again and again during hearings and meetings regarding the termination proposal, Indians and BIA personnel alike remarked that no tribes had complete membership rolls and that many persons appeared on more than one roll.[60]

Petitions pending in the Indian Claims Commission, although meant to facilitate termination, made it even harder to compile final rolls for reservations. Indians feared that the government would relinquish its responsibilities before it paid off old obligations. To allay this fear, the BIA inserted in the termination bills a proviso preserving the tribes' claims against the United States. But as long as ICC claims and termination bills awaited decision, people who held membership both in a tribe that had petitioned the ICC and in an organized reservation community were reluctant to drop one membership in favor of the other.[61]

The ICC may also have fueled opposition to termination when it began issuing awards that were too small to underwrite Indians' transition to full citizenship. The commission's first decisions regarding western Washington, which came in the late 1950s, defined tribal territories restrictively and assigned those territories a paltry value. Convinced that the government had again failed to fulfill century-old promises, people of indigenous descent had a new reason to resist termination.[62]

In 1954 Superintendent Raymond Bitney speculated that Indians of the western Washington agency were trying to talk the termination bill to death.[63] If that was indeed their strategy, it appears to have worked. Even though early BIA reports depicted Bitney's charges as nearly ready for termination, and even though most of those charges declared themselves willing to work toward emancipation, no bill to terminate tribes around Puget Sound passed Congress. Nevertheless, BIA officials continued to assume well into the 1960s that preparing Indians to leave the federal fold was their principal mission. As late as 1963 the assistant director of the BIA's area office in Portland asked superintendents to "[m]ake suggestions for 'guided acculturation'—action which you think would be valuable in helping your Indian people move from their present culture to major culture (either as individuals or as groups)." In response he received a report on the Lummi Tribe that concluded, "[I]t is reasonable to predict that the reservation population will be absorbed into the advancing and aggresive [*sic*] non-Indian dominated community within 20 years. Our job is to accelerate and expand our services in preparing Indian people for successful and graceful assimilation into the changing community."[64]

Much as assimilationists had done at the turn of the century, Commissioner Emmons proposed to prepare Indians for full citizenship by providing them with more BIA services rather than fewer. In 1956 his plans included economic development programs aimed at maximizing the support Indians could glean from their lands and resources.[65] At the same time, however, the bureau was also trying to remove Indians from their reservations. The primary programmatic means of speeding Indians' assimilation during the termination policy era became known as relocation.

The Indian relocation program offered subsidies for vocational training and incentives to move to distant urban areas, where opportunities for employment (and reasons to conform to non-Indian norms) would presumably increase. However, because the program's budget and staff were severely limited, and because off-reservation employment was a long-standing tradition for Indians of Puget Sound, relocation had a negligible impact on the self-definitions and associations of Indians from that region.[66]

The BIA opened a relocation assistance office for western Washington at Olympia in 1957, not long after tribal representatives asked Emmons why they had no access to a program that Indians in eastern Washington already enjoyed. Shortly afterward, a national recession reduced demand for labor. Administrators blamed Indians' awareness of the downturn for the small number of western Washington residents relocated, but they also complained that it was hard to publicize the program to thousands of scattered, loosely organized people. Interest was highest when fishing, sawmills, and logging closed for the season. Yet each year in the program's short life, the BIA helped only a couple dozen families to move to cities in California or to Denver, Dallas, or Cleveland. Moreover, a substantial proportion of those families came back after a few months.

When many of the returnees took jobs off the reservations in the Puget Sound area, BIA staff implied that their services had had the desired effect. More likely the training and relocation services had merely expanded opportunities for Indians to follow their venerable tradition of seeking wealth in short-term, extracommunity activities. Jimmy Cook of Port Angeles, who praised the new program in a letter to the *Post-Intelligencer*, saw relocation not as an ill-conceived effort to detribalize him but as an opportunity for an enterprising person "to start on his own" toward proving his worth.[67]

The most significant effect of relocation and termination programs was an ironic one. The programs aimed to end Indians' peculiar status and rode a wave of rhetoric about common humanity, yet most Indians emerged from the termination era with a heightened sense that they were different from other Americans. Termination policy reflected nationwide pressure for cultural and political conformity, yet it confirmed Indians' abnormality. Applicants for relocation services, even if they hoped to blend into an urban population potpourri, had to identify themselves first as Indians. And people who attended the BIA's many meetings about termination, no matter how they heard themselves characterized there, knew that they were meeting as Indians. By consulting with delegates and councillors from each tribe, the commissioner and his staff also reinforced groupings and institutions that everyone regarded as Indian.

Intertribal organizations were among the groups invigorated. In June 1945 Wilfred Steve notified tribal councils of an effort to form a central organization of Washington Indians. With each letter he enclosed the constitution of the Northwestern Federation of American Indians and asked recipients to suggest changes. Numerous people, he said, saw a need to revive and update the NFAI because "[n]early all the problems dealing with the Indians are somewhat in common." The Tulalip agency superintendent linked this renewed interest in intertribal activity to the visibility of a new organization, the National Congress of American Indians.[68]

Steve announced a meeting that drew representatives from ten tribes—Quinault, Skokomish, Klallam, Lummi, Port Gamble, Tulalip, Duwamish, Nooksack, Snoqualmie, and Swinomish. But a dilemma that had plagued the NFAI for years—the question whether dues should be assessed at a flat rate per tribe or in proportion to tribal populations—apparently proved insoluble. By 1949 the federation had disappeared from the scene.[69]

Undaunted, Steve proposed to address Indians' common problems in a new forum. By 1954 he and other former NFAI members were billing themselves as spokesmen for the Inter-tribal Council of Western Washington Indians. A council of tribes was appropriate because the pressures and incentives of the termination period had also inspired Indians to revitalize the separate tribal organizations they had founded during the teens and twenties. The call to form the umbrella group therefore went to all tribes that had participated in the NFAI and sued in the Court of

Claims in 1927. The purpose of the new organization, according to Joe Hillaire, was to respond to the bill that would terminate all western Washington tribes.

Probably because the new group promptly called for Superintendent Bitney's ouster, Bitney complained to his superiors that the "so-called Intertribal Council" opposed all federal policy and aimed to force the BIA to do Indians' bidding. Nevertheless, while claiming that Indians' interest in the organization was low, Bitney and his successors sent staff to all Intertribal Council meetings, which continued into the 1960s, and often brought questions of policy to the council for discussion.[70]

BIA personnel assumed that they should prepare termination plans not just for people with interests in reservation resources but also for off-reservation Indians who claimed treaty rights. Moreover, the bureau routinely solicited comments about policy and programs from nonreservation groups. The Inter-tribal Council therefore included tribes without reservations as well as reservation governments. Any Indians could be members of the Inter-tribal Council, Joe Hillaire said, if they functioned as a group and traced their origins to some original tribe. At the same table with directors of the federally chartered Tulalip corporation sat delegates from tribes such as Snohomish and Samish, whose members' common attribute was descent from Indians of nineteenth-century bands rather than interest in reservation resources.[71]

But even as federal policy brought Indians from the two types of organizations together to plot joint responses, it highlighted the differences between them. To be sure, the representatives of landless tribes voiced sympathy for the reservation tribes' desire to keep their lands; and all tribes insisted in unison that a proviso preserving treaty-guaranteed rights should be part of any withdrawal bill. However, it was hard to see the relevance of termination legislation to people who had no trust assets. At a meeting to discuss the need for a supratribal organization, a Lummi man advocated separate bills for reservation and nonreservation tribes. Lyman Kavanaugh thought the proposed legislation and the meeting were more pertinent to reservation Indians than to the Samish Indians he represented. Whereas reservation groups wanted to control their land without BIA supervision, Kavanaugh said, the Samish were just fighting for a cash settlement.[72]

Federal officials likewise saw that termination of the landless tribes and termination of the reservations involved different considerations. The BIA's area director, citing the varied conditions and divergent interests of Indians in western Washington, counseled against an omnibus bill. Having heard from BIA staff that the sole basis for the landless tribes' cohesion was the members' desire to share in treaty benefits, a congressional committee expressed hope that mutual termination of the treaties would be sufficient to dispense with such tribes.[73]

In the Inter-tribal Council, reservation-based tribes and so-called aboriginal tribes continued to participate as equivalents. However, even though (or perhaps because) their memberships overlapped and family ties linked many of the tribes' members to each other, relations between leaders of the two kinds of tribes were often awkward and eventually strained. The strain became acute in the early 1950s, when Indians who had not affiliated with the reservation governments, backed by the BIA, challenged the right of those governments to monopolize control of resources reserved by treaty.[74]

Superintendent Bitney contributed to the tension by encouraging the "aboriginal" tribes to claim a share of reservation assets. When the Tulalip tribal corporation demanded an opportunity to lease out land that had long been part of the agency reserve, Bitney—reluctant to grant the request—advanced or approved a theory that the land belonged not to the Tulalip Tribes, Inc., but to the successors of all Indians who endorsed the Point Elliott Treaty. The Tulalip corporation was a post-treaty formation, he reasoned, and had no right to arrogate to itself all the proceeds of land set aside for numerous aboriginal tribes. Bitney's argument called into question the very economic incentives that had made IRA government attractive to some Tulalip residents, and it vindicated people who had retained their membership in the older, landless bands. Indeed, his stance apparently emboldened the Snoqualmie Tribe and a professed chief of the aboriginal Swinomish Tribe to ask for a share of the rent from Tulalip common lands.[75]

Thus, by simultaneously threatening and paying attention to tribal organizations during the 1950s, federal officials breathed new life into them—descent-based and reservation-based tribes alike. None of the organizations enjoyed robust health, however. Along with the uncertainties about their membership, fiscal and jurisdictional conditions poisoned their air. Only two tribal governments had sources of revenue for modest public services. Thanks to fish traps, oyster culture, and a sawmill, the Swinomish Community had $113,555 in income in 1953. That year the Tulalip corporation's take from land leases and a resort was $50,506. Besides employing business managers and providing tribe members with occasional aid, both tribes supported tiny police forces and part-time courts. Elsewhere, however, Indian governments presided over empty treasuries.[76]

None of the governing councils could exert much control over their presumed constituents or over activities within their territories. Besides poverty, their constraints included the fact that the Indians they hoped to govern had scattered "from here to breakfast," as one Suquamish councillor said. At the same time, the reservations harbored a growing number of people who did not believe themselves subject to tribal government regulation. The automobile culture and Americans' postwar migration to the suburbs had stimulated developers' interest in reservation lands; and within the boundaries of several reservations, on fee land and leased trust land, non-Indian residential subdivisions and businesses were springing up.[77]

Some tribal governments admitted and further assured their weakness by inviting state political subdivisions to assume jurisdiction on the reservations. Transfer of jurisdiction from the federal government to the state, permitted by Congress in 1953, was on the terminationists' agenda; and some tribal leaders feared it would mean even greater neglect of their needs. Nevertheless, several reservation councils, citing the law enforcement vacuum created by the BIA's inaction and their own impotence, thought the arrangement worth a try.[78]

It is not surprising, given the tribal governments' lack of resources and limited functions, that few people took an active interest in them. Elections attracted considerably less than half the eligible voters in all tribes except Swinomish. A 1956 Stanford Research Institute study concluded, "Many tribes are loosely organized. In some cases the Tribal Council represents only the resident part of the tribe. These factors make it difficult to deal with some tribal groups in matters pertaining to tribes as a whole."[79]

In sum, American officials' desire to deal with coherent Indian tribal groups in western Washington was little closer to fulfillment in 1956 than in 1856. Policies and conditions of the New Deal and termination eras had prompted people around Puget Sound to create or revive and affiliate with Indian political organizations but had also kept those organizations weak. Both during the period when it succored tribal organizations and during the years when it proposed to "emancipate" tribal organizations, the federal government withheld from those organizations the means to command either strong loyalty from rank-and-file members or respect from powerful non-Indians.

Contrary to the intentions of government officials, federal laws and administrative measures of the 1930s, 1940s, and 1950s had also failed to clarify the parameters of Indian identity in western Washington. In 1960, as before the 1930s, U.S. law and policy gave people two overlapping but sometimes conflicting bases for identifying themselves as Indians and as members of specific tribes; descent from particular ancestors and affiliation with an Indian community. Even after new tribal governments appeared in the 1930s, disparate principles continued to provide grounds for classifying or refusing to classify individuals and groups as Indians. Each organized tribe had criteria for admitting people to membership, but none of the organized tribes employed those criteria to compile definitive rolls of their members. Applying the criteria of membership remained difficult for all kinds of tribes as well as for government agencies, because most potential tribe members also had strong reasons to affiliate with other tribes and even with other racial groups. Consequently, at the end of the 1950s the thousands of people around Puget Sound who considered themselves Indians and tribe members still had varied reasons for doing so.[80]

8 Treaty Fishing Rights
An Emblem Unfurled

After the 1950s one provision of the century-old treaties negotiated by Isaac Stevens became the predominant emblem of Indian identity in western Washington—the provision for off-reservation fishing. To say this is not to assert that fishing and treaties were previously unimportant to descendants of indigenous people. But the twentieth century was more than half over before they focused almost single-mindedly on the treaty-reserved right to fish as the best expression of their relation to non-Indians and thus a cardinal symbol of their Indianness.

Following World War II and particularly by the late 1950s, Indians could see themselves reflected in non-Indians' eyes as poor, backward, and isolated. They responded in typically varied ways. Many sought spiritual and cultural validation of their worth in new or revived religious ceremonies, festivals, and pan-Indian organizations. Many instead or also took pride in the treaties, identifying themselves with the earliest recipients of solemn U.S. promises. Increasingly, the promise they cited was one that Governor Stevens had included in every treaty: "The right of taking fish at usual and accustomed grounds and stations is further secured to said Indians in common with all citizens of the Territory. . . . "[1] Converging pressures spurred diverse people to proclaim this right the definitive element of their Indian heritage. A 1974 victory in federal court subsequently made the emblem official.

Before the 1950s the fishing issue simmered without boiling over. State arrests of Indian fishers and disputes about tribal fish traps prompted BIA superintendents to put the issue on the agenda for their regional meeting in 1940, and the concerns they expressed moved Indian commissioner John Collier to order a study of Washington and Oregon tribes' fishing and hunting rights. The ensuing report of attorney Edward Swindell lamented that whites had curtailed Indian fishing in ways not envisioned at the treaties, but it gave little reason to hope for reduced interference.

The courts, Swindell observed, had approved whites' actions. Indeed, just as Swindell was completing his work in 1942, the Supreme Court issued a ruling that seemed to affirm the states' authority to restrict Indian fishing. On one hand, the decision in *Tulee v. Washington* exempted a Yakima fisher from state license requirements, saying that a venerable rule of law gave Indians the benefit of the doubt when treaty language was ambiguous, that the treaty said nothing about licensing, and that licenses were not "indispensable" to the state's effort to conserve fish. On the other hand, the justices assumed that the state could enforce true conservation regulations against Indians. In Swindell's view, Indians' only recourse after *Tulee* was to plead with lawmakers for pity and special privileges. Noting that Indians' "heritage of the past and its freedom from man-made restrictions is both fresh and uppermost in their minds," he predicted that it would be hard to make them see just how narrow their acknowledged rights were.[2]

Swindell's memorandum gave the BIA an excuse to shove the whole kettle of fish onto a back burner. According to historian Donald Parman, the report had no impact on the administration of Indian affairs. The bureau declined or neglected to petition the Washington state legislature on Indians' behalf. Instead, on the assumption that *Tulee* was the last and best attainable word regarding the treaty right, BIA personnel advised Indians to observe all state laws except license requirements when fishing outside reservations. The 1946 arrest of three Indians who set nets in the Nooksack River roused spokesmen for the Northwestern Federation of American Indians (NFAI) to demand that federal officials try again to alleviate the tensions surrounding state enforcement of hunting and fishing laws. For two subsequent decades, however, federal action consisted of little more than occasionally reminding state officers that Indians had special rights deserving of respect. Whether and how to assert those rights was for Indians—usually individuals—to decide.[3]

Most Indians who wanted to fish enjoyed improved conditions during World War II, thanks to the partial victory in *Tulee* and to an exodus of other harvesters from fishing grounds.[4] No one pretended, however, that the critical issues had been resolved. As Swindell had predicted, some Indians continued to act on an understanding of their rights that differed from the interpretations of state and BIA officials. Often they faced prosecution as a result. In addition, a state ban on traps and other fixed gear ensured that white commercial fishers would pursue migrating salmon in open waters with gear that few Indians could afford, taking most of the fish before they could reach Indian nets in the rivers. Consequently, Indians' proportion of the total catch sank below 10 percent for all species of salmon.[5]

In 1946 state fisheries managers indicated a desire to negotiate with Indians for coordinated conservation measures. More specifically, however, they pressed tribal officers to make Indians follow state rules when fishing on the reservations, where the state government had no jurisdiction. A further reduction in the Indian catch was necessary, they argued, in order to conserve salmon that migrated through the reservations to spawning grounds. While tribal spokesmen were pleased that state officials acknowledged them and their interest in fish, they were irked that the same officials permitted whites to intercept fish bound for reservation waters. The threat to salmon survival, George Adams protested, was not from Indian nets but from state-licensed fishing outside the Sound and from enterprises that despoiled salmon habitat, especially dams and lumber companies.[6]

Galling as it was, the suppression of Indians' fishing had not yet goaded them into concerted resistance, primarily because they were not yet certain that the other staple of their livelihood—wage work—was also failing them. As World War II ended, their newly expanded place in the workforce even gave Indians reason for optimism. In 1944, when the House Subcommittee on Indian Affairs asked tribal leaders to summarize the conditions they faced, the Muckleshoot council responded: "The Muckleshoot people live principally by wage economy and their principal problem is, in general, to maintain working operations. This, for the past few years, has been no difficulty." The federal government could be of most help to Indians, the council concluded, "by maintaining a condition of prosperity which will demand our labor."[7]

A general condition of prosperity did continue. Although Indians lost income when soldiers returned to civilian life and defense contractors laid workers off, the BIA's western Washington agency was officially upbeat about Indians' prospects as late as 1953. (Perhaps a desire to see Indians who could function without federal guardianship prompted BIA staff to don glasses with a rosy tint early in the termination policy period.) Investigators found that living standards had improved since 1934 for Indians in the Puyallup area and on the Muckleshoot, Suquamish, Tulalip, and Swinomish Reservations. The nonreservation Duwamish had earnings comparable to those of non-Indians. Even where there had been no improvement in Indians' economic circumstances, most of them continued to support themselves by wage work. Only in the tiny Nisqually community had conditions deteriorated "due to the reduction in the fish run." Reports such as this justified Commissioner Emmons's 1956 comment that western Washington Indians were "comparatively well off." "'I know of no cases of poverty ... ,'" Emmons told a Seattle newspaper. "'There is a good labor market here and many of them are finding jobs in industry or other places.'"[8]

In reality, many Puget Sound Indians were nearing the base of the slippery economic slope they had been negotiating for most of the century. As Washington's economy had changed, their heavy reliance on unskilled and seasonal wage work had become a liability. In 1963, when the BIA surveyed several reservations in order to determine how fast the Indian residents could move into mainstream society, it saw a more discouraging picture. Employment sufficient for year-round self-support was the exception by then. Ten to 40 percent of Lummis and up to 60 percent of Muckleshoots were unemployed at a time. Between one-quarter and three-quarters of the Indians received welfare payments at least part of the year. On the Tulalip Reservation, according to another report from 1963, fifty-two of ninety-two families lived through the winter on state assistance, and annual family income averaged $1,428—drastically less than the national median of $5,700. In such circumstances, a concurrent loss of fishing opportunities would be frightening and maddening.[9]

How sharply Indians' economic status declined after 1950 is hard to determine. BIA statistics, which were barely more than guesses, profiled different features in different decades, frustrating comparative analysis. Furthermore, the negative emphasis of the bureau's 1963 report could reflect the spirit of the times—the rediscovery of poverty in America—more than a significant deterioration in Indians' material well-being. Although the number of welfare recipients does indicate that a low standard of living was the norm on reservations, welfare statistics are not compelling evidence of an increase in poverty. State public assistance for unemployed Indians, unknown before the war, provided a convenient way to measure poverty that could have existed previously, unacknowledged or undocumented.[10]

Whether Indians actually grew poorer during the 1950s and 1960s does not matter so much here as the fact that virtually everyone thought they did. Both Indians and non-Indians fostered the belief that poverty was endemic in Indian communities. "The Plight of Our Indians: Tribes See Little Hope for Future," announced a *Post-Intelligencer* headline in 1964. A few years later the *Seattle Times* carried stories entitled "Poverty on Indian

Reservations Is Evident at Port Gamble" and "State Indians Worse Off Than Negroes. ... " In response to a *Times* article celebrating Indians' integration into public schools, the editor of *Northwest Indian News* argued that Indians could not hope for equality as long as they began school with material as well as physical and emotional handicaps and quickly became convinced of their inferiority. Muckleshoot leader Annie Garrison complained to a *Times* reporter about a story that characterized her people as poor; but moments earlier she had said that hers was one of the poorest tribes in the state.[11]

Poverty was all the more demoralizing for Indians when contrasted with their wartime employment and the regional postwar boom. As fingers of suburban development reached out to touch the Muckleshoot Reservation, a BIA study noted, "there [was] the incongruous vista of modern housing in the $15,000 to $25,000 range adjacent to very substandard wooden shacks without adequate water or sanitation."[12]

What had gone wrong? Had Indians been pushed off the path to prosperity, voluntarily turned back, or unwittingly taken the wrong fork? Each of these explanations had its adherents. In reporter Robert Browning's opinion, Indians had made choices that doomed them to poverty, particularly the decision to slake their "incurable thirst" for alcohol and the refusal to urge their children to compete with whites at school or work. A Stanford Research Institute survey of 1956 came to a similar conclusion.

> Problems of employment center principally around Indian attitudes and education. While there is no reported general opposition of employers to hiring Indians, the Indians themselves feel that they are not acceptable, and for this reason do not seek employment as aggressively as non-Indians. Where there is discrimination, it is usually based on poor work habits of the individual involved.

Muckleshoot Indians, the Stanford researchers added more caustically, "are generally unwilling to work, show little responsibility, and apparently prefer to subsist on welfare. ... The local employment agency is reluctant to recommend Indians for jobs other than common labor for fear that employers will discontinue use of the service."[13]

Indians and sympathetic non-Indians often laid the blame for Indians' destitution on prejudiced whites. Annie Garrison told Emmons that the taunts of whites contributed to Muckleshoot children's propensity to leave school. Swinomish spokesman Tandy Wilbur said that there were still Indians on the reservations who could not go out "to feel their own way around" and find jobs because "those jobs" were not open to them. Other analysts added that Indians' response to actual or anticipated discrimination reinforced the impact of prejudice, helping to power a vicious cycle of inadequate education, reliance on unskilled labor, poor health, lack of capital, and fear of competing with whites.[14]

The desire to explain and ameliorate Indians' poverty brought special laws and institutions for Indians under public scrutiny once again. Commentators argued about whether reservations kept the vicious cycle spinning or promised to break it. In a 1967 article that described the Port Gamble Klallam community as an eyesore and as Hooverville West, a reporter queried whether rehabilitating the reservation would just make it harder for Indians to give up the "voluntary segregation" that kept them poor. Those who saw reservations as infantilizing wanted to push the Indian residents out into new geographic and occupational territory, where they would learn what it took to survive in the real world. Other observers argued for investment in the reservations on the theory that Indians who managed and worked in their own healthy institutions would gain confidence to deal with the world outside. Sebastian Williams, manager of the Tulalip Tribes' businesses, said he opposed segregation for Indians; yet he wanted to see the reservations "industrialized" for the sake of residents stranded there by the collapse of their traditional mainstays—fishing and lumbering.[15]

Some commentators believed that reservation Indians were the least enterprising of the race, left behind when their more ambitious and capable relatives abandoned the resource-poor enclaves for urban areas. This theory may have been flattering to Indians in the cities, but it did not explain why many of them, too, faced discouraging conditions. Indians in Seattle, surveyed by sociologists in 1971, fared poorly compared with non-Indians. Their unemployment rate was twice and their median income was half that of whites.[16]

The identification of Indians and Indian institutions with poverty, whatever its causes, was humiliating for Indian community representatives. At nineteenth-century intervillage gatherings, well-bred native men had commonly referred to themselves rhetorically as poor, but most had demonstrated their power to be other than poor by lavishing food and gifts on their listeners. Halfway through the twentieth century, self-denigrating rhetoric was still or again a common feature of Indian leaders' formal relations with important outsiders, but it was no longer the rhetoric of people who were confident of their power to attract wealth and win outsiders' respect. Indeed, the modern speakers typically hoped by their words to stimulate listeners to give Indians money rather than accept gifts from them.

If the modern descendants of indigenous people were to take pride in the Indian identity ascribed to them, they would have to base it on something other than an ability to amass wealth or even to maintain independence through the adroit use of resources and opportunities. One long-standing basis for Indian self-assertion and pride was the claimed right to redeem treaty pledges. But to many Indians, the treaties' potential seemed on the wane by the 1950s. Therefore, during this period as in previous eras, Indians also explored other ways to prove themselves worthy of esteem.

Many people, particularly in northern counties of western Washington, found a source of self-esteem in religious activities. Anthropologist June Collins observed that the religious life of Upper Skagit Indians was especially vibrant during the period 1942 to 1969. Not only did Shakers and spirit dancers remain active, but Pentecostals also made converts. Some Indians participated in the ceremonies of all three faiths, each of which gave worshipers a way to demonstrate that they, like their nineteenth-century ancestors, had supernatural assistance. However, rather than ensuring proficiency in exploits that enriched the actor and impressed outsiders, fruitful twentieth-century devotions usually brought good health, power to avoid or survive hardship, and the approval and support of close friends and kin.[17]

Three ethnologists who studied modern spirit dances came to different conclusions about the dances' purpose but agreed that the participants satisfied a need for positive evaluations of their worth—evaluations they rarely received in contacts with non-Indians. John Kew saw status enhancement as the principal purpose of the dances in British Columbia that Tulalip, Swinomish, Lummi, and Nooksack Indians attended during the 1960s. But Joyce Wike, who observed dances on the Swinomish Reservation in the 1930s, and Pamela Amoss, who wrote about dances in the Nooksack Valley during the 1970s, concluded that the dancers' aim was not so much to boost their status in traditional ways as to express their individuality in a supportive context.[18]

If religious displays had the effect of elevating Indians in others' eyes, those eyes were usually Indian. To participate in spirit dancing, individuals had to belong to an Indian community, and their participation confirmed that community members accepted them. The hosts of a successful dance expressed and contributed to the pride of a group that identified itself as Indian. Kew noticed that speeches at the large ceremonials stressed kinship ties and a shared dedication to maintaining Indian traditions—themes that reflected participants' desire for inclusion and recognition both as Indian individuals and as members of particular Indian families or communities.[19]

Some dancers were proud when whites showed interest in or amazement at their performances, but they were also wary of spectators whose respect they could not be sure of. A non-Indian who witnessed dances at north Sound reservations reported in the *Tacoma News Tribune/Sunday Ledger* that visitors were expected to leave after the chief thanked them for coming. "If the whites don't take the hint," he wrote, "there may be a filibuster until they do. There is no great objection to a small number of white visitors if they are genuinely interested in the dances, but large groups of curiosity seekers are definitely discouraged from staying."[20]

Spirit dances and Shaker meetings were not the only Indian gatherings that could boost people's morale and validate positive aspects of their ethnicity. Being recognized at other ceremonial occasions—funerals and namings, for instance—likewise affirmed an individual's place in an estimable group. Harriette Shelton remembered with pleasure being asked to sing her song at a naming ceremony on the Lummi Reservation. "There were people there from all over," she said, "but we all came from the same family." In other words, when those people recognized her, they acknowledged her Indian family tree's noble breadth.[21]

There were also arenas—some of them new—where strangers could celebrate a shared Indian identity. Indians opened a Seattle service center in 1960, and two top staffers told a journalist that such an institution would help Indians from all tribes to realize the best of both the cultures they had to live in. After World War II some reservations revived their summer festivals, attracting Indians from a wide area for activities such as secular dancing, canoe racing, craft sales, and ball games. City powwows, too, nourished assorted Indians' sense of belonging to a self-respecting racial group.[22]

The summer gatherings and powwows are also proof that white bigotry and indifference did not completely discourage Indian efforts to project a better image to outsiders. Indeed, anthropologist John Dewhirst characterized Coast Salish summer festivals of the 1960s as "the direct expression of an Indian identity to large numbers of assembled whites." Powwow organizers advertised their events to whites, involved white dignitaries as special guests, and promoted dances and regalia that met white expectations about Indians. The sponsors were usually Indians who had had frequent contact with whites, had become familiar with whites' stereotypes of Indians, and had even internalized many white middle-class values. At Lummi after the war, the annual Stommish (warrior festival) was a project of the American Legion chapter on the reservation. By appealing to images of Indians that had positive connotations for both whites and Indians, festival leaders sought to "upgrade" their identity, Dewhirst argued. A speaker at the Stommish in 1968 opened his explanation of a public naming ceremony by saying, "The day is upon us when the lowly Indian has to prove his identity."[23]

Some individuals attracted positive attention from whites, as members of an earlier generation had, for their ability to describe Indians of bygone eras. During the late 1940s and 1950s anthropologists June Collins, Wayne Suttles, William Elmendorf, Sally Snyder, and others sought out geriatric Indians willing to talk about the past, recorded the lore they knew, and used it to assemble images of Indian culture before its alleged disintegration.[24] Self-identified authorities on Indian legends and ancient ceremonial life continued to find broader audiences as well. Although a few popular books—for example, Murray Morgan's *Skid Road* and Betty McDonald's novel *The Egg and I*—eschewed romantic depictions of local Indians, there remained a market for tales and performances that evoked Indians unspoiled by modern civilization.[25]

Like her father before her, Harriette Shelton catered to the market, becoming a teacher of Indian language and crafts. For twenty years she held classes, attended mostly by white children, in her home. A *Seattle Times* Sunday magazine in 1958 showed her surrounded by her father's artifacts from many native cultures—beaded buckskin from the Great Plains as well as local cedar carvings. Joe Hillaire, who credited Harriette's father William with teaching him to carve totems, also made energetic efforts to give non-Indians a positive view of Indian culture. In 1965 a *Times* reporter found Hillaire on the Suquamish Reservation, teaching songs to Explorer Scouts who performed them at a nearby tourist attraction.[26]

Hillaire wanted to show that Indians brought an honorable history to their contemporary dealings with whites. In 1954 he promoted a plan to have the Inter-tribal Council and the Washington Department of Parks jointly sponsor a centennial commemoration of the Point Elliott Treaty. He proposed to erect at the treaty conference site a longhouse representing "concepts of primitive life which have seeded themselves fondly in the minds of the American people." While assuring a reporter that the pageant would be a big tourist attraction, Hillaire expounded a version of history that lent Indians' modern circumstances some dignity and an aura of promise.

An idealized account of the treaty was central to Hillaire's image-making. The longhouse, he said, would symbolize the wisdom of the chiefs who chose peace instead of bloodshed when settlers overran their homeland. Realizing without bitterness that " 'the course of human events' " had changed their world and made further change necessary, the Indian treaty makers moved their people onto reservations. With abiding faith that the Great White Father would take care of them as promised, they and their offspring adjusted to a new way of life, accepted American citizenship, and aided the country in wartime. Hillaire expressed a concluding wish that the treaty centennial would prompt everyone to take an inventory of the past, look beyond Indians' immediate problems, and plan for the next hundred years of inevitable change.[27]

If a celebration proceeded as Hillaire proposed, it did not leave a well-marked paper trail. I could find no reference to a local treaty commemoration except in 1961, when Hillaire played the role of Lummi signer Chowitshoot at groundbreaking ceremonies for a commercial Indian theme park.[28] Nevertheless, as the anniversary of the treaty approached, other events were precipitating a reevaluation of Indians' circumstances much like the one Hillaire hoped for. Many people were talking about the treaties, and that talk was pushing more and more residents of western Washington to take inventory of developments since 1855, to consider Indians' contemporary status, and to think about effecting change in the future. The most common focus of discussion was the fishing rights clause.

Although the treaties had long given the descendants of indigenous people a way to understand their relations with white Americans, those understandings had never been uniform or static. To the people who met with reformer Felix Brunot in 1871, the treaties were a U.S. commitment to dispense money and services that would identify Indians as "good." To Thomas Bishop and leaders of the NFAI in 1922, the treaties' most important feature was a promise to boost Indians into first-class citizenship by providing each one with eighty acres of land or the cash equivalent. At a summer festival in the 1960s, Indian speakers were more likely to characterize a treaty as a pledge of mutual respect between races. Dewhirst heard the leader of a Lummi dance troupe say to the crowd at one Stommish:

> "We here in Lummi still exercise the Treaty Day, when the Great White Father sent to our lands a man speaking on his behalf to the Indian people. While our people were meeting with that man, they put on the feathers and wore them proud with honor and dignity, that the marks they placed on this paper that was sent from Washington was gonna be honored and respected among the people. . . ."[29]

Whenever whites' respect for Indians was in question during the 1960s, talk was likely to turn to fishing. Although the topic was hardly a new one, conflict about fishing escalated sharply after 1950, until it nearly preempted other issues between Indians and non-Indians. Tandy Wilbur's 1961 statement to a congressional panel shows the enlarged significance attributed by then to the treaty provision for fishing.

> We the Indians feel that we have paid dearly for this one privilege from which we can earn a living. We have ceded over a vast rich territory which has contributed much to the economy of our country. The only ... concession reserved for us was this right of taking fish which has been a godsend at times to a people in near destitution.[30]

Wilbur emphasized fishing because that was the subject of the hearing. On the other hand, it was Indians' insistence on a generous reading of the treaty fishing provision that had spurred the joint committee on fisheries to devote a day to Indian concerns in the first place.

Several converging developments account for Indians' growing preoccupation with fishing. Non-Indian fishing expanded and salmon populations declined in the 1950s and 1960s—the very time when Indians' economic marginalization magnified salmon's importance for them as a source of food and supplemental income. State fisheries managers responded to a need for conservation measures by enacting regulations that discriminated against those Indians who fished at traditional places along rivers and shorelines.[31] Especially after enjoying prosperity and hearing antifascist propaganda during World War II, many Indians resented the discrepancy between their dwindling opportunities and America's egalitarian ideals. Those who wanted to resist state limitations on their fishing found encouragement in the victories of the civil rights movement and in a general surge of ethnic pride during the 1960s. They also took heart when some courts allowed Indians to raise the treaties as a defense against charges of illegal fishing.[32]

Washington courts and even the Supreme Court had said more than once before the 1950s that the state could make treaty Indians abide by conservation laws when they fished off the reservations. State regulators consequently claimed that virtually all the limits they imposed on times, locations, and methods of fishing were conservation measures. The Department of Fisheries contended, for example, that conserving Hoko River salmon depended on requiring fishers to use hook and line rather than the nets that Indians preferred. But the Makah Tribe, representing the descendants of coastal villagers who had signed a Stevens treaty, disputed the state's contention. When a federal court agreed with the tribe in 1951, it inspired some Indians to set nets in the Puyallup River for the first time in modern memory. And when the state could not make charges against the Puyallup fishers stick in its own courts, more Indians dared to defy the net ban.[33]

Three publications chronicle the twenty-year spiral of action and reaction that followed the Makah Tribe's suit. A 1970 report of the American Friends Service Committee entitled *Uncommon Controversy,* Fay Cohen's *Treaties on Trial,* and 1981 findings of the U.S. Commission on Civil Rights recount that Indians, especially around the south Sound, mounted increasingly militant challenges to restrictions on their fishing. Those Indians both responded to and provoked further state crackdowns.[34]

The courts—that is, the piecemeal nature of the American juridical process—must assume a share of the blame for perpetuating conflict about treaty fishing. Opinions in the Tulee and Makah cases, among others, left it to state fisheries managers to say which regulations were conservation measures. Consequently, when some Indians celebrated their legal victories by fishing in defiance of state laws, the state responded with new regulations that put the brunt of conservation constraints on Indians. In a case arising from Puyallup net fishing, the Washington Supreme Court then split down the middle, prolonging the period when the state Fisheries and Game Departments could claim to lack clear guidelines concerning their obligations under the treaties.[35]

In 1963, six years after the inconclusive Puyallup decision, Washington's high court unequivocally approved the fisheries agencies' broad interpretation of their powers. A solid majority of justices upheld a Swinomish Indian's conviction for fishing in waters closed by state law. Adopting the attorney general's argument that the treaty clause was merely a stopgap agreement to let Indians procure food until they had learned to farm, the court concluded that modern Indians had no basis for expecting special treatment.[36] Triumphant state authorities then closed all of south Puget Sound to off-reservation Indian fishing. This action triggered spontaneous protests centered at Frank's Landing, an Indian settlement downriver from the Nisqually Reservation. State game and fisheries directors, in turn, asked a county court to uphold their regulations.

That request wended its way slowly up the legal ladder, yielding rulings in the state's favor at each level and culminating in a 1968 U.S. Supreme Court decision that seemed to side with the state. In *Puyallup Tribe v. Department of Game,* the Court held that Washington officials could indeed force Indians to obey regulations "reasonable and necessary" for conservation. The next step was for the county court to determine whether the regulations at issue met that ambiguous standard. Meanwhile, on the Nisqually River, angry Indians and their allies staged more demonstrations that met with more paramilitary repression. Judges and juries again refused to convict some of the fishers who cited the treaties as a defense.[37] In 1969 the ball bounced into a federal court in Oregon, which served up an opinion that revived Indians' hopes of avoiding many state regulations. In the case of decorated Yakima war veteran Richard Sohappy, the Oregon judge found that state regulators not only had failed to treat Indians as a group with special federal rights but also had discriminated by allowing others to take the fish before Indians had a chance to try. Because of the treaties, said the judge, states should not restrict Indian fishing unless failing to do so would imperil the salmon's existence. Shortly thereafter the Washington Department of Fisheries agreed to a special season for Indians taking salmon from the Puyallup River. The Department of Game, however, refused to lift its categorical ban on the netting of steelhead trout.[38]

The federal government then entered the fray on the Indians' side—a move that opened the final round of the legal contest and enabled Indians to prevail. It was Sohappy's victory, plus the specter of liability for failing to protect treaty beneficiaries, that finally galvanized the government. In 1970, with the professed hope of putting Washington's regulations to the strict *Sohappy* test, Justice Department lawyers sued the state fisheries agencies in U.S. District Court at Tacoma. The government declared that it was acting as trustee for seven tribes, but those tribes and seven more promptly intervened to argue for a more expansive reading of their rights than government attorneys planned to advocate. Almost four years later, in February 1974, Judge George Boldt ruled for the plaintiffs in *United States et al. v. State of Washington et al.* Although that ruling triggered controversy and violence lasting five more years, it represented the confirmation and renewal of the special relationship with non-Indians that many Indians had long desired.[39]

While conceding that the Supreme Court had allowed states to police Indians who fished outside their reservations, Judge Boldt emphasized that no court decision or act of Congress had annulled what the treaties preserved for Washington Indians. Treaty Indians had rights distinct from and superior to the privileges of other state citizens. After thus validating Indians' depiction of themselves as heirs to a unique and precious legacy, the judge broke new legal ground by quantifying that legacy. When the tribes agreed to fish "in common with" citizens, he declared, they did not acquire a right from non-Indians but instead agreed to share their own most important resource. Common sense and the dictionary suggested that they meant to retain a portion of the fish at least equal to the one they gave up. The modern state therefore had an obligation to regulate its citizens so that half the harvestable migrating salmon could reach the places where Indians fished. Instead, the state had usurped the Indians' legacy. To prevent further expropriation, Boldt forbade the state to regulate Indian fishing in the future unless it first proved that no other measures would preserve the fish.[40]

The judgment in *United States v. Washington* merely construed one treaty clause as it applied to salmon and steelhead fisheries in northwest Washington, yet it had momentous significance for Indians' self-definition. Once the Supreme Court approved the judgment in 1979, *U.S. v. Washington* became the basis not only for peace between the state and Indian fishers but also for the kind of self-representation that many western Washington Indians had come to favor. It even assumed a prominent place among the symbols of a national Indian identity.[41]

In part the litigation's impact derived from its ambitious aim and scope. At the judge's behest, the parties cooperated in framing the issues broadly so that the case would settle all ongoing disputes about the meaning of the treaty language and the extent of state power over Indian fishers. By presenting exhaustive evidence, especially historical evidence, the litigants achieved this objective and more. One result of their efforts was a court opinion that lent coherence and an aura of purpose to Indians' history by summarizing the abundant evidence of Indians' ancient and continuing zeal to fish. In effect, the opinion affirmed that a historical promise of fishing rights was a vital basis of modern Indians' identity.

The decision in *U.S. v. Washington* had momentous implications for Indians' status for a second reason: the parties and much of the public had focused a multitude of hopes and fears on the case. The author of the introduction to *Uncommon Controversy*, for example, hoped that sympathy for Indians' identification with fish would elicit from non-Indian Americans "a more respectful, Indian-like attitude toward nature." Long before the trial, many other people had attributed to the fishing clause, to the controversy about its meaning, and to the anticipated resolution of the controversy an import far broader than the words of the treaty.[42]

To various Indians and their supporters, the fishing rights dispute was a reminder of Indians' need for recognition and respect as a distinct people, the sanctity of American promises to Indians, the need to conserve ancient cultures, the value or indestructibility of cultural differences, and even the imperialistic American subordination of the Third World. In asking whether American Indians were victims of the same "deficient cultural understanding" that underlay the United States' resort to violence in

Vietnam, *Uncommon Controversy* reflected and contributed to a widespread perception that the fishing rights conflict was an allegory about America's treatment of its native peoples and minority groups. Organizations such the American Civil Liberties Union and the National Indian Youth Council weighed in on the Indians' side for this reason.[43]

When Indians prevailed in Judge Boldt's court, idealistic interpretations of the battle for treaty fishing rights gained credibility. A correspondingly positive image of Indians gained credibility as well. Harrison Sachse, an attorney who aided the plaintiffs, told Cohen that the fishers' struggle showed "the lengths that the Indians will go to preserve their culture. It is the opposite of the myths regarding Indians—that they are lazy and don't want to work." Andy Fernando of the Upper Skagit Community thought that Indians saw themselves in a more positive light as a result of *U.S. v. Washington*. "To our elders," he said in Cohen's book, "the court decision is a tribute to the resiliency and tenacity of their ancestors. ... For young Indian boys and girls, the Boldt decision shapes a new image of self."[44]

While the judge's decision appeared to vindicate Indian tenaciousness, it would be an oversimplification to say that it rewarded the efforts of people who united to demand respect for a shared conception of Indian identity. The litigation was a carefully planned undertaking, but it was not the culmination of a concerted campaign by organized tribes. Instead, it came in the course of events that revealed—in fact, the trial itself revealed—western Washington Indians' diversity, internal divisions, and uncertainty about the bases for the identity they claimed.

Although many Indians helped to make the federal litigation a necessity by stubbornly asserting their right to fish, such people often acted spontaneously, without tribal sponsorship or sanction. Often they solicited tribal council support only after they had clashed with state officials. Some people who asserted treaty rights, particularly those at Frank's Landing, fished not just in defiance of state regulations but also against the wishes or regulations of Indian governments. After 1963 some of the loudest voices demanding broad rights to fish came from the Survival of American Indians Association (SAIA), which acted independently of and sometimes in opposition to tribal councils. In 1971 SAIA's founder and two associates even sued the Puyallup tribal council, charging that the tribe's fishing regulations were inconsistent with its own constitution.[45]

A loosely coordinated collection of maverick fishers and pan-Indian activists was able to command state, tribal, and federal attention and thus force the fishing rights issue to a resolution by adapting civil disobedience tactics from black Americans' struggle for civil rights, often to the dismay of other Indians. Rather than hoping to avoid arrest when they fished, they courted arrest as well as publicity. A state court judge reviewing the convictions of several Indian gillnetters said in 1971:

> This was no crime of stealth, for the Muckelshoot [*sic*] Indians had announced days in advance that members of their tribe would drop their gill nets in the upper reaches of the Green River, and thus force an arrest by which means the Muckelshoots could test their claimed right.... Representatives of the newspapers, television stations and the State Game Department were present to record the event.[46]

By the 1960s the tactical repertoire of some treaty rights champions included fish-ins, demonstrations at government facilities, and participation in national protest marches.

Thanks in part to such tactics and in part to the violence with which state authorities and other non-Indians reacted, the press considered the treaty rights conflict newsworthy and provided protesters with a highly visible platform on which to stage their drama. Before long the spotlight attracted nationally prominent sympathizers, including entertainers Marlon Brando and Dick Gregory, who appeared on the rivers to fish and occasionally to suffer arrest with the Indians. Politicized Indian and non-Indian youth, less illustrious but equally willing to join demonstrations or risk arrest, also offered support. While the fish-ins in turn became tactical models for national Red Power organizations in the late 1960s, militance on the rivers escalated.[47]

On the other hand, some leading local Indians shrank from confrontations and publicly disavowed the militants. Two women on the Muckleshoot council said in 1961 that they were reluctant even to sue the non-Indians who had damaged their fisheries for fear of the animosity they would provoke. We "must live compatibly with our white neighbors," they explained, "who possess many legal and financial advantages denied us." When SAIA announced its support for the national Poor People's March in 1968, leaders of the Klallam, Quinault, and Quileute Tribes issued a statement condemning the decision and dissociating themselves from Hank Adams, its most visible advocate. One member of the Lummi Tribe told a reporter in 1968 that he disagreed with the actions of those who battled for fishing rights, even though he considered the right to fish sacred. "'The Indian is known for his patience,'" Joe Washington explained. "'We were told to wait and the promises of the Great Father would come true.'"[48]

Indians who asserted a right to fish disagreed not only about tactics but also about the extent of the right they should claim. Some insisted that no regulation of their fishing, even tribal regulation, was consistent with the understanding of Indians at the treaty conferences. Others, like the Tulalip Tribes' governing council, said they saw no reason to contest the state's power over Indians who ventured off reservation. The Muckleshoot councilwomen complained that one Puyallup Indian's unrestricted fishing had depleted salmon runs on their reservation, and members of the Puyallup council wanted to work with state authorities to curtail the fishing of such notorious tribe members. For reasons like these, the American Friends Service Committee attributed the persistent uncertainty about Indians' rights partly to "the small number of any tribes willing to put energy into" resolving the issue and "the inability of Washington tribes to unite to save fishing rights."[49]

Some champions of fishing rights also provoked controversy among fellow Indians when they purported to speak for tribes listed in the treaties. Hank Adams, a founder of SAIA, was an Assiniboin-Sioux who spent much of his childhood on the Quinault Reservation. By his own account, he took up the cause of the Nisqually and Puyallup Indians only after accompanying Marlon Brando to Frank's Landing and befriending people there. Other conspicuous militants included Sid Mills, who identified his ancestors as Yakima and Cherokee, and Frank's Landing resident Al Bridges, who claimed Puyallup-Nisqually-Duwamish ancestry but could not convince the Nisqually Tribe to enroll him. The *Seattle Times* labeled Bridges "A Prototype of the Outspoken Activist," a renegade, and a man without a country. Bridges, Mills, and Adams all claimed that marriage to Nisqually women gave them a basis to assert Medicine Creek Treaty rights. Their militance, however, may have been in part a reaction to the opposition they met from other Nisqually Indians.[50]

Understandably, officers of tribal governments hoped or expected that they, rather than independent activists, would be recognized as the legitimate spokesmen for Indians with treaty rights. To this end, some tribal councils made efforts to cooperate in pressing for fairer treatment. In the early sixties the Inter-tribal Council of Western Washington Indians formed a Fisheries and Game Commission, with seven members representing the treaty areas, and an adjunct advisory group composed of two members from each tribe. The commission called for tribal regulation to preserve fish runs and scientific studies of the fish and their habitat. Predictably, it was politicians from the Inter-tribal Council and constituent governments who appeared before Congress when lawmakers investigated and proposed solutions to the fishing controversy.[51]

This attempt at intertribal coordination did not move the treaty rights dispute appreciably closer to a resolution, however. Deference to individual and local differences was a long-standing habit among western Washington Indians, and the differences in Indians' situations and interests relating to fish remained considerable. After reciting Swinomish grievances to a Senate subcommittee in 1961, Tandy Wilbur added that his remarks referred only to fishing in the Skagit River and Bay. There might be other areas where Indians had suffered similarly, he said, "but I cannot speak for them."[52]

The divergent interests and understandings of the people who lined up behind the treaty rights banner were apparent even from the few Indians who testified in *U.S. v. Washington*. Rather than presenting numerous witnesses, as they had done in the Court of Claims in 1927, the plaintiff tribes called one or two people each. For the nine tribes from the Medicine Creek, Point Elliott, and Point No Point Treaty areas, sixteen people took the stand to be cross-examined regarding testimony that their lawyers had reduced to writing in advance of trial. Nevertheless, those sixteen people were diverse not only in age, gender, ancestry, and economic status but also in their experience and knowledge of fishing and Indian practices.[53]

Benjamin Wright of the Puyallup Tribe labeled himself a "registered four-fourths Indian," while Squaxin Island witness Calvin Peters claimed but one-eighth Indian ancestry. Both Wright and Peters had fished commercially outside their ancestors' territories and even outside Washington State waters. Louis Starr of Muckleshoot had just fished where his parents and grandparents had, on the Green River, but he had endured multiple prosecutions as a consequence. In contrast, Lena Patrick Smith had not fished for thirty-six years, either on her husband's reservation or in the Stillaguamish Valley where she grew up. "[W]e ain't supposed to," Smith explained. Witnesses who did fish said that it supplemented incomes from assorted occupations. Wright had worked at the state Employment Security Department, while Skokomish witness Joe Andrews was a surveyor.[54]

The plaintiff tribes were as varied as the witnesses who represented them. Tribes differed in degrees of organization, past responses to state interference with fishing, and the objectives they hoped to achieve through the litigation. Calvin Peters testified that he had been an enrolled member of the Squaxin Island Tribe for only fifteen years because the tribe's formal structure was that young. "The tribe has always been a tribe," he elaborated. "It's just that they weren't set up as a council or a group. They had been trying to set up this way for the last thirty years to bring their people together." On the other hand, Esther Ross swore that she had taken minutes at annual councils of the landless Stillaguamish Tribe for forty-six consecutive years. Bill Frank, Jr., feared that the Nisqually Tribe, which had only forty-eight living members, would be terminated if it did not enroll additional people. Meanwhile, Frank said, many other Indians whose tribal affiliations he did not know were fishing at traditional Nisqually grounds. According to Forrest Kinley, the Lummi Tribe maintained a court system and police to enforce regularly enacted fishing regulations. By contrast, the Puyallup Tribe's method of ensuring conservation, as Wright described it, was to send other fishers to talk with anyone who engaged in unwise practices.[55]

The witnesses also had different visions of the opportunities that might follow from a ruling in their favor. Peters hoped to see Squaxins fishing commercially without hindrance anywhere in western Washington, but the Stillaguamish and Sauk-Suiattle witnesses requested only the chance to fish for food in their immediate neighborhoods. In contrast to Wright, who said a lot of Puyallups just wanted to make some extra money fishing, Kinley maintained that Lummis would not have justice unless they could develop fishing into an "economic base" equivalent to that enjoyed by non-Indians. And while Kinley insisted on his tribe's ability to manage the fisheries more wisely than non-Indians, James Enick thought that state regulation of Sauk-Suiattle fishing would be acceptable so long as the regulations acknowledged the treaty right.[56]

 Even though the trial in Judge Boldt's courtroom exposed differences among the people who called themselves treaty Indians, it also represented and promoted a reconciliation of those differences. Much as the Court of Claims had become a forum where people of disparate orientations could fashion a collective Indian history during the 1920s, *U.S. v. Washington* and antecedent events allowed or obliged a wide array of people to claim a shared Indian heritage. People of Indian descent turned the fishing rights controversy into an opportunity to "show themselves to themselves" and to non-Indians, thereby continuing the effort to make sense of the single identity ascribed to them.[57] Such public rituals as congressional hearings, demonstrations, and the trial became occasions for retelling Indians' history and for dramatizing what Indians were and could be.

Like the claims litigation fifty years earlier, this process did not yield a fully integrated, universally endorsed representation of Indians in the Puget Sound region. Nevertheless, from the aggregate of presentations that Indians, their allies, and their lawyers made to the press, to lawmakers, and to Judge Boldt, there emerged an image with some clearly discernible features. All events together, but particularly the trial and the victory in court, confirmed for many people that if they shared nothing else with other Indians, they at least shared a love of fish and a unique relationship—defined by treaty—to the powers-that-be in America.

By the account of several trial witnesses, Indians were people with a carefully cultivated consciousness of their history. Joe Hillaire's wife Lena took the stand wearing regalia that would have marked her as an Indian anywhere: moccasins, beads, and a headband with a feather. "I am talking of the olden days," she volunteered. "I am almost eighty-four years old, and I still know my language and I still know the back history of my people." Fifty-nine-year-old Forrest Kinley had not spoken with anyone who attended the treaty conference, but he was confident nonetheless that he knew what had happened there. "[T]he duty of our old people," he said, "was to inform us about our family and about our rights. I think that this is a tradition that has been as accurate as your history books." According to people who thought as Kinley did, Indians' ancestors had instilled in them a reverence for the treaties as a defining moment in their history.[58]

In the Court of Claims the characterization of Indians as heirs to a bargain between equals had vied for influence with a depiction of the treaty Indians as untutored, weakened people who meekly allowed whites to appropriate their land and assume power over them. In Judge Boldt's courtroom, it was possible to merge these incongruous images into one with positive connotations. To show why the judge should construe ambiguous treaty language in Indians' favor, the plaintiffs conceded that Indians at the treaty were indeed ill equipped to deal with literate, calculating whites. Nevertheless, tribal advocates argued, the old Indians were knowing, self-respecting, and brave enough to insist on the one term that would ensure their survival—access to their foods. And because the promise of access to their foods was the most cherished legacy their ancestors had bequeathed, Indians of the 1970s were justified in demanding that the promise be fulfilled.[59]

Getting non-Indians to agree that modern Indian fishers had a continuing right to special treatment involved judicious appeals to other contrasting ideas about Indians. On one hand, emphasizing that Indians were poor, powerless, and isolated from other Americans sometimes helped to disarm opponents and recruit allies. Frank Wright elicited reassuring remarks from senators when he alleged in 1961 that Indians had little chance of making their side known to the public. And Muckleshoot witness Bernice White said in federal court, "[Y]ou are more or less degraded by being on welfare. But there is no other choice for our people, they lack education and there is no employment. We have no natural resource, the only thing that we can look towards is the fish."[60]

On the other hand, the media coverage and trial also allowed Indians to exploit the more positive traits that many Americans associated with Indians. Judge Boldt made plain his interest and delight when elderly people such as Lena Hillaire spoke of "olden days" Indians living simply and sharing their food. The fishing case also encouraged (indeed required) Indians to portray themselves as wise conservationists, expert in principles of ecology. "We have always lived with nature … ," Forrest Kinley testified. "We can deal with the fishing problems." The judge appeared to agree, at one point inviting Kinley to expound at length about ways to allocate fish resources and later remarking that he doubted anyone's ability to fool Kinley. And there were other opportunities to cite sources of pride. Kinley was one of several witnesses who exulted that Indians were not only skilled fishermen but also top-notch loggers. Seemingly opening to the warmth of the judge's gaze, he added, "Up until five or six years ago … , if you was an Indian, you were something bad. But now, it's something that the attitude of the general public is beginning to look up at the Indian."[61]

Defining Indians as well as describing them was an integral part of mounting the case for liberal fishing rights. The authenticity of asserted Indian or tribal identities was an issue throughout the years of most intense controversy. Before the decision in *U.S. v. Washington,* individuals accused of violating state fishing law could sometimes defend themselves successfully by arguing that they were exercising a treaty-reserved right; but they had to prove their link to a treaty party. Lower state courts therefore considered various kinds of evidence about fishers' Indian affiliations. In some cases they accepted genealogies; in others they relied on evidence that the defendants were regarded as members of modern tribes. Evidence of the second kind persuaded a King County Superior Court judge to dub a man on the Puyallup roll a "constructive Muckleshoot Indian" because he had lived on the Muckleshoot Reservation since he was five.[62]

State officials, particularly in the Department of Game, repeatedly described Indian identity as a vague and arbitrary phenomenon. Their assertions echoed and fostered fears that a liberal reading of the treaties would give thousands of people a material incentive to claim an Indian identity they had previously denied or downplayed. In 1961 the Game Department's chief of enforcement told a congressional investigating committee:

> Enforcement becomes extremely complex when one considers that here in the Northwest there are Indian tribes who have treaties and

reservations, other tribes have treaties but no reservation, other tribes with reservations but no treaties and still other tribes with no treaties or reservations. The next factor to add to this confusion is that many of these Indians have intermarried with other groups of Indians whose tribes may not enjoy a treaty or may be located elsewhere in the United States, Canada, or Mexico. Commonly they marry persons of other races—until the degree of Indian ancestry in some of their members is diluted beyond recognition. The U.S. Bureau of Indian Affairs is unable to inform us who the members of various tribes may be.[63]

Three years later a state lawyer said, "[W]e simply do not know who a treaty Indian is. We do not have any way of knowing."[64] The state raised questions about tribes' authenticity as well. For instance, the Game Department sought to defeat the claim that Indians could net steelhead on the Puyallup River by arguing that the Puyallup Tribe named in the treaty had ceased to exist.

The Puyallup Tribe was an obvious target for those who wanted to limit the number of people with federally protected fishing privileges, because the federal government had tried to disband the tribe in 1903, and many Puyallups had publicly proclaimed their successful assimilation. But the contention that Indians had abandoned the tribal life of their ancestors was one that state lawyers could and did extend to other people who asserted treaty rights. By depicting local Indians as thoroughly adapted to life in a non-Indian society, the state's advocates hoped to undermine the argument that treaties should be interpreted as Indians understood them at the time. Special Indian rights dating from 1855 would seem anachronistic in the 1970s if the state could show that real Indians had disappeared.[65]

In Boldt's courtroom state lawyers attempted to demonstrate that members of the suing tribes were little different from non-Indians who wanted to fish. They wrung concessions from several witnesses similar to the one from Calvin Peters: that most Indians had forsaken the old ways "because of white orientation, involvement, take-over of the Indian people." Peters, Wright, and Joe Andrews agreed with state lawyers that young Indians were adopting an American outlook on life. "Grandma" Hillaire and other elders spoke of Indian ceremonies in the past tense.[66]

To make a persuasive case, those people who claimed that Isaac Stevens's promises were as important to Indians in 1970 as in 1855 had to articulate what continued to set Indians apart. Even before the trial in *U.S. v. Washington*, the American Friends Service Committee undertook to do this. *Uncommon Controversy* described both "old Indian ways" and habits "not themselves derived from a specific tradition" that linked twentieth-century Indians to each other and distinguished them from other people. The AFSC report argued that fishing itself remained "a solid point of identification" for Puget Sound Indians. "Above all," the authors of *Uncommon Controversy* concluded, "attitudes survive[d]"—a different set of values and a stronger orientation to the group than non-Indians had.[67]

When pressed to explain their sense that they remained different from other Americans, some of the Indian trial witnesses hesitated; but none— even those who acknowledged the drastic changes in Indian culture since 1855—were at a complete loss for words. Benjamin Wright insisted that the Puyallup Tribe was more than a mere social organization like the Sons of Norway. Skokomish youth might emulate other young Americans, Joe Andrews said, but they could not lose their identity as Indians. Asked whether the Upper Skagit Tribe practiced any traditional ceremonies, Lawrence Boome replied, "We have a Shaker Church. . . . "[68]

Most often, the witnesses responded to questions about traditional ceremonies by mentioning large social gatherings, salmon feasts, and time-honored methods of cooking fish. Andrews said simply, "[F]ish is pretty sacred to Indians as a whole." The first time Bill Frank, Jr., answered a question about the persistence of ancient ceremonies, he said, "We just have a lot of dinners . . . and a lot of get-togethers. That's a ceremony in itself." The second time a state lawyer asked him the question, Frank thought of his father living in a longhouse as a child, sweat baths, weddings, and berry-picking expeditions to the mountains. "[W]e have got some four generations living on Frank's Landing of our family," he said finally, "and I think that is a ceremony in itself."[69]

Testimony that the descendants of aborigines had forsaken ancestral rites and adopted the same habits and aspirations as their non-Indian neighbors did not sway Judge Boldt. All the plaintiffs in the case, he declared, had established their status as Indian tribes. And even though "employment acculturation" and state law enforcement had drastically reduced the number of Indians who fished, most Indians were distinguished by the fact that the right to fish remained their "single most highly cherished interest and concern."[70]

To resolve issues of Indian and tribal identity, the judge adopted the legal analysis advocated by federal and tribal lawyers. The resulting pronouncements were critical not only to his ruling's practical application but also to its psychological impact on people of Indian descent. Boldt declared that the right reserved by treaty belonged to the collectivities Stevens believed he was dealing with—the tribes. The corporate entities prosecuting the lawsuit were the direct political and legal heirs of tribes or bands named in the treaties. Although the Muckleshoot Tribe had alleged in the Court of Claims that it was not a treaty party, it was able with federal backing and anthropological testimony to convince Boldt that it had succeeded to the rights of bands named in two treaties. Even the Puyallup Tribe, thanks to the federally sanctioned resurrection of its government in the 1930s, persuaded the judge that it was the modern reincarnation of a treaty party.[71]

The judge concluded further that federal law required him to recognize the modern tribes as sovereign polities. He therefore left it to them and their federal guardian to decide how to use the right he had construed. In summarizing the relevant legal principles, Boldt betrayed no suspicion that federal policy had yet to mold all the Indian communities around Puget Sound to fit the model he described.

> Ever since the first Indian treaties were confirmed by the Senate, Congress has recognized that those treaties established self-government by treaty tribes, excepting only as limited in the treaties, judicial interpretation thereof or by Congress. ... There was a period during which Congress enacted legislation limiting the exercise of tribal autonomy in various particulars. However, in the last decade Congressional legislation has definitely been in the contrary direction. ... The philosophy of Congress referred to above and the evidence in this case as a whole clearly indicate to this court that the time has now arrived, and this case presents an appropriate opportunity, to take a step toward applying Congressional philosophy to Indian treaty right fishing. ...[72]

By the judge's logic, individuals had a treaty-ensured right to fish only if they derived that right through a treaty party—that is, only if they were members of a treaty tribe. It was the prerogative of the tribe's government to decide which individuals could exercise the collective right. Boldt accordingly directed all the plaintiff tribes to prepare certified lists of the people they considered members. His opinion thus provided one of the most powerful inducements the descendants of Puget Sound Indians had ever had to align formally and permanently with a tribal organization acknowledged by the U.S. government.[73]

In the year and a half following Boldt's decision, thirteen additional tribes asked him for a declaration that they, too, were the political descendants of treaty parties and therefore eligible to claim fishing rights. When five of the tribes did not get what they requested, the implications of *U.S. v. Washington* for Indian status became clearer. Tribal organizations with governments recognized by the BIA easily passed muster with the judge, but groups that received no federal services did not. Judge Boldt ruled in 1979 that the Samish, Snoqualmie, Snohomish, Duwamish, and Steilacoom Tribes were not successors to any of the entities named in the treaties. By his reasoning, members of those landless, "unrecognized" tribes were not Indians for the purpose that had become central to many people's conception of themselves as Indians.

The five landless intervenors were not the first unrecognized tribal organizations to seek the court's validation of asserted treaty rights, but they were the first to be denied. The original plaintiffs in *U.S. v. Washington* included three tribes—Stillaguamish, Upper Skagit, and Sauk-Suiattle—with no reservations. When the suit began, federal officials did not recognize the three as functioning tribes. Four years later the Upper Skagit and Sauk-Suiattle had secured BIA acknowledgment of their existence as tribes, but neither they nor the Stillaguamish had governments organized under federal law. Although the Interior Department did not challenge the three tribes' assertion that they represented people descended from treaty signers, the state did. Nevertheless, with barely a mention of their difference from the other plaintiffs, Judge Boldt affirmed that the Upper Skagit, Stillaguamish, and Sauk-Suiattle Tribes were the successors to treaty bands with the same names. In upholding this decision, the Court of Appeals said, "Non-recognition of the tribe by the federal government and the failure of the Secretary of the Interior to approve a tribe's enrollment may result in the loss of statutory benefits, but can have no impact on vested treaty rights." Within two years after the court issued its judgment, the BIA had extended formal recognition and limited services to all three tribes.[74]

When the Samish, Snohomish, Snoqualmie, Duwamish, and Steilacoom Tribes asked the court to do for them what it had done for the Stillaguamish, Upper Skagit, and Sauk-Suiattle groups, the response of federal officials and of one federally chartered tribal organization was different. The BIA and the Tulalip Tribes, Inc., urged the court not to let the five landless intervenors share in the newly construed treaty fishing right. On the recommendation of a special master, the judge accepted the BIA lawyers' arguments and denied the five tribes' request.[75]

Boldt acknowledged that members of the five petitioning groups were descended in some degree from Indians of treaty tribes. But by itself, he said, their descent did not entitle them to exercise the right reserved by treaty. They had to prove that they had lived continuously since then in separate, cohesive Indian communities; and this they had failed to do. Except for their voluntary affiliation with organizations whose purpose was to pursue claims against the United States, members of the five tribes had no documented bond of association. Their petitions in the Indian Claims Commission did not prove that they had maintained true tribal ties, since Congress allowed claims on behalf of tribes that had ceased to exist and disbursed judgments to individuals rather than to the councils of such tribes. Boldt found support for his criteria of tribal existence in the Indian Reorganization Act, saying that it applied only to tribes under federal supervision or to Indians of half or more Indian ancestry.[76]

Refusing to second-guess Boldt's understanding of the facts, the Court of Appeals let his decision stand without repudiating the principle that a tribe may retain treaty rights even in the absence of federal recognition.[77] Nevertheless, by declaring the Snoqualmie, Snohomish, Samish, Steilacoom, and Duwamish Tribes ineligible to exercise treaty fishing rights, the courts effectively made BIA recognition a condition of claiming the most desirable prerogative of Indian identity in western Washington. The five spurned tribes therefore petitioned the BIA to recognize them, following Interior Department procedures established in 1978.

Meanwhile, each of the acknowledged tribes developed a membership roll. In virtually all the tribes, by constitutional stipulation, descent from someone on an earlier federal roll or census—often a minimum degree of descent—was the principal or sole qualification for membership. Most tribes also denied membership to anyone enrolled in another Indian tribe.

The desirability of membership in a recognized tribe had been growing even before 1974, largely because federal antipoverty programs enabled tribal governments to offer new employment opportunities and services. The chance to exercise the right affirmed by Judge Boldt was an additional, especially compelling incentive to enroll in a tribe. But the incentive was more than material. As a witness for the Duwamish Tribe told the court, "For a long time people have wanted to identify with a particular group that they derived from, and I think some of it is cultural as well as economic reasons."[78] *U.S. v. Washington* specified a way to identify with people who had exacted a valuable pledge from white Americans in the 1850s. The decision thus enabled many people to fulfill a desire for recognition that being Indian had both "cultural" and economic worth.

The treaty fishing rights litigation demonstrates the power of a particular historical account to define or redefine a social and legal category such as "Indian." In this instance, as is so often true, the account was a creation with many authors, who contributed to it in an extended dialectic of cooperation and conflict, approach and avoidance, comparisons and contrasts. In forums established by non-Indians and according to non-Indian rules,

some citizens of western Washington told a convincing story of their derivation from aboriginal treaty makers. The story gave their past a meaning
that had commendable contemporary utility. It was not the only story
they could have told; for the indigenous people they derived from had
lived many different stories over the course of a century and a half. In the
context of relations with people who repeatedly tried to crowd them into a
single social category, aboriginal people and their descendants had tried diverse ways to organize and to explain themselves. Of the explanations
they tried, however, it was the saga of historic, self-governing tribal communities with an undimmed determination to fish that eventually had the
effect they desired. The plaintiffs whose story captivated Judge Boldt in
1974 had at last fashioned an Indian identity with the power to command
respect from outsiders, including powerful non-Indians.

isn't fishing only a symbolic victory or does it only look that way?

if it only looks that way, isn't it symbolic?

Afterword

The trial

In 1975 the Snohomish Tribe of Indians petitioned the federal government to acknowledge its existence and its direct derivation from the Snohomish Indians named in the Treaty of Point Elliott. When the Interior Department denied the petition, the deputy assistant secretary explained:

> The current petitioner is almost exclusively derived from marriages of early pioneers and Indian women. ... Historically they have been confused with what was at one time a substantial number of Snohomish who were unable or unwilling to move onto the Tulalip Reservation. Later, they were also confused with reservation and non-reservation Indians who were unable to get allotments. They have incorrectly believed themselves to be and have incorrectly been identified by others as descendants of off-reservation members of the historical Snohomish Tribe.[1]

This statement may misuse data from the tribe's petition, as the Snohomish Tribe contends, but it highlights two important lessons of the history recounted in this book. First, ever since English explorers and fur traders slapped the labels "Indian" and "tribe" on indigenous peoples of the Puget Sound area, there have been uncertainty and controversy about the correct use of such labels. Second, different kinds of people with diverse histories have had grounds to call themselves Indians and Indian tribes. Confusion and conflicting beliefs about the historical antecedents that may identify someone as Indian are not surprising in a region where there have been many routes to Indian status.

From the time Europeans and Americans first applied group names to Puget Sound's inhabitants, they had reasons to doubt that those inhabitants understood the names as they did. Hoping they had named categories that Indians used, they asked natives to supply information about the contents of those categories. But the terms and categories were unfamiliar to indigenous people, who gave confusing answers as they strained to determine what the newcomers meant.

The groupings that Britons referred to as tribes in the 1830s did not have political or cultural coherence by European standards, and most of the people associated with those groups also had ties to people in other communities. Because many traders and settlers found partners among indigenous women, they soon had ties to native communities as well; and those ties produced additional cause for disagreements about the proper application of labels such as "Indian" and "tribe." Children born to immigrants and their native wives personified the difficulty of delineating categories.

Reasons for doubts about how to classify indigenous people and their descendants changed in succeeding periods but never disappeared; indeed, they increased in number. Americans thought they could sort Indians into a few tribes and separate them from non-Indians, but their plans foundered because of native people's mobility and propensity to create links between communities. Only after Americans monopolized organized force and gained effective control of economic resources—an achievement that came later than they wished or admitted—could they impose more structure on interracial relations. Shortly thereafter, however, the American government itself made it harder to delineate and segregate Indians. Policy makers of the late 1800s, sure of their civilization's superiority, tried to break up Indian tribes and force tribe members into the general U.S. population. As Americans endeavored to "civilize" Indians and Indians voluntarily mingled with Americans, many descendants of indigenous people changed in ways that blurred the original distinctions between aboriginal and settler societies. "Our Indians," said a federal official in 1889, "seem to us very much like white people."[2]

However, the mingling of natives and immigrants also heightened most people's sense that Indians and non-Indians remained significantly different. Even officials who praised Indians for discarding their old ways believed that persistent traits marked some people as unassimilable Indians. Notwithstanding the government's goal of ending Indians' special status, administrators and judges therefore engaged in an effort to classify some people as Indian wards of the government. But when they realized that diverse kinds of people had reason to count themselves as Indian wards, their reactions were neither unanimous nor consistent. To identify Indians they relied variously on descent, residence, culture, social ties, or combinations of such criteria. By the time that policy changed and the

BIA tried again to sort Indians into tribes—first in order to help them organize governments in the 1930s and then in order to terminate their wardship in the 1950s—the descendants of local natives had developed disparate ideas about what made them members of Indian tribes.

Today, when asserting identity as western Washington Indians, most people cite membership in politically defined tribes. But the transition from a world of interlinked autonomous villages to a world where Indians belong to a handful of such tribes has been halting and remains incomplete. Non-Indians' actions have frustrated as well as effected the transition, often inadvertently. In order to lump people into the category "Indian" and assign them to tribes, non-Indian Americans had to overlook significant differences among presumed Indians; yet the ironic result of their policies was to increase the cultural, social, and genetic diversity of the people classified as Indian. Government measures intended to fuse scattered Indian communities just as often severed or frayed ties among the targeted people.

The strategic choices of aboriginal people and their descendants have also had some surprising results. For example, some people who avoided official Indian enclaves because they declined to mold themselves to government specifications later found themselves classified as less Indian than people on reservations who consciously tried to become like whites.

Since at least the 1880s, U.S. officials have set the parameters of Indian identity for purposes of political and property relations, but they have never monopolized the process of defining "Indian" or "tribe." Such classifications and their meanings have evolved from negotiations between classifiers and classified. Within the framework of laws and federal policies, various descendants of aboriginal people have taken the initiative to define themselves, trying to fashion identities that make sense to them.

The definitions negotiated have never been broad or flexible enough to cover everyone who might expect or be expected to use them. Many people with native ancestry have found themselves in the vaguely defined spaces between races or tribes. Many have not been able to match their own social reference groups to administrative categories for Indians. Esther Hicks Clark was one such person. In the 1920s, when the Interior Department asked Indians of the disbanded Puyallup Tribe to identify themselves, Clark came forward. No one denied that Clark's mother was "full Puyallup." But her father, who identified himself as a Snohomish Indian, had taken Clark to the Nisqually Reservation when she was young. As an adult, she had moved back to the Puyallup vicinity, where she lived off the reservation with men from other tribes. When the enrolling agent refused to include her on the "final" Puyallup roll, he implied that she did not know how to establish a tribal identity. "This applicant and her men," he wrote, "seem to be of the type who pursue Indian benefits instead of taking their places in the community."[3]

The contested or impermanent nature of some people's tribal affiliations does not mean that all tribal affiliations have been arbitrary or unimportant. It does not mean that individuals' reasons for thinking of themselves as Indians have often been spurious. Yet during decades of dialogue about where to draw lines around Indians, there have always been some people who were not sure where to stand, some who resisted pressure to stay inside official lines, and some who faced skepticism or objections when they took up a position. Such people are important not because they have been a majority or typical of Puget Sound's inhabitants but because their existence and the relations that brought them into existence have obliged the creators and users of ethnic categories to define their terms. And the consequent discussions allow us to see how many conceptions of "Indian" and "tribe" there have been.

In the assistant interior secretary's way of thinking, members of the Snohomish Tribe tried to fashion an Indian identity by mistakenly appropriating a historical legacy they had no right to. But the Snohomish Indians' real mistake was not remembering history wrong or concocting a fraudulent history; it was having the wrong kind of history. Their request for recognition failed not because they lack historical continuity with Indians alive in 1855 but because they allegedly did not show the right kind of continuity—the kind that would qualify them under federal law for classification as Indians in tribal association. Like Judge George Boldt, administrators wanted proof that people on the Snohomish roll had lived since treaty times in a geographically and politically defined, indisputably Indian community.[4]

Underlying the Interior Department's standard (and much of Indian history as previously written) is the premise that real Indians have an unshakable core of tradition, a self-definition that resists change. This is an ahistorical concept of identity. The claim that some groups in western Washington can show continuity with a historic Indian tribe while others cannot obscures the fact that all avowed Indians emerged from the same historical maelstrom with self-definitions their ancestors would not recognize. In the 1820s no native societies of the Puget Sound region were corporate groups with government powers and formal memberships based on descent. Members of every tribe today—federally recognized as well as unrecognized—think, speak, support themselves, and organize themselves

[handwritten left margin, top: "existence of nonconforming forced the clear definition of terms like 'Indian' but it seems like a chicken & egg issue"]

[handwritten left margin, bottom: "gov't conception of Indian's ancestry is ahistorical ignoring the many changes forced upon Indian groups."]

[handwritten bottom: "→ also it is based around tribal affiliations that may not have existed in Indian roots."]

in ways that the villagers of 1820 would never have dreamed of. While the modern Snohomish Tribe of Indians gives its name a meaning that would not have occurred to nineteenth-century Snohomish, the same is true of the federally recognized Suquamish Tribe, whose formulation of tribal identity differs in significant respects from that of the Snohomish Tribe.

While some descendants of natives contend that ancestry and limited voluntary affiliation identify them as heirs to a tribal name, others rely on association with a geographically defined community under government protection. Yet all define themselves as Indians and distinguish themselves from people who are not Indians largely on the basis of history. Those who do not have a federal seal of approval, like those who do, account for the identity they claim by a chain of events linking them to Indians of the past. Until recently, most of them have also respected each other's accounts of their links to aboriginal people. Apparently recognizing that there were many routes from the past to the present, they maintained fraternal relations across the political, legal, and geographic lines that officials tried to run around them.

This history of Indians in the Puget Sound region should combat the pernicious and all-too-prevalent assumption that change erodes Indian identity, that Indians are not Indians unless they cling to a traditional core of aboriginal culture. For indigenous people, becoming known as Indians was itself a momentous change; and there have since been many changes in the parameters of Indian identity. Yet unquestionably, there are Indians around Puget Sound, and there will be Indians around Puget Sound for as long as there are people who believe that their own history has made them Indians.

Notes

ABBREVIATIONS

AFSC	American Friends Service Committee
ARCIA	*Annual Report of the Commissioner of Indian Affairs.* Washington, D.C.: Government Printing Office
CCF	Central Classified Files
DIAR	U.S. Department of the Interior. Annual Report. Washington, D.C.: Government Printing Office
NA	National Archives
P-I	*Seattle Post-Intelligencer*
PNR	Pacific Northwest Region
PSAC	Puget Sound Agricultural Company
RG	Record Group
UW	University of Washington
WTSIA	Records of the Washington Territory Superintendency of Indian Affairs

INTRODUCTION

1. *United States and Suquamish Indian Tribe v. Dorwin Aam, et al.,* United States District Court for the Western District of Washington, No. CV 82–1522. I have summarized pleadings, briefs, and evidence in files at the Suquamish Tribal Center.

2. On the difficulty of unseating jurors' notions about Indianness and culture change, see James Clifford, "Identity in Mashpee," in *The Predicament of Culture: Twentieth-Century Ethnography, Literature, and Art* (Cambridge, Mass.: Harvard University Press, 1988), 277–346.

3. *United States et al. v. State of Washington et al.,* 476 Federal Supplement 1101 (United States District Court for the Western District of Washington, 1979).

4. Fredrik Barth, *Ethnic Groups and Boundaries* (Boston: Little, Brown, 1969), 9–38; Manning Nash, *The Cauldron of Ethnicity in the Modern World* (Chicago: University of Chicago Press, 1989); Eugeen E. Roosens, *Creating Ethnicity: The Process of Ethnogenesis* (Newbury Park: Sage, 1989); Joane Nagel, *American Indian Ethnic Renewal: Red Power and the Resurgence of Identity and Culture* (New York: Oxford University Press, 1996), vii, 21, 23, 60; Frank Shuffelton, ed., *A Mixed Race: Ethnicity in Early America* (New York: Oxford University Press, 1993), 7–8; Howard Winant, *Racial Conditions: Politics, Theory, Comparisons* (Minneapolis: University of Minnesota Press, 1994). The essay usually cited for the argument that primordial sentiments bind ethnic groups is Clifford Geertz, "The Integrative Revolution: Primordial Sentiments and Civil Politics in the New States," in *Old Societies and New States: The Quest for Modernity in Asia and Africa*, ed. Clifford Geertz (New York: Free Press, 1963), 105–57. Debate continues about whether universal categories of thought underlie all ethnicities. Charles Keyes, "The Dialectics of Ethnic Change," in *Ethnic Change*, ed. Charles Keyes (Seattle: University of Washington Press, 1981), 4–30.

5. Richard White, "Race Relations in the American West," *American Quarterly* 38 (1986): 396–416; Sarah Deutsch, "Landscape of Enclaves: Race Relations in the West, 1865–1990," in *Under an Open Sky: Rethinking America's Western Past*, ed. William Cronon, Jay Gitlin, and George Miles (New York: Norton, 1992), 110–31; Peggy Pascoe, "Race, Gender, and Intercultural Relations: The Case of Interracial Marriage," *Frontiers* 12 (1991): 5–18; James Gregory, *American Exodus: The Dust Bowl Migration and Okie Culture in California* (New York: Oxford University Press, 1989); George J. Sánchez, *Becoming Mexican American* (New York: Oxford University Press, 1993); Ramón Gutiérrez, *When Jesus Came, the Corn Mothers Went Away: Marriage, Sexuality, and Power in New Mexico, 1500–1846* (Stanford, Calif.: Stanford University Press, 1991), xvii–xviii; James F. Brooks, " 'This Evil Extends Especially ... to the Feminine Sex': Negotiating Captivity in the New Mexico Borderlands," *Feminist Studies* 22, no. 2 (Summer 1996): 279–309. A geographer who describes the process of racialization historically is Kay J. Anderson, *Vancouver's Chinatown: Racial Discourse in Canada, 1875–1980* (Montreal: McGill–Queen's University Press, 1991).

6. Historians of Latin America have led the way. They include John K. Chance, *Race and Class in Colonial Oaxaca* (Stanford, Calif.: Stanford University Press, 1978); Magnus Mörner, *Race Mixture in the History of Latin America* (New York: Little, Brown, 1967); and Richard Graham, ed., *The Idea of Race in Latin America, 1870–1940* (Austin: University of Texas Press, 1990).

7. This predicament has complex origins. Past Indian and non-Indian societies' efforts to incorporate each other produced people with multiple genetic and cultural heritages. People with some basis for accepting the label "Indian" have consequently been diverse. And United States law reserves valuable resources to Indians but lacks a single definition of Indians. In interaction, these

factors have created discrepancies between legal definitions of Indians, unofficial racial ascriptions, and self-identifications. C. Matthew Snipp, "Some Observations about Racial Boundaries and the Experiences of American Indians" (paper presented at University of Washington, April 22, 1993); James A. Clifton, *Being and Becoming Indian: Biographical Studies of North American Frontiers* (Chicago: Dorsey Press, 1989), 17–18, 27.

8. James H. Merrell, *The Indians' New World: Catawbas and Their Neighbors from European Contact through the Era of Removal* (New York: Norton, 1989); J. Leitch Wright, Jr., *Creeks and Seminoles: The Destruction and Regeneration of the Muscogulge People* (Omaha: University of Nebraska Press, 1986); Richard White, *The Middle Ground: Indians, Empires, and Republics in the Great Lakes Region, 1650–1815* (Cambridge: Cambridge University Press, 1991). See also Jacqueline Peterson and Jennifer S. H. Brown, *The New Peoples: Being and Becoming Métis in North America* (Lincoln: University of Nebraska Press, 1985); Melissa L. Meyer, "Signatures and Thumbprints: Ethnicity among the White Earth Anishinaabeg, 1889–1920," *Social Science History* 14 (1990): 305–45. In *The Lumbee Problem: The Making of an American Indian People* (Cambridge: Cambridge University Press, 1980), anthropologist Karen Blu examines issues of Indian identity arising from historic dislocations and relations.

9. White, "Race Relations in the American West."

10. George Vancouver, *A Voyage of Discovery to the North Pacific Ocean and round the World, 1791–1795*, vol. 2, ed. W. Kaye Lamb (London: Hakluyt Society, 1984), 524; Bern Anderson, ed., "The Vancouver Expedition: Peter Puget's Journal of the Exploration of Puget Sound, May 7–June 11, 1792," *Pacific Northwest Quarterly* 30 (April 1939): 199.

11. Barbara Myerhoff, "'Life Not Death in Venice': Its Second Life," in *The Anthropology of Experience*, ed. Victor W. Turner and Edward M. Bruner (Urbana: University of Illinois Press, 1986), 261–86.

12. Barth, *Ethnic Groups and Boundaries*, introduction, 25, 28, 34–35; Nash, *Cauldron of Ethnicity*, 11–16; Keyes, "Dialectics of Ethnic Change," 10. A history showing the uses of ethnicity in economic and political strategy is John Modell's *The Economics and Politics of Racial Accommodation: The Japanese of Los Angeles* (Urbana: University of Illinois Press, 1977).

13. Greg Dening, *Islands and Beaches: Discourse on a Silent Land, Marquesas 1774–1880* (Honolulu: University Press of Hawaii, 1980), 125.

14. Morris W. Foster, *Being Comanche: A Social History of an American Indian Community* (Tucson: University of Arizona Press, 1991).

15. Scholars who acknowledge cultural differences in definitions of power or authority include Thomas Kochman, *Black and White Styles in Conflict* (Chicago: University of Chicago Press, 1981); Eric Wolf, "Facing Power—Old Insights, New Questions," *American Anthropologist* 92 (1990): 585; and Pierre Clastres, *Society against the State: The Leader as Servant and the Humane Uses of Power among the Indians of the Americas* (New York: Urizon Books, 1977). Useful works on different social constructions of reality and

their implications for cross-culture relations include Tzvetan Todorov, *The Conquest of America: The Question of the Other* (New York: Harper & Row, 1984); Marshall Sahlins, *Historical Metaphors and Mythical Realities: Structure in the Early History of the Sandwich Islands Kingdom* (Ann Arbor: University of Michigan Press, 1981), 5–8; Daniel T. Linger, "The Hegemony of Discontent," *American Ethnologist* 20 (1993): 3–24; Stephen Gudeman, *Economics as Culture: Models and Metaphors of Livelihood* (London: Routledge & Kegan Paul, 1986); Roy Wagner, *The Invention of Culture* (Chicago: University of Chicago Press, 1981); Ron Scollon and Suzanne B. K. Scollon, *Narrative, Literacy, and Face in Interethnic Communication* (Norwood, N.J.: Ablex, 1981); and Sergei Kan, *Symbolic Immortality: The Tlingit Potlatch of the 19th Century* (Washington, D.C.: Smithsonian Institution Press, 1989).

16. Richard White, *Land Use, Environment, and Social Change: The Shaping of Island County, Washington* (Seattle: University of Washington Press, 1980), 8 and sources cited there.

17. Although most ethnographies for this region presuppose the existence of the discrete aboriginal peoples whose culture they attempt to reconstruct, they all describe the regional network described here. June McCormick Collins, *Valley of the Spirits: The Upper Skagit Indians of Western Washington* (Seattle: University of Washington Press, 1974); William W. Elmendorf, *The Structure of Twana Culture*, Monographic Supplement No. 2, *Research Studies, a Quarterly Publication of Washington State University* 28 (1960; reprint, Pullman: Washington State University Press, 1992); Erna Gunther, "Klallam Ethnography," *University of Washington Publications in Anthropology* 1 (1927): 171–314; Hermann K. Haeberlin and Erna Gunther, "Indians of Puget Sound," *University of Washington Publications in Anthropology* 4 (1930); Marian W. Smith, "The Coast Salish of Puget Sound," *American Anthropologist* 43 (1941): 197–211; Marian W. Smith, *The Puyallup-Nisqually*, Columbia University Contributions to Anthropology 32 (1940; reprint, New York: AMS, 1969); Sally Snyder, "Skagit Society and Its Existential Basis: An Ethnofolkloristic Reconstruction" (Ph.D. diss., University of Washington, 1964); Bernhard J. Stern, *The Lummi Indians of Northwest Washington* (New York: Columbia University Press, 1934); Wayne Suttles, *Coast Salish Essays* (Seattle: University of Washington Press, 1987); Wayne Suttles and Barbara Lane, "Southern Coast Salish," in *Handbook of North American Indians*, vol. 7, ed. William C. Sturtevant (Washington, D.C.: Smithsonian Institution, 1990), 482–502.

Additional anthropological analyses that support or illustrate points summarized here include E. J. Allen, Jr., "Intergroup Ties and Exogamy among the Northwest Coast Salish," *Northwest Anthropological Research Notes* 10 (1976): 168; Colin Twedell, "A Componential Analysis of the Criteria Defining an Indian 'Tribe' in Western Washington," in *Western Washington Socio-Economics: Papers in Honor of Angelo Anastasio*, ed. Herbert C. Taylor, Jr., and Garland F. Grabert (Bellingham: Western Washington University, 1984), 61–80; Indian Claims Commission, Findings and Opinions, *Coast Salish and*

Western Washington Indians (New York: Garland, 1974); Kenneth D. Tollefson, "Political Organization of the Duwamish," *Ethnology* 28 (1989): 135–49; Bruce G. Miller, "Centrality and Measures of Regional Structure in Aboriginal Western Washington," *Ethnology* 28 (1989): 265–76; Bruce G. Miller and Daniel L. Boxberger, "Creating Chiefdoms: The Puget Sound Case," *Ethnohistory* 41 (1994): 267–93; William W. Elmendorf, "Coast Salish Status Ranking and Intergroup Ties," *Southwestern Journal of Anthropology* 27 (1971): 353–80; Kenneth D. Tollefson, "The Snoqualmie: A Puget Sound Chiefdom," *Ethnology* 26 (1987): 121–36; Astrida Onat, "The Interaction of Kin, Class, Marriage, Property Ownership and Residences with Respect to Resource Locations among the Coast Salish of the Puget Sound Lowland," *Northwest Anthropological Research Notes* 18 (1984): 86–96; June M. Collins, "Multilineal Descent: A Coast Salish Strategy," in *Currents in Anthropology*, ed. Robert Hinshaw (The Hague: Mouton, 1979), 243–54.

18. Ruth M. Underhill, *Indians of the Pacific Northwest* (Riverside, Calif.: Sherman Institute Press, 1945), 10; George Gibbs, "Tribes of Western Washington and Northwestern Oregon," *Contributions to North American Ethnology* 1 (1877): 163; Arthur Ballard, "Some Tales of the Southern Puget Sound Salish," *University of Washington Publications in Anthropology* 2 (1927): 35–41; Erna Gunther, "The Indian Shaker Church," in *Indians of the Urban Northwest*, ed. Marian W. Smith, Columbia University Contributions to Anthropology 36 (1949; reprint, New York: AMS, 1969), 57. Diversity and regional bonds similarly characterized other Northwest Coast Indians. Yvonne P. Hajda, "Regional and Social Organization in the Greater Lower Columbia, 1792–1830" (Ph.D. diss., University of Washington, 1984).

19. Myron Eells, "The Indians of Puget Sound," *American Antiquarian* 9 (1887): 3; Robert F. Berkhofer, Jr., *The White Man's Indian: Images of the American Indian from Columbus to the Present* (New York: Vintage Books, 1978), 3–31; Hazel W. Hertzberg, *The Search for an American Indian Identity: Modern Pan-Indian Movements* (Syracuse, N.Y.: Syracuse University Press, 1971), 1–2.

20. Clifton, *Being and Becoming Indian*, 22; Stephan Palmié, "Spics or Spades? Racial Classification and Ethnic Conflict in Miami," *Amerikastudien/American Studies* 34 (1989): 211–21.

21. Dening, *Islands and Beaches*; Eric R. Wolf, *Europe and the People without History* (Berkeley and Los Angeles: University of California Press, 1982), 388; Pascoe, "Race, Gender, and Intercultural Relations," 10; Deutsch, "Landscape of Enclaves," 112.

22. Studies showing that "white" is also a historical category with evolving content include David R. Roediger, *The Wages of Whiteness: Race and the Making of the American Working Class* (London: Verso, 1991); and Ian F. Haney Lopez, *White by Law: The Legal Construction of Race* (New York: New York University Press, 1996).

23. Recorded reminiscences of Indians born in the mid–nineteenth century reveal that they thought of themselves first and foremost as members of

particular lineages. They discussed social relations in specific personal terms, describing the family ties and particular errands that linked them to other communities. June M. Collins, "John Fornsby: The Personal Document of a Coast Salish Indian," in *Indians of the Urban Northwest*, 287–341; William W. Elmendorf, *Twana Narratives: Native Historical Accounts of a Coast Salish Culture* (Seattle and Vancouver: University of Washington Press and University of British Columbia Press, 1993); Paul Fetzer, "George Swanaset: Narrative of a Personal Document," in the Melville Jacobs Collection, UW Manuscripts 1693–71–13, Box 112; Meeker Family Papers, Notebooks 1–3, UW Manuscripts, Vertical File No. 362 A-C.

24. Indian dialects surely structured and reflected the structure of their users' thought. "To begin to understand the complex relation of language to culture and history, it is imperative that scholars and other readers have an accurate sense of the speaker's language." Greg Sarris, *Keeping Slug Woman Alive: A Holistic Approach to American Indian Texts* (Berkeley and Los Angeles: University of California Press, 1993), 99; Raymond J. DeMallie, " 'These Have No Ears': Narrative and the Ethnohistorical Method," *Ethnohistory* 40 (Fall 1993): 515–38. Distinct peoples often interpret their relations with each other by reference to different metaphors, which determine how they understand or misunderstand each other. Kan, *Symbolic Immortality*; Sahlins, *Historical Metaphors*; Gudeman, *Economics as Culture*. I posit such a miscommunication when I suggest that Puget Sound natives and their colonizers assessed power relations differently. A less speculative analysis would be possible if I knew more about the conceptual assumptions embedded in Indians' original languages.

25. Ethnographers have helped to shape Indians' present sense of themselves. Besides stimulating feelings of pride in people they consulted, as I indicate, ethnographers produced texts and gave public testimony that Indians have incorporated in characterizations of their heritage. Nagel, *American Indian Ethnic Renewal*, 198–200; James Clifford and George E. Marcus, "The Poetics and Politics of Ethnography," in *Writing Culture*, ed. James Clifford and George E. Marcus (Berkeley and Los Angeles: University of California Press, 1989); Robert C. Ulin, *Understanding Cultures* (Austin: University of Texas Press, 1984), chap. 1.

26. Transcript, *United States et al. v. State of Washington et al.* (United States District Court for the Western District of Washington, Civil No. 9213), 3041.

1. FUR TRADERS AND NATIVES

1. Elmendorf, *Twana Narratives*, 108–9. Klallam has often been written with an initial *C* instead of *K*. For the sake of consistency, I use the *K* except for the name of the county and when the *C* appears in a direct quote or title.

2. The first known smallpox epidemic swept through Coast Salish populations in the late 1770s. George M. Guilmet, Robert T. Boyd, David L. Whited,

and Nile Thompson, "The Legacy of Introduced Disease: The Southern Coast Salish," *American Indian Culture and Research Journal* 15 (1991): 9–10, 7. Twana myths use the metaphor "capsizing" (*sp'əláč'*) for a change that replaced the ancient world with the present natural world. Elmendorf, *Twana Narratives*, 115.

3. Hudson's Bay Company, "Journal of the Hudson's Bay Company Kept at Fort Langley during the Years 1827–29," UW Library Microfilm 164, copied from a manuscript in Bancroft Library, Berkeley, California.

4. T. C. Elliott, ed., "The Journal of John Work, November and December, 1824," *Washington Historical Quarterly* 3 (1912): 198–228; Dr. John Scouler, "Journal of a Voyage to N.W. America," *Quarterly of the Oregon Historical Society* 6 (1905): 199, 195–96; Charles Wilkes, *Narrative of the United States Exploring Expedition during the Years 1838, 1839, 1840, 1841, 1842*, vol. 2 (London: Ingram, Cooke, 1852), 178; Vancouver, *Voyage of Discovery*, 565; L. A. Bennett, "Effect of White Contact on the Lower Skagit Indians," *Washington Archaeological Society Occasional Papers* 3 (1972): 10; Erna Gunther, "Vancouver and the Indians of Puget Sound," *Pacific Northwest Quarterly* 51 (1960): 5.

5. Vancouver, *Voyage of Discovery*, 565; Paul Kane, *Wanderings of an Artist among the Indians of North America from Canada to Vancouver's Island and Oregon through the Hudson's Bay Company's Territory and Back Again* (1859; reprint, Toronto: Radisson Society, 1925), 124; Gunther, "Klallam Ethnography," 232, 236; Smith, *Puyallup-Nisqually*, 29; John Peabody Harrington, Papers at the Smithsonian Institution, 1907–1957, UW Microfilm A-6952, Roll 10.

6. Hudson's Bay, "Journal ... Kept at Fort Langley," July 6, 7, 9, 1827; Scouler, "Journal of a Voyage," 199, 195–96; Elliott, "Journal of John Work."

7. Elliott, "Journal of John Work," 208; Hudson's Bay, "Journal ... Kept at Fort Langley;" Scouler, "Journal of a Voyage," 195–97.

8. In 1826–27 HBC's James Douglas produced a census for the Puget Sound region. Without indicating the source of names used, he listed seventeen tribes. In counterclockwise order from the Strait of Juan de Fuca, they were Tlalams, Toannis, Squams, Nisquallus, Pyallups, Sinawamus, Simahooms, Skewhams (inland), Scatchads, Soquimmy, Smallous (inland), Sumamy, Whyllummy, Ossaaks, Noheums, Nahews, Summames. Russel Barsh, "Census Data for the Snohomish Tribe of Indians," Appendix V, Petition of the Snohomish Tribe of Indians for Federal Acknowledgment, 1980 (copy supplied by Snohomish Tribe).

9. E. E. Rich, "Trade Habits and Economic Motivations among the Indians of North America," *Canadian Journal of Economics and Political Science* 26 (1960): 35–53; Sylvia Van Kirk, *Many Tender Ties: Women in Fur-Trade Society, 1670–1870* (Norman: University of Oklahoma Press, 1980), 10; Dorothy O. Johansen and Charles M. Gates, *Empire of the Columbia: A History of the Pacific Northwest* (New York: Harper & Brothers, 1957), 150; David K. Chance, "Influences of Hudson's Bay Company on the Native Cultures of the Colvile District," *Northwest Anthropological Research Notes* 7 (1973): 80, 85, 87.

10. Robin Fisher, *Contact and Conflict: Indian-European Relations in British Columbia, 1774–1890* (Vancouver: University of British Columbia Press, 1977), 24–26; Helen Norton, "Women and Resources of the Northwest Coast: Documentation from the 18th and Early 19th Centuries" (Ph.D. diss., University of Washington, 1985), 207; Rich, "Trade Habits," 42–44.

11. Collins, *Valley of the Spirits*, 31; Albert Reagan, "Some Notes on the Lummi- Nooksack Indians" (1934), UW Special Collections; Samuel Hancock, *The Narrative of Samuel Hancock, 1845–1860* (New York: McBride & Company, 1927), 169–70; Clarence Bagley, "Traditions of Vancouver's Appearance," in *Indian Myths of the Northwest* (Seattle: Lowman & Hanford, 1930), 102–3; Vancouver, *Voyage of Discovery*, 546; Ram Raj Prasad Singh, "Aboriginal Economic System of the Olympic Peninsula Indians, Western Washington" (Ph.D. diss., University of Washington, 1956), 150.

12. Rich, "Trade Habits"; Arthur J. Ray, *Indians in the Fur Trade: Their Role as Trappers, Hunters, and Middlemen in the Lands Southwest of Hudson Bay, 1610–1870* (Toronto: University of Toronto Press, 1974).

13. Hudson's Bay, "Journal ... Kept at Fort Langley," July and August 1827, and September 8, 1827.

14. Edward S. Curtis, *The North American Indian*, vol. 9, *The Salishan Tribes of the Coast*, ed. Frederick Webb Hodge (Cambridge, Mass.: Harvard University Press, 1913; reprint, New York: Johnson Reprint Corporation, 1970), 24–25; Mary Ann Lambert [Vincent], *Dungeness Massacre and Other Regional Tales* (n.p., 1961), 9–12; John McLoughlin, *McLoughlin's Fort Vancouver Letters, 1825–1848*, ed. E. E. Rich (London: Champlain Society for Hudson's Bay Company Society, 1941), 55.

15. F. Ermatinger, "Earliest Expedition against Puget Sound Indians," ed. Eva Emery Dye, *Washington Historical Quarterly* 1 (1907): 22, 28–29.

16. Ibid., 16, 17.

17. Ibid., 21, 23–24.

18. Ibid., 26–29. McLoughlin later described the villagers as ready to give battle and stalling. The Snohomish, he said, were returning from consultations in the village. McLeod suspected that the Klallams on board, who had been requesting a council on shore, fled because they had planned some treachery that would be discovered when the Snohomish boarded. *McLoughlin's Fort Vancouver Letters*, 63–64.

19. Instructive works include Todorov, *Conquest of America*; Dening, *Islands and Beaches*; Sahlins, *Historical Metaphors*; White, *Middle Ground*; Merrell, *Indians' New World*; Gutiérrez, *When Jesus Came*; and Inga Clendinnen, *Ambivalent Conquests: Maya and Spaniard in Yucatan, 1517–1570* (Cambridge: Cambridge University Press, 1987).

20. Sahlins, *Historical Metaphors*, 8; White, *Middle Ground*, x, 50–93.

21. McLoughlin, *McLoughlin's Fort Vancouver Letters*, 55, 63–64.

22. John McLoughlin, *Letters of Dr. John McLoughlin Written at Fort Vancouver*, ed. Burt Brown Parker (Portland, Ore.: Binfords & Mort for Oregon Historical Society, 1948), 83; William Todd to Edward Ermatinger,

July 15, 1829, in *Washington Historical Quarterly* 1 (1907): 257; Ermatinger, "Earliest Expedition," 16–17, 29; *McLoughlin's Fort Vancouver Letters*, 63–4.

23. Elmendorf, *Twana Narratives*, 60–64, 126–153; George P. Castile, ed., *The Indians of Puget Sound: The Notebooks of Myron Eells* (Seattle: University of Washington Press, 1985), 24; Elmendorf, *Structure of Twana Culture*, 467; Collins, *Valley of the Spirits*, 115. Time-consuming discussions were also common. Gunther, "Klallam Ethnography," 266–70.

24. Indian lore is consistent with this supposition. According to Curtis's sources, Klallams later killed many Snohomish to avenge Snohomish men's role in guiding the King George men to Dungeness. A few years later "the leading [Dungeness] warrior redeemed a vow he had made by killing Quaiaks, whose attack on the white men had resulted in the burning of the village." Curtis, *Salishan Tribes*, 24–25; Lambert, *Dungeness Massacre*, 9–12.

25. McLoughlin, *Letters … Written at Fort Vancouver*, 83.

26. Because scores could be evened by supernatural means, Klallams could take credit for any subsequent deaths or disasters among the King George men. Elmendorf, *Twana Narratives*; Elmendorf, *Structure of Twana Culture*, 474. It was common to wait a long time before evening a score. Snyder, "Skagit Society," 428; Joseph Thomas Heath, *Memoirs of Nisqually*, ed. Lucille McDonald (Fairfield, Wash.: Ye Galleon Press, 1979), 105.

27. Pamela Amoss, "The Power of Secrecy among the Coast Salish," in *The Anthropology of Power*, ed. Raymond D. Fogelson and Richard N. Adams (New York: Academic Press, 1977), 134; Pamela Amoss, *Coast Salish Spirit Dancing: The Survival of an Ancestral Religion* (Seattle: University of Washington Press, 1978), 12, 172; Collins, *Valley of the Spirits*, 82; William W. Elmendorf, "Coast Salish Concepts of Power: Verbal and Functional Categories," in *The Tsimshian and Their Neighbors of the North Pacific Coast*, ed. Jay Miller and Carol M. Eastman (Seattle: University of Washington Press, 1984), 282–83; Gunther, "Klallam Ethnography," 291; Smith, *Puyallup-Nisqually*, 56, 71, 153, 167; Suttles, *Coast Salish Essays*, 204; Suttles and Lane, "Southern Coast Salish," 497.

28. Amoss, "The Power of Secrecy," 134, 136; Marian Smith, "The Puyallup of Washington," in *Acculturation of Seven Indian Tribes*, ed. Ralph Linton (New York: Appleton Century Company, 1940), 15; Elmendorf, *Twana Culture*, 508.

29. James G. Swan found Indians of the region suspicious and reserved before strangers, deeming every man an enemy until proved otherwise. Swan, *The Northwest Coast: or Three Years Residence in Washington Territory* (New York: Harper, 1857; reprint, Seattle: University of Washington Press, 1972), 196, 152. Alarm at the approach of strangers also reflects a history of raiding. In 1833, a Suquamish man offered to protect the HBC post at Nisqually from anticipated Klallam attacks by McKenzie's murderer and the son of a person the King George men killed in 1828. William Fraser Tolmie, *The Journals of William Fraser Tolmie, Physician and Fur Trader* (Vancouver, B.C.: Mitchell Press, 1963), 238, 200; McLoughlin to McDonald, June 17, 1829, McLoughlin, *Letters … Written at Fort Vancouver*, 13.

30. Indians of later generations who attributed certain powers to whole communities may have meant that many individuals there had the same powers. Stern, *Lummi Indians,* 97; Harrington Papers, Reel 16, 142; Gunther, "Klallam Ethnography," 291.

31. Gunther mentions the Klallams' reputation in "Klallam Ethnography," 26. References to the prestige of peacemakers and providers appear in Elmendorf, *Structure of Twana Culture,* 465–66; Smith, *Puyallup-Nisqually,* 71; Suttles, *Coast Salish Essays,* 20. Amoss posits that Salish Indians would have respected the religious practices of people who had guns, metals, and textiles. *Coast Salish Spirit Dancing,* 22, 172.

32. Fisher, *Contact and Conflict,* 38–40.

33. Tolmie, *Physician and Fur Trader,* 211, 209, 204, 207–8, 219, 230–32; "Occurrences at Nisqually House," in Works Progress Administration [WPA], *Told by the Pioneers* (Washington Pioneers Project, 1937), vol. 1, 10, 15; Clarence B. Bagley, ed. "Journal of Occurrences at Nisqually House," *Washington Historical Quarterly* 6 (1915): 188–89, 191. To prevent "pilfering," HBC eventually installed pickets to connect the buildings and cover openings. WPA, "Occurrences at Nisqually House," 19–20, 41–42, 50.

34. Hudson's Bay, "Journal ... Kept at Fort Langley," October 3, 1827, and June 25, 1828; Puget Sound Agricultural Company [PSAC], "Journal of Occurrences at Nisqually House," UW Manuscripts, June 13, June 16, and September 27, 1833.

35. Tolmie, *Physician and Fur Trader,* 209, 215; Bagley, *Washington Historical Quarterly* 6: 192; PSAC, "Journal," June 13, 16, 21, and 24, 1833, July 5 and August 5, 1833.

36. PSAC, "Journal," August 5 and October 26, 1834, January 1 and February 19, 1835; Bagley, *Washington Historical Quarterly* 7: 162; Tolmie, *Physician and Fur Trader,* 239, 241; Ray, *Indians in the Fur Trade,* 65–67, 137, 139; Chance, "Influences of Hudson's Bay Company," 91; Norton, "Women and Resources."

37. Karl Polanyi, "Our Obsolete Market Mentality," in *Primitive, Archaic, and Modern Economies,* ed. George Dalton (Garden City, N.Y.: Anchor Books, Doubleday, 1968), 26–37; Nicolas Peterson and Toshio Matsuyama, eds., *Cash, Commoditisation and Changing Foragers* (Osaka, Japan: National Museum of Ethnology, Senri Ethnological Studies, 1991), 2–5.

38. Gunther, "Klallam Ethnography," 213; Barbara Lane, "Political and Economic Aspects of Indian-White Culture Contact in Western Washington in the Mid–Nineteenth Century," report for United States Justice Department, May 1973, 10; Smith, *Puyallup-Nisqually,* 146. Similar observations about tribal peoples elsewhere include Daniel H. Usner, Jr., *Indians, Settlers, and Slaves in a Frontier Exchange Economy: The Lower Mississippi Valley before 1783* (Chapel Hill: University of North Carolina Press, 1992), 26–27, 211; Gudeman, *Economics as Culture;* Kan, *Symbolic Immortality,* 209; Sahlins, *Historical Metaphors,* 31, 44.

39. Gunther, "Klallam Ethnography," 213, 261; Smith, *Puyallup-Nisqually,* 48, 108, 138, 144–45; Stern, *Lummi Indians,* 71; Suttles, *Coast*

Salish Essays, 15–25; T. T. Waterman, "Notes on the Ethnology of the Indians of Puget Sound [1921]," Museum of the American Indian, *Indian Notes and Monographs: Miscellaneous Series,* No. 59 (1973), 76.

40. Hudson's Bay, "Journal ... Kept at Fort Langley," August 20 and October 3, 1827; PSAC, "Journal," June 13, August 15, 21, 22, 27–29, September 27, and October 4, 1833.

41. Tolmie, *Physician and Fur Trader,* 215; PSAC, "Journal," August 6 and 23, December 9, 1833. Babyar's name also appears as Babillard in various journals.

42. Hudson's Bay, "Journal ... Kept at Fort Langley," September 2, 1827. The first crew at Nisqually had only six "effective" men. Tolmie, *Physician and Fur Trader,* 209; McLoughlin to McDonald, June 17, 1829, in *Letters ... Written at Fort Vancouver,* 12; PSAC, "Journal," June 16, 1833, May 29 and June 10, 1835.

43. Tolmie, *Physician and Fur Trader,* 215, 220, 234; PSAC, "Journal," June 21, July 27, September 27, November 15, 1833, September 7, 1834, January 11, 18, 29, and February 18, 1835; Hudson's Bay, "Journal ... Kept at Fort Langley," October 2, 1827; Excerpts from Fort Nisqually Indian Blotters, in Helen Norton, "The Economy and Ecology of the Snohomish Tribe of Indians 1792–1865," report for Snohomish Tribe of Indians, 1990, Appendix 67–81.

44. McLoughlin, *McLoughlin's Fort Vancouver Letters,* 260.

45. Hudson's Bay, "Journal ... Kept at Fort Langley," August 25, September 20, October 1, 3, and 8, 1827, May 11 and July 10, 1828. The traders also cultivated some women's goodwill. Tolmie, *Physician and Fur Trader,* 215; PSAC, "Journal," February 15, 1837.

46. Possession of the gun was more likely a sign of Tslalakum's participation in a ceremonial network than of complicity in murder.

47. Tolmie, *Physician and Fur Trader,* 201.

48. PSAC, "Journal," June 21, 1833, October 4, 1833, September 23, 1835, March 15, 1836, and December 1, 1838; Tolmie, *Physician and Fur Trader,* 219.

49. Smith, *Puyallup-Nisqually,* 153; Wayne Suttles, "Post Contact Culture Change among the Lummi Indians," *British Columbia Historical Quarterly* 18 (1954): 47. For a general discussion of exogamy as a means of creating political alliances, see Clastres, *Society against the State,* 52.

50. Tolmie, *Physician and Fur Trader,* 219, 215.

51. Hudson's Bay, "Journal ... Kept at Fort Langley," November 13, 1828. Tolmie later married the daughter of John Work, whose wife was an Indian. Elliott, "Journal of John Work," editor's preface; Victor J. Farrar, ed., "Diary of Colonel and Mrs. I. N. Ebey," *Washington Historical Quarterly* 7 (1916): 320–21.

52. Jennifer S. H. Brown, *Strangers in Blood: Fur Trade Company Families in Indian Country* (Vancouver: University of British Columbia Press, 1980); Van Kirk, *Many Tender Ties;* McLoughlin, *Letters ... Written at Fort Vancouver,* 185; Hudson's Bay, "Journal ... Kept at Fort Langley," November, 1828; PSAC, "Journal," July 10, 1834, October 22, 1836, July 22, 1850, August 19, 1851; Tolmie, *Physician and Fur Trader,* 238.

53. White, *Middle Ground*.

54. Tolmie, *Physician and Fur Trader*, 240.

55. Ibid., 223–24.

56. Ibid., 213, 219, 221; PSAC, "Journal," December 22, 1833, August 10, 1834, and February 1, 1835.

57. PSAC, "Journal," August 10, 1834, and February 1, 1835; Tolmie, *Physician and Fur Trader*, 219, 221. Kittson also interfered with the observance of menstrual taboos that prevented native women from performing tasks he had hired them for. PSAC, "Journal," November 25–28, 1835, and January 2, 1837.

58. Tolmie, *Physician and Fur Trader*, 221–22, 210, 213; PSAC, "Journal," February 1, 1835.

59. W. S. Phillips, *The Chinook Book* (Seattle: R. L. Davis Printing Company, 1913); F. N. Blanchet, "Pronouncing Dictionary and Jargon Vocabulary to Which Is Added Numerous Conversations Enabling Any Person to Speak the Chinook Jargon" (Portland, Oregon: S. J. M'Cormick, Franklin Book Store, 1853; reprinted as appendix to *Paul Kane, The Columbia Wanderer*, ed. Thomas Vaughan. Portland, Ore.: Oregon Historical Society, 1971); Rev. M[yron] Eells, *Ten Years of Missionary Work among the Indians at Skokomish, Washington Territory, 1874–1884* (Boston: Congregational Sunday-School and Publishing Society, 1886), 34; Swan, *Northwest Coast*, 196.

60. Elmendorf, *Structure of Twana Culture*, 430; Gunther, "Klallam Ethnography," 261, 24; Collins, *Valley of the Spirits*, 36–37; Collins, "John Fornsby," 293; Haeberlin and Gunther, "Indians of Puget Sound," 58; Smith, *Puyallup-Nisqually*, 167; Michael Harkin, "Power and Progress: The Evangelic Dialogue among the Heiltsuk," *Ethnohistory* 40 (1993): 6.

61. Tolmie, *Physician and Fur Trader*, 242; Smith, "Puyallup of Washington," 15; Amoss, *Coast Salish Spirit Dancing*, 22. Blanchet's "Pronouncing Dictionary" defines "Wawa" as to talk, pray, command, and "Sa-ha-le" as heaven, sky, above, high. Inhabitants of the Puget Sound area had probably heard about the Europeans' intriguing religious ideas and practices before they met traders and missionaries. Homer Garner Barnett, *Indian Shakers: A Messianic Cult of the Pacific Northwest* (Carbondale: Southern Illinois University Press, 1957), 301.

62. Francis N. Blanchet and Modeste Demers, *Notices and Voyages of the Famed Quebec Mission to the Pacific Northwest*, trans. Carl Landerholm (Portland, Ore.: Oregon Historical Society, 1956), 63. Blanchet and Demers had a similar conversation with "the great Snohomish chief Schalapahen." Blanchet, *Historical Sketches of the Catholic Church in Oregon during the Past Forty Years (1838–1878)*, UW Microfilm A-2573, Reel 3, 50. Klallam stories about people who obtained power from ships bearing wealth or disease also show belief in Indians' ability to enlist the help of spirits associated with the newcomers. Erna Gunther, "Klallam Folk Tales," *University of Washington Publications in Anthropology* 1 (1925): 154, 122; Gunther, "Klallam Ethnography," 291.

63. PSAC, "Journal," December 22 and 29, 1833, August 10, January 26, and May 25, 1834. Blanchet later noted that Indians of the Puget Sound area

sanctified Sunday "after their fashion, by games and dances to the point of exhaustion." Blanchet and Demers, *Notices and Voyages*, 68. Tolmie referred to the dances by a telling term—Samanowash. Usually spelled with an initial *T* rather than *S*, this is the Chinook jargon word denoting deference to the occult and connoting witchcraft to most Christians. *Physician and Fur Trader*, 222–23; Blanchet, "Pronouncing Dictionary," 28; Phillips, *Chinook Book*, 92.

64. PSAC, "Journal," February 12, 1837, February 6 and 7, 1839.

65. Skagit Valley Indians told Collins in the 1940s that it was easy to get spirit powers in another country or near another people's village. *Valley of the Spirits*, 178. Ethnographers mention the practice of singing power songs upon encountering outsiders. Smith, *Puyallup-Nisqually*, 108; Gunther, "Klallam Ethnography," 306; Collins, "John Fornsby"; Myron Eells, "The Potlatches of Puget Sound," *American Antiquarian* 5 (1883): 135–47; Sally Snyder, "Quest for the Sacred in Northern Puget Sound: An Interpretation of the Potlatch," *Ethnology* 14 (1975): 153. Also, Vancouver, *Voyage of Discovery*, 546.

66. Smith, *Puyallup-Nisqually*, 29; Smith, *Indians of the Urban Northwest*, 13; Collins, "John Fornsby," 302–3; Norton, "Economy and Ecology of the Snohomish." A journal entry for December 3, 1836, mentions people from beyond the Nisqually area who were residing at the fort, thus indicating that some people changed their residence patterns to exploit the trade. Residents of the Snoqualmie River Valley, which does not reach the salt water, did not appear in the Fort Nisqually journal until 1837.

67. Anthropologists do not agree how clear or permeable were the lines between classes in the early nineteenth century. But because most people who obtained wealth power had advice from high-class elders, wealth and prestige tended to correlate with and to perpetuate themselves in certain lineages. Collins, *Valley of the Spirits*, 81, 124; Collins, "Multilineal Descent"; Elmendorf, *Structure of Twana Culture*, 333–34, 325; Smith, *Puyallup-Nisqually*, 48; Snyder, "Skagit Society," 96, 99, 116, 135, 170; Collins, "John Fornsby," 307.

68. PSAC, "Journal," June 13, 1833. It is not possible to say whether all the men HBC identified as chiefs enjoyed high status before their success in the trade. Most probably did; for few would have been able to travel to trading posts or act as brokers without the extensive family ties and name recognition that characterized the well-to-do. Collins, "Multilineal Descent," 251; Martin Sampson, *Indians of Skagit County* (Mount Vernon, Wash.: Skagit County Historical Society, 1972), 20; Suttles, *Coast Salish Essays*, 20; Singh, "Aboriginal Economic System," 139, 149, 207. Scholars who conclude that trade enabled nouveaux riches to found new villages include Collins and Snyder. References to the belief in upward mobility include Underhill, *Indians of the Pacific Northwest*, 206; Betty Uchite'le Randall, "The Cinderella Theme in Northwest Coast Folklore," in Smith, *Indians of the Urban Northwest*, 244–57; and Snyder, "Skagit Society," 131. Along with trade, population loss from epidemics undoubtedly destabilized class status.

69. Collins, "John Fornsby," 311; Collins, *Valley of the Spirits*, 33; PSAC, "Journal," January 21, February 10, and February 18, 1835.

70. Tolmie, *Physician and Fur Trader*, 204, 207–8; PSAC, "Journal," June 22, July 27, and August 3, 1833; McLoughlin, *McLoughlin's Fort Vancouver Letters*, 260. Discussion of intercommunity antagonisms include Elmendorf, *Structure of Twana Culture*, 289; Smith, *Puyallup-Nisqually*, 153, 161; Stern, *Lummi Indians*, 97, 99; Gunther, "Klallam Ethnography," 266; Suttles, *Coast Salish Essays*, 210, 220–21.

71. PSAC, "Journal," August 23, 1833, September 23, 1835; Tolmie, *Physician and Fur Trader*, 223.

72. PSAC, "Journal," January 30, April 5, August 9, and August 13, 1835. The Fort Langley journal mentions raiding parties nearby several times in March, May, and June, and on September 11, 1828.

73. Tolmie, *Physician and Fur Trader*, 220 ("Scetlam the Kaatchet chief having made peace with Chiatsazan [a resident of the nearest village] by a present of two guns, was permitted to visit us. . . . "); PSAC, "Journal," January 11 and 18, April 5, September 6, October 18, 1835, September 7, 1834, February 12, 1837; Hudson's Bay, "Journal . . . Kept at Fort Langley," October 8, 1827. Reports of gambling appear in Tolmie, *Physician and Fur Trader*, 214; PSAC, "Journal," January 29, 1834, August 29, 1835, January 26, 1837, and February 20, 1838.

74. PSAC, "Journal," February 18, March 11, and October 18, 1835, January 2 and February 18, 1837, January 5 and 6 and April 22, 1838. Ethnographic discussions of diplomacy by marriage include Collins, "Multilineal Descent," 251–2; Elmendorf, "Coast Salish Status Ranking," 361; Elmendorf, *Structure of Twana Culture*, 301, 325; Gunther, "Klallam Ethnography," 242; Sampson, *Indians of Skagit County*, 11; Smith, *Puyallup-Nisqually*, 32, 42–43; Stern, *Lummi Indians*, 27.

75. The Langley journal mentions ransoms on August 10 and September 7, 1827.

76. PSAC, "Journal," January 30, April 5, August 9, 11, and 13, September 23, 1835, January 9, 1836, January 15, February 15 and 19, 1837; Hudson's Bay, "Journal . . . Kept at Fort Langley," August 10 and 25, November 15, 1827, May 8, 1828; Bagley, *Washington Historical Quarterly* 7 (1916): 161; Chance, "Influences of Hudson's Bay Company," 87; Kane, *Wanderings of an Artist*, 166.

77. HBC journal entries do not use the term "Indians" for company personnel who were from eastern indigenous societies such as the Iroquois. "Indians" refers to local people.

78. See note 2. Eyewitness accounts of Indian reaction to later epidemics include Hancock, *Narrative of Samuel Hancock*, 181–83; affidavit of Mathew Fleming enclosed with letter to Commissioner of Indian Affairs, January 7, 1922, NA, PNR, RG 75, Western Washington Agency, Box 259.

79. Elmendorf, *Twana Narratives*, 146, 128, 132–36; Curtis, *Salishan Tribes*, 20; Suttles, "Post Contact Culture Change," 45.

80. PSAC, "Journal," July 29, August 29, and September 1, 1837; Scouler, "Journal of a Voyage," 203–4; Hancock, *Narrative of Samuel Hancock*, 183;

PSAC, "Journal," March 15, 1836. A local man told Tolmie that American traders had threatened to send disease among the Indians if they did not bring beaver. *Physician and Fur Trader*, 238. The Salish theory of disease appears in Elmendorf, *Structure of Twana Culture*, 506–7; Swan, *Northwest Coast*, 176; Gunther, "Klallam Ethnography," 300–301; Collins, *Valley of the Spirits*, 172, 206; Smith, *Puyallup-Nisqually*, 86.

81. PSAC, "Journal," July 10 and 20, 1834, March 4, 5, and 10, April 6, 1836, February 21 and May 15, 1837; Tolmie, *Physician and Fur Trader*, 198; Gunther, "Klallam Ethnography," 267; Elmendorf, *Twana Narratives*, 206, 208, 210–11, 213, 215.

82. Harrington Papers, Reel 10, notes of Ruth Greiner interview with John Scalopine. In 1927 Scalopine was an estimated eighty years old. Transcript of Testimony, *Duwamish et al. v. United States* (United States Court of Claims, 1927), 214.

83. Tolmie, *Physician and Fur Trader*, 167. On the ritual treatment of first salmon, see Suttles and Lane, "Southern Coast Salish," 496; Erna Gunther, "An Analysis of the First Salmon Ceremony," *American Anthropologist* 28 (1926): 605–17, and "A Further Analysis of the First Salmon Ceremony," *University of Washington Publications in Anthropology* 2 (1928): 133–73. Elderly Indians told Marian Smith that whites were called birds because they came and went without acquiring identity with a home country. *Puyallup-Nisqually*, 31.

84. Tolmie, *Physician and Fur Trader*, 212, 226, 269. Etiquette is covered in Smith, *Puyallup-Nisqually*, 167; Elmendorf, *Structure of Twana Culture*, 321, 330, 333; Collins, *Valley of the Spirits*, 103, 125; Hancock, *Narrative of Samuel Hancock*, 109; Smith, *Indians of the Urban Northwest*, 9.

85. Collins, *Valley of the Spirits*, 10; John W. Adams, "Recent Ethnology of the Northwest Coast," *Annual Review of Anthropology* 10 (1981): 381; Amoss, *Coast Salish Spirit Dancing*, 21. McDonald noted that everyone, no matter what rank, was eager to trade directly, expecting thereby to be "rewarded like the best of his neighbors." PSAC, "Journal," June 13, 1833.

86. Hudson's Bay, "Journal ... Kept at Fort Langley," July 1828; PSAC, "Journal," May 5, 1835; Bagley, *Washington Historical Quarterly* 7: 149. Economic specialization was common. Smith, *Indians of the Urban Northwest*, 10, 12; Smith, *Puyallup-Nisqually*, 140; Collins, "Multilineal Descent," 250; Underhill, *Indians of the Pacific Northwest*, 158; Collins, *Valley of the Spirits*, 76.

87. Elmendorf, *Structure of Twana Culture*, 325; Hudson's Bay, "Journal ... Kept at Fort Langley," July 1829, November 14, 1828. Mr. Yale's wedding embroiled Fort Langley in tensions between his bride's people and the Skagits. Also, McLoughlin, *Letters ... Written at Fort Vancouver*, 185.

88. Edward Huggins to "My dear sir," December 29, 1900, Edward Huggins Papers, Washington State Historical Society, Tacoma; Johansen and Gates, *Empire of the Columbia*, 151. Upon arriving at Nisqually, Tolmie wrote, "Welcomed by a motley group of Canadians, Owyhees & Indians. ... " *Physician and Fur Trader*, 195. Anthropologist Jennifer Brown calls fur trade society a "partial or incomplete social sphere." *Strangers in Blood*, xvi–xvii.

89. Tolmie, *Physician and Fur Trader*, 240. Desertions were also a problem for the company, and some deserters took refuge with their native in-laws.

2. SETTLERS AND INDIANS

1. Charles Wilkes, *Diary of Wilkes in the Northwest*, ed. Edmond S. Meany (*Washington Historical Quarterly*; reprint, Seattle: University of Washington Press, 1926), 93.

2. Roediger, *Wages of Whiteness*, 21–11; David R. Roediger, "Whiteness and Ethnicity in the History of 'White Ethnics' in the United States," in *Towards the Abolition of Whiteness: Essays on Race, Politics, and Working Class History*, ed. David R. Roediger (London: Verso, 1994), 181.

3. William H. Goetzmann, *New Lands, New Men: America and the Second Great Age of Discovery* (New York: Viking, 1986), 144–45, 168–69, 270; Earl Pomeroy, *The Pacific Slope: A History of California, Oregon, Washington, Idaho, Utah, and Nevada* (New York: Knopf, 1965), 25–28; Fred Wilbur Powell, ed., *Hall J. Kelley on Oregon* (Princeton, N.J.: Princeton University Press, 1932; reprint, New York: DaCapo Press, 1972), vii–xi; Johansen and Gates, *Empire of the Columbia*, 235.

4. Goetzmann, *New Lands*, 272.

5. Wilkes, *Diary of Wilkes*, 13, 21, 27, 87.

6. Ibid., 21.

7. Pierce County Pioneer Association, "Commemorative Celebration at Sequalitchew Lake" (pamphlet, 1906): 13, 14; Wilkes, *Narrative*, vol. 2, 412; George M. Colvocoresses, *Four Years in a Government Exploring Expedition* (New York: Cornish, Lamport, 1852), 236.

8. Ezra Meeker, who arrived in the region in 1853, published a supposedly verbatim rendition of Richmond's speech without indicating his source. *Pioneer Reminiscences of Puget Sound/The Tragedy of Leschi* (Seattle: Lowman & Hanford, 1905), 533–34. Richmond later said of his mission at Nisqually: " 'My part of the work was to represent American citizenship and American enterprise. . . . ' " Quoted from *Daily News*, April 1884, Meeker, *Pioneer Reminiscences*, 513.

9. Pierce County Pioneer Association, "Commemorative Celebration," 33.

10. Meeker, *Pioneer Reminiscences*, 506; Richmond to Editor, *Seattle Weekly Chronicle*, September 11, 1883, in Clarence Bagley Papers, UW Manuscripts, Box 22, vol. 4A.

11. Wilkes, *Narrative*, vol. 2, 178.

12. Ibid., 480; Wilkes, *Diary of Wilkes*, 12–13, 19, 21, 87; Colvocoresses, *Four Years*, 233.

13. Cecilia Svinth Carpenter, *Fort Nisqually: A Documented History of Indian and British Interaction* (Tacoma, Wash.: Tahoma Research, 1986), 81, 97; John S. Galbraith, "The Early History of the Puget's Sound Agricultural Company 1838–1843," *Oregon Historical Quarterly* 55 (1954), 245; "The Nisqually Journal," ed. Victor J. Farrar, *Washington Historical Quarterly* 10

(1919): 205. Wilkes remarked only that Fort Nisqually's manager "was making an experiment with some of [the Indians] to till the land but he found them disinclined to work altho they were more apt than he had given them credit for." Wilkes, *Diary of Wilkes,* 87.

14. PSAC, "Journal," August 4, September 12, 13, and 19, October 28, 1833, July 27, 1835, March 12 and April 2, 1849, July 1850; Tolmie, *Physician and Fur Trader,* 219, 234, 251; Fort Nisqually Blotters for 1844–1855 in Norton, "Economy and Ecology of the Snohomish," Appendix; Anonymous, "Notes Copied from the Hudson's Bay Company Accounts at Fort Nisqually 1833–1850," UW Special Collections; Edward Huggins, "Reminiscences of Puget Sound," collected for Tacoma Public Library by Gary Fuller Reese, 1984, 309–14.

15. Blanchet and Demers, *Notices and Voyages,* 58–59; Blanchet, *Historical Sketches,* paper copy, 83; microfilm copy, 40–41.

16. Blanchet, *Historical Sketches,* paper copy, 83, 100–104; microfilm copy, 40–42; Blanchet and Demers, *Notices and Voyages,* 51; Tolmie, *Physician and Fur Trader,* 221–22.

17. Blanchet and Demers, *Notices and Voyages,* 44, and Blanchet, *Historical Sketches,* microfilm copy, 41, 42; Hancock, *Narrative of Samuel Hancock,* 109.

18. Blanchet and Demers, *Notices and Voyages,* 103, 46, 66, 99; Blanchet, *Historical Sketches,* microfilm copy, 41.

19. Blanchet and Demers, *Notices and Voyages,* 102, 60, 99, 197; Blanchet, *Historical Sketches,* paper copy, 97.

20. Blanchet, *Historical Sketches,* microfilm copy, 40–42.

21. Galbraith, "Early History," 234–35; Heath, *Memoirs of Nisqually,* introduction; Carpenter, *Fort Nisqually,* 128–30.

22. Heath, *Memoirs of Nisqually,* 88. Parenthetical material supplied by Lucille McDonald, editor.

23. Ibid., 25, 14–15, 18, 21, 28, 34, 36, 64.

24. Ibid., 80–84.

25. Ibid., 140, 23, 28, 40, 52, 55, 88.

26. Ibid., 19, 17, 28, 41, 85, 90, 109, 153.

27. Ibid., 45, 18. Samuel Hancock mentions daily baths in "Thirteen Years Residence on the Northwest Coast" (1860), UW Manuscripts, Vertical File No. 70.

28. Collins, *Valley of the Spirits,* 111; Elmendorf, *Structure of Twana Culture,* 312; Suttles, *Coast Salish Essays,* 20–21, 57; Smith, "Puyallup of Washington," 11, 13; Smith, *Puyallup-Nisqually,* 35, 49, 54; Snyder, "Skagit Society," 72–76; Stern, *Lummi Indians,* 32.

29. Anonymous, "Notes Copied from the Hudson's Bay Company," November 11, 1845; Johansen and Gates, *Empire of the Columbia,* 266–67; PSAC, "Journal," March 12, 27, 29, and 31, 1847, and April 6, 1847; Huggins, "Reminiscences of Puget Sound," 314–15.

30. Washington Centennial Association, "1845–1945: A Washington Centennial Commemoration" (1945), 8–9; A. B. Rabbison [Bancroft's spelling],

"Growth of Towns," in Hubert H. Bancroft ms. collection, UW Microfilm 155; "Edward Sylvester's Narrative," in Bancroft collection, Microfilm 20; PSAC, "Journal," April 12 and 13, 1847; Robert A. Bennett, *A Small World of Our Own* (Walla Walla, Wash.: Pioneer Press Books, 1985), 205.

31. WPA, "Narrative of James Longmire, A Pioneer of 1853," in *Told by the Pioneers*, vol. 1, 134; Edward Huggins, "A Trip to 'Alki' Point Near Duwamsh Bay ... 1852," 1901, UW Special Collections, 1; John M. Swan, "The Colonisations around Puget Sd," in Bancroft collection, UW Microfilm 223; "Edward Sylvester's Narrative," in Bancroft collection.

32. George Gibbs, *Indian Tribes of Washington Territory* (House Exec. Doc. 91, 33d Cong., 2d sess., 1854; reprint, Fairfield, Wash.: Ye Galleon Press, 1967), 27.

33. PSAC, "Journal," March 16, 20, and 21, August 12 and 28, 1846, March 4, 5, 6, and 9, 1847, March 24 and 27, 1849; Anonymous, "Notes Copied from Hudson's Bay Company," February 7, 1845, and November 23, 1847 ("1 green blanket to Tamatlutaiah—expected to die, and as a mark of respect customary on the death of friendly Indians of note").

34. Tolmie, *Physician and Fur Trader*, 198; PSAC, "Journal," August 9, 1834, September 9, 1838; Carpenter, *Fort Nisqually*, 8; Smith, *Puyallup-Nisqually*, 7–14, 247–52; June McCormick Collins, "Growth of Class Distinctions and Political Authority among the Skagit Indians during the Contact Period," *American Anthropologist* 52 (1950), 332, 336.

35. Heath, *Memoirs of Nisqually*, 55; PSAC, "Journal," February 6, 1846, and March 10, 1847; Smith, "Puyallup of Washington," 25; Carpenter, *Fort Nisqually*, 143.

36. Hancock, *Narrative of Samuel Hancock*, 58; Johansen and Gates, *Empire of the Columbia*, 283–85; William Fraser Tolmie, "History of Puget Sound and the Northwest Coast" (manuscript preserved at the Bancroft Library, 1878), UW Microfilm 190, 31, 32; Tolmie to Rodk Finlayson, January 8, 1848, and Tolmie to Board of Management, April 13, 1848, in PSAC, "Journal." Rabbeson's oft-repeated story of the Snoqualmie chief appears in *Washington Standard*, March 21, 1868, 2; Hubert Howe Bancroft, *History of Oregon* (San Francisco: History Company, 1888), 11; George Albert Kellogg, "A History of Whidbey's Island" (series in *Island County Farm Bureau News*, 1933–34; scrapbook in UW Library), 11.

37. Tolmie to Peter Skeen Ogden, July 24, 1848, PSAC, "Journal"; Tolmie, "History of Puget Sound," 32.

38. Bancroft, *History of Oregon*, 47; Washington Centennial, "1845–1945," 8–9; Rabbison, "Growth of Towns"; PSAC, "Journal," May 1, 1849.

39. PSAC, "Journal," May 1, 1849; Tolmie, "History of Puget Sound," 33–34. Saying that Snoqualmie and Skykomish targeted Nisqually Indians or HBC rather than Americans are Emily Denny, *Blazing the Way* (Seattle: Rainier Printing, 1909), 398; Bancroft, *History of Oregon*, 67; and Rabbison, "Growth of Towns," in Bancroft collection. Herbert Hunt and Floyd C. Kaylor claim the Snoqualmies aimed to chase whites from the country. *Washington West of the Cascades*, vol. 1 (Seattle: S.J. Clark, 1917), 106.

40. Hunt and Kaylor, *Washington West of the Cascades,* 106; Report of Joseph Lane, October 13 and 22, 1849, *Report of the Commissioner of Indian Affairs,* Senate Exec. Doc. 1, Paper E, p. 156, Serial 587. The source of the ultimatum tale appears to be Rabbeson, who was in California at the time, "Growth of Towns." PSAC, "Journal" shows that American fears were unfounded. One Snoqualmie headman soon dissociated himself from the troublemakers and pledged his friendship; days later, the headmen gathered peacefully to hear a letter of remonstrance from Oregon Territory's governor; and in early June a prominent Snoqualmie apologized for the shooting. May 14 and 18, June 8, 1849.

41. Report of Joseph Lane, 156; PSAC, "Journal," May 18, 1849.

42. PSAC, "Journal," August 7, 1849.

43. Report of Joseph Lane, 163; Tolmie, "History of Puget Sound," 35; PSAC, "Journal," August 21 and 22, September 3, 1849. For the U.S. policy regarding Indians who killed whites, see Francis Paul Prucha, *The Great Father* (Lincoln: University of Nebraska Press, 1984), 104. The practice of trying such Indians antedates the United States. White, *Middle Ground,* 76–77.

44. PSAC, "Journal," September 5, 1849. Tolmie gave blankets to the relatives of two Indians killed May 1, perhaps because the dead men worked at the fort. PSAC, "Journal," September 6, 1849. References to compensatory payments appear in E. A. Starling to Commissioner, December 10, 1853, WTSIA, Roll 9, Reel 17; *Columbian,* October 8, 1853, p. 2, c. 2; Snyder, "Skagit Society," 397; Elmendorf, *Structure of Twana Culture,* 476–77; Haeberlin and Gunther, "Indians of Puget Sound," 59; Stern, *Lummi Indians,* 99–100. Thom Hess, *Dictionary of Puget Salish* defines $g^w\acute{\imath}halik^w$ as "asking for whatever can be gotten equal to murdered man's station in life."

45. Report of Joseph Lane, 166; PSAC, "Journal," September 1, 5, and 13 and October 2, 1849. The latter journal entry, Lane's report, and Tolmie's "History of Puget Sound" are the only records of the trial.

46. Lawrence Friedman, "The Development of American Criminal Law," in *Law and Order in American History,* ed. Joseph M. Hawes (Port Washington, N.Y.: Kennikat Press, 1979), 14. French historian Michel Foucault says that a public execution can both represent and activate the sovereign's power. *Discipline and Punish: The Birth of the Prison* (New York: Vintage Books, 1979), 48–50.

47. Arthur Armstrong Denny, *Pioneer Days on Puget Sound* (1888; Fairfield, Wash.: Ye Galleon Press, 1979), 68; Ezra Meeker, *Pioneer Reminiscences,* 547.

48. W. W. Elmendorf, "Skokomish Sorcery, Ethics, and Society," in *Systems of North American Witchcraft and Sorcery,* ed. Deward E. Walker, Jr. (Moscow: University of Idaho Press, 1970), 147–82; Smith, *Puyallup-Nisqually,* 62; Suttles and Lane, "Southern Coast Salish," 495; Snyder, "Skagit Society," 98; Stern, *Lummi Indians,* 99–100; Collins, "John Fornsby," 321.

49. Tolmie, "History of Puget Sound," 36.

50. This contradiction also occurs to Karen Anderson in *Changing Woman: A History of Racial Ethnic Women in Modern America* (New York: Oxford University Press, 1996), 31.

51. Pomeroy, *Pacific Slope*, 34–35, 64, 70; Johansen and Gates, *Empire of the Columbia*, 270–71, 293–94, 301. The settlers of 1845 included George Washington Bush, a man of African descent who had located north of the Columbia because he arrived in the Willamette Valley shortly after a provisional American government there voted to exclude blacks. Oregon's law in 1849 prohibited men of Bush's ancestry from sitting on a jury. Sid White and S. E. Solberg, eds., *Peoples of Washington: Perspectives on Cultural Diversity* (Pullman: Washington State University Press, 1989), 79, 81; Gordon B. Dodds, *The American Northwest: A History of Oregon and Washington* (Arlington Heights, Ill.: Forum Press, 1986), 82–83.

52. E. A. Starling to Anson Dart, *ARCIA* (1852), 172; William Petit Trowbridge, "Journal of a Voyage on Puget Sound in 1853," *Pacific Northwest Quarterly* 33 (1942): 395; Farrar, "Diary of Colonel and Mrs. I. N. Ebey," 139–40; Meeker, *Pioneer Reminiscences*, 57.

53. Swan, "The Colonisations around Puget Sd," in Bancroft collection; Charles Miles and O. B. Sperlin, eds., *Building a State, 1889–1939* (Tacoma, Wash.: Washington State Historical Society, 1940), 404; Johansen and Gates, *Empire of the Columbia*, 290–91.

54. Trowbridge, "Journal of a Voyage," 397; *Columbian* (Olympia), November 6, 1852, 2, and January 15, 1853; Rabbison, "Growth of Towns" and "Capt. Henry Roder's Narrative," in Bancroft collection; Meeker, *Pioneer Reminiscences*, 43, 54. Cf. James G. Swan, who came in 1852 as a "moral refugee," turning his back on economic security in New England for an unorthodox life out West. *The Northwest Coast*, v.

55. Hall J. Kelley, an early promoter of Oregon settlement, wanted to teach Indians American habits of industry and give them plots of land in pioneer colonies. Powell, *Hall J. Kelley on Oregon*, 63–64, 85.

56. *Columbian*, May 21, 1853, 2.

57. Tolmie, "History of Puget Sound," 36.

58. WPA, *Told by the Pioneers*, vol. 1, 151, 135, 166; Gibbs, *Indian Tribes of Washington Territory*, 38; E. Denny, *Blazing the Way*, 312; Farrar, "Diary of Colonel and Mrs. I. N. Ebey," 134; A. Denny, *Pioneer Days*, 36; Trowbridge, "Journal of a Voyage," 396–97, 402; Frances Kautz, ed., "Extracts from the Diary of Gen. A. V. Kautz," *Washington Historian* 2 (1900): 14; Meeker, *Pioneer Reminiscences*, 129; E. A. Starling to Isaac I. Stevens, December 4, 1853, WTSIA, Letters Received, Microfilm A-171, Roll 9, Reel 17. Criteria for aboriginal village and camp sites appear in Collins, *Valley of the Spirits*, 55, 81; Elmendorf, *Structure of Twana Culture*, 258–59; Suttles, *Coast Salish Essays*, 23; Gunther, "Klallam Ethnography," 195, 199; Smith, "Puyallup of Washington," 5; Smith, *Indians of the Urban Northwest*, 3.

59. Catherine Blaine to her family, August 4, 1854, and May 31, 1854, and David E. Blaine to Mother, August 5, 1854, Blaine Family Papers, UW Manuscripts; "Diary of Colonel and Mrs. I. N. Ebey," 132; WPA, *Told by the Pioneers*, vol. 2, 33; vol. 1, 169; Trowbridge, "Journal of a Voyage," 393, 394, 396, 403; excerpt from diary of customs house at Olympia, November 19, 1851, in

Washington Centennial, "1845–1945," 38; Hancock, "Thirteen Years Residence;" H. A. G. to I. F. A., in *Columbian,* September 11, 1852, 3.

60. A. Denny, *Pioneer Days,* 51, 36; Robert C. Hill, in WPA, *Told by the Pioneers,* vol. 2, 115; E. Denny, *Blazing the Way,* 70, 74; Kautz, "Diary of Gen. A. V. Kautz," 117; Meeker, *Pioneer Reminiscences,* 129; WPA, *Told by the Pioneers,* vol. 1, 168; Gibbs, *Indian Tribes of Washington Territory,* 36; Theodore Winthrop, *The Canoe and Saddle, or Klalam and Klickatat,* ed. John H. Williams (Tacoma, Wash.: John H. Williams, 1913), 70; J. W. McCarthy, in Bennett, *Small World,* 195.

61. Gibbs, *Indian Tribes of Washington Territory,* 33; Farrar, "Diary of Colonel and Mrs. I. N. Ebey," *Washington Historical Quarterly* 7 (1916): 311, and 8 (1917): 57, 129; A. Denny, *Pioneer Days,* 65; Kautz, "Diary of Gen. A. V. Kautz," 12; Winthrop, *Canoe and Saddle,* 11; Abby J. Hanford, "Seattle and Its Indian War" and "Capt. Henry Roder's Narrative," in Bancroft collection; PSAC, "Journal," January 1, 1850; Hancock, *Narrative of Samuel Hancock,* 158.

62. Rabbison, "Growth of Towns"; Meeker, *Pioneer Reminiscences,* 47–48, 216; Hancock, *Narrative of Samuel Hancock,* 95, 112, 131; Swan, *Northwest Coast,* 152; Washington Centennial, "1845–1945," 8–9. For westward migrants' expectations, see Glenda Riley, *Women and Indians on the Frontier, 1825–1915* (Albuquerque: University of New Mexico Press, 1984).

63. Rabbison, "Growth of Towns."

64. *Columbian,* January 8, 1853, 2; January 15, 1853, 1 and 2; February 26, 1853, 2; March 5, 1853, 1; Bennett, *Small World,* 170, 150, 206; Swan, *Northwest Coast,* 317; Meeker, *Pioneer Reminiscences,* 47; Trowbridge, "Journal of a Voyage," 403; David Blaine to Mother, August 4, 1854; Hancock, *Narrative of Samuel Hancock,* 113, 124; A. Denny, *Pioneer Days,* 49; "Autobiography of Edwin Chalcraft," Manuscript 039, Washington State Library; DeL. Floyd Jones to Major E. D. Townsend, September 1, 1853, in *Indian Affairs of the Pacific–Puget Sound,* 1857, House Exec. Doc. 76, 34th Cong., 3d sess., Serial 906.

65. Rabbison, "Growth of Towns"; Farrar, "Diary of Colonel and Mrs. I. N. Ebey," 135.

66. *Columbian,* October 29, 1853, 2, and November 16, 1853, 2.

67. Miles and Sperlin, *Building a State,* 461, 462; Bennett, "Effect of White Contact," 12; Swan, "The Colonizations around Puget Sd," in Bancroft collection; Harry W. Deegan, *History of Mason County, Washington* (n.p., [1957]), 23; A. Denny, *Pioneer Days,* 45, 47, 85; Washington Centennial, "1845–1945," 38; Daniel L. Boxberger, *To Fish in Common: The Ethnohistory of Lummi Indian Salmon Fishing* (Lincoln: University of Nebraska Press, 1989), 24–5; Clarence Bagley, "Chief Seattle and Angeline," *Washington Historical Quarterly* 22 (October 1931): 245; Meeker, *Pioneer Reminiscences,* 504; L. L. Langness, "A Case of Post-Contact Reform among the Clallam" (M.A. thesis, University of Washington, 1959), 20; *Washington Pioneer* (formerly the *Columbian*), August 27, September 10, and November 26, 1853; Trowbridge, "Journal of a Voyage," 402, 404; Kautz, "Diary of Gen. A. V. Kautz," 13.

68. Farrar, "Diary of Colonel and Mrs. I. N. Ebey," 139–40; Catherine Blaine to Family, March 7, 1854; Meeker, *Pioneer Reminiscences*, 57; *ARCIA* (1852), 172; Trowbridge, "Journal of a Voyage," 395; Gibbs, *Indian Tribes of Washington Territory*, 37.

69. Hancock, *Narrative of Samuel Hancock*, 59, 119, 121, 130; Swan, *Northwest Coast*, 166; Bagley, "Chief Seattle and Angeline," 244–45; Cornelius H. Hanford, *Seattle and Environs* (Chicago: Pioneer Historical Publishing, 1924), vol. 1, 144; A. Denny, *Pioneer Days*, 37; Jonathan J. Bishop, "Why the 'Duke of York' was Friendly to the Whites," in WPA, *Told by the Pioneers*, unpublished manuscripts (Jefferson County), Washington State Library.

70. James G. McCurdy, *By Juan de Fuca's Strait, Pioneering along the Northwestern Edge of the Continent* (Portland, Ore.: Metropolitan Press, 1937), 26; Swan, *Northwest Coast*, 166; WPA, *Told by the Pioneers*, vol. 2, 83; "Capt. Henry Roder's Narrative," in Bancroft collection.

71. Gibbs, *Indian Tribes of Washington Territory*, 37.

72. E. Denny, *Blazing the Way*, 114; WPA, *Told by the Pioneers*, vol. 1, 166, 172; Bennett, *Small World*, 9; Kellogg, "History of Whidbey's Island," 11; Kautz, "Diary of Gen. A. V. Kautz," 14; Meeker, *Pioneer Reminiscences*, 118; PSAC, "Journal," August 19, 1851; Miles and Sperlin, *Building a State*, 405; Greg Russell Hubbard, "The Indian under the White Man's Law in Washington Territory, 1853–1889" (M.A. thesis, University of Washington, 1972), 48.

73. Bennett, *Small World*, 150–51.

74. Letter of Catherine Blaine, November 14, 1854.

75. Farrar, "Diary of Colonel and Mrs. I. N. Ebey," 132. All misspellings appear in original text. Also, WPA, *Told by the Pioneers*, vol. 1, 170, and vol. 2, 86; E. Denny, *Blazing the Way*, 46; Kellogg, "History of Whidbey's Island," 27; Winthrop, *Canoe and Saddle*, 22, 48; Hancock, *Narrative of Samuel Hancock*, 110, 112–13.

76. McCurdy, *By Juan de Fuca's Strait*, 38; "Capt. Henry Roder's Narrative," in Bancroft collection; A. Denny, *Pioneer Days*, 67–68; *Columbian*, October 8, 1853, 2; Letter of Catherine Blaine to unknown correspondent, March 7, 1854; Farrar, "Diary of Colonel and Mrs. I. N. Ebey," 44–45, 130.

77. *ARCIA* (1852), 168, 169–70.

78. Starling to I. I. Stevens, December 4 and 10, 1853, WTSIA, Roll 9, Reel 17; Jones, *Indian Affairs of the Pacific-Puget Sound*, Serial 906, 5; Kautz, "Diary of Gen. A. V. Kautz," *Washington Historian* 1, 118, and 2, 14–15; George Gibbs to George McClellan, March 23, 1854, UW Microfilm A-142; Gibbs, *Indian Tribes of Washington Territory*, 31; *ARCIA* (1853), 213–17; Charles H. Gates, *Messages of the Governors of the Territory of Washington to the Legislative Assembly, 1854–1889* (Seattle: University of Washington Publications in the Social Sciences, 1940), 11; *ARCIA* (1854–55), 451. When a citizen complained that Superintendent of Indian Affairs Anson Dart had been in office two years without deigning to visit Puget Sound, Dart replied that he had no means to visit—not one dollar for presents or travel. H. A. G. to I. F. A., *Columbian*, September 11, 1852, 3; Anson Dart to H. A. G., *Columbian*, October 9, 1852, 3.

79. Meeker, *Pioneer Reminiscences*, 119, 87, 65; Catherine Blaine to Friends, May 3, 1854. Allusions to squatters and merchants who harried the HBC appear in "The Nisqually Journal," *Washington Historical Quarterly* 11 (1920): 62, 141; 14 (1923): 229; 15 (1924): 139, 292. In the Bancroft collection, H. L. Yesler's "Settlement of Washington Territory" and Swan's "The Colonisations around Puget Sd" mention rivalries between town founders.

80. David E. Blaine to Father, June [illegible], 1854, and D. E. Blaine to Mother, August 4, 1854; Gibbs to McClellan, May 1, 1854; Meeker, *Pioneer Reminiscences*, 91, 119, 121; Gibbs, *Indian Tribes of Washington Territory*, 32; *ARCIA* (1852), 173; Starling to Stevens, December 5, 1853, WTSIA; Michael T. Simmons to Isaac I. Stevens, July 1, 1854, WTSIA, Roll 9, Reel 17; *Columbian*, August 27, 1853, 2; Capt. J. G. Parker, "Puget Sound," UW Microfilm 37, Rabbison, "Growth of Towns," and William A. Bell, "Settlement of Seattle," all in Bancroft collection, UW Microfilm 21.

81. Farrar, "Diary of Colonel and Mrs. I. N. Ebey," *Washington Historical Quarterly* 8 (1917), 139; *Columbian*, April 9, 1853, 2; Winthrop, *Canoe and Saddle*, 43; Hancock, *Narrative of Samuel Hancock*, 96–102; Gibbs, "Tribes of Western Washington and Northwestern Oregon," 188–89; *ARCIA* (1852), 172; *ARCIA* (1854–55), 452; Trowbridge, "Journal of a Voyage," 398; E. Denny, *Blazing the Way*, 312.

82. Hancock, *Narrative of Samuel Hancock*, 98, 108; Gibbs, *Indian Tribes of Washington Territory*, 36–37, 27, 29; McCurdy, *By Juan de Fuca's Strait*, 38; *ARCIA* (1852), 172, (1854–55), 451; Collins, "John Fornsby," 311; Huggins, "Reminiscences of Puget Sound," 314; *ARCIA* (1852), 169; Washington Centennial, "1845–1945," 21, 38; Wilkes, *Diary of Wilkes*, 88; Farrar, "Diary of Colonel and Mrs. I. N. Ebey," *Washington Historical Quarterly* 8: 57, 125, 134; PSAC, "Journal," September 23, 1850, and January 15, 1851; *Columbian*, April 30, 1853, 2; G. A. Barnes, "Oregon and California in 1849," in Bancroft Collection, UW Microfilm 36; Letter of Catherine Blaine, March 7, 1854; Meeker, *Pioneer Reminiscences*, 72.

83. Hancock, "Thirteen Years Residence," 200; Parker, "Puget Sound," and Yesler, "Settlement of Washington Territory," in Bancroft collection; Huggins, "Reminiscences of Puget Sound," 262; WPA, *Told by the Pioneers*, vol. 3, 24.

84. Starling to Stevens, December 4, 1853, WTSIA; Jones, *Indian Affairs of the Pacific-Puget Sound*, 9; Gibbs, *Indian Tribes of Washington Territory*, 29; Swan, *Northwest Coast*, 381; WPA, *Told by the Pioneers*, vol. 1, 172; Kellogg, "A History of Whidbey's Island," 28; "Capt. Henry Roder's Narrative," in Bancroft collection; *Columbian*, September 11, 1852; April 30, 1853, 2; October 8, 1853, 2.

85. Winthrop, *Canoe and Saddle*, 14, 15, 19; Hancock, "Thirteen Years Residence," 196; Gibbs, *Indian Tribes of Washington Territory*, 28, 36; McCurdy, *By Juan de Fuca's Strait*, 38; *ARCIA* (1852), 172; E. Denny, *Blazing the Way*, 374; Kane, *Wanderings of an Artist*, 138.

86. Edward Huggins to Ezra Meeker, April 15, 1903, Ezra Meeker Papers, Washington State Historical Society, Box 5, Folder 17; Gibbs to McClellan, March

23 and May 1, 1854; Huggins, "Reminiscences of Puget Sound," 262; Meeker, *Pioneer Reminiscences*, 45; PSAC, "Journal," January 1, 1834, November 18, 1849, June 27 and September 11, 1851, May 1 and June 25, 1852; Tolmie, *Physician and Fur Trader*, 235–36; Trowbridge, "Journal of a Voyage," 393–94; Gibbs, *Indian Tribes of Washington Territory*, 36–37; "Capt. Henry Roder's Narrative," in Bancroft collection; WPA, *Told by the Pioneers*, vol. 2, 86; M. T. Simmons to I. I. Stevens, July 1, 1854, WTSIA, Roll 9; Winthrop, *Canoe and Saddle*, 8–9, 5.

87. A surveyor named Hunt also died by violence in Swinomish country, and several Americans reportedly died at Indian hands in the Bellingham Bay area. E. Denny, *Blazing the Way*, 102; A. Denny, *Pioneer Days*, 67; *Columbian*, October 8, 1853, 2; *Pioneer and Democrat*, March 11, 1854, 2; March 25, 1854, 2; December 9, 1854, 2; Isaac I. Stevens to Major Chas. H. Larnard, February 9, 1854, WTSIA, Roll 1; Gibbs, *Indian Tribes of Washington Territory*, 37; Gibbs to McClellan, May 1, 1854; Starling to Stevens, December 4 and December 16, 1853, WTSIA.

88. Catherine Blaine to Friends, March 7, 1854.

89. Starling to Stevens, December 10, 1853, WTSIA, Roll 9.

90. *Seattle Sunday Star*, October 29, 1887, 3. This is the only known record of the speech. The approximate date must be surmised from a report in the *Washington Pioneer*, January 28, 1854, p, 2, c. 5, that the governor had just returned to Olympia from a trip down the Sound to ascertain the populations and conditions of the various tribes.

91. E. A. Starling to I. I. Stevens, December, 10, 1853, WTSIA, Roll 9, Reel 17; Gibbs, *Indian Tribes of Washington Territory*, 29; Caroline C. Leighton, *Life at Puget Sound with Sketches of Travel in Washington Territory, British Columbia, Oregon, and California, 1865–1881* (Boston: Lee and Shepard, 1884), 156. According to some sources, many Indians had already concluded that their own spirit powers could not reach the whites. Swan, *Northwest Coast*, 148, 174, 192–3; Smith, "Puyallup-Nisqually," 84.

92. John A. Rich obtained this information from a lawyer for Vivian Carkeek, who told on his own deathbed about hearing Smith's deathbed statement. *Seattle's Unanswered Challenge* (1947; reprint, Fairfield, Wash.: Ye Galleon Press, 1970), 45.

93. M. Eells, *Ten Years of Missionary Work*, 33–34; Letter of D. E. Blaine to Mother, August 4, 1854; George Gibbs, *Dictionary of the Chinook Jargon* (New York: Cramoisy Press, 1863; reprint, New York: AMS Press, 1970), vii; WPA, *Told by the Pioneers*, vol. 2, 83; H. A. Smith, "Our Aborigines," *Seattle Weekly Intelligencer*, August 30, 1873, p. 1, c. 4–6. For counterarguments and speculations on this topic, see Rudolf Kaiser, "Chief Seattle's Speech(es): American Origins and European Reception," in *Recovering the Word: Essays on Native American Literature*, ed. Brian Swann and Arnold Krupat (Berkeley and Los Angeles: University of California Press, 1987), 497–536; Howard Hanson, "Chief Seattle's Great Oration" (speech delivered to Washington State Historical Society, 1939; in UW Library, Special Collections), 14, citing Roberta F. Watt, *The Story of Seattle* (Seattle, 1932), 177.

94. Kaiser, "Chief Seattle's Speech(es)"; David Buerge and Vi Hilbert in Timothy Egan, "Chief's 1854 Speech Given New Meaning (and Text)," *New York Times,* April 21, 1991, p. 1, c. 1–2 and ff. Rich calls Smith an accomplished writer and poet. *Seattle's Unanswered Challenge.* In the article that included the famous speech, Smith himself said that Seattle was always flattered by marked attention from white men "and never so much as when seated at their tables."

95. Brian Dippie, *The Vanishing American: White Attitudes and U.S. Indian Policy* (Middletown, Conn.: Wesleyan University Press, 1982).

96. Snyder, "Skagit Society," 167; Snyder, "Quest for the Sacred in Northern Puget Sound," 154–55; Stern, *Lummi Indians,* 73.

97. After Seattle died in 1866, the non-Indians who placed a marker at his grave estimated his birthdate as 1786, apparently on the strength of his statement that he remembered seeing Vancouver when he was a boy. Bagley, "Chief Seattle and Angeline," 244.

3. TREATIES AND WAR

1. *Columbian,* May 7, 1853, and the following dates and pages in 1853: April 30, 2; July 9, 2; July 23, 2; October 17, 1; December 3, 1; December 17, 2.

2. Ezra Meeker, "Address delivered at Olympia March 2d 1903 upon the occasion of celebrating Creation day of Washington Territory fifty years before," Bagley Papers, Box 22, vol. 9; *Columbian,* April 30, 1853, 2; "Captain John E. Burns," in Bennett, *Small World,* 82.

3. James G. Swan, "Scenes in Washington Territory" (from *San Francisco Bulletin,* May 19, 1859, UW Special Collections); Winthrop, *Canoe and Saddle,* 19; Trowbridge, "Journal of a Voyage," 396; Transcript, *State v. Alexis* (Superior Court of Whatcom County, Washington, 1915), 36 (appended to Report of Daniel L. Boxberger, "The Ethnohistory of Western Washington Indians in the Nineteenth Century, with Reference to Shellfish Use and Control," May 1993, in records of Evergreen Legal Services, Seattle); WPA unpublished ms., Bishop, "Why the 'Duke of York' Was Friendly to Whites"; Edmond Meany, "Chief Patkanim," *Washington Historical Quarterly* 15 (1924): 192–93.

4. Elmendorf, *Twana Narratives,* 39–41, 88–91, 94–99, 108–10, 64–87; Waterman, "Notes on the Ethnology," 78–79; Stern, *Lummi Indians,* 55; Adams, "Recent Ethnology," 373; Gunther, "Klallam Ethnography," 307; Smith, "Puyallup of Washington," 19; Snyder, "Quest for the Sacred in Northern Puget Sound," 152.

5. Collins, "Growth of Class Distinctions," 335–37; Miller, "Centrality and Measures of Regional Structure," 271; Snyder, "Quest for the Sacred," 155; Twedell, "Componential Analysis," 68–69; Warren A. Snyder, "Southern Puget Sound Salish: Texts, Place Names and Dictionary," Sacramento Anthropological Society Paper 9 (1968): 134; *ARCIA* (1854–55), 452; *Columbian,* April 9, 1853, 2; Collins, "John Fornsby," 299–301; Elmendorf, *Twana Narra-*

tives, 128, 130–41, 143–53, 39–41, 60–63, 92–99. Regarding whites' catalytic effect on potlatching, see Miller and Boxberger, "Creating Chiefdoms"; Adams, "Recent Ethnology," 381; Collins, *Valley of the Spirits,* 10.

6. *ARCIA* (1852), 172; Kane, *Wanderings of an Artist,* 152–54; Farrar, "Diary of Colonel and Mrs. I. N. Ebey," 57; George A. Blankenship, *Lights and Shades of Pioneer Life on Puget Sound* (Olympia, Wash., 1923), 82; J. A. Costello, *The Siwash, Their Life, Legends and Tales* (Seattle: Calvert Company, 1895; reprint, Everett, Wash.: The Printers, 1974), 105; Albert Reagan, "Chief Cha-me-tsot's Potlatch Hall," in "Traditions of West Coast Indians" (1911), Washington State Library, Manuscript 219; Gibbs, Journal, Records of Boundary Claims, Commissions, and Arbitrations, 1853–1901, Records relating to Northwest Boundary Survey, NA, RG 76; notes of interview with Polan, Edmond S. Meany Papers, UW Manuscripts, Accession No. 106–70–12, Box 86, Folder 86–2; Elmendorf, "Coast Salish Status Ranking," 362, 364; Smith, *Puyallup-Nisqually,* 108; Elmendorf, *Structure of Twana Culture,* 313–14.

7. *Washington Pioneer,* December 3, 1853, 1; Starling to Stevens, December 10, 1853, WTSIA, Roll 9, Reel 17; *Pioneer and Democrat* (formerly the *Columbian*), July 8, 1854, 2.

8. *Pioneer and Democrat,* April 8, 1854, 1; Starling to Stevens, December 4, 1853, WTSIA, Roll 9, Reel 17; A. Denny, *Pioneer Days,* 68.

9. Bell, "Settlement of Seattle," in Bancroft collection; Gibbs to McClellan, May 1, 1854; letters of Catherine Blaine, March 7, 1854, and October 30, 1854; A. Denny, *Pioneer Days,* 67–68; E. Denny, *Blazing the Way,* 102–4; Swan, *Northwest Coast,* 381; Starling to Stevens, December 4, 1853, WTSIA, Roll 9, Reel 17. Early settlers appointed to judgeships are named in *Pioneer and Democrat,* April 8, 1854, 1; *Washington Pioneer,* December 3, 1853, 1.

10. Jefferson County cases numbers 2, 3, 4, and 5 against Sawinum, Tootoosh, Jack, and Watsersmi [Watsissimi], *Territory v. Slaham,* Jefferson County case number 9, and *Territory v. Tom Taylor,* Jefferson County case number 11, all in Territory District Court Files, Washington State Archives; Letter of G. B. Moore, *Columbian,* October 8, 1853, 2; George Gibbs, Journal, March 9–22, 1854. Of the first thirty-three cases on the docket of the First Judicial Circuit—which then embraced Klallam territory, Whidbey Island, and lands from the Stillaguamish River to the international boundary—the defendants in twenty-one were either Indians or persons accused of selling liquor to Indians. Territory District Court Case Files, Jefferson County Clerk, 1854–1889.

11. Stevens to Major Chas. H. Larnard, February 9, 1854, WTSIA, Roll 1; *Columbian,* October 8, 1853, 2; *Pioneer and Democrat,* March 18, 1854, 2; Gibbs to McClellan, March 23, 1854. This mayhem had an equally violent sequel. *Pioneer and Democrat,* December 9, 1854, 2.

12. Gibbs, Journal in Records of Boundary Claims; Gibbs to McClellan, March 23, 1854.

13. Indians could testify only against other Indians. Laws of Washington, 1st session (1854), Act to Regulate the Practice and Proceedings in Civil Ac-

tions, and Act to Regulate the Practice and Pleadings in Prosecutions for Crimes; Hubbard, "Indian under the White Man's Law," 41, 44.

14. *Pioneer and Democrat*, March 25, 1854, 1.

15. Comments of Mr. Biles, *Pioneer and Democrat*, March 25, 1854, 1; comments of Mr. Chenoweth, *Pioneer and Democrat*, April 22, 1854, 1; Catherine Blaine to Friends, May 3, 1854.

16. *Pioneer and Democrat*, April 22, 1854, 3, and March 25, 1854, 1; Laws of Washington, 2d session (1855); Hubbard, "Indian under the White Man's Law," 48. Studies of whites' attitudes toward people of white and Indian ancestry include Dippie, *Vanishing American*, 260–61; Robert E. Bieder, *Science Encounters the Indian, 1820–1880: The Early Years of American Ethnology* (Norman: University of Oklahoma Press, 1986), 166–67, 230–31; Van Kirk, *Many Tender Ties*, 201–42.

17. Robert A. Trennert, Jr., *Alternative to Extinction: Federal Indian Policy and the Beginnings of the Reservation System, 1846–51* (Philadelphia: Temple University Press, 1975), 3, 29, 56; Prucha, *Great Father*, 403, 326–27.

18. Trennert, *Alternative to Extinction*, 39, 53; Albert L. Hurtado, *Indian Survival on the California Frontier* (New Haven, Conn.: Yale University Press, 1988), 125–26, 135, 141; John M. Findlay, "An Elusive Institution: The Birth of Indian Reservations in Gold Rush California," in *State and Reservation*, ed. George P. Castile and Robert L. Bee (Tucson: University of Arizona Press, 1992), 13–35; James J. Rawls, *Indians of California: The Changing Image* (Norman: University of Oklahoma Press, 1984), 148; Kent D. Richards, *Isaac I. Stevens, Young Man in a Hurry* (Provo, Utah: Brigham Young University Press, 1979), 170, 190–92, 194–95.

19. Stevens to Manypenny, December 26, 1853, Senate Exec. Doc. No. 34, 33rd Cong., 1st sess., Serial 698, 6–7; Stevens to Manypenny, December 29, 1853, ibid., 13–14; Manypenny to Robert McClelland, February 6, 1854, ibid., 1–2; Record of the Proceedings of the Commission to Hold Treaties with the Indian Tribes in Washington Territory and the Blackfoot Country, December 7, 1854–March 3, 1855, WTSIA, Roll 26; 10 *United States Statutes* 330; Prucha, *Great Father*, 402–3.

20. *ARCIA* (1854–55), 456; Starling to Stevens, December 10, 1853, WTSIA; Gibbs, *Indian Tribes of Washington Territory*, 29–30.

21. Amoss, *Coast Salish Spirit Dancing*, 149; Smith, "Puyallup of Washington," 5; Smith, *Puyallup-Nisqually*, 35, 108; Snyder, "Quest for the Sacred in Northern Puget Sound," 151, 153; Collins, *Valley of the Spirits*, 136; Elmendorf, *Twana Narratives*, 92–99; McCurdy, *By Juan de Fuca's Strait*, 26; Swan, *Northwest Coast*, 166; A. Denny, *Pioneer Days*, 68; *ARCIA* (1852), 169; Gibbs, *Indian Tribes of Washington Territory*, 29.

22. Smith, *Puyallup-Nisqually*, 142, 108; Elmendorf, *Structure of Twana Culture*, 267–70, 332; Smith, "Puyallup of Washington," 14; Collins, "John Fornsby," 301, 305.

23. Entries of January 21 and 12, 1855, Record of the Proceedings ... to Hold Treaties, WTSIA, Roll 26; Collins, "John Fornsby," 308; *Pioneer and De-*

mocrat, February 3, 1855, 2; Swan, *Northwest Coast,* 334; Richards, *Isaac I. Stevens,* 203.

24. Richards, *Isaac I. Stevens,* 199. Raymond J. DeMallie argues that the rituals of treaty councils are as important to reconstructing the parties' understandings as are speeches. "Touching the Pen: Plains Indian Treaty Councils in Ethnohistorical Perspective," in *Ethnicity on the Great Plains,* ed. Frederick C. Luebke (Lincoln: University of Nebraska Press, 1980), 38–41.

25. Record of Proceedings, December 25–26, 1854; January 22 and January 25–26, 1855; Swan, *Northwest Coast,* 341–45.

26. While Stevens was negotiating treaties at Point Elliott and Point No Point, the territorial legislature was voiding marriages between Indians and non-Indians. Gates, *Messages of the Governors,* 16.

27. Record of the Proceedings, December 7 and 10, 1854; Stevens to Manypenny, December 30, 1854, in Documents Relating to the Negotiation of Indian Treaties, Ratified Treaty No. 281, UW Microfilm A-8207, Reel 5.

28. Record of the Proceedings, December 26, 1854.

29. Record of the Proceedings, January 25, 1855, and December 10, 1854.

30. Record of the Proceedings, January 22, 1855.

31. Prucha, *Great Father,* xxvii; White, *Middle Ground,* 84–85; DeMallie, "Touching the Pen," 42, 50–51; Amoss, *Coast Salish Spirit Dancing,* 8; Smith, *Puyallup-Nisqually,* 32; Elmendorf, *Structure of Twana Culture,* 312; Vi Hilbert and Crisca Bierwert, *Ways of the Lushootseed People: Ceremonies and Traditions of Northern Puget Sound Indians* (Seattle: United Indians of All Tribes Foundation, 1980), 37. Twanas used the terms for parents only in an actual parental relationship but considered it "nice" and "careful" to address respected elders by the terms for uncles, aunts, or grandparents. Elmendorf, *Structure of Twana Culture,* 390. Klallams customarily addressed and referred to people by names rather than kinship terms. Gunther, "Klallam Ethnography," 259. Minutes of the various proceedings vary considerably in the amount of dialogue they purport to reproduce verbatim. Minutes of the Medicine Creek conference say only that the Indians had some discussion, while records of debates at Point No Point are detailed.

32. Record of the Proceedings, January 25, 1855.

33. Record of the Proceedings, January 25–26, 1855. Recollections that treaty gifts were few and cheap are in Transcript, *Duwamish et al. v. United States,* United States Court of Claims (1927), UW Microfilm A-7374, 596, 612, 641; Meeker, *Pioneer Reminiscences,* 236; Elizabeth Shackleford, "A History of the Puyallup Indian Reservation, Tacoma"(thesis, College of Puget Sound, 1918), 10. Standards for a potlatch host's generosity appear in Collins, *Valley of the Spirits,* 139; Snyder, "Quest for the Sacred in Northern Puget Sound"; Snyder, "Skagit Society," 81–83; Elmendorf, *Structure of Twana Culture,* 343.

34. Snyder, "Skagit Society," 167, 468; Collins, *Valley of the Spirits,* 120; Elmendorf, *Structure of Twana Culture,* 333; Smith, "Puyallup of Washington," 20.

35. Meeker, *Pioneer Reminiscences*, 244, 151; Swan, *Northwest Coast*, 345; Adams, "Recent Ethnology," 373; Smith, "Puyallup of Washington," 20. A Skagit-Swinomish historian asserts that Indians signed the treaties with misgivings but a recognition of the inevitable. Sampson, *Indians of Skagit County*, 31.

36. Two men present at Point Elliott claimed much later that the Indians conferred before meeting Stevens and agreed on a single Indian negotiating strategy. Testimony of Henry Kwina and Tom Squiqui, *State v. Alexis*, 13, 42.

37. 10 *United States Statutes* 1132; 12 *United States Statutes* 927; 12 *United States Statutes* 933. See also *ARCIA* (1854–55), 457–58 (census prepared in anticipation of treaties); Indian Claims Commission, *Coast Salish and Western Washington Indians*, 32, 34, 92, 112.

38. Testimony of Wapato John, *Duwamish et al. v. U.S.*, 662; Meeker, *Pioneer Reminiscences*, 236, 241, 242; Depositions of Jack Wheeler, 6, and Bill Kanim, 9, In the Matter of the Claims of Indian Tribes and Individual Indians against the Government Arising Out of the Treaty of Point Elliott, NA PNR RG75, Tulalip Box 96, Folder 60, p. 6.

39. *ARCIA* (1858), 576–77; Smith, "Puyallup-Nisqually," 29, 31; Marian W. Smith, "The Coast Salish of Puget Sound," *American Anthropologist* 43 (1941): 198–99. In 1994 the government of the Yakima Indian Nation changed the spelling of its name to Yakama. *Seattle Times*, January 24, 1994, B2. I use the former spelling because it was preferred during the period covered in this book. Spellings of Klickitat also vary. I adopt the current spelling for geographic features.

40. William Fraser Tolmie to His Excellency Fayette McMullin, January 12, 1858, in Bagley Papers, Box 22; Gibbs to Swan, January 7, 1857, in Swan, *Northwest Coast*, Appendix, 426–29; Richard White, "The Treaty at Medicine Creek: Indian-White Relations on Upper Puget Sound, 1830–1880" (M.A. thesis, University of Washington, 1972), 41, 65; Thomas W. Prosch, "The Indian Wars in Washington Territory," *Quarterly of the Oregon Historical Society* 16 (1915): 6; Smith, *Puyallup-Nisqually*, 31–32.

41. Simmons to Stevens, March 26, 1855, WTSIA, Roll 9, Reel 17; Granville O. Haller, "The Indian War of 1855–56, in Washington and Oregon," Bagley Papers, Box 22, vol. 7; David Blaine to Parents, January 24, 1855; *Pioneer and Democrat*, December 30, 1854, 2; February 3, 1855, 2; May 5, 1855; White, "Treaty at Medicine Creek," 59, 93. Sources for the "land of darkness" story include Tolmie to McMullin, Bagley Papers; J. Ross Browne, *Indian War in Oregon and Washington Territories*, House Exec. Doc. 38, 35th Cong., 1st sess., 11; Roy N. Lokken, "Frontier Defense in Washington Territory, 1853–1861" (M.A. thesis, University of Washington, 1951), 40; W. B. Gosnell, "Indian War in Washington Territory," *Washington Historical Quarterly* 17 (1926): 294.

42. Tolmie to McMullin, Bagley Papers; E. Denny, *Blazing the Way*, 67; Tolmie, "History of Puget Sound," 40; WPA, *Told by the Pioneers*, vol. 1, 176–80; *Puget Sound Courier*, August 24, 1855; *Pioneer and Democrat*, September 28, 1855, and October 12, 1855, 2; Haller, "The Indian War of

1855–56," in Bagley papers; Bennett, *Small World*, 185, 196; Lokken, "Frontier Defense," 40.

43. *Pioneer and Democrat*, October 19, 1855, 2, and November 9, 1855, 2; United States Navy, Log of the *Decatur*, October 25 and 31, 1855, UW Microfilm 58; Jerry A. Eckrom, *Remembered Drums: A History of the Puget Sound Indian War* (Walla Walla, Wash.: Pioneer Press Books, 1989), 20–21; Lokken, "Frontier Defense," 43–47; White, "Treaty at Medicine Creek," 72; Tolmie to McMullin, Bagley Papers; Bennett, *Small World*, 14, 149, 151–52, 186–88, 197.

44. U.S. Navy, *Decatur* Log, October 31 and November 3, 1855.

45. *Pioneer and Democrat* on following dates and pages: December 14, 1855, 2; February 1, 1856, 2; February 15, 1856, 2; March 7, 1856, 2; June 27, 1856, 2; September 12, 1856, 2; Gates, *Messages of the Governors*, January 21, 1856, and December 3, 1856, 23–39; Indian Council, August 4, 1856, in Bagley Papers, Box 22, vol. 3; Jones, *Indian Affairs of the Pacific-Puget Sound*, 220 and ff.; Erasmus D. Keyes, *Fighting Indians in Washington Territory*, originally *Fifty Years' Observation of Men and Events* (New York: Scribner, 1884; reprint, Fairfield, Wash.: Ye Galleon Press, 1988), 7–16; Eckrom, *Remembered Drums*, 44, 49–53, 63–64, 73–79, 95, 107, 122, 124–25, 133–34, 139, 141–47, 150; Lokken, "Frontier Defense," 50, 53, 78, 88, 102, 132, 158–60, 168; Prosch, "Indian Wars"; White, "Treaty at Medicine Creek," 66, 92; Hubert Howe Bancroft, *History of Washington, Idaho, and Montana, 1845–1889* (San Francisco: History Company, 1890), 123, 164; Gosnell, "Indian War," 297; Elmendorf, *Twana Narratives*, 153; Meeker Family Papers, Notebook II, 13, UW Manuscripts Vertical File No. 362A-C.

46. *Puget Sound Courier*, August 24, 1855; *Pioneer and Democrat* on following dates and pages: August 31, 1855, 2; October 26, 1855, 2; December 7, 1855, 2; March 28, 1856, 2 and 3; April 11, 1856, 2; August 8, 1856, 3; September 5, 1856, 2; September 12, 1856, 1; February 27, 1857, 1; Gates, *Messages of the Governors*, January 21 and December 3, 1856; Browne, *Indian War*, 2, 4–13; Gosnell, "Indian War," 294–96; Haller, "Indian War of 1855–56"; U.S. Navy, Log, November 3, 1855; Richards, *Isaac I. Stevens*, 241.

47. Report of George Gibbs and H. A. Goldsborough, June 6, 1856, in *Message from the President of the United States*, Senate Exec. Doc. 41, 34th Cong., 3d sess., Serial 881, 26; Tolmie to McMullin, Bagley Papers; Tolmie, "History of Puget Sound"; Proceedings of Military Commission, April 14–15, 1856, NA, RG 393, Records of U.S. Army Continental Commands, 1821–1920, Fort Steilacoom, pp. 21, 24, 26; "The Widow's Story" (interview with Leschi's widow), in Papers of Ezra Meeker, Washington State Historical Society (copy of typescript provided by Jerry A. Eckrom); notes of interview with Henry Martin (cousin of Leschi), Edmond S. Meany Papers, UW Manuscripts, Folder 86–2.

48. Gates, *Messages of the Governors*, 25; *Pioneer and Democrat*, March 28, 1856, 2; Haller, "Indian War of 1855–56"; Browne, *Indian War*, 9–12; Bancroft, *History of Washington, Idaho, and Montana*, 276; Eckrom, *Remembered Drums*, 110, 161, 162; Hunt and Kaylor, *Washington West of the Cas-*

cades, 144, 163; Meeker, *Pioneer Reminiscences,* 205, 446; Prosch, "Indian Wars," 6; Bennett, *Small World,* 86.

49. "The Widow's Story," Meeker papers; Gibbs and Goldsborough, Senate Exec. Doc. 41, Serial 881, 24; Tolmie, "History of Puget Sound," 41; Tolmie to McMullin, Bagley Papers; Proceedings of Military Commission of April, 1856, pp. 7, 13–14, 28; *Pioneer and Democrat,* November 9, 1855, 2, and February 27, 1857, 1; *ARCIA* (1856), 185; Hanford, "Seattle and Its Indian War," in Bancroft collection; Meeker, *Pioneer Reminiscences,* 209–10; Eckrom, *Remembered Drums,* 9, 21, 24, 74; White, "Treaty at Medicine Creek," 36, 41–42; Richards, *Isaac I. Stevens,* 259.

50. A. Denny, *Pioneer Days,* 74. Also, Gates, *Messages of the Governors,* 16–17; Meeker, *Pioneer Reminiscences,* 12–13.

51. Elmendorf, *Twana Narratives,* 126–64; Suttles and Lane, "Southern Coast Salish," 495; Elmendorf, *Structure of Twana Culture,* 465–70; Smith, *Puyallup-Nisqually,* 154, 161; Smith, "Puyallup of Washington," 26; Collins, *Valley of the Spirits,* 115; R. Brian Ferguson and Neil L. Whitehead, eds., *War in the Tribal Zone: Expanding States and Indigenous Warfare* (Santa Fe, N.M.: School of American Research Press, 1992), 19, 142–43.

52. Thomas Stowell Phelps, "The Indian Attack on Seattle January 26, 1856" (originally "Reminiscences of Seattle, Washington Territory," in *The United Service Magazine* 5, no. 6 [1881]; reprint, Seattle: Farwest Lithograph & Printing, 1932), 41. Other accounts of Indian fighters' "superstitions" appear in Keyes, *Fighting Indians,* 10, 13; Bell, "Settlement of Seattle," and Hanford, "Seattle and Its Indian War," in Bancroft collection.

53. J. W. Wiley to *Pioneer and Democrat,* November 9, 1855, 2; Keyes, *Fighting Indians,* 2, 13; Hanford, "Seattle and Its Indian War." There is abundant evident that Americans retaliated by indiscriminately killing Indians. *ARCIA* (1856), 186; *Pioneer and Democrat,* February 27, 1857, 1; Letter of David Blaine, June 20, 1856; Bell, "Settlement of Seattle"; Phelps, "Indian Attack on Seattle," 52, 54; PSAC, "Journal," May 23, 1856; Bennett, *Small World,* 190–92. Documenting the use of native auxiliaries are Phelps, "Indian Attack on Seattle," 50, 52; *Pioneer and Democrat,* February 8, 1856, 2, and February 15, 1856, 2; James Tilton to Capt. E. Lander, February 12, 1856, Adjutant General Correspondence, Outgoing, Washington State Archives RG 82/1–1; Nathan D. Hill to Stevens, February 2 and 21 and March 31, 1856, WTSIA, Roll 10, Reel 21; D. S. Maynard to Stevens, February 19, 1856, ibid.; E. S. Fowler to Stevens, March 7, 1856, WTSIA, Roll 10, Reel 22; Richards, *Isaac I. Stevens,* 265. Natives lent assistance but on their own terms. They suspended war activity when they wished and otherwise resisted integration into the American military hierarchy.

54. *Pioneer and Democrat,* November 9, 2–3. On war's tendency to polarize, see Elaine Scarry, *The Body in Pain* (New York: Oxford University Press, 1985), 88.

55. Gates, *Messages of the Governors,* 32; Gibbs and Goldsborough, Serial 881, including Doc. A, pp. 48–50; Gosnell, "Indian War," 295; Browne, *Indian*

War, 10–11; PSAC, "Journal," May 21, 1856; Bennett, *Small World*, 94; Eckrom, *Remembered Drums*, 143–44; Lokken, "Frontier Defense," 93, 123–28. Whites also resisted the relocation of Indians who worked for them. D. S. Maynard to M. T. Simmons, September 19, 1856, WTSIA, Roll 10, Reel 20. Volunteer militia members bickered among themselves and often did not cooperate with the army. Richards, *Isaac I. Stevens*, 261, 263.

56. Indian Council, August 4, 1856, Bagley Papers.

57. Ibid. The next month Ford told Stevens that formerly hostile Indians showed in other talks that they were fully satisfied "as to the superiority of the white race." Ford to Stevens, September 30, 1856, WTSIA, Roll 10, Reel 21.

58. Records of U.S. Army Continental Commands, 1821–1920, Fort Steila-coom, NA RG 393; *ARCIA* (1856), 186–7; *ARCIA*, (1857), 339; Proceedings of a Military Commission Convened at Seattle, May, 1856, Washington State Archives (copy provided by Jerry A. Eckrom); Samuel McCaw to I. I. Stevens, April 12, 1856, WTSIA, Roll 10, Reel 21; *Pioneer and Democrat* on following dates and pages: September 12, 1856, 2; February 27, 1857, 1; April 1, 1859, 3; *Territory v. Wahoolit alias Nisqually or Yelm Jim*, Thurston County Clerk's Records, Case 262, Washington Territorial Court Records; *Territory v. Leschi*, Pierce County Clerk's Records, Case No. 140, ibid.; Yesler, "Settlement of Washington Territory," in Bancroft Collection.

59. *Pioneer and Democrat*, February 27, 1857, 1; *Territory v. Wahoolit*; Jones, *Indian Affairs*; Richards, *Isaac I. Stevens*, 310. According to Phelps, a military commission in Seattle acquitted twenty-one Indians because "the evidence proved them only guilty of legitimate warfare." But evidence at the trial was consistent with the claim that some defendants were coerced to accompany hostile Indians. Phelps, "Indian Attack on Seattle," 52; Proceedings of a Military Commission, May, 1856, Washington State Archives.

60. Meeker, *Pioneer Reminiscences*, 416; Richards, *Isaac I. Stevens*, 280. From 1853 to 1861, judges were appointed by the Democrats, Stevens's party. J. J. McGilvra, "Reminiscences of the Early Days of the Washington Bar," UW Special Collections.

61. *Territory v. Leschi*, Pierce County Case No. 140; Butler P. Anderson [to Isaac I. Stevens?], May 4, 1858, *Washington Historical Quarterly* 1 (1907): 59; *Leschi v. Washington Territory*, Washington Territorial Reports 1 (1857): 13. Also, M. T. Simmons to Stevens, December 31, 1856, WTSIA, Roll 9, Reel 17.

62. Simmons to Stevens, December 31, 1856, and April 4, 1857, WTSIA, Roll 9, Reel 17; WPA, *Told by the Pioneers*, vol. 1, 143; Letter of Theodore O. Williams, March 13, 1904, in *Washington Historical Quarterly* 2 (1934): 300; Richards, *Isaac I. Stevens*, 309.

63. Starling to Stevens, December 10, 1853, WTSIA, Roll 9, Reel 17; Gibbs, "Tribes of Western Washington and Northwestern Oregon," 189; Elmendorf, "Skokomish Sorcery," 161–62; Smith, *Puyallup-Nisqually*, 161. Cf. John Phillip Reid, *A Law of Blood: The Primitive Law of the Cherokee Nation* (New York: New York University Press, 1970), 70.

64. Elmendorf, *Twana Narratives,* 153; Smith, *Puyallup-Nisqually,* 154; Smith, "Puyallup of Washington," 26. Indians on trial for acts of war no doubt recognized many of their judges and jurors as men who had recently faced them in battle.

65. Ford to Stevens, December 31, 1856, WTSIA, Roll 10, Reel 21; Meeker, *Pioneer Reminiscences,* 451; R. C. Fay to M. T. Simmons, December 31, 1857, WTSIA, Roll 10, Reel 22; Simmons to J. W. Nesmith, December 31, 1857, WTSIA, Roll 9, Reel 17. Seattle told American officials about an attempt by Yakima Indians to recruit chiefs on the Sound for an uprising in the event of Leschi's execution. G. A. Paige to I. I. Stevens, April 14, 1857, WTSIA, Roll 20, Reel 20.

66. Elmendorf, *Twana Narratives,* 153–61.

67. Wahoolit's belief that the important conflicts for Indians were those with other Indians shows an inward deflection of anger common among oppressed groups and may reflect conditions late in the century, when Frank Allen heard this story.

68. James Tilton to Isaac Stevens, September 8, 1856, Washington Territorial Volunteers Papers, Indian War Correspondence, Washington State Archives, RG 1/A-3, Box 4, Folder 16; Simmons to Nesmith, December 31, 1857, WTSIA, Roll 9, Reel 17; Journal of S. S. Ford, Jr., May 30, 1856, WTSIA, Roll 10, Reel 21; Ford to Simmons, September 30, 1856, ibid.; Gosnell, "Indian War," 293; "The Widow's Story," Meeker Papers; Proceedings of Military Commission at Fort Steilacoom, December 17, 1855, and Proceedings of Military Commission, April 14–15, 1856, Records of U.S. Army Continental Command.

69. Stevens to R. C. Fay, December 29, 1856, NA PNR RG 75, M-2011, Reel 1; following documents in WTSIA, Roll 10, Reel 21: Samuel McCaw to Stevens, April 12, 1856; Ford to Stevens, May 3, 1856; Ford to Stevens, May 16, 1856; Ford's journal, June 15 and September 30, 1856; Letters of Nathan D. Hill to Stevens, 1856; D. S. Maynard to Stevens, February 9, 1856; Letters of H. Haley to Stevens, spring 1856, WTSIA, Roll 10, Reel 20; G. A. Paige to Simmons, September 26, 1856, ibid.; following documents in WTSIA, Roll 10, Reel 22: E. S. Fowler to Simmons, September 23, 1856; Fay to Stevens, November 30, 1856; Fay to Simmons, September 1856; Gosnell to Stevens, April 2, 1856; Gosnell, "Indian War," 292; *Pioneer and Democrat,* November 6, 1857, 1; Simmons to Nesmith, November 27, 1857, WTSIA, Roll 9, Reel 17; *ARCIA* (1858), 587; Fitzhugh to Simmons, March 5, 1858, NA PNR RG 75, M-1011; Charles Edwin Garretson, " A History of the Washington Superintendency of Indian Affairs, 1855–1865" (M.A. thesis, University of Washington, 1962), 79.

70. Browne, *Indian Affairs,* 2–3; Mary Brown to Sister Almida, September 29, 1861, Brown Family Papers, Washington State Library Manuscript 071; Charles Prosch, *Reminiscences of Washington Territory* (Seattle: n.p., 1904), 13, 42; Jas. H. Goudy to Simmons, January 6, 1861, NA PNR RG 75, M-2011; *Washington Standard,* January 19, 1861, 2, and July 9, 1864, 1; Ezra Meeker, "Uncle Ezra's Short Stories for Children" (Tacoma, Wash., n.d.); Bell, "Settlement of

Seattle," in Bancroft collection; McGilvra, "Reminiscences of the Early Days," 1; John R. Watt, "Introduction to Economic and Labor History of Western Washington" (M.A. thesis, University of Washington, 1942), 52, 55, 62.

71. Fay to Stevens, April 31, 1857, WTSIA, Roll 10, Reel 22; Fowler to Stevens, March 29, 1856, ibid.; Simmons to Stevens, April 4 and May 1, 1857, WTSIA, Roll 9, Reel 17; Fitzhugh to Stevens, February 8, 1856, WTSIA, Roll 10, Reel 20; Paige to Stevens, May 13, 1857, ibid.; Ford to Stevens, November 22, 1856, WTSIA, Roll 10, Reel 21; *Pioneer and Democrat*, November 6, 1857, 1; Diary of James Swan, May 20, 1859, James G. Swan Papers, UW Manuscripts, Box 5; Kellogg, "History of Whidbey's Island," 42; Elmendorf, *Twana Narratives*, 132–36.

72. Simmons to Stevens, May 1, 1857, WTSIA; Ford to Stevens, December 31, 1856, WTSIA, Roll 10, Reel 21.

73. Simmons to Nesmith, December 31, 1857, WTSIA, Roll 9, Reel 17; *ARCIA* (1857), 317; *ARCIA* (1858), 586; Simmons to C.H. Mott, October 10, 1858, NA PNR RG 75, M-2011.

74. Simmons to Nesmith, August 14, 1858, WTSIA, Roll 9, Reel 18; Simmons to Edward R. Geary, August 18 and 20, 1859, ibid.; Ford to Stevens, December 1, 1856, WTSIA, Roll 20, Reel 21; N. D. Hill to Stevens, March 17, 1857, ibid.; Paige to Simmons, August 8, 1858, WTSIA, Roll 10, Reel 20.

75. Simmons to Stevens, December 29, 1856, WTSIA, Roll 10, Reel 20; Hill to Stevens, December 31, 1856, WTSIA, Roll 10, Reel 21; Fay to Stevens, January 1, 1857, WTSIA, Reel 22; *ARCIA* (1857), 334; *ARCIA* (1858), 223; Gates, *Messages of the Governors*, 58; report of William M. Morrow, June 30, 1861, WTSIA, Roll 9, Reel 19; Fitzhugh to Simmons, January 12, 1856, NA PNR RG 75, M-2011.

76. Simmons to Nesmith, September 16 and December 22, 1858, WTSIA, Roll 9, Reel 18; Simmons to Geary, September 1, 1860, ibid.; Agent to Nesmith, September 30, 1857, NA PNR RG 75, M-2011; Geary to Simmons, August 31, 1860, ibid.; Annual Report, Tulalip Reservation, September 30, 1862, ibid.; *ARCIA* (1859), 391; *ARCIA* (1860), 198–99; *ARCIA* (1861/62), 386, 389, 410; *ARCIA* (1864), 80; *ARCIA* (1870), 17.

77. *ARCIA* (1861/1862), 384; *ARCIA* (1870), 17; Simmons to Geary, January 1, 1861, WTSIA, Roll 9, Reel 19; Gosnell to William Miller, July 26, 1861, ibid.; Annual report of W. B. Gosnell, August 18, 1861, ibid.; *Washington Standard* on following dates and pages: July 27, 1861, 1; February 14, 1863; September 17, 1864, 3; October 19, 1868, 3; *Territorial Republican*, October 19, 1868, 3.

78. Simmons to Geary, December 13, 1859, WTSIA, Roll 9, Reel 18; *ARCIA* (1860), 199; *ARCIA* (1862), 462; *ARCIA* (1863), 4; *ARCIA* (1864/65), 60. One agent said, "An Indian will very readily live anywhere, if there is any inducement for doing so." *ARCIA* (1864/65), 457.

79. *ARCIA* (1862/63), 439; *ARCIA* (1861/62), 390, 405–6; *ARCIA* (1864/65), 75; Simmons to Geary, January 1, 1861, WTSIA, Roll 9, Reel 19; Annual report of E. C. Chirouse, September 30, 1862, ibid.; Howe to Hale, Jan-

uary 18, 1863, ibid.; Chirouse to Howe, February 25, 1865, NA PNR RG 75, M-2011, Reel 1.

80. Browne, *Indian Affairs*, 6, 4; E. C. Fitzhugh, Annual Report, September 1, 1856, WTSIA, Roll 10, Reel 20; H. Haley to Stevens, May 2, 1856, WTSIA, Roll 10, Reel 20; *ARCIA* (1861/62), 387; *ARCIA* (1864/65), 74; Annual Report of W. B. Gosnell, WTSIA, Roll 9, Reel 19. For several years officials failed to fulfill the treaty promise to provide doctors. *ARCIA* (1858), 579; Simmons to Nesmith, October 15, 1857, and August 15, 1858, WTSIA, Roll 9, Reel 17.

81. Fay to Stevens, April 25, 1856, WTSIA, Roll 10, Reel 22; Fay to Simmons, June 30, 1860, NA PNR RG 75, M-2011; Hill to Stevens, April 20, May 20, and June 24, 1856, WTSIA, Roll 10, Reel 21; following documents in WTSIA, Roll 10, Reel 20: Fitzhugh to Stevens, February 7, 1858; Haley to Stevens, April 7, 22, and 27, 1856; D. S. Maynard to Simmons, September 19, 1856; Paige to Simmons, September 26, 1856; Paige to Stevens, December 24, 1856, and May 13, 1857; *ARCIA* (1858), 576.

82. *ARCIA* (1858), 580; *ARCIA* (1857), 329–30; *ARCIA* (1859), 402; Fay to Stevens, March 17, 1856, WTSIA, Roll 10, Reel 22; Fay to Stevens, January 1, 1857, ibid.; A. J. Simmons to Stevens, February 19, 1856, ibid.; Fay to M. T. Simmons, June 30, 1860, NA PNR RG 75, M-2011; C. C. Finkboner to S. D. Howe, January 18, 1863, and May 2, 1864, ibid.; Finkboner to G. D. Hill, March 30, 1870, ibid.; Simmons to Stevens, December 29, 1856, WTSIA, Roll 9, Reel 17; Simmons to Nesmith, December 31, 1857, ibid.; Capt. G. E. Pickett to Simmons, June 19, 1860, WTSIA, Roll 9, Reel 18; Fitzhugh to Stevens, December 12, 1856, WTSIA, Roll 10, Reel 20; Report of William Morrow, June 30, 1861, WTSIA, Reel 19; T. Hubbard to Stephens [*sic*], May 26, 1856, WTSIA, Roll 10, Reel 21; Hill to Stevens, March 17, 1857, ibid.

83. Browne, *Indian Affairs*, 4; Paige to Stevens, November 30, 1856, WTSIA, Roll 10, Reel 20; *ARCIA* (1857), 326; *ARCIA* (1859), 402; *Pioneer and Democrat*, November 6, 1857, 1; Finkboner to Geo. D. Hill, September 28, 1869, NA M-2011, Reel 2; Diary of John Campbell, UW Manuscripts; Meeker Family Papers, Notebooks I–III; Accounts of Mill Hands, A. J. Miller Company (1860–62), UW Manuscripts, Vertical File No. 94; WPA, *Told by the Pioneers*, vol. 2, 179, 181; Collins, "John Forsnby," 295, 307; Thomas Somerville, "The Mediterranean of the Pacific," *Harper's New Monthly Magazine* 41 (1870): 487; Swan, Diary of James Swan, June 26, 1859, and July 12, 1860.

84. Swan, Diary of James G. Swan, May 2, 1859; also February 20, 1859, and March 4, 1860; C. Prosch, *Reminiscences*, 43, 10, 26; Simmons to Nesmith, July 27, 1858, WTSIA, Roll 9, Reel 18; Simmons to Geary, July 1, 1859, NA PNR RG75, M-2011, Reel 1; Fitzhugh to Simmons, June 13, 1858, ibid.; Wm. Hammond to S. D. Howe, May 3, 1864, ibid.; *ARCIA* (1857), 335; *ARCIA* (1858), 582, 587; Swan, "Scenes in Washington Territory," no. 2 (May 10, 1859); Leighton, *Life at Puget Sound*, 19–23; Mrs. George Lotzgesell, "Pioneer Days at Old Dungeness," *Washington Historical Quarterly* 24 (1933): 265; Allen Weir, "Roughing It on Puget Sound in the Early Sixties," *Washington Historian* 3 (1900): 120; WPA, *Told by the Pioneers*, vol. 2, 53, 58, 125, 129,

221; Kellogg, "History of Whidbey's Island," 50, 59; H. A. Swift, "Notes on Whidby Island History" (typescript of article from *Island County Times,* December, 13, 1913), UW Special Collections.

85. Collins, "John Fornsby," 306–7, 320; Hubbard, "Indian under the White Man's Law," 48, 49; Washington Territory District Court Case Files, Jefferson County Cases No. 1036, 1037 and Thurston County Cases No. 34, 157, 158; House Journal, Washington Territorial Legislature, 1866, UW Manuscripts Accession No. 4284, Box 2, Folders 2–10 and 2–11; WPA, *Told by the Pioneers,* vol. 2, 179, 221; C. Prosch, *Reminiscences,* 27–29; Swan, Diary of James Swan, December 29, 1862, and October 10, 1868; Affidavit of John Montgomery, 1864, NA PNR RG 75, M-2011, Reel 1; Campbell, Diary of John Campbell, January 7 and October 26, 1869; Robert Emmett Hawley, *Skqee Mus, or Pioneer Days on the Nooksack,* ed. P. R. Jeffcott (Bellingham, Wash.: n.p., 1945), 31.

86. John A. Tennant to B. F. Kendall, November 15, 1861, Bion F. Kendall Papers, UW Manuscripts. Also, Bagley, "Chief Seattle and Angeline," 260; Swan, Diary of James Swan, February 9 and December 25, 1860; Journal of S. S. Ford, May 31, 1856; *ARCIA* (1862/63), 469; Finkboner to Friend Howe, December 9, 1863, and August 1, 1865, NA M-2011, Reel 1.

87. G. Allen to Governor, May 20, 1856, Washington Territorial Volunteers Papers, Box 2, Folder 9; Petition from Island County, May 20, 1856, ibid.; Fitzhugh to Simmons, June 13, 1858, NA M-2011, Reel 1; W. Hammond to Howe, May 2, 1864, ibid.; Finkboner to Mr. Alvey, October 6, 1867, ibid., Reel 2.

88. Simmons to Stevens, December 31, 1856, and April 4, 1857, WTSIA, Roll 9, Reel 17; Simmons to Nesmith, December 31, 1857, ibid.; Simmons to Nesmith, September 10, 1859, WTSIA, Roll 9, Reel 18; Journal of S. S. Ford, May 30 and June 10, 1856; Paige to Simmons, August 8, 1858, WTSIA, Roll 10, Reel 20; Gosnell to Stevens, December 1, 1856, WTSIA, Roll 10, Reel 22; Fay to Stevens, November 15, 1856, ibid.; Hill to Stevens, June 18, 1856, WTSIA, Roll 10, Reel 21; Commander of U.S. Naval Force in Puget Sound to Stevens, July 7, 1856, Washington Territorial Volunteers Papers, Box 4, Folder 9; *Washington Standard,* July 16, 1864, 1; *ARCIA* (1860), 188–89; *ARCIA* (1863/64), 62, 69–70; Howe to Waterman, August 1, 1865, NA M-2011, Reel 1; Thos. J. Hanna to Simmons, September 18 and 21, 1857, ibid.; Tennant to Simmons, August 8, 1859, ibid.; Hammond to Howe, May 2, 1864, ibid.; Meeker Family Papers, Notebook III; McGilvra, "Reminiscences of the Early Days," 3, 15; C. Prosch, *Reminiscences,* 69; McCurdy, *By Juan de Fuca's Strait,* 124; Kellogg, "History of Whidbey's Island," 50; Weir, "Roughing It on Puget Sound," 121.

89. *ARCIA* (1863/64), 61.

90. Fitzhugh to Simmons, December 7, 1857, NA M-2011, Reel 1; Finkboner to Howe, January 10, 1863, ibid.; Report of Fitzhugh, September 1, 1856, WTSIA, Roll 10, Reel 20; Swan, "Scenes in Washington Territory," No. 8; Report of Simmons, December 14, 1860, WTSIA, Roll 9, Reel 17; Fitzhugh to Stevens, September 8, 1856, WTSIA, Roll 10, Reel 20; *ARCIA* (1861/62), 407–8; *ARCIA* (1863/64), 61, 70; *ARCIA* (1865), 67; Swan, Diary of James

Swan, March 16, 1861, and October 12, 1868; Chirouse to Hale, April 1869, NA M-2011, Reel 2; *Territorial Republican,* June 28, 1869, 2; C. Prosch, *Reminiscences,* 85; McGilvra, "Reminiscences of the Early Days," 1, 17.

91. Petition forwarded by E. C. Chirouse to Mister Simmons, August 16, 1859, Records of the Bureau of Indian Affairs, Tulalip Agency Papers, Washington State University Manuscripts, Cage 256, Folder 6.

92. Ford to Stevens, December 31, 1856, WTSIA, Roll 10, Reel 21; Swan, "Scenes in Washington Territory," no. 4 (May 24, 1859); Fitzhugh to Simmons, September 27, 1857, NA M-2011, Reel 1; Simmons to Nesmith, September 30, 1857, ibid.; Fay to Simmons, June 5, 1860, ibid.; Chirouse to McKenney, May 3, 1871, ibid., Reel 2; *ARCIA* (1861/62), 404–5, 409; Leighton, *Life at Puget Sound,* 24–25, 35, 113–14; Meany Papers, Folder 86–2 (Chowitshoot's potlatches); Collins, "John Fornsby," 316; Swan, Diary of James Swan for following dates: April 26, 1859; May 21, 1859; May 23, 1859; April 20, 1860; May 19, 1860; August 24, 1860; February 15, 1861; September 3, 1868.

93. *ARCIA* (1861/62), 409; Leighton, *Life at Puget Sound,* 24–25; Simmons to Geary, June 22, 1860, WTSIA, Roll 9, Reel 18.

94. Collins, "John Fornsby," 296, 307; Fay to Stevens, February 3, 1856, WTSIA, Roll 10, Reel 22; Roll of Indians, May 20, 1856, ibid.

95. Simmons to Nesmith, August 29, 1858, and September 10, 1859, WTSIA, Roll 9, Reel 18; Simmons to Geary, December 14, 1860, ibid.; Swan, Diary of James Swan, January 30 and February 3–6, 1860.

96. Swan, Diary of James Swan, January 31–February 6, 1860.

4. REFORMERS AND INDIANS

1. Somerville, "Mediterranean of the Pacific," 483–93.

2. Carl Herbert Mapes, "A Map Interpretation of Population Growth and Distribution in the Puget Sound Region" (Ph.D. diss., University of Washington, 1943), 11, 16, 26; Watt, "Introduction to Economic and Labor History," 123, 158; Johansen and Gates, *Empire of the Columbia,* 343; Smith, "Puyallup of Washington," 31.

3. Mapes, "Map Interpretation," 39; Johansen and Gates, *Empire of the Columbia,* 368–82, 383–84, 389–92; Robert E. Ficken, *The Forested Land: A History of Lumbering in Western Washington* (Seattle: University of Washington Press, 1987), 55, 68–69; Dodds, *American Northwest,* 137–38. Financial crisis slowed railroad construction and immigration for a few years in the 1870s. William Sidney Schiach, ed., *An Illustrated History of Skagit and Snohomish Counties* (Chicago: Interstate Publishing Company, 1906), 112.

4. Smith, "Our Aborigines," 1; *ARCIA* (1872), 332; Myron Eells, "The Twana Indians of the Skokomish Reservation in Washington Territory," *U.S. Geological Survey Bulletin* 3 (1877): 60; M. Eells, "The Indians of Puget Sound," 271; *ARCIA* (1870), 17; *ARCIA* (1877), 198; Reports of Inspector Pollock, March 28 and April 16, 1881, NA M-1070, Roll 31; Swan, Diary of James

Swan, December 2, 1859; *ARCIA* (1883), 149; W. H. Talbott to Commissioner of Indian Affairs, August 15, 1889, NA PNR RG 75, Tulalip Agency, Box 25; *ARCIA* (1889), 289; Census of the Tulalip Agency, 1885, NA M-595, Roll 582.

5. Watt, "Introduction to Economic and Labor History," 125–26, 117, 121; Johansen and Gates, *Empire of the Pacific,* 384–99; Ethel Van Fleet Harris, "Early Historical Incidents of Skagit County" (1926), UW Special Collections, 5, 26; Natalie Andrea Roberts, "A History of the Swinomish Tribal Community" (Ph.D. diss., University of Washington, 1975), 158; Collins, *Valley of the Spirits,* 39; Bancroft, *History of Washington, Idaho, and Montana,* 338–39, 344–49; Swan, Diary of James Swan, December 2, 1877.

6. Meeker Family Papers, Notebook III, I, 8.

7. Collins, "John Fornsby," 306; *ARCIA* (1861/62), 411; J. Goudy to Simmons, May 27, 1860, NA M-2011, Reel 1; Myron Eells, "Justice to the Indian" (July 14, 1883), UW Special Collections excerpt from unidentified periodical, 44; *ARCIA* (1872), 348–49; Hawley, *Skqee Mus,* 35; *Washington Standard,* January 4, 1873, 3; Swan, Diary of James Swan, February 28, 1877; Patricia Slettvet Noel, *Muckleshoot Indian History* (Auburn, Wash.: Auburn School District No. 408, 1980), 11; Statement of William Hicks, Skagit Roll, Applications for Enrollment and Allotment of Washington Indians, NA M-1343, Roll 4; testimony of Mary Jerry Dominick, *Duwamish et al. v. United States,* 170.

8. Collins, "John Fornsby," 307, 295; *ARCIA* (1872), 346; Lotzgesell, "Pioneer Days," 269; Buckley to H. Price, September, 1883, and January 5, 1884, NA PNR RG 75, Tulalip Box 24; WPA, *Told by the Pioneers,* vol. 2, 179, 182; *Washington Standard,* June 12, 1875, 2, and September 29, 1877, 4; Roberts, "History of the Swinomish," 240–42; Boxberger, *To Fish in Common,* 36; White, "Treaty at Medicine Creek," 172.

9. *Washington Standard,* September 11, 1875, 2, and September 9, 1876, 2; Thompson and Meade, General Merchandise and Puget Sound Hops, to Father Chirusch [*sic*], August 28, 1875, NA M-2011; Report of Inspector Ward, March 8, 1884, NA M-1070, Roll 53; Johansen and Gates, *Empire of the Columbia,* 384; Watt, "Introduction to Labor and Economic History," 33–35; Meeker, *Pioneer Reminiscences,* 222, 224; Alfred N. Marion to E. A. Hayt, November 7, 1878, NA PNR RG 75, Tulalip Box 24; John O'Keane to Hayt, September 1, 1879, ibid.; *ARCIA* (1877), 199; Records of Hop Growers' Association of Snoqualmie, 1885–89, UW Manuscripts, Vertical File 1387. In 1885 it was apparently harder for Indians to laugh off competition from Chinese pickers. Several Indians joined whites in a lethal attack on Chinese hop harvesters. Hunt and Kaylor, *Washington West of the Cascades,* 297; Schiach, *Illustrated History,* 137.

10. Jim Lightner by friend to Charley Artemus, May 29, 1873, NA PNR RG 75, Tulalip Boxes 2–4 (on M-2011); *ARCIA* (1872), 346; Ann Nugent, ed., *Lummi Elders Speak* (Lynden, Wash.: Lynden Tribune, 1982), Aurelia Balch Celestine, 37. Also, Finkboner to Hill, June 28, 1870, NA M-2011; *ARCIA* (1861/62), 407; Hawley, *Skqee Mus,* 26 (most longshoring at Seattle docks done by Indians in 1872).

11. E. C. Johnson to Mr. Cambers [*sic*], June 24, 1869, Papers of Thomas McCutcheon Chambers, 1838–1876, Washington State Historical Society.

12. *Territorial Republican*, January 1, 1870, 2; "H. A." in *Daily Pacific Tribune*, August 22, 1871, 1, 2; Smith, "Our Aborigines"; *Territorial Republican*, September 14, 1868, 3.

13. Petition to Col. Ross, November, 1869, and Franklin Mathias to Hill, November 29, 1869, NA M-2011, Reel 2; E. Carr to Ross, November 3, 1869, ibid.; Letter of Edwin Richardson, *Commercial Age*, January 22, 1870, 1; Letter of Edmund Carr, ibid., 2; *ARCIA* (1870/71), 271.

14. Prucha, *Great Father*, 481–83, 492, 562; Paul Stuart, *The Indian Office: Growth and Development of an American Institution, 1865–1900* (Ann Arbor: University Microfilms International, 1978), 1, 17, 77. The idea of isolating Indians in order to teach them "civilized" ways was not new. James Axtell, *The European and the Indian: Essays in the Ethnohistory of Colonial America* (New York: Oxford University Press, 1981), 62–63.

15. *Daily Pacific Tribune*, August 22, 1871, 1, 2; Smith, "Our Aborigines," 1; Prucha, *Great Father*, 532; *Cherokee Nation v. Georgia*, 5 Peters 1, 15–20 (1831); *United States v. Kagama*, 118 United States Reports 375 (1886).

16. Prucha, *Great Father*, 481–82, 512, 517–18, 526–27; Stuart, *Indian Office*, 13, 32, 38; *ARCIA* (1876/77), 3; *ARCIA* (1872), 333; Sister Mary Louise, "Eugene Casimir Chirouse" (M.A. thesis, University of Washington, 1932), 41, 68; Castile, *Indians of Puget Sound*, ix; Robert H. Ruby and John A. Brown, *Myron Eells and the Puget Sound Indians* (Seattle: Superior Publishing, 1976), 8–9; Cesare Marino, "History of Western Washington since 1846," in *Handbook of North American Indians*, vol. 7, ed. William C. Sturtevant (Washington, D.C.: Smithsonian Institution, 1990), 173; Edwin Eells Papers, Washington State Historical Society; M. Eells, "Justice to the Indian," 39, 46; *ARCIA* (1883), 149.

17. *ARCIA* (1876/77), 1; Frederick Hoxie, *A Final Promise: The Campaign to Assimilate the Indians, 1880–1920* (Lincoln: University of Nebraska Press, 1984), 10–11.

18. Prucha, *Great Father*, 501–3, and Stuart, *Indian Office*, 32, describe the Board of Indian Commissioners, an unpaid advisory group charged with assessing how well the Indian Office met the humanitarian goals of the Peace Policy.

19. Excerpt from *Third Annual Report of the Board of Indian Commissioners* (Washington, D.C.: Government Printing Office, 1871), Appendix A, on NA M-2011, Reel 2. Speeches made during Brunot's meeting at Skokomish appear in Castile, *Indians of Puget Sound*, 268–69.

20. At Skokomish Big John told Brunot, "You come to get the Indian's [*sic*] hearts, You ought to take time." Collins notes the custom of allowing everyone to voice an opinion at deliberations. *Valley of the Spirits*, 112–13.

21. *Third Annual Report of the Board of Indian Commissioners*.

22. Castile, *Indians of Puget Sound*, 268.

23. Collins, *Valley of the Spirits*, 81; Smith, *Puyallup-Nisqually*, 48; Elmendorf, "Skokomish Sorcery," 162. Hess, *Dictionary of Puget Salish*, at 184, gives a single word for the English terms "good," "well," and "happy."

24. Prucha, *Great Father,* 477, 492; *ARCIA* (1872), 337.

25. Prucha, *Great Father,* 481–82, 509–10.

26. E. Eells to McKenny [*sic*], August 31, 1871, Edwin Eells Papers; E. Eells, Speech regarding history of Cushman School, June 16, 1910, ibid., Box 3, Folder 2; *ARCIA* (1872), 349; *ARCIA* (1870), 18–20; *ARCIA* (1870/71), 289; White, "Treaty at Medicine Creek," 169. It was common for new reservation administrators to deplore the conditions bequeathed to them by predecessors, thus deliberately or subconsciously laying a basis for claiming dramatic improvements during their tenure.

27. Stuart, *Indian Office,* 8, 49, 55, 70, 74, 119; *ARCIA* (1876/77), 1, 199–200; *ARCIA* (1872), 358; *ARCIA* (1873), 299; *ARCIA* (1874), 327; *ARCIA* (1875/76), 138; *ARCIA* (1880/81), 166, 172; *ARCIA* (1883), 147–48; Report of Inspector Bannister, February 20, 1886, NA M-1070, Roll 31; Report of Inspector Pollock, March 28, 1881, ibid.; Marion to Hayt, February 4, 1879, and November 6, 1878, NA PNR RG75, Tulalip Agency, Box 24; O'Keane to Commissioner, June 7, 1881, ibid.

28. Milroy to Chirouse, February 21, 1873, NA M-2011; Eells to McKinney [*sic*], August 30, 1871, Eells Papers; *ARCIA* (1872), 352; McKenny [*sic*] to Hill, January 14, 1871, NA M-2011.

29. Eells to McKinney, August 30, 1871, Eells Papers; E. Eells to Milroy, April 16, 1873, ibid.; E. Eells to E. P. Smith, December 2, 1873, ibid.; William H. Reeves to Father Chirouse, March 8, 1874, NA M-2011; Chirouse to Smith, August 17 and December 1, 1876, ibid.; Chirouse to Milroy, April 12, 1874, ibid.; Milroy to Chirouse, June 24, 1874, ibid.; Chalcraft, "Autobiography of Edwin Chalcraft," 16; *ARCIA* (1886), 244; Elmendorf, *Twana Narratives,* 4–5.

30. *ARCIA* (1874), 338; Eells to unknown correspondent, November 24, 1879, Eells Papers, Box 3, Folder 8; *Indians in Washington Territory,* House Exec. Doc. 87, 43d Cong., 2d sess., 1875.

31. 10 *United States Statutes* 1132, Article 6; 12 *United States Statutes* 927; 12 *United States Statutes* 933; *ARCIA* (1872), 329–30, 337; *ARCIA* (1874), 338; *ARCIA* (1876/77), 190; *ARCIA* (1883), 148–49; Chalcraft, "Autobiography of Edwin Chalcraft"; Dippie, *Vanishing American,* 161–64; Prucha, *Great Father,* 659–71.

32. Finkboner to Chirouse, March 10, 1873, NA M-2011, Reel 2; Charley Jules and Charley Shelton to our dear Fathers at Washington, March 10, 1879, NA PNR RG75, Tulalip Box 24; excerpts of speeches by Big John, Jackman and Chehalis Jack and letter of unidentified schoolboy in Castile, *Indians of Puget Sound,* 269–73; *ARCIA* (1873), 306; *ARCIA* (1874), 338.

33. *ARCIA* (1874), 78, 80; *ARCIA* (1878), 137; *ARCIA* (1876/77), 198; Chirouse to Smith, December 1, 1874, NA M-2011, Reel 2; E. Eells to unknown correspondent, March 15, 1878, Eells Papers, Box 3, Folder 8; Report of J. Pollock, March 28, 1881, NA M-1070, Roll 31; Report of Inspector Thomas, February 16, 1887, NA M-1070, Roll 53; Council of Chiefs, Puyallup Indians, to Hon. H. Price, February 13, 1884, copy attached to Kent Richards, "Federal Indian Policy, Isaac Stevens, and the Western Washington Treaties," 1993, in

files of Evergreen Legal Services, Seattle; J. B. Harrison, *The Latest Studies on Indian Reservations* (Philadelphia: Indian Rights Association, 1887), 92.

34. Minutes of meeting with Brunot, NA M-2011; Elmendorf, *Twana Narratives*, 5–6; Stella Lane Nickolsen in Nugent, *Lummi Elders Speak*, 73; Marion to Hayt, December 11, 1878, NA PNR RG75, Tulalip Box 24; Chirouse to Milroy, March 10 and April 10, 1874, NA M-2011, Reel 2; A Boston Tillicum, Esq. [James Wickersham], "A Monograph on the Puyallup Indians of the State of Washington," 1892, 13, UW Special Collections.

35. Annual Report, August 18, 1872, NA M-2011; *ARCIA* (1872), 349; *Seattle Weekly Intelligencer*, September 4, 1871, 2, and March 29, 1873, 3; Chirouse to Hon. Delano, January 20, 1874, WTSIA, Roll 10, Reel 20; Chirouse to Blinn, February 11, 1874, ibid.; Report of J. M. Kelley, September 1, 1869, Eells Papers, Box 3, Item 8 (letter book); *ARCIA* (1870), 19, 43; Chirouse to Milroy, December 7, 1872, and April 12, 1874, NA M-2011; *ARCIA* (1876/77), 190; E. Mallet to Commissioner, August 18, 1877, quoted in Indian Claims Commission, *Coast Salish and Western Washington Indians*, 428; permit issued to Dan Leighton, May 12, 1876, NA M-2011; Report of Inspector Pollock, March 22, 1881, NA PNR M-1070, Roll 53; Marion to Hayt, November 6, 1878, NA PNR RG75, Tulalip Box 24.

36. Indian Census Rolls (1885), NA PNR M-595, Rolls 302 and 582. The 1890 census counted 103 on the Muckleshoot Reservation.

37. E. Eells to unknown correspondent, March 15, 1878, Eells Papers; *ARCIA* (1876/77), 196–97; *ARCIA* (1879), 171, 242–43; Myron Eells, "Census of the Clallam and Twana Indians of Washington Territory," *American Antiquarian* 6 (1884): 36–38; Special Census, Tenth Census of the United States, Indian Division, 1880, NA PNR RG29, Microfilm I-34, Rolls 1 and 2, and Microfilm P-2193; Tribal Census Rolls, 1880–1921, NA PNR RG75, Puyallup Box 70; O'Keane to Hayt, March 31, 1879, NA PNR RG75, Tulalip Box 24; *ARCIA* (1878), 135; *ARCIA* (1880), 163; *ARCIA* (1882), 167; *ARCIA* (1883), 149.

38. Castile, *Indians of Puget Sound*, 271–74; O'Keane to Hayt, March 10, 1879, enclosing letter "To our dear Fathers at Washington," NA PNR RG75, Tulalip Box 24.

39. "Observer" in *Seattle Weekly Intelligencer*, September 4, 1871, 2; Report of Chirouse, August 18, 1872, NA M-2011; *ARCIA* (1862/63), 461–62; *Washington Standard*, November 26, 1864, 3; Collins, "John Fornsby," 311; Blankenship, *Lights and Shades*, 47; O'Keane to R. E. Trowbridge, July 5, 1880, NA PNR RG75, Tulalip Box 24.

40. Collins, "John Fornsby," 314; O'Keane to Hayt, March 31 and December 9, 1879, NA PNR RG75, Tulalip Box 24; Chirouse to Milroy, March 12, 1873, NA M-2011; Buckley to Henry Quina, May 20, 1884, NA PNR RG75, Tulalip Box 123; Sampson, *Indians of Skagit County*, 33.

41. *ARCIA* (1876/77), 196–97; Chirouse to Milroy, December 7, 1872, NA M-2011, Reel 2; Milroy to Chirouse, February 7, 1873, December 15, 1872, and April 4, 1874, ibid.; To whom it may concern from McKenny, November 25, 1868, ibid.; Summary of "trial" of Jim Spakwak and Jacob for death of In-

dian Watchman at Utsalady, April 10, 1874, ibid.; Marion to Hayt, November 7, 1878, NA PNR RG75, Tulalip Box 24.

42. E. Eells to J. A. Smith, February 14, 1877, Eells Papers. Eells also had the chief of a Klallam village, 130 miles from the agency, arrested for disobeying instructions and leading his band into anarchy. Eells to Hayt, August 7, 1879, ibid.

43. E. Eells to E. P. Smith, December 2, 1873, Eells Papers; Milroy to Chirouse, April 4, 1874, NA M-2011; Chirouse to Milroy, April 10, 1874, ibid.; Milroy to O'Keane, June 14, 1881, ibid.; *ARCIA* (1886), 244–45; Buckley to Ben Stretch, Sheriff, October 25, 1883, NA PNR RG75, Tulalip Box 123; Harrison, *Latest Studies*, 98; Edward Bristow to C. B. Buchanan, October 21, 1903, NA PNR RG75, Tulalip Box 99.

44. Chirouse to Smith, June 10, 1875, NA M-2011; O'Keane to Hayt, November 30, 1880, NA PNR RG75, Tulalip Box 24; M. Eells, "Potlatches of Puget Sound," 137; M. Eells, answers to questions posed by General Howard attached to letter of E. Eells, March 15, 1878, Eells Papers, Box 3, Folder 8; M. Eells, essay on 1876 potlatch, Eells Papers, Box 1, Folder 17; Finkboner to Hill, November 8, 1869, NA M-2011.

45. Michel Foucault, *Power/Knowledge: Selected Interviews and Other Writings by Michel Foucault, 1972–1977*, ed. Gordon Colin (New York: Pantheon Books, 1980), 98.

46. Shortly after quashing Billy Clams's rebellion, Eells argued that Indians could hardly learn what it meant to live in a society ruled by laws while they were subject to agents' despotism. *ARCIA* (1876/77), 196–97; Marion to Hayt, November 30, 1878, NA PNR RG75, Tulalip Box 24; Indian Police Record Book, 1878–1884, NA PNR RG75, Tulalip Box 504; Records of T. R. Wilson, Chief of Police, Puyallup, 1881, Eells Papers, Box 3; Talbott to Michael J. Clark, November 25, 1889, NA PNR RG75, Tulalip Box 25; Buckley to Kwina, October 24, 1883, NA PNR RG75, Tulalip Box 123; Buckley to Whome [sic] it may concern, December 5, 1883, ibid.; E. Eells to unknown correspondent, March 15, 1878, Eells Papers; Chirouse to J. Q. Smith, May 2, 1876, NA M-2011; Milroy to O'Keane, June 14, 1881, ibid.; Talbott to Joe Snohomish, November 9, 1886, ibid.; Finkboner to Hill, November 8, 1869, NA M-2011, Reel 2; Buckley to Quina, May 20, 1884, NA PNR RG75, Tulalip Box 123; D. C. Govan to Judges of Court of Indian Offenses at Lummi Reservation, March 6, 1897, NA PNR RG75, Tulalip Box 26.

47. Eells to Sir, July 29, 1878, Eells Papers. At Puyallup, the council of chiefs abolished tamanous (aboriginal doctoring and religious ceremonies), gambling, and payments for brides. Milroy crowed that Indian enforcement of the bans had turned that reservation into the most orderly community in the territory. *ARCIA* (1879), 152. When Jerry Meeker was a subchief of the Puyallup Reservation, chiefs' duties included judging prosecutions under regulations they themselves had promulgated. As captain of police, Meeker persuaded Eells to boost officers' pay (and the incentive to abuse their power) by assigning them the fines from liquor cases. Meeker Family Papers, Notebook III; Milroy to O'Keane, June 14, 1881, NA M-2011.

48. Chirouse to McKenney, May 3? [illegible], 1871, NA M-2011; Finkboner to Hill, November 8, 1869, ibid.; Report of E. C. Chirouse, March 27, 1872, ibid.; O'Keane to Commissioner, August 2, 1881, NA PNR RG75, Tulalip Box 24; Buckley to Price, February 4, 1885, ibid.; John Baldwin to Buckley, November 9 and 15, 1883, NA M-2011, Reel 3; Sam Crockett to Buckley, June 1, 1885, ibid.; Records of T. R. Wilson, Eells Papers, Box 3, December 27. Also, William McCluskey to C. B. Buchanan, July 8, 1905, NA PNR RG75, Tulalip Box 99.

49. Chalcraft, "Autobiography of Edwin Chalcraft"; *ARCIA* (1876/77), 196–97; Milroy to O'Keane, October 30, 1879, and July 1, 1880, NA M-2011; Summary of proceedings, April 10, 1874, NA M-2011; E. Eells to H. D. Gibson, March 19, 1875, Eells Papers; E. Eells to W. H. Boyle, March 16, 1875, ibid.; *ARCIA* (1879), 152.

50. Anthony Giddens, *The Nation-State and Violence* (Berkeley and Los Angeles: University of California Press, 1985), 10–11.

51. Ben Solomon to Buckley, June 1, 1886, NA M-2011, Reel 3; Chirouse to Smith, November 13, 1874, NA M-2011, Reel 2; Chirouse to McKenney, May 3?, 1871, ibid.; E. Eells to Sir, July 29, 1878, Eells Papers; Marion to Hayt, November 30, 1878, NA PNR RG75, Tulalip Box 24; Finkboner to Howe, November 6, 1864, NA M-2011, Reel 1.

52. *ARCIA* (1883), 149, 169; Report of Inspector Frank C. Armstrong, July 15, 1887, NA M-1070, Roll 31; Report of Inspector R. S. Gardner, November 19, 1887, NA M-1070, Roll 53; O'Keane to Hayt, March 31, 1879, NA PNR RG75, Tulalip Box 24; O'Keane to Trowbridge, June 2, 1880, ibid.; *ARCIA* (1880/81), 166; *ARCIA* (1885), 193; *Washington Standard*, April 1, 1887, 1; M. Eells, "Indians of Puget Sound," 7; Milroy to Chirouse, March 14, 1873, NA M-2011; Chirouse to Smith, August 2, 1876, ibid.; Chirouse to Rev. J. B. Brouillet, March 6, 1876, ibid.; Chirouse to Rev. A. M. A. Blanchet, March 28, 1876, ibid.

53. Harrison, *Latest Studies*, 90; *ARCIA* (1885), 193; *ARCIA* (1876/77), 196–98; *ARCIA* (1880/81), 171; *ARCIA* (1879), 155; reports of Inspector J. Pollock, March 22 and 28 and April 16, 1881, NA M-1070, Rolls 53 and 31; Jno. McGlinn to Chirouse, February 28, 1874, NA M-2011, Reel 2. Later observations to the same effect include Edwin Eells to Governor Miles C. Moore, August 29, 1889, Washington State Archives, RG 1/P-1, Box 2; *ARCIA* (1900), 397.

54. M. Eells, "Indians of Puget Sound," 6–7. Also, M. Eells, "Census of the Clallam and Twana Indians," 35; Elmendorf, *Twana Narratives*, 64; *ARCIA* (1872), 349; *ARCIA* (1879), 148; *ARCIA* (1880/81), 171; E. Eells to unknown correspondent, March 15, 1878, Eells Papers; Aurelia Balch Celestine in Nugent, *Lummi Elders Speak*, 37.

55. Undated form listing off-reservation bands at Lake Washington, on the upper Skagit, lower Skagit, Samish, Nooksack, Stillaguamish, Snohomish, White, Black, and Cedar Rivers, on Orcas, Guemes, and Whidbey Islands, and at Port Orchard, in NA M-2011; O'Keane to Hayt, January 31, 1880, NA PNR RG75, Tulalip Box 24; O'Keane to Trowbridge, November 4, 1880, ibid.; O'Keane to Commissioner, April 6, 1881, ibid.; O'Keane to Fred Dyer, March

6, 1880, NA PNR RG75, Tulalip Box 123; C. C. Thornton to Commissioner, December 2, 1893, NA PNR RG 75, Tulalip Box 25; *ARCIA* (1870), 43; Hunt and Kaylor, *Washington West of the Cascades*, vol. 1, 426; Schiach, *Illustrated History*, 109, 119, 122, 132, 471–73.

56. McGlinn to Chirouse, February 28, 1874, NA M-2011; Chirouse to J. Q. Smith, April 12, 1876, ibid.; WPA, *Told by the Pioneers*, vol. 2, 179, 53.

57. Old Man Olie and others to the Commissioner, February 15, 1875, NA M-2011. There is no indication who wrote this petition for the Indians, who were probably illiterate, or whether the writer had a personal stake in the Indians' remaining off the reservation. Also, *ARCIA* (1878), 138.

58. Chirouse to Milroy, September 22, 1873, NA M-2011; Agent to Milroy, April 12, 1874, ibid.; Chirouse to J. Q. Smith, April 12, 1876, ibid.; Buckley to Jno. D. L. Atkins, February 5, 1886, NA PNR RG75, Tulalip Box 24; *ARCIA* (1880/81), 171; E. Eells to E. P. Smith, December 2, 1873, Eells Papers.

59. *ARCIA* (1883), 169; Collins, "John Fornsby," 319; M. Eells, "Census of the Clallam and Twana Indians," 35, 37; Applications for Enrollment and Allotment, NA M-1343; Chirouse to Smith, June 10 1875, NA M-2011.

60. Meeker Family Papers, Notebooks I and III; Collins, "John Fornsby," 307, 311, 315, 319.

61. Nels Bruseth, *Indian Stories and Legends of the Stillaguamish, Sauks and Allied Tribes* ([Arlington, Wash., 1926]; reprint, Fairfield, Wash.: Ye Galleon Press, 1972), 5, 9; WPA, *Told by the Pioneers*, vol. 2, 52, 181, 221; Kellogg, "History of Whidbey's Island," 8, 27, 30, 59–60, 72; Hawley, *Skqee Mus*, 26, 31, 36, 40, 44, 53, 77–78, 108; Swift, "Notes on Whidby Island History," July 4 and December 13, 1913; Collins, "John Fornsby," 313; Harris, "Early Historical Incidents," 3, 26; Phoebe Goodell Judson, *A Pioneer's Search for an Ideal Home* (Bellingham, Wash.: Union Printing, 1925; reprint, Lincoln: University of Nebraska Press, 1984); M. Eells, "Potlatches of Puget Sound," 145; Hunt and Kaylor, *Washington West of the Cascades*, vol. 1, 394–95, 397, 399; Schiach, *Illustrated History*, 103–6, 109, 137, 270–71, 459; Thomas Prosch, "Later Celebrations," in Pierce County Pioneer Association, "Commemorative Celebration"; Fetzer, "George Swanaset."

62. Collins, "John Fornsby," 307, 311, 312, 317, 320, 334, 306.

63. Campbell, Diary, 1869–1894; O'Keane to Commissioner, April 6, 1881, NA PNR RG75, Tulalip Box 24; Statistical report on Skagit River, 1881, NA M-2011, Reel 3; *Indian Jimmie, Yen Tey, Indian Charlie, et al. v. W.B. Moore*, Civil Case No. 1991, King County Clerk's Records, Territory District Court Files; *Territory v. Dr. Jack*, District Court Case No. 2700, ibid.; Swan, Diary of James Swan, Book 22 (1877); *Washington Standard*, January 11 and 18, 1879, 1; *Puget Sound Weekly Courier*, January 9, 1880, 1; E. Eells to unknown correspondent, March 15, 1878, Eells Papers; Chirouse to Milroy, March 12, 1873, NA M-2011; *ARCIA* (1880/81), 167.

64. Edward Harper Thomas, *Chinook: A History and Dictionary of the Northwest Coast Trade Jargon* (Portland, Ore.: Metropolitan Press, 1935), 27; testimony of Wapato John and Augustus Kautz, *Duwamish et al. v. United*

States, 667, 679; Report of Inspector Robert Gardner, February 6, 1883, NA M-1070, Roll 53; Hawley, *Skqee Mus*, 53; Harris, "Early Historical Incidents," 10; Kellogg, "History of Whidbey's Island," 59; James Wickersham, "Notes on the Indians of Washington," *American Antiquarian* 21 (1891): 370; Myron Eells, "The Chinook Jargon," *American Anthropologist* 7 (1894): 303; M. Eells, "Twana Indians," 98; M. Eells, *Ten Years of Missionary Work*, 33–34; Chalcraft, "Autobiography of Edwin Chalcraft"; Bruseth, *Indian Stories*; Chirouse to W. B. Gosnell, July 1, 1861, WTSIA, Roll 9, Reel 19; [Tacoma] *Daily Ledger*, May 23, 1889, 4, and November 28, 1890, 2; Thornton to Commissioner, December 2, 1893, NA PNR RG75, Tulalip Box 25; Affidavits of John Elwood and Kate Waller in *United States et al. v. The Chicago Fishing Company*, U.S. District Court for the District of Washington (1895), NA PNR RG21, Box 82, Case No. 481; transcript of *Hatch v. Ferguson et al.*, ibid., Box 20, Case No. 151, 10, 15, 44, 58.

65. M. Eells, "Indians of Puget Sound," 1.

66. Federal officials briefly considered relinquishing guardianship altogether when the payments ordained by the Medicine Creek treaty ended in 1876. Believing that "the Indians could demand nothing further of the Government," the commissioner terminated all services in the south Sound area except three small schools. However, by the time the Point Elliott and Point No Point treaty payments lapsed five years later, officials knew they had continuing responsibility for property set aside by treaty and for people with a claim to that property. "Half-civilized" Indians on protected land still needed a federal guardian. M. Eells, "Indians of Puget Sound," 104; E. Eells, speech on history of Cushman school, 1910, Eells Papers; *ARCIA* (1883), 147–48; *Puget Sound Weekly Courier*, February 11, 1881, 1; White, "Treaty at Medicine Creek," 177.

67. *ARCIA* (1872), 348; *ARCIA* (1874), 79; E. Eells to Brown, Register, December 8, 1879, Eells Papers; E. Eells to R. S. Greene, December 12, 1879, ibid.; *ARCIA* (1886), 244; Chirouse to Smith, August 2, 1876, NA M-2011; W. B. Hall to O'Keane, February 19, 1881, ibid.; Chirouse to J. Q. Smith, April 12 and May 2, 1876, ibid.; Richard Jeffs to O'Keane, May 15, 1882, ibid.; Buckley to U.S. District Attorney, June 30, 1886, NA PNR RG75, Tulalip Box 24; DeShaw, Papers of William DeShaw, Box 1, File 13.

68. Buckley to Whome [*sic*] this may concern, November 19, 1883, NA PNR RG75, Tulalip Box 123; O'Keane to Hayt, September 1, 1879, NA PNR RG75, Tulalip Box 24; Milroy to Superintendent, March 14, 1874, NA M-2011; Buckley to Whome it may concern, December 5, 1883, NA PNR RG75, Tulalip Box 123; Edward Bristow to C. B. Buchanan, January 16, 1902, NA PNR RG75, Tulalip Box 98.

69. Milroy to Joseph and Elizabeth To-la-walh, July 12, 1873, NA M-2011; Chalcraft, "Autobiography of Edwin Chalcraft"; Citizen of White River to Tulalip Agent, May 18, 1873, NA M-2011; F. Tarbell to Chirouse, February 15, 1874, ibid.; Buckley to C. H. Hanford, October 8, 1883, NA PNR RG75, Tulalip Box 123.

70. Marion to Hayt, December 11 and November 7, 1878, NA PNR RG75, Tulalip Box 24; *ARCIA* (1874), 338; Annual Report, March 27, 1872, NA

M-2011; E. Eells to Hayt, May 10, 1879, Eells Papers; Harrison, *Latest Studies*, 168–69; *Territory v. John Kilcup* and *Territory v. Arthur Petit*, Whatcom County Justice Court Cases No. 157 and 158, respectively (1885), Territory District Court Case Files; Charley Jules *et al.* to our dear Fathers at Washington, March 10 1879, NA PNR RG75, Tulalip Box 24.

71. M. Eells, "Potlatches of Puget Sound," 136–37; *Puget Sound Weekly Courier*, November 3, 1876, 1; O'Keane to Trowbridge, November 30, 1880, NA PNR RG75, Tulalip Box 24; McGlinn to Chirouse, February 28, 1874, NA M-2011; Elmendorf, *Twana Narratives*, 29–37, 64–87; Leighton, *Life at Puget Sound*, 24–25, 3–36. A sign of Indian sensitivity to white attitudes is the report that Twanas and Klallams tolerated whites at their potlatches only so long as the whites did not laugh. M. Eells, "Potlatches of Puget Sound," 145.

72. DeShaw to Chirouse, April 16, 1876, NA M-2011.

73. M. Eells, "Potlatches of Puget Sound," 136–37; M. Eells, answers to request of General Howard, Eells Papers; *ARCIA* (1874), 337; Buckley to Commissioner, *ARCIA* (1884), 171; *Puget Sound Weekly Argus*, November 26, 1878, 8; *ARCIA* (1864), 461–62; Castile, *Indians of Puget Sound*, 248.

74. Collins, "John Fornsby," 295; Meeker Family Papers, Notebook III.

75. T. T. Waterman, "Puget Sound Geography" [ca. 1920], UW Special Collections, 70; Lida W. Quimby, "Puget Sound Indian Shakers," *The State* 7 (January 1902): 188; Notes (1930s), Erna Gunther Papers, UW Manuscripts, Accession No. 614–70–20, Box 2, Folder 16, and Box 3, Folder 2; notes of interviews at Squaxin Island (1905), Edmond S. Meany Papers, UW Manuscripts, Accession No. 106–70–12, Box 86, Folder 2; *P-I*, October 22, 1905, Magazine, 5; M. Eells, "Indians of Puget Sound," 5; Deegan, *History of Mason County*, 30–31; Barnett, *Indian Shakers*, 349, 351; George P. Castile, "The 'Half-Catholic' Movement: Edwin and Myron Eells and the Rise of the Indian Shaker Church," *Pacific Northwest Quarterly* 73 (1982): 171.

76. Gunther Papers; account of beginning of Shaker faith told by Annie James to Frank F. Bennett (1944), Records of the Indian Shaker Church of Washington and the Northwest, 1892–1945, UW Microfilm A-4547; Chalcraft, "Autobiography of Edwin Chalcraft"; Castile, "The 'Half-Catholic' Movement," 168; Erna Gunther, "The Shaker Religion of the Northwest," in Smith, *Indians of the Urban Northwest*, 55–56; Barnett, *Indian Shakers*, 53; Lummi History Record Center, *Nooh-whLummi, A Brief History of the Lummi* (n.p., 1974), 15; William W. Elmendorf, "An Almost Lost Culture," *Washington State Review* 2 (1958): 6; June McCormick Collins, "The Indian Shaker Church," *Southwestern Journal of Anthropology* 6 (1950): 405.

77. Castile, "The 'Half-Catholic Movement,'" 170–71; Barnett, *Indian Shakers*, 46, 48–49, 51–52; *P-I*, October 22, 1905, Magazine, 5; Gunther, "Shaker Religion," 70.

78. Eells Papers, Box 1, Folder 17; Castile, "The 'Half-Catholic' Movement," 171; Gunther, "Shaker Religion," 70; Barnett, *Indian Shakers*, 56; M. Eells, *Ten Years of Missionary Work*, 185; *Daily Ledger*, November 28, 1890, 2.

79. Chalcraft, "Autobiography of Edwin Chalcraft"; Castile, "The 'Half-Catholic' Movement," 172; Barnett, *Indian Shakers*, 91, 93; Quimby, "Puget Sound Indian Shakers," 189; *Daily Ledger*, November 28, 1890, 2.

80. Gunther, "Shaker Religion," 41–42, 59; Collins, *Valley of the Spirits*, 43; Langness, "Case of Post-Contact Reform," 40; Lummi History Record Center, *Nooh-whLummi*, 15; Smith, *Puyallup-Nisqually*, 86; Albert B. Reagan, "The Shaker Church of the Indians," *Alaska-Yukon Magazine* 5 (1908): 82–83; Elmendorf, "An Almost Lost Culture," 6; Collins, "Indian Shaker Church," 405.

81. Shakers insisted that they formed their own church without borrowing from whites. *P-I*, October 22, 1905, Magazine, 5.

82. Gunther, "Shaker Religion," 41–42; Collins, *Valley of the Spirits*, 43; Barnett, *Indian Shakers*, 338–39; Roberts, "History of the Swinomish," 254–55; Elmendorf, *Twana Narratives*, 224–26, 216–17; June McCormick Collins, "An Interpretation of Skagit Intragroup Conflict during Acculturation," *American Anthropologist* 54 (1952): 347–55; Smith, "Puyallup of Washington," 7. Ethnographers say aboriginal villages rarely had more than one shaman. Yet Eells counted five medicine men at the Skokomish Reservation in 1880, and this was undoubtedly an incomplete tally of people who claimed shamanic power. Special Census, 1880–81, NA Mic P-2193.

83. Stephen Cornell, *The Return of the Native: Native American Political Resurgence* (New York: Oxford University Press, 1988), 62–67; Dippie, *Vanishing American*, 202. Religious innovation and zeal were not peculiar to Indian societies during the late nineteenth century. Paul A. Carter, *The Spiritual Crisis of the Gilded Age* (DeKalb: Northern Illinois University Press, 1971); T. J. Jackson Lears, *No Place of Grace: Anti-Modernism and the Transformation of American Culture, 1880–1920* (New York: Pantheon, 1981).

84. Chalcraft, "Autobiography of Edwin Chalcraft."

85. Sahlins, *Historical Metaphors*, 33, 35; Foster, *Being Comanche*, 14, citing Loretta Fowler, *Shared Symbols, Contested Meanings: Gros Ventre Culture and History, 1778–1984* (Ithaca, N.Y.: Cornell University Press, 1987).

86. This reference to boundaries does not mean that the Shaker church provided Indians with a formal, organizational means of proclaiming their identity. The Shakers, who valued spontaneity and the individual's personal relation to the holy spirit, did not constitute an association with a defined membership.

5. INDIANS

1. *P-I*, May 22, 1892, 5.

2. Data supplied by Russel Barsh, University of Lethbridge, Alberta. Barsh counts as mixed-ancestry people those who so identified themselves, the children of couples with different racial identifications, and a few people whose

ancestry he infers from other genealogical data. In 1877 Tulalip special agent Edmund Mallet estimated that one-eighth of Indians in his jurisdiction had some white ancestors. *ARCIA* (1876/77), 198. Censuses in 1910 for Tulalip Agency reservations and five communities in the Cushman (Puyallup) Agency jurisdiction show 707 of 2,107 people, or 33 percent, with mixed ancestry. Indian Census Rolls, NA PNR M-595, Rolls 93, 582, and 583. Of thirty-seven marriages recorded by Tulalip Agency officials in 1907 and 1908, sixteen joined an acknowledged Indian to a non-Indian or to someone with substantial non-Indian ancestry. Marriage Registers, 1907–1918, NA PNR RG75, Tulalip Box 472.

3. Census takers in 1900 identified as white everyone on the Port Madison and Lummi Reservations who had one white and one Indian parent. Barsh census data. Also, Special Census, Indian Division (1880), NA PNR RG29, Microfilm I-34, Roll 1, Port Madison Reservation, and Roll 2, Lummi Reservation; Special Census of Indians Not Taxed, 1880–81, NA PNR Microfilm P-2193, Twana Tribe; *ARCIA* (1880/81), 164. Edwin Eells dropped from his censuses those Indian women who married whites and lived with them off the reservation. Eells to E. A. Hayt of March 1, 1878, Eells Papers, Box 1, Folder 17.

4. Mapes, "Map Interpretation," 11–12, 47; Johansen and Gates, *Empire of the Columbia*, 383, 400, 407, 491–92; Miles and Sperlin, *Building a State*, 84, 87, 90, 93, 97.

5. Johansen and Gates, *Empire of the Columbia*, 389, 397–99, 461–63, 476, 479, 482–83, 486–87; Miles and Sperlin, *Building a State*, 85, 87–88; Schiach, *Illustrated History*, 166, 317; Boxberger, *To Fish in Common*, 45; Annual Report of Charles M. Buchanan, October 24, 1901, 5, NA PNR, RG75, Tulalip Box 311. The *P-I* implied that Charles Kelley's lawsuit was the brainchild of white "friends" who knew that the boom had driven the value of Michael's estate up 4,000 percent in two decades. *P-I*, May 12, 1892, 5.

6. Shackleford, "History of the Puyallup," 18–23; *Washington Standard*, September 26, 1890, 1, and January 8, 1892, 1; Boston Tillicum [James Wickersham], "Monograph," 5–6; Hon. John B. Allen, "Puyallup Indian Reservation Lands," speech in U.S. Senate, July 20, 1892, 14–15, UW Special Collections; Pierce County Commissioners, Memorial, Senate Misc. Doc. 62, 52d Cong., 1st sess., 1892; Mayor and Council of Tacoma, Memorial, Senate Misc. Doc. 73, 52d Cong., 1st sess., 1892; Commercial Club of Tacoma, Memorial, Senate Misc. Doc. 78, 52d Cong., 1st sess., 1892; Elwood Evans, "Puyallup Indian Reservation Lands," speech to Tacoma Chamber of Commerce, May 17, 1892, UW Special Collections; Miles and Sperlin, *Building a State*, 10. Ross, a non-Indian, had an Indian wife and children. Applications for Enrollment and Allotment, NA M-1343. Some of the many newspaper articles on this subject appear in the *Daily Ledger* on March 24, 1889, 6; March 25, 1889, 3; August 1, 1889, 5; December 3, 1889, 4; January 14, 1890, 3.

7. *Ross v. Eells*, 56 Federal Reporter 855–59 (U.S. Circuit Court for District of Washington, 1893); *Eells v. Ross*, 64 Federal Reporter 417, 420 (U.S. Court of Appeals, Ninth Circuit, 1894); Shackleford, "History of the Puyallup,"

22–23. Litigation about Puyallup lands included *Meeker et al. v. Winyear et al.*, 48 Washington Reports 27 (1907); *Bird v. Terry*, 129 Federal Reporter 472, 473 (U.S. Circuit Court for District of Washington, 1903); *Meeker v. Kaelin*, 173 Federal Reporter 216, 222 (U.S. Circuit Court for District of Washington, 1909); and *Terry v. Sicade*, 37 Washington Reports 249 (1905).

8. Reports of demands for reservation land include Talbott to Commissioner, March 28, 1890, NA PNR RG75, Tulalip Box 25; C. B. Buchanan to A. A. Bartow, April 9, 1906, NA PNR RG75, Tulalip Box 103; *P-I*, October 1, 1905, Magazine, 6; *P-I*, October 6, 1906, 8; F. H. Abbott to Chas. E. McChesney, October 20, 1909, NA RG75 CCF, Entry 121, Tulalip File 84430–1909–150. Information on trespass cases includes *P-I*, November 9, 1903, 7; *United States v. O'Brien*, 170 Federal Reporter 508 (U.S. Circuit Court for District of Washington, 1903); Susan Olsen and Mary Randlett, *An Illustrated History of Mason County* (Shelton, Wash.: Mason County Senior Center, 1978), 31–32; William McCluskey to Buchanan, February 13, 1906, NA PNR RG75, Tulalip Box 99; Chas. A. Reynolds to Buchanan, September 26, 1903, NA PNR RG75, Tulalip Box 100; Chas. H. Baker to Buchanan, August 11, 1904, ibid.; Affidavit of Chas. Reynolds, February 25, 1905, NA PNR RG75, Tulalip Box 101; Bartow to Jesse A. Frye, January 31, 1905, NA PNR RG75, Tulalip Box 102; Farmer, Swinomish Reservation, to Buchanan, May 1901 and ff., NA PNR RG75, Tulalip Box 104; Buchanan to State Fish Commissioner, July 17, 1901, NA PNR RG75, Tulalip Box 123; *ARCIA* (1904), 359; *United States v. Ashton*, 170 Federal Reporter 509 (U.S. Circuit Court for District of Washington, 1908); *Corrigan v. Brown*, 169 Federal Reporter 477 (U.S. District Court for Western District of Washington, 1909); Nugent, *Lummi Elders Speak*, 19–20.

9. *Josephine Hatch et al. v. Ferguson et al.*, 57 Federal Reporter 959 (U.S. Circuit Court for District of Washington, 1893); Miles and Sperlin, *Building a State*, 85–87. The judge in the Hatch case was the same who later approved Ross's deals with the Puyallups.

10. *Kelley v. Kitsap County*, 5 Washington Reports 521 (1893); *In re Estate of John T. Wilbur*, 14 Washington Reports 242, 245 (1896); *P-I*, March 17, 1913, 8; Hubbard, "Indian under the White Man's Law," 48. Kitty Wilbur later married John Fornsby, who recalled the lawsuit. Collins, "John Fornsby," 320.

11. McCluskey to Jesse E. Flanders, January 16, 1909, NA PNR RG75, Tulalip Box 99; Philip John to McCluskey, March 27, 1906, ibid.; Nugent, *Lummi Elders Speak*, 66; P. Gard to Buchanan, March 26, 1903, NA PNR RG75, Tulalip Box 116; Johnson Williams to Buchanan, April 16, 1903, ibid.; Buchanan to Moses Pike, November 21, 1901, NA PNR RG75, Tulalip Box 123; *P-I*, October 22, 1905, Magazine, 5; Reynolds to Buchanan, December 18, 1902, NA PNR RG75, Tulalip Box 100; Annual Report, October 24, 1901, 5, NA PNR RG75, Tulalip Box 311; Johansen and Gates, *Empire of the Columbia*, 446, 452–54; *ARCIA* (1903), 336; 24 *U.S. Statutes* 388.

12. D. C. Govan to Commissioner, November 20, 1895, NA PNR RG75, Tulalip Box 25. People of uncertain affiliation are mentioned in Reynolds to Buchanan, October 9, 1901, and April 9, 1902, NA PNR RG75, Tulalip Box

100; Bartow to Buchanan, January 19, 1903, and November 13, 1901, NA PNR RG75, Tulalip Box 102; statements of Chas. J. Thompson and Charles Keokuke, April 28, 1902, ibid.; C. B. Pickrell to Buchanan, September 11, 1908, NA PNR RG75, Tulalip Box 103; Pickrell to Flanders, January 26, 1909, ibid. Some non-Indian men had lived for years on reservation, complying with Indian regulations; others were outsiders who apparently instigated their wives' requests in hope of profiting when allowed to sell the land. Pickrell to Buchanan, October 27, 1908, ibid. Other correspondence about women married to non-Indians includes Thornton to Commissioner, January 29, 1891, NA PNR RG75, Tulalip Box 25; Talbott to Commissioner, April 12, 1887, ibid.; Pickrell to Buchanan, October 12, 1908, NA PNR RG75, Tulalip Box 103; Neil Spithill to Buchanan, May 12, 1903, NA PNR RG75, Tulalip Box 116.

13. N. D. Hill to Isaac Stevens, February 2, April 20, and May 28, 1856, WTSIA, Roll 10, Reel 21; *ARCIA* (1857), 326, 329–30, 340; *ARCIA* (1860), 202; *ARCIA* (1860/62), 386, 389, 410; *ARCIA* (1862/63), 457; *ARCIA* (1873), 310; *ARCIA* (1877), 190; *ARCIA* (1878), 133; Milroy to Chirouse, March 25, 1873, NA PNR RG75, M-2011, Roll 2; R. C. Fay to Mr. Taylor, August 28, 1861, ibid.; annual report from Tulalip, September 30, 1862, ibid.; Finkboner to Howe, November 6, 1864, ibid.; Haley to Stevens, April 7, 1856, WTSIA, Roll 10, Reel 20. The special Indian census of 1880 indicates that most residents at Tulalip had been there since the treaty or before.

14. Milroy to Chirouse, March 14, 1873, NA PNR RG75, M-2011; Bartow to Buchanan, March 31, 1902, NA PNR RG75, Tulalip Box 102; Statement of Charlie Moses, Applications for Enrollment, NA M-1343, Roll 3.

15. M. Eells, "Census of the Clallam and Twana Indians," 35, 37; M. Eells, "Indians of Puget Sound," 4–5, 271; Talbott to Daniel Dorchester, October 19, 1890, NA PNR RG75, Tulalip Box 25; Report of Tulalip Superintendent, 1915, NA RG75 CCF, Entry 121, Tulalip File 39946–033; Tenth Census of the United States, Indian Division, 1880, NA PNR RG29, Microfilm I-34, Rolls 1 and 2.

16. The reservation system of the 1860s and 1870s was supposed to protect Indians from harmful interracial contact until they could cope with it. E. Eells to T. P McKinney, August 30, 1871, Eells Papers; E. Eells to Blinn, January 20, 1874, ibid.; McGlinn to Chirouse, February 28, 1874, NA PNR RG75, M-2011; Chirouse to J. B. Brouillet, March 6, 1876, ibid.; Chirouse to J. Q. Smith, August 17, 1876, ibid.; *ARCIA* (1874), 336–37; Trennert, *Alternative to Extinction*, 195. But by the late 1880s Indian policy reform aimed to effect Indians' assimilation into American society by dismantling reservations. Hoxie, *Final Promise*, 10–11, 66–67, 190; Dippie, *Vanishing American*, 247–50; Helen Marie Bannan, "Reformers and the 'Indian Problem,' 1878–1887 and 1922–1934" (Ph.D. diss., Syracuse University, 1976), 177–78; Alexandra Harmon, "When Is an Indian Not an Indian? The 'Friends of the Indian' and the Problems of Indian Identity," *Journal of Ethnic Studies* 18 (Summer 1990): 100 and notes 27–30. Local support for acculturation by contact appears in *ARCIA* (1883), 148–49; *ARCIA* (1885), 193; O. O. Howard in *P-I*, January 4, 1891, 9; *Seattle Mail and Herald*, July 11, 1903, 10, c. 3–4; interview with D. C.

Govan, *P-I*, January 2, 1897, 7; Charles Milton Buchanan, "The Indian: His Origin and Legendary Lore," *Overland Monthly* 36 (1900): 118; *ARCIA* (1904), 355; Lida W. Quimby, "Indian Education," *The State* 5 (March 1900): 80; Report of Bartow, June 30, 1905, NA PNR RG75, Tulalip Box 311; Meeker, *Pioneer Reminiscences*, 226. An interest in encouraging Indians to interact with exemplary whites gave officials a rationale for bringing whites onto reservations as lessees and purchasers of land. F. H. Abbott to Chas. E. McChesney, October 20, 1909, NA RG75 CCF, Entry 121, Tulalip File 84430–1909–150; Buchanan to Commissioner, February 15, 1910, ibid.; Report of Tulalip Superintendent, 1915, NA RG75 CCF, Entry 121, Tulalip File 39946–033.

17. Felix S. Cohen, *Felix S. Cohen's Handbook of Federal Indian Law* (Washington, D.C.: U.S. Government Printing Office, 1942; reprint, Albuquerque: University of New Mexico Press, n.d.), 154, citing 24 *United States Statutes* 288, 289; Article 6 of Treaty with the Nisqualli, etc., 10 *United States Statutes* 1132; Treaty with the D'Wamish, etc., 12 *United States Statutes* 927; Treaty with the S'Klallam, etc., 12 *United States Statutes* 933; *ARCIA* (1876/77), 190; *ARCIA* (1885), 192; Allen, "Puyallup Indian Reservation Lands," 10.

18. *ARCIA* (1888/89), 286; *ARCIA* (1892), 498–99; *Daily Ledger*, February 18, 1891, 4; *ARCIA* (1891), 451; *ARCIA* (1890), 227; Eells to Hayt, May 10, 1879, Eells Papers; Eells to H. Himes, March 17, 1910, Eells Papers, Box 3, Folder 17; Report of Inspector McCormick, March 11, 1894, NA PNR RG75, M-1070, Roll 31; Report of Govan, August 20, 1895, NA PNR RG75, Tulalip Box 311; Report of Buchanan, August 6, 1906, ibid.; Reynolds to Buchanan, May 2, 1905, NA PNR RG75, Tulalip Box 101; Bartow to Buchanan, September 7, 1901, NA PNR RG75, Tulalip Box 102; Thornton to Commissioner, August 24, 1892, NA PNR RG75, Tulalip Box 25; Letter from Ezra Meeker, *P-I*, November 15, 1903, 30; *Daily Ledger*, March 24, 1889, 6.

19. 18 *United States Statutes* 402, 420; 23 *United States Statutes* 76, 96; Cohen, *Cohen's Handbook*, 259–60.

20. Talbott to Commissioner, February 6, 1890, NA PNR RG75, Tulalip Box 25; Talbott to Patrick Halloran, June 10, 1890, ibid.; Thornton to Commissioner, December 2, 1893, ibid.; Edward Bristow to Edward Mills, January 29, 1901, ibid., Box 26; McCluskey to Flanders, January 16, 1909, NA PNR RG75, Tulalip Box 99; Bristow to Buchanan, May 7, 1903, NA PNR RG75, Tulalip Box 104; Agent, Tulalip Reservation, to James Moore, October 31, 1901, NA PNR RG75, Tulalip Box 115.

21. Buchanan to Commissioner, August 19, 1901, NA PNR RG75, Tulalip Box 123.

22. Reynolds to Buchanan, November 4, 1901, NA PNR RG75, Tulalip Box 100; Bristow to Buchanan, June 5, 1902, NA PNR RG75, Tulalip Box 104; McCluskey to Buchanan, June 27, 1906, NA PNR RG75, Tulalip Box 99. Evidence of difficulties compiling censuses includes Reynolds to Buchanan, n.d., regarding circular of April 5, 1902, NA PNR RG75, Tulalip Box 100; Bartow to

Buchanan, November 13, 1901, NA PNR RG75, Tulalip Box 102; Birth and Death Certificates and Reports, 1897–1939, NA PNR RG75, Tulalip Box 470; Notes from Book of Indian Offences, 1908–1912, Suquamish Tribal Archives. Sources for McCluskey's background are *P-I*, October 1, 1905, Magazine, 6; Sister Mary Louise, "Eugene Casimir Chirouse," 91–92.

23. Buchanan to Commissioner, February 15, 1910, NA RG75 CCF, Entry 121, Tulalip File 93127–07–311; Bristow to Buchanan, June 5, 1902, NA PNR RG75, Tulalip Box 104; Buchanan to Superintendent, Puyallup Indian School, October 22, 1908, Attachment to Report of Inspector Davis, NA RG75 CCF, Entry 121, Tulalip File 24323–1908–150.

24. Report of Inspector Davis, NA RG75 CCF, Entry 121, Tulalip File 24323–1908–150.

25. Memorandum Decision (1907), *Spithill et al. v. McLean et al.*, United States Circuit Court for Western District of Washington, Case No. 1194, NA PNR RG75, Tulalip Box 503; Record in *Spithill v. McLean*, NA PNR RG21, Civil and Criminal Case Files, 1890–1911, Box 184; Alexander Spithill to Buchanan, August 13, 1901, NA PNR RG75, Tulalip Box 115; Hunt and Kaylor, *Washington West of the Cascades*, 404; Applications for Enrollment, Snohomish Roll, NA PNR RG75, M-1343; Patrick Buckley to Commissioner, July 20, 1886, NA PNR RG75, Tulalip Box 24; Buchanan to S. T. Smith, September 13, 1901, NA PNR RG75, Tulalip Box 123; Buchanan to Talbott, September 21, 1901, ibid.; Buchanan to Govan, November 26, 1901, ibid. Besides Buchanan, the Spithills sued the half-white, half-Skagit man to whom Buchanan proposed to assign the land.

26. Transcript, *Spithill v. McLean*, NA PNR RG21, Box 184, pp. 55, 61, 63, 70, 77, 205, 215–16, 232.

27. Acting Commissioner to Buckley, in *Spithill v. McLean*; Memorandum Decision, *Spithill v. McLean*, October 23, 1907; Transcript, *Spithill v. McLean*, 210.

28. Transcript, *Spithill v. McLean*, 14, 31, 33, 7, 91, 93, 103, 148, 181, 190–91, 195.

29. Ibid., 289, 292, 18–31, 183.

30. Ibid., 79–80, 40–41, 323–24.

31. Ibid., 80, 205.

32. Boston Tillicum [James Wickersham], "Monograph," 6–13.

33. Ibid., 21, 25, 28, 33–41. Some people did settle and receive land on the Puyallup Reservation despite a lack of known previous ties to people in that area. Application of August Kautz, Duwamish Roll, Applications for Enrollment, NA M-1343, Roll 3; George Sloan, ibid., Roll 4; Charles Satiacum, ibid., Roll 5.

34. Criminal prosecutions also contributed to the formulations, because racial classifications determined which jurisdiction could punish offenders or whether certain laws applied to them. When the defendants or their ancestors had crossed racial boundaries, courts had to define "Indian" or tribal membership. Some who faced trial as Indians under federal law argued that white an-

cestry or lack of ties to a reservation community made them non-Indians who could be tried only in state courts, while some with equivalent backgrounds tried to dodge state charges by emphasizing descent from or association with Indians. *State v. Williams*, 13 Washington Reports 339 (1895); *State v. Tommy Santiago Howard*, 33 Washington Reports 251, 254 (1903); *State v. Jack Smokalem*, 37 Washington Reports 91 (1905); *State v. Nicolls*, 61 Washington Reports 142 (1910); *United States v. Hadley*, 99 Federal Reporter 437–38 (U.S. Circuit Court for District of Washington, 1900). Courts wrestled with similar questions throughout the United States. Prucha, *Great Father*, 773, 783; *Waldron v. United States*, 143 Federal Reporter 413 (1905); *United States v. Gardner*, 189 Federal Reporter 690 (1911); *Alberty v. United States*, 162 United States Reports 499 (1896); *Montoya v. United States*, 180 United States Reports 261 (1901); *United States v. Ward*, 42 Federal Reporter 320 (1890); *Keith v. United States*, 8 Oklahoma Reports 466 (1899); *United States v. Higgins*, 103 Federal Reporter 348 (1900). Their efforts came in an era when courts were defining the "white race" by ruling on the racial identities of people from a variety of nations and ancestries. Peggy Pascoe, "Miscegenation Law, Court Cases, and Ideologies of 'Race' in Twentieth-Century America," *Journal of American History* 83 (June 1996): 44–70; Lopez, *White by Law*.

35. My data do not support a systematic quantitative analysis, but sources cited in the pages that follow are evidence of the volume of articles concerning Indians, as are indexes for local newspapers at the Tacoma and Seattle Public Libraries.

36. *P-I* articles include January 4, 1891, 9 (potlatch); January 2, 1897, 7; May 20, 1898, 5; July 4, 1897, 20 (treaties); May 11, 1898, 8 (Shakers); May 24, 1898, 9 (Lummi "feast"); September 17, 1899, 22; April 5, 1901, 9 (government policy); June 16, 1901, 35 (treaties); August 14, 1904, 9 ("Injun Dan"); September 13, 1905, 8 (Shakers). Meany's *P-I* stories appeared July 30, 1905, Magazine, 13 (Tulalip); August 13, 1905, sec. 2, 11 (Muckleshoot); October 1, 1905, Magazine, 6 (Lummi); October 8, 1905, Magazine, 6 (Swinomish); October 22, 1905, Magazine, 5 (Twana and Klallam); October 29, 1905, Magazine, 6 (Port Madison); November 5, 1905, Magazine, 6. Also, *Washington Standard*, January 8, 1892, 1; Thomas Nelson Strong, "Indians of the Northwest," *Pacific Monthly* 16 (1906): 169–77; James Wickersham, "Nusqually Mythology: Studies of the Washington Indians," *Overland Monthly* 32 (1898): 345–51.

37. *P-I*, May 31, 1904, 9; *Seattle Mail and Herald*, November 29, 1902, 6; October 6, 1906, 5; December 8, 1906, 5; *Patriarch* 15 (May 13, 1911): 2; *P-I* on following dates and pages: July 4, 1891, 8; September 10, 1899, 6; June 22, 1904, 9; June 26, 1904, 10; December 30, 1904, 9; December 10, 1905, 7; May 29, 1906, 1; October 1, 1906, 16. Anecdotes about Indians who seemed comical because of näiveté about whites or ignorance of technology appear in the *P-I*, November 5, 1905, Magazine, 6; *Mail and Herald*, August 2, 1902, 10. UW Special Collections Library houses a large number of photographs of Indians around Puget Sound taken during the period 1890 to 1910, some of which il-

lustrated articles cited above. Many, such as numbers 1337, 869, 743, 707, and 1501, feature Indians on city streets.

38. Dippie, *Vanishing American*, 199–200, 202–7; Hoxie, *Final Promise*, 85–90; Barbara A. Davis, *Edward S. Curtis: The Life and Times of a Shadow Catcher* (San Francisco: Chronicle Books, 1985), 31, 33–34; Lee Clark Mitchell, *Witnesses to a Vanishing America: The Nineteenth-Century Response* (Princeton, N.J.: Princeton University Press, 1981); Werner Sollors, *Beyond Ethnicity: Consent and Descent in American Culture* (New York: Oxford University Press, 1986), 118–19.

39. Bennett, *Small World*, xi, 365–68; Meeker, *Pioneer Reminiscences*, 47; Weir, "Roughing It on Puget Sound"; Clarence B. Bagley, *In the Beginning* (Tacoma, Wash.: Lowman & Hanford, 1905); Meeker, "Uncle Ezra's Short Stories"; E. Denny, *Blazing the Way;* Orange Jacobs, *Memoirs of Orange Jacobs* (Seattle: Hanford & Lowman, 1908); C. Prosch, *Reminiscences;* Swift, "Notes on Whidby Island"; *P-I,* July 22, 1906, Magazine, 6; Edward Huggins, "The Story of 'Bill' or 'Sclousin'" (1900) and "A Trip to 'Alki' Point Near Duwamsh Bay" (1901), UW Special Collections; A. Denny, *Pioneer Days;* Leighton, *Life on Puget Sound;* M. Eells, *Ten Years of Missionary Work;* Keyes, *Fighting Indians;* Henry Yesler, "The Daughter of Old Chief Seattle," *Washington Magazine* 1, no. 3 (1889): 25–27; Judson, *Pioneer's Search;* Bruseth, *Indian Stories;* Blankenship, *Lights and Shades;* Kellogg, "History of Whidbey's Island"; Lotzgesell, "Pioneer Days"; McCurdy, *By Juan de Fuca's Strait;* WPA, *Told by the Pioneers* (1937). Histories that drew heavily on elicited memories of pioneer settlers include Bancroft, *History of Oregon* and *History of Washington, Idaho, and Montana;* Elwood Evans and Edmond Meany, *The State of Washington: A Brief History* (Tacoma, Wash.: Tacoma Daily News, 1893); Edmond Meany, *History of the State of Washington* (New York: Macmillan, 1909); William F. Prosser, *A History of the Puget Sound Country* (New York: n.p., 1908); Hunt and Kaylor, *Washington West of the Cascades;* Schiach, *Illustrated History.*

40. E. Denny, *Blazing the Way,* 260; Barbara Allen, "Shaping History: The Creation of a Collective Pioneer Experience," *Columbia* 7, no. 4 (Winter 1993/94), 6–13; Clyde A. Milner II, "The Shared Memory of Montana Pioneers," *Montana* 37 (1987): 4–7; Meeker, *Pioneer Reminiscences*, 205–6; Meeker in *P-I,* June 16, 1901, 35.

41. Benjamin F. Shaw, "Medicine Creek Treaty," speech, December 20, 1903, *Proceedings of the Oregon Historical Society* (1906), Appendix C, 24–32; A. Denny, *Pioneer Days,* 18, 38, 47; E. Denny, *Blazing the Way,* 51, 57, 67, 175; Ezra Meeker, "Address delivered at Olympia March 2d 1903 upon the occasion of celebrating Creation day of Washington Territory fifty years before," Bagley Papers, Box 22, vol. 9, 3, 8, 12–13; Parker, "Puget Sound," in Bancroft collection. Tales of narrow escapes from Indian murder plots include WPA, *Told by the Pioneers,* vol. 2, 92; Hancock, *Narrative of Samuel Hancock,* 110, 112–13.

42. *P-I,* November 9, 1903, 7; *United States v. O'Brien; United States v. Ashton; United States et al. v. Alaska Packers' Association et al.,* 70 Federal

Reporter 152 (U.S. Circuit Court for District of Washington, 1897); *P-I*, March 13, 1897, 5.

43. *P-I*, November 15, 1903, 30; Meeker, *Pioneer Reminiscences*, 172, 208, 213–14, 223–24, 226, 228, 232; Yesler, "Settlement of Washington Territory."

44. *P-I*, July 4, 1897, 20; *P-I*, June 16, 1901, 35; *P-I*, July 30, 1905, Magazine, 13; Shaw, "Medicine Creek Treaty"; "Did Leschi Sign the Medicine Creek Treaty?" *P-I*, January 31, 1904, 25; Editorial, *P-I*, March 3, 1904, 4; Evans, "Puyallup Indian Reservation," 4–5. A later positive characterization of the treaties is Samuel A. Eliot, *Report upon the Conditions and Needs of the Indians of the Northwest Coast* (Washington, D.C.: Government Printing Office, 1915).

45. Shaw, "Medicine Creek Treaty," 25–26; Emily Inez Denny, "Types and Characteristics of Puget Sound Indians," *Northwest Magazine* 12 (September 1894): 4–6; E. Denny, *Blazing the Way*, 56; Meeker, *Pioneer Reminiscences*, 129, 222–24; Meeker in *P-I*, June 16, 1901, 35; M. Eells, "Indians of Puget Sound," 276.

46. Denny, "Types and Characteristics," 5; *P-I*, October 29, 1905, Magazine, 6; "Princess Angeline," *Midland Monthly*, October 2, 1897, reprinted in the *Ballard News*, [n.d.], 3, UW Microfilm 212; Smith, *Seattle Sunday Star*, October 29, 1887, 3; Frederic James Grant, *History of Seattle, Washington* (New York: American Publishing and Engraving, 1891), 432 and ff.; Costello, *The Siwash*, 29, 31, 105. In 1912 leading citizens of Seattle erected a bust of Chief Seattle in a city park. At the ceremonies were white members of the Tilikums Club, organized in three "tribes." Otherwise unidentified 1912 newspaper article in Meany Papers; Miles and Sperlin, *Building a State*, 99. Descriptions of other "friendly" Indians include McCurdy, *By Juan de Fuca's Strait*, 126; *P-I*, August 13, 1905, sec. 2, 11.

47. Meeker, *Pioneer Reminiscences*, 180, 205–10, 215, 220, 242, 246, 446, 455–57; Shaw, "Medicine Creek Treaty," 30–32.

48. Buchanan, "The Indian," 114, 118; Dippie, *Vanishing American*, 208–9; Davis, *Edward S. Curtis*, 33–34; *P-I* on following dates and pages: September 17, 1899, 22; February 17, 1903, 8; April 15, 1907, 20; May 30, 1907; August 11, 1907, 9; *P-I*, December 9, 1909, cited in Noel, *Muckleshoot Indian History*, 87; Strong, "Indians of the Northwest," 169; Meeker, *Pioneer Reminiscences*, 172. D. C. Govan denied that Indians were dying out. *P-I*, January 2, 1897, 7.

49. "Princess Angeline," *Midland Monthly*; Bagley, "Chief Seattle and Angeline," 273, 275; E. Denny, *Blazing the Way*, 378–81; *P-I*, October 29, 1905, Magazine, 6. To Edward Huggins, Angeline was "not by any means worthy of so much gush and blarney as has been written about her." Letter to E. N. Fuller, September 11, 1900, Huggins Papers. A Klallam woman said that white merchants tolerated Angeline's shoplifting because they knew that whites had driven her out of her home. Harrington Papers, Reel 10, 1107. Portraits of other aged, living "relics" of the aboriginal past include Lucius Grant Folsom, "An Hour with a Queen," *Overland Monthly* 61 (1913): 502–4; *P-I*, August 14, 1904, 9 ("Injun Dan"); *P-I*, May 29, 1906, 1 (Indian John); UW Native American Collection photographs 1056, 591, 1184–85, 1359–60, 1174, 1175.

50. *P-I*, April 15, 1907, 20. Inhabitants of the village, the author said, came from several nearby reservations, British Columbia, and the Columbia River. UW Native American Collection photographs of young Indians making use of commodities and conveniences introduced by non-Indians include Nos. 1362, 1126, 1366–67, 1173, and 662. Regarding the tendency to see Indians who accept cultural change as heading for extinction, see Clifford, *Predicament of Culture*, 5.

51. Diary, Tulalip Agency, 1909–1913, NA PNR RG75, Tulalip Box 310; programs from commencement, Christmas, and dedication ceremonies at Tulalip School, 1905–1916, Meany Papers, Folder 85–16; Bartow to Buchanan, July 31, 1902, and September 9, 1903, NA PNR RG75, Tulalip Box 102; Liza Whitaker to Buchanan, May 19, 1902, NA PNR RG75, Tulalip Box 104; Bristow to Buchanan, June 30, 1904, ibid.; Buchanan to Emma Jules, [December?] 1901, NA PNR RG75, Tulalip Box 123; *ARCIA* (1895), 320; *ARCIA* (1896), 399; Annual Report of 1908, NA PNR RG75, Tulalip Box 311; Stella Nickolsen in Nugent, *Lummi Elders Speak*, 96; Report of Chas. L. Davis, NA RG75 CCF, Tulalip File 24323–1908–150; Lawrence Rygg, "The Continuation of Upper Class Snohomish Coast Salish Attitudes and Deportment as Seen through the Life History of a Snohomish Coast Salish Woman" (M.A. thesis, Western Washington College, 1977), 118, 140–41; Noel, *Muckleshoot Indian History*, 43. Information on the curricula at the Indian schools appears in Quimby, "Indian Education," 79; H. H. Johnson to Commissioner, March 21, 1910, NA PNR RG75, Puyallup Box 2, Book 3.

52. *P-I*, October 1 and 29, 1905, Magazine, 6; H. H. Johnson to Commissioner, July 17, 1909, NA PNR RG75, Puyallup Box 2, Book 2. Also, Henry Sicade, "The Indians' Side of the Story," in Miles and Sperlin, *Building a State*, 490–503 (paper read at meeting of the Research Club of Tacoma, April 10, 1917); Johnson Williams, "Black Tamanous, the Secret Society of the Clallam Indians," *Washington Historical Quarterly* 7 (1916): 296–300.

53. *P-I*, July 4, 1891, 8; *P-I*, August 11, 1907, 9; F. I. Vassault, "Patsy's Potlatch," *Overland Monthly* 19 (1892): 461–64; Castile, *Indians of Puget Sound*, 326; *P-I* on following dates and pages: June 22, 1904, 9; June 26, 1904, 10; December 30, 1904, 9; May 29, 1906, 1 and 10; December 24, 1906, 16; May 5, 1907, 9, and May 6, 1907, 1; notes regarding potlatch of Peter John at Oyster Bay in 1904, Meany Papers, Folder 86–3; Waterman, "Notes on the Ethnology," 77; Jacobs, *Memoirs*, 161–62; UW Native American photographs Nos. 831–33, 861, 864.

54. Edward Mills to Buchanan, May 7, 1902, NA PNR RG75, Tulalip Box 115; clipping from *Seattle Times*, September 16, 1903, in Meany Papers, Folder 85–12; Bristow to Buchanan, May 14, 1903, NA PNR RG75, Tulalip Box 104; Bristow to Buchanan, July 8, 1906, NA PNR RG75, Tulalip Box 105; UW Native American photographs 1176–79. Indians also gave craft and culture demonstrations at the Alaska-Yukon Exposition of 1909. Diary, August 23 and October 16, 1909, NA PNR RG75, Tulalip Box 310.

55. Bartow to Buchanan, July 16 and September 9, 1903, NA PNR RG75, Tulalip Box 102; Mills to E. P. Edson, June 27, 1899, NA PNR RG75, Tulalip Box

26; Diary, January 23, 1910, and January 22, 1913, NA PNR RG75, Tulalip Box 310; *P-I*, January 23, 1913, 1; Program for Chief Seattle Day, August 26, 1911, Meany Papers, Folder 85–12; notes, Suquamish Oral History interviews H.8.01 (Holmes Hyland, December 23, 1981) and W.1.18 (Lawrence Webster, July 1, 1982). Whites also invited elderly Indians to collaborate in representing a shared past. In 1894 the principal orator at Oak Harbor's Independence Day was Indian resident Billy Barlow; in 1903 presumed descendants of Chief Seattle came from Port Madison to help the city of Seattle celebrate its golden anniversary; and in 1906, when the Pierce County Pioneer Association commemorated the Wilkes Expedition, Slugamus Koquilton was a featured speaker. Kellogg, "History of Whidbey's Island," 72; Pierce County, "Commemorative Celebration," 9; Miles and Sperlin, *Building a State*, 99. In the 1970s elderly Lummis recalled that their families joined whites for pre–World War I pioneer picnics and Fourth of July festivities. Nugent, *Lummi Elders Speak*, 108–9.

56. A reference to Indians paid "for services rendered" during Seattle's Potlatch Week appears in W. J. Egbert to John F. Pace, August 4, 1911, Notes from Book of Indian Offences, Suquamish Tribal Archives. Katherine McCurdy described one Indian's expectation of a monetary reward for being picturesque. *Seattle Mail and Herald*, April 28, 1906, 4.

57. *P-I*, November 9, 1903, 7; Meeker, *Pioneer Reminiscences*, 210. Indian Office personnel often purported to relay Indians' views of themselves, as in interviews for articles published in the *P-I* on January 2, 1897, 7; March 21, 1898, 3; May 20, 1898, 5; February 13, 1899, 5; September 17, 1899, 22; April 5, 1901, 9; and Meany's 1905 series cited above. Also Myron Eells, "Treatment of Indians by Whites," *Seattle Argus*, December 29, 1899; *P-I*, August 20, 1899, 16; *P-I*, September 16, 1899, 32; Buchanan, "The Indian"; Quimby, "Puget Sound Shakers"; Quimby, "Indian Education"; Reagan, "Shaker Church of the Indians." Although government officials transmitted Indian assertions selectively, they did pass on complaints and inquiries about rights guaranteed in the treaties. Indian Agent [Buchanan] to State Fish Commissioner, July 17, 1901, NA PNR RG75, Tulalip Box 123; Govan to Governor John R. Rogers, January 28, 1898, NA PNR RG75, Tulalip Box 26; Govan to U.S. Attorney F. C. Robertson, July 23, 1897, ibid.; Reynolds to Buchanan, July 4, 1904, NA PNR RG75, Tulalip Box 100; Bristow to Buchanan, May 1, 1902, and March 2, 1903, NA PNR RG75, Tulalip Box 104; Bristow to Buchanan, October 17, 1905, NA PNR RG75, Tulalip Box 105; *ARCIA* (1895), 318; Govan to Commissioner, August 20, 1895, NA PNR RG75, Tulalip Box 311.

58. Ann Nugent, "Regulation of the Lummi Indians by Governmental Officials between 1900–1920," 1977, UW Special Collections; Annual Report for 1914, NA PNR RG75, M-1011, Roll 153.

59. Collins, "John Fornsby," 322–23; Nugent, *Lummi Elders Speak*, 82; Deposition of William Shelton, *Duwamish v. United States*, 254; Suquamish Oral History interview G.1.01 (Martha George, March 13, 1982).

60. Bristow to Buchanan, December 24, 1901, NA PNR RG75, Tulalip Box 98; James Moore to Tulalip Agent, October 30, 1901, NA PNR RG75, Tulalip

Box 115; *Daily Ledger,* May 20, 1891, 6; "To Whom It Concerns," signed with marks by Louis and Lucy Napoleon, Port Madison, October 10, 1902, NA PNR RG75, Tulalip Box 102; Bartow to Buchanan, October 20, 1902, ibid.; Suquamish Oral History Interviews W.1.07 and J.3.03; Bremner to Buchanan, December 15, 1903, NA PNR RG75, Tulalip Box 98; Bristow to Mills, July 11, 1900, ibid.; Bartow to Buchanan, January 30, 1903, and November 13, 1901, NA PNR RG75, Tulalip Box 102; Bristow to Buchanan, September 20, 1906, NA PNR RG75, Tulalip Box 105.

61. *Daily Ledger,* April 16, 1892, 4; July 30, 1889, 5; August 1, 1889, 5; Meeker Family Papers, Notebook III; Thornton to Commissioner, December 2, 1893, NA PNR RG75, Tulalip Box 25; Bristow to Mills, January 29, 1901, NA PNR RG75, Tulalip Box 26; McCluskey to Flanders, January 16, 1909, NA PNR RG75, Tulalip Box 99.

62. *ARCIA* (1896), 315; Govan to Commissioner, August 20, 1895, NA PNR RG75, Tulalip Box 311; Report of C. Buchanan, 1906, ibid.; Report on Homes Visited, 1907, NA PNR RG75, Tulalip Boxes 324–25 combined; Buchanan to Estelle Reel, September 19, 1903, NA PNR RG75, Tulalip Box 106; Indian Census Rolls, NA PNR M-595, Roll 583; Suquamish Oral History Interviews G.1.01 and G.1.06, W.1.10 and W.1.12; Nugent, *Lummi Elders Speak,* 83, 87; *ARCIA* (1899), 359–60; Meeker Family Papers, Notebook III; Report of Inspector John Lane, December 17, 1896, NA PNR M-1070, Roll 31; Johnson to Commissioner, September 9, 1909, NA PNR RG75, Puyallup Box 2, Book 2; Thornton to Commissioner, October 14, 1892, NA PNR RG75, Tulalip Box 25; Bristow to Mills, July 11, 1900, NA PNR RG75, Tulalip Box 98; Amelia Thomas to Buchanan, December 3, 1907, NA PNR RG75, Tulalip Box 99; Fetzer, "George Swanaset."

63. References to differences between generations appear in Nugent, *Lummi Elders Speak,* 70, 80–81; *P-I,* January 2, 1897, 7; *P-I,* September 17, 1899, 22; Suquamish Oral History Interview G.1.04; Report of Govan, 1895, NA PNR RG75, Tulalip Box 311; Folsom, "An Hour with a Queen," 503. As of 1900 about half the children counted as Indians were attending school. *P-I,* February 13, 1899, 5; *ARCIA* (1900), 397; Notes from Book of Indian Offences. That people of the same generation had contrasting childhood socializations can be seen in Suquamish Oral History Interviews J.3.03, G.1.05, W.1.07, W.1.10; Nugent, *Lummi Elders Speak,* 68, 80–81, 87, 92, 95, 96, 98, 103. For a general treatment of this subject, see Anderson, *Changing Woman,* 40, 59.

64. Meeker Family Papers, Notebook III; J. B. Boulet to Mr. Mills, June 20, 1900, NA PNR RG75, Tulalip Box 115; McCluskey to Buchanan, August 21, 1905, NA PNR RG75, Tulalip Box 99.

65. "Tulalip Tribal Customs Prevail against the White Man's Methods of Dealing Justice," *P-I,* July 7, 1901, 35.

66. This summary is based on documents labeled "Subject Series: Murder of David Teuse" in the Charles M. Buchanan Papers, UW Manuscripts, Accession No. 3907. Included are notes of interviews and inquest testimony as well as the undated transcript of a hearing where Mills took testimony under oath.

The *P-I* identified Shelton as the reservation farmer, but Buchanan's papers indicate that he worked in the sawmill until shortly before the murder. Although Buchanan said Shelton left in a huff when his salary was reduced, several witnesses referred to Shelton's anger at being fired. Hook said that Shelton's father and aunt had been killed "up the river" but denied knowledge of the killers' identities. Shelton, who was born at his father's village on Whidbey Island, identified himself in 1900 as Snohomish. The 1880 Tulalip census identifies Te-use or David as Skiwhomish—that is, from the inland Skykomish River Valley. Special Census, NA PNR RG29 Microfilm I-34, Roll 1. Later, Shelton's daughter spoke of fearing that her father was in mortal danger from Snoqualmies and recalled her father and mother speaking bitterly about Indian judges' arbitrary use of power, accusing them of stealing to augment their wealth. Rygg, "Continuation of . . . Attitudes," 60–61, 63, 66.

67. Several people said they saw Hook "mammucking his temaniwas [using his spirit powers]" shortly before the murder. They also attributed several earlier deaths to his supernatural power. When Mills asked witnesses whether they were afraid of the medicine man, he got negative as well as positive answers; but it is evident that most people fit the description that one informant gave of Jim Snoqualmie: "scared both of the tamanamus man and of the Agent and he does not know what to do between the two fears." Unable to pin Teuse's death on Shelton or Hook, Mills and Buchanan turned the hearing into an attempt to discredit the shaman and shamanic power. They put Hook on the stand, where he said that for fear of the law he used his power only off the reservation. By threatening him with jail if he used his power anywhere, they then wrung from him a public statement that his power had grown weak.

68. *ARCIA* (1900), 400.

69. *P-I*, July 7, 1901, 35.

70. By 1905, Shelton was again the Tulalip millwright. *P-I*, July 30, 1905, Magazine, 13. His subsequent career as a government-endorsed representative of Tulalip Indians is summarized in the *Everett Herald*, February 11, 1938, Appendix G-13, Reply, Snohomish Petition for Federal Acknowledgement. Also, Rygg, "Continuation of . . . Attitudes." Loretta Fowler's study of the Fort Belknap Reservation shows how conflict among people with different histories and cultures has been a key to their development of an understanding of themselves as Indians. *Shared Symbols, Contested Meanings.*

71. Chief George Nelson, Joe Snohomish, Bob James, Justin Joseph, and Joe Billy to Buchanan, November 20, 1903, NA PNR RG75, Tulalip Box 100 (all misspellings in original text). Like Indian courts, reservation schools were common lightning rods for the energy of people who sought to unite Indians in opposition to whites' agenda. Thornton to Commissioner, October 14, 1892, NA PNR RG75, Tulalip Box 25; Govan to Thomas Jefferson, November 4, 1895, ibid.; "We the Indians" to Buchanan, January 14, 1902, NA PNR RG75, Tulalip Box 102; Bartow to Buchanan, February 12, 1902, ibid.; Thornton to Commissioner, May 26, 1893, ibid.; George Bremner to Buchanan, September 28, 1904, NA PNR RG75, Tulalip Box 98.

72. Agent to Mr. [   ] [   ], May 25, 1899, NA PNR RG75, Tulalip Box 26; *P-I* on following dates and pages: May 24, 1898, 9; September 10, 1899, 6; June 22, 1904, 9; December 30, 1904, 9; May 5, 1907, 9; August 11, 1907, 4; August 23, 1907, 8; *Tacoma Morning Union*, December 30, 1896, 3; *Daily Ledger*, May 4, 1898, 3; Fetzer, "George Swanaset," 9, 11, 12; Nugent, *Lummi Elders Speak*, 107; Suquamish Oral History Interviews W.1.20, H.8.01, J.3.03, G.1.04; Noel, *Muckleshoot Indian History*, 50–51.

73. *P-I*, May 11, 1898, 8; Barnett, *Indian Shakers*, 8; Gunther, "Shaker Religion," 61.

74. WPA, *Told by the Pioneers*, vol. 2, 180; Rygg, "Continuation of … Attitudes," 147; Suquamish Oral History interview J.4.06; list of mixed-blood children living off reservations but attending boarding school at Puyallup, appended to report of Inspector McCormick, March 11, 1894, NA PNR M-1070, Roll 31; K. Tsianina Lomawaima, "Domesticity in the Federal Indian Schools: The Power of Authority over Mind and Body," *American Ethnologist* 20 (May 1993): 236.

75. Meeker, *Pioneer Reminiscences*, 209, 242, 255; *P-I*, November 15, 1903, 30; Suquamish Oral History Interview W.1.11. See also chapter 6.

76. Foster, *Being Comanche*, 14, 20, 28–30.

77. Minutes of Convention at Yakima Reservation, October 18, 1912, and other Records of the Indian Shaker Church of Washington and the Northwest, 1892–1945, UW Microfilm A-4547.

78. The remaining material in this chapter is found in *United States et al. v. Alaska Packers' Association et al.*, 70 Federal Reporter (1897),152, 155–56; *P-I*, March 13, 1897, 5. Testimony in the form of affidavits is in the records of Cases No. 481 and 482, NA PNR RG21, Box 82.

6. INDIANS AND THE UNITED STATES

1. Hoxie, *Final Promise*; Helen M. Bannan, "The Idea of Civilization and American Indian Policy Reformers in the 1880s," *Journal of American Culture* 1 (Winter 1978): 787–99.

2. Hoxie, *Final Promise*, 113, 85, 95–98, 108, 116–44; Thomas N. Holm, "Indians and Progressives: From Vanishing Policy to the Indian New Deal" (Ph.D. diss., University of Oklahoma, 1978), 153–54, 176; Herbert Welsh, *How to Bring the Indian to Citizenship and Citizenship to the Indian* (Philadelphia: Indian Rights Association, 1892), 5–6.

3. As an explanation of racial differences, orthodox evolutionism lost ground to theories that fed skepticism about Indians' ability to progress. Some theorists thought that early environment and social tradition stamped themselves indelibly on Indians' minds. Others posited that race or inherited culture retarded Indians' advancement. The doctrine of racial determinism had gained widespread acceptance in the United States by the end of the nineteenth century. At the same time, nostalgia about past American frontiers, a nativistic reaction to immigration, and the flowering of modern anthropology

contributed to some whites' interest in conserving rather than destroying aboriginal cultural features. Dippie, *Vanishing American*, 94, 200; Hoxie, *Final Promise*, 85. See also chapter 5.

4. Francis Ellington Leupp, *The Indian and His Problem* (New York: Scribner's, 1910), 46, 43–44, 50–51, 53; F. E. Leupp, "Outlines of an Indian Policy," *Outlook* 79 (1905): 946; Buchanan, "The Indian," 122; Annual Report (1915), NA RG75 CCF, Tulalip File 89946–033; Annual Report (1914), NA PNR RG75, M-1011, Roll 153, 137–38.

5. *ARCIA* (1895), 318–19; *ARCIA* (1902), 359; Dippie, *Vanishing American*, 185–86; Prucha, *Great Father*, 717; Reginald Horsman, *Race and Manifest Destiny: The Origins of American Racial Anglo-Saxonism* (Cambridge, Mass.: Harvard University Press, 1981), 156–57; Hoxie, *Final Promise*, 95–98, 106, 164, 193; Michael Banton, *The Idea of Race* (London: Tavistock, 1977), 27; Thomas F. Gossett, *Race: The History of an Idea in America* (Dallas: Southern Methodist University Press, 1963), 244, 155; Editorial, *Sunday Portland Oregonian*, November 24, 1901, 4.

6. Hoxie, *Final Promise*, 160–238; Dippie, *Vanishing American*, 190–91.

7. 34 *United States Statutes* 182; Cohen, *Cohen's Handbook*, 168; Prucha, *Great Father*, 875–77.

8. 34 *United States Statutes* 1015; 36 *United States Statutes* 855, sections 1, 2, 4; Prucha, *Great Father*, 671–73, 759; Cohen, *Cohen's Handbook*, 212–14, 229–36; Holm, "Indians and Progressives," 166.

9. *United States v. Celestine*, 215 United States Reports 278, 290 (1909); *United States v. Nice*, 241 United States Reports 591 (1916); Superintendent of Tulalip Reservation to Roy A. Darling, November 25, 1922, NA PNR RG75, Tulalip Box 503; Cohen, *Cohen's Handbook*, 156–57; Hoxie, *Final Promise*, 229, 238; Dippie, *Vanishing American*, 178–79, 192–96. An 1897 law prohibited all Indians with trust lands or federal protection from acquiring liquor. The Supreme Court first ruled that citizenship protected Indians from prosecution under this statute, but *U.S. v. Nice* reversed that holding. 29 *United States Statutes* 506–7; Prucha, *Great Father*, 655.

10. 36 *United States Statutes* 855; *ARCIA* (1917), 3–4; Cohen, *Cohen's Handbook*, 25–26; Hoxie, *Final Promise*, 176–81; Prucha, *Great Father*, 881–82. Statutes reflecting the presumption that admixtures of "white blood" tend to make Indians competent include 34 *United States Statutes* 1015, 1034, and 35 *United States Statutes* 312. A federal court agreed that "blood" was an appropriate way to demarcate noncompetent Indians. *United States v. Shock*, 187 Federal Reporter 862, 870 (Eastern District of Oklahoma, 1911).

11. *Laws of Washington* (1901), Chapter 135, Sec. 1, 284; *Laws of Washington* (1911), Chapter 89, Sec. 4960; Annual Report (1914), 155, Tulalip Agency, and Report of William J. Egbert, NA PNR RG75, M-1011, Roll 153; W. V. Tanner to R. A. Lathrop, June 15, 1916, NA PNR RG75, Tulalip Box 503; Annual Report (1916), 4, NA RG75 CCF, Tulalip File 39946–033; H. H. Johnson to Commissioner, April 15, 1912, NA PNR RG75, Puyallup Box 3, Book 6; Lewis H. St. John, "The Present Status and Probable Future of the In-

dians of Puget Sound," *Washington Historical Quarterly* 5 (1914): 12–13; *Laws of Washington* (1909), Chapter 140, Sec. 1, 537; Norman H. Clark, *The Dry Years: Prohibition and Social Change in Washington* (Seattle: University of Washington Press, 1965), 91. The legal category "Indians not taxed" derived from a provision of the Washington constitution in which the state, as required by Congress, disclaimed jurisdiction over lands owned and held by Indians who had not severed tribal relations and taken fee patents. Washington State Constitution, Article 26, Section 2. On May 28, 1939, at page 8, *Seattle Argus* reported a state attorney general's ruling that the ban on voting by "Indians not taxed" was invalid.

12. *P-I*, April 21, 1903, 9; E. H. Hammond to Local Board of Pierce County, January 16, 1918, and Daniel Howell to Hammond, March 20, 1918, NA PNR RG75, Puyallup Box 17.

13. Annual Report (1914), 129, NA PNR RG75, M-1011; *Survey of Conditions of the Indians in the United States*, Senate Committee on Indian Affairs, 72nd Cong., 1st sess., 1934, part 32, pp. 17196–213; Nugent, "Regulation of the Lummi," 12.

14. Johnson to Commissioner, July 14, 1911, NA PNR RG75, Puyallup Box 3, Book 5; Annual Report, Tulalip (1914), 129, NA PNR RG75, M-1011; Bristow to Buchanan, February 10, 1903, NA PNR RG75, Tulalip Box 104; Nugent, "Regulation of the Lummi," 13; Johnson to Commissioner, October 13, 1908, NA PNR RG75, Puyallup Box 2, Book 1.

15. Johansen and Gates, *Empire of the Columbia*, 528–29; Report of Inspector McConnell, October 15, 1897, NA PNR RG75, M-1070, Roll 53; Annual Report, Tulalip (1914), 86, NA PNR RG75, M-1011. According to a Tulalip report for 1922, few whites were locating on lands acquired from Indians. NA PNR RG75, M-1011. Sales of allotted lands around Puget Sound were slower before allotment ended in 1934 than elsewhere in the country. Senate Subcommittee, *Survey of Conditions*, 17196–201.

16. Annual Report, Tulalip (1916), 1, NA PNR RG75, M-1011; Superintendent to United States Attorney, January 19, 1917, NA PNR RG75, Puyallup Box 17. Even in the 1930s, Felix Cohen doubted whether the federal government had jurisdiction on allotments that Indians owned outright. Cohen, *Cohen's Handbook*, 8.

17. *Tulalip Bulletin* (May 1916): 2, NA PNR, M-1011, Roll 153; Annual Report, Tulalip (1916), Sec. VII, 1, NA M-1011, Roll 153; Superintendent to Commissioner, September 4, 1918, NA PNR RG75, Puyallup Box 5; Cohen, *Cohen's Handbook*, 226.

18. Superintendent to Chas. A. Reynolds, February 14, 1917, NA PNR RG75, Puyallup Box 17; Reynolds to T. B. Wilson, January 3, 1915, NA PNR RG75, Puyallup Box 15; Andrew P. Peterson to H. H. Johnson, May 18, 1909, NA PNR RG75, Puyallup Box 2, Book 2; Nugent, "Regulation of the Lummi," 1, 12–21.

19. *ARCIA* (1890), 230; Superintendent to Commissioner, June 19, 1915, and April 24, 1918, NA PNR RG75, Puyallup Box 5; Barsh census materials; Cohen, *Cohen's Handbook*, 229–30; Annual Report (1913), Puyallup, NA

PNR RG75, Puyallup Box 4, Book 8; Johnson to Commissioner, January 16 and March 21, 1912, NA PNR RG75, Puyallup Box 3, Book 6; Annual Report, Tulalip (1917), Sales, NA PNR RG75, M-1011; Annual Report, Tulalip (1920), 18, ibid.; Annual Report, Tulalip (1919), Sales, ibid.; Eliot, *Report upon the Conditions*, 19. Later references to differences among owners of undivided allotments appear in Report of Earl Y. Henderson, January 25, 1929, NA RG75 CCF, Entry 121, Taholah File 7962–1929–150; Annual Report, Tulalip (1927), NA PNR RG75, M-1011, Roll 155.

20. Annual Reports, Tulalip (1914), 23–33, and Tulalip (1922), Narrative, NA PNR RG75, M-1011; *Tulalip Bulletin* (July 1917); Superintendent to Commissioner, August 18, 1918, NA PNR RG75, Puyallup Box 5. Although other Indian Service personnel approved of the Shakers, they were equally paternalistic, encouraging the Shakers' abstinence from alcohol and gambling in the hope of moving them toward conformity with other white middle-class values. Johnson to Commissioner, September 9, 1909, NA PNR RG75, Puyallup Box 2, Book 2; Quimby, "Puget Sound Indian Shakers," 189.

21. Buchanan to Commissioner, April 18, 1917, NA PNR RG75, Tulalip Box 94, File 1H–12H; E. B. Merritt to Richard Squiqui, May 18, 1917, ibid.; C. F. Hauke to Mr. Hadley, March 19, 1918, ibid.; McCluskey to Superintendent, November 22, 1917, ibid.; J. B. Boulet to Buchanan, February 5, 1918, ibid.; Annual Report (1922), Narrative, NA PNR RG75, M-1011; Rygg, "Continuation of ... Attitudes," 143, 62, 13–14, 117. Rather than ritual representations of Indians' past, the Office of Indian Affairs promoted agricultural fairs as a means "to put the Indians on a par with their white neighbors." Annual Tulalip Indian fairs began in 1915. NA PNR RG75, Tulalip Box 492.

22. Prucha, *Great Father*, 833–34; C. F. Hauke to all superintendents, March 15, 1924, Records of Tulalip Court of Indian Offenses, NA PNR RG75, Tulalip Box 503; Statement of Louis and Lucy Napoleon, October 18, 1902, NA PNR RG75, Tulalip Box 102; Suquamish Museum, *The Eyes of Chief Seattle* (Suquamish, Wash.: Suquamish Indian Tribe, 1985), 40–41; Suquamish Oral History Interview J.4.06 (Clara Jones, September 23, 1982); Report of Chas. L. Davis, 1908, NA RG75 CCF, Entry 121, Tulalip File 24323–1908–150; Rygg, "Continuation of ... Attitudes," 118, 141; correspondence with parents or reservation employees on behalf of parents, NA PNR RG75, Tulalip Box 99; Nugent, "Regulation of the Lummi," 3; Speech on History of Cushman School, June 16, 1910, Eells Papers, Box 3, Folder 12; Sister Mary Louise, "Eugene Casimir Chirouse," 43, 49, 62, 68–69; *P-I*, April 5, 1901, 9; Annual Report, August 6, 1906, NA PNR RG75, Tulalip Box 311; Hunt and Kaylor, *Washington West of the Cascades*, 502; Report of Fred A. Baker, December 6, 1910, NA RG75 CCF, Entry 121, Tulalip File 100544–1910–150; Superintendent to Archie M. Taylor, September 13, 1918, NA PNR RG75, Puyallup Box 50; Charles Roberts, "The Cushman Indian Trades School and World War I," *American Indian Quarterly* 11 (1987): 222; Bristow to Buchanan, December 24, 1901, NA PNR RG75, Tulalip Box 98; *ARCIA* (1902), 359; Johnson to Commissioner, April 15, 1912, NA PNR RG75, Puyallup Box 3, Book 6; St.

John, "Present Status," 15–16. Buchanan estimated in 1914 that 74.5 percent of school-age children in his jurisdiction actually attended school—a proportion exceeding that for all children (56 percent) and for Indians (42 percent) nationwide. Annual Report (1914), NA PNR RG75, Tulalip M-1011. Government boarding schools usurped the functions of Indian parents in order to implant values the parents presumably failed to teach. Quimby, "Indian Education," 79; Roberts, "Cushman Indian Trades School," 222.

23. James Moore to Superintendent, October 30, 1901, NA PNR RG75, Tulalip Box 115; Addie Caldwell to Commissioner, October 20, 1917, NA PNR RG75, Puyallup Box 50; Mrs. H. Anderson to Chushman [*sic*] school, March 27, 1918, ibid.; Superintendent to Archie M. Taylor, Sequim, September 13, 1918, ibid.; Roberts, "Cushman Indian Trades School," 226.

24. Annual Report, Tulalip (1914), 125, NA PNR RG75, M-1011; Annual Report, Puyallup (1913), NA PNR RG75, Puyallup Box 4, Book 8.

25. *Tulalip Bulletin* (November 1917): 4, NA PNR RG75, M-1011. From the 1870s into the early twentieth century, Indian agents took cognizance of and provided some services to off-reservation people identified as Klallam Indians. *ARCIA* (1881), 171; *ARCIA* (1895), 399; *ARCIA* (1900), 397; Eells, "Census of the Clallam and Twana Indians"; Correspondence, Eells Papers; Indian Census Rolls, 1916+, NA PNR M-595, Roll 93; Reports of John Lane, December 13 and 17, 1896, NA PNR RG75, M-1070, Roll 31. Yet the Puyallup superintendent said in 1918, "The Clallam tribe no longer exists except in name. The Indians consider themselves citizens. ... Only the old or indigent Indians seek aid in any way from our Bureau." Superintendent to Commissioner, January 26, 1918, NA PNR RG75, Puyallup Box 50.

26. Johnson to Commissioner, March 21, 1910, NA PNR RG75, Puyallup Box 2, Book 3; Eliot, *Report upon the Conditions*, 20; Superintendent to Commissioner, March 19, 1918, NA PNR RG75, Puyallup Box 5.

27. Annual Report, Tulalip (1914), 124, NA PNR RG75, M-1011; Malcolm McDowell, *Fifty-second Annual Report of the Board of Indian Commissioners* (Washington, D.C.: Government Printing Office, 1921), Appendix K, 81; Applications for Enrollment, NA M-1343, Skagit Roll.

28. Applications for Enrollment, NA M-1343, Roll 5 (Thomas G. Bishop); Barsh, Census of 1900, Jefferson County; Helen Norton, "Social, Marital, Economic and Political Relationships of the Snohomish Tribe of Indians in the Late 19th and Early 20th Centuries," 1992, Records of the Snohomish Tribe of Indians, 39.

29. Sells to Roblin, November 27, 1916, Applications for Enrollment, NA M-1343.

30. Ibid.; Charles E. Roblin, Schedule of Unenrolled Indians, 1919, NA PNR, Reading Room; Hauke to Buchanan, November 15, 1916, NA RG75 CCF, Entry 121, Tulalip File 117342–1916–053; McChesney to Commissioner, March 6, 1914, NA PNR RG75, Puyallup Box 4, Book 9. Roblin's list includes people who wished to be enrolled in tribes not included in this study, such as Cowlitz, Chinook, and Chehalis.

31. Eliot, *Report upon the Conditions,* 21; Roblin, Schedule of Unenrolled Indians (report); Buchanan to Sells, February 10, 1916, NA PNR RG75, Tulalip Box 71; McDowell, *Fifty-second Annual Report,* Appendix K, 78, 82.

32. Buchanan to Sells, February 10, 1916, NA PNR RG75, Tulalip Box 71; Annual Report, Tulalip (1922), NA PNR RG75, M-1011, Roll 154. McDowell noted that the count of western Washington Indians under federal jurisdiction grew by one thousand between 1910 and 1919. Either the government had taken more people under control, he reasoned, or it had counted more accurately, or the mixed-blood population had grown. Apparently ignorant of Roblin's work, McDowell urged a special canvass of non-reservation Indians aimed at getting children into school and aid to the indigent. *Fifty-second Annual Report,* Appendix K, 77, 78. Also, petition from members of Stillaguamish Tribe, August 12, 1929, NA RG75 CCF, Entry 121, Tulalip File 41499–1929–059; F. F. Duclos to Commissioner, August 15, 1929, ibid.

33. Report of Inspector Gardner, September 22, 1890, NA PNR RG75, M-1070, Roll 53.

34. McDowell, *Fifty-second Annual Report,* Appendix K, 82–83; Johnson to Commissioner, October 28, 1909, NA PNR RG75, Puyallup Box 2, Book 2; Johnson to Commissioner, September 28, 1910, NA PNR RG75, Puyallup Box 2, Book 3; Annual Report, Puyallup (1913), NA PNR RG75, Puyallup Box 4, Book 8; *ARCIA* (1883), 151; *ARCIA* (1898), 303; Report of Inspector Lane, December 17, 1896, NA PNR RG75, M-1070, Roll 31; Reynolds to Buchanan, July 22, 1904, NA PNR RG75, Tulalip Box 311; St. John, "Present Status," 15; Eugene Hill to Commissioner, November 19, 1920, NA RG75 CCF, Entry 121, Taholah File 86457–1920–150; Mathew Fleming to Commissioner, January 7, 1922, NA PNR RG75, Western Washington Box 259; Quimby, "Indian Education," 80; Eells, "Census of the Clallam and Twana Indians," 36–37; Census Rolls, NA PNR RG75, Tulalip Box 474.

35. Applications for Enrollment and Allotment, Dwamish, NA M-1343, Roll 3; Norton, "Social, Marital, Economic and Political Relationships," 37.

36. Eliot, *Report upon the Conditions,* 17; Annual Reports, Tulalip (1920, 1921, and 1927), NA PNR RG75, M-1011, Roll 154; Roberts, "History of the Swinomish," 238–42; Report of Eugene Hill (1920), NA RG75 CCF, Entry 121, Taholah File 86457–1920–150; Hauke to Buchanan, June 13, 1917, NA RG75 CCF, Entry 121, Tulalip File 59910–1917–920; Report of Flora Warren Seymour, July 11, 1925, NA RG75 CCF, Entry 121, Tulalip File 50598–1925–150; Rygg, "Continuation of ... Attitudes," 18; U.S. Department of Commerce, *State Personal Income: 1929–1982* (Washington, D.C.: Government Printing Office, 1984), 258. No statistics before 1929 permit comparison of Indians' incomes with non-Indians', and even the later statistics are principally for reservation Indians.

37. Meeker Family Papers, Notebook III; Fetzer, "George Swanaset," 9, 11–15, 22; Nugent, *Lummi Elders Speak,* 19–20, 37, 38–40; Suquamish Oral History Interview W.1.04.

38. Agent to Fidalgo Island Cannery Company, July 3, 1897, NA PNR RG75, Tulalip Box 26; Bristow to Buchanan, December 2, 1905, and August 31, 1907, NA PNR RG75, Tulalip Box 105; Boxberger, *To Fish in Common*, 36, 44–45, 56.

39. Report of Buchanan, August 6, 1906, NA PNR RG75, Tulalip Box 311; Annual Report, Tulalip (1914), 73, NA PNR RG75, M-1011; *ARCIA* (1902), 358; Norton, "Social, Marital, Economic and Political Relationships," 37; St. John, "Present Status," 15; Annual Report, Tulalip (1917), NA PNR RG75, M-1011; Eliot, *Report upon the Conditions,* 17; Suquamish Oral History Interviews W.1.04, W.1.20; Johansen and Gates, *Empire of the Columbia,* 527–29. Even for Indians with land and capital, farming was rarely practical in the Puget Sound region. One official remarked that allottees who could earn cash as laborers balked at spending one hundred dollars an acre to prepare poor, stump-studded fields for cultivation. *ARCIA* (1902), 358; Report of Buchanan (1906), NA PNR RG75, Tulalip Box 311; Superintendent to Commissioner, June 10, 1915, NA PNR RG75, Puyallup Box 5; telegram from Hauke to Buchanan and reply, June 13, 1917, NA RG75 CCF, Entry 121, Tulalip File 59910–1917–920; Sells to Mr. Hadley, June 23, 1917, ibid.; Acting Commissioner to Superintendent, Puyallup Indian School, January 12, 1907, NA PNR RG75, Tulalip Agency Decimal Files 053; George Vaux, Jr., *Forty-ninth Annual Report of the Board of Indian Commissioners* (Washington, D.C.: Government Printing Office, 1918), Appendix P, 75.

40. *ARCIA* (1895), 318; testimony of Henry Kwina and Tom Squiqui, *State v. Alexis,* in Boxberger, "Ethnohistory"; *ARCIA* (1896), 315; Charles M. Buchanan, "Rights of the Puget Sound Indians to Game and Fish," *Washington Historical Quarterly* 6 (1915), 110–13; Annual Report, Tulalip (1914), 11–13, and (1915), 2, NA PNR RG75, M-1011; Annual Report, Tulalip (1917), 8, and Port Madison Industries Narrative, ibid.; *Tulalip Bulletin* (September 1916): 2; Eliot, *Report upon the Conditions,* 17; Nugent, *Lummi Elders Speak,* 23, 26–8; Superintendent to Reynolds, November 4, 1919, NA PNR RG75, Puyallup Box 17; Boxberger, *To Fish in Common,* 40, 55; Noel, *Muckleshoot Indian History,* 71–72; Miles and Sperlin, *Building a State,* 91, 94; *ARCIA* (1901), 391; Reynolds to Buchanan, September 26, 1903, NA PNR RG75, Tulalip Box 100; affidavit of Reynolds, February 25, 1905, NA PNR RG75, Tulalip Box 101; Bristow to Buchanan, October 17, 1905, NA PNR RG75, Tulalip Box 105; Andrew Peterson to Johnson, May 18, 1909, NA PNR RG75, Puyallup Box 2, Book 2; Bob James et al. to Honorable Commissioner of Indian Affairs, May 15, 1916, NA PNR RG75, Puyallup Box 15; Fay G. Cohen, *Treaties on Trial: The Continuing Controversy over Northwest Indian Fishing Rights* (Seattle: University of Washington Press, 1986), 42.

41. Annual Report, Tulalip (1914), 52, NA PNR RG75, M-1011; Annual Report (1917), Swinomish Narrative, ibid.; Annual Report, Tulalip (1932), ibid., Roll 155; Superintendent to Commissioner, August 15, 1918, NA PNR RG75, Puyallup Box 5; Acting Commissioner to Superintendent, January 12, 1907, NA PNR RG75, Tulalip Decimal File 053; Suquamish Oral History In-

terviews G.6.01 (Ben George, Jr., March 10, 1982), J.4.06 (Clara Jones, September 23, 1982).

42. Johnson to Commissioner, October 28, 1909, NA PNR RG75, Puyallup Box 2, Book 2; Johnson to Commissioner, September 28, 1910, NA PNR RG75, Puyallup Box 2, Book 3; Annual Report, Puyallup (1913), NA PNR RG75, Puyallup Box 4, Book 8; Annual Report, Tulalip (1916), Lummi Schools and Lummi Industries, NA PNR RG75, M-1011; Suquamish Oral History Interviews W.1.07 (Webster, March 15, 1982) and A.4.03 (Bernard Adams, April 13, 1982); Russel Lawrence Barsh, "Puget Sound Indian Demography, 1900–1920: Migration and Economic Integration," *Ethnohistory* 43 (Winter 1996): 89.

43. Superintendent to Commissioner, May 21, 1918, NA PNR RG75, Puyallup Box 5; Hauke to Buchanan and reply, June 13, 1917, NA RG75 CCF, Tulalip File 59910–1917–920; Sells to Mr. Hadley, June 23, 1917, ibid.; Annual Report, Tulalip (1917 and 1918), Port Madison Industries Narrative, NA PNR RG75, M-1011; Annual Report, Tulalip (1919), Tulalip Industries, Swinomish Narrative, 11, ibid.; Report of E. M. Sweet, Jr., March 26, 1918, NA RG75 CCF, Entry 121, Tulalip File 29966–1918–150; Daniel Howell to E. H. Hammond, March 20, 1918, NA PNR RG75, Puyallup Box 17; Roberts, "Cushman Indian Trades School," 221, 224; Annual Report, Tulalip (1927), NA PNR RG75, M-1011, Roll 154; Johansen and Gates, *Empire of the Columbia,* 543–48; Mapes, "Map Interpretation," 14.

44. Boxberger, *To Fish in Common,* 60; Annual Report, Tulalip (1924), M-1011, Roll 155; W. F. Dickens to Commissioner, February 20, 1923, NA RG75 CCF, Entry 121, Tulalip File 88710–1922–150; Report of Flora Seymour, July 11, 1925, NA RG75 CCF, Entry 121, Tulalip File 50598–1925–150; Annual Report, Tulalip (1924), NA PNR RG75, M-1011, Roll 155.

45. Annual Report, Tulalip (1918), 6, 8; Roberts, "Cushman Indian Trades School," 224; Superintendent to Commissioner, December 28, 1917, NA PNR RG75, Puyallup Box 5; Superintendent to Commissioner, June 28 and August 8, 1918, ibid.

46. Conscription, which required determination of Indians' status, revealed the arbitrary nature of that status. According to Indian Service guidelines for draft boards, wardship did not depend on a man's actual relationship to federal authorities but on accidents of timing. Men who received allotments before the Burke Act were citizens whether or not the government still controlled the disposition of their property. Their sons' status followed theirs unless the sons had received allotments after the Burke Act. Most other Indians were noncitizens. Under this reading of the law, officials approved the conscription of some reservation residents who had never exercised citizenship rights but exempted men who had never been under the government's wing. For instance, a superintendent concluded that one youth on the Puyallup roll was a noncitizen—despite the fact that U.S. guardianship of tribe members had ceased in 1903—because neither the youth nor his father had taken an allotment. Circular to all Indians from Cushman School, December 19, 1917, NA PNR RG 75, Puyallup Box 17; Superintendent to Commissioner, No-

vember 28, 1917, NA PNR RG75, Puyallup Box 5; letters of November 26 and December 28, 1917, ibid.; Correspondence Regarding Indians in Military Service, NA PNR RG75, Puyallup Box 17; Lummi Annual Report, Law and Order Narrative (1918), NA PNR RG75, M-1011, Roll 153. See also Russel L. Barsh, "American Indians in the Great War," *Ethnohistory* 38 (1991): 280–81, 277.

47. Vaux, *Forty-ninth Annual Report*, 80; Nugent, "Regulation of the Lummi," 17–18; Annual Report, Tulalip (1918), Lummi Law and Order Narrative, NA PNR RG75, M-1011, Roll 153.

48. *Tulalip Bulletin* (September 1917): 2. See samples of similar Indian reasoning in Barsh, "American Indians in the Great War," 288–89.

49. *Tulalip Bulletin* (September, 1918); Charles M. Buchanan, "The Evolution of an Indian Hero in France," *Washington Historical Quarterly* 9 (July 1918): 163–68; Superintendent to Local Board, October 6, 1917, NA PNR RG75, Puyallup Box 17; Barsh, "American Indians in the Great War," 286–88. Agents also pressured Indians to buy war bonds. Superintendent to Commissioner, October 9, 1917, NA PNR RG75, Puyallup Box 5.

50. Vaux, *Forty-ninth Annual Report*, 73; Roberts, "Cushman Indian Trades School," 221, 225–26, 229–30.

51. 43 *United States Statutes* 253; Prucha, *Great Father*, 793; Dippie, *Vanishing American*, 194–96; Barsh, "American Indians in the Great War," 295.

52. F. S. Hall, "The Vanishing Race," *Seattle Woman* 2, no. 1 (1924): 12.

53. Annual Report, Tulalip (1922), NA PNR RG75, M-1011, Roll 154; Annual Report, Tulalip (1924), Roll 155; Dickens to Commissioner, February 20, 1923, NA RG75 CCF, Entry 121, Tulalip File 88710–1922–150; Vaux, *Forty-ninth Annual Report*, 74–79. Dickens disposed of lands he deemed useless to Indian owners. At the same time he strengthened reservation institutions such as the courts. The principal policy change of the 1920s was letting the state educate all Indian children except those living far from public schools or in need of firm discipline. Yet even in public schools, Dickens said, Indians needed federal protection. Annual Reports, Tulalip (1924, 1927, 1928); Dickens to Loomis W. Baldrey, May 5, 1922, NA PNR RG75, Tulalip Box 503; Report of Inspector Hill, November 19, 1920, NA RG75 CCF, Entry 121, Taholah File 86457–1920–150; Report of Earl Y. Henderson, January 25, 1929, ibid., File 7962–1929–150.

54. Buchanan, "Rights of the Puget Sound Indians"; Annual Reports, Tulalip (1915 and 1917), NA PNR RG75, M-1011; Jerry Kanim to F. A. Gross, April 21, 1927, NA PNR RG75, Tulalip Decimal File 920; Merritt to Dickens, May 26, 1926, ibid.; Superintendent to Kanim, April 26, 1927, ibid.; Superintendent to Reynolds, October 5, 1926, ibid.; *Tulalip Bulletin* (September 1916): 2.

55. Report of Flora Seymour, July 11, 1925, NA RG75 CCF, Entry 121, Tulalip File 50598–1925–150; Superintendent to Commissioner, May 4, 1926, NA PNR RG75, Tulalip Decimal File 173.1; Henry Sicade to Charles Burke, February 18, 1928, NA PNR RG75, Puyallup Box 276.

56. Annual Report, Tulalip (1922), NA PNR RG75 M-1011, Roll 154; Annual Reports, Tulalip (1924 and 1926), Roll 155; Report of Seymour, July 11, 1925.

57. Report of Earl Y. Henderson, March 7, 1929, NA RG75 CCF, Entry 121, Tulalip File 13931–1929–150; Report of Henderson, January 25, 1929, NA RG75 CCF, Entry 121, Taholah File 7962–1929–150; Annual Report, Tulalip (1926), 13, NA PNR RG75, M-1011, Roll 155; Annual Report, Tulalip (1928), Census, ibid.; Report of Seymour, July 11, 1925.

58. Chief George Swamaset [*sic*], Louis George, William Hunt to Charley H. Burk [*sic*], n.d., NA PNR RG75, Tulalip Decimal File 060.

59. Superintendent to Commissioner, March 9, 1928, NA PNR RG75, Tulalip Decimal File 072–3.

60. Joyce Annabel Wike, "Modern Spirit Dancing of Northern Puget Sound" (M.A. thesis, University of Washington, 1941), 58, 69, 37; Collins, *Valley of the Spirits,* 118; Fetzer, "George Swanaset"; Superintendent to Commissioner, June 27, 1925, NA PNR RG75, Western Washington Box 259; McCluskey to Gross, December 21, 1926, NA PNR RG75, Tulalip Decimal File 045.

61. Minutes of meeting on the Swinomish Reservation, February 21, 1928, NA PNR RG75, Tulalip Decimal File 072–73.

62. Report of Seymour, July 11, 1925; Annual Report, Tulalip (1926), Narrative, 10.

63. Superintendent to Secretary, Spokane Betterment Organization, April 6, 1926, NA PNR RG75, Tulalip Decimal File 047; District Superintendent, Lapwai, to Dickens, June 4, 1926, ibid.; Superintendent to V. H. Johnson, June 23, 1926, ibid.

64. "Scenes at Potlatch at Tulalip," *P-I*, January 23, 1913, 1; *Everett Herald*, February 11, 1938, Petition for Acknowledgement of Snohomish Tribe, Reply Appendix G-13; Hertzberg, *Search for an American Indian Identity*, 31.

65. Bishop and others founded the NFAI shortly after the question of allotments at Quinault arose. Fetzer, "George Swanaset," 17; Suquamish Oral History Interview W.1.07; Roblin to Commissioner, January 31, 1919, Schedule of Unenrolled Indians; Sells to Roblin, November 27, 1916, NA PNR RG75, Western Washington Box 259, file labeled "Indian Claims Commissioners Suiattle & Other Tribes 1922–23"; Eliot, *Report upon the Conditions,* 21. Ages of early NFAI representatives inferred from census of 1900 and Fetzer, "George Swanaset."

66. Hertzberg, *Search for an American Indian Identity,* 19, 26–27, 59, 65, 67, 103; Charles A. Eastman, *The Soul of the Indian* (Boston: Houghton Mifflin, 1911); Charles A. Eastman, *The Indian To-day* (Garden City, N.Y.: Doubleday Page, 1915).

67. *P-I*, November 20, 1911, Sec. 2, p. 2; *P-I*, January 12, 1912, 2; Hertzberg, *Search for an American Indian Identity,* 190, 193.

68. Constitution of NFAI, NA PNR RG75, Western Washington Box 259; Hertzberg, *Search for an American Indian Identity,* 72, 80–81.

69. Hertzberg, *Search for an American Indian Identity,* 96; Annual Report, Tulalip (1918), Swinomish Narrative, NA PNR RG75, M-1011, Roll 154; Annual Report, Tulalip (1924), NA M1011, Roll 155; Superintendent to Commissioner, June 27, 1925, NA PNR RG75, Western Washington Box 259; Su-

perintendent to Commissioner, January 29, 1923, ibid.; Superintendent to Commissioner, February 15, 1922, ibid.; Questionnaire regarding tribal organization, Indian Reorganization Act Records, NA RG75, Entry 1012, Taholah 068, File 9748-A; Thomas Bishop to Dear Friend, February 26, 1916, DeShaw Papers, Box 1A, File 3, Miscellany.

70. Superintendent to Commissioner, February 15, 1922, NA PNR RG75, Western Washington Box 259; Constitution, NFAI, ibid.; Minutes of meeting at Tulalip, December 10, 1921, ibid.; Testimony of Wilfred Steve and Peter James, *Indian Tribes of Washington,* House Committee on Indian Affairs, 68th Cong., 1st sess., 1924, H.342–4, pp. 19, 21, 28; Suquamish Oral History Interviews W.1.11 (Webster, March 25, 1982) and G.1.05 (Martha George, November 4, 1982); Fetzer, "George Swanaset," 17, 27; DeShaw Papers. In 1914 Buchanan claimed there were no governing councils on reservations under his supervision, but the Lummi farmer reported that business councils met there several times in 1916. Annual Report, Tulalip (1914), 127, and (1916), NA PNR RG75, M-1011. Later BIA records date the organization of tribal councils to the 1920s. Questionnaires regarding tribal organization, Indian Reorganization Act Records, NA RG75. However, it is clear from Dickens's letter to the Commissioner of June 27, 1925, that many groups were already well organized when he met with them in the 1920s. NA PNR RG75, Western Washington Box 259.

71. "The Meeting of the Snoqualmie Indians held at Tolt, on the 2d. of June 1916," NA PNR RG75, Tulalip Box 474; Memorandum, December 22, 1915, in Indian Census Rolls, NA PNR M-595, Roll 584.

72. Applications for Enrollment and Allotment, NA M-1343, Roll 4; Webster to Dickens, July 18, 1922, NA PNR RG75, Tulalip Box 473; Ve Van Houten to Mr. Duclos, April 29, 1930, NA PNR RG75, Tulalip Decimal File 054. Numerous people who applied for enrollment with the Puyallups in 1929 had applied for enrollment with other tribes when Roblin conducted his survey. Virtually all produced evidence of connections to tribal communities besides Puyallup. NA RG75, Entry 615, Puyallup Boxes 1–5.

73. Probably Roblin, rather than the applicants, decided to list most people with their fathers' tribes, thus applying federal law as he understood it. However, he apparently allowed people to take exception to this rule. Letter to son of Kate Stevens Grady Johnson, May 29, 1918, Clallam Roll, NA M-1343.

74. Bishop to Dear Friend, February 26, 1916, DeShaw Papers; correspondence from applicants for a share of tribal entitlements in NA PNR RG75, Tulalip Decimal File 060, and NA RG75 CCF, Entry 121, Tulalip Files 62204–1923–053, 53155–1927–053, 52780–1927–053. An act of June 30, 1919, 41 *United States Statutes* 3, 9, authorized a final roll of any tribe's members for purposes of segregating tribal funds. Officials invoked this act in the 1920s to assemble a list of Indians entitled to share in assets remaining from the Puyallup Reservation. Records and Evidence concerning Puyallup Enrollment, NA RG75, Entry 615, Puyallup Boxes 1–5; Files of Tribal Operations Branch, NA PNR RG75, Western Washington Box 276.

75. Suquamish Oral History Interview W.1.18.

76. Testimony of John Sam and William Bagley, *Duwamish v. United States*, 203, 197; Nugent, *Lummi Elders Speak*, 83, 116; Rygg, "Continuation of ... Attitudes," 85; Suquamish Oral History Interview W.1.11; Testimony, *United States v. Alaska Packers' Association;* Testimony of Henry Kwina and Tom Squiqui, *State v. Alexis,* in Boxberger, "Ethnohistory"; *United States v. Romaine,* 255 Federal Reporter 256 (Ninth Circuit Court of Appeals, 1919). Eliot said the Indians' complaints were misunderstandings or "old grievances which have really been adjusted but which are handed down in families as counts against the government." *Report upon the Conditions,* 19.

77. Thomas G. Bishop, "An Appeal to the Government to Fulfill Sacred Promises Made 61 Years Ago," 1915, UW Special Collections.

78. Bishop, "Appeal to the Government"; Superintendent to Commissioner, February 15, 1922, and Memorandum, n.d., and resolution appended to Minutes of meeting at Tulalip Reservation, December 10, 1921, NA PNR RG75, Western Washington Box 259; Minutes of same meeting, NA PNR RG75, Tulalip Box 96, File 60.

79. McDowell, *Fifty-second Annual Report,* Appendix K, 78; 43 *United States Statutes* 886.

80. Buchanan to Sells, February 10, 1916, NA PNR RG75, Tulalip Box 71; Buchanan to Bishop, February 1916, ibid.; Minutes of meeting, December 10, 1921, NA PNR RG75, Tulalip Box 96, File 60; Dickens to Commissioner, July 30, 1921, NA RG75 CCF, Entry 121, Tulalip File 62672–1921–054; Superintendent to Commissioner, February 15, 1922, NA PNR RG75, Western Washington Box 259; Minutes, executive committee meeting of December 12, 1921, ibid.; Superintendent to Commissioner, January 29, 1923, ibid.

81. Telegram, Dickens to Commissioner, July 29, 1921, and Dickens to Commissioner, July 30, 1921, NA RG75 CCF, Tulalip File 62672–1921–054; Superintendent to Commissioner, June 27, 1925, NA PNR RG75, Western Washington Box 259; Proceedings of NFAI Advisory Board, October 3, 1925, ibid.; Rygg, "Continuation of ... Attitudes," 90.

82. Fetzer, "George Swanaset," 18. Swanaset told Congress that Nooksacks sent a chief named Humclalim to the treaty, but the chief took a Frenchman's advice not to sign. *Indian Tribes of Washington,* H.342–4, p. 54. At trial three years later, a Nooksack witness testified that no Nooksacks went down to the treaty. Transcript of Testimony, *Duwamish et al. v. U.S.,* 504.

83. 43 *United States Statutes* 886 and 1102. A fourth nontreaty group named in these statutes—the Suattle [*sic*]—did not file suit with the others. Instead they "submitted a written statement in which they said that they did not want money but they wanted their land back." Superintendent to Commissioner, June 27, 1925, NA PNR RG75, Western Washington Box 259.

84. Hearing transcript, NA PNR RG75, Tulalip Box 96, Folder 60; *Duwamish v. U.S.,* testimony of Johnnie Scalopine, 218, Lucy Gurand, 646, and Tom Milroy, 674.

85. Transcript, *Duwamish v. United States,* 252–57, 627, 244, 402, 407–8.

86. Ibid., 189.

87. Ibid., 291–92, 431, 500.

88. *The Duwamish, Lummi, Whidby Island Skagit, Upper Skagit, Swinomish, Kikiallus, Snohomish, Snoqualmie, Stillaguamish, Suquamish, Samish, Puyallup, Squaxin, Skokomish, Upper Chehalis, Muckelshoot, Nooksack, Chinook, and San Juan Islands Tribes of Indians v. the United States,* 79 Court of Claims 530–613 (1934).

89. Myerhoff, "'Life Not Death in Venice,'" 261–68; Rygg, "Continuation of ... Attitudes," 89–90. Indians had other occasions during the 1920s to display a past that a variety of people could admire. Boasian ethnographers were recording Indians' language and memories of their ancestors' culture. Elaine Mills, ed. *A Guide to the Field Notes of John Peabody Harrington* (Washington, D.C.: Smithsonian Institution, 1981), xxv, in Harrington Papers; Fetzer, "George Swanaset," 22; Thelma Adamson, *Folk-Tales of the Coast Salish* (New York: American Folk-Lore Society, 1934); Ballard, "Some Tales of the Southern Puget Sound Salish," 57–81; Arthur C. Ballard, "Mythology of Southern Puget Sound," *University of Washington Publications in Anthropology* 3 (1929) 31–150; Gunther, "Klallam Ethnography"; Gunther, "Klallam Folk Tales," 113–70; Hermann Haeberlin, "Mythology of Puget Sound," *Journal of American Folklore* 37 (1924): 371–438; Haeberlin and Gunther, "Indians of Puget Sound"; Waterman, "Notes on the Ethnology." Although local press interest in Indians apparently waned after World War I, a market for Indian crafts and literature remained. Annual Report, Tulalip (1926), NA PNR RG75, M-1011; H. W. Shipe to Dickens, July 12, 1926, NA PNR RG75, Tulalip Decimal File 045; W. J. Henry to Dickens, March 27, 1925; ibid., Rygg, "Continuation of ... Attitudes," 110, 59, 81; Chief William Shelton, *The Story of the Totem Pole: Early Indian Legends Handed Down from Generation to Generation* (Everett, Wash.: Kane and Harcus, 1935), 6.

90. Transcript, *Duwamish v. United States,* 345, 183, 229, 266, 327, 351, 377, 472.

91. Deposition of Skookum George, NA PNR RG75, Tulalip Box 96, Folder 60; Transcript, *Duwamish v. United States,* 320, 493, 620.

92. Suquamish Oral History Interview W.1.07.

93. Testimony of Snoqualmie Jim and Skookum George, In the Matter of the Claims of Indian Tribes, NA PNR RG75, Tulalip Box 96, Folder 60; *Indian Tribes of Washington,* H.320–7, 24; *Indian Tribes of Washington,* H.342–4, 43; Petition, *Duwamish v. United States,* 6; Transcript, *Duwamish v. United States.,* 670, 348, 356, 391, 620, 641.

94. Transcript, *Duwamish v. United States,* 354, 342.

7. TRIBES

1. Histories focused on policy in this period include Larry Burt, *Tribalism in Crisis: Federal Indian Policy, 1953–1961* (Albuquerque: University of New Mexico Press, 1982); Donald Fixico, *Termination and Relocation: Federal In-*

dian Policy, 1945–1966 (Albuquerque: University of New Mexico Press, 1986); Alvin M. Josephy, Jr., "Modern America and the Indian," in *Indians in American History,* ed. Frederick E. Hoxie (Arlington Heights, Ill.: Harlan Davidson, 1988), 251–72; Kenneth R. Philp, *John Collier's Crusade for Indian Reform, 1920–1934* (Tucson: University of Arizona Press, 1977); Graham D. Taylor, *The New Deal and American Indian Tribalism* (Lincoln: University of Nebraska Press, 1980).

2. U.S. Senate, *Survey of Conditions of the Indians in the United States,* 71st Cong., 3d sess., 1931, S.545–8-A, 11759–874.

3. R. Douglas Hurt, *Indian Agriculture in America* (Lawrence: University Press of Kansas, 1987), 159, 164, 172; Richard Lowitt, *The New Deal and the West* (Bloomington: Indiana University Press, 1984), 123; Taylor, *New Deal,* 7; Johansen and Gates, *Empire of the Columbia,* 555.

4. Senate, *Survey of Conditions,* S.545–8-A, 11779–783; Narrative, Annual Report, Tulalip (1931), NA PNR RG75, M-1011, Roll 155; Narrative, Annual Report, Tulalip (1934), NA PNR RG75, M-1011, Roll 156.

5. Suquamish Oral History Interviews W.1.04 (Webster, September 30, 1981); W.1.20 (Webster, July 29, 1982); A.4.02, A.4.03 (Bernard Adams, March 24, 1982); A.1.01 (Margaret Adams, April 4, 1982); G.6.01 (Ben George, Jr., March 10, 1982); Rygg, "Continuation of . . . Attitudes," 218–22, 256; O. C. Upchurch to Commissioner, December 16, 1936, NA PNR RG75, Tulalip Box 509.

6. Statistics (1929 and 1930), Tulalip Agency, NA PNR RG75, M-1011, Roll 155; Department of Commerce, *State Personal Income,* 258; Economic Land Surveys (1934–35), Tulalip and Taholah Agencies, NA RG75, Entry 793; Annual Reports of Extension Workers, NA PNR RG75, Taholah Decimal File 052.2, Box 75; Suquamish Oral History Interview J.04.09 (Clara Jones, March 30, 1985).

7. Economic and Social Surveys (1933–34), NA PNR RG75, Tulalip Boxes 498–499; Narrative and Statistics, Annual Reports (1934 and 1935), NA PNR RG75, M-1011, Roll 156; Annual Report of Gladys McIlveen for December 1, 1933, to December 31, 1934, NA PNR RG75, Tulalip Decimal File 904; Reports of Extension Workers (1934); George P. LaVatta to Commissioner, March 16, 1937, NA PNR RG75, Tulalip Box 486; Narrative, Annual Report, Tulalip (1931), NA PNR RG75, M-1011, Roll 155; McCormick Lumber Company Papers, UW Manuscripts Accession No. 4286; Pope and Talbot Payroll Records, UW Manuscripts Accession No. 1130; Indian Census Rolls (1930), NA PNR M-595, Roll 589; LaVatta to Commissioner, March 19, 1938, Petition for Acknowledgement of Snohomish Tribe, Reply Appendix J-3. By 1938 the McCormick mill was operating only two days a week. Walter J. Rue to Homer T. Bone, April 13, 1938, NA PNR RG75, Tulalip Box 486.

8. John Collier, *From Every Zenith* (Denver: Sage Books, 1963), 187; DIAR (1933), 69–70; Donald H. Parman, "The Indian and the Civilian Conservation Corps," *Pacific Historical Review* 40 (February 1971): 41, 45–46; Emergency Conservation Work Authorizations (1933), NA PNR RG75, Taholah Decimal File 980, Box 173; ECW and CCC Employee Cards (1937–43), NA PNR RG75,

Taholah Box 339; Testimony of Sam George and O. C. Upchurch, U.S. Senate, Committee on Indian Affairs, *Survey of Conditions of Indians in the United States* (Washington, D.C.: Government Printing Office, 1934), 17179–80; N. O. Nicholson to Mr. Daiker, January 14, 1935, NA RG75 CCF, Entry 121, Taholah File 9283–1935–150; Works Progress Administration Project Files (1935–40), NA PNR RG75, Taholah Box 342; Upchurch to Commissioner, May 4, 1934, Economic and Social Surveys (1933–34), NA PNR RG75, Tulalip Box 498; Records of CCC (1934–41), NA PNR RG75, Tulalip Boxes 467, 468; Social and Economic Survey (1934), NA RG75, Entry 792, Taholah Agency; Annual Reports, Tulalip (1933–1935), NA PNR RG75, M-1011, Rolls 155–156; Nicholson to Upchurch, November 17, 1936, NA PNR RG75, Western Washington Box 257; Resolution of Tulalip Indian Protective Association, June 12, 1935, NA PNR RG75, Tulalip Decimal File 052.1; Upchurch to Commissioner, May 9, 1934, NA PNR RG75, Tulalip Decimal File 921; Robert Lane Sicade to Taholah Agency, January 23, 1940, NA PNR RG75, Taholah Decimal File 980, Box 174; Noel, *Muckleshoot Indian History,* 133; Suquamish Oral History Interviews W.1.06, A.4.03, and B.4.01 (Floyd Buber, August 4, 1982). The Indian Emergency Conservation Work program was renamed the Civilian Conservation Corps–Indian Division in 1937. Parman, "The Indian and the Civilian Conservation Corps," 41, 45–46; Taylor, *New Deal,* 132.

9. Collier, *From Every Zenith,* 187; DIAR (1933), 69–70; *Indians at Work* 2 (December 1, 1934): 34; Parman, "The Indian and the Civilian Conservation Corps," 41, 44, 47–49; U.S. Senate, *Survey of Conditions* (1934), 17182; William H. Zeh, *Indians at Work* (July 1, 1936): 39; Lowitt, *New Deal and the West,* 124–25, 130, 132–34; Taylor, *New Deal,* 131, 150; Richard White, *The Roots of Dependency: Subsistence, Environment, and Social Change among the Choctaws, Pawnees, and Navajos* (Lincoln: University of Nebraska Press, 1983), 256.

10. Civil Works Administration Project Files (1933–34), NA PNR RG75, Taholah Box 341; WPA Files (1935–40), NA PNR RG75, Taholah Box 342; Resolution of Lummi Tribal Council, Records Relating to Tribal Reorganization, February 18, 1938, NA PNR RG75, Tulalip Box 478–79; Sam Ulmer to John Collier, March 1938, NA RG75 CCF, Entry 121, Tulalip File 18916–1938–931. Natalie Roberts argues that WPA projects strengthened ties among Indians on the Swinomish Reservation. "History of the Swinomish," 309–11. When residents of Swinomish and a few other reservations undertook collective protection or exploitation of their resources later in the 1930s, their inspiration was the Indian Reorganization Act and non-Indian encroachment on subsistence resources more than federal work programs. Upchurch to Commissioner, July 18, 1936, NA PNR RG75, Tulalip Box 509; Upchurch to Commissioner, May 9, 1934, NA PNR RG75, Tulalip Decimal File 921; Upchurch to Commissioner, July 21, 1937 ibid.; Martin J. Sampson to Lewis B. Schwellenbach, August 2, 1937, ibid.

11. Annual Reports, Tulalip (1933, 1934, 1935, 1936), NA PNR RG75, M-1011; Economic and Social Surveys (1933–34), NA PNR RG75, Tulalip

Box 498; Annual Statistical Report (1939), NA PNR RG75, Tulalip Decimal File 052.1; Suquamish Oral History Interview W.1.20; Rygg, "Continuation of . . . Attitudes," 159.

12. U.S. Senate, *Survey of Conditions* (1934), 17158–86, 17150, 17171, 17175, 17185, 17188–89, 17183; Resolutions of June 14, 1933, NA RG75 CCF, Entry 121, Tulalip File 34035–1934–059.

13. 48 *United States Statutes* 984; Prucha, *Great Father*, 957–963; Lawrence C. Kelly, "John Collier and the Indian New Deal: An Assessment," in *Indian-White Relations: A Persistent Paradox*, ed. Jane F. Smith and Robert M. Kvasnicka (Washington, D.C.: Howard University Press, 1981), 233–38; Dippie, *Vanishing American*, 315, 319. Movement toward the changes enacted in 1934 was evident in the 1920s. Institute for Government Research, *The Problem of Indian Administration* (Washington, D.C.: Institute for Government Research, 1928); Dippie, *Vanishing American*, 299–302. Whether the IRA fundamentally departed from the assimilationist tradition is an issue scholars still debate. Cf. Kelly, "John Collier and the Indian New Deal," 240; Prucha, *Great Father*, 917; D'Arcy McNickle, *Native American Tribalism: Indian Survivals and Renewals* (New York: Oxford University Press, 1973), 93.

14. Prucha, *Great Father*, 954–55; Kenneth R. Philp, "John Collier and the Controversy over the Wheeler-Howard Bill," in Smith and Kvasnicka, *Indian-White Relations*, 171, 173, 179, 192–94; Dippie, *Vanishing American*, 307–8, 312–13; Taylor, *New Deal*, 7, 22–23.

15. Taylor, *New Deal*, 13, 23, 30, 40; Philp, "John Collier and the Controversy," 172–73; Philp, *John Collier's Crusade*, 97, 161; Kelly, "John Collier and the Indian New Deal," 228; DIAR (1941), 408; DIAR (1938), 210; Collier, *From Every Zenith*, 114, 119, 123, 126.

16. Philp, "John Collier and the Controversy," 174; Prucha, *Great Father*, 955.

17. Minutes of the Northwest Indian Congress, March 8, 1934, NA PNR RG75, Western Washington Box 257. All quotations in the succeeding discussion of the Chemawa conference are from this source.

18. Tulalip Agency delegates at Chemawa wrote down questions that do not appear in the minutes. They included: How will the bill affect landless, nonreservation Indians and Indians living on public domain lands? How will the bill affect pending treaty rights? Does the department intend to do anything for Indians forced from reservations for economic reasons and now dependent on local charity? How will the bill affect Indian suffrage? Reactions to the Indian Reorganization Act, NA RG75, 066–4894–1934, Box 3.

19. N. O. Nicholson to Commissioner, March 6, 1934, NA PNR RG75, Western Washington Box 257a.

20. Memorandum of Muckleshoot Business Council, received at Tulalip May 18, 1934, NA PNR RG75, Western Washington Box 257a; Tulalip Chair and Tribal Committee to Commissioner, February 1, 1934, ibid.; Minutes of Meeting at Nisqually March 1, enclosed with Nicholson to Commissioner, March 6, 1934, ibid.; Memorandum of "Suquamish Tribe of Indians in council assembled," NA RG75, Reactions to the IRA, Box 4.

21. Dippie, *Vanishing American,* 317; Upchurch to Nicholson, April 19, 1935, NA PNR RG75, Western Washington Box 277; Final Results of IRA Referenda, NA PNR RG75, Western Washington Box 258. Voters at Lummi rejected the IRA even though their tribal council endorsed the bill. Resolution of Lummi Tribal Council, May 13, 1934, NA PNR RG75, Western Washington, Box 257a.

22. Taylor, *New Deal,* 52, 60; Philp, "John Collier and the Controversy," 175, 177, 185 and ff.; Dan McDowell to Collier, March 27, 1934, NA RG75, Reactions to the IRA, Box 5; J. R. Hillaire to Collier, March 15, 1934, ibid.; Collier to Peter James, n.d., ibid., Box 2; Chester M. Williams to Collier, received April 20, 1934, and Jerry Kenum to Collier, n.d., and Record of Tribal Council of Duwamish Tribe of Indians, ibid., Box 4; Rygg, "Continuation of . . . Attitudes," 232; Memo of Muckleshoot Business Council.

23. George LaVatta to Commissioner, November 8, 1938, NA PNR RG75, Western Washington Box 277; Meeker and Cross to Collier, April 16, 1934, NA RG75, Reactions to the IRA, Box 4; Kenum to Collier, May 4, 1934, and Collier to Kenum, May 31, 1934, NA RG75, Reactions to the IRA, Box 7; Upchurch to Collier, April 9, 1934, NA RG75, Reactions to the IRA, Box 3.

24. Roberts, "History of the Swinomish," 307; Indian Reorganization Act General Records, NA RG75, Entry 1012, Tulalip and Taholah. Information on councils formed during the NFAI's early years appears in chapter 6 and in Questionnaires on Tribal Organization, NA PNR RG75, Western Washington Box 257a; Andrew Joe to Duclos, April 5, 1929, NA PNR RG75, Tulalip Decimal File 064–69; Duclos to Commissioner, March 26, 1930, ibid.; Farmer to Duclos, April 6, 1929, ibid.; Minutes of meeting at Suquamish, February 12, 1916, DeShaw Papers; Minutes, Committee of Five, Puyallup Tribe, February 12, 1929, NA PNR RG75, Western Washington Box 276; Henry C. Sicade to F. A. Gross, May 2, 1927, ibid.; correspondence between Skokomish Reservation policemen and superintendent of Taholah Agency, 1922–24, NA PNR RG75, Taholah Decimal File 173.04; Narrative, Annual Report, Tulalip (1928), NA PNR RG75, M-1011; Gross to Commissioner, February 28, 1928, NA RG75 CCF, Tulalip File 52780–1927–053; Dickens to Commissioner, July 30, 1921, NA RG75 CCF, Tulalip File 62672–1921–054; Eugene Hill to Commissioner, November 19, 1920, NA RG75 CCF, Entry 121, Taholah File 86457–1920–150; Fetzer, "George Swanaset," 16–17; Nugent, *Lummi Elders Speak,* 111. Indian workers had even organized strikes. Suquamish Oral History Interview J.4.04 (Clara Jones, July 27, 1982) and W.1.04 (Lawrence Webster, September 30, 1981); *The Real American,* April 27, 1922, in Meany Papers.

25. Hillaire to Collier, March 15, 1934. NFAI activists' desire for government recognition complemented the government's desire to deal with individuals who could influence and relay Indians' opinions. The BIA as well as federation officers therefore expected the NFAI to lead the response to the IRA. But the NFAI did not have a strong presence in every Indian community and did not monopolize discussions about self-government. Resolutions of June 14, 1933, NA RG75 CCF, Tulalip File 34035–1934–059; Memorandum of O. C.

Upchurch, July 14, 1934, NA PNR RG75, Tulalip Decimal File 072–3; Martin Sampson to members of NFAI, April 28, 1933, ibid.; Don McDowell to J. C. Cavill, November 13, 1933, ibid.; Resolution endorsing Wheeler-Howard Act, May 8, 1934, ibid.

26. 48 *United States Statutes* 984.

27. Memorandum, n.d., enclosed with letter from Collier to Nicholson, September 29, 1934, NA PNR RG75, Western Washington Box 257. "Final rolls" listed people entitled to share in the distribution of a disbanding tribe's assets. 41 *United States Statutes* 3, 9. In 1934 two Puget Sound tribes had such rolls—Puyallup and Klallam. Records in NA PNR RG75, Western Washington Box 276, and Records and Evidence Concerning Puyallup Enrollment, NA RG75, Entry 615, Boxes 1–5; correspondence between O. C. Upchurch and Mrs. Arthur Newman, May and June, 1934, NA RG75 CCF, Entry 121, Tulalip File 23543–1934–053.

28. U.S. Senate, *Survey of Conditions* (1934), 17216–18; Duclos to William Dunstan, January 29, 1929, NA PNR RG75, Tulalip Decimal File 921; Petition, August 12, 1929, NA RG75 CCF, Entry 121, Tulalip File 41499–1929–059; Duclos to Commissioner, August 15, 1929, ibid.; Scattergood to Duclos, September 10, 1929, ibid.

29. William Zimmerman to Silas Meeker, December 14, 1934, NA PNR RG75, Western Washington Box 257a; "Land Acquisition Program for the Tulalip Jurisdiction," September 5, 1934, Tulalip Reorganization Files, 1934–40, NA PNR RG75, Tulalip Box 293; Narrative, Annual Report, Tulalip (1934), NA PNR RG75, M-1011, Roll 156; Memorandum attached to letter of Joe Jennings to O. C. Upchurch, December 9, 1937, ibid.; Upchurch to Foster Jones, Sr., October 9, 1935, NA PNR RG75, Western Washington Decimal File 103.3, Box 15.

30. Zimmerman to Nicholson, October 26, 1934, NA PNR RG75, Western Washington Box 257, File 105.1; Frank D. Beaulieu to Nicholson, October 29, 1934, NA PNR RG75, Western Washington Box 286; Collier to Edward Percival, March 27, 1935, Petition for Acknowledgement of Snohomish Tribe, Reply Appendix H-8; Upchurch to Commissioner, January 29, 1937, Indian Reorganization Act General Records, NA RG75, Entry 1012, Tulalip 066, File 9691; Daiker to LaVatta, August 6, 1940, ibid. CWA surveys of 1933–34 permit an estimate of the number of adults on each reservation and show individuals' tribal affiliations. Tabulations of Surveys, NA PNR RG75, Tulalip Box 498.

31. Questionnaire on Tribal Organization, Tulalip (1934), NA PNR RG75, Western Washington Box 257a; Upchurch to Commissioner of Internal Revenue, December 2, 1937, NA PNR RG75, Tulalip Box 293; Frank W. Porter III, "Without Reservation: Federal Indian Policy and the Landless Tribes of Washington," in *State and Reservation*, ed. George P. Castile and Robert L. Bee (Tucson: University of Arizona Press, 1992), 121–22. In 1938 Upchurch told the commissioner of internal revenue that the pre-IRA Snohomish Tribe "was largely a social organization" and had not been active for two or three years.

Upchurch to Commissioner, October 6, 1938, NA PNR RG75, Tulalip Box 293. At Swinomish, where organizing under the IRA also meant confederating prereservation bands, BIA advisors knew that the IRA government was not the same as the "aboriginal" Swinomish Tribe. Charlot Westwood to Mr. Heacock, September 9, 1935, Indian Reorganization Act General Records, NA RG75, Tulalip 068, File 9764-A; Questionnaire on Tribal Organization; Roberts, "History of the Swinomish," 333–35.

32. Upchurch to Sacramento Land Field Agent, March 31, 1936, NA PNR RG75, Tulalip Box 486; LaVatta to E. M. Johnston, March 16, 1937, in Questionnaires on Tribal Organization (1953), NA PNR RG75, Western Washington Box 16; Porter, "Without Reservation," 121–22. Upchurch, concerned about the applicability of the liquor act of 1897 (29 *U.S. Statutes* 506), told the commissioner's office about two to three hundred persons "of less than one-half Indian blood" living in the San Juan Islands. "It seems that I should either take steps to enroll and organize these Indians of the San Juan tribe, or that they should be dismissed as white citizens. I would favor the latter procedure." Upchurch to Daiker, April 30, 1938, replying to an inquiry of April 25, 1938, NA PNR RG75, Western Washington Box 257.

33. Narrative, Annual Reports, Tulalip (1934 and 1936), NA PNR RG75, M-1011; "Land Acquisition Program for the Tulalip Jurisdiction"; LaVatta to Upchurch, August 29, 1935, ibid.; Upchurch to Commissioner, December 3, 1934, NA PNR RG75, Tulalip Box 486; Collier to Upchurch, August 3, 1935, ibid.; Walter J. Rue to Homer T. Bone, April 13, 1938, ibid.; Data on "Clallam Free State," March 26, 1934, Indian Reorganization Act General Records, NA RG75, Entry 1012, Tulalip 068, File 9548-A.

34. La Vatta to Commissioner, March 17, 1937, Indian Reorganization Act General Records, NA RG75, Entry 1012, Tulalip 068, File 9548-A; LaVatta to Commissioner, March 21 and September 9, 1938, NA PNR RG75, Tulalip Box 486; Memorandum of Kenneth Meiklejohn, n.d., Indian Reorganization Act Records, NA RG75, Tulalip 068, File 9568-A; LaVatta to Commissioner, March 19, 1938, Petition for Acknowledgement of Snohomish Tribe, Reply Appendix J-3; Daiker to LaVatta, September 28, 1940, ibid., Appendix J-4. Since many Klallams on the 1928 roll had less than half Indian blood, one officer argued in 1953 that they were not Indians as defined in the IRA and the government's acquisition of their lands was invalid. Recommendations of Program Office, June 24, 1953, "Government Withdrawal Program 1953," Lower Elwha report, NA PNR RG75, Western Washington Decimal File 103.3, Box 15.

35. Following letters in NA PNR RG75, Taholah Decimal File 064, Box 85: Ray Gruhlke to Nicholson, July 26, 1936; LaVatta to Gruhlke, October 13, 1936; Gruhlke to Nicholson, September 28, 1936; Daiker to LaVatta, April 23, 1937; Nicholson to Commissioner, June 10, 1937. Also, Frank D. Beaulieu to Nicholson, October 13, 1936, NA PNR RG75, Taholah Box 277; Porter, "Without Reservation," 122–23.

36. Minutes of Nisqually Tribal Meeting, July 20, 1940, NA PNR RG75, Taholah Decimal File 064, Box 85; Floyd H. Phillips to Commissioner, October

7, 1944, NA PNR RG75, Western Washington Box 257; Correspondence in file entitled "Chief Peter Kalama v. B. M. Brennan et al.," NA PNR RG75, Taholah Decimal File 173.04, Box 113. The secretary of the interior finally approved a Nisqually Tribe constitution on September 9, 1946. It specified that members would include all persons on a BIA census of 1945 and children of those members if born on the reservation. American Friends Service Committee (AFSC), *Uncommon Controversy: Fishing Rights of the Muckleshoot, Puyallup and Nisqually Indians* (Seattle: University of Washington Press, 1970), 57.

37. Suquamish Oral History Interview W.1.06; Beaulieu to Nicholson, February 21, 1938, NA PNR RG75, Taholah Decimal File 064; Memorandum of Upchurch, November 18, 1938, NA PNR RG75, Tulalip Box 477. As of May 1940, the only Puget Sound groups with IRA constitutions were the Tulalip Tribes, Swinomish Tribal Community, Puyallup Tribe, Skokomish Tribe, and Port Gamble Indian Community. Cohen, *Cohen's Handbook*, 129. It is especially hard to imagine a tribal government's making a positive difference at Nisqually. During World War I the U.S. Army had acquired two-thirds of the reservation lands. Allottees there scattered. By 1929 officials believed the tribe's membership had shrunk to sixty-six. That year Earl Henderson described Nisqually as "a picture of an Indian reservation in the last stages of abandonment," with poor soil, a few shacks, and few jobs in the surrounding area. Report of Henderson, January 25, 1929, NA RG75 CCF, Taholah File 7962–1929–150. Tribes elsewhere were slow to take advantage of the IRA's self-government provisions. Taylor, *New Deal*, 85, 106–7, 141.

38. Following documents in NA PNR RG75, Western Washington Box 277: Upchurch to Commissioner, February 8, 1936; Frank Wrolson to Collier, October 5, 1937; Upchurch to Commissioner, July 7, 1937; Puyallup Tribal Council to John M. Coffee, April 20, 1940; La Vatta to Commissioner, November 8, 1938. Also, Indian Reorganization Act Records, NA RG75, Tulalip 068, File 9698-A; Upchurch and La Vatta to Commissioner, August 15, 1935, NA PNR RG75, Western Washington Box 293; Upchurch to Commissioner, November 25, 1935, ibid.; Records of the Tulalip Board of Directors, NA PNR RG75, Tulalip Box 477, File 105.1; Minutes of Tulalip Board of Directors, December 1936 through March 11, 1939, NA PNR RG75, Western Washington Box 293.

39. Daiker to La Vatta, September 28, 1940, Petition for Acknowledgement of the Snohomish Tribe, Reply Appendix J-4; Lester Jackson to La Vatta, November 22, 1938, NA PNR RG75, Tulalip Box 486; Zimmerman to La Vatta, January 13, 1939, ibid.; Meiklejohn memo, Indian Reorganization Act Records, NA RG75, Tulalip 068, File 9548-A; memorandum of Felix Cohen, November 18, 1935, ibid., File 9567-A; Daiker to La Vatta, August 6, 1940, ibid., File 9691; memorandum, n.d., suggesting revisions to Puyallup constitution, ibid., File 9698-A. As of 1953 the Nooksack Tribe still had no BIA-approved written constitution. Questionnaire on Tribal Organization, May 15, 1953, NA PNR RG75, Western Washington Box 16.

40. "Report on W.W. Reservation Statistical Data for Informational Bulletin—2/11–60," NA PNR RG75, Western Washington Decimal File 050.1;

"Skokomish Correspondence Minutes, 1931–45," NA PNR RG75, Tribal Operations Branch Files, Western Washington Box 286.

41. House Subcommittee on Indian Affairs, *Investigate Indian Affairs*, 78th Cong., 2d sess., 1944, H.1051–0, 686. The Nooksack witness said his people were "known as the public-domain Indians" who had voted on the IRA but then concluded that it could not be applied to them. Ibid., 691–92.

42. Kelly, "John Collier and the Indian New Deal," 238–40; Prucha, *Great Father*, 993–1005.

43. Gross to Commissioner, March 19, 1946, NA PNR RG75, Tulalip Decimal File 620; "Swinomish Tribe Is Proud of Part It Plays in War," *Seattle Times*, September 17, 1944, 10; "Northwest Indians on Warpath Again: Contributions to War Effort," *Seattle Times*, September 5, 1943, Magazine, 3; Alison R. Bernstein, *American Indians and World War II: Toward a New Era in Indian Affairs* (Norman: University of Oklahoma Press, 1991); Prucha, *Great Father*, 1005–9; Taylor, *New Deal*, 139.

44. Gross to H. D. McCullough, May 18, 1945, NA PNR RG75, Tulalip Decimal File 922; memorandum on Swinomish Indian Tribal Community letterhead, n.d., NA PNR RG75, Tulalip Decimal 620; Suquamish Oral History interviews W.1.11 (Webster, March 25, 1982), S.7.02 (Ethel Sam, June 22, 1982), A.4.02 (Bernard Adams, March 24, 1982), A.4.03 (B. Adams, April 13, 1982), A.1.01 (Margaret Adams, April 4, 1982), A.7.01 (Evelyn Armstrong, August 2, 1982), G.1.03 (Martha George, January 27, 1982); Rygg, "Continuation of . . . Attitudes," 262–64, 271; *Bellingham Herald*, November 23, 1959, 1.

45. House of Representatives, *Investigate Indian Affairs*, H. 1051–0, 702, 685, 687, 690.

46. Prucha, *Great Father*, 1000–2; Burt, *Tribalism in Crisis*, 5–6, 19–20.

47. Prucha, *Great Father*, 1013–16; Burt, *Tribalism in Crisis*, 5, 46.

48. Suquamish Oral History Interview W.1.11; "Government Withdrawal Program 1953," NA PNR RG75, Western Washington Decimal File 103.3, Box 15; letters from Emmons to Snoqualmie Tribe, et al., January 21, 1954, ibid.; draft termination bill, September 15, 1953, NA PNR RG75, Western Washington Box 32; Prucha, *Great Father*, 1041–44; Burt, *Tribalism in Crisis*, 22–25. Other statements in favor of terminating western Washington tribes include Resolution of Northwest Superintendents' Council, NA PNR RG75, Western Washington Box 257; Wesley D'Ewart to House Committee on Interior and Insular Affairs, *Washington State Indian Problems*, unpublished U.S. House of Representatives Committee Hearings, 83d Cong., 1953, HIni-t-549. BIA-drafted termination legislation had several standard provisions: each tribe member was to receive an interest in tribal assets; the government would prepare a final roll of people entitled to share; members could choose whether to sell everything, organize a state corporation, or install a private trustee in the BIA's stead; allotments would go out of trust status; and the secretary of the interior could sell or partition heirship lands. Burt, *Tribalism in Crisis*, 30.

49. "Minutes of Tribal Meetings with Commissioner Emmons 9/13–14/56," NA PNR RG75, Western Washington Decimal File 109. Similar

reasoning appears in comments of Congressman A. L. Miller, U.S. House, *Washington State Indian Problems.*

50. Minutes, Tulalip Planning Committee, June 28, 1952, NA PNR RG75, Western Washington Decimal File 103.3, Box 15; "Intertribal Council WW Indians, Minutes 1–15/16–54," ibid., File 103.31; comments of Frank Wrolson, ibid.; testimony of Steve, U.S. House, *Washington State Indian Problems.* In some records the word "Inter-tribal" appears as "Intertribal."

51. Adams was commenting on a bill that would have denied enrollment to persons with less than half Indian ancestry. Raymond H. Bitney to Morgan Pryse, February 9, 1954, describing proceedings of Inter-tribal Council on February 6, NA PNR RG75, Western Washington Decimal File 060, Box 260; Minutes, meeting of Inter-tribal Council, January 12, 1957, ibid.; Questionnaires on Tribal Organization, May 15, 1953, NA PNR RG75, Western Washington Box 16; Martin Hopie to Emmons, January 19, 1955, NA PNR RG75, Western Washington Decimal File 109, Box 17; "Intertribal Council WW Indians, Minutes 1–15/16–54," NA PNR RG75, Western Washington Decimal File 103.31; Eva Greenslit Anderson, *George Adams, Indian Legislator* (Olympia, Wash.: n.p., [1955]).

52. "Minutes of Tribal Meetings with ... Emmons 9/13–14/56."

53. U.S. House, *Washington State Indian Problems,* HIni-T-549.

54. "Minutes of Tribal Meetings with ... Emmons 9/13–14/56."

55. "Notes of Meeting with Commissioner Emmons and Delegates of Various Tribes," October 9, 1953, NA PNR RG75, Western Washington Decimal File 103.3, Box 15; Questionnaires on Tribal Organization, May 15, 1953, NA PNR RG75, Western Washington Box 16; U.S. House, *Washington State Indian Problems.*

56. Resolution of Lower Elwha Tribe Council, February 12, 1958, in "Government Withdrawal Program 1953," NA PNR RG75, Western Washington Decimal File 103.3, Box 15; U.S. House, *Investigate Indian Affairs,* 700; Gross to Commissioner, October 23, 1945, NA PNR RG75, Tulalip Decimal File 610; Bitney to Pryse, February 9, 1954, letter furnished by Snohomish Tribe; statement on juvenile delinquency, in file of surveys dated 1956, NA PNR RG75, Western Washington Decimal File 024, Box 6. The Lower Elwha Klallam council eventually reversed its position on termination, thereby killing a pending bill to terminate the band. Secretary to Mr. Aspinall, April 13, 1960, and Hopie to Sam Reyburn [*sic*], April 27, 1960, NA PNR RG75, Western Washington Decimal File 103.3, Box 15. The consolidated Western Washington Agency maintained rolls of 7,185 Indians in thirty-two tribes, although it refused to serve 2,000 of those people. Its jurisdiction included eighteen reservations and 107 public domain allotments in sixteen counties. "Report of Eric Stork—Mgt Planning Withdrawal Program 1952," NA PNR RG75, Western Washington Decimal File 103.3, Box 15; Bitney to Pryse, September 10, 1952, ibid. Reports of this agency show how little information it had on the Indians it served. "Report on W.W. Reservation Statistical Data for Informational Bulletin—2/11/60," NA PNR RG75, Western Washington Decimal

File 050.1, Box 8; Superintendent to R. D. Holtz, July 20, 1965, NA PNR RG75, Western Washington Decimal File 052.9, Box 260.

57. Statements of Swinomish Tribal Community, n.d., and November 7 and 9, 1955, in "Government Withdrawal Program 1953," NA PNR RG75, Western Washington Decimal File 103.3, Box 15; Statement of Tulalip Tribes, January 20, 1955, ibid.

58. U.S. House, *Washington State Indian Problems.*

59. Ibid.

60. Bitney to Edith Riley, January 19, 1954, NA PNR RG75, Western Washington Decimal File 052.9, Box 260; "Report on Meeting Held with Tulalip Tribes, Inc., etc. and Representatives of 18 other Tribes, Bands or Groups, November 14, 1953, for the Purpose of Discussing Proposed Government Withdrawal Legislation, Western Washington Agency," 2, copy furnished by Snohomish Tribe; Bitney to Pryse, February 9, 1954, NA PNR RG75, Western Washington Decimal File 060, Box 260; "Report on W.W. Reservation Statistical Data," NA PNR RG75, Western Washington Decimal File 050.1; report on Duwamish tribal organization, May 15, 1953, NA PNR RG75, Western Washington Box 16; clipping from *Everett Daily Herald*, February 1956, furnished by Snohomish Tribe.

61. Prucha, *Great Father*, 1017–19; Bitney to Pryse, October 13, 1950, furnished to the Snohomish Tribe by Barbara Lane; Bitney to Pryse, February 9, 1954, ibid.; Indian Claims Commission, *Coast Salish and Western Washington Indians*, 518.

62. Wilfred Steve to Dear Friend, June 21, 1945, NA PNR RG75, Records of Portland Area Office Tribal Operations Branch, Series 56, Box 1503; "Report on Meeting Held with Tulalip Tribes, etc ... November 14, 1953," 3; *Seattle Times*, July 23, 1958, 22; *Seattle Argus*, September 12, 1958, 1. Nineteen groups asserting aboriginal title to lands in the vicinity of the Puget Sound and Hood Canal filed petitions in the Indian Claims Commission: Duwamish, Kikiallus, Lummi, Muckleshoot, Nisqually, Nooksack, Puyallup, Samish, Skagit, Upper Skagit, S'Klallam, Skokomish, Snohomish, Snoqualmie, Squaxin, Steilacoom, Stillaguamish, Suquamish, and Swinomish. Indian Claims Commission, *Coast Salish and Western Washington Indians*, 67, 70, 116, 128; U.S. House, *Investigate Indian Affairs*, 695–97, 706–7.

63. Bitney to Pryse, January 27, 1954, NA PNR RG75, Western Washington Decimal File 103.3.

64. "Acculturation Reports, May 1, 1963," memorandum of Richard Balsiger, March 9, 1963, and Lummi Study, NA PNR RG75, Western Washington Decimal File 024.1, Box 6.

65. BIA press release, January 12, 1955, NA PNR RG75, Western Washington Decimal File 109, Box 17; memorandum of Melvin Robertson to all tribes, January 4, 1955, ibid.; Portland Area Office to Superintendent, August 24, 1956, NA PNR RG75, Western Washington Decimal File 109, Box 18; clipping from *Seattle Times*, September 13, 1956, ibid.; Burt, *Tribalism in Crisis*, 75.

66. "Minutes of Tribal Meetings with ... Emmons"; *Bellingham Herald*, November 23, 1959, 1; Burt, *Tribalism in Crisis*, 56–58.

67. Employment Assistance Case Files (1957–1961), NA PNR RG75, Western Washington, Box 186, including: Report to Area Director, December 17, 1959; "Relocation 1957"; Fiscal Year 1962 Evaluations; Statistical and Narrative Report, November 9, 1960; and clipping from *Seattle P-I*, April 27, 1959.

68. Wilfred Steve to Dear Friend, June 21, 1945, NA PNR RG75, Portland Area Series 56, Box 1503.

69. Minutes, NFAI meeting, July 3, 1945, and July 15, 1939, NA PNR RG75, Tulalip Decimal File 090; F. A. Gross to several BIA offices, June 19, 1945, ibid., with a newspaper clipping and minutes of the meeting of June 15; Porter, "Without Reservation," 126.

70. Notes of Meeting with Commissioner Emmons, October 9, 1953, NA PNR RG75, Western Washington Decimal File 103.3; Bitney to Pryse, February 9 and January 27, 1954, ibid.; Joseph Hillaire to members, House Committee, Interior and Insular Affairs, February 10, 1954, NA PNR RG75, Western Washington, Box 15; "Sebastian Williams Named President of Intertribal Group at Renton Sessions," *Everett Daily Herald*, February 1956, copy of clipping supplied by Snohomish Tribe; Inter-tribal Council of Western Washington Indians Resolution No. 1, November 14, 1953, NA PNR RG75, Western Washington Decimal File 060, Box 260; Porter, "Without Reservation," 129.

71. "Intertribal Council WW Indians, Minutes 1–15/16–54," NA PNR RG75, Western Washington Decimal File 103.31; Indian Affairs Task Force, *Are You Listening, Neighbor? and The People Speak, Will You Listen?* (Olympia: State of Washington, 1978), 85; attendance list for meeting with commissioner, January 20, 1955, NA PNR RG75, Western Washington Box 17, Folder 109; list of tribal delegates appointed to meet with commissioner, attached to notes on meeting with Commissioner Emmons, November 7, 1953, copy furnished by Barbara Lane via Snohomish Tribe; Bitney to Pryse, September 30, 1953, ibid.; Bitney to Chairman of Snohomish Tribal Council, April 2, 1951, Petition for Acknowledgement of Snohomish Tribe, Reply Appendix G-14; Bitney to Forrest Elwell, ibid., Appendix G-15; Bitney to Dessie McDermott, November 19, 1951, ibid., Appendix G-16; File of tribal council rosters, 1946–1949, NA PNR RG75, Western Washington Box 257. A draft termination bill dated September 15, 1953, defines "tribe" as "tribes, bands, communities, organizations or groups: Chehalis, Chinook, Clallam, Cowlitz, Dwamish [*sic*], Hoh, Humptulips, Jamestown Tribal Organization, Kikiallus Tribe, Lower Elwha Tribal Community, Lower Skagit, Lummi, Makah, Muckelshoot [*sic*], Nisqually, Nooksak [*sic*], Ozette Tribes, Port Gamble Community, Puyallup, Quileute, Quinault, Samish, San Juan Island, Satsop, Shoalwater Bay and Georgetown, Skagit, Skokomish, Snohomish, Snoqualmie, Squaxin, Steilacoom, Stillaguamish, Suiattle, Suquamish, Swinomish Tribe and Tulalip Tribes, Inc." NA PNR RG75, Western Washington Box 32.

72. Minutes of meeting of Inter-tribal Council of Western Washington Indians, November 14, 1953, NA PNR RG75, Western Washington Decimal File

060; Resolutions of Snoqualmie, Skagit, and Snohomish Tribes, 1955, NA PNR RG75, Western Washington Decimal File 109, Box 17.

73. House Report 2680, 83d Cong., 2d sess., September 20, 1954, cited in Indian Claims Commission, *Coast Salish*, 512; Questionnaire on Tribal Organization in report for Committee on Interior and Insular Affairs, May 15, 1953, NA PNR RG75, Western Washington Agency, Box 16; Porter, "Without Reservation," 126; minutes of Samish Tribe of Indians in BIA Tribal Operations Branch Files for Western Washington Agency, NA PNR RG75, Box 286; Bitney to Mary McDowell Hansen, August 28, 1953, ibid.; Hansen to Bitney, October 3, 1953, ibid.; Minutes, San Juan Islands Indian Tribe, April 14, 1951, NA PNR RG75, Western Washington Decimal File 064.23, Box 11.

74. Testimony of Tandy Wilbur, U.S. House, *Investigate Indian Affairs*, 713; Porter, "Without Reservation," 127–31.

75. Bitney to Pryse, October 17, 1950, copy supplied by Barbara Lane via the Snohomish Tribe; Bitney to Commissioner, September 30, 1953, enclosing "Congressional Hearing ... Sept. 25, 1953," NA PNR RG75, Western Washington Decimal File 024.1, Box 6; U.S. House, *Washington State Indian Problems*; Bitney to Commissioner, November 28, 1953, furnished by Snohomish Tribe; Bitney to Pryse, February 9, 1954, NA PNR RG75, Western Washington Decimal File 060, Box 260; "Intertribal Council WW Indians, Minutes 1–15/16–54," NA PNR RG75, Western Washington Decimal 103.31; Porter, "Without Reservations," 129–30. It is possible that Indians originated the argument Bitney made. Minutes of Tulalip Board of Directors, June 18, 1937, NA PNR RG75, Western Washington Box 293.

76. Questionnaires on Tribal Organization, May 15, 1953, NA PNR RG75, Western Washington Decimal Files, Box 16; "Government Withdrawal Program 1953," NA PNR RG75, Western Washington Decimal File 103.3, Box 16; Surveys of Lower Elwha, Lummi, Muckleshoot, Nisqually, Port Gamble, Port Madison, Puyallup, Skokomish, Squaxin, Swinomish, and Tulalip Tribes in Report for Committee on Interior and Insular Affairs, 1956, NA PNR RG75, Western Washington Decimal File 024, Box 6; Minutes of individual tribal delegates' meetings with Emmons, 1956, NA PNR RG75, Western Washington Decimal File 109, Box 18; "Acculturation Reports, May 1, 1963," NA PNR RG75, Western Washington Decimal File 024.1; "Indians in the Real-Estate Business," *Seattle Times*, November 28, 1954, Magazine, 10.

77. Minutes of tribal delegates' meetings with Emmons, 1956, NA PNR RG75, Western Washington Decimal File 109, Box 18; agency statement regarding juvenile delinquency on reservations, 1956, NA PNR RG75, Western Washington Decimal File 024, Box 6; "Acculturation Reports, May 1, 1963"; *Seattle Times*, November 13, 1949, Magazine. BIA officials stepped up sales and leases of Indian lands during the 1950s. Burt, *Tribalism in Crisis*, 59–61. Congress approved long-term leases on Washington reservations, making it possible to develop housing for numerous non-Indians at Tulalip and Port Madison. Minutes of delegates' meetings with Emmons, 1956. For a summary of national trends stimulating growth of suburbs and highway-dependent

businesses, see Richard Polenberg, *One National Divisible: Class, Race, and Ethnicity in the United States since 1938* (New York: Penguin Books, 1960), 127–35; Michael Schaller, Virginia Scharff, and Robert D. Schulzinger, *Present Tense: The United States since 1945* (Boston: Houghton Mifflin, 1992), 125–29.

78. *67 United States Statutes* 588–90; Prucha, *Great Father,* 1044–46; statement regarding juvenile delinquency, 1956; *Bellingham Herald,* July 12, 1959, 1; "Government Withdrawal Program 1953," NA PNR RG75, Western Washington Decimal File 103.3, Box 15; "Intertribal Council WW Indians, Minutes 1–15/16–54," NA PNR RG75, Western Washington Decimal File 103.31; "State to Rule Muckleshoots," *Seattle Times,* August 27, 1957; "Tulalips Put under State Jurisdiction," *Seattle Times,* May 8, 1958; "Civil-Court Jurisdiction over Indians Is Problem for State," *Seattle Times,* November 11, 1959, 3; "Law Enforcement Problems Plague Pacific N.W. Reservation Indians," *Seattle Times,* March 20, 1960, Magazine 7; *Seattle Times,* October 5, 1958, 47.

79. Minutes of delegates' meetings with Emmons, 1956; "Stanford Research Institute Report June 1, 1956," NA PNR RG75, Western Washington Decimal File 052.9, Box 9.

80. Questionnaires on Tribal Organization, 1953, NA PNR RG75, Western Washington Decimal Files, Box 16; Bitney to Riley, January 19, 1954, NA PNR RG75, Western Washington Decimal File 060; Minutes of delegates' meetings with Emmons, 1956; Roger Patrick Karrigan, "A Study of the Scholastic Performance of the Indian Pupils in the Marysville (Washington) School District" (M.A. thesis, University of Washington, 1961), 7; "When Is an Indian Not an Indian?" *Seattle Times,* July 22, 1956, Magazine, 10.

8. TREATY FISHING RIGHTS

1. This language from Article 3 of the Treaty of Medicine Creek—the first that Stevens negotiated—appears in each treaty subsequently concluded with tribes in western Washington. *10 United States Statutes* 1132, *12 United States Statutes* 927 (Article 5), *12 United States Statutes* 933 (Article 4).

2. U.S. Department of the Interior, Office of Indian Affairs, Division of Forestry and Grazing (Edward G. Swindell, Jr.), *Report on Source, Nature and Extent of the Fishing, Hunting and Miscellaneous Related Rights of Certain Indian Tribes in Washington and Oregon,* July 1942, UW Microfilm A-941; cover letter of August 26, 1942, 66, 75–78; *Tulee v. Washington,* 315 United States Reports 681 (1942).

3. Donald L. Parman, "Inconstant Advocacy: The Erosion of Indian Fishing Rights in the Pacific Northwest, 1933–1956," *Pacific Historical Review* 53 (1984): 177; F. A. Gross to all organized tribes in Tulalip Agency jurisdiction, August 14, 1946, NA PNR RG75, Tulalip Decimal File 922; Report of Assistant Secretary of the Interior and statement of Deputy Attorney General of the U.S., in *Indian Fishing Rights,* Hearing of Senate Subcommittee on Indian Affairs, 88th Cong., August 5–6, 1964, S.1641–8, pp. 3–8; Sebastian Williams and Tandy Wilbur to U.S. Attorney General, April 12, 1946, and other correspon-

dence regarding the case of Henry Cooper, NA PNR RG75, Tulalip Decimal File 171–77; U.S. House of Representatives, *Investigate Indian Affairs,* H.1051–0, 695–96. The courts had already ruled that Washington State had no power to affect Indians' fishing inside reservation boundaries. *Pioneer Packing Company v. Winslow,* 159 Washington Reports 655 (1930).

4. By directing Indians into the military or war-related jobs, World War II also reduced the number who needed to fish out of season. U.S. House, *Investigate Indian Affairs,* 698–99, 714, 695–96; Boxberger, *To Fish in Common,* 117–25, 104.

5. Swindell, *Report on . . . Fishing,* 96; Boxberger, *To Fish in Common,* 104–5, 111, 119, 138, 147–48; AFSC, *Uncommon Controversy,* 121–25, 126–29; testimony of Wayne Williams and Forrest Kinley, *Northwest Salmon Fisheries Resources,* Senate Committee on Commerce and House Merchant Marine and Fisheries Committee, 87th Cong., 1961, S.1493–3, pp. 88–94; Indian Affairs Task Force, *Are You Listening, Neighbor?,* 26.

6. Minutes of meeting of Northwestern Federation of American Indians with Milo Moore, State Director of Fisheries, January 8, 1946, NA RG75, Entry 121, Tulalip File 931. Since most Indians fished close to spawning grounds and used relatively efficient gear, many non-Indians accepted uncritically the state's argument that "unregulated" Indian fishing threatened the fish resource. Indians in turn commonly responded as Adams did. *Seattle Times,* October 5, 1958, 47; February 10, 1959, 19; December 10, 1959, 39; March 3, 1964, 14; testimony of Tandy Wilbur, U.S. Senate, *North Pacific Fisheries Problems,* 87th Cong., 1961, S.1493–1, 221–22; testimony of Frank Wright, U.S. Senate, *Northwest Salmon Fisheries Resources,* 64; Cohen, *Treaties on Trial,* 70–71; Boxberger, *To Fish in Common,* 132.

7. U.S. House, *Investigate Indian Affairs,* 690. Similar testimony appears at 689, 691–92, 704.

8. "Government Withdrawal Program 1953," NA PNR RG75, Western Washington Decimal File 103.3, Box 15; *P-I,* September 15, 1956, clipping in NA PNR RG75, Western Washington Decimal File 109, Box 18. A summary of the nationwide postwar decline in Indians' income appears in Bernstein, *American Indians and World War II,* 141, 148–50.

9. "Acculturation Reports, May 1, 1963," NA PNR RG75, Western Washington Decimal File 024.1, Box 6; "The Plight of Our Indians" *P-I,* April 20, 1964, 1, 7; Memorandum to files, October 2, 1962, NA PNR RG75, Western Washington Decimal File 050.1, Box 8; Schaller, Scharff, and Schulzinger, *Present Tense,* 126. In 1970 the BIA estimated that two-thirds of employable adults in the Muckleshoot, Puyallup, and Tulalip Tribes were either unemployed or holding temporary jobs. Catherine E. Reaugh, "Muckleshoot, Port Gamble, Puyallup and Tulalip: Four Puget Sound Indian Communities Today" (senior thesis, University of Washington, 1970), 8, 38, 49; "Colorful Lummi Festival Hides Poverty," *Seattle Times,* July 4, 1968, 57, and July 3, 1968, 35.

10. Public assistance may have helped to perpetuate Indians' concentration in seasonal occupations by providing income not previously available

during the off-season. Regarding the rediscovery of poverty in the early 1960s, see Polenberg, *One Nation Divisible,* 193–202; Schaller, Scharff, and Schulzinger, *Present Tense,* 229–30, 243.

11. Browning, *P-I,* April 20, 1964, 1, 7; *Seattle Times* on the following dates and pages: Don Hannula, "Poverty on Indian Reservations ... ," February 12, 1967, 33; "State Indians Worse off ... ," July 26, 1968, 9; Mrs. Robert G. Fleagle, "State Indian Children Still Are Handicapped," February 20, 1958, 8; June 1, 1961, 3; June 2, 1961, 9; Hannula, "The Indian Problem," June 30, 1968, 92; Hannula, "Dwindling Nisquallys Face a Bleak Future," June 30, 1968, 93; "Colorful Lummi Festival Hides Poverty," July 4, 1968, 57; "Muckleshoots Have Few Resources," July 2, 1968, 4.

12. "Acculturation Reports." Cf. a report of the State Department of Public Assistance in Skagit County that a "considerably lower" proportion of Indians than non-Indians received welfare there in 1956. Administrator to Superintendent, August 24, 1956, NA PNR RG75, Western Washington Decimal File 024, Box 6.

13. "Stanford Research Institute Report June 1, 1956," NA PNR RG75, Western Washington Decimal File 052.9, Box 9; *P-I,* April 20, 1964.

14. Minutes of tribal delegates' meetings with the commissioner, 1956, NA PNR RG75, Western Washington Decimal File 109, Box 18; "Intertribal Council WW Indians, Minutes 1–15/16–54," NA PNR RG75, Western Washington Decimal File 103.31, Box 15; remarks of social worker Martha Muckey in *Seattle Times,* June 2, 1961, 9; Bruce A. Chadwick and Joseph H. Stauss, "The Assimilation of American Indians into Urban Society: The Seattle Case," *Human Organization* 34 (Winter 1975): 365; *Seattle Times,* November 9, 1962, 4; John Dewhirst, "Coast Salish Summer Festivals: Rituals for Upgrading Social Identity," *Anthropologica* 18 (1976): 234–35; Lummi Reservation study, "Acculturation Reports"; Capt. Florence Ross to Superintendent, August 28, 1956, NA PNR RG75, Western Washington Decimal File 024, Box 6; Susan Schwartz, *Seattle Times,* March 19, 1969, 25; Amelia Louise Schultz, "Indian Unmarried Mothers" (M.S.W. thesis, University of Washington, 1947), 4, 26, 108, 111.

15. *Seattle Times,* June 2, 1961, 9; Hannula, *Seattle Times,* February 12, 1967, 33, and June 30, 1968, 92; *Bellingham Herald,* November 23, 1959, 1, 3.

16. Chadwick and Stauss, "Assimilation of American Indians," 366, 368; Hannula, *Seattle Times,* July 5, 1968, 27; "Indians Face Bias," *P-I,* July 23, 1972, C8. Bernstein includes income and employment statistics for Indians in all U.S. cities. *American Indians and World War II,* 149–50.

17. Collins, *Valley of the Spirits,* 243, 44; Collins, "Indian Shaker Church," 405; Wike, "Modern Spirit Dancing," 9, 13, 37; Amoss, *Coast Salish Spirit Dancing,* 27, 149, 157; "Acculturation Reports"; Suquamish Oral History Interviews S.7.01 and J.4.01.

18. Wike, "Modern Spirit Dancing," 9, 136; Amoss, *Coast Salish Spirit Dancing,* 27, 149, 157; John Edward Michael Kew, "Coast Salish Ceremonial Life: Status and Identity in a Modern Village" (Ph.D. diss., University of Washington, 1970), 1, 80, 317, 325, 340, 349–50.

19. Two white men, both married to Indian women, were initiated as spirit dancers in the 1960s. Although white observers were not excluded, they rarely attended dances, which were invitational events. Kew, "Coast Salish Ceremonial Life," 205, 200. According to Collins, Upper Skagits worshiped with whites in Pentecostal churches. *Valley of the Spirits,* 44. As described by Kew and Suttles, the large ceremonials were occasions to bestow hereditary names, display mementos of the dead, give away wealth, and make speeches, thus combining features of aboriginal spirit dancing and potlatches and enhancing the reputations of those who participated. Suttles, *Coast Salish Essays,* 223–27; Kew, "Coast Salish Ceremonial Life," 145, 149, 205, 326, 341. Suttles speculates that the Shaker Church network provided a link between people in the northern winter dancing circuit, Indian groups to the south, and groups such as the Yakima who continued other forms of native ceremonialism. *Coast Salish Essays,* 229. See also Kew, "Coast Salish Ceremonial Life," 244.

20. David Richardson, "N.W. Indians Continue Spirit Dance Ritual," *Tacoma News Tribune/Sunday Ledger,* March 10, 1957, Magazine, 3.

21. Rygg, "Continuation of . . . Attitudes," 334, 339; Kew, "Coast Salish Ceremonial Life," 80.

22. *Seattle Times,* August 17, 1960, 3; Walt Woodward, "Indians Begin to Find Own Voices," *Seattle Times,* April 27, 1966, 11; Dewhirst, "Coast Salish Summer Festivals"; Gross to Lucile McDonald, December 17, 1947, NA PNR RG75, Tulalip Box 492; Gross to Commissioner, February 28, 1950, ibid.; Kew, "Coast Salish Ceremonial Life," 277 and ff. Of the Seattle Indians in the sample that Chadwick and Stauss studied, 74 percent attended powwows. "Assimilation of American Indians," 363.

23. Dewhirst, "Coast Salish Summer Festivals," 232, 256; Kew, "Coast Salish Ceremonial Life," 289–97; "Indian Water Carnival," *Seattle Times,* July 12, 1953, Pictorial, 45; "Intertribal Indian Days," *Seattle Times,* August 4, 1971, E18; "Indian Fete Revives Old Customs," *Seattle Times,* July 2, 1950, Rot., 14–15.

24. Collins, *Valley of the Spirits;* Elmendorf, *Structure of Twana Culture;* Kew, "Coast Salish Ceremonial Life"; Langness, "Case of Post-Contact Reform"; Snyder, "Skagit Society"; Suttles, *Coast Salish Essays.* Many of the anthropologists were gathering evidence for use in the Indian Claims Commission.

25. *Seattle Times,* June 18, 1950, Magazine, 1; January 24, 1954, Magazine, 2; May 15, 1966, Magazine, 5; "Susie Sampson Peter, Oldest of the Kikiallus," *Seattle Times,* November 2, 1958, Magazine, 7; *Mercer Islander,* April 10, 1952, 1, and May 1, 1952, 1; Mary Ann Lambert Vincent, *House of the Seven Brothers: A Genealogical Story of Olympic Peninsula Indians* (n.p., 1960), foreword; Lambert, *Dungeness Massacre;* Murray Morgan, *Skid Road: An Informal Portrait of Seattle* (New York: Viking Press, 1951), 20; Betty McDonald, *The Egg and I* (Philadelphia: Lippincott, 1945), 12, 22, 202.

26. "Relics of a Proud Past," *Seattle Times,* September 14, 1958, Magazine, 46–47; Rygg, "Continuation of . . . Attitudes," 304, 317–78; Don Duncan,

Seattle Times, July 25, 1965, clipping in NA PNR RG75, Western Washington Decimal File 040, Box 7.

27. Charlotte D. Widrig, "Point Elliott Treaty Centennial," *Seattle Times*, October 31, 1954, Magazine, 4.

28. "Point Elliott Treaty-Signing Re-enacted," *Seattle Times*, May 3, 1961, 53. The *Times* did cover a ceremony in Walla Walla to commemorate the centennial of the treaty with the Yakimas and other eastern Washington Indians. "Whites Join Indians in Treaty Fete," *Seattle Times*, June 8, 1955.

29. Dewhirst, "Coast Salish Summer Festivals," 246.

30. U.S. Senate, *Northwest Salmon Fisheries Resources*, 96.

31. "Fishing in Western Washington—A Treaty Right, a Clash of Cultures," in U.S. Commission on Civil Rights, *Indian Tribes: A Continuing Quest for Survival* (Washington, D.C.: Government Printing Office, June 1981), 61, 64 and ff.; Parman, "Inconstant Advocacy"; AFSC, *Uncommon Controversy*, 72–106; Cohen, *Treaties on Trial*, especially 41–65; Boxberger, *To Fish in Common*, 98–140.

32. "Minutes of Tribal meetings with … Emmons 9/13–14/56," NA PNR RG75, Western Washington Decimal File 109, Box 18; Cohen, *Treaties on Trial*, 75; Harold J. Plaster to Stewart L. Udall, n.d. [received February 13 or 18, 1962], NA PNR RG75, Western Washington Decimal File 060; comments of Joe Teao, "Intertribal Council WW Indians, Minutes 1–15/16–54," NA PNR RG75, Western Washington Decimal File 103.31; Testimony of Benjamin Wright, *United States, Quinault Tribe, et al. v. State of Washington, Thor Tollefson, et al.* (United States District Court, Western District of Washington at Tacoma, September 1973), Civil No. 9213, Transcript, 2904 (hereafter *U.S. v. Washington* Transcript); "Indians, Like Negroes, Step Up Rights Fight," Sunday *Oregonian*, February 23, 1964, 25; "Indians Begin to Find Own Voices," *Seattle Times*, April 27, 1966, 11; "Program Opening New Doors for Area Tribes," *Everett Herald*, March 6, 1970, 9B; "Indians Urge Self-Help, Change of Image," *Seattle Times*, April 13, 1961, 6; "Tribal Members Respond to Indianness Question," *Bremerton Sun*, April 14, 1973, 1; Nagel, *American Indian Ethnic Renewal*, 122.

33. U.S. Commission on Civil Rights, *Indian Tribes*, 66–67; *Makah Indian Tribe v. Schoettler*, 192 Federal Reporter 2d 224 (Ninth Circuit Court of Appeals, 1951); *State v. Satiacum*, 50 Washington Reports 2d 513 (1957); Cohen, *Treaties on Trial*, 67–68; "Intertribal Council of WW Indians, Minutes 1–15/16–54"; written testimony of Washington Department of Fisheries, U.S. Senate, *Northwest Salmon Fisheries Resources*, 5.

34. See also Sid Mills, "A Choice of Allegiance," in *Chronicles of American Indian Protest*, ed. Council on Interracial Books for Children (Greenwich, Conn.: Fawcett Publications for the Council on Interracial Books for Children, 1971), 280–83.

35. *State v. Satiacum*, 530, 534.

36. *Washington v. McCoy*, 387 Pacific Reporter 2d 942, 949, 951 (Washington Supreme Court, 1963).

37. *Puyallup Tribe v. Department of Game*, 391 United States Reports 392, 398, 401–3 (1968); U.S. Commission on Civil Rights, *Indian Tribes*, 67. A small sampling of the coverage of this long story might include the following articles from the *Seattle Times*: "More Indians Defy Bans," March 4, 1964, 4B; "State to File Case against Indian Fishing," August 10, 1964, 36; "Plan Fish-In as Nisqually Protest," February 16, 1964, 14; "Indians Win 'Um Fight over Fish," January 10, 1965, Magazine, 2; "State Regulation of Indian Fishing Upheld," May 27, 1968, S4; "State Indians Plan to Protest High Court Ruling on Fishing," June 12, 1968, 12; "Indian Camp-In on Capitol Lawn Grows," June 24, 1968, 3; "46 Days of Confrontation on Nisqually," October 20, 1968, 7; "Indian Suit Challenges New Rules," July 26, 1968, 72; as well as "Restraining Order Halts Indian Fishing," *Tacoma News Tribune*, November 13, 1963; "Indians to Stage Fish-Ins Today," *P-I*, June 13, 1968, 3; "Protestors Stage Demonstration," *P-I*, September 6, 1968, 29; "Indian War Starts at Frank's Landing," *Everett Herald*, October 18, 1968, 1.

38. *Sohappy v. Smith*, 302 Federal Supplement 899, 904 (U.S. District Court for the District of Oregon, 1969); U.S. Commission on Civil Rights, *Indian Tribes*, 68.

39. AFSC, *Uncommon Controversy*, 86–87; U.S. Commission on Civil Rights, *Indian Tribes*, 70; "U.S. to Defend Indians in Fish Disputes," *Seattle Times*, May 5, 1966, 9; "Legal Struggle Has Been Long," *Seattle Times*, September 28, 1970, A16; "U.S. Sues State," *P-I*, September 19, 1970, 1; "Attorneys for Tribes Join U.S. Suit," *P-I*, January 17, 1971, 14; *United States v. Washington*, 384 Federal Supplement 312 (U.S. District Court, Western District of Washington, 1974).

40. *U.S. v. Washington*, 384 Federal Supplement 312, 335–39. When the Ninth Circuit Court of Appeals agreed that Judge Boldt could retain jurisdiction in order to ensure implementation of his decision, a concurring judge laid the blame for the "fish wars" at the state's feet: "The record in this case, and the history set forth in [other cases] make it crystal clear that it has been recalcitrance of Washington State officials (and their vocal non-Indian commercial and sports fishing allies) which produced the denial of Indian rights requiring intervention by the district court. This responsibility should neither escape notice nor be forgotten." 520 Federal Reporter 2d 693 (Burns, J., concurring).

41. "Legal Struggle," *Seattle Times*, September 28, 1970, A16; *U.S. v. Washington*, 384 Federal Supplement 328, 330; affirmed at 520 Federal Reporter 2d 676 (Ninth Circuit Court of Appeals, 1975); certiorari denied at 423 United States Reports 1006 (1976). The Supreme Court modified the District Court's ruling slightly but affirmed its most important holdings. *Washington v. Washington State Commercial Passenger Fishing Vessel Association*, 443 United States Reports 658–708 (1979).

42. AFSC, *Uncommon Controversy*, xxvi.

43. Ibid., xx–xxi, 71; "Hank Adams Dedicated to His People's Fight," *Seattle Times*, January 24, 1971, A16; Robert Johnson, "Northwest Indians: Our Invisible Society," *P-I*, July 28, 1969, Northwest Today, 7–11.

44. Cohen, *Treaties on Trial*, 179, 186–87, xxiii, xxv.

45. AFSC, *Uncommon Controversy*, 108; "3 Indians Sue Puyallup Tribe," *P-I*, October 14, 1971, A10.

46. *State v. Robert Moses et al.*, opinion of Washington State Supreme Court *en banc*, Docket No. 40267 (1971); AFSC, *Uncommon Controversy*, 108–13; Cohen, *Treaties on Trial*, 66–67, 70–77. Some of the many newspaper accounts of fish-ins and other protests are cited in note 37. Others include "Indians Call Nisqually Raid a Nazi Trick," *Tacoma News Tribune*, January 12, 1962, 1, and the following *Seattle Times* articles: "Plan Fish-In at Nisqually," February 27, 1964, I58; March 1, 1964, 39; March 3, 1964, 14; "More Indians Defy Bans," March 4, 1964, 4B; "Indian Women Dare Fishing Arrests," March 11, 1964, 7; "Fishing Hearing Picketed by Indians," March 20, 1964, 42; "Indians Parade Here," October 26, 1965, 46; "Fewer Than 50 Begin March for Fishing Rights," May 13, 1966, 2; "Indians Plan Fishing Rights Appeal at The Hague," August 13, 1968, I58.

47. Cohen, *Treaties on Trial*, 73, 75; "Marlon Brando, San Francisco Cleric Arrested," *Seattle Times*, March 2, 1964, 1, and March 16, 1964, 3; *P-I*, July 18, 1968, 3; *Seattle Times*, August 13, 1970, B4; Nagel, *American Indian Ethnic Renewal*, 129, 162.

48. Statement of Bernice White and Annie Garrison, U.S. Senate, *Northwest Salmon Fisheries Resources*, 114–16; testimony of Forrest Kinley, *U.S. v. Washington* Transcript, 3008; "Indians Reject Marches, Sit-Ins," *P-I*, February 16, 1964, 10; *Seattle Times*, March 1, 1964, 39; April 28, 1968, 25; June 30, 1968, 92; July 4, 1968, 57; "Indians Tell Negroes to Stay Out of Case," *Seattle Times*, March 1, 1964, 39; *Seattle Times*, March 1, 1964, 39; AFSC, *Uncommon Controversy*, 116–17; "Indian Leader Opposes U.S. Suit," *P-I*, March 3, 1971, 2.

49. Statement of Tulalip Tribe, *Indian Fishing Rights*, Senate Subcommittee on Indian Affairs, 88th Cong., 1964, S. 1641–8, 181–182; Testimony of Wayne Williams, U.S. Senate, *Northwest Salmon Fisheries Resources*, 89–90; Swindell, *Report*, 112, 137; *Seattle Times*, October 5, 1958, 47; "Tulalip Indians Support State Fishing Rules," *Seattle Times*, April 11, 1962, 53; "Non-Treaty Indians Back Set-Net Ban," *Seattle Times*, January 9, 1962, 11; Cohen, *Treaties on Trial*, 69; AFSC, *Uncommon Controversy*, 105, 115–16.

50. *Seattle Times*, January 24, 1971, A16, and June 30, 1968, 92; *P-I*, October 14, 1971, A10; Cohen, *Treaties on Trial*, 66.

51. Inter-tribal Council to Stewart Udall, January 5, 1962, NA PNR RG75, Western Washington Decimal File 060; Resolution of Inter-tribal Council, October 14, 1961, ibid.; "Top Northwest Indian Officials Join Fishing Rights Fight," *P-I*, September 13, 1970, 66; AFSC, *Uncommon Controversy*, 113–14. The difficulty of mobilizing a unified defense of treaty fishing rights is evident in the four-year gap between the Inter-tribal Council's first efforts to address the issue and its actual establishment of a Fish and Game Commission. Minutes, Inter-tribal Council, January 12, 1957, NA PNR RG75, Western Washington Decimal File 060.

52. Swindell, *Report on ... Fishing*, 112; U.S. Senate, *North Pacific Fisheries Problems*, 222; James Jackson in U.S. Senate, *Northwest Salmon Fisheries Resources*.

53. The tribes were Squaxin Island, Skokomish, Nisqually, Stillaguamish, Puyallup, Lummi, Muckleshoot, Sauk-Suiattle, and Skagit. *U.S. v. Washington* Transcript.

54. *U.S. v. Washington* Transcript, 2870, 2698, 2600; Findings, Conclusions, and Order, *State v. James Starr, Louis Starr, et al.* (Superior Court for State of Washington in King County, No. 37072). Information regarding Peters's genealogy appears in "Puyallup—1929 Payment Roll," NA PNR RG75, Western Washington Box 276.

55. *U.S. v. Washington* Transcript, 2486–87, 2711–12, 2718, 2635, 2659, 2591, 2604, 2883.

56. Ibid., 2489, 2713, 2894, 3065, 3020–21, 3232.

57. Myerhoff, " 'Life Not Death in Venice.' "

58. *U.S. v. Washington* Transcript, 2559–60, 3004, 3023, 2710; *Seattle Times*, September 12, 1973, A10; Cohen, *Treaties on Trial*, xxiii, 65; AFSC, *Uncommon Controversy*, 113; Lane, "Political and Economic Aspects," 41–42. Calvin Peters confessed to very little knowledge about Squaxin Island Indians' past practices. *U.S. v. Washington* Transcript, 2499–2500.

59. Testimony of Frank Wright, U.S. Senate, *Northwest Salmon Fisheries Resources*, 68; Testimony of Tandy Wilbur, ibid., 95–96; Lane, "Political and Economic Aspects," 29; Testimony of Malcolm McLeod, U.S. Senate, *Indian Fishing Rights*, 95; AFSC, *Uncommon Controversy*, 20–25.

60. U.S. Senate, *Northwest Salmon Fisheries Resources*, 66, 94, 96; U.S. Senate, *Indian Fishing Rights*, 80, 93; *U.S. v. Washington* Transcript, 3179, 3049.

61. *U.S. v. Washington* Transcript, 3021, 3041, 3148–52 and ff., 2861, 3025, 3081, 3189; Testimony of Al Ziontz, U.S. Senate, *Indian Fishing Rights*, 80; *Seattle Times*, September 12, 1973, A5, A10.

62. *Seattle Times*, March 28, 1962, 26; Plaster to Udall, NA PNR RG75, Western Washington Decimal File 060; Findings, Conclusions, Order of Dismissal, *State v. James Starr, Louie Starr, Leonard Wayne* (Superior Court for the State of Washington in King County, No. 37072); U.S. Senate, *North Pacific Fisheries Problems*, 113–14; U.S. Senate, *Indian Fishing Rights*, 4; Murray Morgan, "State Fights Indians; Fishing Rights Questioned," *Seattle Argus*, May 18, 1962, 9; AFSC, *Uncommon Controversy*, 79. Also, "3 Indians Sue Puyallup Tribe," *P-I*, October 14, 1971, A10.

63. U.S. Senate, *Northwest Salmon Fisheries Resources*, 37.

64. U.S. Senate, *Indian Fishing Rights*, 35, 38.

65. AFSC, *Uncommon Controversy*, 67, 95; Mills, "Choice of Allegiance," 280–83; E. M. Benn, Chief Inspector, to Gross, April 18, 1950, NA PNR RG75, Tulalip Decimal File 922; Gross to Emoore W. George, May 4, 1950, ibid.

66. *U.S. v. Washington* Transcript, 2507–8, 2599–2600, 2655, 2688–89, 2859–60, 2891–93, 2978, 3241, 3268.

67. AFSC, *Uncommon Controversy*, 66–70. Also Lane, "Political and Economic Aspects," 41–42.

68. *U.S. v. Washington* Transcript, 3268.

69. *U.S. v. Washington* Transcript, 2507, 2516–17, 2598, 2655, 2688–89, 2978, 3268.

70. *U.S. v. Washington*, 384 Federal Supplement 358, 339–40.

71. 384 Federal Supplement 314, 360 (Lummi Tribe) and ff.

72. 384 Federal Supplement 339–40.

73. 384 Federal Supplement, 360 and ff., 341; Russel L. Barsh, "Backfire from Boldt: The Judicial Transformation of Coast Salish Proprietary Fisheries into a Commons," *Western Legal History* 4 (1991): 85–102.

74. Indian Affairs Task Force, *Are You Listening, Neighbor?*, 28, 86; *U.S. v. Washington*, 384 Federal Supplement 328, 376, 378–79; 520 Federal Reporter 2d 692–93.

75. Findings of Fact, *U.S. v. Washington*, 476 Federal Supplement 1101 (U.S. District Court for the Western District of Washington, 1979).

76. 476 Federal Supplement, 1104–5. According to Indian Affairs Task Force (*The People Speak*, 82, 87), several of the landless tribes requested in vain that their ICC judgment funds be used to purchase land in trust or disbursed in a lump sum for use in tribal programs.

77. *United States v. State of Washington*, 641 Federal Reporter 2d 1368 (1981), certiorari denied, 102 Supreme Court Reporter 1001.

78. Testimony of Willard Bill, Hearing before Magistrate Robert Cooper, December 18, 1974, *United States v. Washington* (United States District Court for the Western District of Washington at Tacoma, Civil No. 9213), 142; Nagel, *American Indian Ethnic Renewal*, 126.

AFTERWORD

1. Deputy Assistant Secretary—Indian Affairs (Operations), Recommendation and Summary of Evidence for Proposed Finding against Federal Acknowledgment of the Snohomish Tribe of Indians, Inc., Pursuant to 25 CFR 83, March 16, 1983; copy furnished by Snohomish Tribe.

2. Edwin Eells to Governor Miles C. Moore, August 29, 1889, Washington State Archives, Record Group 1/P-1, Box 2.

3. Records and Evidence Concerning Puyallup Enrollment, NA RG 75, Hill Entry 615, Box 2; Files on Puyallup Reorganization, NA PNR RG 75, Western Washington Box 277.

4. 25 *Code of Federal Regulations* Sec. 83.7; Sharon O'Brien, "Tribes and Indians: With Whom Does the United States Maintain a Relationship?" *Notre Dame Law Review* 66 (1991), 1475.

Bibliography

BOOKS AND BOOKLETS

Adamson, Thelma. *Folk-Tales of the Coast Salish*. New York: American Folk-Lore Society, 1934.

American Friends Service Committee. *Uncommon Controversy: Fishing Rights of the Muckleshoot, Puyallup and Nisqually Indians*. Seattle: University of Washington Press, 1970.

Amoss, Pamela. *Coast Salish Spirit Dancing: The Survival of an Ancestral Religion*. Seattle: University of Washington Press, 1978.

Anderson, Eva Greenslit. *Chief Seattle*. Caldwell, Idaho: Caxton Printers, 1943.

———. *George Adams, Indian Legislator*. [Olympia, Wash.: n.p., ca. 1955].

Anderson, Karen. *Changing Woman: A History of Racial Ethnic Women in Modern America*. New York: Oxford University Press, 1996.

Anderson, Kay J. *Vancouver's Chinatown: Racial Discourse in Canada, 1875–1980*. Montreal: McGill–Queen's University Press, 1991.

Axtell, James. *The European and the Indian: Essays in the Ethnohistory of Colonial America*. New York: Oxford University Press, 1981.

Bagley, Clarence B. *In the Beginning*. Tacoma, Wash.: Lowman & Hanford, 1905.

Bancroft, Hubert H. *History of the Northwest Coast*. 2 vols. San Francisco: A. L. Bancroft, 1884, 1886.

———. *History of Oregon*. San Francisco: History Company, 1888. Also published as volumes 29 and 30 of *The Works of Hubert Howe Bancroft*.

———. *History of Washington, Idaho and Montana 1845–1889*. San Francisco: History Company, 1890. Also published as volume 31 of *The Works of Hubert Howe Bancroft*.

Banton, Michael. *The Idea of Race*. London: Tavistock, 1977.

Barnett, Homer Garner. *Indian Shakers: A Messianic Cult of the Pacific Northwest*. Carbondale: Southern Illinois University Press, 1957.

Barry, J. Neilson. *Redskin and Pioneer, Brave Tales of the Great Northwest.* New York: Rand McNally, 1932.

Barth, Fredrik. *Ethnic Groups and Boundaries.* Boston: Little, Brown, 1969.

Bennett, Robert A., ed. *A Small World of Our Own: Authentic Pioneer Stories of the Pacific Northwest from the Old Settlers Contest of 1892.* Walla Walla, Wash.: Pioneer Press Books, 1985.

Berkhofer, Robert F., Jr. *The White Man's Indian: Images of the American Indian from Columbus to the Present.* New York: Vintage Books, 1978.

Bernstein, Alison R. *American Indians and World War II: Toward a New Era in Indian Affairs.* Norman: University of Oklahoma Press, 1991.

Bieder, Robert E. *Science Encounters the Indian, 1820–1880: The Early Years of American Ethnology.* Norman: University of Oklahoma Press, 1986.

Blanchet, Francis N. *Historical Sketches of the Catholic Church in Oregon, during the Past Forty Years (1838–1878).* Portland, Ore.: n.p., 1878; and microcopied edition, n.p., University of Washington Library Microfilm A-2573.

Blanchet, Francis N., and Modeste Demers. *Catholic Church Records of the Pacific Northwest, Vancouver, and Stellamaris Mission.* Translated by Mikell De Lores Wormell Warner; annotated by Harriet Duncan Munnick. St. Paul, Ore.: French Prairie Press, 1972.

———. *Notices and Voyages of the Famed Quebec Mission to the Pacific Northwest.* Translated by Carl Landerholm. Portland: Oregon Historical Society, 1956.

Blankenship, George A. *Lights and Shades of Pioneer Life on Puget Sound.* Olympia, Wash.: n.p., 1923.

Blu, Karen I. *The Lumbee Problem: The Making of an American Indian People.* Cambridge: Cambridge University Press, 1980.

Boxberger, Daniel L. *To Fish in Common: The Ethnohistory of Lummi Indian Salmon Fishing.* Lincoln: University of Nebraska Press, 1989.

Brown, Jennifer S. H. *Strangers in Blood: Fur Trade Company Families in Indian Country.* Vancouver: University of British Columbia Press, 1980.

Bruseth, Nels. *Indian Stories and Legends of the Stillaguamish, Sauks and Allied Tribes.* [Arlington, Wash., 1926]; reprint, Fairfield, Wash.: Ye Galleon Press, 1972.

Burt, Larry. *Tribalism in Crisis: Federal Indian Policy, 1953–1961.* Albuquerque: University of New Mexico Press, 1982.

Carpenter, Cecilia Svinth. *Fort Nisqually: A Documented History of Indian and British Interaction.* Tacoma, Wash.: Tahoma Research, 1986.

———. *They Walked Before: The Indians of Washington State.* Tacoma: Washington State American Revolution Bicentennial Commission, 1977.

Carter, Paul A. *The Spiritual Crisis of the Gilded Age.* DeKalb: Northern Illinois University Press, 1971.

Castile, George P., ed. *The Indians of Puget Sound: The Notebooks of Myron Eells.* Seattle: University of Washington Press, 1985.

Chance, John K. *Race and Class in Colonial Oaxaca.* Stanford, Calif.: Stanford University Press, 1978.

Clark, Norman H. *The Dry Years: Prohibition and Social Change in Washington.* Seattle: University of Washington Press, 1965.

Clastres, Pierre. *Society against the State: The Leader as Servant and the Human Uses of Power among Indians of the Americas.* New York: Urizon Books, 1977.

Clendinnen, Inga. *Ambivalent Conquests: Maya and Spaniard in Yucatan, 1517–1570.* Cambridge: Cambridge University Press, 1987.

Clifford, James. *The Predicament of Culture: Twentieth-Century Ethnography, Literature, and Art.* Cambridge, Mass.: Harvard University Press, 1988.

Clifford, James, and George E. Marcus. *Writing Culture: The Poetics and Politics of Ethnography.* Berkeley and Los Angeles: University of California Press, 1989.

Clifton, James A. *Being and Becoming Indian: Biographical Studies of North American Frontiers.* Chicago: Dorsey Press, 1989.

Cohen, Fay G. *Treaties on Trial: The Continuing Controversy over Northwest Indian Fishing Rights.* Seattle: University of Washington Press, 1986.

Cohen, Felix S. *Felix S. Cohen's Handbook of Federal Indian Law.* Washington, D.C.: U.S. Government Printing Office, 1942; reprint, Albuquerque: University of New Mexico Press, n.d.

Collier, John. *From Every Zenith.* Denver: Sage Books, 1963.

Collins, June McCormick. *Valley of the Spirits: The Upper Skagit Indians of Western Washington.* Seattle: University of Washington Press, 1974.

Colvocoresses, George M. *Four Years in a Government Exploring Expedition to . . . the Northwest Coast.* New York: Cornish, Lamport, 1852.

Cornell, Stephen. *The Return of the Native: American Indian Political Resurgence.* New York: Oxford University Press, 1988.

Costello, J. A. *The Siwash, Their Life, Legends and Tales.* Seattle: Calvert Company, 1895; reprint, Everett, Wash.: The Printers, 1974.

Curtis, Edward. *The Salishan Tribes of the Coast.* Volume 9 of *The North American Indians.* Edited by Frederick Webb Hodge. Cambridge, Mass.: Harvard University Press, 1913; reprint, New York: Johnson Reprint Corporation, 1970.

Davis, Barbara A. *Edward S. Curtis: The Life and Times of a Shadow Catcher.* San Francisco: Chronicle Books, 1985.

Deegan, Harry W. *History of Mason County, Washington.* N.p., 1957.

Dening, Greg. *Islands and Beaches: Discourse on a Silent Land, Marquesas 1774–1880.* Honolulu: University Press of Hawaii, 1980.

Denny, Arthur Armstrong. *Pioneer Days on Puget Sound.* 1888; Fairfield, Wash.: Ye Galleon Press, 1979.

Denny, Emily I. *Blazing the Way.* Seattle: Rainier Printing, 1909.

Dippie, Brian. *The Vanishing American: White Attitudes and U.S. Indian Policy.* Middletown, Conn.: Wesleyan University Press, 1982.

Dixon, Joseph Kossuth. *The Vanishing Race: The Last Great Indian Council.* Philadelphia: National American Indian Memorial Association Press, 1925.

Dodds, Gordon B. *The American Northwest: A History of Oregon and Washington.* Arlington Heights, Ill.: Forum Press, 1986.

Eastman, Charles A. *The Indian To-day.* Garden City, N.Y.: Doubleday Page, 1915.
————. *The Soul of the Indian.* Boston: Houghton Mifflin, 1911.
Eckrom, Jerry A. *Remembered Drums: A History of the Puget Sound Indian War.* Walla Walla, Wash.: Pioneer Press Books, 1989.
Eells, Myron. *The Indians of Puget Sound: The Notebooks of Myron Eells.* Edited by Pierre Castile. Seattle: University of Washington Press, 1985.
————. *Ten Years of Missionary Work among the Indians at Skokomish, Washington Territory, 1874–1884.* Boston: Congregational Sunday-School and Publishing Society, 1886.
Elmendorf, William W. *The Structure of Twana Culture.* Monographic Supplement No. 2 of *Research Studies, a Quarterly Publication of Washington State University,* vol. 28, 1960; reprint, Pullman: Washington State University Press, 1992.
————. *Twana Narratives: Native Historical Accounts of a Coast Salish Culture.* Seattle and Vancouver: University of Washington Press and University of British Columbia Press, 1993.
Emmons, Della Gould. *Leschi of the Nisquallies.* Minneapolis: T. S. Denison, 1965.
Evans, Elwood, and Edmond Meany. *The State of Washington: A Brief History.* Tacoma, Wash.: Tacoma Daily News, 1893.
Ficken, Robert E. *The Forested Land: A History of Lumbering in Western Washington.* Seattle: University of Washington Press, 1987.
Ficken, Robert E., and Charles P. LeWarne. *Washington: A Centennial History.* Seattle: University of Washington Press, 1988.
Fisher, Robin. *Contact and Conflict: Indian-European Relations in British Columbia, 1774–1890.* Vancouver: University of British Columbia Press, 1977.
Fixico, Donald L. *Termination and Relocation: Federal Indian Policy, 1945–1960.* Albuquerque: University of New Mexico Press, 1986.
Foster, Morris W. *Being Comanche: A Social History of an American Indian Community.* Tucson: University of Arizona Press, 1991.
Foucault, Michel. *Discipline and Punish: The Birth of the Prison.* New York: Vintage Books, 1979.
————. *Power/Knowledge: Selected Interviews and Other Writings by Michel Foucault, 1972–1977.* Edited by Gordon Colin. New York: Pantheon Books, 1980.
Fowler, Loretta. *Shared Symbols, Contested Meanings: Gros Ventre Culture and History, 1778–1984.* Ithaca, N.Y.: Cornell University Press, 1987.
Gates, Charles H. *Messages of the Governors of the Territory of Washington to the Legislative Assembly, 1854–1889.* Seattle: University of Washington Publications in the Social Sciences, 1940.
Gibbs, George. *Dictionary of the Chinook Jargon, or, Trade Language of Oregon.* New York: Cramoisy Press, 1863; reprint, New York: AMS Press, 1970.
————. *Indian Tribes of Washington Territory.* House Exec. Doc. 91, 33rd Cong., 2d sess., 1854; reprint, Fairfield, Wash.: Ye Galleon Press, 1967.
Giddens, Anthony. *The Nation-State and Violence.* Berkeley and Los Angeles: University of California Press, 1985.

Goetzmann, William H. *New Lands, New Men: America and the Second Great Age of Discovery.* New York: Viking, 1986.

Gossett, Thomas F. *Race: The History of an Idea in America.* Dallas: Southern Methodist University Press, 1963.

Graham, Richard, editor. *The Idea of Race in Latin America, 1870–1940.* Austin: University of Texas Press, 1990.

Grant, Frederic James. *History of Seattle, Washington.* New York: American Publishing and Engraving, 1891.

Gregory, James. *American Exodus: The Dust Bowl Migration and Okie Culture in California.* New York: Oxford University Press, 1989.

Gudeman, Stephen. *Economics as Culture: Models and Metaphors of Livelihood.* London: Routledge & Kegan Paul, 1986.

Gutiérrez, Ramón A. *When Jesus Came, the Corn Mothers Went Away: Marriage, Sexuality, and Power in New Mexico, 1500–1846.* Stanford, Calif.: Stanford University Press, 1991.

Hale, Horatio. *A Manual of the Oregon Trade Language or "Chinook Jargon."* London: Whittaker & Company, 1890.

Hancock, Samuel. *The Narrative of Samuel Hancock, 1845–1860.* New York: McBride & Company, 1927.

Hanford, Cornelius H. *Seattle and Environs.* Chicago: Pioneer Historical Publishing Company, 1924.

Harrison, J. B. *The Latest Studies on Indian Reservations.* Philadelphia: Indian Rights Association, 1887.

Hawley, Robert Emmett. *Skqee Mus, or Pioneer Days on the Nooksack.* Edited by P. R. Jeffcott. Bellingham, Wash.: n.p., 1945.

Heath, Joseph. *Memoirs of Nisqually.* Edited by Lucille McDonald. Fairfield, Wash.: Ye Galleon Press, 1979.

Hertzberg, Hazel W. *The Search for an American Indian Identity: Modern Pan-Indian Movements.* Syracuse, N.Y.: Syracuse University Press, 1971.

Hess, Thom. *Dictionary of Puget Salish.* Seattle: University of Washington Press, 1976.

Hess, Thom, and Vi Hilbert. *Lushootseed.* Seattle: Daybreak Star Center, 1980.

Hilbert, Vi. *Haboo: Native American Stories from Puget Sound.* Seattle: University of Washington Press, 1985.

Hilbert, Vi, and Crisca Bierwert. *Ways of the Lushootseed People: Ceremonies and Traditions of Northern Puget Sound Indians.* Seattle: United Indians of All Tribes Foundation, 1980.

Horsman, Reginald. *Race and Manifest Destiny: The Origins of American Racial Anglo-Saxonism.* Cambridge, Mass.: Harvard University Press, 1981.

Hoxie, Frederick E. *A Final Promise: The Campaign to Assimilate the Indians, 1880–1920.* Lincoln: University of Nebraska Press, 1984.

Hunt, Herbert, and Floyd Kaylor. *Washington West of the Cascades,* vol. 1. Seattle: S. J. Clarke, 1917.

Hurt, R. Douglas. *Indian Agriculture in America.* Lawrence: University Press of Kansas, 1987.

Hurtado, Albert L. *Indian Survival on the California Frontier.* New Haven, Conn.: Yale University Press, 1988.

Indian Affairs Task Force. *Are You Listening, Neighbor? and The People Speak. Will You Listen?* Olympia: State of Washington, 1978.

Indian Claims Commission. *Coast Salish and Western Washington Indians.* 5 vols. New York: Garland, 1974.

Institute for Government Research. *The Problem of Indian Administration.* Washington, D.C.: Institute for Government Research, 1928.

Jacobs, Orange. *Memoirs of Orange Jacobs.* Seattle: Hanford & Lowman, 1908.

Johansen, Dorothy O., and Charles M. Gates. *Empire of the Columbia: A History of the Pacific Northwest.* New York: Harper & Brothers, 1957.

Jorgenson, Joseph G. *Salish Language and Culture.* Bloomington: Indiana University Press, 1969.

Judson, Katherine Berry. *Myths and Legends of the Pacific Northwest (Especially of Washington and Oregon).* 2d ed. Chicago: A. C. McClurg, 1912.

Judson, Phoebe Goodell. *A Pioneer's Search for an Ideal Home.* Bellingham, Wash.: Union Printing, 1925; reprint, Lincoln: University of Nebraska Press, 1984.

Kan, Sergei. *Symbolic Immortality: The Tlingit Potlatch in the 19th Century.* Washington, D.C.: Smithsonian Institution Press, 1989.

Kane, Paul. *Wanderings of an Artist among the Indians of North America from Canada to Vancouver's Island and Oregon through the Hudson's Bay Company's Territory and Back Again.* 1859; reprint, Toronto: Radisson Society, 1925.

Keyes, Erasmus D. *Fighting Indians in Washington Territory.* Originally *Fifty Years' Observation of Men and Events.* New York: Scribner, 1884; reprint, Fairfield, Wash.: Ye Galleon Press, 1988.

Kitsap County Historical Society Book Committee. *Kitsap County History: A Story of Kitsap County and Its Pioneers.* Seattle: Dinner & Klein, 1977.

Kochman, Thomas. *Black and White Styles in Conflict.* Chicago: University of Chicago Press, 1981.

Lambert, Mary Ann [Vincent]. *Dungeness Massacre and Other Regional Tales.* N.p., 1961.

Lansing, Ronald B. *Juggernaut: The Whitman Massacre Trial, 1850.* San Francisco: Ninth Judicial Circuit Historical Society, 1993.

Lears, T. J. Jackson. *No Place of Grace: Anti-Modernism and the Transformation of American Culture, 1880–1920.* New York: Pantheon, 1981.

Leighton, Caroline. *Life at Puget Sound, with Sketches of Travel in Washington Territory, British Columbia, Oregon, and California, 1865–1881.* Boston: Lee and Shepard, 1884.

Leupp, Francis Ellington. *The Indian and His Problem.* New York: Scribner, 1910.

Lewis, Claudia. *Indian Families of the Northwest Coast.* Chicago: University of Chicago Press, 1970.

Lopez, Ian F. Haney. *White by Law: The Legal Construction of Race.* New York: New York University Press, 1996.

Lowitt, Richard. *The New Deal and the West.* Bloomington: Indiana University Press, 1984.

Lummi History Record Center. *Nooh-whLummi, A Brief History of the Lummi.* N.p., 1974.

Marriott, Elsie Frankland. *Bainbridge through Bifocals.* Seattle: Gateway Printing Company, 1941.

MacDonald, Betty. *The Egg and I.* Philadelphia: Lippincott, 1945.

McCurdy, James G. *By Juan de Fuca's Strait; Pioneering along the Northwestern Edge of the Continent.* Portland, Ore.: Metropolitan Press, 1937.

McLoughlin, John. *Letters of Dr. John McLoughlin Written at Fort Vancouver.* Edited by Burt Brown Parker. Portland, Ore.: Binfords & Mort for Oregon Historical Society, 1948.

———. *McLoughlin's Fort Vancouver Letters, 1825–1848.* Edited by E. E. Rich. London: Champlain Society for Hudson's Bay Company Society, 1941.

McNickle, D'Arcy. *Native American Tribalism: Indian Survivals and Renewals.* New York: Oxford University Press, 1973.

Meany, Edmond. *History of the State of Washington.* New York: Macmillan, 1909.

Meeker, Ezra. *Pioneer Reminiscences of Puget Sound and The Tragedy of Leschi.* Seattle: Lowman & Hanford, 1905.

Merrell, James. *The Indians' New World: Catawbas and Their Neighbors from European Contact through the Era of Removal.* New York: Norton, 1989.

Miles, Charles, and O. B. Sperlin, eds. *Building a State, 1889–1939.* Tacoma: Washington State Historical Society, 1940.

Mitchell, Lee Clark. *Witnesses to a Vanishing America: The Nineteenth-Century Response.* Princeton, N.J.: Princeton University Press, 1981.

Modell, John. *The Economics and Politics of Racial Accommodation: The Japanese of Los Angeles.* Urbana: University of Illinois Press, 1977.

Morgan, Murray. *Skid Road: An Informal History of Seattle.* New York: Viking, 1951.

Mörner, Magnus. *Race Mixture in the History of Latin America.* New York: Little, Brown, 1967.

Murray, David. *Forked Tongues: Speech, Writing, and Representation in North American Indian Texts.* London: Pinter, 1991.

Nagel, Joane. *American Indian Ethnic Renewal: Red Power and the Resurgence of Identity and Culture.* New York: Oxford University Press, 1996.

Nash, Manning. *The Cauldron of Ethnicity in the Modern World.* Chicago: University of Chicago Press, 1989.

Noel, Patricia Slettvet. *Muckleshoot Indian History.* Auburn, Wash.: Auburn School District No. 408, 1980.

Nugent, Ann, ed. *Lummi Elders Speak.* Lynden, Wash.: Lynden Tribune, 1982.

Olsen, Susan, and Mary Randlett. *An Illustrated History of Mason County.* Shelton, Wash.: Mason County Senior Center, 1978.

Persons, Stow. *American Minds: A History of Ideas.* Malabar, Fla.: Robert E. Krieger, 1983.

Peterson, Jacqueline, and Jennifer S. H. Brown. *The New Peoples: Being and Becoming Métis in North America*. Lincoln: University of Nebraska Press, 1985.

Peterson, Nicolas, and Toshio Matsuyama, eds. *Cash, Commoditisation and Changing Foragers*. Osaka, Japan: National Museum of Ethnology, Senri Ethnological Studies, 1991.

Phillips, W. S. *The Chinook Book*. Seattle: R. L. Davis Printing, 1913.

Philp, Kenneth R. *John Collier's Crusade for Indian Reform, 1920–1934*. Tucson: University of Arizona Press, 1977.

Polenberg, Richard. *One Nation Divisible: Class, Race, and Ethnicity in the United States since 1938*. New York: Penguin Books, 1980.

Pomeroy, Earl. *The Pacific Slope: A History of California, Oregon, Washington, Idaho, Utah, and Nevada*. New York: Knopf, 1965.

Powell, Fred Wilbur, ed. *Hall J. Kelley on Oregon*. Princeton, N.J.: Princeton University Press, 1932; reprint, New York: Da Capo Press, 1972.

Prosch, Charles. *Reminiscences of Washington Territory*. Seattle: n.p., 1904.

Prosser, William F. *A History of the Puget Sound Country*. New York: n.p., 1908.

Prucha, Francis Paul. *The Great Father*. Lincoln: University of Nebraska Press, 1984.

Rawls, James J. *Indians of California: The Changing Image*. Norman: University of Oklahoma Press, 1984.

Ray, Arthur J. *Indians in the Fur Trade: Their Role as Trappers, Hunters, and Middlemen in the Lands Southwest of Hudson Bay, 1660–1870*. Toronto: University of Toronto Press, 1974.

Reid, John Phillip. *A Law of Blood: The Primitive Law of the Cherokee Nation*. New York: New York University Press, 1970.

Rich, John A. *Seattle's Unanswered Challenge*. 1947; reprint, Fairfield, Wash.: Ye Galleon Press, 1970.

Richards, Kent D. *Isaac I. Stevens, Young Man in a Hurry*. Provo, Utah: Brigham Young University Press, 1979.

Riley, Glenda. *Women and Indians on the Frontier, 1825–1915*. Albuquerque: University of New Mexico Press, 1984.

Roediger, David R. *The Wages of Whiteness: Race and the Making of the American Working Class*. London: Verso, 1991.

———, ed. *Towards the Abolition of Whiteness: Essays on Race, Politics, and Working Class History*. London: Verso, 1994.

Roosens, Eugeen E. *Creating Ethnicity: The Process of Ethnogenesis*. Newbury Park, Calif.: Sage, 1989.

Ruby, Robert H., and John A. Brown. *Myron Eells and the Puget Sound Indians*. Seattle: Superior Publishing, 1976.

Ruffner, W. H. *Report on Washington Territory*. New York: Seattle, Lakeshore & Eastern Railway, 1889.

Sahlins, Marshall. *Historical Metaphors and Mythical Realities: Structure in the Early History of the Sandwich Islands Kingdom*. Ann Arbor: University of Michigan Press, 1981.

Sampson, Martin. *Indians of Skagit County*. Mount Vernon, Wash.: Skagit County Historical Society, 1972.

Sánchez, George J. *Becoming Mexican American*. New York: Oxford University Press, 1993.

Sarris, Greg. *Keeping Slug Woman Alive: A Holistic Approach to American Texts*. Berkeley and Los Angeles: University of California Press, 1993.

Scarry, Elaine. *The Body in Pain*. New York: Oxford University Press, 1985.

Schaller, Michael, Virginia Scharff, and Robert D. Schulzinger. *Present Tense: The United States since 1945*. Boston: Houghton Mifflin, 1992.

Schiach, William Sidney, ed. *An Illustrated History of Skagit and Snohomish Counties*. Chicago: Interstate Publishing, 1906.

Scollon, Ron, and Suzanne B. K. Scollon. *Narrative, Literacy, and Face in Interethnic Communication*. Norwood, N.J.: Ablex, 1981.

Sequim Bicentennial Committee. *Dungeness: The Lure of a River*. Port Angeles, Wash.: The Daily News at Olympic Printers, 1976.

Shelton, Chief William. *The Story of the Totem Pole: Early Indian Legends as Handed Down from Generation to Generation*. Everett, Wash.: Kane & Harcus, 1935.

Shuffelton, Frank, ed. *A Mixed Race: Ethnicity in Early America*. New York: Oxford University Press, 1993.

Simmons, William S. *Spirit of the New England Tribes: Indian History and Folklore, 1620–1984*. Hanover, N.H.: University Press of New England, 1986.

Smith, Marian W. *Indians of the Urban Northwest*. Columbia University Contributions to Anthropology, 1949; reprint, New York: AMS, 1969.

———. *The Puyallup-Nisqually*. Columbia University Contributions to Anthropology, 1940; reprint, New York: AMS, 1969.

Sollors, Werner. *Beyond Ethnicity: Consent and Descent in American Culture*. New York: Oxford University Press, 1986.

Stern, Bernhard J. *The Lummi Indians of Northwest Washington*. New York: Columbia University Press, 1934.

Stuart, Paul. *The Indian Office: Growth and Development of an American Institution, 1865–1900*. Ann Arbor, Mich.: University Microfilms International, 1978.

Suquamish Museum. *The Eyes of Chief Seattle*. Suquamish, Wash.: Suquamish Indian Tribe, 1985.

Suttles, Wayne. *Coast Salish Essays*. Seattle: University of Washington Press, 1987.

Swan, James G. *The Northwest Coast: or Three Years Residence in Washington Territory*. New York: Harper, 1857; reprint, Seattle: University of Washington Press, 1972.

Taussig, Michael. *Mimesis and Alterity*. New York: Routledge, 1993.

Taylor, Graham D. *The New Deal and American Indian Tribalism*. Lincoln: University of Nebraska Press, 1980.

Thomas, Edward Harper. *Chinook: A History and Dictionary of the Northwest Coast Trade Jargon*. Portland, Ore.: Metropolitan Press, 1935.

Thwaites, Reuben Gold, ed. *Original Journals of the Lewis and Clark Expedition, 1804–1806*, vol. 3. New York: Dodd, Mead, 1905.

Todorov, Tzvetan. *The Conquest of America: The Question of the Other*. New York: Harper & Row, 1984.

Tolmie, William Fraser. *The Journals of William Fraser Tolmie, Physician and Fur Trader*. Vancouver, B.C.: Mitchell Press, 1963.

Trennert, Robert A. *Alternative to Extinction: Federal Indian Policy and the Beginnings of the Reservation System, 1846–51*. Philadelphia: Temple University Press, 1975.

Ulin, Robert C. *Understanding Cultures*. Austin: University of Texas Press, 1984.

Underhill, Ruth M. *Indians of the Pacific Northwest*. Riverside, Calif.: Sherman Institute Press, 1945; reprint, New York: AMS, 1978.

Usner, Daniel H., Jr. *Indians, Settlers, and Slaves in a Frontier Exchange Economy: The Lower Mississippi Valley before 1783*. Chapel Hill: University of North Carolina Press, 1992.

Vancouver, George. *A Voyage of Discovery to the North Pacific Ocean and Round the World, 1791–1795*, vol. 2. Edited by W. Kaye Lamb. London: Hakluyt Society, 1984.

Van Kirk, Sylvia. *Many Tender Ties: Women in Fur-Trade Society, 1670–1870*. Norman: University of Oklahoma Press, 1980.

Vincent, Mary Ann Lambert. *House of the Seven Brothers: A Genealogical Story of Olympic Peninsula Indians*. N.p., 1960.

Wagner, Roy. *The Invention of Culture*. Chicago: University of Chicago Press, 1981.

Welsh, Herbert. *How to Bring the Indian to Citizenship and Citizenship to the Indian*. Philadelphia: Indian Rights Association, 1892.

White, Richard. *Land Use, Environment, and Social Change: The Shaping of Island County, Washington*. Seattle: University of Washington Press, 1980.

———. *The Middle Ground: Indians, Empires, and Republics in the Great Lakes Region, 1650–1815*. Cambridge: Cambridge University Press, 1991.

———. *The Roots of Dependency: Subsistence, Environment, and Social Change among the Choctaws, Pawnees, and Navajos*. Lincoln: University of Nebraska Press, 1983.

White, Sid, and S. E. Solberg, eds. *Peoples of Washington: Perspectives on Cultural Diversity*. Pullman: Washington State University Press, 1989.

Wilkes, Charles. *Diary of Wilkes in the Northwest*. Edited by Edmond S. Meany. *Washington Historical Quarterly*, 1925–1926; reprint, Seattle: University of Washington Press, 1926.

———. *Narrative of the United States Exploring Expedition during the Years 1838, 1839, 1840, 1841, 1842*. 5 vols. London: Ingram, Cooke, 1852.

Winant, Howard. *Racial Conditions: Politics, Theory, Comparisons*. Minneapolis: University of Minnesota Press, 1994.

Winthrop, Theodore. *The Canoe and Saddle, or Klalam and Klickatat*. Edited by John H. Williams. Tacoma, Wash.: John H. Williams, 1913.

Wolf, Eric R. *Europe and the People without History.* Berkeley and Los Angeles: University of California Press, 1982.

Works Progress Administration. *Told by the Pioneers.* 3 vols. Edited by F. I. Trotter, F. H. Loutzenhiser, and J. R. Loutzenhizer. Olympia: Washington Pioneers Project, 1937.

Wright, J. Leitch, Jr. *Creeks and Seminoles: The Destruction and Regeneration of the Muscogulge People.* Lincoln: University of Nebraska Press, 1986.

ARTICLES AND PAMPHLETS

Adams, John W. "Recent Ethnology of the Northwest Coast." *Annual Review of Anthropology* 10 (1981), 361–392.

Allen, Barbara. "Shaping History: The Creation of a Collective Pioneer Experience." *Columbia* 7, no. 4 (Winter 1993/94), 6–13.

Allen, E. J., Jr. "Intergroup Ties and Exogamy among the Northwest Coast Salish." *Northwest Anthropological Research Notes* 10 (1976), 161–172.

Amoss, Pamela. "The Power of Secrecy among the Coast Salish." In *The Anthropology of Power,* edited by Raymond D. Fogelson and Richard N. Adams, 131–140. New York: Academic Press, 1977.

Anderson, Bern, ed. "The Vancouver Expedition: Peter Puget's Journal of the Exploration of Puget Sound, May 7–June 11, 1792." *Pacific Northwest Quarterly* 30 (April 1939), 177–217.

Anonymous. "Skokomish Potlatch." *Overland Monthly* 19 (May 1892), 461.

Bagley, Clarence. "Chief Seattle and Angeline." *Washington Historical Quarterly* 22 (October 1931), 243–275.

———. "Traditions of Vancouver's Appearance." In *Indian Myths of the Northwest,* 102–3. Seattle: Lowman & Hanford, 1930.

———, ed. "Journal of Occurrences at Nisqually House." *Washington Historical Quarterly* 6 (1915), 179–197, 264–278, and *Washington Historical Quarterly* 7 (1916), 144–168.

Bahr, Howard M., Bruce A. Chadwick, and Joseph H. Stauss. "Discrimination against Urban Indians in Seattle." *Indian Historian* 5 (Winter 1972), 4–11.

Ballard, Arthur C. "Mythology of Southern Puget Sound." *University of Washington Publications in Anthropology* 3 (1929), 31–150.

———. "Some Tales of the Southern Puget Sound Salish." *University of Washington Publications in Anthropology* 2 (1927), 35–41,57–81.

Bannan, Helen M. "The Idea of Civilization and American Indian Policy Reformers in the 1880s." *Journal of American Culture* 1 (Winter 1978), 787–799.

Barry, J. Neilson, ed. "Broughton's Reconnaissance of the San Juan Islands in 1792." *Washington Historical Quarterly* 21 (1930), 55–60.

Barsh, Russel Lawrence. "American Indians in the Great War." *Ethnohistory* 38 (1991), 276–303.

———. "Backfire from Boldt: The Judicial Transformation of Coast Salish Proprietary Fisheries into a Commons." *Western Legal History* 4 (1991), 85–102.

———. "Puget Sound Indian Demography, 1900–1920: Migration and Economic Integration." *Ethnohistory* 43 (Winter 1996), 65–97.

Bennett, L. A. "Effects of White Contact on the Lower Skagit Indians." *Washington Archaeological Society Occasional Papers* 3 (1972).

Bishop, Thomas G. "An Appeal to the Government to Fulfill Sacred Promises Made 61 Years Ago." 1915. University of Washington Library, Special Collections.

Blanchet, Francis N. "Pronouncing Dictionary and Jargon Vocabulary to Which Is Added Numerous Conversations Enabling Any Person to Speak the Chinook Jargon." Portland, Ore.: S. J. M'Cormick, Franklin Book Store, 1853; reprinted as Appendix of *Paul Kane, The Columbia Wanderer*, ed. Thomas Vaughan. Portland, Ore.: Oregon Historical Society, 1971.

Boit, John. "John Boit's Log of the Columbia—1790–1793." *Oregon Historical Quarterly* 22 (1921), 257–356.

Boxberger, Daniel L. "In and Out of the Labor Force: The Lummi Indians and the Development of the Commercial Salmon Fishery of North Puget Sound, 1880–1900." *Ethnohistory* 35 (1988), 161–190.

———. "The Introduction of Horses to the Southern Puget Sound Salish." In *Western Washington Indian Socio-Economics: Papers in Honor of Angelo Anastasio*, edited by Herbert C. Taylor, Jr., and Garland F. Grabert, 103–119. Bellingham: Western Washington University, 1984.

Boyd, Robert T. "Demographic History, 1774–1874: Northwest Coast." In *Handbook of North American Indians*, vol. 7, 135–148. Washington, D.C.: Smithsonian Institution, 1990.

Brooks, James F. "'This Evil Extends Especially . . . to the Feminine Sex': Negotiating Captivity in the New Mexico Borderlands." *Feminist Studies* 22 (Summer 1996), 279–309.

Buchanan, Charles M. "The Evolution of an Indian Hero in France." *Washington Historical Quarterly* 9 (1918), 163–168.

———. "The Indian: His Origin and Legendary Lore." *Overland Monthly* 36 (1900), 114–122.

———. "Rights of the Puget Sound Indians to Game and Fish." *Washington Historical Quarterly* 6 (1915), 109–118.

Carpenter, Cecilia Svinth. "Leschi, Last Chief of the Nisquallies." *Pacific Northwest Forum* 1, no. 1 (January 1976); reprint, 1986.

Castile, George P. "The 'Half-Catholic' Movement: Edwin and Myron Eells and the Rise of the Indian Shaker Church." *Pacific Northwest Quarterly* 73 (1982), 165–174.

Chadwick, Bruce A., and Joseph H. Stauss. "The Assimilation of American Indians into Urban Society: The Seattle Case." *Human Organization* 34 (Winter 1975), 359–369.

Chance, David K. "Influences of Hudson's Bay Company on the Native Cultures of the Colvile District." *Northwest Anthropological Research Notes* 7 (1973).

Coan, C. F. "The Adoption of the Reserve Policy in the Pacific Northwest, 1849–1855." *Quarterly of the Oregon Historical Society* 23 (1922), 1–38.

Collins, June McCormick. "Growth of Class Distinctions and Political Authority among the Skagit Indians during the Contact Period." *American Anthropologist* 52 (1950), 331–342.

———. "The Indian Shaker Church." *Southwestern Journal of Anthropology* 6 (1950), 399–411.

———. "An Interpretation of Skagit Intragroup Conflict during Acculturation." *American Anthropologist* 54 (1952), 347–355.

———. "John Fornsby: The Personal Document of a Coast Salish Indian." In *Indians of the Urban Northwest*, edited by Marian W. Smith, 287–341. New York: Columbia University Press, 1949.

———. "Multilineal Descent: A Coast Salish Strategy." In *Currents in Anthropology*, edited by Robert Hinshaw, 243–254. The Hague: Mouton, 1979.

DeMallie, Raymond J. "'These Have No Ears': Narrative and the Ethnohistorical Method." *Ethnohistory* 40 (Fall 1993), 515–538.

———. "Touching the Pen: Plains Indian Treaty Councils in Ethnohistorical Perspective." In *Ethnicity on the Great Plains*, edited by Frederick C. Luebke, 38–53. Lincoln: University of Nebraska Press, 1980.

Denny, Emily Inez. "Types and Characteristics of Puget Sound Indians." *Northwest Magazine* 12 (September 1894), 4–6.

Deutsch, Sarah. "Landscape of Enclaves: Race Relations in the West, 1865–1990." In *Under an Open Sky: Rethinking America's Western Past*, edited by William Cronon, Jay Gitlin, and George Miles, 110–131. New York: Norton, 1992.

Dewhirst, John. "Coast Salish Summer Festivals: Rituals for Upgrading Social Identity." *Anthropologica* 18 (1976), 231–273.

Eells, Myron. "Census of the Clallam and Twana Indians of Washington Territory." *American Antiquarian* 6 (1884), 35–38.

———. "The Chinook Jargon." *American Anthropologist* 7 (July 1894), 300–311.

———. "The Indians of Puget Sound." *American Antiquarian* 9 (1887), 1–9, 97–104, 211–219, 271–276.

———. "Justice to the Indian." 1883. Copy from unidentified periodical, in University of Washington Library, Special Collections.

———. "The Potlatches of Puget Sound." *American Antiquarian* 5 (1883), 135–147.

———. "Traditions and History of the Puget Sound Indians." *American Antiquarian* 9 (1887), 1, 97, 211, 271.

———. "The Twana, Chemakum and Klallum Indians of Washington Territory." *Annual Report of the Smithsonian Institution for 1887* 1; reprint, Seattle: Shorey Publications, 1971.

———. "The Twana Indians of the Skokomish Reservation in Washington Territory." *U.S. Geological Survey Bulletin* 3 (1877), 57–114.

Elliott, T. C., ed. "The Journal of John Work, November and December, 1824." *Washington Historical Quarterly* 3 (1912), 198–228.

Elmendorf, William W. "An Almost Lost Culture." *Washington State Review* 2 (1958), 2–6.

———. "Coast Salish Concepts of Power: Verbal and Functional Categories." In *The Tsimshian and Their Neighbors of the North Pacific Coast,* edited by Jay Miller and Carol M. Eastman, 281–291. Seattle: University of Washington Press, 1984.

———. "Coast Salish Status Ranking and Intergroup Ties." *Southwestern Journal of Anthropology* 27 (1971), 353–380.

———. "Skokomish and Other Coast Salish Tales." *Research Studies: A Quarterly Publication of Washington State University* 29, nos. 1–3 (1961).

———. "Skokomish Sorcery, Ethics, and Society." In *Systems of North American Witchcraft and Sorcery,* edited by Deward E. Walker, Jr., 147–182. Moscow: University of Idaho Press, 1970.

Ermatinger. F. "Earliest Expedition against Puget Sound Indians." Edited by Eva Emery Dye. *Washington Historical Quarterly* 1 (1907), 16–29.

Farrar, Victor J., ed. "Diary of Colonel and Mrs. I. N. Ebey." *Washington Historical Quarterly* 7 (1916), 307–341, and 8 (1917), 40–62, 124–152.

———. "The Nisqually Journal." *Washington Historical Quarterly,* vol. 10 (1919), 205–230; vol. 11 (1920), 59–65, 136–149, 218–229, 294–302; vol. 12 (1921), 68–70, 137–148, 219–228, 300–303; vol. 13 (1922), 57–60, 131–141, 225–232, 293–299; vol. 14 (1923), 145–148, 223–234, 299–306; vol. 15 (1924), 63–66, 215–226, 289–298.

Ferguson, R. Brian, and Neil L. Whitehead. "The Violent Edge of Empire." In *War in the Tribal Zone: Expanding States and Indigenous Warfare,* edited by R. Brian Ferguson and Neil L. Whitehead, 13–14. Santa Fe, N.M.: School of American Research Press, 1992.

Ferndale Record. "A Look at the Lummis." Reprint, Bellingham, Wash.: Goliard, 1972.

Findlay, John M. "An Elusive Institution: The Birth of Indian Reservations in Gold Rush California." In *State and Reservation,* edited by George P. Castile and Robert L. Bee, 13–37. Tucson: University of Arizona Press, 1992.

Folsom, Lucius Grant. "An Hour with a Queen." *Overland Monthly* 61 (1913), 502–504.

Friedman, Lawrence. "The Development of American Criminal Law." In *Law and Order in American History,* edited by Joseph M. Hawes, 6–24. Port Washington, N.Y.: Kennikat Press, 1979.

Galbraith, John S. "The Early History of the Puget's Sound Agricultural Company 1838–1843." *Oregon Historical Quarterly* 55 (1954), 234–259.

Galloway, Brent D. "A Phonology, Morphology, and Classified Word List for the Samish Dialect of Straits Salish." Canadian Museum of Civilization, *Canadian Ethnology Service Mercury Series,* Paper No. 116, 1990.

Gates, Charles M. "The Indian Treaty of Point No Point." *Pacific Northwest Quarterly* 41 (1955), 52–58.

Geertz, Clifford. "The Integrative Revolution: Primordial Sentiments and Civil Politics in the New States." In *Old Societies and New States: The*

Quest for Modernity in Asia and Africa, edited by Clifford Geertz, 105–157. New York: Free Press, 1963.

Gibbs, George. "Tribes of Western Washington and Northwestern Oregon." *Contributions to North American Ethnology* 1 (1877), 157–361.

Gosnell, W. B. "Indian War in Washington Territory." *Washington Historical Quarterly* 17 (1926), 289–299.

Guilmet, George M., Robert T. Boyd, David L. Whited, and Nile Thompson. "The Legacy of Introduced Disease: The Southern Coast Salish." *American Indian Culture and Research Journal* 15 (1991), 1–32.

Gunther, Erna. "An Analysis of the First Salmon Ceremony." *American Anthropologist* 28 (1926), 605–617.

———. "A Further Analysis of the First Salmon Ceremony." *University of Washington Publications in Anthropology* 2 (1928), 133–173.

———. "The Indian Background of Washington History." *Pacific Northwest Quarterly* 41 (1950), 189–202.

———. "Klallam Ethnography." *University of Washington Publications in Anthropology* 1, no. 5 (1927), 171–314.

———. "Klallam Folk Tales." *University of Washington Publications in Anthropology* 1 (August 1925), 113–170.

———. "Vancouver and the Indians of Puget Sound." *Pacific Northwest Quarterly* 51 (1960), 1–12.

Haeberlin, Hermann. "Mythology of Puget Sound." *Journal of American Folklore* 37 (1924), 371–438.

Haeberlin, Hermann K., and Erna Gunther. "The Indians of Puget Sound." *University of Washington Publications in Anthropology* 4, no. 1 (1930).

Hagan, Thomas. "Full Blood, Mixed Blood, Generic, and Ersatz, the Persisting Problem of Indian Identity." *Arizona and the West* 28 (1986), 309–326.

Hale, Horatio. "Ethnography and Philology." In *United States Exploring Expedition, 1839–1842,* 635–650. Philadelphia: Lea & Blanchard, 1846.

———. "Hale's Indians of North-west America." In *Transactions of the American Ethnological Society,* vol. 2. New York: Bartlett & Welford, 1848.

Hall, F. S. "The Vanishing Race." *Seattle Woman* 2, no. 1 (1924), 12.

Harkin, Michael. "Power and Progress: The Evangelic Dialogue among the Heiltsuk." *Ethnohistory* 40 (1993), 1–33.

Harmon, Alexandra. "Lines in Sand: Shifting Boundaries between Indians and Non-Indians in the Puget Sound Region." *Western Historical Quarterly* 26 (Winter 1995), 428–453.

———. "When Is an Indian Not an Indian? The 'Friends of the Indian' and the Problems of Indian Identity." *Journal of Ethnic Studies* 18 (Summer 1990), 95–123.

Hayner, Norman, and Una Hayner. "Three Generations of Pacific Northwest Indians." *American Sociological Review* 8 (1943), 650–656.

Herberg, Ruth. "Princess Angeline, Pawn of Two Worlds." *Frontier Times Magazine* 49, no. 5 (1975), 55–56.

Howay, F. W. "The Introduction of Intoxicating Liquors amongst the Indians of the Northwest Coast," *British Columbia Historical Quarterly* 6 (1942), 157–169.

Hudson's Bay Company. "Documents." *Washington Historical Quarterly* 1 (1907), 256–266, and 2 (1908), 161–168.

Jacobs, Melville. "Texts in Chinook Jargon." *University of Washington Publications in Anthropology* 7 (1936), 1–27.

Jenness, Diamond. "The Faith of a Coast Salish Indian." *Anthropology in British Columbia*, Memoir 3 (1955).

Josephy, Alvin M., Jr. "Modern America and the Indian." In *Indians in American History*, edited by Frederick E. Hoxie, 251–272. Arlington Heights, Ill.: Harlan Davidson, 1988.

Kaiser, Rudolf. "Chief Seattle's Speech(es): American Origins and European Reception." In *Recovering the Word: Essays on Native American Literature*, edited by Brian Swann and Arnold Krupat, 497–536. Berkeley and Los Angeles: University of California Press, 1987.

Kautz, Frances, ed. "Extracts from the Diary of Gen. A. V. Kautz." *Washington Historian* 1 (1900), 115–119, and 2 (1900), 12–15.

Kellogg, George Albert. "A History of Whidbey's Island." Weekly columns published in *Island County Farm Bureau News*, 1933–34; in scrapbook in University of Washington Library, Special Collections.

Kelly, Lawrence C. "The Indian Reorganization Act: The Dream and the Reality." *Pacific Historical Review* 44 (1975), 291–312.

———. "John Collier and the Indian New Deal: An Assessment." In *Indian-White Relations: A Persistent Paradox*, edited by Jane F. Smith and Robert M. Kvasnicka, 227–241. Washington, D.C.: Howard University Press, 1981.

Keyes, Charles. "The Dialectics of Ethnic Change." In *Ethnic Change*, edited by Charles Keyes, 4–31. Seattle: University of Washington Press, 1981.

Langness, L. L. "Individual Psychology and Cultural Change: An Ethnohistorical Case from the Klallam." In *The Tsimshian and Their Neighbors of the North Pacific Coast*, edited by Jay Miller and Carol M. Eastman, 255–280. Seattle: University of Washington Press, 1984.

Leechman, John D. "Bibliography of the Anthropology of the Puget Sound Indians." *Washington Historical Quarterly* 11 (1920), 266–273.

Leupp, F. E. "Outlines of an Indian Policy." *Outlook* 79 (1905), 946.

Linger, Daniel T. "The Hegemony of Discontent." *American Ethnologist* 20 (1993), 3–24.

Lomawaima, K. Tsianina. "Domesticity in the Federal Indian Schools: The Power of Authority over Mind and Body." *American Ethnologist* 20 (1993), 227–240.

Lotzgesell, Mrs. George. "Pioneer Days at Old Dungeness." *Washington Historical Quarterly* 24 (1933), 264–270.

Marino, Cesare. "History of Western Washington since 1846." In *Handbook of North American Indians*, vol. 7, edited by William C. Sturtevant, 169–179. Washington, D.C.: Smithsonian Institution, 1990.

McBride, Delbert J. "Viewpoints and Visions in 1792." *Columbia* 4, no. 2 (Summer 1990), 21–27.

Meany, Edmond S. "Chief Patkanim." *Washington Historical Quarterly* 15 (1924), 187–198.

Meeker, Ezra. "Uncle Ezra's Short Stories for Children." Tacoma, Wash., n.d. In University of Washington Library.

Meyer, Melissa L. "Signatures and Thumbprints: Ethnicity among the White Earth Anishinaabeg, 1889–1920." *Social Science History* 14 (1990), 305–345.

Miller, Bruce G. "Centrality 'and Measures of Regional Structure in Aboriginal Western Washington." *Ethnology* 28 (1989), 265–276.

Miller, Bruce G., and Daniel L. Boxberger. "Creating Chiefdoms: The Puget Sound Case." *Ethnohistory* 41 (Spring 1994), 267–293.

Mills, Sid. "A Choice of Allegiance." In *Chronicles of American Indian Protest*, edited by the Council on Interracial Books for Children, 290–295. Greenwich, Conn.: Fawcett Publications, 1971.

Milner, Clyde A., II. "The Shared Memory of Montana Pioneers." *Montana* 37 (1987), 4–7.

Mooney, Kathleen. "Social Distance and Exchange: The Coast Salish Case." *Ethnology* 15 (1976), 323–346.

Myerhoff, Barbara. "'Life Not Death in Venice': Its Second Life." In *The Anthropology of Experience*, edited by Victor W. Turner and Edward M. Bruner, 261–286. Urbana: University of Illinois Press, 1986.

Nugent, Ann. "Regulation of the Lummi Indians by Government Officials between 1900–1920." Lummi Communications, 1979. In University of Washington Library, Special Collections.

O'Brien, Sharon. "Tribes and Indians: With Whom Does the United States Maintain a Relationship?" *Notre Dame Law Review* 66 (1991), 1461–1494.

Onat, Astrida. "The Interaction of Kin, Class, Marriage, Property Ownership and Residences with Respect to Resource Locations among the Coast Salish of the Puget Sound Lowland." *Northwest Anthropological Research Notes* 18 (1984), 86–96.

Palmié, Stephan. "Spics or Spades? Racial Classification and Ethnic Conflict in Miami." *Amerikastudien/American Studies* 34 (1989), 211–221.

Parman, Donald L. "Inconstant Advocacy: The Erosion of Indian Fishing Rights in the Pacific Northwest, 1933–1956." *Pacific Historical Review* 53 (1984), 163–189.

———. "The Indian and the Civilian Conservation Corps." *Pacific Historical Review* 40 (February 1971), 39–56.

Pascoe, Peggy. "Miscegenation Law, Court Cases, and Ideologies of 'Race' in Twentieth-Century America." *Journal of American History* 83 (June 1996), 44–70.

———. "Race, Gender, and Intercultural Relations: The Case of Interracial Marriage." *Frontiers* 12 (1991), 5–18.

Pearsall, Marion. "Contributions of Early Explorers and Traders to Northwest Ethnography." *Pacific Northwest Quarterly* 40 (1949), 316–326.

Phelps, Thomas Stowell. "The Indian Attack on Seattle January 26, 1855." Originally "Reminiscences of Seattle, Washington Territory," in *United Service Magazine* 5, no. 6 (1881); reprint, Seattle: Farwest Lithograph & Printing, 1932.

Pierce County Pioneer Association. "Commemorative Celebration at Sequalitchew Lake." 1906. In University of Washington Library.

Polanyi, Karl. "Our Obsolete Market Mentality." In *Primitive, Archaic, and Modern Economies*, edited by George Dalton, 26–37. Garden City, N.Y.: Anchor Books, 1968.

Porter, Frank W., III. "Without Reservation: Federal Indian Policy and the Landless Tribes of Washington." In *State and Reservation*, edited by George P. Castile and Robert L. Bee, 110–135. Tucson: University of Arizona Press, 1992.

Prosch, Thomas W. "The Indian Wars in Washington Territory." *Quarterly of the Oregon Historical Society* 16 (1915), 1–23.

Quimby, Lida W. "Indian Education." *The State* 5 (March 1900), 79–81.

———. "Puget Sound Indian Shakers." *The State* 7 (January 1902), 188–189.

Reagan, Albert B. "The Shaker Church of the Indians." *Alaska-Yukon Magazine* 5 (1908), 82–86.

Rich, E. E. "Trade Habits and Economic Motivations among the Indians of North America." *Canadian Journal of Economics and Political Science* 26 (1960), 35–53.

Roberts, Charles. "The Cushman Indian Trades School and World War I." *American Indian Quarterly* 11 (1987), 221–239.

Scott, Leslie M. "Indian Diseases as Aids to Pacific Northwest Settlement." *Oregon Historical Quarterly* 29 (1928), 144–161.

Scouler, John. "Journal of a Voyage to N.W. America." *Quarterly of the Oregon Historical Society* 6 (1905), 159–205.

Seammon, C. M. "Old Seattle and His Tribe." *Overland Monthly* 4 (April 1870), 297–302.

Shaw, B. F. "Medicine Creek Treaty." In *Proceedings of the Oregon Historical Society* (1906), Appendix C, 24–32.

Smith, Marian W. "The Coast Salish of Puget Sound." *American Anthropologist* 43 (1941), 197–211.

———. "The Cultural Development of the Northwest Coast." *Southwestern Journal of Anthropology* 12 (1956), 272–294.

———. "The Puyallup of Washington." In *Acculturation of Seven Indian Tribes*, edited by Ralph Linton, 3–36. New York: Appleton Century, 1940.

Snyder, Sally. "Quest for the Sacred in Northern Puget Sound: An Interpretation of Potlatch." *Ethnology* 14 (1975), 149–161.

Snyder, Warren A. "Southern Puget Sound Salish: Texts, Place Names and Dictionary." Sacramento Anthropological Society Paper No. 9 (Fall 1968).

Somerville, Thomas. "The Mediterranean of the Pacific." *Harper's New Monthly Magazine* 41 (1870), 481–498.

St. John, Lewis H. "The Present Status and Probable Future of the Indians of Puget Sound." *Washington Historical Quarterly* 5 (1914), 12–21.

Stevens, Hazard. "The Pioneers and Patriotism." *Pacific Northwest Quarterly* 8 (1917), 172–179.

Stevens, Isaac I. "Notes and Documents: Letters of Governor Isaac I. Stevens, 1857–1858." Edited by Ronald Todd. *Pacific Northwest Quarterly* 31 (1940), 403–459.

Strong, Thomas Nelson. "Indians of the Northwest." *Pacific Monthly* 16 (1903), 169–177.

Suttles, Wayne, "Post Contact Culture Change among the Lummi Indians." *British Columbia Historical Quarterly* 18 (1954), 29–102.

Suttles, Wayne, and Barbara Lane. "Southern Coast Salish." In *Handbook of North American Indians,* vol. 7, edited by William C. Sturtevant, 482–502. Washington, D.C.: Smithsonian Institution, 1990.

Swan, James G. "Scenes in Washington Territory." Series in *San Francisco Bulletin* (May–July 1859). Collected in University of Washington Library, Special Collections.

Swift, H. A. "Notes on Whidby Island History." Originally "Ancutty Tillicum, The Indians in the 60s," in *Island County Times.* 1913. In University of Washington Library, Special Collections.

Tollefson, Kenneth D. "Political Organization of the Duwamish." *Ethnology* 28 (1989), 135–149.

———. "The Snoqualmie: A Puget Sound Chiefdom." *Ethnology* 26 (1987), 121–136.

Trowbridge, William Petit. "Journal of a Voyage on Puget Sound in 1853." *Pacific Northwest Quarterly* 32 (1942), 391–407.

Twedell, Colin E. "A Componential Analysis of the Criteria Defining an Indian 'Tribe' in Western Washington." In *Western Washington Indian Socio-Economics: Papers in Honor of Angelo Anastasio,* edited by Herbert C. Taylor, Jr., and Garland F. Grabert, 61–80. Bellingham: Western Washington University, 1984.

Upchurch, O. C. "The Swinomish People and Their State." *Pacific Northwest Quarterly* 27 (1936), 283–310.

Vassault, F. I. "Patsy's Potlatch." *Overland Monthly* 19 (1892), 461–464.

Walker, Anna Sloan. "History of the Liquor Laws of the State of Washington." *Washington Historical Quarterly* 5 (April 1914), 116–120.

Washington Centennial Association. "1845–1945, A Washington Centennial Commemoration." 1945. University of Washington Library, Special Collections.

Waterman, T. T. "Notes on the Ethnology of the Indians of Puget Sound [1921]." Museum of the American Indian, *Indian Notes and Monographs, Miscellaneous Series* No. 59 (1973).

Weir, Allen. "Roughing It on Puget Sound in the Early Sixties." *Washington Historian* 1 (1900), 70–75, 120–124.

White, Richard. "Race Relations in the American West." *American Quarterly* 38 (1986), 396–416.

[Wickersham, James] A Boston Tillicum, Esq. "A Monograph on the Puyallup Indians of the State of Washington." 1892. In University of Washington Library, Special Collections.

Wickersham, James. "Notes on the Indians of Washington." *American Antiquarian* 21 (1899), 369–375.

———. "Nusqually Mythology, Studies of the Washington Indians." *Overland Monthly* 32 (1898), 345–351.

———. "Pueblos on the Northwest Coast." *American Antiquarian* 18 (1896), 21–24.

Wike, Joyce Annabel. "The Role of the Dead in Northwest Coast Culture." In *Indian Tribes of Aboriginal America: Selected Papers of the Twenty-ninth International Congress of Americanists,* edited by Sol Tax, 97–103. Chicago: University of Chicago Press, 1952.

Williams, Johnson. "Black Tamanous, the Secret Society of the Clallam Indians." *Washington Historical Quarterly* 7 (1916), 296–300.

Wolf, Eric R. "Facing Power—Old Insights, New Questions." *American Anthropologist* 92 (1990), 585–596.

Yesler, Henry. "The Daughter of Old Chief Seattle." *Washington Magazine* 1, no. 3 (1889), 25–27.

Zanger, Martin. "Conflicting Concepts of Justice: A Winnebago Murder Trial on the Illinois Frontier." *Journal of the Illinois Historical Society* 73 (1980), 263–276.

UNPUBLISHED MANUSCRIPTS

[Anonymous.] "Notes Copied from the Hudson's Bay Company Accounts at Fort Nisqually 1833–1850." In University of Washington Library, Special Collections.

Bagley, Clarence B. Papers. University of Washington, Manuscripts, Box 22.

Bancroft, Hubert H. Narratives of and interviews with early settlers. 1878. Originals at Bancroft Library, Berkeley, California; uncataloged microfilm copies at University of Washington, cited as Bancroft collection.

Bannan, Helen Marie. "Reformers and the 'Indian Problem,' 1878–1887 and 1922–1934." Ph.D. dissertation, Syracuse University, 1976.

Barsh, Russel. "Census Data for the Snohomish Tribe of Indians." Appendix V of Petition of the Snohomish Tribe of Indians for Federal Acknowledgment. 1980.

Barsh, Russel. Data and analysis based on U.S. Census, Western Washington, 1900. Copy furnished by author.

Blaine Family Papers, 1848–1862. University of Washington Library, Manuscripts.

Boxberger, Daniel L. "The Ethnohistory of Western Washington Indians in the Nineteenth Century, with Reference to Shellfish Use and Control." May 1993. From records of Evergreen Legal Services, Seattle.

Brown Family Papers, 1861. Washington State Library, Manuscript 071.

Buchanan, Charles M. Papers. University of Washington Library, Manuscripts, Accession No. 3907.

Campbell, John. Diary, 1869–1894. University of Washington Library, Manuscripts.

Chalcraft, Edwin. "Autobiography of Edwin Chalcraft." Washington State Library, Manuscript 039.

Chambers, Thomas McCutcheon. Papers. Washington State Historical Society.

DeShaw, William. Papers. 1852–1898. University of Washington Library, Manuscripts, Accession No. 387.

Dubuar Scrapbooks. University of Washington Library, Special Collections.

Eells, Edwin. Papers. 1841–1916. Washington State Historical Society.

Eells, Myron. "Justice to the Indian." University of Washington Library, Special Collections.

Evans, Elwood. "Puyallup Indian Reservation Lands." Speech to Tacoma Chamber of Commerce. May 17, 1892. University of Washington Library, Special Collections.

Fetzer, Paul. "George Swanaset: Narrative of a Personal Document." 1951. In Melville Jacobs Collection, University of Washington Library, Manuscripts, Accession No. 1693–71–13, Box 112.

Fitzpatrick, Darleen. "We Are Cowlitz: Traditional and Emergent Ethnicity." Ph.D. dissertation, University of Washington, 1986.

Garretson, Charles Edwin. "A History of the Washington Superintendency of Indian Affairs, 1855–1865." M.A. thesis, University of Washington, 1962.

Gibbs, George. Letters to Captain George McClellan, 1854. University of Washington Microfilm A-142.

Ginn, Edward. Papers. 1861. University of Washington Library, Manuscripts, Vertical File 31.

Gunther, Erna. Papers. University of Washington Library, Manuscripts, Accession No. 614–70–20.

Hajda, Yvonne P. "Regional Social Organization in the Greater Lower Columbia, 1792–1830." Ph.D. dissertation, University of Washington, 1984.

Hancock, Samuel. "Thirteen Years Residence on the Northwest Coast." 1860. University of Washington Library, Manuscripts, Vertical File 70.

Hansen, Jane. "Attitudes of Tulalip Indians Regarding Relations with Public Assistance Agencies." M.A. thesis, University of Washington, 1960.

Hansen, Karen T. "American Indians and Work in Seattle: Associations, Ethnicity, and Class." Ph.D. dissertation, University of Washington, 1979.

Hanson, Howard. "Chief Seattle's Great Oration." 1939. Transcript of speech to Washington State Historical Society. University of Washington Library, Special Collections.

Harrington, John Peabody. Papers at the Smithsonian Institution, 1907–1957. University of Washington Microfilm A-6952.

Harris, Ethel Van. "Early Historical Incidents of Skagit County." 1926. University of Washington Library, Special Collections.

Holm, Thomas N. "Indians and Progressives: From Vanishing Policy to the Indian New Deal." Ph.D. dissertation, University of Oklahoma, 1978.

Hop Growers' Association of Snoqualmie. Records, 1885–89. University of Washington Library, Manuscripts, Vertical File 1387.

Hubbard, Greg Russell. "The Indian under the White Man's Law in Washington Territory, 1853–1889." M.A. thesis, University of Washington, 1972.

Hudson's Bay Company. "Journal of the Hudson's Bay Company Kept at Fort Langley during the Years 1827–29." University of Washington Library Microfilm 164.

Huggins, Edward. Papers. Washington State Historical Society.

———. "A Trip to 'Alki' Point Near Duwamsh Bay...1852." 1901. University of Washington Library, Special Collections.

———. "Reminiscences of Puget Sound." Writings collected by Gary Fuller Reese for Tacoma Public Library, 1984.

———. "The Story of 'Bill' or 'Sclousin.'" 1900. University of Washington Library, Special Collections.

Indian Shaker Church Records, 1892–1945. University of Washington Library, Microfilm A-4547.

Karrigan, Roger Patrick. "A Study of the Scholastic Performance of the Indian Pupils in the Marysville (Washington) School District." M.A. thesis, University of Washington, 1961.

Kew, John Edward Michael. "Coast Salish Ceremonial Life: Status and Identity in a Modern Village." Ph.D. dissertation, University of Washington, 1970.

Lane, Barbara. "Political and Economic Aspects of Indian-White Culture Contact in Western Washington in the Mid–Nineteenth Century." Report prepared at request of United States Justice Department, May 1973.

Langness, L. L. "A Case of Post-Contact Reform among the Clallam." M.A. thesis, University of Washington, 1959.

Lokken, Roy N. "Frontier Defense in Washington Territory, 1853–1861." M.A. thesis, University of Washington, 1951.

Longtin, Mary Michelle. "The Duwamish Tribe: Evidence for the Persistence of a Duwamish Community and an Assessment of Tribal Status." M.A. thesis, University of Washington, 1980.

Louise, Sister Mary. "Eugene Casimir Chirouse." M.A. thesis, University of Washington, 1932.

Luark, Patterson. Journal, 1853–1858. Washington State Library, Manuscript 103.

Mapes, Carl Herbert. "A Map Interpretation of Population Growth and Distribution in the Puget Sound Region." Ph.D. dissertation, University of Washington, 1943.

McCormick Lumber Company Papers. University of Washington Library, Manuscripts, Accession No. 4286.

McGilvra, J.J. "Reminiscences of the Early Days of the Washington Bar." N.d. University of Washington Library, Special Collections.

Meany, Edmond S. Papers. University of Washington Library, Manuscripts, Accession No. 106–70–12.

———. "A Prophecy Fulfilled: Address to Tulalip School." 1920. University of Washington Library, Special Collections.

Meeker, Ezra. Papers. Washington State Historical Society.

Meeker Family Papers. University of Washington Library, Manuscripts, Vertical File No. 362 A-C.

Meyers, Samuel, Director. *Listening to Indians*. Oral History project of St. Louis Community College, 1974–77.

Miller, A.J., Company Papers. University of Washington Library, Manuscripts, Vertical File 94.

Native Americans of the Pacific Northwest. Photographs. University of Washington Library, Special Collections.

Northwest Intertribal Court System. "Traditional and Informal Dispute Resolution Processes in Tribes of the Puget Sound and Olympic Peninsula Region." 1991.

Norton, Helen. "The Economy and Ecology of the Snohomish Tribe of Indians 1792–1865." 1990. Records of Snohomish Tribe of Indians.

———. "The Snohomish Tribe of Indians, Their History, Ecology, Economics, Genealogy, Social and Political Relationships in the 19th and 20th Centuries." 1993. Records of Snohomish Tribe of Indians.

———. "Social, Marital, Economic and Political Relationships of the Snohomish Tribe of Indians in the Late 19th and Early 20th Centuries." 1992. Records of Snohomish Tribe of Indians.

———. "Women and Resources of the Northwest Coast: Documentation from the 18th and Early 19th Centuries." Ph.D. dissertation, University of Washington, 1985.

Pope and Talbot Company Papers, 1930–35. University of Washington Library, Manuscripts, Accession No. 1130.

Puget Sound Agricultural Company. Journal, 1835–1857. University of Washington Library, Manuscripts.

Reagan, Albert. "Some Notes on the Lummi-Nooksack Indians." 1934. University of Washington Library, Special Collections.

———. "Traditions of West Coast Indians." 1911. Washington State Library, Manuscript 219.

Reaugh, Catherine E. "Muckleshoot, Port Gamble, Puyallup, and Tulalip: Four Puget Sound Indian Communities Today." Senior thesis, University of Washington, 1970.

Reese, Gary Fuller. "A Documentary History of Fort Steilacoom, Washington." Document compilation for Tacoma Public Library, 1984.

———. "Leschi, the Officers and the Citizens." Document compilation for Tacoma Public Library, 1984.

Richards, Kent D. "Federal Indian Policy, Isaac I. Stevens, and the Western Washington Treaties." 1993. Records of Evergreen Legal Services, Seattle.

Roberts, Natalie Andrea. "A History of the Swinomish Tribal Community." Ph.D. dissertation, University of Washington, 1975.

Rygg, Lawrence. "The Continuation of Upper Class Snohomish Coast Salish Attitudes and Deportment as Seen through the Life History of a Snohomish Coast Salish Woman." M.A. thesis, Western Washington College, 1977.

Schultz, Amelia Louise. "Indian Unmarried Mothers." M.S.W. thesis, University of Washington, 1947.

Shackleford, Elizabeth. "A History of the Puyallup Indian Reservation, Tacoma." Thesis, College of Puget Sound, 1918.

Singh, Ram Raj Prasad. "Aboriginal Economic System of the Olympic Peninsula Indians, Western Washington." Ph.D. dissertation, University of Washington, 1956.

Snipp, C. Matthew. "Some Observations about Racial Boundaries and the Experiences of American Indians." Paper presented at a seminar entitled "Comparative Study of Ethnicity and Nationalism," University of Washington, April 22, 1993.

Snyder, Sally. "Skagit Society and Its Existential Basis: An Ethnofolkloristic Reconstruction." Ph.D. dissertation, University of Washington, 1964.

Swan, James G. Diaries, 1868–1887. University of Washington Library, Manuscripts.

———. Letters. University of Washington Library, Special Collections.

Tolmie, William Fraser. "History of Puget Sound and the Northwest Coast." 1878. University of Washington Library, Microfilm 190.

Waterman, T. T. "Puget Sound Geography." N.d. [ca. 1920] Copy of Smithsonian Institution Manuscript No. 1864, University of Washington Library, Special Collections.

Watt, John R. "Introduction to Economic and Labor History of Western Washington." M.A. thesis, University of Washington, 1942.

White, Richard. "The Treaty at Medicine Creek: Indian-White Relations on Upper Puget Sound, 1830–1880." M.A. thesis, University of Washington, 1972.

Wike, Joyce Annabel. "Modern Spirit Dancing of Northern Puget Sound." M.A. thesis, University of Washington, 1941.

Works Progress Administration. "Told by the Pioneers." Washington State Library Manuscripts.

NEWSPAPERS

Bellingham Herald, 1950–60

Columbian (Olympia, Washington), 1851–53

Commercial Age (Olympia), 1869–70

Daily Ledger (Tacoma), 1884–1920s

Daily Pacific Tribune (Olympia), 1871

Indians at Work, 1934–36

Patriarch, 1909–11

Pioneer and Democrat (Olympia), 1854–59

Puget Sound Weekly Courier (Olympia), 1876–82

Seattle Argus, 1899–1963

Seattle Mail and Herald, 1901–6

Seattle Post-Intelligencer, 1891–1980

Seattle Times, 1940–80

Seattle Weekly Intelligencer, 1871–73

Sunday Oregonian (Portland), 1890–1970

Tacoma Morning Union, 1896

Tacoma News Tribune, 1950–60

Territorial Republican (Olympia), 1868–69

Tulalip Bulletin, 1916–19

Washington Pioneer (Olympia), 1853–54

Washington Standard (Olympia), 1861–87

GOVERNMENT REPORTS AND DOCUMENTS

Allen, John B. "Puyallup Indian Reservation Lands." Speech in United States Senate, July 20, 1892. In University of Washington Library, Special Collections.

Alvord, B. *Indians of Puget Sound and the Straits, with Statistics of Population.* 34th Cong., 3d sess., 1857, House Exec. Doc. 76, 1–22. Serial 906.

Browne, J. Ross. *Indian War in Oregon and Washington Territories.* 35th Cong., 1st sess., 1857, House Exec. Doc. 38.

Browne, J. Ross. *Indian Affairs in the Territories of Oregon and Washington.* 35th Cong., 1st sess., 1857, House Exec. Doc. 39.

Commercial Club of Tacoma, Washington. Memorial. 52nd Cong., 1st sess., 1892, Senate Misc. Doc. 78.

Doty, James. *Journal of Operations of Governor Isaac Ingalls Stevens of Washington Territory in 1855.* 1855; reprint, Fairfield, Wash.: Ye Galleon Press, 1978.

Eliot, Samuel A. *Report upon the Conditions and Needs of the Indians of the Northwest Coast.* Washington, D.C.: Government Printing Office, 1915.

Gibbs, George. Journal, March 9–22, 1854. Records relating to Northwest Boundary Survey in Records of Boundary Claims, Commissions, and Arbitrations, 1853–1901. National Archives, Record Group 76.

Indian Agency Reports to Governor Miles C. Moore, 1889. Washington State Archives, Record Group 1/P-1.

Jones, DeL. Floyd. *Indian Affairs of the Pacific-Puget Sound.* 34th Cong., 3d sess., 1857, House Exec. Doc. 76, 4–10. Serial No. 906.

Lane, Joseph. In *Report of the Commissioner of Indian Affairs.* 31st Cong., 2d sess., 1850, Senate Exec. Doc. 1, Paper E, 156–167. Serial 587.

Mayor, Council of Tacoma, Washington. Memorial. 52nd Cong., 1st sess, 1892, Senate Misc. Doc. 73.

McClellan, George B. *Report of Exploration of a Route for the Pacific Railroad from St. Paul to Puget Sound.* 33rd Cong., 1st sess., 1854, House Exec. Doc. 129. Serial 736.

McDowell, Malcolm. *Fifty-second Annual Report of the Board of Indian Commissioners,* Appendix K. Washington, D.C.: Government Printing Office, 1921.

Pierce County Commissioners. Memorial. 52nd Cong., 1st sess., 1892, Sen. Misc. Doc. 62.

Pierce, Franklin. *Message from the President of the United States.* 34th Cong., 3d sess., 1857, Senate Exec. Doc. 41. Serial 881.

Roblin, Charles E. Schedule of Unenrolled Indians. United States Department of the Interior, Office of Indian Affairs, 1919. National Archives, Pacific Northwest Region.

Special Census of Indians Not Taxed. 1880–81. National Archives, Pacific Northwest Region, Microfilm P-2193.

Stevens, I. I., and others. *Indian Habits and Customs with Statistics and Notes on the Population.* 33rd Cong., 2d sess., 1854, Senate Exec. Doc. 1, 392–506. Serial 746.

———. *Indian Tribes, Chiefs and Missions of Puget Sound.* 33d Cong., 2d sess., 1853, Senate Exec. Doc. 78. Serial 758.

Tenth Census of the United States, Indian Division. 1880. Record Group 29, National Archives Microfilm I-34, Rolls 1 and 2.

U.S. Commission on Civil Rights. *Indian Tribes: A Continuing Quest for Survival.* Washington, D.C.: Government Printing Office, 1981.

U.S. Congress. *Indian Fishing Rights: Hearings on S.J.R. 170 and 171.* 88th Cong., 2d sess., 1964. Serial 1641–8.

———. Public Documents Regarding Indian Affairs, 1854–1906. In University of Washington Library, Special Collections.

U.S. Court of Claims. *Duwamish et al. v. United States.* University of Washington Library, Microfilm A-7374.

U.S. Department of Commerce. *State Personal Income: 1929–1982.* Washington, D.C.: Government Printing Office, 1984.

U.S. Department of the Interior. *Annual Report of the Commissioner of Indian Affairs.* Washington, D.C.: Government Printing Office, 1856–1932.

———. *Annual Reports.* Washington, D.C.: Government Printing Office, 1933–1960.

———. *Annual Reports of the Board of Indian Commissioners.* Washington, D.C.: Government Printing Office, 1918, 1921.

———. *Compendium of Eleventh Census.* 52nd Cong., 1st sess., 1890, House Misc. Doc. 340. Serial 3013.

U.S. Department of the Interior, Deputy Assistant Secretary for Indian Affairs. "Recommendation and Summary of Evidence for Proposed Finding Against Federal Acknowledgment of the Snohomish Tribe of Indians." 1983.

U.S. Department of the Interior, Office of Indian Affairs, Division of Forestry and Grazing (Edward G. Swindell, Jr.). *Report on Source, Nature and Extent of Fishing, Hunting and Miscellaneous Related Rights of Certain In-*

dian Tribes in Washington and Oregon. July 1942. University of Washington Library, Microfilm A-941.

U.S. House of Representatives. *Indians in Washington Territory.* 43d Cong., 2d sess., 1875. House Exec. Doc. 87.

U.S. House of Representatives, Committee on Indian Affairs. *Indian Tribes of Washington* (hearing on H.R. 2694). 68th Cong., 1924. H.342–4.

U.S. House of Representatives, Committee on Interior and Insular Affairs. *Washington State Indian Problems.* 83d Cong., 1953. H.Ini-T-549.

U.S. House of Representatives, Subcommittee on Indian Affairs. *Indian Tribes of Washington.* 67th Cong., 2d sess., 1922. H.320–7.

———. *Investigate Indian Affairs* (hearings on H.R. 166). 78th Cong., 2d sess., 1944. H.1051-O.

U.S. Navy. Log of the *Decatur,* July 24, 1855-October 24, 1856. University of Washington Library, Microfilm 58.

U.S. Senate. *Puyallup Indian Lands.* 50th Cong., 1st sess., 1888, Senate Exec. Doc. 274.

U.S. Senate. Committee on Commerce, Merchant Marine and Fisheries Subcommittee. *North Pacific Fisheries Problems.* 87th Cong., 1961. S.1493–1.

U.S. Senate. Committee on Commerce, with House Merchant Marine Fisheries Committee. *Northwest Salmon Fisheries Resources.* Hearings, 87th Cong., 1961, S.1493–3.

U.S. Senate, Committee on Indian Affairs. *Survey of Conditions of Indians in the United States.* Washington, D.C.: Government Printing Office, 1934.

U.S. Senate, Subcommittee on Indian Affairs. *Survey of Conditions of the Indians in the United States.* 71st Cong., 3d sess., 1931. S.545–8-A.

U.S. Senate, Subcommittee on Indian Affairs of the Committee on Interior and Insular Affairs. *Indian Fishing Rights.* 88th Cong., 1964. S. 1641–8.

Vaux, George, Jr. *Forty-ninth Annual Report of the Board of Indian Commissioners.* Washington, D.C.: Government Printing Office, 1918. Appendix P.

Washington Territorial Legislature, House Journal, 1866. University of Washington, Manuscripts, Accession No. 4284, Box 2.

Watkins, E. C. *Proposed Consolidation of Reservations.* 45th Cong., 2d sess., 1877, Senate Exec. Doc. 20, 1–8. Serial 1780.

Wright, George. *Report of the Secretary of War.* 36th Cong., 2d sess., 1860, Senate Exec. Doc. 1, 138–40. Serial 1079.

ARCHIVAL RECORD COLLECTIONS

National Archives and Records Service, Pacific Northwest Region:
Applications for Enrollment and Allotment of Washington Indians, 1911–1919, Microfilm M-1343.
Records of the Bureau of Indian Affairs, Hoquiam/Taholah Indian Agency, Record Group 75.
Records of the Bureau of Indian Affairs, Portland Area Office, Record Group 75.

Records of the Bureau of Indian Affairs, Puyallup Indian Agency, Record Group 75.

Records of the Bureau of Indian affairs, Tulalip Indian Agency, Record Group 75.

Records of the Bureau of Indian Affairs, Western Washington Agency, Record Group 75.

Records of the Office of Indian Affairs, Indian Census Rolls, Microfilm M-595, Rolls 93, 302, 406, 565–569, 582–593.

Records of the United States Circuit Court for the District of Washington, Record Group 21.

Reports of the Office of Indian Affairs, Inspection of Field Jurisdictions, 1881–99, Microfilm M-1070.

National Archives and Records Service, Washington, D.C.:

Records of the Bureau of Indian Affairs, Central Classified Files for Puyallup, Tulalip, Taholah Agencies, Record Group 75.

Records of the Bureau of Indian Affairs, Indian Organization Division, Record Group 75.

Records of the Bureau of Indian Affairs, Industries Section, Record Group 75.

Records of the Bureau of Indian Affairs, Social and Economic Surveys, Tulalip and Taholah Agencies, Record Group 75.

Records of the Bureau of Indian Affairs, Special Case Files, Puyallup and Tulalip Agencies, Record Group 75.

Records of the United States Army, Continental Commands, 1821–1890. Records Relating to Military and Civilian Trials, Fort Steilacoom, 1855–1859, Record Group 393.

Snohomish Tribe of Indians, Arlington, Washington. Office Records

Suquamish Indian Tribal Archives, Suquamish, Washington

University of Washington, Seattle, Washington:

Records of the Office of Indian Affairs. Documents Relating to the Negotiation of Indian Treaties, Microfilm A-8207, reels 5–6.

Records of the Washington Superintendency of Indian Affairs, Microfilm A-171.

Washington State Archives:

Records of Washington Territory Adjutant General, Correspondence, Record Group 82/1-1.

Records of Washington Territory Courts, 1854–1889.

Washington Territorial Volunteers Papers, Indian War Correspondence, 1854–57, Record Group 1/A-3.

Washington State University, Pullman, Washington:

Records of Bureau of Indian Affairs, Tulalip Agency.

Index

Illustrations (ill.) can be found in unnumbered plate section.

Compositor:	Impressions Book and Journal Services, Inc.
Text:	10/13 Aldus
Display:	Aldus
Printer and Binder:	Edward Brothers, Inc.